Postcolonial Discourses
An Anthology

To Camille

Postcolonial Discourses
An Anthology

Edited by

GREGORY CASTLE

Copyright © Blackwell Publishers Ltd 2001
Editorial matter, selection and organization copyright © Gregory Castle 2001

First published 2001

2 4 6 8 10 9 7 5 3 1

Blackwell Publishers Ltd
108 Cowley Road
Oxford OX4 1JF
UK

Blackwell Publishers Inc.
350 Main Street
Malden, Massachusetts 02148
USA

British Library Cataloguing in Publication Data

A CIP catalogue record for this book is available from the British Library.

Library of Congress Cataloging-in-Publication Data is available for this book.

ISBN 0–631–21004–0 (Hbk)
ISBN 0–631–21005–9 (Pbk)

Typeset in 10 on 12.5pt Photina
by Kolam Information Services Pvt. Ltd., Pondicherry, India
Printed in Great Britain by Biddles Ltd, Guildford, Surrey

This book is printed on acid-free paper

Contents

IV. Caribbean Encounters: Revolution, Hybridity, Diaspora

V. Rump Commonwealth: Settler Colonies and the "Second World"

VI. The Case of Ireland: Inventing Nations

Thematic Contents

Nationalism

Complicity and Ambivalence

Diaspora and Identity

Race

Gender and the Rights of Women

Literary Interpretations

New Historicist Approaches

Colonial Discourse Analysis

Acknowledgments

I would like to thank my graduate students, Jeremy Meyer and Amanda Yeates, who helped me sift through the incredible amount of critical and theoretical work in postcolonial studies. I would also like to thank the students in my seminars on postcolonial theory, especially Edmond Brosnan, who willingly discussed with me at length the issues and problems illustrated in the essays in *Postcolonial Discourses*. I would like to express my gratitude for the constructive comments made early in the process of creating this anthology by D. J. Walder, Sangeeta Ray, Ali Bedad, Ania Loomba and Suvir Kaul, Robert Young and R. Radhakrishnan. My editor, Andrew McNeillie, was unstinting in his support of this project and I want to thank him for a pleasant and instructive experience. Sarah Dancy, Alison Dunnett, and Margaret Walsh, all at Blackwell, were a pleasure to work with – sympathetic, thorough, and thoroughly professional. All editors should have it so good. I would like to thank Jodie Milam at the Arizona State University Library for her professionalism and patience as I tracked down the texts from which these essays are derived, and the College of Liberal Arts and Sciences at Arizona State, which funded early stages of the *Anthology*'s preparation. Finally, I would like to express my love for Camille Angeles-Castle, whose laughter kept me going.

With the publishers, I gratefully acknowledge permission to reprint copyright material in this book from the following: Achebe, Chinua, "An Image of Africa: Racism in Conrad's *Heart of Darkness*," *The Massachusetts Review* 18, 1977; Appiah, Kwame Anthony, *In my Father's House: Africa in the Philosophy of Culture* (London: Methuen, 1992); Bhabha, Homi K.,"Unsatisfied: Notes on Vernacular Cosmopolitanism," from Laura Garcia Moreno and Peter C. Pfeiffer (eds.), *Text and Nation: Cross-Disciplinary Essays on Cultural and National Identities* (Columbia, SC: Camden House Inc., 1996); Bourke, Angela, "Reading a Woman's Death: Colonial Text and Oral Tradition in Nineteenth-Century Ireland," *Feminist Studies* 21, 1995; Chatterjee, Partha, "The Nationalist Resolution of the Women's Question," from Kumkum Sangari and Sudesh Vaid (eds.), *Recasting Women: Essays in Indian Colonial History* (New Brunswick, NJ: Rutgers University Press, 1990); Crane, Ralph J., "Out of the Center: Thoughts on the Post-colonial Literatures of Australia and New Zealand," from Radhika Mohanram and Gita Rajan (eds.), *English Postcoloniality: Literatures from around the World* (Westport: Greenwood Publishing Inc., 1996); Fanon, Frantz, "Spontaneity: Its Strength and Weakness," from *The Wretched of the Earth*, trans. Constance Farrington (London: Grove Weidenfeld, 1963); Ferguson, Moira, *Colonialism and Gender Relations from Mary Wollstonecraft to Jamaica Kincaid: East Caribbean Connections* (© 1993 Columbia University Press; reprinted by permission of the publisher); Gibbons, Luke, *Transformations in Irish Culture* (Notre Dame: University of Notre Dame Press, and Cork: Cork University Press, 1996); Guha, Ranajit, "The Prose of Counter-Insurgency," from Ranajit Guha and Gayatri Chakravorty Spivak (eds.), *Selected Subaltern Studies* (Delhi and New York: Oxford University Press, 1988; reprinted by permission of Oxford University Press, New Delhi, India); Hall, Stuart, "Negotiating Caribbean Identities," *New Left Review* 209, January 1995; Hodge, Bob and Vijay Mishra, *Dark Side of the Dream: Australian Literature and the Postcolonial Mind* (North Sydney: Allen & Unwin, 1990); Hulme, Peter, "Survival and Invention: Indigeneity in the Caribbean," from Laura Garcia Moreno and Peter C. Pfeiffer (eds.), *Text and Nation: Cross-Disciplinary Essays on Cultural and National Identities* (Columbia, SC: Camden House Inc., 1996); Kiberd, Declan, *Inventing Ireland* (Cambridge, MA: Harvard University Press, 1996, and London: Jonathan Cape); Lamming, George, *In the Castle of My Skin* (University of Michigan Press, 1991; © George Lamming); Lazarus, Neil, " 'Unsystematic Fingers at the Conditions of the Times': 'Afropop' and the Paradoxes of Imperialism," from Jonathan White (ed.), *Recasting the World: Writing after Colonialism* (© Baltimore: The Johns Hopkins University Press, 1994), pp. 137–60; Lloyd, David, "Adulteration and the Nation," from *Anomalous States: Irish Writing and the Post-Colonial Moment* (Durham, NC: Duke University Press, 1993); Mama, Amina, "Sheroes and Villains: Conceptualizing Colonial and Contemporary Violence Against Women in Africa," from © 1996 M. Jacqui Alexander and Chandra Talpade Mohanty (eds.), *Feminist Genealogies, Colonial Legacies, Democratic Futures* (reproduced by permission of Taylor & Francis, Inc./Routledge, Inc., http://www.routledgeny.com); Radhakrishnan, R., *Diasporic Mediations: Between Home and Location* (University of Minnesota Press, Minneapolis, 1996); Rajan, Rajeswari Sunder, "Representing Sati: Continuities and Discontinuities," from Sarah Webster Goodwin and Elizabeth Bronfen (eds.), *Death and Representation* (© Baltimore: The Johns Hopkins University Press, 1993), pp. 285–311; Said, Edward W., *Culture and Imperialism* (New York: Alfred Knopf, 1993); Schaffer, Kay, "Colonizing Gender in Colonial Australia: The Eliza Fraser Story," from *Writing Women and Space: Colonial and Post-Colonial Geographies* (New York: Guilford Publications Inc., 1994); Slemon, Stephen, "Post-colonial Critical Theories," from Bruce King (ed.), *New National and Post-Colonial Literatures: An Introduction* (Oxford: Clarendon Press, 1996); Spivak, Gayatri Chakravorty, "The Burden of English," from Carol A. Breckenridge and Peter van der Veer (eds.), *Orientalism and the Postcolonial Predicament: Perspectives on South Asia* (Philadelphia: University of Pennsylvania Press, 1993); Tiffin, Helen, "The Body in the Library: Identity, Opposition and the Settler-Invader Woman," from Marc Delrez and Bénédicte Ledent (eds.), *The Contact and the Culmination* (L3-Liège Language and Literature, 1997); Young, Robert J. C., "Colonialism and the Desiring Machine," from *Colonial Desire: Hybridity in Theory, Culture and Race* (Routledge, London, 1995).

Editor's Introduction:
Resistance and Complicity in
Postcolonial Studies

I

Postcolonial Discourses is intended to fill a gap left vacant by anthologies whose principal aim has been to represent an array of thematic approaches by which postcolonial studies theorizes its subject-matter, whether that subject-matter is a political movement, a social condition, a literary text, or a concept like "postcolonialism." Such anthologies typically attempt to give a broad view of the field of postcolonial studies, suggesting by their thematic arrangement a certain homogenization of the "postcolonial" as a concept.[1] Another strategy has been to assemble a collection of essays around one or two concepts like gender, nationalism, textuality, postmodernism;[2] sometimes collections emerge out of important academic events, such as the 1991 University of Essex symposium on "Colonial Discourse/Postcolonial Theory."[3] This symposium resulted in a collection of essays that sums up the main trends and critical junctures in colonial discourse analysis and postcolonial critical theory as they appeared at the beginning of the 1990s.

This *Anthology* attempts to do something quite different. The regional approach I have adopted here is intended to emphasize a strong tendency in postcolonial studies in the last two decades of the twentieth century toward an increasingly regional or national (if not always nationalist) approach to the legacies of colonialism. An early and very influential regional approach can be found in *The Empire Writes Back: Theory and Practice in Post-colonial Literatures*. According to Stephen Slemon, the editors of *The Empire Writes Back* put forward "a theory of literary resistance that has to do with an inevitable hybridization within and 'continuity of preoccupations' between, those cultures 'affected by the imperial process'" (108).[4] My regional approach is meant to build on the innovations of *The Empire Writes Back* but also to disrupt the "continuity of preoccupations" that its editors, W. D. Ashcroft, Gareth Griffiths, and Helen Tiffin, call upon to strengthen an argument for postcolonial literature as a collective mode of "reading for resistance." One way of disrupting the tendency toward a collectivist postcolonialism, a tendency grounded in a Commonwealth studies tradition of antagonism toward Anglocentric academic programs, is to consider a broader array of theoretical writings that attempt to articulate the political, aesthetic, social, and historical dimensions of local conditions. The selections I have made tend to emphasize the ways that local responses to theoretical issues reconceptualize and repoliticize post-colonialism's complicit relations with colonial discourse. The inclusion of a section on Ireland (which is not discussed in *The Empire Writes Back* or any of the other readers and anthologies[5]) underscores the extent to which resistance to empire is not always as radical as it seems, that it is predicated on a principled complicity, an ambivalence that is foundational. Complicity is, paradoxically, post-colonialism's "radical" edge.

As the title of this *Anthology* indicates, it is concerned primarily with postcolonial discourses rather than with colonial discourse analysis, though separating these two species of intellectual work is a very difficult task. Colonial discourse analysis typically considers the larger structural framework from which historical documents emanate, the Foucauldian "social formations" that generate attitudes and "fantasies" about the Other. But it is, today, only one of many approaches to the problem of what some have called the "postcolonial condition." Many critics now at work in postcolonial studies might be accurately called historical materialists or historicists, and many of them have challenged the assumptions made in colonial discourse analysis, with Edward Said's *Orientalism* coming in for a good deal of criticism for failing to address the problem of the subaltern as a *class* possessing a revolutionary agency and function. Some have emerged as sympathetic and influential literary critics. I have therefore avoided in my title the term "theory," wishing to group under the plural term "discourses" an array of written responses to colonialism that includes theoretical reflection, meta-discursive critique, discourse analysis, historical analysis, and literary criticism.

If *Postcolonial Discourses* has a general orientation, it is toward an articulation of what Homi K. Bhabha, in his contribution, calls the "temporality of continuance" (39). In Bhabha's reading of a passage from Frantz Fanon's "Spontaneity: Its Strength and Weakness" (also included here), temporality is dynamic and future orientated, rather than static and past (or tradition) orientated; it sustains the paradox of a historical perspective that is essentially palimpsestic: an overlay of interpretations that includes the multiplicitous versions of the colonized in varying degrees of complicity, whether by cooperation or co-optation, with imperialist master narratives of history and bureaucratic organization. Bhabha's term "vernacular cosmopolitanism," like the perspectives of many of the writers collected here, reinforces the fundamental importance of *location*, the felt experience of the local, which is not collectivized or sublated in a universal historical narrative, but coexists, with all of its local, even marginal character, within putatively universal narratives, challenging that universality by their very coexistence.[6] Many of the essays offered in this *Anthology* are critical of schemes to do away with such universalizing tendencies, which inevitably founder on the hope of every accomplishing such a goal and are weakened, when they succeed at all, by the substitution of a new revolutionary universalism that reinscribes a strictly dialectical attitude toward material social relations.

From the start, postcolonial literatures – especially novels such as James Joyce's *Finnegans Wake*, Rushdie's *Midnight's Children* or J. M. Coetzee's *Foe* – have underscored the necessity for the coexistence of mutually exclusive narrative forms that unsettle dialectical thinking (as well as traditional notions of historical continuity). It is this necessity that keeps the local relevant within a globalized capital market and a transnational politics in which "third- and fourth-world" countries find their futures determined by international agencies such as the UN, NATO, the World Bank, and the International Monetary Fund. Some of the essays in this *Anthology* critique the forms of neocolonialism (especially the political and economic policies of European and US governments) that global capitalism has engendered. These critical interventions reveal something of the manner in which specific regions respond to the necessity for continuing the struggle for postcolonial self-determination, and they do so by sustaining a more sharply critical mode of colonial discourse analysis, one actuated by new concerns for gender, class, race, nationalism, and a "fourth world" of migrants and refugees. The postcolonial critic enters into what Mary Louise Pratt calls an "auto-ethnographic" engagement with imperialism,[7] a specific form of writing or talking back that fashions complicity into a form of textual insurgency (see Spivak in this volume). It is a process in which the native intellectual crafts or *forges* a new discourse, a new literary style, a way of singing or dancing that expresses a native point of view in contest with colonial discourse. It is an agonistic mode of national self-fashioning that does not, in the end, succumb to the seduction of neocolonialist solutions to native problems. Thus, the essays in this *Anthology* elaborate on Fanon's paradoxical insight that "[n]ational consciousness, which is not nationalism, is the only thing that will give us an international dimension."[8] The regional approach I take here is, I submit, the most productive way to guide the student toward a historical understanding of Fanon's insight.

II

As many postcolonial commentators have made evident, it is difficult to say what exactly postcolonial theory is. As anyone who has studied or taught postcolonial theory soon discovers, there is no "tradition" per se for such a theory – as we might say there is a philosophical tradition for deconstruction, a psychoanalytical tradition for Lacan's "return to Freud," a Marxian tradition for cultural materialism, and so on. Indeed, we might say that it is a strong tradition that permits these theoretical orientations to become universalized by those who use them. Said's *Orientalism*, with its magisterial mode of colonial discourse analysis, can be said to have founded one possible tradition of postcolonial theory – and this *despite* the critiques lodged against it. Patrick Williams and Laura Chrisman, in *Colonial Discourse and Post-Colonial Theory*, effectively canonized Said's text as central to postcolonial theory precisely by devoting space to a suite of critical responses to it. Another tradition might proceed from Fanon's critique of "national consciousness," while still another might start from the colonial discourse analysis of Gayatri Chakravorty Spivak's "Can the Subaltern Speak?" or Bhabha's "Signs Taken for Wonders," in order to emphasize the affiliations of postcolonialism with post-structuralist theory. My point here is that there is a multiplicity of origins or theoretical foundations for postcolonial theory that is sometimes masked by the tendency of anthologies (as well as much of the criticism emanating from postcolonial studies) to refer to a singular theory. I do not mean to imply that editors and critics advocate universalist or hegemonic conceptions of postcolonial theory; for it is often the case that arguments conducted under the aegis of such a "postcolonial theory" belie any singular foundation or methodology. As Anne McClintock writes, "[i]f post-colonial *theory* has sought to challenge the grand march of Western historicism and its entourage of binaries (self–other, metropolis–colony, centre–periphery, etc.), the *term* post-colonialism nonetheless reorients the globe once more around a single binary opposition: colonial–post-colonial" (quoted in Slemon, 103). It is this condition of interrelation, which Vijay Mishra and Bob Hodge call "complicit postcolonialism," that *Postcolonial Discourses* seeks to diagnose through heterogeneous points of view whose commonality is an irreducibly local difference, the *pre*condition of any interrelation (critical or otherwise) with a global or globalizing point of view.[9]

As the foregoing suggests, the very term "postcolonial" has come under considerable pressure by critics who seek to undermine any simple understanding of "postcolonialism," especially its relations (temporal and ideological) with colonialism, since many anti-colonial and nationalist movements have their origin in colonial epochs and are often implicated in the structure of colonial discourse in complicated ways. At the same time, these critics are also wary of any parallelism that would place "postcolonialism" alongside postmodernism, since many writers and critics from postcolonial regions overtly reject Western models of epistemology and ontology, including the so-called radical approaches of post-structuralist critique.[10] Postcolonial theory, therefore, ought to be concerned with what we might call indigenous solutions to colonial problems; but it is often the case that the term "postcolonial" stands as a roadblock to any progress toward this goal precisely because it implies affiliations with Western intellectual traditions. Complicating this picture is the fact that at the textual level such affiliations are vital to postcolonial analysis, especially those that take a "new historical" approach to colonial discourse. Colonial discourse analysis, for example, though it is only one mode of postcolonial critique, has acquired a signal importance by establishing the historical context in which a postcolonial position or condition can make sense. The "ur-text" of this mode of analysis, for Slemon and others, is Said's *Orientalism*, a text that has provided a useful model for subsequent postcolonial theorists, such as Ranajit Guha and others in the Subaltern Studies Group, whose objective is to analyze the discursive hegemony of colonial power.

What these general remarks about the term "postcolonial" make clear is that postcolonial theory is far from singular and coherent and that the *location* of the theorist (or the location theorized) is of central importance. For these reasons, I have chosen to organize the essays selected for this *Anthology* according to *region*. In this way I hope to give readers a sense of the heterogeneity and historical embeddedness of postcolonial discourses in specific geographical locations. Additionally, because *Postcolonial Discourses* is designed in part to supplement courses on British literature and postcolonialism, I have restricted coverage to the former British colonial territories, principally South Asia, the Caribbean, Africa, Ireland, and settler colonies, mainly Australia and New Zealand. My justification for this approach is based on an argument that is rapidly gaining favor in postcolonial studies – the argument that theorizing postcoloniality is ineluctably tied to specific geographical, social, and historical conditions. Many of the issues dealt with in the essays collected here – nationalism, gender, language, identity, violence – while they may be universal in the sense that they crop up in nearly every postcolonial context, are far from universal in the sense that each region raises these issues in the same ways and offers the same solutions. Consider, for example, the problem of gender, which is addressed differently in the Indian context, where the practice of *sati* (ritualistic self-immolation of widows) serves as an important trope for the role of women in a caste society, from how it is in, say, Africa, where genital mutilation serves as an equally important trope for the status of women's bodies in a tribal society.

This is not to say that there are no common elements transcending regional differences – for example, the notion that identity is constituted in a struggle between indigenous and colonizing forces is well-nigh universal in postcolonial studies – but it *is* a way of insisting on the pre-eminence of location for any understanding of the issues and problems facing postcolonial critics and writers. Robert Young's critique of postcolonialism's "Holy Trinity" (Said, Spivak, Bhabha) ends with a cautionary note that sums up the dangers and benefits of the regional approach:

> Fanon points out how colonialism itself was "separatist and regionalist," a technique designed to reinforce separation and quietism. Those who today emphasize its geographical and historical differences may in effect be only repeating uncritically colonialism's own partitioning strategies. Yet at this point in the postcolonial era, as we seek to understand the operation and effects of colonial history, the homogenization of colonialism does also need to be set against its historical and geographical particularities. The question for any theory of colonial discourse is whether it can maintain, and do justice to, both levels (79).

It is, I think, one of the many virtues of the essays in this *Anthology* that they attempt to maintain both levels of inquiry: situated in a theoretical context that transcends regional boundaries, they articulate concerns that are dictated by those boundaries. In the articulation of specific regional concerns, postcolonial critics can find the best chance of avoiding the dangers of "separation and quietism" and resist, at the level of textual practice, the monolithic character and authority of colonialism that permits such "divide and conquer" tactics in the first place. The twofold responsibility of "postcolonial theory" – articulation and resistance – has origins in both Marxist and Fanonian thought and is reflected in many of the essays in *Postcolonial Discourses*.

By arranging essays under regional rubrics, I emphasize the separate development of different postcolonial experiences with respect to nationalism, language, gender, cultural production, and national politics (which are, after all, highly volatile, weirdly contingent on both local and neocolonial imperatives); at the same time, it is my hope that the student will be able to appreciate the regional differences reflected in these essays and to apply the theoretical or historical lessons they offer to literary texts from the regions in question. Students will be able to draw from these very different approaches some general conclusions about the "postcolonial condition" – that strangely atemporal, strangely historical "space" of linguistic and cultural development, marked by the violence and ambivalence of colonialism – and to use those conclusions as the basis for asking new questions about texts from quite different regions. To this end, I have provided headnotes for each essay that will help students draw such conclusions without losing sight of the regional distinctions that make these essays such valuable contributions to postcolonial studies.

III

I would like now to consider briefly the essays in Part I, "Postcolonial Discourses: Complicity and Critique," in order to highlight certain arguments and indicate how they might be useful to the student in making his or her way through the regional sections. The first section features essays that consider general problems within the field of postcolonial studies, with an emphasis on the ever-present possibility, signaled in the very term "postcolonial," of both critical intervention in and complicity with colonial discourse. Fanon's "Spontaneity: Its Strength and Weakness" argues that a recognition of both possibilities is necessary not only for the continuation of the struggle against colonialism but also for the process of creating genuine national independence. The significance of this essay lies principally in Fanon's concentration on the role of native intellectuals and national leaders in periods of colonial struggle and the importance of recognizing the revolutionary potential of the people who occupy the countryside and shantytowns. This potential, which Fanon calls "spontaneity," "gives concrete form to the general insecurity, and colonialism takes fright and either continues the war or negotiates" (8). But it must be channeled and directed; the people must be educated politically if the immediate violence of an uprising is to sustain itself as a revolutionary war. The education of the people, the building up of awareness of the pitfalls as well as the triumphs of "spontaneous" anti-colonial violence, which intellectuals and national leaders must take on as their historical responsibility, lead ultimately to a realization that simple Manichean distinctions between settler and native, black and white, do not exist in reality. Care must be taken, Fanon argues, that the people recognize the dangers of spontaneity, for the "springing wolf" and "rising gust of wind which was to have brought about a real revolution run the risk of becoming quite unrecognizable if the struggle continues: and continue it does" (21). Fanon's conclusions are echoed in essays reprinted here by Partha Chatterjee, Amina Mama, and Angela Bourke – essays that in very different ways explore the fissures within native populations due in large measure to the inadequate political education of the people.

Fanon's work is especially pertinent for Bhabha's consideration of the "temporality of continuance" in which a "cosmopolitan community envisaged in a *marginality*" carries on the revolutionary struggle of nationalism within an international community. In Western European traditions, cosmopolitanism is associated with a form of universality; however, Bhabha's "vernacular cosmopolitanism" develops the discontinuous temporality of postcolonial spaces and margins and "stops short of the transcendent universal." He reads Adrienne Rich's poetic meditations on the paradoxical universality of local utterances – "I am" spoken from a variety of locations, expressing an array of experiences: pain, dislocation, death – and through this reading challenges not only the Manichaeism of an earlier generation of colonial discourse analysis but also the tendency in his own early work to posit a dualistic structure of colonial disavowal.[11] It is perhaps more accurate to regard this self-critical impulse as a function of a continuance in Bhabha's own anti-colonial project. We might say the same of Spivak's contribution, "The Burden of English," which explores the complicated and complicit structures of native Indian texts (60). Concentrating on the "implied reader" of colonial texts, and the "alienating assent" (56) that she is so often moved to make while reading such texts – an assent to class, race, or gender models that may not conform with her own experience – Spivak describes an emancipatory complicity, a "productive and chosen contradiction" within colonial texts, which leads to a recognition of their heterogeneity and of the complex relations that ensue between "British and colonial/Commonwealth literatures."

Spivak's emphasis on pedagogy demonstrates the pragmatic implications of post-colonial theory for students of colonial and postcolonial literatures as well as for the teachers who attempt to guide them as they make (or refuse to make) their "alienated assent." Her essay is a precise and precisely articulated example of the political education that Fanon prescribes as necessary for the successful continuance of the colonial struggle in the era of independence. Helen Tiffin, in her contribution to this *Anthology*, makes a similar point about the work of the Antiguan writer Jamaica Kincaid: "Kincaid addresses the foreign reader not from a position of an essentialist local identity, but from one deliberately, i.e., narratively, adopted to enable her to accuse the murderers [i.e., colonialists] clearly and directly" (376). Other women, like Kay Schaffer and Angela Bourke, who write about the stake of women in colonial and postcolonial discourses, suggest that the idea of the local is not an essentialist one, it does not require assent to traditional notions of gender, though such notions linger as strong residual imperatives. For these critics, as for so many others, the idea of the local, especially as it impinges on the experience of women, entails a commitment to *in*authenticity, and strategies of discursive (or performative) self-fashioning that will enable subaltern women to negotiate between and among competing visions of postcolonial history that all too often carry on the iconographic sexism that characterized both the old colonial regimes and the anti-colonial nationalist movements ranged against them.[12]

Said's *Culture and Imperialism*, which continues the project of colonial discourse analysis he inaugurated in *Orientalism*, advances a concept of "discrepant experiences" remarkably similar to Spivak's emancipatory complicity. The "difficulty with theories of essentialism and exclusiveness," which Said finds in many postcolonial situations that have allowed nativism to triumph over the kind of cosmopolitanism of which Bhabha speaks, "is that they give rise to polarizations that absolve and forgive ignorance and demagogy more than they enable knowledge" (27). A comparative or "contrapuntal" perspective – like those offered by Spivak and Bhabha – Said's "discrepant experiences" afford the postcolonial intellectual a genuine chance to over-come the hegemony of the Western "super-subject, whose historicizing and disciplinary rigor either takes away or, in the post-colonial period, restores history to people and cultures" presumed to be without it (30). In an analysis of some contemporary examples – the Desert Storm operation staged by the United States and other instances of prejudice against Arabs – Said implicitly revises his own powerful interpretation of Orientalist discourse, joining his voice, as well as those of a new generation of native intellectuals, to Fanon's in a call to move beyond "the reified polarities of East and West" (35).

The essays by Said, Spivak, and Bhabha represent a new emphasis (though hardly a new presence) in postcolonial studies, one that appears to reflect both a return to Fanon's foundational ideas about the role of the native intellectual and a turn to context-specific discourses. For Spivak and Bhabha, however, it might be more accurate to say that it is a *return* or *reiteration* of local concerns that have always occupied them but which have been forgotten by many of their followers who have formulated theories of postcolonialism based on their work.

Essays by Young and Slemon round out Part I of the *Anthology* and serve two functions: they sum up the main currents of postcolonial studies at the end of the millennium and call our attention to the need for modes of analysis and critique better suited to the commingling, in a postcolonial sphere, of local, national, international, and "migrant" interests. Young usefully considers the enormous influence of Said, Bhabha, and Spivak, writing that their contributions to colonial discourse analysis have provided a "significant framework" for the work of critics and theorists who follow them. By "emphasizing that all perspectives on colonialism share and have to deal with a common discursive medium which was also that of colonialism itself," they call attention to the chief danger of postcolonial theorizing, the fact that colonial discourse, if it goes unchallenged, will determine every mode of analysis by which it is criticized. The failure to issue such a challenge results, as Young sees it, in "the 'alienation effect' of much of the language of postcolonial criticism" (77). He calls for a "critical ethnography of the West," a meta-critical project of cultural analysis, which, I would argue, is precisely what many of the contributors to *Postcolonial Discourses* are already doing.

Young himself offers a model of analysis based on the theories of Gilles Deleuze and Felix Guattari, one capable of challenging the hegemonic tendencies of "discursive models" such as Said's *Orientalism*. Deleuze and Guattari regard colonialism as a "desiring machine" which "deterritorializes" and "reterritorializes" local landscapes and structures of power. For Young, the "social formations" that emerge in the process of de- and reterritorialization constitute a form of "writing geography" – a model of colonial discourse analysis that posits a system of ideological and military-adminis-trative "flows" that restructure native space in terms congenial to colonial and capitalist expansion. The operation of colonialism, in this view, is a form of ambivalent desire grounded in a "doubled logic": "While providing an overall theoretical para-digm, the desiring machine also allows for the specificity of incommensurable, compet-ing histories forced together in unnatural unions by colonialism" (86). This "forcing together" is most powerfully expressed in the "double fear" of racial mixing: on the one hand, the colonialist fears racial integration and miscegenation, refusing any scheme that might bring different races together; but, on the other hand, he obsessively tabulates the possibilities of racial mixture, revealing an ambivalent desire for the Other. In seeking to understand the contradictory desires and incommensurate prac-tices of postcolonialism, Young discovers "a way of theorizing the material geopolitics of colonial history, as at the same time, an agonistic narrative of desire" (86).

Stephen Slemon's essay is valuable not only for offering a short critical summary of the field, including a discussion of the problem of the term "postcolonial," but for reminding students that the critical emphasis in postcolonial studies on non-realist writing and on "writing for resistance" has its origin in "Commonwealth literary studies" and its battle against the Anglocentric English departments. Defying the "representational contract" of realism is a common strategy in postcolonial literature still, and it may be responsible for the "difficulty" of some postcolonial theory. Since "realist writing is tied to a naturalizing drive in language," it poses a special problem for postcolonial writing of all kinds dedicated to finding ways to escape the "disempowering cognitive legacies of imperialism" (106–7). The problem is that anti-realist strategies too often employ linguistic and narrative theories borrowed from Western traditions of post-structuralism and postmodernism; rather than "decolonizing the mind," anti-realist postcolonial writing threatens to *recolonize* it.[13] Another element of Commonwealth studies that contributes to postcolonialism offsets this danger of recolonization, and that is what Slemon calls "reading for resistance," a practice he associates strongly with Bill Ashcroft, Gareth Griffiths, and Helen Tiffin (the editors of *The Empire Writes Back*). This practice essentially involves the "'abrogation' or refusal of the normative standards of the imperial culture – the standards of 'correct' grammar, syntax, and pronunciation, for example – and then by an 'appropriation' of the colonizer's language, appropriately adapted, to the cultural and political ends of the colonized" (107). A wide variety of national literatures and critical practices were held together by collectivist theories of resistance to an "Anglocentric, English-department monologue." Though some, like George Lamming, are profoundly collectivist in imagination if not in politics, many others resist the tendency in collectivism to idealize the "will of the people." Postcolonial writers such as R. Radhakrishnan, Chatterjee, Lamming, David Lloyd, and Bob Hodge and Vijay Mishra continue to make increasingly sophisticated interventions into imperial structures of power, particularly in the areas of family and gender relations, nationalist politics, and education.

The analysis of the role of history within postcolonialism with which Slemon concludes his essay is especially important and can serve as a general starting point for understanding the historical points of view represented in the essays that follow. One of the dominant modes of new historical critique within postcolonial studies is that practiced by the Subaltern Studies Group (represented here by Ranajit Guha's "The Prose of Counter-Insurgency"). Because it concentrates on the documents of colonialism in order to arrive at some sense of the felt reality of subaltern peoples, the Subaltern Studies Group underscores the dynamic and dialogical process by which history is made and by which it might be written as a *counter*-history, since it becomes clear that colonial discourse makes sense only when we consider the reality of subaltern experience. And that experience, according to Slemon, ambivalent and "in-between": "neither fully subjected to power nor fully agential, in the sense of having full self-knowledge, and will, and purpose" (110). Guha's analysis of colonialist documents indicates the hidden assumptions about race and "primitive" peoples inscribed in colonial discourse which reveal themselves in the often hysterical representations they offer up of the Other (or, as many critics prefer, the "subaltern").[14] The problem, as Spivak and others have demonstrated, is that the "reality" of the subaltern is always already mediated by the very colonialist discourse that comes to the aid of the postcolonial historian seeking to write a *counter*-history. It is an impossible position, but the native intellectual must nevertheless strive for it as the condition of any possible discourse of subalternity. As many of the essays in *Postcolonial Discourses* demonstrate, much can be learned in the process of attempting the impossible.

Slemon concludes his remarks about the state of postcolonial studies by alluding to progress made in the field of colonial discourse analysis. If Said's theory of Orientalism made little allowance for the voice of the native, for a kind of "talking back," other modes of colonial discourse analysis, like that practiced by Peter Hulme, make just such allowances. As Slemon points out in his essay (112), Hulme discloses the ways in which "discursive regulations" between colonizers and the colonized govern not only "how Europe understands its Others but also, foundationally, how European 'sovereign' subjects understand themselves." He goes further in his essay included here when he argues that "what Europeans perceived in Native American actions was a distorted *self*-image projected onto their indigenous antagonists" (296). The dislocations created by new modes of historical critique in colonial discourse analysis as well as in other areas within postcolonial studies have necessitated what Bhabha calls "a space for a new discursive temporality" (quoted in Slemon, 114). And it is in this space that the essays in *Postcolonial Discourses* unfold.

IV

As I have indicated above, the essays in *Postcolonial Discourses* reflect the hetero-geneity of postcolonial projects that emanate from or direct their attentions to specific localities and adapt Western theoretical models in order to look at widely different social and cultural phenomena; they also give evidence of an array of strategies for avoiding the traps of "universalizing" theories of race, gender, religion, ethnicity, and nationalism. Rather than conceiving of "tradition" as a monolithic or hegemonic system of forces for the organization of knowledge and theory, the postcolonial writer draws on a plurality of traditions, where local particularities map out strategies of theoretical resistance and (re)construction, where local voices articulate a response not only to colonial discourse but to what we might call the first wave of postcolonial theory, one dominated by Said's concept of Orientalism and by South Asian theorists such as Bhabha and Spivak. A greater emphasis on historical and regional awareness characterizes the theoretical work of the 1990s, which has led to increasingly differentiated attitudes toward race, gender, nationalism, and other local manifesta-tions of what too often become globalized or totalizing theoretical categories.

By the same token, I want to emphasize that the regions as they are conceived in *Postcolonial Discourses* are not monolithic or coherent "areas" in the sense that we might find it used in "area studies" of the sort favored by US intelligence agencies during the Cold War. They are, rather, contingent sites of significant cultural activity; as I conceive them, the regions are material realities and geographical "formations" (many of which were imperially "mapped") that have very real effects on individuals; at the same time, these regions are ideas, powerful tropes for nationhood and self-hood, the property of both native intellectuals and migrant university scholars, the native bourgeoisie and the refugees. It is no surprise that the exile should figure so prominently in postcolonial literature or that so many postcolonial writers became exiles themselves, living with the feeling of being, as Salman Rushdie puts it, "buffeted by too much history."[15]

Each region is represented by four essays that give the student a good sense of the variety of style, method, and theme of postcolonial discourses. I have tried to include in each section essays that feature literary interpretation, as well as essays that explore the hidden corners of imperial archives. In each section, I feature essays that address the problem of effective local responses to colonial discourse, essays that to some degree theorize or thematize or criticize the idea of *location*. There are many commonalties, shared methods and theories, shared themes, shared concerns for language, gender, race, and national identity. A strong sense of historicism as a force in both nation-building and critical intervention can be found in every essay here, though the regional arrangement will, I hope, underscore the precise nature of the contingencies that make postcolonial experiences of history so different from those recorded in the West – contingencies based on the material realities of national politics and opposition movements, migration and emigration, regional and civil wars, economic fluctuations, and the ever-present pressure of international organizations. To some degree, as colonial discourse analysis has shown, there is always on the part of postcolonial writers a certain complicity with colonialism, one that cannot be avoided and has in fact been embraced as the site of genuine revolutionary progress, especially in the realm of local politics, education, scholarship, the rights of women and children, and the evolving role postcolonial nations play in international politics. The essays collected here are part of an ongoing response to colonial discourse, unfolding in the space of Bhabha's "temporality of continuance," an emancipatory complicity that overcomes the historical arrogance of colonialism, overcomes the "reality" of having never played a meaningful role in history, never having possessed the basic freedoms that constitute subjectivity and thus make history possible.

Brief headnotes at the beginning of each section will sum up the main thematic and theoretical currents in the region, provide the student with relevant historical, biographical, or technical information, identify key terms, and cross-reference each essay with othe similar essays for purposes of class discussion and research. A glossary of important critical and theoretical terms will help the student with some of the technical difficulties that inevitably arise in the interdisciplinary, often ideologically resistant, discourses found in postcolonial studies. I have also included a table of contents organized by theme and theoretical approach in order to demonstrate how these essays might be grouped together for discussion or analysis. In this supplementary table of contents, the essays are arranged under the following headings: Nationalism, Complicity and Ambivalence, Diaspora and Identity, Race, Gender and the Rights of Women, Literary Interpretations, New Historicist Approaches, and Colonial Discourse Analysis. For further study, students may wish to consult the Select Bibliography, a short list of important works in postcolonial studies published in the last quarter century.

NOTES

1   See, for example, Padmini Mongia, ed., *Contemporary Postcolonial Theory: A Reader* (London: Arnold, 1996); Patrick Williams and Laura Chrisman, eds., *Colonial Discourse and Post-Colonial Theory: A Reader* (New York: Columbia University Press, 1994); W. D. Ashcroft, Gareth Griffiths, and Helen Tiffin, *The Post-colonial Studies Reader* (London and New York: Routledge, 1995).

2   Collections with a strong conceptual orientation include Chris Tiffin and Alan Lawson,
    eds., *De-Scribing Empire: Post-Colonialism and Textuality* (London: Routledge, 1994);
    Andrew Parker, Mary Russo, Doris Sommer, and Patricia Yaeger, eds., *Nationalisms and
    Sexualities* (New York: Routledge, 1992); Alison Blunt and Gillian Rose, eds., *Writing
    Women and Space: Colonial and Post-Colonial Geographies* (New York: Guilford, 1994); Ian
    Adam and Helen Tiffin, eds., *Past the Last Post: Theorizing Post-Colonialism and Post-
    Modernism* (Calgary: University of Calgary Press, 1990); M. Jacqui Alexander and Chandra
    Talpade Mohanty, eds., *Feminist Genealogies, Colonial Legacies, Democratic Futures* (New
    York: Routledge, 1997); Anne McClintock, Aamir Mufti, and Ella Shohat, eds., *Dangerous
    Liaisons: Gender, Nation, and Postcolonial Perspectives* (Minneapolis: Minnesota University
    Press, 1997).

3   Francis Barker, Peter Hulme, and Margaret Iversen, eds., *Colonial Discourse/Postcolonial
    Theory* (Manchester: Manchester University Press, 1994).

4   Parenthetical page references in this introduction are to the versions of those texts
    reprinted in this *Anthology*.

5   This is not true of essay collections. See, for example, Radhika Mohanram and Gita Rajan,
    eds., *English Postcoloniality: Literatures from around the World* (Westport, CT: Greenwood,
    1996); Blunt and Rose, *Writing Women and Space*.

6   For a number of influential discussions on the problem of narrative in a postcolonial
    context, see Homi K. Bhabha, ed., *Nation and Narration* (London: Routledge, 1990).

7   Mary Louise Pratt, *Imperial Eyes: Travel Writing and Transculturation* (London and New
    York: Routledge, 1992), 6.

8   Frantz Fanon, *The Wretched of the Earth*, trans. Constance Farrington (New York: Grove
    Weidenfeld, 1963), 247.

9   On "complicit postcolonialism," see Mishra and Hodge, "What Is Post(-) Colonialism?"
    and Stephen Slemon, "Post-colonial Critical Theories," in Bruce King, ed., *New National
    and Post-Colonial Literatures: An Introduction* (Oxford: Clarendon Press, 1996), 178–97.

10 The complications disclosed by analysis of the term "postcolonialism" constitute a valu-
    able trend of disciplinary self-criticism that reflects an equally valuable refusal to allow
    "postcolonialism" to congeal into a single orientation. The debate is lively. Slemon and
    Young present it here, but the student is invited to consult Simon During, "Postmodern-
    ism: Or, Post-Colonialism Today," in Thomas Docherty, ed., *Postmodernism: A Reader* (New
    York: Columbia University Press, 1993), 448–62; Stuart Hall, "When Was the 'Post-
    Colonial'? Thinking at the Limit," in Iain Chambers and Lidia Curti, eds., *The Post-Colonial
    Question: Common Skies, Divided Horizons* (London and New York: Routledge, 1996), 242–
    60; Kwame Anthony Appiah, "Is the Post- in Postmodernism the Post- in Postcolonial?"
    Critical Inquiry 17 (1991): 336–57; Arun P. Mukherjee, "Whose Post-Colonialism and
    Whose Postmodernism," *World Literature Written in English* 30.2 (1990): 1–9; Anne
    McClintock, "The Angel of Progress: Pitfalls of the Term 'Postcolonialism,'" *Social Text*
    10.2–3 (1992): 84–98, reprinted in McClintock, *Imperial Leather: Race, Gender and Sexu-
    ality in the Colonial Contest* (New York: Routledge, 1995); Barker, Hulme, and Iversen,
    Colonial Discourse/Postcolonial Theory, "Introduction," 2–6; Vijay Mishra and Bob Hodge,
    "What is Post(-) Colonialism?" *Textual Practice* 5 (1991): 399–414.

11 See Bhabha, *The Location of Culture* (London and New York: Routledge, 1994).

12 See Jenny Sharpe, *Allegories of Empire: The Figure of Woman in the Colonial Text* (Minnea-
    polis: University of Minnesota Press, 1993); Richard Kearney, "Myth and Motherland," in
    Ireland's Field Day: Field Day Theatre Company (London: Hutchinson, 1985), 61–80; Denis
    Kandiyoti, "Identity and its Discontents: Women and the Nation," in Patrick Williams and
    Laura Chrisman, eds., *Colonial Discourse and Post-Colonial Theory: A Reader* (New York:
    Columbia University Press, 1994).

13   See Ngugi wa Thiong'o, *Decolonizing the Mind: The Politics of Language in African Literature* (1981; rpt. Westport, CT: Greenwood, 1996).
14   See, for example, Sharpe's discussion, in *Allegories of Empire*, of E. M. Forster's *A Passage to India* in the context of colonialist responses to the Indian Mutiny of 1857.
15   Salman Rushdie, *Midnight's Children* (New York: Penguin, 1991), 37.

Selected Bibliography

The list of key works below reflects mainly the regions emphasized in the *Anthology*, though I have tried to give a fair sense of the diversity of theme and theoretical orientation that exists within postcolonial studies generally. Students and teachers alike are invited to use the *Anthology* as a starting point for researching and discussing the array of critical and theoretical problems reflected in these works.

Alexander, M. Jacqui and Chandra Talpade Mohanty, eds. *Feminist Genealogies, Colonial Legacies, Democratic Futures*. New York: Routledge, 1997.

Ashcroft, W. D., Gareth Griffiths, and Helen Tiffin, eds. *The Empire Writes Back: Theory and Practice in Post-colonial Literatures*. London and New York: Routledge, 1989.

Bhabha, Homi K. *The Location of Culture*. London and New York: Routledge, 1994.

Cairns, David and Shaun Richards. *Writing Ireland: Colonialism, Nationalism and Culture*. Manchester: Manchester University Press, 1988.

Chambers, Iain and Lidia Curti, eds. *The Post-Colonial Question: Common Skies, Divided Horizons*. London: Routledge, 1996.

Chatterjee, Partha. *The Nation and its Fragments: Colonial and Post-Colonial Histories*. Princeton: Princeton University Press, 1993.

Fanon, Frantz. *The Wretched of the Earth*. Trans. Constance Farrington. New York: Grove Weidenfeld, 1963.

Guha, Ranajit, and Gayatri Spivak, eds. *Selected Subaltern Studies*. Delhi and New York: Oxford University Press, 1988.

Hulme, Peter. *Colonial Encounters: Europe and the Native Caribbean, 1492–1797*. London: Methuen, 1986.

Kiberd, Declan. *Inventing Ireland*. Cambridge, MA: Harvard University Press, 1996.

King, Bruce, ed. *New National and Post-Colonial Literatures: An Introduction*. Oxford: Clarendon Press, 1996.

Lazarus, Neil. *Resistance in Postcolonial African Fiction*. New Haven: Yale University Press, 1990.

Lloyd, David. *Anomalous States: Irish Writing and the Post-Colonial Moment*. Durham, NC: Duke University Press, 1993.

McClintock, Anne. *Imperial Leather: Race, Gender and Sexuality in the Colonial Contest*. New York: Routledge, 1995.

McClintock, Anne, Aamir Mufti, and Ella Shohat, eds. *Dangerous Liaisons: Gender, Nation, and Postcolonial Perspectives*. Minneapolis: Minnesota University Press, 1997.

Memmi, Albert. *The Colonizer and the Colonized*. New York: Orion, 1965.

Minh-ha, Trinh T. *Woman, Native, Other: Writing Postcoloniality and Feminism.* Bloomington, IN: Indiana University Press, 1989.

Ngugi wa Thiong'o. *Decolonizing the Mind: The Politics of Language in African Literature.* Westport, CT: Greenwood, 1996.

Radhakrishnan, R. *Diasporic Mediations: Between Home and Location.* Minneapolis: University of Minnesota Press, 1996.

Rajan, Rajeswari Sunder. *Real and Imagined Women: Gender, Culture and Postcolonialism.* London: Routledge, 1993.

Said, Edward W. *Orientalism.* London: Penguin, 1985.

Sharpe, Jenny. *Allegories of Empire: The Figure of Woman in the Colonial Text.* Minneapolis: University of Minnesota Press, 1993.

Spivak, Gayatri Chakravorty. *A Critique of Postcolonial Reason: Toward a History of the Vanishing Present.* Cambridge, MA; London: Harvard University Press, 1999.

Young, Robert J. C. *Colonial Desire: Hybridity in Theory, Culture and Race.* London: Routledge, 1995.

Part I

Postcolonial Discourses: Complicity and Critique

Frantz Fanon, "Spontaneity: Its Strength and Weakness"
Edward W. Said, "Discrepant Experiences"
Homi K. Bhabha, "Unsatisfied: Notes on Vernacular Cosmopolitanism"
Gayatri Chakravorty Spivak, "The Burden of English"
Robert J. C. Young, "Colonialism and the Desiring Machine"
Stephen Slemon "Post-colonial Critical Theories"

Spontaneity: Its Strength and Weakness

FRANTZ FANON

Frantz Fanon's work has proven to be seminal in the development of postcolonial studies. *Black Skin, White Masks*, his study of race and the effects of racism in colonial and postcolonial contexts, was instrumental in the formation of **Homi Bhabha**'s theory of disavowal and has contributed greatly to our understanding of the racial politics of colonialism. *The Wretched of the Earth*, from which this essay is taken, may justly be regarded as foundational for postcolonial theory. Its analysis of violence and national consciousness has influenced nearly every significant theory of postcolonialism that seeks to move beyond simplistic, binary conceptions of the struggle against colonialism. This essay features an exploration of the idea of "spontaneity," the violent expression of injustice and the desire for freedom that lie, according to Fanon, at the heart of all anti-colonial movements. Fanon willingly confronts the possibility of complicity between nationalist leaders and colonial powers and champions "the people" (by which term Fanon means both the rural peasantry and the shantytown dwellers of urban centers) who are all too often overlooked by nationalist movements. The emphasis on nationalism and the role it plays in the formation of postcolonial states has made Fanon's work consistently relevant – a fact made abundantly clear in the essays by **Bhabha**, **Luke Gibbons**, and **Declan Kiberd**.

Spontaneity: Its Strength and Weakness

[The] consideration of violence has led us to take account of the frequent existence of a time lag, or a difference of rhythm, between the leaders of a nationalist party and the mass of the people. In every political or trade-union organization there is a traditional gap between the rank-and-file, who demand the total and immediate bettering of their lot, and the leaders, who, since they are aware of the difficulties which may be made by the employers, seek to limit and restrain the workers' demands. This is why you often are aware of a dogged discontentment among the rank-and-file as regards their leaders. After a day spent in demonstrating for their demands, the leaders celebrate the victory, whereas the rank-and-file have a strong suspicion that they have been cheated. It is through a multiplicity of demonstrations in support of their claims and through an increase in trade-union demands that the rank-and-file achieve their political education. A politically informed trade-union member is a man who knows that a local conflict is not a decisive settlement between himself and the employers. The native intellectuals, who have studied in their respective "mother countries" the working of political parties, carefully organize similar institutions in order to mobilize the masses and bring pressure to bear on the colonial administration. The birth of nationalist parties in the colonized countries is contemporary with the formation of an intellectual elite engaged in trade. The elite will attach a fundamental importance to organization, so much so that the fetish of organization will often take precedence over a reasoned study of colonial society. The notion of the party is a notion imported from the mother country. This instrument of modern political warfare is thrown down just as it is, without the slightest modifica-tion, upon real life with all its infinite variations and lack of balance, where slavery, serfdom, barter, a skilled working class, and high finance exist side by side.

The weakness of political parties does not only lie in the mechanical application of an organization which was created to carry on the struggle of the working class inside a highly industrialized, capitalist society. If we limit ourselves to the *type* of organiza-tion, it is clear that innovations and adaptations ought to have been made. The great mistake, the inherent defect in the majority of political parties in underdeveloped regions has been, following traditional lines, to approach in the first place those elements which are the most politically conscious: the working classes in the towns, the skilled workers, and the civil servants – that is to say, a tiny portion of the population, which hardly represents more than 1 per cent.

Taken from *The Wretched of the Earth*, trans. Constance Farrington (New York: Grove Weidenfeld, 1963), pp. 107–48.

But although this proletariat has read the party publications and understood its propaganda, it is much less ready to obey in the event of orders being given which set in motion the fierce struggle for national liberation. It cannot be too strongly stressed that in the colonial territories the proletariat is the nucleus of the colonized population which has been most pampered by the colonial regime. The embryonic proletariat of the towns is in a comparatively privileged position. In capitalist countries, the working class has nothing to lose; it is they who in the long run have everything to gain. In the colonial countries the working class has everything to lose; in reality it represents that fraction of the colonized nation which is necessary and irreplaceable if the colonial machine is to run smoothly: it includes tram conductors, taxi drivers, miners, dockers, interpreters, nurses, and so on. It is these elements which constitute the most faithful followers of the nationalist parties, and who because of the privileged place which they hold in the colonial system constitute also the "bourgeois" fraction of the colonized people.

So we understand that the followers of the nationalist political parties are above all town-dwellers – shop stewards, industrial workers, intellectuals, and shopkeepers all living for the most part in the towns. Their way of thinking is already marked in many points by the comparatively well-to-do class, distinguished by technical advances, that they spring from. Here "modern ideas" reign. It is these classes that will struggle against obscurantist traditions, that will change old customs, and that will thus enter into open conflict with the old granite block upon which the nation rests.

The overwhelming majority of nationalist parties show a deep distrust toward the people of the rural areas. The fact is that as a body these people appear to them to be bogged down in fruitless inertia. The members of the nationalist parties (town workers and intellectuals) pass the same unfavorable judgment on country districts as the settlers. But if we try to understand the reasons for this mistrust on the part of the political parties with regard to the rural areas, we must remember that colonialism has often strengthened or established its domination by organizing the petrification of the country districts. Ringed round by marabouts, witch doctors, and customary chieftains, the majority of country-dwellers are still living in the feudal manner, and the full power of this medieval structure of society is maintained by the settlers' military and administrative officials.

So now the young nationalist middle class, which is above all a class interested in trade, is going to compete with these feudal lords in many and various fields. There are marabouts and medicine men who bar the way to sick people who otherwise could consult the doctor, oracles which pass judgment and thus render lawyers useless, caids who make use of their political and administrative powers to set up in trade or to start a transport service, customary chiefs who oppose, in the name of religion and tradition, the setting up of businesses and the introduction of new goods. The rising class of native traders and wholesalers needs the disappearance of these prohibitions and barriers in order to develop. The native customers, the preserve of feudal lords, who now become aware that they are more or less forbidden to buy the new products, therefore become a market to be contended for.

The feudal leaders form a screen between the young Westernized nationalists and the bulk of the people. Each time the elite tries to get through to the country people, the tribal chieftains, leaders of confraternities, and traditional authorities intensify their warnings, their threats and their excommunications. These traditional author-ities who have been upheld by the occupying power view with disfavor the attempts made by the elite to penetrate the country districts. They know very well that the ideas which are likely to be introduced by these influences coming from the towns call in question the very nature of unchanging, everlasting feudalism. Thus their enemy is not at all the occupying power with which they get along on the whole very well, but these people with modern ideas who mean to dislocate the aboriginal society, and who in doing so will take the bread out of their mouths.

The Westernized elements experience feelings with regard to the bulk of the peasantry which are reminiscent of those found among the town workers of indus-trialized countries. The history of middle-class and working-class revolutions has shown that the bulk of the peasants often constitute a brake on the revolution. Generally in industrialized countries the peasantry as a whole are the least aware, the worst organized, and at the same time the most anarchical element. They show a whole range of characteristics – individualism, lack of discipline, liking for money, and propensities toward waves of uncontrollable rage and deep discouragement which define a line of behavior that is objectively reactionary.

We have seen that the nationalist parties copy their methods from those of the Western political parties; and also, for the most part, that they do not direct their propaganda toward the rural masses. In fact, if a reasoned analysis of colonized society had been made, it would have shown them that the native peasantry lives against a background of tradition, where the traditional structure of society has remained intact, whereas in the industrialized countries it is just this traditional setting which has been broken up by the progress of industrialization. In the colonies, it is at the very core of the embryonic working class that you find individualist behavior. The landless peasants, who make up the *lumpenproletariat*, leave the coun-try districts, where vital statistics are just so many insoluble problems, rush toward the towns, crowd into tin-shack settlements, and try to make their way into the ports and cities founded by colonial domination. The bulk of the country people for their part continue to live within a rigid framework, and the extra mouths to feed have no other alternative than to emigrate toward the centers of population. The peasant who stays put defends his traditions stubbornly, and in a colonized society stands for the disciplined element whose interests lie in maintaining the social structure. It is true that this unchanging way of life, which hangs on like grim death to rigid social structures, may occasionally give birth to movements which are based on religious fanaticism or tribal wars. But in their spontaneous movements the country people as a whole remain disciplined and altruistic. The individual stands aside in favor of the community.

The country people are suspicious of the townsman. The latter dresses like a European; he speaks the European's language, works with him, sometimes even lives in the same district; so he is considered by the peasants as a turncoat who has betrayed everything that goes to make up the national heritage. The townspeople are "traitors and knaves" who seem to get on well with the occupying powers, and do their best to get on within the framework of the colonial system. This is why you often hear the country people say of town-dwellers that they have no morals. Here, we are not dealing with the old antagonism between town and country; it is the antagonism which exists between the native who is excluded from the advantages of colonialism and his counterpart who manages to turn colonial exploitation to his account.

What is more, the colonialists make use of this antagonism in their struggle against the nationalist parties. They mobilize the people of the mountains and the up-country dwellers against the townsfolk. They pitch the hinterland against the seaboard, they rouse up the tribes-people, and we need not be surprised to see Kalondji crowned king of Kasai, just as it was not surprising to see, some years ago, the assembly of the chiefs of Ghana making N'kruma dance to their tune.

The political parties do not manage to organize the country districts. Instead of using existing structures and giving them a nationalist or progressive character, they mean to try and destroy living tradition in the colonial framework. They believe it lies in their power to give the initial impulse to the nation, whereas in reality the chains forged by the colonial system still weigh it down heavily. They do not go out to find the mass of the people. They do not put their theoretical knowledge to the service of the people; they only try to erect a framework around the people which follows an a priori schedule. Thus from the capital city they will "parachute" organizers into the villages who are either unknown or too young, and who, armed with instructions from the central authority, mean to treat the *douar* or village like a factory cell.

The traditional chiefs are ignored, sometimes even persecuted. The makers of the future nation's history trample unconcernedly over small local disputes, that is to say the only existing national events, whereas they ought to make of village history – the history of traditional conflicts between clans and tribes – a harmonious whole, at one with the decisive action to which they call on the people to contribute. The old men, surrounded by respect in all traditional societies and usually invested with unquestionable moral authority, are publicly held up to ridicule. The occupying power's local authorities do not fail to use the resentment thus engendered, and keep in touch with the slightest decisions adopted by this caricature of authority. Police repression, well-informed because it is based on precise information, strikes. The parachuted leaders and the consequential members of the new assembly are arrested.

Such setbacks confirm the "theoretical analysis" of the nationalist parties. The disastrous experience of trying to enroll the country people as a whole reinforces their distrust and crystallizes their aggressiveness toward that section of the people. Even after the struggle for national freedom has succeeded, the same mistakes are made and such mistakes make for the maintenance of decentralizing and autonomist tendencies. Tribalism in the colonial phase gives way to regionalism in the national phase, and finds its expression as far as institutions are concerned in federalism.

But it may happen that the country people, in spite of the slight hold that the nationalist parties have over them, play a decisive part either in the process of the maturing of the national consciousness, or through working in with the action of nationalist parties, or, less frequently, by substituting themselves purely and simply for the sterility of these parties. For the propaganda of nationalist parties always finds an echo in the heart of the peasantry. The memory of the anti-colonial period is very much alive in the villages, where women still croon in their children's ears songs to which the warriors marched when they went out to fight the conquerers. At twelve or thirteen years of age the village children know the names of the old men who were in the last rising, and the dreams they dream in the *douars* or in the villages are not those of money or of getting through their exams like the children of the towns, but dreams of identification with some rebel or another, the story of whose heroic death still today moves them to tears.

Just when the nationalist parties are trying to organize the embryonic working class in the towns, we notice certain seemingly completely inexplicable explosions in the country districts. Take for example the famous rebellion of 1947 in Madagascar. The colonial authorities were categorical: it was a peasant rising. In fact we now know that as usual things were much more complicated than that. During the Second World War the big colonial companies greatly increased their power and became the possessors of all the land that up to then was still free. At the same time there was talk of planting the island eventually with Jewish, Kabylian, and West Indian refugees. Another rumor was equally rife – that the whites of South Africa were soon going to invade the island with the collusion of the settlers. Thus, after the war the candidates on the nationalist list were triumphantly elected. Immediately after, organized repression began of the cells of the Mouvement Democratique de la Rénovation Malgache (Democratic Movement for Madagascan Restoration). Colonialism, in order to reach its ends, used the usual traditional methods: frequent arrests, racist propaganda between tribes, and the creation of a party out of the unorganized elements of the *lumpenproletariat*. This party, with the name of the Disinherited Madagascans, gave the colonial authorities by its distinctly provocative actions the legal excuse to maintain order. It happened that this very frequent operation of liquidating a party which had been set up in advance took on in this context gigantic proportions. The rural masses, on the defensive for the last three or four years, suddenly felt themselves in deadly peril and decided to oppose colonialist forces savagely. Armed with spears, or more often simply with sticks and stones, the people flung themselves into the general revolt for national liberty. We know the end of the story.

Such armed rebellions only represent one of the means used by the country-dwellers to join in the national struggle. Sometimes when the nationalist party in the towns is tracked down by police repression the peasants carry on the tradition of urban agitation. News of the repression comes to the country districts in a grossly exaggerated form; the tale runs that the leaders are arrested, that machine-gunning is rife, that the town is running red with the blood of Negroes, or that the small settlers are bathing in Arab blood. Thereupon the accumulated, exacerbated hate explodes. The neighboring police barracks is captured, the policemen are hacked to pieces, the local school-master is murdered, the doctor only gets away with his life because he was not at home, etc. Pacifying forces are hurried to the spot and the air force bombards it. Then the banner of revolt is unfurled, the old warriorlike traditions spring up again, the women cheer, the men organize and take up positions in the mountains, and guerrilla war begins. The peasantry spontaneously gives concrete form to the general insecurity; and colonialism takes fright and either continues the war or negotiates.

What is the reaction of the nationalist parties to this eruption of the peasant masses into the national struggle? We have seen that the majority of nationalist parties have not written into their propaganda the necessity for armed intervention. They do not oppose the continuing of the rebellion, but they content themselves with leaving it to the spontaneous action of the country people. As a whole they treat this new element as a sort of manna fallen from heaven, and pray to goodness that it'll go on falling. They make the most of the manna, but do not attempt to organize the rebellion. They don't send leaders into the countryside to educate the people politically, or to increase their awareness or put the struggle onto a higher level. All they do is to hope that, carried onward by its own momentum, the action of the people will not come to a standstill. There is no contamination of the rural movement by the urban movement; each develops according to its own dialectic.

The nationalist parties do not attempt to give definite orders to the country people, although the latter are perfectly ready to listen to them. They offer them no objective; they simply hope that this new movement will go on indefinitely and that the bombardments will not put an end to it. Thus we see that even when such an occasion offers, the nationalist parties make no use at all of the opportunity which is offered to them to integrate the people of the countryside, to educate them politically, and to raise the level of their struggle. The old attitude of mistrust toward the countryside is criminally evident.

The political leaders go underground in the towns, give the impression to the colonialists that they have no connection with the rebels, or seek refuge abroad. It very seldom happens that they join the people in the hills. In Kenya, for example, during the Mau-Mau rebellion, not a single well-known nationalist declared his affiliation with the movement, or even tried to defend the men involved in it.

The different strata of the nation never have it out with each other to any advantage; there is no settling of accounts between them. Thus, when independence is achieved, after the repression practiced on the country people, after the entente between colonialism and the national parties, it is no wonder that you find this incomprehension to an even greater degree. The country-dwellers are slow to take up the structural reforms proposed by the goverment; and equally slow in following their social reforms, even though they may be very progressive if viewed objectively, precisely because the people now at the head of affairs did not explain to the people as a whole during the colonial period what were the aims of the party, the national trends, or the problems of international politics.

The mistrust which country-dwellers and those still living within the feudal system feel toward nationalist parties during the colonial period is followed by a similarly strong hostility during the national period. The colonial secret services which were not disbanded after independence keep up the discontentment and still manage to make serious difficulties for the young governments. All in all, the government is only being made to pay for its laziness during the period of liberation, and its unfailing mistrust of the country people. The nation may well have a reasonable, even progressive, head to it; its body will remain weak, stubborn, and non-cooperative.

The temptation therefore will be to break up this body by centralizing the administration and surrounding the people by a firm administrative framework. This is one of the reasons why you often hear it said that in underdeveloped countries a small dose of dictatorship is needed. The men at the head of things distrust the people of the countryside; moreover, this distrust takes on serious proportions. This is the case for example of certain governments which, long after national independence is declared, continue to consider the interior of the country as a non-pacified area where the chief of state or his ministers only go when the national army is carrying out maneuvers there. For all practical purposes, the interior ranks with the unknown. Paradoxically, the national government in its dealings with the country people as a whole is reminiscent of certain features of the former colonial power. "We don't quite know how the mass of these people will react" is the cry; and the young ruling class does not hesitate to assert that "they need the thick end of the stick if this country is to get out of the Middle Ages." But as we have seen, the offhand way in which the political parties treated the rural population during the colonial phase could only prejudice national unity at the very moment when the young nation needs to get off to a good start.

Sometimes colonialism attempts to dislocate or create diversions around the upward thrust of nationalism. Instead of organizing the sheiks and the chiefs against the "revolutionaries" in the towns, native committees organize the tribes and confraternities into parties. Confronted with the urban party which was beginning to "embody the national will" and to constitute a danger for the colonial regime, splinter groups are born, and tendencies and parties which have their origin in ethnic or regional differences spring up. It is the entire tribe which is turning itself into a political party, closely advised by the colonialists. The conference table can now be pulled out. The party which advocates unity will be drowned in the computations of the various splinter groups, while the tribal parties will oppose centralization and unity, and will denounce the party of unity as a dictatorship.

Later on, the same tactics will be used by the national opposition. The occupying power has made its choice from among the two or three nationalist parties which led the struggle for liberation. The ways of choosing are well-known: when a party has achieved national unanimity and has imposed itself on the occupying power as the sole spokesman of the nation, the colonial power starts complicated maneuverings and delays the opening of negotiations as much as ever it can. Such a delay will be used to fritter away the demands of this party or get its leaders to put certain "extremist" elements into the background.

If on the other hand no party really succeeds in imposing itself, the occupying power is content to extend privileges to the party which it considers to be the most "reasonable." The nationalist parties which have not taken part in the negotiations engage in denunciations of the agreement reached between the other party and the occupying power. The party which takes over the reins from the colonialists, conscious of the danger with which the extremely demagogical and confused attitude of the rival party threatens it, tries to disband its competitor and to condemn it to illegality. The persecuted party has no alternative but to seek refuge in the outskirts of the towns and in the country districts. It tries to rouse the people of the country against the "traitors of the seaboard and the corrupt politicians of the capital." Any excuse is good enough: religious feeling, innovations made by the new government which break from tradition, and so on. The obscurantist tendencies of the country-dwellers are exploited to the full. The so-called revolutionary doctrine in fact rests on the retrograde, emotional, and spontaneous nature of the country districts. Here and there it is whispered that the mountain is moving, that the countryside is discontented. It's said that in a certain place the police have opened fire on the peasantry, that reinforcements have been sent out, and that the government is on the point of falling. The parties in opposition, since they have no clear program, have no other end in view but to take the place of the governing party; and with this as their goal they place their destiny in the hands of the obscure, spontaneous mass of the peasantry.

Inversely, it sometimes happens that the opposition no longer relies for support on the country people, but rather on the progressive elements found in the trade unions of the young nation. In this case the government calls upon the countryfolk to oppose the demands of the workers, which they denounce as the maneuvers of anti-traditionalist adventurers. The facts we have established regarding the political parties are once more observed, *mutatis mutandis*, on the level of the trade unions. In the beginning the trade-union organizations in colonial territories are regularly local branches of the trade unions of the mother country, and their orders are the echo of those given in the mother country.

Once the decisive phase of the struggle for liberation emerges, some native trade unionists will decide upon the creation of national unions. The old structure, imported from the mother country, will suffer heavy losses as the native members desert it. This creating of new unions is a fresh element of pressure in the hands of the populations of the towns upon colonialism. We have seen that the working class in the colonies is in an embryonic state and represents that fraction of the people which is the most favored. The national unions are born out of the struggle for independence organized in the towns, and their program is above all a political program and a nationalist program. Such a national union which comes into being during the decisive phase of the fight for independence is in fact the legal enlistment of conscious, dynamic nationalist elements.

The mass of the country-dwellers, looked down upon by the political parties, continue to be kept at a distance. Of course there will be an agricultural workers' union there, but its creation is simply to supply an answer to the categorical necessity to "present a united front to colonialism." The trade-union officials who have won their colors in the field of the union organizations of the mother country have no idea how to organize the mass of country people. They have lost all contact with the peasantry and their primary preoccupation is to enlist dockers, metallurgists, and state-employed gas and electricity workers in their ranks.

During the colonial phase, the nationalist trade-union organizations constitute an impressive striking power. In the towns, the trade unionists can bring to a standstill, or at any rate slow down at any given moment, the colonialist economy. Since the European settlement is often confined to the towns, the psychological effects of demonstrations on that settlement are considerable: there is no electricity, no gas, the dust bins are left unemptied, and goods rot on the quays.

These little islands of the mother country which the towns constitute in the colonial structure are deeply conscious of trade-union action; the fortress of colonialism which the capital represents staggers under their blows. But the "interior" – the mass of country-dwellers – knows nothing of this conflict.

Thus we see that there is a lack of proportion from the national point of view between the importance of the trade unions and the rest of the nation. After independence, the workers who have joined the unions get the impression that they are living in a vacuum. The limited objective that they set themselves turns out to be, at the very moment that it is attained, extremely precarious, having regard to the immensity of the task of national reconstruction. When faced with the national middle class whose connections with the government are often closely linked, the trade-union leaders discover that they can no longer limit themselves to working-class agitation. Isolated by their very nature from the country people, and incapable of giving directions once outside the suburbs, the unions become more and more political in their attitude. In fact, the unions become candidates for governmental power. They try by every means to corner the middle classes: they protest against the maintenance of foreign bases on the national territory, they denounce trade agreements, and they oppose the national government's foreign policy. The workers, now that they have their "independence," do not know where to go from there. For the day after independence is declared the trade unions realize that if their social demands were to be expressed, they would scandalize the rest of the nation: for the workers are in fact the most favored section of the population, and represent the most comfortably off fraction of the people. Any movement starting off to fight for the bettering of living conditions for the dockers and workmen would not only be very unpopular, but would also run the risk of provoking the hostility of the disinherited rural population. The trade unions, to whom all trade-union activity is forbidden, merely mark time.

This unhealthy state of affairs simply shows the objective necessity of a social program which will appeal to the nation as a whole. Suddenly the unions discover that the back-country too ought to be enlightened and organized. But since at no time have they taken care to establish working links between themselves and the mass of the peasants, and since this peasantry precisely constitutes the only spontaneously revolutionary force of the country, the trade unions will give proof of their inefficiency and find out for themselves the anachronistic nature of their programs.

The trade-union leaders, steeped in working-class political action, automatically go from there to the preparation of a *coup d'état*. But here again the back-country is left out; this is a limited settling of accounts only, between the national middle class and the union workers. The national middle class, taking up the old traditions of colonialism, makes a show of its military and police forces, while the unions organize mass meetings and mobilize tens of thousands of members. The peasants confronted with this national middle class and these workers, who after all can eat their fill, look on, shrugging their shoulders; and they shrug their shoulders because they know very well that both sides look on them as a makeweight. The unions, the parties, or the government in a kind of immoral Machiavellian fashion all make use of the peasant masses as a blind, inert tactical force: brute force, as it were.

On the other hand, in certain circumstances the country people are going to intervene in decisive fashion both in the struggle for national freedom and in the way that the future nation marks out for itself. This phenomenon takes on a fundamental importance for underdeveloped countries; this is why we propose to study it in detail.

We have seen that inside the nationalist parties, the will to break colonialism is linked with another quite different will: that of coming to a friendly agreement with it. Within these parties, the two processes will sometimes continue side by side. In the first place, when the intellectual elements have carried out a prolonged analysis of the true nature of colonialism and of the international situation, they will begin to criticize their party's lack of ideology and the poverty of its tactics and strategy. They begin to question their leaders ceaselessly on crucial points: "What is nationalism? What sense do you give to this word? What is its meaning? Independence for what? And in the first place, how do you propose to achieve it?" They ask these questions, and, at the same time, require that the problems of methodology should be vigorously tackled. They are ready to suggest that electoral resources should be supplemented by "all other means." After the first skirmishes, the official leaders speedily dispose of this effervescence which they are quick to label as childishness. But since these demands are not simply effervescence, nor the sign of immaturity, the revolutionary elements which subscribe to them will rapidly be isolated. The official leaders, draped in their years of experience, will pitilessly disown these "adventurers and anarchists."

The party machine shows itself opposed to any innovation. The revolutionary minority finds itself alone, confronted with leaders who are terrified and worried by the idea that they could be swept away by a maelstrom whose nature, force, or direction they cannot even imagine. The second process concerns the main leaders, or their seconds in command, who were marked out for police repression under the colonialists. It must be emphasized that these men have come to the head of the party by their untiring work, their spirit of sacrifice, and a most exemplary patriotism. Such men, who have worked their way up from the bottom, are often unskilled workers, seasonal laborers, or even sometimes chronically unemployed. For them the fact of militating in a national party is not simply taking part in politics; it is choosing the only means whereby they can pass from the status of an animal to that of a human being. Such men, hampered by the excessive legalism of the party, will show within the limits of the activities for which they are responsible a spirit of initiative, courage, and a sense of the importance of the struggle, which mark them out almost automatically as targets for colonialist repression. Arrested, condemned, tortured, finally amnestied, they use their time in prison to clarify their ideas and strengthen their determination. Through hunger strikes and the violent brotherhood of the prisons' quicklime they live on, hoping for their freedom, looking on it as an opportunity to start an armed struggle. But at one and the same time outside the prison walls colonialism, attacked from all sides, is making advances to the nationalist moderates.

So we can observe the process whereby the rupture occurs between the illegal and legal tendencies in the party. The illegal minority is made to feel that they are undesirables and are shunned by the people that matter. The legal members of their party come to their aid with great precaution, but already there is a rift between the two tendencies. The illegalists, therefore, will get in touch with the intellectual elements whose attitude they were able to understand a few years back; and an underground party, an offshoot of the legal party, will be the result of this meeting. But the repression of these wayward elements intensifies as the legal party draws nearer to colonialism and attempts to modify it "from the inside." The illegal minority thus finds itself in a historical blind alley.

Boycotted by the towns, these men first settle in the outskirts of the suburbs. But the police network traps them and forces them to leave the towns for good, and to quit the scenes of political action. They fall back toward the countryside and the mountains, toward the peasant people. From the beginning, the peasantry closes in around them, and protects them from being pursued by the police. The militant nationalist who decides to throw in his lot with the country people instead of playing at hide-and-seek with the police in urban centers will lose nothing. The peasant's cloak will wrap him around with a gentleness and firmness that he never suspected. These men, who are in fact exiled to the backwoods, who are cut off from the urban background against which they had defined their ideas of the nation and of the political fight, these men have in fact become "Maquisards." Since they are obliged to move about the whole time in order to escape from the police, often at night so as not to attract attention, they will have good reason to wander through their country and to get to know it. The cafés are forgotten; so are the arguments about the next elections or the spitefulness of some policeman or other. Their ears hear the true voice of the country, and their eyes take in the great and infinite poverty of their people. They realize the precious time that has been wasted in useless commentaries upon the colonial regime. They finally come to understand that the changeover will not be a reform, nor a bettering of things. They come to understand, with a sort of bewilderment that will from henceforth never quite leave them, that political action in the towns will always be powerless to modify or overthrow the colonial regime.

These men get used to talking to the peasants. They discover that the mass of the country people have never ceased to think of the problem of their liberation except in terms of violence, in terms of taking back the land from the foreigners, in terms of national struggle, and of armed insurrection. It is all very simple. These men discover a coherent people who go on living, as it were, statically, but who keep their moral values and their devotion to the nation intact. They discover a people that is generous, ready to sacrifice themselves completely, an impatient people, with a stony pride. It is understandable that the meeting between these militants with the police on their track and these mettlesome masses of people, who are rebels by instinct, can produce an explosive mixture of unusual potentiality. The men coming from the towns learn their lessons in the hard school of the people; and at the same time these men open classes for the people in military and political education. The people furbish up their weapons; but in fact the classes do not last long, for the masses come to know once again the strength of their own muscles, and push the leaders on to prompt action. The armed struggle has begun.

The rising disconcerts the political parties. Their doctrine, in fact, has always affirmed the uselessness of a trial of force, and their very existence is a constant condemnation of all rebellion. Secretly, certain political parties share the optimism of the settlers, and congratulate themselves on being well away from this act of madness which, it's said, will be put down with bloodshed. But once the match is lit, the blaze spreads like wildfire through the whole country. The armored cars and the airplanes do not win through with unqualified success. Faced with the full extent of the trouble, colonialism begins to reflect on the matter. At the very core of the oppressing nation voices are raised, and listened to, which draw attention to the gravity of the situation.

As for the people, they join in the new rhythm of the nation, in their mud huts and in their dreams. Under their breath and from their hearts' core they sing endless songs of praise to the glorious fighters. The tide of rebellion has already flooded the whole nation. Now it is the parties' turn to be isolated.

The leaders of the rising, however, realize that some day or another the rebellion must come to include the towns. This awareness is not fortuitous; it is the crowning point of the dialectic which reigns over the development of an armed struggle for national liberation. Although the country districts represent inexhaustible reserves of popular energy, and groups of armed men ensure that insecurity is rife there, colonialism does not doubt the strength of its system. It does not feel that it is endangered fundamentally. The rebel leaders therefore decide to bring the war into the enemy's camp, that is to say into his grandiose, peaceful cities.

The organizing of the rising in the centers of population sets the leaders some difficult problems. We have seen that the greater part of the leaders, born or brought up in the towns, have fled from their normal background because they were wanted by the colonialist police and were in general unappreciated by the cautious, reasonable administrators of the political parties. Their retreat into the country was both a flight from persecution and a sign of their distrust for the old political structure. The natural receiving stations in the towns for these leaders are well-known nationalists who are in the thick of the political parties. But we have seen that their recent history was precisely an offshoot from these timid, nervous officials who spend their time in ceaseless lamentation over the misdeeds of colonialism.

Moreover, the first overtures which the men of the Maquis make toward their former friends – precisely those whom they consider to be the most toward the Left – will confirm their fears and will take away even the wish to see their old companions again. In fact the rebellion, which began in the country districts, will filter into the towns through that fraction of the peasant population which is blocked on the outer fringe of the urban centers, that fraction which has not yet succeeded in finding a bone to gnaw in the colonial system. The men whom the growing population of the country districts and colonial expropriation have brought to desert their family holdings circle tirelessly around the different towns, hoping that one day or another they will be allowed inside. It is within this mass of humanity, this people of the shanty towns, at the core of the *lumpenproletariat*, that the rebellion will find its urban spearhead. For the *lumpenproletariat*, that horde of starving men, uprooted from their tribe and from their clan, constitutes one of the most spontaneous and the most radically revolutionary forces of a colonized people.

In Kenya, in the years preceding the Mau-Mau revolt, it was noticeable how the British colonial authorities multiplied intimidatory measures against the *lumpenproletariat*. The police forces and the missionaries coordinated their efforts, in the years 1950–51, in order to make a suitable response to the enormous influx of young Kenyans coming from the country districts and the forests, who when they did not manage to find a market for their labor took to stealing, debauchery, and alcoholism. Juvenile delinquency in the colonized countries is the direct result of the existence of a *lumpenproletariat*. In parallel fashion, in the Congo, Draconian measures were taken from 1957 onward to send back to the countryside the "young hooligans" who were disturbing the social order. Resettlement camps were opened and put under the charge of evangelical missions, protected, of course, by the Belgian army.

The constitution of a *lumpenproletariat* is a phenomenon which obeys its own logic, and neither the brimming activity of the missionaries nor the decrees of the central government can check its growth. This *lumpenproletariat* is like a horde of rats; you may kick them and throw stones at them, but despite your efforts they'll go on gnawing at the roots of the tree.

The shantytown sanctions the native's biological decision to invade, at whatever cost and if necessary by the most cryptic methods, the enemy fortress. The *lumpen-proletariat*, once it is constituted, brings all its forces to endanger the "security" of the town, and is the sign of the irrevocable decay, the gangrene ever present at the heart of colonial domination. So the pimps, the hooligans, the unemployed, and the petty criminals, urged on from behind, throw themselves into the struggle for liberation like stout working men. These classless idlers will by militant and decisive action discover the path that leads to nationhood. They won't become reformed characters to please colonial society, fitting in with the morality of its rulers; quite on the contrary, they take for granted the impossibility of their entering the city save by hand grenades and revolvers. These workless less-than-men are rehabilitated in their own eyes and in the eyes of history. The prostitutes too, and the maids who are paid two pounds a month, all the hopeless dregs of humanity, all who turn in circles between suicide and madness, will recover their balance, once more go forward, and march proudly in the great procession of the awakened nation.

The nationalist parties do not understand this new phenomenon which precipitates their disintegration. The outbreak of the rebellion in the towns changes the nature of the struggle. Whereas before the colonialist troops were entirely concerned with the country districts, we now see them falling back in haste on the towns in order to ensure the safety of the town population and their property. The forces of repression spread out; danger is present everywhere; now it's the very soil of the nation, the whole of the colony, which goes into a trance. The armed groups of peasants look on while the mailed fist loses its grip. The rising in the towns is like an unhoped-for gas balloon.

The leaders of the rising who see an ardent and enthusiastic people striking decisive blows at the colonialist machine are strengthened in their mistrust of traditional policy. Every success confirms their hostility toward what in future they will describe as mouthwash, wordspinning, blather, and fruitless agitation. They feel a positive hatred for the "politics" of demagogy, and that is why in the beginning we observe a veritable triumph for the cult of spontaneity.

The many peasant risings which have their roots in the country districts bear witness wherever they occur to the ubiquitous and usually solidly massed presence of the new nation. Every native who takes up arms is a part of the nation which from henceforward will spring to life. Such peasant revolts endanger the colonial regime; they mobilize its troops, making them spread out, and threaten at every turn to crush them. They hold one doctrine only: to act in such a way that the nation may exist. There is no program; there are no speeches or resolutions, and no political trends. The problem is clear: the foreigners must go; so let us form a common front against the oppressor and let us strengthen our hands by armed combat.

So long as the uncertainty of colonialism continues, the national cause goes on progressing, and becomes the cause of each and all. The plans for liberation are sketched out; already they include the whole country. During this period spontaneity is king, and initiative is localized. On every hill a government in miniature is formed and takes over power. Everywhere – in the valleys and in the forests, in the jungle and in the villages – we find a national authority. Each man or woman brings the nation to life by his or her action, and is pledged to ensure its triumph in their locality. We are dealing with a strategy of immediacy which is both radical and totalitarian: the aim and the program of each locally constituted group is local liberation. If the nation is everywhere, then she is here. One step further, and only here is she to be found. Tactics are mistaken for strategy. The art of politics is simply transformed into the art of war; the political militant is the rebel. To fight the war and to take part in politics: the two things become one and the same.

This people that has lost its birthright, that is used to living in the narrow circle of feuds and rivalries, will now proceed in an atmosphere of solemnity to cleanse and purify the face of the nation as it appears in the various localities. In a veritable collective ecstasy, families which have always been traditional enemies decide to rub out old scores and to forgive and forget. There are numerous reconciliations. Long-buried but unforgettable hatreds are brought to light once more, so that they may more surely be rooted out. The taking on of nationhood involves a growth of awareness. The national unity is first the unity of a group, the disappearance of old quarrels and the final liquidation of unspoken grievances. At the same time, forgiveness and purification include those natives who by their activities and by their complicity with the occupier have dishonored their country. On the other hand, traitors and those who have sold out to the enemy will be judged and punished. In undertaking this onward march, the people legislates, finds itself, and wills itself to sovereignty. In every corner that is thus awakened from colonial slumber, life is lived at an impossibly high temperature. There is a permanent outpouring in all the villages of spectacular generosity, of disarming kindness, and willingness, which cannot ever be doubted, to die for the "cause." All this is evocative of a confraternity, a church, and a mystical body of belief at one and the same time. No native can remain unmoved by this new rhythm which leads the nation on. Messengers are despatched to neighboring tribes. They constitute the first system of intercommunication in the rebellion, and bring movement and cadence to districts which are still motionless. Even tribes whose stubborn rivalry is well known now disarm with joyful tears and pledge help and succour to each other. Marching shoulder to shoulder in the armed struggle these men join with those who yesterday were their enemies. The circle of the nation widens and fresh ambushes to entrap the enemy hail the entry of new tribes upon the scene. Each village finds that it is itself both an absolute agent of revolution, and also a link in the chain of action. Solidarity between tribes and between villages, national solidarity, is in the first place expressed by the increasing blows struck at the enemy. Every new group which is formed, each fresh salvo that bursts out is an indication that each is on the enemy's track, and that each is prepared to meet him.

This solidarity will be much more clearly shown during the second period, which is characterized by the putting into operation of the enemy offensive. The colonial forces, once the explosion has taken place, regroup and reorganize, inaugurating methods of warfare which correspond to the nature of the rising. This offensive will call in question the ideal, Utopian atmosphere of the first period. The enemy attacks, and concentrates large forces on certain definite points. The local group is quickly over-run, all the more so because it tends to seek the forefront of the battle. The optimism which reigned in the first period makes the local group fearless, or rather careless. It is persuaded that its own mountain peak is the nation, and because of this it refuses to abandon it, or to beat a retreat. But the losses are serious, and doubts spring up and begin to weigh heavily upon the rebels. The group faces a local attack as if it were a decisive test. It behaves as if the fate of the whole country was literally at stake, here and now.

But we should make it quite clear that this spontaneous impetuosity which is determined to settle the fate of the colonial system immediately is condemned, in so far as it is a doctrine of instantaneity, to self-repudiation. For the most everyday, practical realism takes the place of yesterday's effusion, and substitutes itself for the illusion of eternity. The hard lesson of facts, the bodies mown down by machine guns: these call forth a complete reinterpretation of events. The simple instinct to survive engenders a less rigid, more mobile attitude. This modification in fighting technique characterized the first months of the war of liberation of the people of Angola. We may remember that on March 15, 1961, a group of two or three thousand Angolan peasants threw themselves against the Portuguese positions. Men, women, and children, armed and unarmed, afire with courage and enthusiasm, then flung themselves in successive waves of compact masses upon the districts where the settler, the soldier, and the Portuguese flag held sway. Villages and airports were encircled and subjected to frequent attacks, but it must be added that thousands of Angolans were mown down by colonialist machine guns. It did not take long for the leaders of the Angolan rising to realize that they must find some other methods if they really wanted to free their country. So during the last few months[1] the Angolan leader Holden Roberto has reorganized the National Angolan Army, using the experience gained in various other wars of liberation, and employing guerrilla techniques.

The fact is that in guerrilla warfare the struggle no longer concerns the place where you are, but the place where you are going. Each fighter carries his warring country between his bare toes. The national army of liberation is not an army which engages once and for all with the enemy; it is rather an army which goes from village to village, falling back on the forests, and dancing for joy when in the valley below there comes into view the white column of dust that the enemy columns kick up. The tribes go into action, and the various groups move about, changing their ground. The people of the north move toward the west; the people of the plains go up into the mountains. There is absolutely no strategically privileged position. The enemy thinks he is pursuing us; but we always manage to harry his rearguard, striking back at him at the very moment when he thinks he has annihilated us. From now on, it is *we* who pursue *him*; in spite of all his technical advantages and his superior artillery power the enemy gives the impression that he is floundering and getting bogged down. And as for us, we sing, we go on singing.

Meantime, however, the leaders of the rising realize that the various groups must be enlightened; that they must be educated and indoctrinated, and that an army and a central authority must be created. The scattering of the nation, which is the manifestation of a nation in arms, needs to be corrected and to become a thing of the past. Those leaders who have fled from the useless political activity of the towns rediscover politics, no longer as a way of lulling people to sleep nor as a means of mystification, but as the only method of intensifying the struggle and of preparing the people to undertake the governing of their country clearly and lucidly. The leaders of the rebellion come to see that even very large-scale peasant risings need to be controlled and directed into certain channels. These leaders are led to renounce the movement in so far as it can be termed a peasant revolt, and to transform it into a revolutionary war. They discover that the success of the struggle presupposes clear objectives, a definite methodology, and above all the need for the mass of the people to realize that their unorganized efforts can only be a temporary dynamic. You can hold out for three days – maybe even for three months – on the strength of the admixture of sheer resentment contained in the mass of the people; but you won't win a national war, you'll never overthrow the terrible enemy machine, and you won't change human beings if you forget to raise the standard of consciousness of the rank-and-file. Neither stubborn courage nor fine slogans are enough.

Moreover, as it develops the war of liberation can be counted upon to strike a decisive blow at the faith of the leaders. The enemy, in fact, changes his tactics. At opportune moments he combines his policy of brutal repression with spectacular gestures of friendship, maneuvers calculated to sow division, and "psychological action." Here and there he tries with success to revive tribal feuds, using *agents provocateurs* and practicing what might be called counter-subversion. Colonialism will use two types of natives to gain its ends; and the first of these are the traditional collaborators – chiefs, caids, and witch doctors. The mass of the peasantry is steeped, as we have seen, in a changeless, ever-recurring life without incident; and they continue to revere their religious leaders who are descended from ancient families. The tribe follows, as one man, the way marked out for it by its traditional chief. Colonialism secures for itself the services of these confidential agents by pensioning them off at a ransom price.

Colonialism will also find in the *lumpenproletariat* a considerable space for maneuvering. For this reason any movement for freedom ought to give its fullest attention to this *lumpenproletariat*. The peasant masses will always answer the call to rebellion, but if the rebellion's leaders think it will be able to develop without taking the masses into consideration, the *lumpenproletariat* will throw itself into the battle and will take part in the conflict – but this time on the side of the oppressor. And the oppressor, who never loses a chance of setting the niggers against each other, will be extremely skillful in using that ignorance and incomprehension which are the weaknesses of the *lumpenproletariat*. If this available reserve of human effort is not immediately organized by the forces of rebellion, it will find itself fighting as hired soldiers side by side with the colonial troops. In Algeria, it is the *lumpenproletariat* which furnished the harkis and the messalists;[2] in Angola, it supplied the road openers who nowadays precede the Portuguese armed columns; in the Congo, we find once more the *lumpenproletariat* in regional manifestations in Kasai and Katanga, while at Leopoldville the Congo's enemies made use of it to organize "spontaneous" mass meetings against Lumumba.

The enemy is aware of ideological weaknesses, for he analyzes the forces of rebellion and studies more and more carefully the aggregate enemy which makes up a colonial people; he is also aware of the spiritual instability of certain layers of the population. The enemy discovers the existence, side by side with the disciplined and well-organized advance guard of rebellion, of a mass of men whose participation is constantly at the mercy of their being for too long accustomed to physiological wretchedness, humiliation, and irresponsibility. The enemy is ready to pay a high price for the services of this mass. He will create spontaneity with bayonets and exemplary floggings. Dollars and Belgian francs pour into the Congo, while in Madagascar levies against Hova increase and in Algeria native recruits, who are in fact hostages, are enlisted in the French forces. The leaders of the rebellion literally see the nation capsizing. Whole tribes join up as harkis, and, using the modern weapons that they have been given, go on the warpath and invade the territory of the neighboring tribe, which for this occasion has been labeled as nationalist. That unanimity in battle, so fruitful and grandiose in the first days of the rebellion, undergoes a change. National unity crumbles away; the rising is at a decisive turning of the way. Now the political education of the masses is seen to be a historic necessity.

That spectacular volunteer movement which meant to lead the colonized people to supreme sovereignty at one fell swoop, that certainty which you had that all portions of the nation would be carried along with you at the same speed and led onward by the same light, that strength which gave you hope: all now are seen in the light of experience to be symptoms of a very great weakness. While the native thought that he could pass without transition from the status of a colonized person to that of a self-governing citizen of an independent nation, while he grasped at the mirage of his muscles' own immediacy, he made no real progress along the road to knowledge. His consciousness remains rudimentary. We have seen that the native enters passionately into the fight, above all if that fight is an armed one. The peasants threw themselves into the rebellion with all the more enthusiasm in that they had never stopped clutching at a way of life which was in practice anti-colonial. From all eternity, by means of manifold tricks and through a system of checks and balances reminiscent of a conjurer's most successful sleight-of-hand, the country people had more or less kept their individuality free from colonial impositions. They even believed that colonialism was not the victor. The peasant's pride, his hesitation to go down into the towns and to mingle with the world that the foreigner had built, his perpetual shrinking back at the approach of the agents of colonial administration: all these reactions signified that to the dual world of the settler he opposed his own duality.

Racial feeling, as opposed to racial prejudice, and that determination to fight for one's life which characterizes the native's reply to oppression are obviously good enough reasons for joining in the fight. But you do not carry on a war, nor suffer brutal and widespread repression, nor look on while all other members of your family are wiped out in order to make racialism or hatred triumph. Racialism and hatred and resentment – "a legitimate desire for revenge" – cannot sustain a war of liberation. Those lightning flashes of consciousness which fling the body into stormy paths or which throw it into an almost pathological trance where the face of the other beckons me on to giddiness, where my blood calls for the blood of the other, where by sheer inertia my death calls for the death of the other – that intense emotion of the first few hours falls to pieces if it is left to feed on its own substance. It is true that the never-ending exactions of the colonial forces reintroduce emotional elements into the struggle, and give the militant fresh motives for hating and new reasons to go off hunting for a settler to shoot. But the leader realizes, day in and day out, that hatred alone cannot draw up a program. You will only risk the defeat of your own ends if you depend on the enemy (who of course will always manage to commit as many crimes as possible) to widen the gap, and to throw the whole people on the side of the rebellion. At all events, as we have noticed, the enemy tries to win the support of certain sectors of the population, of certain districts, and of certain chiefs. As the struggle is carried on, instructions are issued to the settlers and to the police forces; their behavior takes on a different complexion: it becomes more "human." They even go as far as to call a native "Mister" when they have dealings with him. Attentions and acts of courtesy come to be the rule. The native is in fact made to feel that things are changing.

The native, who did not take up arms simply because he was dying of hunger and because he saw his own social forms disintegrating before his eyes, but also because the settler considered him to be an animal, and treated him as such, reacts very favorably to such measures. Hatred is disarmed by these psychological windfalls. Technologists and sociologists shed their light on colonialist maneuvers, and studies on the various "complexes" pour forth: the frustration complex, the belligerency complex, and the colonizability complex. The native is promoted; they try to disarm him with their psychology, and of course they throw in a few shillings too. And these miserable methods, this eyewash administered drop by drop, even meet with some success. The native is so starved for anything, anything at all that will turn him into a human being, any bone of humanity flung to him, that his hunger is incoercible, and these poor scraps of charity may, here and there, overwhelm him. His consciousness is so precarious and dim that it is affected by the slightest spark of kindliness. Now it is that the first great undifferentiated thirst for light is continually threatened by mystification. The violent, total demands which lit up the sky now become modest, and withdraw into themselves. The springing wolf which wanted to devour every-thing at sight, and the rising gust of wind which was to have brought about a real revolution run the risk of becoming quite unrecognizable if the struggle continues: and continue it does. The native may at any moment let himself be disarmed by some concession or another.

The discovery of this instability inherent in the native is a frightening experience for the leaders of the rebellion. At first they are completely bewildered; then they are made to realize by this new drift of things that explanation is very necessary, and that they must stop the native consciousness from getting bogged down. For the war goes on; and the enemy organizes, reinforces his position, and comes to guess the native's strategy. The struggle for national liberation does not consist in spanning the gap at one stride; the drama has to be played out in all its difficulty every day, and the sufferings engendered far out-measure any endured during the colonial period. Down in the towns the settlers seem to have changed. Our people are happier; they are respected. Day after day goes by; the native who is taking part in the struggle and the people who ought to go on giving him their help must not waver. They must not imagine that the end is already won. When the real objectives of the fight are shown to them, they must not think that they are impossible to attain. Once again, things must be explained to them; the people must see where they are going, and how they are to get there. The war is not a single battle, but rather a series of local engage-ments; and to tell the truth, none of these are decisive.

So we must be sparing of our strength, and not throw everything into the scales once and for all. Colonialism has greater and wealthier resources than the native. The war goes on; the enemy holds his own; the final settling of accounts will not be today, nor yet tomorrow, for the truth is that the settlement was begun on the very first day of the war, and it will be ended not because there are no more enemies left to kill, but quite simply because the enemy, for various reasons, will come to realize that his interest lies in ending the struggle and in recognizing the sovereignty of the colonized people. The objectives of the struggle ought not to be chosen without discrimination, as they were in the first days of the struggle. If care is not taken, the people may begin to question the prolongation of the war at any moment that the enemy grants some concession. They are so used to the settler's scorn and to his declared intention to maintain his oppression at whatever cost that the slightest suggestion of any generous gesture or of any good will is hailed with astonishment and delight, and the native bursts into a hymn of praise. It must be clearly explained to the rebel that he must on no account be blindfolded by the enemy's concessions. These concessions are no more than sops; they have no bearing on the essential question; and from the native's point of view, we may lay down that a concession has nothing to do with the essentials if it does not affect the real nature of the colonial regime.

For, as a matter of fact, the more brutal manifestations of the presence of the occupying power may perfectly well disappear. Indeed, such a spectacular disappearance turns out to be both a saving of expense to the colonial power and a positive way of preventing its forces being spread out over a wide area. But such a disappearance will be paid for at a high price: the price of a much stricter control of the country's future destiny. Historic examples can be quoted to help the people to see that the masquerade of giving concessions, and even the mere acceptance of the principle of concessions at any price, have been bartered by not a few countries for a servitude that is less blatant but much more complete. The people and all their leaders ought to know that historical law which lays down that certain concessions are the cloak for a tighter rein. But when there has been no work of clarification, it is astonishing with what complacency the leaders of certain political parties enter into undefined com- promises with the former colonialist. The native must realize that colonialism never gives anything away for nothing. Whatever the native may gain through political or armed struggle is not the result of the kindliness or good will of the settler; it simply shows that he cannot put off granting concessions any longer. Moreover, the native ought to realize that it is not colonialism that grants such concessions, but he himself that extorts them. When the British government decides to bestow a few more seats in the National Assembly of Kenya upon the African population, it needs plenty of effrontery or else a complete ignorance of facts to maintain that the British govern- ment has made a concession. Is it not obvious that it is the Kenyan people who have made the concession? The colonized peoples, the peoples who have been robbed, must lose the habits of mind which have characterized them up to now. If need be, the native can accept a compromise with colonialism, but never a surrender of principle.

All this taking stock of the situation, this enlightening of consciousness, and this advance in the knowledge of the history of societies are only possible within the framework of an organization, and inside the structure of a people. Such an organiza- tion is set afoot by the use of revolutionary elements coming from the towns at the beginning of the rising, together with those rebels who go down into the country as the fight goes on. It is this core which constitutes the embryonic political organization of the rebellion. But on the other hand the peasants, who are all the time adding to their knowledge in the light of experience, will come to show themselves capable of directing the people's struggle. Between the nation on a wartime footing and its leaders there is established a mutual current of enlightenment and enrichment. Traditional institutions are reinforced, deepened, and sometimes literally transformed. The tribunals which settle disputes, the *djemmas* and the village assemblies turn into revolutionary tribunals and political and military committees. In each fighting group and in every village hosts of political commissioners spring up, and the people, who are beginning to splinter upon the reefs of misunderstanding, will be shown their bearings by these political pilots. Thus the latter will not be afraid to tackle problems which if left unclarified would contribute to the bewilderment of the people. The rebel in arms is in fact vexed to see that many natives go on living their lives in the towns as if they were strangers to everything taking place in the mountains and as if they failed to realize that the essential movement for freedom has begun. The towns keep silent, and their continuing daily humdrum life gives the peasant the bitter impression that a whole sector of the nation is content to sit on the side line. Such proofs of indifference disgust the peasants and strengthen their tendency to condemn the townsfolk as a whole. The political educator ought to lead them to modify this attitude by getting them to understand that certain fractions of the population have particular interests and that these do not always coincide with the national interest. The people will thus come to understand that national independence sheds light upon many facts which are sometimes divergent and antagonistic. Such a taking stock of the situation at this precise moment of the struggle is decisive, for it allows the people to pass from total, indiscriminating nationalism to social and economic awareness. The people who at the beginning of the struggle had adopted the primitive Manicheism of the settler – Blacks and Whites, Arabs and Christians – realize as they go along that it sometimes happens that you get Blacks who are whiter than the Whites and that the fact of having a national flag and the hope of an independent nation does not always tempt certain strata of the population to give up their interests or privileges. The people come to realize that natives like themselves do not lose sight of the main chance, but quite on the contrary seem to make use of the war in order to strengthen their material situation and their growing power. Certain natives continue to profiteer and exploit the war, making their gains at the expense of the people, who as usual are prepared to sacrifice everything, and water their native soil with their blood. The militant who faces the colonialist war machine with the bare minimum of arms realizes that while he is breaking down colonial oppression he is building up automatically yet another system of exploitation. This discovery is unpleasant, bitter, and sickening: and yet everything seemed to be so simple before: the bad people were on one side, and the good on the other. The clear, unreal, idyllic light of the beginning is followed by a semi-darkness that bewilders the senses. The people find out that the iniquitous fact of exploitation can wear a black face, or an Arab one; and they raise the cry of "Treason!" But the cry is mistaken; and the mistake must be corrected. The treason is not national, it is social. The people must be taught to cry "Stop thief!" In their weary road toward rational knowledge the people must also give up their too-simple conception of their overlords. The species is breaking up under their very eyes. As they look around them, they notice that certain settlers do not join in the general guilty hysteria; there are differences in the same species. Such men, who before were included without distinction and indiscriminately in the monolithic mass of the foreigner's presence, actually go so far as to condemn the colonial war. The scandal explodes when the prototypes of this division of the species go over to the enemy, become Negroes or Arabs, and accept suffering, torture, and death.

Such examples disarm the general hatred that the native feels toward the foreign settlement. The native surrounds these few men with warm affection, and tends by a kind of emotional over-valuation to place absolute confidence in them. In the mother country, once looked upon as a blood-thirsty and implacable stepmother, many voices are raised, some those of prominent citizens, in condemnation of the policy of war that their government is following, advising that the national will of the colonized people should be taken into consideration. Certain soldiers desert from the colonialist ranks; others explicitly refuse to fight against the people's liberty and go to prison for the sake of the right of that people to independence and self-government.

The settler is not simply the man who must be killed. Many members of the mass of colonialists reveal themselves to be much, much nearer to the national struggle than certain sons of the nation. The barriers of blood and race-prejudice are broken down on both sides. In the same way, not every Negro or Moslem is issued automatically a hallmark of genuineness; and the gun or the knife is not inevitably reached for when a settler makes his appearance. Consciousness slowly dawns upon truths that are only partial, limited, and unstable. As we may surmise, all this is very difficult. The task of bringing the people to maturity will be made easier by the thoroughness of the organization and by the high intellectual level of its leaders. The force of intellect increases and becomes more elaborate as the struggle goes on, as the enemy increases his maneuvres and as victories are gained and defeats suffered. The leaders show their power and authority by criticizing mistakes, using every appraisal of past conduct to bring the lesson home, and thus insure fresh conditions for progress. Each local ebb of the tide will be used to review the question from the standpoint of *all* villages and of *all* political networks. The rebellion gives proof of its rational basis and expresses its maturity each time that it uses a particular case to advance the people's awareness. In defiance of those inside the movement who tend to think that shades of meaning constitute dangers and drive wedges into the solid block of popular opinion, the leaders stand firm upon those principles that have been sifted out in the national struggle, and in the worldwide struggle of mankind for his freedom. There exists a brutality of thought and a mistrust of subtlety which are typical of revolutions; but there also exists another kind of brutality which is astonishingly like the first and which is typically anti-revolutionary, hazardous, and anarchist. This unmixed and total brutality, if not immediately combated, invariably leads to the defeat of the movement within a few weeks.

The nationalist militant who had fled from the town in disgust at the demagogic and reformist maneuvers of the leaders there, disappointed by political life, discovers in real action a new form of political activity which in no way resembles the old. These politics are the politics of leaders and organizers living inside history who take the lead with their brains and their muscles in the fight for freedom. These politics are national, revolutionary, and social and these new facts which the native will now come to know exist only in action. They are the essence of the fight which explodes the old colonial truths and reveals unexpected facets, which brings out new meanings and pinpoints the contradictions camouflaged by these facts. The people engaged in the struggle who because of it command and know these facts, go forward, freed from colonialism and forewarned of all attempts at mystification, inoculated against all national anthems. Violence alone, violence committed by the people, violence organized and educated by its leaders, makes it possible for the masses to understand social truths and gives the key to them. Without that struggle, without that knowledge of the practice of action, there's nothing but a fancy-dress parade and the blare of the trumpets. There's nothing save a minimum of readaptation, a few reforms at the top, a flag waving: and down there at the bottom an undivided mass, still living in the middle ages, endlessly marking time.

Notes

1   This was written in 1961 (*Trans.*).
2   Algerians enlisted in the French army (*Trans.*).

Discrepant Experiences

EDWARD W. SAID

Edward Said is one of the most influential practitioners of colonial discourse analysis, the critical practice of understanding and countering the discursive hegemony of imperial cultures. His *Orientalism* is a magisterial account of the scope and character of a colonial discourse that sought, through theoretical, artistic, and scholarly means, to represent and thus contain the "Otherness" of non-Western cultures. It has profoundly affected the work of many critics and scholars, and places him, along with **Frantz Fanon**, at the foundation of post-colonial studies. The piece reprinted here is taken from his *Culture and Imperialism*, a text that furthers the project of colonial discourse analysis begun in *Orientalism*. The concept of "discrepant experience" is, in some ways, a response to critics who find fault with Said's analysis of Orientalist discourse, who argue that it leaves little room for genuine dialogue and constructive interaction between non-Western subaltern peoples and the Western centers of cultural and political power. Discrepant experiences open up potential for dialogue and interaction between East and West beyond the limits of a binary or "Manichean" opposition in which the West maintains a near-total discursive hegemony over colonial and postcolonial territories in the East. Indeed, such experiences expose the limitations of such abstract conceptions as "East" and "West" and suggest the possibility of a "world order" that would respect differences of all kinds rather than use them to construct artificial barriers to political and cultural understanding.

Discrepant Experiences

Let us begin by accepting the notion that although there is an irreducible subjective core to human experience, this experience is also historical and secular, it is accessible to analysis and interpretation, and – centrally important – it is not exhausted by totalizing theories, not marked and limited by doctrinal or national lines, not confined once and for all to analytical constructs. If one believes with Gramsci that an intellectual vocation is socially possible as well as desirable, then it is an inadmissible contradiction at the same time to build analyses of historical experience around exclusions, exclusions that stipulate, for instance, that only women can understand feminine experience, only Jews can understand Jewish suffering, only formerly colonial subjects can understand colonial experience.

I do not mean what people mean when they say glibly that there are two sides to every question. The difficulty with theories of essentialism and exclusiveness, or with barriers and sides, is that they give rise to polarizations that absolve and forgive ignorance and demagogy more than they enable knowledge. Even the most cursory look at the recent fortunes of theories about race, the modern state, modern nationalism itself verifies this sad truth. If you know in advance that the African or Iranian or Chinese or Jewish or German experience is fundamentally integral, coherent, separate, and therefore comprehensible only to Africans, Iranians, Chinese, Jews, or Germans, you first of all posit as essential something which, I believe, is both historically created and the result of interpretation – namely the existence of Africanness, Jewishness, or Germanness, or for that matter Orientalism and Occidentalism. And second, you are likely as a consequence to defend the essence or experience itself rather than promote full knowledge of it and its entanglements and dependencies on other knowledges. As a result, you will demote the different experience of others to a lesser status.

If at the outset we acknowledge the massively knotted and complex histories of special but nevertheless overlapping and interconnected experiences – of women, of Westerners, of Blacks, of national states and cultures – there is no particular intellectual reason for granting each and all of them an ideal and essentially separate status. Yet we would wish to preserve what is unique about each so long as we also preserve some sense of the human community and the actual contests that contribute to its formation, and of which they are all a part. An excellent example of this approach is one I have already referred to [in *Culture and Imperialism*], the essays in *The Invention of Tradition*, essays which consider invented traditions that are highly specialized and

Taken from *Culture and Imperialism* (New York: Knopf, 1993), pp. 31–43.

local (e.g., Indian durbars and European football games) yet, even though they are very different, share similar characteristics. The point of the book is that these quite various practices can be read and understood together since they belong to comparable fields of human experience, those Hobsbawm describes as attempting "to establish continuity with a suitable historic past."[1]

A comparative or, better, a contrapuntal perspective is required in order to see a connection between coronation rituals in England and the Indian durbars of the late nineteenth century. That is, we must be able to think through and interpret together experiences that are discrepant, each with its particular agenda and pace of development, its own internal formations, its internal coherence and system of external relationships, all of them co-existing and interacting with others. Kipling's novel *Kim*, for example, occupies a very special place in the development of the English novel and in late Victorian society, but its picture of India exists in a deeply antithetical relationship with the development of the movement for Indian independence. Either the novel or the political movement represented or interpreted without the other misses the crucial discrepancy between the two given to them by the actual experience of empire.

One point needs further clarification. The notion of "discrepant experiences" is not intended to circumvent the problem of ideology. On the contrary, no experience that is interpreted or reflected on can be characterized as immediate, just as no critic or interpreter can be entirely believed if he or she claims to have achieved an Archimedean perspective that is subject neither to history nor to a social setting. In juxtaposing experiences with each other, in letting them play off each other, it is my interpretative political aim (in the broadest sense) to make concurrent those views and experiences that are ideologically and culturally closed to each other and that attempt to distance or suppress other views and experiences. Far from seeking to reduce the significance of ideology, the exposure and dramatization of discrepancy highlights its cultural importance; this enables us to appreciate its power and understand its continuing influence.

So let us contrast two roughly contemporary early nineteenth-century texts (both date from the 1820s): the *Description de l'Égypte* in all its massive, impressive coherence, and a comparatively slender volume, 'Abd al-Rahman al-Jabarti's *'Aja'ib al-Athar*. The *Description* was the twenty-four-volume account of Napoleon's expedition to Egypt, produced by the team of French scientists which he took with him. 'Abd al-Rahman al-Jabarti was an Egyptian notable and *'alim*, or religious leader, who witnessed and lived through the French expedition. Take first the following passage from the general introduction to the *Description* written by Jean-Baptiste-Joseph Fourier:

> Placed between Africa and Asia, and communicating easily with Europe, Egypt occupies the center of the ancient continent. This country presents only great memories; it is the homeland of the arts and conserves innumerable monuments; its principal temples and the palaces inhabited by its kings still exist, even though its least ancient edifices had already been built by the time of the Trojan War. Homer, Lycurgus, Solon, Pythagoras, and Plato all went to Egypt to study the sciences, religion, and the laws. Alexander founded an opulent city there, which for a long time enjoyed commercial supremacy and

which witnessed Pompey, Caesar, Mark Antony, and Augustus deciding between them the fate of Rome and that of the entire world. It is therefore proper for this country to attract the attention of illustrious princes who rule the destiny of nations.

No considerable power was ever amassed by any nation, whether in the West or in Asia, that did not also turn that nation toward Egypt, which was regarded in some measure as its natural lot.[2]

Fourier speaks as the rationalizing mouthpiece of Napoleon's invasion of Egypt in 1798. The resonances of the great names he summons, the placing, the grounding, the normalizing of foreign conquest within the cultural orbit of European existence – all this transforms conquest from a clash between a conquering and a defeated army into a much longer, slower process, obviously more acceptable to the European sensibility enfolded within its own cultural assumptions than the shattering experience could have been for an Egyptian who endured the conquest.

At almost the same time Jabarti records in his book a series of anguished and perceptive reflections on the conquest; he writes as an embattled religious notable recording the invasion of his country and the destruction of his society.

This year is the beginning of a period marked by great battles; serious results were suddenly produced in a frightening manner; miseries multiplied without end, the course of things was troubled, the common meaning of life was corrupted and destruction overtook it and the devastation was general. [Then, as a good Muslim, he turns back to reflect on himself and his people.] "God," says the Koran (xi, 9) "does not unjustly ruin cities whose inhabitants are just."

The French expedition was accompanied by a whole team of scientists whose job it was to survey Egypt as it had never been surveyed before – the result was the gigantic *Description* itself – but Jabarti has eyes for, and only appreciates, the facts of power, whose meaning he senses as constituting a punishment for Egypt. French power bears upon his existence as a conquered Egyptian, an existence for him compressed into that of a subjugated particle, barely able to do more than record the French army's comings and goings, its imperious decrees, its overwhelmingly harsh measures, its awesome and seemingly unchecked ability to do what it wants according to imperatives that Jabarti's compatriots could not affect. The discrepancy between the politics producing the *Description* and that of Jabarti's immediate response is stark, and highlights the terrain they contest so unequally.

Now it is not difficult to follow out the results of Jabarti's attitude, and generations of historians have in fact done this, as I shall do to some extent later in this book. His experience produced a deep-seated anti-Westernism that is a persistent theme of Egyptian, Arab, Islamic, and Third World history; one can also find in Jabarti the seeds of Islamic reformism which, as promulgated later by the great Azhar cleric and reformer Muhammad 'Abdu and his remarkable contemporary Jamal al-Din al-Afghani, argued either that Islam had better modernize in order to compete with the West, or that it should return to its Meccan roots the better to combat the West; in addition, Jabarti speaks at an early moment in the history of the immense wave of national self-consciousness that culminated in Egyptian independence, in Nasserite

theory and practice, and in contemporary movements of so-called Islamic fundamentalism.

Nevertheless, historians have not so readily read the development of French culture
and history in terms of Napoleon's Egyptian expedition. (The same is true of the
British reign in India, a reign of such immense range and wealth as to have become a
fact of nature for members of the imperial culture.) Yet what later scholars and critics
say about the European texts literally made possible by the *Description*'s consolidation
of the conquest of the Orient is also, interestingly, a somewhat attenuated and highly
implicit function of that earlier contest. To write today about Nerval and Flaubert,
whose work depended so massively upon the Orient, is to work in territory originally
charted by the French imperial victory, to follow in its steps, and to extend them into
150 years of European experience, although in saying this one once again highlights
the symbolic discrepancy between Jabarti and Fourier. The imperial conquest was not
a one-time tearing of the veil, but a continually repeated, institutionalized presence in
French life, where the response to the silent and incorporated disparity between
French and subjugated cultures took on a variety of forms.

The asymmetry is striking. In one instance, we assume that the better part of
history in colonial territories was a function of the imperial intervention; in the other,
there is an equally obstinate assumption that colonial undertakings were marginal
and perhaps even eccentric to the central activities of the great metropolitan cultures.
Thus, the tendency in anthropology, history, and cultural studies in Europe and the
United States is to treat the whole of world history as viewable by a kind of Western
super-subject, whose historicizing and disciplinary rigor either takes away or, in the
post-colonial period, restores history to people and cultures "without" history. Few
full-scale critical studies have focused on the relationship between modern Western
imperialism and its culture, the occlusion of that deeply symbiotic relationship being a
result of the relationship itself. More particularly, the extraordinary formal and
ideological dependence of the great French and English realistic novels on the facts
of empire has also never been studied from a general theoretical standpoint. These
elisions and denials are all reproduced, I believe, in the strident journalistic debates
about decolonization, in which imperialism is repeatedly on record as saying, in effect,
You are what you are because of us; when we left, you reverted to your deplorable
state; know that or you will know nothing, for certainly there is little to be known
about imperialism that might help either you or us in the present.

Were the disputed value of knowledge about imperialism merely a controversy
about methodology or academic perspectives in cultural history, we would be justified
in regarding it as not really serious, though perhaps worth notice. In fact, however,
we are talking about a compellingly important and interesting configuration in the
world of power and nations. There is no question, for example, that in the past decade
the extraordinarily intense reversion to tribal and religious sentiments all over the
world has accompanied and deepened many of the discrepancies among polities that
have continued since – if they were not actually created by – the period of high
European imperialism. Moreover, the various struggles for dominance among states,
nationalisms, ethnic groups, regions, and cultural entities have conducted and
amplified a manipulation of opinion and discourse, a production and consumption
of ideological media representations, a simplification and reduction of vast complex-

ities into easy currency, the easier to deploy and exploit them in the interest of state policies. In all of this intellectuals have played an important role, nowhere in my opinion more crucial *and* more compromised than in the overlapping region of experience and culture that is colonialism's legacy where the politics of secular interpretation is carried on for very high stakes. Naturally the preponderance of power has been on the side of the self-constituted "Western" societies and the public intellectuals who serve as their apologists and ideologists.

But there have been interesting responses to this imbalance in many formerly colonized states. Recent work on India and Pakistan in particular (e.g., *Subaltern Studies*) has highlighted the complicities between the post-colonial security state and the intellectual nationalist elite; Arab, African, and Latin American oppositional intellectuals have produced similar critical studies. But I shall focus here more closely on the unfortunate convergence that uncritically propels the Western powers into action against ex-colonial peoples. During the time I have been writing this book, the crisis caused by Iraq's invasion and annexation of Kuwait has been in full flower: hundreds of thousands of the United States' troops, planes, ships, tanks, and missiles arrived in Saudi Arabia; Iraq appealed to the Arab world (badly split among the United States' supporters like Mubarak of Egypt, the Saudi royal family, the remaining Gulf Sheikhs, Moroccans, and outright opponents like Libya and Sudan, or caught-in-the-middle powers like Jordan and Palestine) for help; the United Nations was divided between sanctions and the United States' blockade; and in the end the United States prevailed and a devastating war was fought. Two central ideas clearly were held over from the past and still hold sway: one was the great power's right to safeguard its distant interests even to the point of military invasion; the second was that lesser powers were also lesser peoples, with lesser rights, morals, claims.

Perceptions and political attitudes molded and manipulated by the media were significant here. In the West, representations of the Arab world ever since the 1967 War have been crude, reductionist, and coarsely racialist, as much critical literature in Europe and the United States has ascertained and verified. Yet films and television shows portraying Arabs as sleazy "camel-jockeys," terrorists, and offensively wealthy "sheikhs" pour forth anyway. When the media mobilized behind President Bush's instructions to preserve the American way of life and to roll Iraq back, little was said or shown about the political, social, cultural actualities of the Arab world (many of them deeply influenced by the United States), actualities that made possible both the appalling figure of Saddam Hussein and at the same time a complex set of other, radically different configurations – the Arabic novel (whose preeminent practitioner, Naguib Mahfouz, won the 1988 Nobel Prize) and the many institutions surviving in what was left of civil society. While it is certainly true that the media is far better equipped to deal with caricature and sensation than with the slower processes of culture and society, the deeper reason for these misconceptions is the imperial dynamic and above all its separating, essentializing, dominating, and reactive tendencies.

Self-definition is one of the activities practiced by all cultures: it has a rhetoric, a set of occasions and authorities (national feasts, for example, times of crisis, founding fathers, basic texts, and so on), and a familiarity all its own. Yet in a world tied together as never before by the exigencies of electronic communication, trade, travel, environmental and regional conflicts that can expand with tremendous speed, the assertion of identity is by no means a mere ceremonial matter. What strikes me as especially dangerous is that it can mobilize passions atavistically, throwing people back to an earlier imperial time when the West and its opponents championed and even embodied virtues designed not as virtues so to speak but for war.

One perhaps trivial example of this atavism occurred in a column written for *The Wall Street Journal* on May 2, 1989, by Bernard Lewis, one of the senior Orientalists working in the United States. Lewis was entering the debate about changing the "Western canon." To the students and professors at Stanford University who had voted to modify the curriculum to include texts by more non-Europeans, women, and so on, Lewis – speaking as an authority on Islam – took the extreme position that "if Western culture does indeed go, a number of things would go with it and others would come in their place." No one had said anything so ludicrous as "Western culture must go," but Lewis's argument, focused on much grander matters than strict accuracy, lumbered forward with the remarkable proposition that since modifications in the reading list would be equivalent to the demise of Western culture, such subjects (he named them specifically) as the restoration of slavery, polygamy, and child marriage would ensue. To this amazing thesis Lewis added that "curiosity about other cultures," which he believes is unique to the West, would also come to an end.

This argument, symptomatic and even a trifle comic, is an indication not only of a highly inflated sense of Western exclusivity in cultural accomplishment, but also of a tremendously limited, almost hysterically antagonistic view of the rest of the world. To say that without the West, slavery and bigamy would return is to foreclose the possibility that any advance over tyranny and barbarism could or did occur outside the West. Lewis's argument has the effect of driving the non-Westerner into a violent rage or, with equally unedifying consequences, into boasting about the achievements of non-Western cultures. Rather than affirming the interdependence of various histories *on* one another, and the necessary interaction of contemporary societies *with* one another, the rhetorical separation of cultures assured a murderous imperial contest between them – the sorry tale is repeated again and again.

Another example occurred in late 1986, during the broadcast and subsequent discussion of a television documentary called *The Africans*. Originally commissioned and mostly funded by the BBC, this series was written and narrated by a distinguished scholar and professor of political science at the University of Michigan, Ali Mazrui, a Kenyan and a Muslim, whose competence and credibility as a first-rank academic authority were unquestioned. Mazrui's series had two premises: one, that for the first time in a history dominated by Western representations of Africa (to use the phrase from Christopher Miller's book *Blank Darkness*, by a discourse that is thoroughly Africanist in every instance and inflection)[4] an African was representing himself and Africa before a Western audience, precisely that audience whose societies for several hundred years had pillaged, colonized, enslaved Africa; second, that African history was made up of three elements or, in Mazrui's language, concentric circles: the native African experience, the experience of Islam, and the experience of imperialism.

For a start, the National Endowment for the Humanities removed its financial support for the broadcast of the documentaries, although the series ran on PBS anyway. Then *The New York Times*, the leading American newspaper, ran consecutive attacks on the series in articles (September 14, October 9 and 26, 1986) by the (then) television correspondent John Corry. To describe Corry's pieces as insensate or semi-hysterical would not be an exaggeration. Mostly, Corry accused Mazrui personally of "ideological" exclusions and emphases, for example, that he nowhere mentioned Israel (in a program about African history Israel may have appeared to Mazrui as not relevant) and that he vastly exaggerated the evils of Western colonialism. Corry's attack especially singled out Mazrui's "moralistic and political ordinates," a peculiar euphemism implying that Mazrui was little more than an unscrupulous propagandist, the better to be able to challenge Mazrui's figures about such things as the number of people who died in building the Suez Canal, the number killed during the Algerian war of liberation, and so on. Lurking near the turbulent and disorderly surface of Corry's prose was the (to him) disturbing and unacceptable reality of Mazrui's performance itself. Here at last was an African on prime-time television, in the West, daring to accuse the West of what it had done, thus reopening a file considered closed. That Mazrui also spoke well of Islam, that he showed a command of "Western" historical method and political rhetoric, that, in fine, he appeared as a convincing model of a real human being – all these ran contrary to the reconstituted imperial ideology for which Corry was, perhaps inadvertently, speaking. At its heart lay the axiom that non-Europeans should not represent their views of European and American history as those histories impinged on the colonies; if they did, they had to be very firmly resisted.

The entire legacy of what can metaphorically be called the tension between Kipling, who finally saw only the politics of empire, and Fanon, who tried to look past the nationalist assertions succeeding classical imperialism, has been disastrous. Let us allow that, given the discrepancy between European colonial power and that of the colonized societies, there was a kind of historical necessity by which colonial pressure created anti-colonial resistance. What concerns me is the way in which, generations later, the conflict continues in an impoverished and for that reason all the more dangerous form, thanks to an uncritical alignment between intellectuals and institutions of power which reproduces the pattern of an earlier imperialist history. This results, as I noted earlier, in an intellectual politics of blame and a drastic reduction in the range of material proposed for attention and controversy by public intellectuals and cultural historians.

What is the inventory of the various strategies that might be employed to widen, expand, and deepen our awareness of the way the past and present of the imperial encounter interact with each other? This seems to me a question of immediate importance, and indeed explains the idea behind [*Culture and Imperialism*]. Let me very briefly illustrate my idea with two examples that are usefully presented, I think, in anecdotal form; in subsequent pages I shall present a more formal and methodological account of the issues and of the cultural interpretations and politics that follow.

A few years ago I had a chance encounter with an Arab Christian clergyman who had come to the United States, he told me, on an exceedingly urgent and unpleasant mission. As I myself happened to be a member by birth of the small but significant minority he served – Arab Christian Protestants – I was most interested in what he had to say. Since the 1860s there has been a Protestant community comprising a few sects scattered throughout the Levant, largely the result of the imperial competition for converts and constituents in the Ottoman Empire, principally in Syria, Lebanon, and Palestine. In time of course these congregations – Presbyterian, Evangelical, Episcopalian, Baptist, among others – acquired their own identities and traditions, their own institutions, all of which without exception played an honorable role during the period of the Arab Renaissance.

Roughly 110 years later, however, the very same European and American synods and churches which had authorized and indeed sustained the early missionary efforts appeared, quite without warning, to be reconsidering the matter. It had become clear to them that Eastern Christianity was really constituted by the Greek Orthodox Church (from which, it should be noted, the overwhelming majority of Levantine converts to Protestantism came: the nineteenth-century Christian missionaries were totally unsuccessful in converting either Muslims or Jews). Now, in the 1980s, the Western principals of the Arab Protestant communities were encouraging their acolytes to return to the Orthodox fold. There was talk of withdrawing financial support, of disbanding the churches and schools, of cancelling the whole thing in a sense. The missionary authorities had made a mistake one hundred years ago in severing Eastern Christians from the main church. Now they should go back.

To my clergyman friend this was a truly drastic eventuality; were it not for the genuinely aggrieved sensibility involved, one might have considered the whole matter merely a cruel joke. What struck me most strongly, however, was the way in which my friend put his argument. This was what he was in America to say to his ecclesiastical principals: he could understand the new doctrinal point being put forward, that modern ecumenism ought generally to go in the direction of dissolving small sects and preserving the dominant community, rather than encouraging these sects to remain independent from the main church. That you could discuss. But what seemed horrendously imperialist and entirely of the realm of power politics was, he said, the total disregard with which over a century of Arab Protestant experience was simply scratched off as if it had never happened. They do not seem to realize, my gravely affected friend told me, that while once we were their converts and students, we have in fact been their partners for well over a century. We have trusted them and our own experience. We have developed our own integrity and lived our own Arab Protestant identity within our sphere, but also spiritually within theirs. How do they expect us to efface our modern history, which is an autonomous one? How can they say that the mistake they made a century ago can be rectified today by a stroke of the pen in New York or London?

One should note that this touching story concerns an experience of imperialism that is essentially one of sympathy and congruence, not of antagonism, resentment, or resistance. The appeal by one of the parties was to the value of a mutual experience. True, there had once been a principal and a subordinate, but there had also been dialogue and communication. One can see in the story, I think, the power to give or withhold attention, a power utterly essential to interpretation and to politics. The implicit argument made by the Western missionary authorities was that the Arabs had gotten something valuable out of what had been given them, but in this relationship of historical dependence and subordination, all the giving went one way, the value was mainly on one side. Mutuality was considered to be basically impossible.

This is a parable about the area of attention, greater or lesser in size, more or less equal in value and quality, that is furnished for interpretation by the post-imperial situation.

The second general point I want to make can also be made by example. One of the canonical topics of modern intellectual history has been the development of dominant discourses and disciplinary traditions in the main fields of scientific, social, and cultural inquiry. Without exceptions I know of, the paradigms for this topic have been drawn from what are considered exclusively Western sources. Foucault's work is one instance and so, in another domain, is Raymond Williams's. In the main I am in considerable sympathy with the genealogical discoveries of these two formidable scholars, and greatly indebted to them. Yet for both the imperial experience is quite irrelevant, a theoretical oversight that is the norm in Western cultural and scientific disciplines except in occasional studies of the history of anthropology – like Johannes Fabian's *Time and the Other* and Talal Asad's *Anthropology and the Colonial Encounter* – or the development of sociology, such as Brian Turner's *Marx and the End of Orientalism*.[5] Part of the impulse behind what I tried to do in my book *Orientalism* was to show the dependence of what appeared to be detached and apolitical cultural disciplines upon a quite sordid history of imperialist ideology and colonialist practice.

But I will confess that I was also consciously trying to express dissatisfaction at the consolidated walls of denial that had been built around policy studies passing themselves off as uncontroversial, essentially pragmatic scholarly enterprises. Whatever effect my book achieved would not have occurred had there not also been some readiness on the part of a younger generation of scholars, in the West and in the formerly colonized world, to take a fresh look at their collective histories. Despite the acrimony and recriminations that followed their efforts, many important revisionary works have appeared. (Actually, they started to appear as early as one hundred years ago, during the resistance to empire all through the non-Western world.) Many of these more recent works, which I discuss elsewhere in [*Culture and Imperialism*], are valuable because they get beyond the reified polarities of East versus West, and in an intelligent and concrete way attempt to understand the heterogenous and often odd developments that used to elude the so-called world historians as well as the colonial Orientalists, who have tended to herd immense amounts of material under simple and all-encompassing rubrics. Examples worth mentioning include Peter Gran's study on the Islamic roots of modern capitalism in Egypt, Judith Tucker's research on Egyptian family and village structure under the influence of imperialism, Hanna Batatu's monumental work on the formation of modern state institutions in the Arab world, and S. H. Alatas's great study *The Myth of the Lazy Native*.[6]

Yet few works have dealt with the more complex genealogy of contemporary culture and ideology. One notable effort has been the recently published work of a Columbia doctoral student from India, a trained scholar and teacher of English literature whose historical and cultural research has, I think, uncovered the political origins of modern English studies and located them to a significant extent in the system of colonial education imposed on natives in nineteenth-century India. A great deal about Gauri Viswanathan's work, *The Masks of Conquest*, has unusual interest, but her central point alone is important: that what has conventionally been thought of as a discipline created entirely by and for British youth was first created by early nineteenth-century colonial administrators for the ideological pacification and re-formation of a potentially rebellious Indian population, and then imported into England for a very different but related use there.[7] The evidence, I think, is incontrovertible and free from "nativism," an especially besetting hobble of most post-colonial work. Most important, though, this kind of study maps out a varied and intertwined archeology for knowledge whose actualities lie considerably below the surface hitherto assumed to be the true locus, and textuality, of what we study as literature, history, culture, and philosophy. The implications are vast, and they pull us away from routinized polemics on the superiority of Western over non-Western models.

There is no way of dodging the truth that the present ideological and political moment is a difficult one for the alternative norms for intellectual work that I propose in [*Culture and Imperialism*]. There is also no escape from the pressing and urgent calls many of us are likely to respond to from embattled causes and turbulent fields of battle. The ones that involve me as an Arab are, alas, perfect cases in point, and they are exacerbated by pressures exerted on me as an American. Nevertheless, a resistant, perhaps ultimately subjective component of oppositional energy resides in the intellectual or critical vocation itself, and one has to rely on mobilizing this, particularly when collective passions seem mostly harnessed to movements for patriotic domination and nationalist coercion, even in studies and disciplines that claim to be humanistic. In standing up to and challenging their power, we should try to enlist what we can truly comprehend of other cultures and periods.

For the trained scholar of comparative literature, a field whose origin and purpose is to move beyond insularity and provincialism and to see several cultures and literatures together, contrapuntally, there is an already considerable investment in precisely this kind of antidote to reductive nationalism and uncritical dogma: after all, the constitution and early aims of comparative literature were to get a perspective beyond one's own nation, to see some sort of whole instead of the defensive little patch offered by one's own culture, literature, and history. I suggest that we look first at what comparative literature originally was, as vision and as practice; ironically [. . .] the study of "comparative literature" originated in the period of high European imperialism and is irrecusably linked to it. [W]e can draw out of comparative literature's subsequent trajectory a better sense of what it can do in modern culture and politics, which imperialism continues to influence.

NOTES

1 Eric Hobsbawm, "Introduction," in Eric Hobsbawm and Terence Ranger, eds., *Invention of Tradition* (Cambridge: Cambridge University Press, 1983), p. 1.
2 Jean-Baptiste-Joseph Fourier, *Préface historique*, Vol. 1 of *Description de l'Égypte* (Paris: Imprimerie royale, 1809–1828), p. 1.
3 'Abd al-Rahman al-Jabarti, *'Aja'ib al-Athar fi al-Tarajum wa al-Akhbar*, Vol. 4 (Cairo: Lajnat al-Bayan al-'Arabi, 1958–1967), p. 284.
4 See Christopher Miller, *Blank Darkness: Africanist Discourse in French* (Chicago: University of Chicago Press, 1985), and Arnold Temu and Bonaventure Swai, *Historians and Africanist History: A Critique* (Westport: Lawrence Hill, 1981).

5   Johannes Fabian, *Time and the Other: How Anthropology Makes Its Object* (New York: Columbia University Press, 1983); Talal Asad, ed., *Anthropology and the Colonial Encounter* (London: Ithaca Press, 1975); Brian S. Turner, *Marx and the End of Orientalism* (London: Allen & Unwin, 1978). For a discussion of some of these works, see Edward W. Said, "Orientalism Reconsidered," *Race and Class* 27, No. 2 (Autumn 1985), 1–15.

6   Peter Gran, *The Islamic Roots of Capitalism: Egypt, 1760–1840* (Austin: University of Texas Press, 1979); Judith Tucker, *Women in Nineteenth Century Egypt* (Cairo: American University in Cairo Press, 1986); Hanna Batatu, *The Old Social Classes and the Revolutionary Movements of Iraq* (Princeton: Princeton University Press, 1978); Syed Hussein Alatas, *The Myth of the Lazy Native: A Study of the Image of the Malays, Filipinos, and Javanese from the Sixteenth to the Twentieth Century and Its Function in the Ideology of Colonial Capitalism* (London: Frank Cass, 1977).

7   Gauri Viswanathan, *The Masks of Conquest: Literary Study and British Rule in India* (New York: Columbia University Press, 1989).

Unsatisfied: Notes on Vernacular Cosmopolitanism

Homi K. Bhabha

Homi K. Bhabha's essay represents a further development of his work in *The Location of Culture*, the collection of essays that made him one of the most respected voices in postcolonial studies today. His groundbreaking synthesis of deconstruction, psychoanalysis, and literary and historical criticism has gone a long way toward defining the tone of intellectual combativeness and urbanity that characterizes the best postcolonial criticism. The notorious difficulty of his work, like that of **Gayatri Chakravorty Spivak**'s, should be understood in the context of a theoretical project that seeks both to deconstruct colonial discourse and to construct alternatives to it that do not simply replicate or invert its characteristic expressions of discursive authority. The concept of "vernacular cosmopolitanism" proceeds from **Frantz Fanon**'s insistence on the "continuance" of an anti-colonial struggle that combines local concerns with international political relevance. Cosmopolitanism, in Bhabha's paradoxical formulation, reconstitutes a seemingly complicit relation with colonial and neocolonial discourses as a form of geopolitics that grants real political power to postcolonial subjects. The alternative "temporalities" in which postcolonial subjects articulate their concerns no longer constitute a non- or prehistorical space; the postcolonial subject becomes historical precisely in the sense that he or she becomes "contemporary," and his or her local situation begins to exert an international influence. The confounding of space and time, of the temporal and the local, represents one of Bhabha's signal contributions to the postcolonial critique of imperial historiography.

Unsatisfied: Notes on Vernacular Cosmopolitanism

The springing wolf which wanted to devour everything at sight, and the rising gust of wind which was to have brought about a real revolution run the risk of becoming unrecognizable if the struggle continues: and continue it does. The native may at any moment let himself be disarmed by some concession or another.

Frantz Fanon, 'Spontaneity: Its Strength and Weakness'[1]

Why invoke Frantz Fanon today, quite out of historical context? Why invoke Fanon when the ardor of emancipatory discourse has seemingly yielded to fervent, ferocious pleas for "the end of history," the end of the struggle? Why invoke Fanon, who spoke out most pertinently and passionately at that historical moment when, as he said, it was "a question of the Third World starting a new history of Man"?[2] To answer these questions by pointing to historical parallels, or by asking "Who carries the torch of struggle now, who is the sheep in wolf's clothing?" is, I believe, to miss the subtlety and the power of the phrase "the struggle continues." To grasp its meaning we must get beyond the rhetoric of continuance and inheritance in which the articulation of past and present is effected; we must resist what Walter Benjamin describes as the historicist (not histori*cal*) causality represented in "a sequence of events like the beads of a rosary"[3] – an essentially additive process of "events" enacted in a homogeneous empty time. Such a perspective yields a utopic, atopic discourse driving towards a synchronous future: as Fanon puts it elsewhere, "What we want is to go forward all the time, night and day, in the company of Man, in the company of all men."[4] But the temporality of continuance, the transformation, displacement, even transfiguration of struggle through continuity into something unrecognizable that I am drawing attention to, uncannily shadows that historicist hope and introduces another *chiasmatic* historical time and another form of social causality that Fanon names "the knowledge of the *practice* of action."[5] Continuance is not an additive time nor an apocalyptic time: it is calculative time, the time of the "day to day" that has to negotiate the undecidability, the indeterminacy of political direction – history's promise – as it turns into an ethical "affect" that splits and situates the subject's agency – the political imperative. The notion of continuance, as it relates to "taking stock of the situation at the precise moment of struggle," is similar to what Gramsci, in a famous passage on the subaltern subject, defines as the importance of "knowing all the truths, even the

Taken from Laura Garcia Moreno and Peter C. Pfeiffer (eds.), *Text and Nation: Cross-Disciplinary Essays on Cultural and National Identities* (Columbia, SC: Camden House, 1996).

unpleasant ones which entails grasping the complex of superstructures in their *rapid transience*" – a form of contradiction, Gramsci informs us, that is often found *outside* the "formally dialectical" structures, because we need to grasp the dialectic as it is *forming in the process of* becoming itself in history.[6]

This is the anti-historicist Fanon representing what I have called the *temporality of continuance* that informs the "day to day" quotidian struggle for survival:

> They [the people] must not imagine that the end is already won, [but at the same time]...they must not think that the "objectives" are impossible to attain....The war is not a single battle but rather a series of local engagements...and none of these are decisive....Consciousness slowly dawns upon truths that are only partial, limited and unstable....Each local ebb and tide will be used to review the question from the standpoint...of all political networks.[7]

To grasp this everyday form of "continuance" in the cataclysm of struggle – Fanon called it "living inside History" – we have to eschew the springing wolf's instinct of total annihilation and the messianic blast of the revolutionary gust of wind. But what are we left with, or are we, indeed, stranded? Fanonian "continuance" is the temporality of the practice of action: its performativity or agency is constituted from its emphasis on the singularity of the "local"; and iterative structuring of the historical event and political pedagogy; and ethical sense constructed from truths that are partial, limited, unstable. What is formally at stake here resounds with Derrida's reading of the "spectrality" of Marxist messianism; in particular, his insight that the promise of futurity – the world-wide struggle of mankind for its freedom – has "at its heart, this eschatological relation to the *to-come* of an event and of a singularity, of an alterity that can't be anticipated."[8] Fanon's promise drives such "singularity" towards an anticipation, perhaps an inti-mation, that he inscribes as his credo: "National consciousness, *which is not national-ism*, is the only thing that will give us an international dimension."[9] It is this Fanonian paradox that is both enigmatic and essential for the continuance of discourses of cultural globality and transnationality to which we, too often, accede or concede without a necessary struggle. Consider this complexity: the eschatological "to come" of Nationalist struggle is, at the same time, both the emergence and erasure of the consciousness of nationness in the anticolonial struggle, a move not dissimilar to the Derridian promise of emancipation which "retain[s] the temporal form of a *future present* of a future modality of the *living present*."[10] And the psychic and social condition of that erasure is the alterity, the difference, of the international or transnational dimension that is at once a continuance of the nationalist struggle and, in keeping with that *temporality of continuance*, the international is a structure of specification, of singularization, that is partial, limited, and unstable. How do we *think* this relation of locality whose every ebb and flow requires the re-inscription of global relations? What representational form of struggle – psychic, social, discursive – informs such an iterative causality that, in Gramsci's words, must be sought outside "formal dialec-tics"?[11] What is the sign of "humanness" in the category of the transnational "cos-mopolitan"? Where does the subject of global inquiry or injury stand or speak from? To what does it bear relation; from where does it claim responsibility? It is to a brief, *unsatisfied* consideration of these issues that I want to turn today.

For Martha Nussbaum, whose essay "Patriotism and Cosmopolitanism" has generated widespread debate in the United States, the "identity" of cosmopolitanism demands a *spatial* imaginary: the "self" at the center of a series of concentric circles that move through the various cycles of familial, ethnic, and communal affiliation to "the largest one, that of humanity as a whole." The task of the citizen of the world, she writes, lies in making human beings more like our "fellow city dwellers," basing our deliberations on "that interlocking commonality."[12]

In her attempt to avoid nationalist or patriotic sovereignty, Nussbaum embraces a "universalism" that is profoundly provincial in a specific, early imperial sense. Nussbaum too readily assumes the "givenness" of a commonality that centers on a particular image of the "empathetic self" – as the Satrap of a belated liberal benevolence – as it generates its "cosmopolitan" concentric circles, of equal measure and comparable worth. If Nussbaum's philosophical genealogy reaches back to the Stoics and Kant, the ethical urgency for revising cosmopolitanism for the contemporary world order takes its geopolitical bearings from global dialogue about global planning, global knowledge, and the recognition of a shared future – ecology, food supply, and population. But who are our "fellow city dwellers" in the global sense? The 18 or 19 million refugees who lead their unhomely lives in borrowed and barricaded dwellings? The 100 million migrants, of whom over half are women, fleeing poverty and forming part of an invisible, illegal workforce? The 20 million who have fled health and ecological disasters?[13] Are the Stoic values of a respect for human dignity and the opportunity for each person to pursue happiness adequate cosmopolitan proposals for this scale of global economical and ecological disjuncture?

These extreme conditions – or awkward questions – do not constitute the limits of the cosmopolitan ideal. It has been one of the tensions internal to Enlightenment and post-Enlightenment cosmopolitanism – as Schlereth pointed out long ago in his classic study of Franklin, Hume, and Voltaire – to attempt to grasp the unity of mankind without working through the relation of the part to the whole.[14] In Nussbaum's argument such a tension becomes emphasized as a certain liminality in the identity or subject of cosmopolitan process. It is a subject peculiarly free of the complex "affect" that makes possible social identification and affiliation. She neglects "those identities...[that] arise from fissures in the larger social fabric," as Richard Sennett suggests in his response to Nussbaum, "[containing] its contradictions and injustices...remaining necessarily incomplete versions of any individual's particular experience."[15]

What is the relevant – or responsible – community in the context of global interconnectedness? "Whose consent is necessary and whose participation is justified in decisions concerning AIDS, or acid rain, or the use of nonrenewable resources?" The consensual language of these questions – whose consent / whose participation – as posed by David Held in his new book on the *Democracy and the Global Order* alerts us to a problem.[16] Despite Held's influential attempts to transform the sovereignty of the Westphalian order and the nation-state, he inadvertently assumes a model of an individuated, democratic "national" citizenry (either prevalent or projected), as the very basis of the "local" in the global order. It is not that Held does not make space for regional parliament and inter-state institutions; the problem is his concept of the civil sphere, *post-transnational cosmopolitanism*, which is an unexceptional array of free and equal public spheres, neither planned nor simply market-orientated, "but open to organizations and agencies pursuing their own projects, subject to democratic restraint and a *common structure of action.*"[17] If, in an age of global interconnectedness and technological connectivity – the interchange of cultures and the flow of people – international politics unfolds with "uncertainty and indeterminateness," then what permits him to assume, at the level of "local" community, a *common, non-contingent* structure of action? What Held fails to engage with is the "culture" of community that has resulted from the transnational flows of cultures and peoples which have disaggregated (and disarticulated) that mechanism of the national imaginary – Benedict Anderson's "imagined community": the ability to visualize in the nation's *homogeneous empty time,* "in a general way the existence of thousands and thousands like themselves... of whose existence they are confident, yet of whose identity they have not the slightest notion."[18] In the context of increased cultural diversity, space and culture have [a less definitive or determinate] relation" – as Paul Hirst has recently observed in "Globalization and the Nation State"[19] – and not only for the diasporic, the migrant, and the refugee, but also for the increasingly impoverished national working class or underclass of the South, which suffer from restricted practices in the domestic markets.

If we return to the critical responses to Nussbaum's cosmopolitan proposals, with these disjunctions of space, time, and culture in mind, we observe an engaging paradox in the notion of "cosmopolitan" community. As the rhetoric of globality becomes more vaunting and all-embracing, there emerges an indeterminate, uncertain discourse of community that, nevertheless, provides a moral measure against which transnational *cultural* claims are measured. It is surprising how little we learn from those of Nussbaum's critics who provide us with narratives that assume a universal ethic or subject. For instance, Harvey Mansfield defends patriotism against cosmopolitanism on the grounds that "The Declaration of Independence is not jingoistic... it is the result of the consent of the people... a right they have in virtue of their human nature... so the particular is not arbitrary, but rooted in the universal."[20] This is a wide-eyed, wide-angled view where the horizon of the community blends totally with the haze of humanity, but what I am proposing is not a moralism of the local against the global, or a materialism of ever-increasing specificity against ever inflating generality. I am interested in cosmopolitan community envisaged in a *marginality,* even metonomy, that I find in Anthony Appiah's vision of a certain postcolonial translation of the relation between the patriotic and the cosmopolitan, the home and the world: "It is because humans live best on a smaller scale that we should defend not just the state, but the country, the town, the street, the business, the craft, the profession... as circles among the many circles narrower than the human horizon, that are the appropriate spheres of moral concern."[21]

It is precisely this border – narrower than the human horizon – that attracts me; this space that somehow stops short (not falls short) of the transcendent human universal, and for that very reason provides an ethical entitlement to, and enactment of, the sense of community. I see something related in Richard Sennett's sketch for an affective identification with a darker cosmopolitanism where concern for "others arises from recognizing the insufficiencies of the self... the fractures, self-destructiveness and irresolvable conflicts of desires within ourselves which ... will prompt us to cross boundaries. ... Openness to the needs of others comes from ceasing to dream of the world made whole."[22] And although I distance myself from its ecological "holism," I see something of this marginal cosmopolitanism in Vandana Shiva's statements on environmental sustainability: "Just as ecological recovery begins from centers of diversity which are gene pools, Third World women and those tribals and peasants left out of maldevelopment ... offer the best promise [and ethic] for survival ... because they have knowledge of what it means to be the victims of progress."[23]

In each of these instances there is a "vernacular cosmopolitan" negotiation: between a morally arbitrary sense of the nation (*pace* Herder) and a necessary postcolonial state (Appiah); between the "insufficiency of the self" derived from early Christian ethics and the needs of modern, urban communities of interest and inquiry (new social movements) (Sennett); between contemporary, postcolonial Third World feminism, the unsustainable commodification of the world, and the old, dying earth itself (Shiva). Their concepts of community come from a precarious sense of survival: on the liminal borders of the homogenizing discourses of nationality; in contention with the domineering narratives of civil society; effecting salutary acts of cultural translation between here and there, private and public, past and present. Are these forms of communal life part of the potentially subversive, subterranean concept of community that Partha Chatterjee has located for us in the unsurpassed contradiction between capital and community at the very end of his recent book, *The Nation and its Fragments?*[24] A community that seeks to articulate itself at a "level of immediacy," surviving in an interstitial zone of the indeterminate, between the private and the public, the family and civil society, always in danger of being peremptorily "nationalized," or being considered an atavistic minoritarian voice.

In a revisionary reading of Hegel's section on "Ethical Life," in the *Philosophy of Right*, Chatterjee revives an avowedly "fuzzy" concept of community that leads a subservient, subterranean, even subversive existence in nationalized and colonized societies. It is a form of marginal or partial interpellation that opens up a space occupied by those who seek to establish an ethic of community that is "many circles narrower than the human horizon" (Appiah) and ceases to dream of "the world made whole" (Sennett). Derived from such an experience of emancipation comes that experience of modern living that Julia Kristeva has called "the cosmopolitanism of those who have been flayed"[25] or what I shall tentatively name a "vernacular cosmopolitanism." But is it possible to be "culturally particularist" without being patriotic? Committed to the specificity of event and yet linked to a transhistorical memory and solidarity?

Here lies, I believe, the difference in Adrienne Rich's cosmopolitical meditations. Her poetic evocation does not provide us with pedagogical proposals for the good society or virtuous world, as Nussbaum attempts to do. What she allows us to envisage is a certain affective and ethical identification with globality premised on the need to establish a subject of transhistorical memory. In some severe sense she is concerned to address that problem of imagined and unimagined communities from the place where the specific memory of traumatic historical events accede to what Toni Morrison has called a re-memorization:

I'm a canal in Europe where bodies are floating
I'm a mass grave I'm the life that returns
I'm a table set with room for the Stranger
I'm a field with corners left for the landless
[...]
I'm a man-child praising God he's a man
I'm a woman bargaining for a chicken
I'm a woman who sells for a boat ticket
I'm a family dispersed between night and fog
I'm an immigrant tailor who says *A coat*
is not a piece of cloth only I sway
in the learning of the master-mystics
I have dreamed of Zion I've dreamed of world revolution
[...]
I'm a corpse dredged from a canal in Berlin
a river in Mississippi I'm a woman standing
[...]
I am standing here in your poem unsatisfied[26]

For Rich, the boundaries and territories of the so-called cosmopolitan "concentric" world are profoundly, and painfully, underscored and overdetermined. The "I" that speaks – its place of enunciation – is iteratively and interrogatively staged. It is poised at the point at which, in recounting historical trauma, the incommensurable "localities" of experience and memory bear witness, side by side, but there is no easy ethical analogy or historical *parallelism*: as, for instance, in the deaths by water – Rosa Luxemburg once, now the Turkish *Gastarbeiter* – offered up in the *Landwehrkanal* in Berlin, or the lynched body floating in the Mississippi. What we have is a form of repetition that provides a *parallaxal shift in the subject of the event as the enunciating I shifts its geopolitical location and rhetorical locution*. It is this realignment of memory and the present as an "atlas of the difficult world," that articulates a defiant and transformative "dissatisfaction," a dissonance at the heart of that complacent circle that constitutes "our fellow city dwellers." For it is precisely there, in the ordinariness of the day to day, in the intimacy of the indigenous, that, unexpectedly, we become unrecognizable strangers to ourselves in the very act of assuming a more worldly, or what is now termed "global," responsibility.

The subject of "unsatisfaction" which Rich poetically prefigures out of the tattered materials of historical crisis and trauma – like the migrant tailor restitching the tattered coat that is not a piece of cloth only – keeps setting new, disjunctive scenes of repetition for the recognition, perhaps misrecognition, of the speaking "I." It is both a situational form of ethical-political discourse and a kind of identity or identification, that in its *iterative* field of address – *I'm a table ... a field ... a man-child ... a woman ... an immigrant* – attenuates the sovereignty of a "representative" human or world-subject authorized in its mastery of events. This does not mean that we are being offered some postmodern *soufflé* of identity (renowned for its lightness of being) nor some benevolent pluralism or perspectivalism that is equally, reasonably visible from the empyrean heights and the top deck of the Clapham omnibus (so beloved of ethical philosophers).

Rich's mode of address attempts to open up an intervening space, a space of translation as transformation particularly apposite to the difficult, transnational world. And it is an approach that resonates with Walter Benjamin's description in "On Language As Such and the Language of Man," of that particular temporality of translation that ensues in the move between, what he calls "media of varying densities.... Translation passes through *continua* of transformation, not abstract ideas of identity and similarity."[27] In emphasizing the mediated nature of both identity and event, while stressing the crucial differential "densities" that are involved in the process of designating a historical transformation, Benjamin alerts us to a way of reading and being or dwelling "in" History. He insists on the need to recognize the "human" (or the historical) as always in need of translation, or mediation, in order to accede to its historicity: the human as the cultural "sign" of a social or discursive event, not simply the assumed abstract idea or symbol of the universal similitude of all Humanity.

The *continua* of identification that we hear in Rich's work, both here and elsewhere, does not attempt to harmonize the local and general, the poetic and the political as an abstract identity. Historical memory, which she likens variously to film and photography, is a material "medium" that must be "restored and framed," cut and edited: its ethical importance lies in its being at once a form of presence – an "exposure" – and a technology of "processing," remembering, repeating, and working through. It eschews the easy equivalence of social "victimage," or the abstract identification with universalizing human worth. It is the agony of her ethical and political "unsatisfaction" that is marked in the *continua* of the poem's iterative agency. Its rhetoric of repetition articulates varying social densities and personal destinies that haunt the event of history – death by bloating, beating water, survival by mere tailor's stitch – but they contain no strong sense of the global cosmopolitan universalism that Nussbaum describes as "learning to recognize humanity... undeterred by traits that are strange... to learn about the [culturally] 'different' [in order to]... recognize common aims instantiated... in many cultures and histories."[28]

In my view it would be a minimal reading of Rich's transnational events, individuals, and communities, rendered through the poetic "media" of memory, that would reduce the address of her verse to some identitarian sense of a "common humanity," or some Whitmanesque celebration of manifold, naturalistic destiny. For that would erase the tropic force of the verses themselves. The iterative "I'm a / I'm a... I'm a" – as in some bleak counting song of a monstrous child of our times – finds its spatial extension in an object, an attribute, or an event of world historical significance – Slavery, War, Holocaust, migration, diaspora, revolution. The "I'm a" is less the instantiation of the commonality of history and culture (*pace* Nussbaum) than the emphasizing, through insistent repetition, of starting again, re-visioning, so that the process of being subjected to, or the subject of, a particular historicity or system of cultural difference and discrimination has to be, as they say, *"recounted"* or reconstituted as a historical sign in a continua of transformation – not abstract ideas of identity and similarity (to echo Benjamin) once more.

The position Rich stakes out is an intervention into the flow of "history that stops for no one" (to use one of her essay titles) and the iterative "I" attempts to articulate the constant motion of what it means to be "torn between ways."[29] Rich interrupts the flow just long enough to behold

> the random and various shapes of death and survival ... mourning the dead and survivor alike, in a poem where everything is made concrete and there are no cloudy generalities or abstract pronouncements. ... A borderland poem ... from the consciousness of being of no one geography, time-zone or culture, of moving inwardly as well as outwardly between continents, landmasses, eras of history. ... A consciousness that cannot be and refuses to be assimilated. A consciousness that tries to claim all its legacies: courage, endurance, vision, fierceness of human will and also the underside of oppression.[30]

Within the iterative poetic line – its *continua* of transformation, the movement within and without – lies the articulation of a problem in the representation or signification of the historical "time" of the global or the transnational as it is experienced today. According to the sociologist Anthony Giddens, the essence of "global cosmopolitanism" consists in a "transformation of space and time ... *action at a distance.*"[31] An unassimilated agent that wants to claim its legacies, exert its human ethical will and "recount" its spectral memories can no longer survive within what ethical philosophers of "public life" call the "concentric-circle picture."[32] The causality that subtends "action at a distance" is wired through a structure of contingency that theorists of the circuitry of the techno-tele-media forms of global culture have described as manufactured "uncertainty." Rich's attempt to maintain the *singularity* of each event and person she inscribes – World War, starvation, Indian landless peasants, migrant labor, religious custom, Vietnamese boat people, feminist solidarity – is made possible by her attention to the varying, differential density of the "media" and "image structure" that signify these subjects – there can be no easy egalitarianism. What makes them representative of the cosmopolitan contingency, or the transnational uncertainty, is that in iterative flow of the verse, each "installation of the image," each institution of subjecthood or citizenship become contiguously and contingently related. They are not correlated because they share the same historical "cause" or are mediated by the same sign: their relationship is performative, part of the actuality of praxis: "intrusive, inappropriate bitter flashing."[33] And if I may move swiftly between the law of language to the rule of transnational citizenship, then it is intriguing to see that the form of performative contingency/contiguity that I have just described is replicated by Etienne Balibar in his description of the articulation of social divisions and differences in the transnational "national" space. In "Propositions for Citizenship," his influential essay on "political duties beyond borders,"[34] the French political philosopher acquaints us with a hybridized form of knowledge that is crucial for understanding the very nature of citizenship in the transnational social relation. There is no structural causality that necessarily links, for instance, the limits of private and public in the gendered world of labor and work, with the issue of "social rights" in the class struggle and the "national / foreigner distinction" in citizenship rights: in Benjaminian terms, their mediatic differences resist abstract similarity. However, Balibar's argument combines the performative character of social praxis and the ethics of public choice: they have to be thought of together – but with the proviso that there can be no determinate a priori causality that will *synchronously articulate* the transformation in each of these spheres of public interest. This must not be confused with the structure of post-Althusserian "over-determination" with which we are familiar, for there the contingent and the non-synchronous are symptomatic of, and finally regulated by and representative of, the structural causality of capital. In the structure of causality that I am describing for the transnational or global "cosmopolitical," there is an incommensurability between media of the historical as "event" and the means of discursive representation and inscription: the moment of abstract systemic causality that produces a singular mode of difference – race, gender, class at the (pedagogical) level and the performative articulation of the social as an *ensemble or problematic of differentiation*. These two levels have to be kept separate and conjugated at the same *historical* time in different *discursive* spaces. This accords with Ben Lee's recent formulation of a critical inter-nationalism which, in the sphere of cultural criticism, proceeds through a mode of comparative judgment that he names "conditional universals."[35] These are, signific-antly, signifying systems whose norms and codes do not presuppose affinity or articulation; the bases for cultural comparison emerge through the praxis of con-tingent articulation and it is through that performative mode that the rules or norms of connection are established *in practice*.

What does it mean, *for us*, to occupy the space of the "unsatisfied" – which Adrienne Rich has poetically performed, rather than propositionally prescribed? I have talked of the human as a "translational" sign but what becomes of the social object in this process? Now this is not just an abstract problem for over-excited literary theorists such as myself. It has become one of the main areas of discussion and contention in the debate around "what it means to be a citizen," between the communitarians and the cosmopolitans in America today. One of the most influential contributions to this debate by Berkeley law professor Jeremy Waldron, explores the cosmopolitan perspective by taking his bearings from Salman Rushdie's explication of the sense of "self" displayed in *The Satanic Verses*:

> *The Satanic Verses* celebrates hybridity, impurity, intermingling, the transformation that comes of new and unexpected human beings, cultures, ideas, politics, movies, songs... [*Mélange*]... is *how newness enters the world*. It is the great possibility that mass migration gives to the world and I have tried to embrace it.[36]

Waldron particularly alights, as we have done, on the hybridization of identity as an effect of the articulation of an "unexpected transformation" in the very structure of selfhood. Waldron is fair in suggesting, contra Michael Snadel and Will Kymlicka, that it hardly addresses the complex forms of social differentiation that constitute contemporary society, to suggest that "the coherence that makes a particular com-munity a single cultural entity will confer a corresponding degree of integrity on the individual self that is constituted under its auspices."[37] However, does Waldron himself provide a more adequate "image" of the cosmopolitan self when he celebrates its limitless diversity of character and its variety and open texture? Is this not in its own way gratuitous, when we remember the agonistic, iterative self, the "I" in Rich's poem that sought to articulate a cosmopolitan identification with transnational/transhistorical memory? To return finally to the satisfaction of the "unsatisfied," however briefly, leads us to concur with Judith Butler's response to Martha Nussbaum (with whom, you remember, we began) which focuses on the task of translation in the constitution of a new cosmopolitanism as a form of transnationality. She writes: "The *movement* of the *unanticipated transformation* establishes the universal which is yet to be achieved and which in order to *resist domestication* may never be fully or finally achievable."[38]

> You cannot live on me alone
> you cannot live without me
> [...]
> [...] I can't be restored or framed
> I can't be still I'm here
> in your mirror pressed leg to leg beside you
> intrusive inappropriate bitter flashing[39]

Judith Butler's decisive, descriptive link between the movement of the media of historical representation and the establishment of the ethical universal as an "unsatisfied" futurity draws together one theoretical / discursive moment of my argument and opens up another phase or location of my argument. What is the scope and scale of the entity that we are talking about? (Waldron). How do we conceive of the "object" of identification – the transnational or global differential – as the ground of a new cosmopolitanism, if cultural / social agency is positioned within the ethics of an unsatisfied "universal"? Unsatisfied, not because it is mimetically in / non-adequate, but because "unsatisfaction" is a sign of the movement or relocation of revision of the "universal" or the general, such that it is producing a process of "unanticipated transformation" of what is local and what is global. Can we ever resist (*pace* Butler) the "domestication" of the universal; or is it precisely our task to turn the movement of "unsatisfaction" towards the "domestic" to reveal it as an *uncanny* site / sign of the native, the indigenous, as a kind of vernacular "cosmopolitanism"? Bear in mind, of course, that the "vernacular" shares an etymological root with the "domestic" but adds to it – like the "Un" that turns *heimlich* into *unheimlich* – the process and indeed the performance of translation, the desire to make a dialect: to vernacularize is to "dialectize" as a process; it is not simply *to be* in a dialogic relation with the native or the domestic, but it is to be on the border, *in between*, introducing the global-cosmopolitan "action at a distance" into the very grounds – now displaced – of the domestic. But such resistance is not a "negation" of the rule of the universal or the dereliction of either representation, responsibility or judgment. As we learnt from Rich and a number of sociologists, political theorists, and ethical philosophers who work on "globalization" or transnationality, it is to take your position at the point in space and time of the "unexpected transformation." Remember the immigrant tailor who says, in the vernacular dialect of the poem, somewhat ungrammatically: *A coat is not a piece of cloth only* . . .

As I conclude, I want to briefly effect such an "unexpected transformation" in the liberal democratic discourse on secularism as it is in the process of being "translated" in the context of the situational ethics and "singular" politics of migrant communities in the metropolis. The trouble with concepts like secularism is that we understand them too well. These are ideas, and ideals, that are increasingly complicit with a self-reflective claim to a culture of modernity, whether it is held by the elites of the East and West, or the North and South. We may define them in different ways, assume different political or moral positions in relation to them, but they seem "natural" to us: it is as if they are instinctive to our sense of what civil society or a civic consciousness must be. Despite their limitations, they have a certain universal historical resonance: a universality that comes from the origins of these concepts in the value-system of the European Enlightenment. It is such universality, argues Eric Hobsbawm, the greatest socialist historian of our own era, that stands as bulwark between civility and "an accelerated descent into darkness."[40]

I would like to suggest that these concepts of a modern political and social lexicon have a more complex history. If they are immediately, and accurately, recognizable as belonging to the European Enlightenment, we must consider them in relation to the colonial and imperial enterprise which was an integral part of that same Enlightenment. For example, if liberalism in the West was rendered profoundly ambivalent in its avowedly egalitarian project, when confronted with class and gender difference, then, in the colonial world, the famous virtue of liberal "tolerance" could not easily extend to the demand for freedom and independence when articulated by native subjects of racial and cultural difference. Instead of Independence, they were offered the "civilizing mission"; instead of power, they were proffered paternalism.

I want to suggest that it is this complex, self-contradictory history of universal concepts like Liberalism, transformed through their colonial and postcolonial contexts, that is particularly important to our current social and cultural debates in a multicultural, multi-ethnic society. In order to understand the cultural conditions and the rights of migrant and minority populations, we have to turn our minds to the colonial past, not because those are the countries of our "origins," but because the values of many so-called "western" ideals of government and community are *themselves* derived from the colonial and postcolonial experience.

The problems of secularism which we confront today, particularly in relation to censorship, blasphemy, and minority rights, may have a long history, but they have had a very specific postcolonial resonance since the *fatwah* against Rushdie. They are problems that have arisen through the cultural and political impact of migrant and minority communities on the British state and nation. We must be very cautions and circumspect in our use of the term "secularism" after its abuse by many spokespersons of the Eurocentric liberal "arts" establishment, who have used it to characterize the "backwardness" of migrant communities in the post-*Satanic Verses* cataclysm. Great care must be taken to separate secularism from the unquestioned adherence to a kind of ethnocentric and Eurocentric belief in the self-proclaimed values of modernization.

The traditional or classic claim to secularism is grounded in an unreconstructed liberalism of the kind I described above – a liberalism devoid of the *crucial interpolation* of its colonial history. So secularism often "imagines" a world of equal individuals who determine their lives, and the lives of others, rationally and commonsensically. This is a secularism of the privileged, a perspective far removed from the cultural and national context in which various minority groups like Women Against Fundamentalism in England, are demanding an adherence to secularism. The secularism that is demanded by WAF, for instance, is a secularism that is based on an awareness of the gendered critique of rationalism (emphatically not "rationality"), and the passion that is provoked by racism and sexism in the control of minorities – this control may be exerted by state institutions against minority groups, or by patriarchal and class structures within minority communities themselves. What we need is a "subaltern" secularism that emerges from the limitations of "liberal" secularism and "*keeps faith*" with those communities and individuals who have been denied and excluded from the egalitarian and tolerant values of liberal individualism. I am not using the word "subaltern" in its militaristic application. I am using it in the spirit of the Italian Marxist, Gramsci, who used the term to define oppressed, minority groups whose presence was crucial to the self-definition of the majority group: subaltern social groups were also in a position to subvert the authority of those who had hegemonic power.

Now my attempt to "translate" secularism for the specific experiential purposes of marginalized or minority communities who are struggling against various oppressions of race, class, gender, generation – what I have called "subaltern secularism" – is brought to life brilliantly in a few pages in Gita Saghal's essay "Secular Spaces: The Experience of Asian Women Organizing":

> Many women's centers are secular in their conduct rather then specifically in their aims or their constitution. Welcoming women from different religious backgrounds, they create the space to practice religion as well as challenge it. This is peculiarly difficult for multi-culturalist policy makers to grasp. Having abandoned the egalitarian ideal for a policy of recognizing cultural differences, they tend to have to codify, implement and reinforce their differences (as British colonialism did in relation to family law). For instance, a well-meaning social worker, inquiring into cooking arrangements, was told there were two kitchens. "Ah yes," she said knowledgeably. "One vegetarian and one non-vegetarian." "No," we said, "one upstairs and one downstairs".... The difficulty for secularists, particularly those who have embraced a pluralist ideology rather than being complete atheists, is that they cannot offer a complete identity to people in search of their roots. With the breaking down of the traditional distinctions between public and private spheres, the idea itself is in the process of redefinition. Secularists can, however, raise awkward questions: for instance, about how the experience of domestic violence and the challenge to family values have radicalized many women. But their involvement in Southall Black sisters or the Brent Asian Women's Refuge has not made women into clones of the feminists who run these projects. The engagement with the complexity of the response to religion is just beginning. It is only in a secular space that women can conduct the conversation between atheist and devotee, belief and unbelief, sacred and profane, the grim and the bawdy.[41]

What Gita Saghal articulates through the space of the refuge, which becomes a metaphor for the idea of an emergent secular community, is an ethical moment of choice. Fundamentalism limits choice to a pre-given authority or a protocol of precedence and tradition. Secularism of the liberal variety, which I have criticized, suggests that free choice is inherent in the individual. This, as I have argued, is based on an unquestioned egalitarianism and a utopian notion of individualism which bears no real relation to the history of minorization.

But the secularism – the subaltern secularism – that I see played out in Saghal's exposition of the politics of the "everyday," and the politics of the "experiential," is not a presupposed or prescribed value. The process of choice and the ethics of coexistence come from the social space which has to be communally shared with others, and from which solidarity is not simply based on similarity but on the recognition of difference. It is a community of the putative and subversive or subterranean kind that Partha Chatterjee established; for choice in those circumstances is less inherent in the subjective will and more an act of shared solidary responsibility. Such a secularism does not assume that the value of freedom lies within the "goodness" of the individual; freedom is much more the testing of boundaries and limits as part of a communal, collective process, so that choice is less an individualistic internal desire than it is a public demand and duty. Secularism at its best, I believe, enshrines this public, ethical duty of choice, precisely because it often comes from the most private experiences of suffering, doubt, and anxiety. We need to "secularize" the public sphere so that, paradoxically, we may be free to follow our strange gods or pursue our much maligned monsters, as part of a collective and collaborative "ethics" of choice.

NOTES

Parts of this essay appeared, in different context, in "Unpacking My Library...Again," *The Postcolonial Question: Common Skies, Divided Horizons*, ed. Ian Chambers, Lidia Curti (New York: Routledge, 1996), 199–211.

1   Frantz Fanon, "Spontaneity: Its Strength and Weakness," in his *The Wretched of the Earth* (New York: Grove Weidenfeld, 1963), 140 [p. 21 in this vol.].
2   Fanon, "Conclusion," in his *The Wretched of the Earth*, 315.
3   Walter Benjamin, "Theses on the Philosophy of History," in his *Illuminations*, ed. Hannah Arendt, trans. Harry Zorn (New York: Schoken Books, 1968).
4   Fanon, "Conclusion," 315.
5   Fanon, "Spontaneity," 147 [p. 24 in this vol.].
6   Antonio Gramsci, *A Gramsci Reader*, ed. David Forgacs (London: Lawrence and Wishart, 1988), 197.
7   Fanon, "Spontaneity," 141 and 146 [p. 21 and 24 in this vol.].
8   Jacques Derrida, *Specters of Marx: The State of the Debt, the Work of Mourning and the New International*, trans. Peggy Kamuf (New York: Routledge, 1994), 65.
9   Fanon, "On National Culture," in his *The Wretched of the Earth*, 247.
10   Derrida, *Specters of Marx*, 65.
11   Gramsci, *A Gramsci Reader*, 197.
12   Martha Nussbaum, "Patriotism and Cosmopolitanism," *Boston Review* XIX.5 (Oct/Nov 1994).
13   Herbert Gintis, "A Defense of Communal Values," *Boston Review* XIX.5 (Oct/Nov 1994).
14   Thomas J. Schlereth, *The Cosmopolitan Ideal* (Notre Dame, IN: University of Notre Dame Press, 1977), 12.
15   Richard Sennett, "Christian Cosmopolitanism," *Boston Review* XIX.5 (Oct/Nov 1994).
16   David Held, *Democracy and the Global Order: From the Modern State to Cosmopolitan Governance* (Cambridge: Polity Press, 1995).

17   David Held, "Democracy: From City-States to a Cosmopolitan Order?" *Political Studies* XL, special issue (1992): 10–39.

18   Benedict Anderson, *Imagined Communities* (London: Verso, 1983), 74 and 39.

19   Paul Hirst, "Globalization and the Nation State" (unpublished manuscript), 11.

20   Harvey Mansfield, "Foolish Cosmopolitanism," *Boston Review* XIX.5 (Oct/Nov 1994).

21   Anthony Appiah, "Loyalty to Humanity," *Boston Review* XIX.5 (Oct/Nov 1994).

22   Sennett, "Christian Cosmopolitanism."

23   Vandana Shiva, *Staying Alive: Women, Ecology and Development* (London: Zed Books, 1988), 46–7.

24   Partha Chatterjee, *The Nation and its Fragments: Colonial and Post-Colonial Histories* (Princeton NJ: Princeton University Press, 1993), 220–39.

25   Julia Kristeva, *Strangers to Ourselves*, trans. Leon S. Roudiez (New York: Columbia University Press, 1991), 13.

26   Adrienne Rich, "Eastern Wartime," in her *Atlas of a Difficult World: Poems 1988–1991* (New York: W. W. Norton, 1991), 35–44; here 44.

27   Walter Benjamin, "On Language As Such and the Language of Man," in his *One-Way Street and Other Writings*, trans. Edmund Jephcott and Kingsley Shorter (London: NLB, 1979), 107–23.

28   Nussbaum, "Patriotism and Cosmopolitanism."

29   Adrienne Rich, *What is Found There: Notebooks on Poetry and Politics* (New York: Norton, 1994), 139 – a quote by Gloria Anzaldúa, unreferenced in Rich's text.

30   Rich, *What is Found There*, 139.

31   Anthony Giddens, *Beyond Left and Right: The Future of a Radical Politics* (Stanford, CA: Stanford University Press, 1994), 4.

32   Shue, "Mediating Duties," *Ethics: An International Journal of Social, Political and Legal Philosophy* 98.4 (July 1988): 693.

33   Rich, "Eastern Wartime," 43.

34   See Etienne Balibar, "Propositions on Citizenship," *Ethics: An International Journal of Social, Political and Legal Philosophy* 98.4 (July 1988): 723–30.

35   Ben Lee, unpublished manuscript.

36   Salman Rushdie, "In Good Faith," in his *Imaginary Homelands* (Harmondsworth: Granta/ Penguin, 1992), 394; italics are Rushdie's.

37   Jeremy Waldron, "Minority Cultures and the Cosmopolitan Alternative," *University of Michigan Journal of Law Reform* 25.3, 4 (Spring and Summer 1992).

38   Judith Butler, "Kantians in Every Culture?" *Boston Review* XIX.5 (Oct/Nov 1994).

39   Rich, "Eastern Wartime," 43.

40   Eric Hobsbawm, "Barbarism: A User's Guide," *New Left Review* 206 (1994): 44–54.

41   Gita Saghal, "Secular Spaces: The Experience of Asian Women Organizing," in *Refusing Holy Orders: Women and Fundamentalism in Britain*, ed. Gita Saghal and Nira Yuval-Davis (London: Virago Press, 1992), 192 and 197.

The Burden of English

GAYATRI CHAKRAVORTY SPIVAK

Gayatri Chakravorty Spivak's previous work – especially the seminal essay "Can the Subaltern Speak?" – established her as one of the most controversial and influential theorists of postcolonial studies. The difficulty of her work, like **Homi Bhabha**'s, to some degree threatens to overwhelm the reader and obscure the originality and the importance of her contribution to postcolonial studies and literary criticism. Her willingness, in "Can the Subaltern Speak?," to pursue a critique of representation beyond the limits understood in the West, to ask the hard question whether the subaltern subject can speak if she can find no space from which to articulate that is not determined in advance by a discourse designed to silence her – all of this has made Spivak a formidable theorist and an unrelenting critic of the project of "theory." "The Burden of English" continues this mode of critical deconstruction (as a translator of the French philosopher Jacques Derrida, Spivak has a firm grounding in Western modes of philosophical critique), and advances a concept of "emancipatory complicity" that opens up possibilities of assent to literary texts that enable the postcolonial subject to come to terms with the gender, racial, class, and ethnic differences that have historically constituted the struggle between East and West. Like **Edward Said**, Spivak calls for a greater degree of appreciation for and acceptance of differences; she also specifies how we, as teachers and students, might be able to model this appreciation and difference in the classroom.

The Burden of English

What I have called a "new orientalism" in the discipline of English constructs an object of study called "third world" or "postcolonial" literature. In this essay I suggest some ways in which this interested construction can be actively undone in the teaching of English – the "burden" of English – in India.

I use the word "burden" in at least its two chief senses. First, as the content of a song or account: in this case, expanding the metaphor, the import of the task of teaching and studying English in the colonies. And, second, as a singular load to carry, in a special way.

I am speaking not of English language policy but of the teaching, specifically, of English literature. Let me start with a passage from *Decolonizing the Mind* by the Kenyan writer Ngugi wa Thiong'o to show how much, in spite of obvious differences, the predicament of the teaching of English literature in postcolonial India has in common with the situation, say, in postcolonial Kenya:[1]

> [A] lot of good work on Kenyan and African languages has been done at the Department of Linguistics and African languages at the University of Nairobi.... They acknowledge ...the reality of there being three languages for each child in Kenya, a reality which many patriotic and democratic Kenyans would not argue should be translated into social and official policy. Kiswahili would be the all-Kenya national and official language; the other nationality languages would have their rightful places in the schools; and English would remain Kenya people's language of international communication. But...I am not dealing so much with the language policies as with the language practice of African writers.[2]

I, too, am dealing with practice, not policies. But I am not dealing with the language practice of Indian writers either. To repeat, my topic here is the situation of the Indian teachers of English.

What is the basic difference between teaching a second language as an instrument of communication and teaching the same language so that the student can appreciate literature? It is certainly possible to argue that in the most successful cases the difference is not easy to discern. But there is a certain difference in orientation between the language classroom and the literature classroom. In the former, the goal is an active and reflexive use of the mechanics of the language. In the latter, the goal is at least to shape the mind of the student so that it can resemble the mind of

Taken from Carol A. Breckenridge and Peter van der Veer (eds.), *Orientalism and the Postcolonial Predicament: Perspectives on South Asia* (Philadelphia: University of Pennsylvania Press, 1993).

the so-called implied reader of the literary text, even when that is a historically distanced cultural fiction.

The figure of an implied reader is constructed within a consolidated system of cultural representation. The appropriate culture in this context is the one supposedly indigenous to the literature under consideration. In our case, the culture of a vague space called Britain, even England, in its transaction with Europeanness (meaning, of course, *Western* Europe), Hellenism and Hebraism, the advent of Euramericanism, the trendiness of Commonwealth literature, and the like. Our ideal student of British literature must so internalize this play of cultural self-representation that she can, to use the terms of the most naive kind of literary pedagogy, "relate to the text," "identify" with it. However naive these terms, they describe the subtlest kind of cultural and epistemic transformation, a kind of upward race mobility, an entry, however remote, into a geopolitical rather than merely national "Indian"-ness. It is from this base that R. K. Narayan can speak of "English In India" as if it were a jolly safari arranged by some better-bred version of the India Tourist Board; conversely, it is also on this base that a critical study of colonial discourse can be built.[3]

It is with this in mind that many decolonized intellectuals feel that the straightforward ideal of teaching English literature in the theater of decolonization continues the process of producing an out-of-date British Council style colonial bourgeoisie in a changed global context.

I am not suggesting for a moment that, given the type of student who chooses English as a field of study in the general Indian context of social opportunity (whatever that might be), this kind of ideological production is successfully achieved. The demand for a "general cultural participant" in the colonies has at any rate changed with the dismantling of actual territorial imperialism. Today, the student of English literature who is there because no other more potentially lucrative course of study is open to him is alienated from his work in a particular way.

It cannot be ignored that there is a class argument lurking here, although it is considerably changed from my student days in the mid- to late 1950s. The reasons why a person who obviously takes no pleasure in English texts chooses English Honors are too complex to explore here. At any rate, the class value of the choice of English Honors is gendered, and is different according to the hierarchy of institutions – in the metropolitan, urban, suburban, and rural centers. The same taxonomy as it operates among students of English literature as a Pass subject, and the teacher's accommodation within it as Brit. Lit. becomes less and less normative, are much more demographically and politically interesting. I have not the skills to study this area and so will turn to a more literary-critical topic and return to the "implied reader."

The implied reader is imagined, even in the most simple reading, according to rudimentary or sophisticated hypotheses about persons, places, and times. You cannot make sense of anything written or spoken without at least implicitly assuming that it was destined for you, that you are its implied reader. When this sense of latent destiny of the texts of a literary tradition is developed along disciplinary lines, even the students (mostly women) who come to English studies in a self-consciously purposive way – all students at elite institutions would have to be included here – might still be open, under the best circumstances, to an alienating cultural indoctrination that is out of step with the historical moment. This becomes all the more dubious when the best of them become purveyors of native culture abroad.

I should like to look first at a few literary figurations of this alienation. I want next to plot some ways of negotiating with the phenomenon. As I have already suggested, this alienation is a poison *and* a medicine, a base on which both elitism and critique can be built. The institutional curriculum can attempt to regulate its use and abuse.

I will discuss a few literary figurations of the gradual cultural alienation that might become a persistent accompaniment to the successful teaching of English literature in India. I employ the word "figure" here from the word "figurative" as opposed to "literal." When a piece of prose reasonably argues a point, we understand this as its *literal* message. When it advances this point through its form, images, and metaphors, and indeed its general rhetoricity, we call it figuration or figuring forth. Rhetoric in this view is not mere *alamkāra*. The literal and the figurative depend on each other even as they interrupt each other. They can be defined apart but they make each other operate.

Indeed, literature might be the best complement to ideological transformation. The successful reader learns to identify implicitly with the value system figured forth by literature through learning to manipulate the figures, rather than through (or in addition to) working out the argument explicitly and literally, with a view to reasonable consent. Literature buys your assent in an almost clandestine way, and therefore it is an excellent instrument for a slow transformation of the mind, for good or for ill; as medicine or as poison, perhaps always a bit of both. The teacher must negotiate and make visible what is merely clandestine.

To emphasize my point that the assent the implied reader gives to literature is more than merely reasonable, indeed perhaps clandestine, my first example is a text where I am perhaps myself the type-case. To make of "myself," written into a cultural text, the example of alienating assent is a direct challenge to the hegemonic notion of the "willing suspension of disbelief," still an active orthodoxy coming via such influential figures as the Anglo-American T. S. Eliot and I. A. Richards, and the Euramerican Herbert Marcuse.

The text is the short story "Didi" (1895) or "The Elder Sister" by Rabindranath Tagore.[4] It is not a text written in English, although many of you have read it in a rather indifferent English translation. My point here is to illustrate how the implied reader is drawn into patterns of cultural value as she assents to a text and says "yes" to its judgments, in other words, as she reads it with pleasure. When we teach our students to read with pleasure texts where the implied reader is culturally alien and hegemonic, the assent might bring a degree of alienation.[5]

It is a simple story. Shoshi was the only daughter of an elderly couple. Her husband Joygopal was hoping to inherit their property. The elderly couple had a son in late middle age. After their death, Shoshi takes her orphaned infant brother to her bosom almost in preference to her own sons. Joygopal, enraged by the loss of his inheritance, does everything to take it away from the orphan boy and indeed tries to precipitate his death by neglecting a serious illness. At this point, the English magistrate for the area comes on tour. Shoshi delivers her brother over to the magistrate. She soon dies mysteriously and is cremated overnight.

I have read this story many times. I am not only its implied reader, but its *successful* implied reader. Even after all these readings, my throat catches at the superb senti-mental ending: "Shoshi had given her word to her brother at parting, we will meet again. I don't know where the word was kept" (p. 290). This assent is so strong that the analysis of it that I will now begin and that I have performed before cannot seriously interfere with it. This is why literature is such an excellent vehicle of ideological transformation – for good or for ill, as medicine or as poison.

Literature, for women of any class and inclination (*pravritti*), is a major ingredient in the centering of the subject that says "yes," first to reading, and then to reading something, so that more of that subject can be consolidated and sedimented; so that it can go on saying "yes" indefinitely. (There are different systems of representation that facilitate this centering for different classes or *varnas*, different inclinations. And the weave – the *text*-ile – of the system is interrupted with the patchwork of intervention and contingency. To give an example of a different class, a different history, a different set of inclinations: it is "religion" thrown into the potential sign-system of "citizen-ship" as concept and metaphor that wins the assent of the young woman whose class-family *pravritti* insert her into the Rashtriya Sevika Samiti.)

How then is my assent given to this story? To what do I assent? How am I, or indeed how *was* I, historically constructed as its implied reader so that I was able to read it with pleasure within my cultural self-representation?

Many of Tagore's short stories are *about* emancipated women. This story is about a village woman whose love for her brother emancipates her to the extent that she can see that the impartial white colonial administrator will be a better *ma-baap* than her self-interested Indian kin. Yet, as a woman, she cannot choose to give herself over to him. Does she choose to remain behind? Or is she, for herself, a prisoner of the patriarchal system from which she delivers her brother by assigning the Englishman as his father? (This is, of course, a central patriarchal theme, this giving of the name of the father to the Englishman, for the issue is inheritance and the passage of property.) At any rate, the implied reader, whose position I occupy for the moment as the daughter of upper middle-class female emancipation in urban Bengal, cannot be sure whether Shoshi chooses to remain with or is a prisoner of patriarchy, and, indeed, still cannot be sure where she stands within this situation. This must remain what Meenakshi Mukherjee has called an "interesting but elusive and unver-ifiable statement" for the moment. I will speak of the thrill of ambivalence later. Here all I need to say is that, in order to assent to the story, to derive pleasure from a proper reading, one must somehow see the entire colonial system as a way out of indigenous patriarchy.[6] I have written elsewhere about the cultural politics of this conviction in the matter of the abolition of the self-immolation of widows in 1829.[7]

In most of his prose writing, Rabindranath Tagore is not simply telling a story or making a point but also fashioning a new Bengali prose. You will therefore accept the suggestion that the texture of the levels of prose plays a strong part in the fabrication of the implied reader's assent. In "Didi," Tagore endows only Shoshi with full-fledged subjectivity. It is in the service of building that subject that Tagore deploys that stunning mixture of Sanskritized and colloquial Bengali that marks his writing of this period.

There is some cultural discrepancy in creating Shoshi as the subject-agent of a romantic love or *prem* that is still not the legitimate model of the cementing emotion of the institution of the Indian marriage. Rabindranath brings this about through an expert manipulation of the model of *biraho* or love-in-absence abundantly available in classical Sanskrit. Any careful reader will see the marks of this in the construction of Shoshi's subjectivity.

The discrepancy involved in the Sanskritization of Shoshi's subjectivity as the agent of *prem* is never treated ironically by Tagore. It is in the interest of constructing Shoshi as the subject or agent of *sneho* or affection that a benevolent irony makes its appearance, but always only at the expense of her brother Nilmoni. There are many instances of this. I will quote a tiny fragment simply to remind myself of the pleasure of the text:

কৃষকায় বৃহৎমস্তক গম্ভীরমুখ শ্যামবর্ণ ছেলেটী

This fantastic collection of epithets, reading which it is almost impossible to depart from pure Sanskrit phonetics, is a measure of the registers of irony and seriousness with which Tagore can play the instrument of his prose. The available English translation, "the heavy-pated, grave-faced, dusky child," is, of course, hopeless at catching these mechanics.

Why read a high-culture vernacular text as we think of the burden of teaching English? Let us backtrack. The goal of *teaching* such a thing as literature is epistemic: transforming the way in which objects of knowledge are constructed. One such object, perhaps the chief object, is the human being, inevitably gendered. It is always through such epistemic transformations that we begin to approximate the implied reader. In our case, the approximation is mediated by the new vernacular literatures secreted by the encounter described, for this writer with a profound imperialist irony, as "the Bengal Renaissance." That particular mediation has been commented on ad nauseam and is indeed a cliché of Indian cultural history. Like most clichés, this one has become part of the "truth," of Indian cultural self-representation. And in the fabrication of this truth, Tagore's role is crucial.

Some of Tagore's most significant epistemic meddling is with women. Women constituted by, and constituting, such "minds" become the culturally representative "implied reader." Therefore the problem of the teaching of English literature is not separated from the development of the colonial subject. And as women are notoriously the unfixed part of cultural subjectivity as it is represented by men, the construction of the feminine subject in colonial vernacular literature can give us a sense of the classroom molding of minds preserved in literary form. To read vernacular colonial literature in this way, as preparing the ground for, as it is prepared by, British literature in the colonies, is to challenge the contrast often made, in "western" colonial discourse studies, between western literature as "central" and third world literature – in this case "Indian"(!) – as "marginal" or "emergent." Expanding Ashis Nandy's idea of the "intimate enemy," or my own notion of "violating enablement," it seems more productive to consider the heterogeneity on both sides.[8]

In order to make systemic changes we need systemic taxonomies. It bears repeating here that two discontinuous ways in which the opposition center / margin or dominant / emergent is undone are gender and class. Thus it seems important to look at Tagore's participation in the project of epistemic transformation by way of a rural woman. This is more interesting in this business of the construction of the implied reader precisely because Shoshi, the central character, does not belong to the class of women who will read the story felicitously, "in its own time." This class separation allows for a feeling of identity-in-difference that seems a much more flexible instrument of epistemic transformation as a site of negotiations. What happens when an exceptional underclass woman is herself a creative reader of British literature will be considered in the next section.

Shoshi is developed as an agent of romantic love in elegant Sanskritic prose in descriptive third person with no hint of indirect free style.[9] In other words, rhetorically she is given no access to a Sanskritized subjectivity. In her case, what will be shown is the subordination of love or *prem* for her husband to affection or *sneho* for her orphan brother. The entire network of *Indian* patriarchy, including colonial functionaries, would like to keep Shoshi in the gendered private sphere, as her husband's adjunct. Shoshi enters the public sphere by establishing direct contact with the British colonial authority and *chooses* to re-enter the patriarchal enclosure. She is destroyed by this choice, since the story strongly suggests that she dies by foul play and is therefore cremated as quickly as possible.

Keeping within the allegory of the production of the colonial subject, with something like a relationship with the implied reader of British literature, we see the orphaned brother as the full-fledged future colonial subject, mourning his sister – his personal past – but encircled by the sahib's left arm, the right implicitly pointing to a historical future. But it is Shoshi who supplements the picture, choosing to remain in the static culture, while sending the young unformed male into the dynamic colonial future. A gendered model, this, of the colonial reader, not quite identical with the "real" reader and therefore, in a patriarchal system of reckoning, more like a "woman."

How, then, can we construct a model of the woman and man of the urban middle class, themselves woven and patched as well by the same strands, of the same stuff, reading, in the exciting identity-in-difference frame of mind, the subject laid out in the pages of the story? A richly constructed, richly praised female subject chooses to remain within the indigenous patriarchal structure; she places her confidence in the Magistrate as foster-father, another mark of her heroism. This is the complex of attitudes that is the condition and effect of any appropriate reading of the story. The structure survives; Madhu Kishwar of the *Manushi* collective will not call herself a "feminist" because the word is too much marked by the West, but will work for (other) women's rights.[10]

The Magistrate is constructed as a subject who might be privy to the thrill of this ambivalence. The possibility is lodged in this exchange: "The saheb asked, 'Where will you go.' Shoshi said, 'I will return to my husband's house, I have nothing to worry about.' The saheb smiled a little and, seeing no way out ...'" By contrast, the neighbor Tara, who opposes husbands if they are scoundrels at the beginning of the story, and roars out her rage at the end, is displeased when Shoshi leaves her husband's house to look after her sick brother: "If you have to fight your husband why not sit at home and do it; what's the point in leaving home? A husband, after all" (p. 288).

The Magistrate (Brit. Lit.) (perhaps) understands best of all that Shoshi must sacrifice herself to her own culture, but takes charge of Nilmoni (the indefinite future): a crude but recognizable model of what the "best" students manage – saying "yes" and "no" to the Shoshi-function, as it were – in our Brit. Lit. classes.

I want now to show how this necessarily limited and divided assent to implied readership is parodied in Kipling's *Kim*, published within five years of the publication of "Didi." Thus it is particularly necessary today not to differentiate British and Indian literatures as "central" and "marginal" in a benevolent spirit; that differentiation is a mere legitimation by reversal of the colonial cliché whose real displacement is seen in the turbulent mockery of migrant literature – Desani or Rushdie. Here is Kipling's

> Hurree Chunder Mookerjee, ... an M.A. of Calcutta University, [who] would explain the advantages of education. There were marks to be gained by due attention to Latin and Wordsworth's *Excursion* ... also a man might go far, as he himself had done, by strict attention to plays called *Lear* and *Julius Caesar*; the book cost four annas, but could be bought second-hand in Bow Bazar for two. Still more important than Wordsworth, or the eminent authors Burke and Hare, was the art and science of mensuration.... "How am I to fear the absolutely non-existent?" said Hurree Babu, talking English to reassure himself. It is an awful thing still to dread the magic that you contemptuously investigate – to collect folklore for the Royal Society with a lively belief in all the Powers of Darkness.[11]

What Tagore is performing in the narrative, through the epistemic transformation of the central *female* character, is a productive and chosen contradiction: a self-sacrifice to culture while bequeathing the future to the colonist *in loco parentis*. Kipling describes an identical phenomenon in this minor male character as an unproductive contradiction: a bondage to a superstitious and mercenary indigenous culture while mouthing sublime doctrine, the distinctive failure of the colonial subject. (We know that Kipling understood the good Indian within an earlier, feudal, semiotic system and was incapable of bringing to life an Indian woman as subject or agent of profound inner change.)

At least two kinds of point can be made here. By contrast to Kipling – of course Kipling is an interested choice on my part – Tagore's complicated and complicit structure remains preferable as a mode of assent in the colonies. In the frame of indigenous class alliances and gendering the Tagorean structure becomes dubious. The activist teacher of English can negotiate this only if she works to undo the divide between English and vernacular literatures laid down in our institutions. The teacher can use her own native language skills and draw on the multilingual skills of the students. More important, departments of Modern Indian Literatures, of Literature in the State Vernacular, of Comparative Literature must work together so that the artificial divide between British and Native is undone.

I should like to make clear that I am not *conflating* British and colonial / Commonwealth literatures. Nor am I suggesting a collapsing of boundaries. I am proposing rather that the complexity of their relationship, collaborative / parasitical / contrary /

resistant, be allowed to surface in literary pedagogy. They are different but complicit. I will recite this refrain again, for it is a common misunderstanding.[12]

As contrast to Tagore's class-divisive gendering I will draw on Binodini Dasi's *Amar Katha* (*My Story*).[13] First, to contrast Kipling's dismissal of the agency of a productive contradiction in the colonial subject, I will point at Tagore's *Gora* as a counter to *Kim*.[14]

Gora ("Whitey" – the word applied to the British tommy is here a perfectly acceptable diminutive from Gaurmohan) appeared five years after the publication of *Kim*. The heroes of both novels are Irish orphans of the Indian Mutiny, turned Indian. But there the resemblance ends. Gora becomes both a nationalist Indian and a tremendously orthodox Brahman. At the end of the novel he finds out that he is not only not a Brahman, but not even a Hindu or an Indian by birth. It is then that he realizes that he is most truly Indian, because he chooses to be so. His realization is embedded in a discourse of woman. First his identification of India with his (foster) mother who, unlike his (foster) father, did not observe caste difference: "Ma, you have no caste rules, no loathing, no contempt. You are my India." Then the summons to the hitherto spurned untouchable servant: "Now call your Lachchmia. Ask her to bring me a glass of water." And finally the mother's request to him to acknowledge the love of the emancipated Brahmo heroine, expressed obliquely as a request to summon a male friend: "Gora, now send for Binoy" (p. 572).[15] This ending is rather different in historical "feel" from *Kim* (which ends with Kim O'Hara and the Lama on a hilltop).

If I were commenting on the thematics of the half-caste as "true" Indian, I should contrast Gora with Mahasweta Devi's Mary Oraon, and again the registers of class and gender (and of course coloniality and *post*coloniality) would come into play.[16] In contrasting it to Kipling's Irish-as-Indian hero, however, one would have to notice there the feudal and here the nationalist axiomatic: the codified past as opposed to a possible dynamic future. Kim's return is acted out again by E. M. Forster's Fielding; their futures are not seriously marked by the colonies. For Gora, agency is bestowed by the colony as nation. The theme of choice is important here as well.

But Gora is not a divided subject in the same way as Shoshi is; if he chooses a return to culture, he is also the inheritor of the future. The theme of sacrifice is less ambivalent and therefore less interesting in *Gora*. The colonial reader is as race- and gender-divided from Gora as she would be class-divided from Shoshi. And from that race- and gender-distanced position, the system of representations the reader assents to is again not quite accessible to the staging of her own identity, but this time "from below," not, as in the case of the indigenous woman, "from above."[17] The cultural choice and bequest of the future can inhere in the same fantasmatic character: the white man turned Indian by choice.[18] The development of readership thrives in the difference and deferment staged between hero and reader, whether from above or below. In a former colony, the institutional teacher of imperialist and colonial literature can open this space of difference only by way of persistently undoing the institutional difference between that literature and the literature(s) in the mother tongue(s). It is then that the active vectors of these differences, negotiating gender, class, and race, would begin to appear.[19]

Let us now consider a performance of this undoing, in the very house of performance, during the colonial era. I am referring to the Calcutta professional theater at the
end of the nineteenth century. To give an example of the undoing of institutional
difference, I will quote from Binodini's *Amar Katha* at length:

> Girishbabu [the eminent actor Girishchandra Ghosh (1844–1912)] taught me with great
> care the performance of parts. His teaching method was superb. First he explained the
> essence [*bhab* – *bhava*] of the part. Then he would ask us to memorize it. Then when he
> had time he would sit in our house, with Amrita Mitra, Amritababu and others, and tell
> us the writings of many different British actresses, of eminent British poets such as
> Shakespeare, Milton, Byron, Pope, as if they were stories. Sometimes he would read the
> books aloud and explain. He taught various moves and gestures [*hab-bhab*] one by one.
> Because of this care I started learning the work of acting with knowledge and intelli-
> gence. What I had learnt before was like the cleverness of parrots, I had experienced little.
> I had not been able to say or understand anything with argument or reasoning. From
> now on I could understand my own performance-selected part. When big British *actors* or
> *actresses* came I would be eager to see their acting. And the directors of the theatre would
> accompany me with infinite care to see English theatre. When we returned home
> Girishbabu would ask, "How was it?" (pp. 33–4).

Here indeed is teaching to perform. Men teaching women the trick of the "inside" of
their captors, as the captors themselves code that "inside," with instruments supposedly generated in a deeper "inside," for general decipherment in an "outside," the
British audience, who supposedly possess "insides" that are resolutely considered
quite different from those held by these men and women. But the devout colonial
subject, decent dupe of univeralism, thinks to learn the trick perfectly. The performance of the teaching and of the learning is not mere mimicry. Deliberate, canny,
wholesale epistemic transformation is what we are witnessing here. This is not the
Natya Sastra warmed over. The idea that apprenticeship with the West introduces
analytic learning in place of rote learning is a sentiment that thoroughly informed the
debates on education in the nineteenth century and continues to this day: it was
heard in February 1991 from an Indian woman dancer who learnt her stuff from an
old-fashioned Indian male master but went on to collaborate with a European male
director whose method was not unlike Girishbabu's.[20]

A later passage allows us to sense how completely the principle of reasonable
learning affected the episteme:

> I had no taste for other topics of conversation. I liked only the accounts of the great
> British actors and actresses that respected Girishbabu gave me, the books he read to me.
> When Mrs. Sidnis [Siddons?] left theatre work, spent ten years in the married state and
> then returned to the stage, where in her acting the critics noticed what fault, where she
> was excellent, where lacking, all this he read and explained to me from books. He would
> also tell me which British actress practised her voice by mingling it with birdsong in the
> woods, this too he would tell me. How Ellen Terry dressed, how Bandman made himself
> up as Hamlet, how Ophelia dressed in flowers, what book Bankimchandra's *Durgeshnan-
> dini* imitated, in what English book *Rajani* found its idea [*bhab* = thoughts], so many
> things of this nature, I do not know where to begin. Thanks to the loving care of
> respected Girishbabu and other affectionate friends, I cannot recount how many tales

by what great English, Greek, French, and German authors I have heard. I did not only listen, I collected ideas [*bhab* = mood] from them and reflected upon them ceaselessly. As a result of this my nature [*shabhab – swabhava*] became such that, when I went to visit a garden, I did not like the buildings there, I would search out the secluded spots resplendent with wild flowers. I would feel that perhaps I lived in those woods, ever-nurtured by them! My heart would throw itself down as it witnessed beauty so intimately mingled with every plant and bud. It was as if my soul would start to dance with joy! When I sometimes went to a riverbank it would seem as if my heart would fill with waves, I would feel as if I had played in the waves of this river forever. Now these waves have left my heart and are throwing themselves about. The sand on the banks of the river at Kuchbihar is full of mica, most lovely, I would often go alone to the riverbank, which was quite far from my living quarters, lie down on the sand and watch the waves. I would feel as if they spoke to me. (pp. 35–6)

The rhetoric of this extended passage lays out the construction of the colonial subject as contradictory implied reader of the imperial text. Binodini was indeed receiving an education in English and European literature in a way that no university student does. To be sure, to learn to read well is to say "yes, yes" to the text, if only in order to say "no," in other words to perform it, if only against the grain. But between that general sense of performance and the narrow sense of performing in order to simulate there is an immense difference in degree. Binodini was not obliged to get her information right; the proper names are often askew. (Ellen Terry comes out "Ellentarry" in Bengali, a single word; and "Ophelia" inhabits the same register of reality as Mr. Bandman and Mrs. Sidnis.) Yet here we see the difference between knowing and learning. Binodini identifies with Bankim, the master-creator recognized as the successful colonial subject by the very *babu*-culture of Bengal that Kipling mocks. If Bankim had taken the *bhab* of British Literature, so would she; he to write, she to interpret through performance. Reading-in-performance *is* a species of writing, as Bankim himself recognized:

One day Bankimbabu came to see the performance of his *Mrinalini*, and I was playing the part of "Manorama" at that time. Having seen the part of Manorama being played, Bankimbabu said: "I only wrote the character of Manorama in a book, I had never thought to see it with my own eyes, seeing Manorama today I thought I was seeing my Manorama in front of me." (p. 36)[21]

The public sphere of professional theater and the private sphere of the self interpenetrate in the longer passage in a clearer and more intense model of what *can* happen in the classroom. In the consummate rhetoric of this gifted craftswoman, the epistemic simulacrum is obstinately sustained. The translator has taken care to preserve every "as if," every "perhaps." (It would have been possible to construct the Bengali sentences without them.) It is not a "real" nature that Binodini imagines as the place of eternal nurture. It is rather the planted woods in a garden house. In the passage about the waves, the *location* of the waves is made nicely indeterminate; but in fact the waves, ostensibly the vehicle of union, preserve separation between river and heart, displacing it from figure to figure. This rhetorical effusion does not break step with the ritual language celebrating her dead protector within which the autobiography is framed. It seems appropriate that we, in search of a model for the colonial subject as implied reader, should be implicated in the reader function of this thoroughly benevolent and utterly dominant male.

Binodini was no rural subaltern. In her own words:

> I was born in this great city of Calcutta, in a family without resource and property. But not to be called poverty-stricken, for, however painfully, we scratched together a living. … My grandmother, my mother, and the two of us, brother and sister. (p. 14)

Binodini is in a family of women, quite within the other discursive formation that can look upon marriage as a socio-economic institution of exchange for consumption.

> But with our sentience our sufferings from poverty increased, and then our grandmother perpetrated a marriage between my infant brother of five years and a girl of two and a half [the play between infant *shishu* – and girl – *balika* – is her own] and brought home a negligible quantity of ornaments. Then our livelihood was earned through the sale of ornaments.

It is not only the play between *shishu* and *balika* that signals that Binodini, writing at the age of forty-seven, after her brilliant and thwarted attempt at staging herself, in every sense, as female individualist, is still unemphatically at ease with the pragmatic patriarchal culture that thwarted her; although her expressed sentiments will not draw from it. The next few sentences quietly emphasize this, for it is the love (*sneho*) of the older women rather than the unconsummated child marriage that remains in memory: "My grandmother and respected Mother were most affectionate [*sneho-moyee*]. They would sell the ornaments one by one at the goldsmith's shop and give us all kinds of food stuff. They never regretted the ornaments."

The brother died soon after the marriage. What happened to the child bride deprived of her ornaments for the subsistence of the other women? We cannot know. But there can be no doubt that the tragedy of feminism is played out not only in the obvious and visible masculist suppression of Binodini's ambitions but also in the widening gap between the obscurity of the unremembered child widow and the subtle and layered memoir of the autobiographer.[22]

The male suppression of the competitive female is a poignant story, where the politically correct judgment is trivially obvious, but it is not the only story in coloniality. The feminist has the dubious task of marking the division in womanspace. Tagore may have found it difficult to stage the estranged wife Shoshi as the full-fledged colonial subject, insert her fully into the contradiction of implied readership, make her the agent of both *sneho* and *prem*, but the prostitute-performer Binodini straddles the gap with ease. In prostitution, sublated through performance on the colonially fractured stage, the old lesson in *lasya* is destroyed and preserved on another register as *prem*.[23] Although Binodini is bitter and contemptuous about the men's refusal to let her own a part of her beloved Star Theatre, and indeed to keep their promise of preserving her proper name by naming it "B-Theatre" – curious synecdoche, known only to the knowing – her extraordinary language of exalted devotion to her dead protector, her companion in the long years after her departure from the stage, rings with greater affect, as does the explicit (auto-)eroticism of her singular love poems, where the agency of the male lover is only present to the extent that it is necessary for the topos of male inconstancy. Marriage may be an institution that crumples when the woman is epistemically fractured, but residential (rather than itinerant) prostitution can be recoded as a peculiar liberty. How far do we want to take this as an allegory of colonial reading?

In the Brit. Lit. classroom today, an answer might be concocted in terms of Hanif Kureishi's *The Buddha of Suburbia*.[24] The shifts are: a century in time, coloniality through postcoloniality to migrancy, a literary representation by a male author who "read philosophy at King's College London" (jacket blurb). Here too an uncomfortable opposition between native and migrant can be undone or put under erasure (crossed out while leaving visible.)[25] Again, this is not conflation; perhaps the very shock of the reconstellation lets "truth"(s) flash forth.

The central character Karim will not be allowed to be English, even as Binodini was not allowed to be entrepreneurial professional individualist, although she carried bricks on her head for the building of the theater, he is

> Englishman born and bred, almost.... Englishman I am (though not proud of it), from the South London suburbs and going somewhere. Perhaps it is the odd mixture of continents and blood, of here and there, of belonging and not, that makes me restless and easily bored. (p. 3)

This is the flip side of Binodini's restless self-separation on the glittering sand of the Kuchbihar river; the style difference may be that between Romanticism (capital R) and existentialist modernism (small e, small m: *Catcher in the Rye, Under the Net*), rather than only that between India and Britain. Let the student notice that Karim, as he learns performance from British and American directors, is being asked to be "Indian," or to portray migrants favorably. He must dye his skin browner (his mother is working-class English) as he is given Mowgli's part in Kipling's *The Jungle Book*, and produce "an Indian accent," which he finally, during performance, begins to "send up" with occasional lapses into Cockney. Yet outside the theater, he lives in the incredible violence of racism in contemporary London, which is also vividly described in the novel.

Karim's father, a Muslim, becomes a Buddhist from do-it-yourself books and finds fulfillment with an "artist" woman. Yet there is real good sense in him, real unworld-liness, and there is love between them, however sweetly sexist.

Dominant British society shuttles between racist violence and approval of the "real" Indian. Once again, it is the productive epistemic fracture of the colonial, postcolonial, hybrid subject that is denied. The benevolent expectations are Kipling's Mowgli, or the Buddha of Suburbia. The transformation of the father is given in the third person. Let us consider what the son says, in the first person, about learning to act.

"India" is an imagined ingredient with material vestiges in the son's account, important in the survival technique of the fabrication of a hybrid identity. With a different political impulse from the malevolent racist British underclass, or the benevolent racist British artist, we too would like to keep alive the divide between "real" Indian and migrant "Indian." Without collapsing the difference, what if we attended to the fact that Binodini's imagined "England" and the representation of Karim's imagined "India" are both "created" under duress? We would begin, then, to plot an alternative literary historiography. Binodini thought of the duress as imaginative freedom. We are not surprised that Karim is represented as creatively happy when he puts together his stage Indian. Both are the intimate enemy, a violation that enables. The teacher of British literature in the former colonies must look at this phenomenon carefully, to let the differences appear in their entanglements.

Here, then, are the passages from *The Buddha of Suburbia*. Karim is rethinking the Indian character, having been criticized for his initial negative representation of an Indian immigrant:[26]

> At night, at home, I was working on Changez's shambolic walk and crippled hand, and on the accent, which I knew would sound, to white ears, funny and characteristic of India. (p. 188)

He is at his father's best friend Anwar's funeral (the two had come to Britain from Bombay many years ago):

> There was a minor row when one of the Indians pulled out a handy compass and announced that the hole hadn't been dug facing in the right direction, towards Mecca. . . . But I did feel, looking at these strange creatures now – the Indians – that in some way these were my people, and that I'd spent my life denying or avoiding that fact. I felt ashamed and incomplete at the same time, as if half of me were missing, and as if I'd been colluding with my enemies, those whites who wanted Indians to be like them. Partly I blamed Dad for this. After all, like Anwar, for most of his life he'd never shown any interest in going back to India. He was always honest about this: he preferred England in every way. Things worked; it wasn't hot; you didn't see terrible things on the street that you could do nothing about [this is contradicted by the graphic descriptions of racist violence in London]. He wasn't proud of his past, but he wasn't unproud of it either; it just existed, and there wasn't any point in fetishizing it, as some liberals and Asian radicals like to do. So if I wanted the additional personality bonus of an Indian past, I would have to create it. (pp. 212–13)

How very different from the "uncreative" sacrificial choice thrust on the rural woman or the unfetishized choice of a culture without the bonus of a past accessible to the "white migrant" imagined in the colonial context! Again, leisurely classroom consideration of the difference will show how the representations of "race," of "gendering," of "religion / culture" construct the chain of displacements on which these examples may be plotted. "Nation" and "class" relate to these links on other levels of abstraction.

For Binodini, the professional theater had promised an access to feminist individualism that residential prostitution denied. Along a chain of displacements, casual prostitution and the stage have become confused for Kureishi's character Karim, although in the "real" world, professional prostitution still has a confining relationship to the media. At any rate, the identity forged in the theater had come to organize Binodini's own staging of her identity in honorable residential prostitution recalled in later life. "The acting bit of her lost its moorings and drifted out into real life."[27] There is no such bleeding over in the representation of Karim. The character who plays the sexual field is the Paki. When he "wants the additional personality bonus of an Indian past," he reverses the demands of his protector, and "creates":

> There were few jobs I relished as much as the invention of Changez / Tariq....I uncovered notions, connections, initiatives I didn't even know were present in my mind....I worked regularly and kept a journal [*Amar Katha?*];...I felt more solid myself, and not as if my mind were just a kind of cinema for myriad impressions and emotions to flicker through. This was worth doing, this had meaning, this added up the elements of my life. And it was this that Pyke [the director] had taught me: what a creative life could be....I was prepared to pay the price for his being a romantic, an experimenter. He had to pursue what he wanted to know and follow his feelings wherever they went, even as far as my arse and my girlfriend's cunt. (p. 217)

Karim is a character in a book. The fact that this passage about creativity and the discovery of a coherent identity is much less gripping than Binodini's passage about divided self-creation cannot be taken as representative of the difference between the colonial reader's longing for the metropolis and the migrant's fancy for his roots. It is simply that our students might be encouraged to place it on that chain of displacements that will include *Gora* and *Kim* and *The Jungle Book*. Through attention to the rhetorical conduct of each link on the chain, the student might be encouraged, to belabor the by now obvious, neither to conflate nor oppose, but to figure out gender and class difference in complicity. I draw attention, again, to the moment when the half-caste tribal woman in "The Hunt" fabricates identity for the object (rather than the individualist subject) by intoning a word that would allow the indigenous exploiter to be constructed within the script of Oraon performance. Mahasweta offers a link in the chain away from migrancy into subalternity.

What I am suggesting, then, is that, in the postcolonial context, the teaching of English literature can become critical only if it is intimately yoked to the teaching of the literary or cultural production in the mother tongue(s). In that persistently asymmetrical intimacy, the topos of language learning, in its various forms, can become a particularly productive site. I am not speaking here of becoming an "expert" of the mother tongue, for the benefit of those who are thoroughly ignorant of it in the metropolis, a temptation to which many of us have given in. I am speaking of a much less practical thing: becoming "inter-literary," not "comparative," in the presence of long-established institutional divides and examination requirements. It is a kind of homoeopathic gesture: scratching at the epistemic fracture by awkwardly assuming a language to be an "epistemic system" and staging a collision between Kipling and Tagore, "Didi" and Binodini, "Mary Oraon" and "Karim." The authority of cultivating the felicitous implied readership is questioned in such teaching and learning. Any number of "correct" readings can be scrupulously taught here, with some degree of assurance that the reader's space of the mother tongue will secure the quotation marks by way of repeated colonial and postcolonial encounters, among them the one in the classroom.

Great clumps of topics are pulled up with this style of teaching: access to subjectivity, access to the other's language are among them. Such topics allow us to float into Commonwealth Literature, even without access to the various native traditions or emergences. The peculiar authority in this floating reading is of the contingent reader who *might* have that access. An interruptive authority, for the text is in English.

Let us consider an example: the last scene of Nadine Gordimer's *July's People*.[28]

Successful black insurgency in South Africa. A family being protectively steered into the village of their former servant, July. Barriers falling, people learning about being human, the nature of power, being gendered, the master–servant dialectic. The emergence of July's proper name – Mwawate – in itself the kind of topic that rocks the centralized place of the "implied reader." As if Man Friday should have a history. When people have been pared down a good bit, we encounter an event impossible to conceive earlier in the book. Mwawate speaks to his former mistress, the central character in the book, in his own language, with authority, dignity, and irritation. I will first quote the preparatory moments: "She knew those widened nostrils. Go, he willed, go up the hill to the hut; as he would to his wife. . . . The only way to get away from her was . . . to give up to her this place that was his own . . ." (p. 152).

Then a furious exchange in English about why had he stolen little things; why had she given him only rubbish; why had he accepted rubbish; almost frantically resembling what Jan Nederveen Pieterse has called "the dialects of terror": "*Not* discussed is the *initial* . . . terror, which includes the institutional violence of the denial of . . . human rights and [of imperialist] occupation."[29]

It is in response to this frustrating exchange that Mwawate speaks:

> You – He spread his knees and put an open hand on each. Suddenly he began to talk at her in his own language, his face flickering powerfully. The heavy cadences surrounded her; the earth was fading and a thin, far radiance from the moon was faintly pinkening parachute-silk hazes stretched over the sky. She understood although she knew no word. Understood everything: what he had had to be, how she had covered up to herself for him, in order for him to be her idea of him. But for himself – to be intelligent, honest, dignified for *her* was nothing; his measure as a man was taken elsewhere and by others. She was not his mother, his wife, his sister, his friend, his people. He spoke in English what belonged in English – Daniel he's go with those ones like in town. He's join. – The verb, unqualified, did for every kind of commitment: to a burial society, a hire purchase agreement, their thumbprints put to a labour contract for the mines or sugar plantations. (p. 152)

Gordimer is playing a whole set of variations on the topos of languages as epistemes. To begin with, the imperious gesture of the pronominal address as imperative: "You." But even before that, and surreptitiously, the sudden incursion of Mwawate's "inside" into the novel: "Go, *he willed*" (emphasis mine). It remains paratactic – cannot be staged as becoming syntactic in the hands of this white author woman writing about a female white protagonist, precisely because both are painfully politically correct. The sentences can start only after that enabling shifter, "you," (staged by the writer as) pronounced by the imperfect speaker of English. Put this on a spectrum of contemporary artists using this topos in many different ways: Toni Morrison, J. M. Coetzee, Guillermo Gomes-Pena, Jamelie Hassan.[30]

In the hands of a radical Creole writer like Gordimer, the implied black reader of a white text cannot be in a subject position, not even a compromised one like Shoshi's. The text belongs to the native speaker. But the rhetorical conduct of the text undermines and complicates this. The desire of the radical native speaker of English is in the sentence: "She understood although she knew no word." How fragile the logic of that sentence is; there are no guarantees. It is as if the white magistrate in "The Elder Sister" should enunciate the desire for understanding Shoshi's ambivalence, which the writer as classed male colonial subject articulates by way of the representation of his slight smile. And, in Gordimer's text there is the strong suggestion that rather than understand the "burden" of Mwawate's words, the peculiar situation of being addressed by him in his tongue produces in her an understanding of a narrative of, precisely, the infelicity of their communication. His utilization of this uneven bilinguality was elsewhere. "He spoke in English what belonged in English."

Just as Mwawate's subject space is syntactically inaccessible in the rhetoric of the novel, so is the dubious assertion of "understanding" unmoored from the passage that tells you *what* she understood. In addition, the man speaking his mother tongue – the other tongue from English – is deliberately distanced by a metonym with nature: Mwawate flickering, adjacent to the moon and the parachute silk clouds. Put this on a spectrum with the neat divisive locatives of nature and mind in Binodini's *self*-staging!

What is it that Mwawate says in English? It is the matter of public organizations: "he's join." This is not a "mistake," just as Dopdi Mejhen's "counter" is not.[31] In its profound ungrammaticality, it undoes the dominant language and pushes its frontiers as only pidgin can. Put this calm approach on a spectrum with Kipling's mockery, Rushdie's teratology, and Tagore's colonial prose.

It is not possible for an "expatriate English Professor," as Madhu Jain described me in a December 1990 issue of *India Today*, to produce a thick analysis of the burden of English teaching in India. Let me remind my readers that I have not attempted to comment on the importance of English as an international medium of exchange. (For the record, the proportion of Honors to Pass students in English at Delhi University is 602/13,900, 580/15,700, 660/17,300, 748/18,800 and 845/19,800 – for 1986–90 respectively.[32]) All I seem to have done is offered impractical suggestions: to undo the imported distinction between center and periphery as well as some indigenous institutional divisions by looking at literature as the staged battleground of epistemes.

These suggestions may not be altogether as impractical as they seem, at first glance, to the embattled local teacher. I am speaking, after all, of disturbing the arrangement of classroom material as well as our approach to it. Predictably, this would be against the interest of the student, who would have to sit for an examination that expects ferocious loyalty to a colonial curricular arrangement. (This is an argument we daily face, *mutatis mutandis*, in terms of bilingualism in the United States; in the 1960s and 1970s it was black English.) Can one share the dilemma with the students while preparing them for the regular exam papers? We have a time-honored strategy of politicization through pedagogy. The counter-argument here is the cynicism of students in a demoralized society, where English learning does not occupy center stage; also the difficulty of learning the language for those students who would be most susceptible to such politicization. (In the United States, this translates, as imperfectly as all translations, to the justified cynicism of the urban underclass student toward the smorgasbord of Cultural Studies.) Alas, the answers to that one are lost or found, lost *and* found, in the transactions in the classroom. It is to the most practical aspect of our trade that I dedicate these ruminations.

Would such a technique of teaching work outside of modern literature? And if so, with Adivasi creation-myths and the reclaiming of "African" mythic traditions by writers and filmmakers of contemporary Africa? Or only with *Beowulf* and the *Mahabharata*? One looks forward to an alternative literary historiography of postcoloniality critical of the hierarchical imprint of "the Commonwealth."

NOTES

This paper was delivered in a shorter form at Miranda House on February 13, 1987. I thank Gyan Pandey for giving the present version of the paper a first reading.

1 Ngugi wa Th'iongo, *Decolonizing the Mind: The Politics of Language in African Literature* (Portsmouth, NH: Heinemann, 1986).
2 Ngugi, *Decolonizing the Mind*, p. xi.
3 R. K. Narayan, "English in India," in *A Story-Teller's World* (New Delhi: Penguin India, 1989), pp. 20–3.
4 Rabindranath Tagore, "Didi," in *Galpaguchchha* (Calcutta: Visva-Bharati, 1975), vol. 2. Translations are my own.
5 I have given a historical account of this alienation outside of the classroom in "Once Again a Leap into the Post-Colonial Banal," *Differences* III, 3 (Fall 1991): 139–70.
6 David Hardiman comments on the peasants' misplaced belief that the British would give them direct access to vengeance as justice (discussion after "The Peasant Experience of Usury: Western India in the Nineteenth Century," paper delivered at the Davis Center for Historical Studies, Princeton University, April 12, 1991). In response to my query to Hardiman as to whether there is any documentary evidence that indigenous collaborators with the colonial authorities saw through this peasant belief, Gyan Prakash advises me to look in Bengali tract literature. Until I can undertake that research, I mark this place with the question: what are the cultural politics of Tagore's rhetorical representation of this belief or faith, at a later date, and on the woman's part?
7 Spivak, "Can the Subaltern Speak?," in Cary Nelson and Lawrence Grossberg, eds., *Marxism and the Interpretation of Culture: Limits, Boundaries, Frontiers* (Urbana: University of Illinois Press, 1988).
8 Ashis Nandy, *The Intimate Enemy: Loss and Recovery of the Self Under Colonialism* (Delhi: Oxford University Press, 1983).
9 For the importance of the assignment of reported, direct, and indirect speech and style, see V. N. Volosinov, *Marxism and the Philosophy of Language*, tr. Ladislav Matejka and I. R. Titunik (Cambridge, MA: Harvard University Press, 1986), Part III.
10 Madhu Kishwar, "Why I Do Not Call Myself a Feminist," *Manushi* 61 (Nov–Dec 1990).
11 Rudyard Kipling, *Kim* (reprint New York: Viking Penguin, 1987), pp. 210–11.
12 For an example of such a misunderstanding, with reference to the relationship between philosophy and literature, and based on minimal documentation, see the chapter on Derrida in Jurgen Habermas, *The Philosophical Discourse of Modernity: Twelve Lectures* (Cambridge, MA: MIT Press, 1987).

13 Binodini Dasi, *Amar Katha o Anyanyo Rachona*, ed. Saumitra Chattopadhyaya et al. (Calcutta: Subarnorekha, 1988). Translations mine. For a reading of this text in the context of women's autobiographies, see Partha Chatterjee, "In Their Own Words? Women's Autobiographies in Nineteenth-Century Bengal" (forthcoming).

14 Rabindranath Tagore, *Gora*, in *Rabindra Rachanabali* (Calcutta: Biswa-Bharati, 1955), vol. 6. Sujit Mukherjee is supervising a new translation of *Gora*.

15 I am grateful to Ranes Chakravorty for reading this paragraph to me, when my own *Gora* was inaccessible and the library did not have one.

16 Mahasweta Devi, "The Hunt," *Women in Performance* V, 1 (1990): 80–92.

17 The elegantly staged representation of Sarada Devi as the rural woman denoting cultural choice and victory in the general text of imperialist seduction is a complex variation on the thematics we are discussing (Swami Gambhirananda, *Srima Sarada Devi* (Calcutta: Udbodhan, 1st edn, 1954), pp. 1–6).

18 There are a handful of prominent whites of this genre who receive a great deal of publicity (on a less exalted register, like middle-class husbands who cook). They offer an eagerly grasped standby for cultural representation as alibi. One thinks of their role in Richard Attenborough's film *Gandhi* and, more recently, in the conception of the hero of *Dances with Wolves*.

19 The artificial separation between colonial (roughly British) and neocolonial (roughly US), migrant and postcolonial, covers a wide field. Howard Winant, for example, makes the claim that "*in the postmodern political framework of the contemporary United States, hegemony is determined by the articulation of race and class*" (Howard Winant, "Postmodern Racial Politics in the United States: Difference and Inequality," *Socialist Review* XX, 1 (Jan–Mar 1990): 137; author's emphasis. "Postmodern" is used here in the to me unsatisfactory sense of neocolonialism as being not only after the phase of modernization but also entering a phase after orthodox socialist radicalism.) A curricular reconstellation as is being proposed here might have broader implications than one imagines.

20 For a sober accounting of the debates, see J. P. Naik and Syed Nurullah, *A History of Education in India* (2nd rev. edn, London: Macmillan, 1951). The recent reference is to Samjukta Panigrahi, discussion after lecture demonstration with Eugenio Barba, at a Conference on Inter-Cultural Performance, Bellagio, February 20, 1991. The denigration of "rote" learning as opposed to "analytic" knowing is no longer as clearly on the agenda and shows evidence of an unquestioning ideological (and therefore often unwitting) acceptance of nineteenth-century imperialist universalism. The project would be to reinscribe the presuppositions – of knowledge before understanding – proposed in some Indian Speech Act linguistics that challenge British speech act theory (Bimal Krishna Matilal, "Knowledge from Linguistic Utterances," in *The Word and the World* (Delhi: Oxford University Press, 1990)).

21 For the contrast between Binodini's testimonial and Tagore's literary representation of the insulted wife playing, precisely, Manorama, see "Giribala" (see note 4, above).

22 It is not to denigrate feminism to point out that feminist ambition in the colonial nineteenth century must involve competition and class ambition. For a discussion of this in the western context, see Elizabeth Fox-Genovese, *Feminism Without Illusions: A Critique of Individualism* (Chapel Hill: University of North Carolina Press, 1991). Here too the relationship between colony and the West is complex, not merely oppositional. The fact that powerful men suppressed Binodini's ambition points at another complex relationship between feminism and the critique of capitalism.

23 The connection between the dramatic representation of lust and drama proper is available in reverse in Damodargupta's *Kuttinimatam* (see Mandakranta Basu, "*Lasya*: A Dramatic

Art?" in Bimal Krishna Matilal and Bilimoriya, eds., *Sanskrit and Related Studies* (Albany: State University of New York Press, 1992).)

24   Hanif Kureishi, *The Buddha of Suburbia* (New York: Viking Penguin, 1991).

25   Sensitively argued in "Location, Intervention, Incommensurability: A Conversation with Homi Bhabha," *Emergences* I (1989).

26   The criticism comes from Tracey, a politically mature African-British woman. In our classroom, we would have to develop the point of this criticism, significantly different from the desire of the white.

27   Martin Amis, *London Fields* (New York: Harmony Books, 1989). I quote this from a trendy English novelist somewhat bloody-mindedly, because Amis too is in a world transformed by migrants. His villain is "multiracial" in his choice of women. But the staging of identity in migrancy is not Amis's burden. Hence this sentence about life and acting does not attach to a multiracial character. They remain victims. Our best students will have to come to grip with the fact that the epistemic fracturing of the colonial reader is no longer a marginal event.

28   Nadine Gordimer, *July's People* (New York: Viking Penguin, 1981).

29   Jan Nederveen Pieterse, *Israel's State Terrorism and Counterinsurgency in the Third World* (Kingston: NECEF Publications, 1986), p. 4. My extrapolations refer to the specific case of Israel and Palestine. Again, the student can link the international press with autobiography, Brit. Lit., and vernacular literature if the teacher fills in Pieterse's passage. The pedagogic interest is, always, to globalize and politicize the burden by pointing at linked differences rather than divisive turf battles.

30   I have discussed this cluster in Spivak, "Acting Bits/Identity Talk," *Critical Inquiry* XVIII, 4 (1992): 770–803. Lars Engle makes a persuasive case for this passage as the characteristic irruption of the Freudian "uncanny" (Lars Engle, "The Political Uncanny: The Novels of Nadine Gordimer," *Yale Journal of Criticism* II, 2 (1989): 120–1). I think, however, it is more fruitful to consider the "uncanny" as inhabiting the past and the present and the future – always under the skin of the familiar everyday – rather than only a "post-revolutionary" future conceived as a future present in sequential narrative time. I also think that we should take note of "July"'s real name. The uncanny lurks under the skin of the everyday as Mwawate always lives in the skin that is always called July by his masters.

31   See Spivak, " 'Draupadi' by Mahasveta Devi," in *In Other Worlds: Essays in Cultural Politics* (New York: Routledge, 1987).

32   Figures received from University Grants Commission, May 9, 1991. For an excellent analysis of who studies English, see Yasmeen Lukmani, "Attitudinal Orientation Toward Studying English Literature in India" and Lola Chatterji, "Landmarks in Official Educational Policy" in Rajeswari Sunder Rajan, ed., *The Lie of the Land: English Literary Studies in India* (Delhi: Oxford University Press, 1992), pp. 156–86, 300–8.

Colonialism and the Desiring Machine

ROBERT J. C. YOUNG

Robert Young might be described as one of the "second wave" of postcolonial theorists who has attempted both to explain the important work of writers such as **Edward Said**, **Homi K. Bhabha**, and **Gayatri Chakravorty Spivak**, and to put forward his own contribution to the growing field of postcolonial studies. His first book, *White Mythologies*, critiques the work of these theorists and situates them within a general project of postcolonial historiography. The essay included here is the concluding chapter of Young's *Colonial Desire: Hybridity in Theory, Culture and Race* and explores the conjunction of Western philosophical theory and the "geography" of postcolonialism. Young adopts the controversial ideas of Gilles Deleuze and Felix Guattari (the former a philosopher, the latter a psychoanalyst) – especially the idea of "deterritorialization," which refers to the breakdown of existing physical, psychical, and conceptual boundaries and limits – in order to advance a theory of "desiring machines" which articulate and regulate power and discourse. By regarding colonial power and discourse, especially the discourse of race, in terms of energy "flows" and a fluid series of discursive connections and consolidations, Young suggests that we might be able to overcome the tyranny of structures (Oedipal and geopolitical) that sustained colonial power and continue to sustain neocolonial interventions in postcolonial countries. Like **Frantz Fanon** and **Bhabha**, Young brings a psychoanalytic acuity to bear on the political problems of postcolonialism and suggests that psychic structures, like political and geographical ones, must be changed before lasting and genuine social change can be effected.

Colonialism and the Desiring Machine

Colonial discourse analysis was initiated as an academic sub-discipline within literary and cultural theory by Edward Said's *Orientalism* in 1978.[1] This is not to suggest that colonialism had not been studied before then, but it was Said who shifted the study of colonialism among cultural critics towards its discursive operations, showing the intimate connection between the language and forms of knowledge developed for the study of cultures and the history of colonialism and imperialism. This meant that the kinds of concepts and representations used in literary texts, travel writings, memoirs and academic studies across a range of disciplines in the humanities and social sciences could be analysed as a means for understanding the diverse ideological practices of colonialism. Said's Foucauldian emphasis on the way in which Orientalism developed as a discursive construction, so that its language and conceptual structure determined both what could be said and what recognized as truth, had three main theoretical implications. First, Said showed how Foucault's notion of discourse offered an alternative way of thinking about the operations of ideology, both as a form of consciousness and as a lived material practice. If discourse comes close to Althusser's definition of ideology as the "representation of the imaginary relationship of individuals to their real conditions of existence", Said extended the implication to be found in Althusser that a cultural construction could be historically determining.[2] *Orientalism* thus challenged the traditional self-devaluation in deference to the economic of orthodox Marxist cultural criticism. And though doubtless the Western expansion into the East was determined by economic factors, Said argued that the enabling cultural construction of Orientalism was not simply determined by them, and thus established a certain autonomy of the cultural sphere.

The second implication of the charting of the complicity of Western literary and academic knowledge with the history of European colonialism was that it emphasized the ways in which seemingly impartial, objective academic disciplines had in fact colluded with, and indeed been instrumental in, the production of actual forms of colonial subjugation and administration. *Orientalism* provided powerful evidence of the complicity between politics and knowledge. In recent years it has been augmented by Martin Bernal's *Black Athena* (1987), which has provided the most detailed and comprehensive demonstration to date of the way in which the allegedly objective historical scholarship of an apparently non-political academic discipline, Classics, was in fact determined by its own cultural and political history – in this case, of racism and eurocentrism. Bernal's book suggests that the parameters that have already been set

Taken from *Colonial Desire: Hybridity in Theory, Culture and Race* (London: Routledge, 1995).

up defining the limits of colonial discourse need to be extended much more widely into the history of academic disciplines. *Black Athena* holds out the much more disturbing possibility that all Western knowledge is, directly or indirectly, a form of colonial discourse.

This can be related to the third, most controversial, contention of Said's book, namely that the discursive construction of Orientalism was self-generating, and bore little, if any, relation to the actuality of its putative object, "the Orient". The important point here is that Western knowledge of the Other can be seen to be constructed as a part of the whole system of Orientalist discourse: "such texts can *create* not only knowledge but also the very reality that they appear to describe" (94). This knowledge has no necessary relation to the actual at all. It is for this reason that there is no *alternative* to the Western construction of the Orient, no "real" Orient, because the Orient is itself an Orientalist concept. Orientalism, according to Said, is simply "a kind of Western projection onto and will to govern over the Orient" (95). This has been the most disputed aspect of his thesis and the most difficult for his critics to accept.

At the same time, it has been one which, at worst, has allowed a certain lack of historical specificity. After all, if Orientalist discourse is a form of Western fantasy that can say nothing about actuality, while at the same time its determining cultural pressure means that those in the West cannot but use it, then any obligation to address the reality of the historical conditions of colonialism can be safely discarded. Such colonial-discourse analysis has meant that we have learnt a lot about the fantasmatics of colonial discourse, but at the same time it has by definition tended to discourage analysts from inquiring in detail about the actual conditions such discourse was framed to describe, analyse or control. Said's emphasis on the question of representation has at best been balanced by attention to the reality which that representation missed or excluded: not only the suppressed "voice of the Other", but also the history of the subaltern, both in terms of the objective history of subaltern or dominated, marginalized groups, and in terms of the subjective experience of the effects of colonialism and domination, an area most searchingly investigated by the founding father of modern colonial critique, Frantz Fanon.[3] The most productive revisions of Said's work have therefore focused on the question of representation, mediated with analyses of counter-histories or the effects of colonialism on colonial subjects and the forms of their subjectivity.

The totalizing aspect of Said's argument in *Orientalism* was quickly challenged by Homi K. Bhabha, who maintained that Said assumed too readily that an unequivocal intention on the part of the West was always realized through its discursive productions.[4] Bhabha focused on Said's claim that Orientalist knowledge was instrumental and always worked successfully when put into practice. In theoretical terms Bhabha's move was to add psychoanalysis to Said's Foucauldian analysis, and he did this neatly by finding it already in Said. Bhabha called attention to the moment in which Said briefly, but in an undeveloped way, set up the possibility of Orientalism working at two conflictual levels, and in a significant but uncharacteristic invocation of psycho-analysis, distinguished between a "manifest" Orientalism, the conscious body of "scientific" knowledge about the Orient, and a "latent" Orientalism, an unconscious positivity of fantasmatic desire. Bhabha's outstanding contribution has been to develop the implications of this idea by emphasizing the extent to which the two levels fused and were, in operation, inseparable; he has shown how colonial discourse of whatever kind operated not only as an instrumental construction of knowledge but also according to the ambivalent protocols of fantasy and desire. Ambivalence is a key word for Bhabha, which he takes from psychoanalysis where it was first developed to describe a continual fluctuation between wanting one thing and its opposite (also "simultaneous attraction toward and repulsion from an object, person or action"). In making ambivalence the constitutive heart of his analyses, Bhabha has in effect performed a political reversal at a conceptual level in which the periphery – the borderline, the marginal, the unclassifiable, the doubtful – has become the equivocal, indefinite, indeterminate ambivalence that characterizes the centre.

Bhabha has subsequently extended this idea of a constitutive ambivalence resting at the heart of colonial discursive production, an ambivalence that its appearance in a non-European context only accentuated. He has exhibited through a series of analyses the ways in which European colonial discourse – whether it be governmental decree, district officers' reports or missionary accounts – is effectively decentred from its position of power and authority. We have already seen how Bhabha shows that this occurs when authority becomes hybridized when placed in a colonial context and finds itself layered against other cultures, very often through the exploitation by the colonized themselves of its evident equivocations and contradictions that are all too apparent in the more hostile and challenging criteria of alien surroundings. An example of the different kind of framing that Western culture receives when translated into different contexts would be Bhabha's illustration of a Christian missionary trying to teach Indian Hindus about the Christian communion service: the missionary is quite confounded when he finds that the vegetarian Hindus react with horror to the idea of eating Christ's body and drinking his blood. Suddenly it is the white English culture that betrays itself, and the English missionary who is turned into a cannibalistic vampire.[5] If Said shows that misrelation is the anagrammatic secret of Orientalism, then Bhabha demonstrates that oscillation is that of the colonialist.

By contrast, Gayatri Chakravorty Spivak has been concerned to emphasize, against Said, the possibility of counter-knowledges such as those constructed around the criteria of the journal *Subaltern Studies*.[6] The desire of today's anti-colonial historian is to retrieve a subaltern history that rewrites the received account both of the colonizing academics and of the native ruling elite, a history of the excluded, the voiceless, of those who were previously at best only the object of colonial knowledge and fantasy. Spivak seeks to analyse the effects of colonial violence and denial of subjectivity on subjectivity. She stresses the pitfalls and aporias that even radical historiography can fall into, drawing particular attention to examples of histories that continue to be ignored even today by revisionist historians, particularly those of native subaltern women. Such women were subject to what is today often called a "double colonization" – that is, in the first instance in the domestic sphere, the patriarchy of men, and then, in the public sphere, the patriarchy of the colonial power.[7] This has led to increasing comparisons being made between patriarchy and colonialism. Spivak argues that taken always as an object of knowledge, by colonial and indigenous rulers who are as masculist as each other, the subaltern woman is written, argued about, even legislated for, but allowed no discursive position from which to speak herself.[8] She therefore tends to be absent from the documentary archives, and to write her history has to involve a particular effort of retrieval, or, in the case of fiction such as Toni Morrison's *Beloved*, a particular effort of historical imagination.

This focus on the kinds of exclusion produced not only by colonialism itself but even by current forms of understanding is typical of Spivak's more general concern with what she considers to be the continuing epistemic violence that is practised in the exercise of Western forms of thought upon the East. Equally importantly, Spivak has championed with a remarkable degree of success the cause of minority groups excluded or neglected by contemporary academic, particularly feminist, practices. It is typical of the relentlessly questioning nature of her work, however, that she has recently been concerned with an interrogation of, as she sees it, the increasing commodification in academia of the category of "marginality" itself.[9] Yet in her own work she has, through her own hybridizing, syncretic method which juxtaposes the political priorities of gender, class and race through a constant theoretical modulation, brilliantly forced the disruption of the marginal through the mainstream of contemporary academic presuppositions, pushing them to their unrecognizable limits.

Aspects of these positions have been elaborated and developed by a number of other critics, but it would be true to say that Said, Bhabha and Spivak constitute the Holy Trinity of colonial-discourse analysis, and have to be acknowledged as central to the field. While there has been a remarkable, indeed quite staggering, growth of analysts researching in this area, an increasing tendency has been to produce new archival material rather than to develop further the theoretical parameters set up by Said et al. The main challenge has come from critics such as Chandra Talpade Mohanty, Benita Parry or Aijaz Ahmad, who have criticized a certain textualism and idealism in colonial-discourse analysis which, they allege, occurs at the expense of materialist historical enquiry.[10] There is considerable cogency to many of these objections, but it could be also argued that they also involve a form of category mistake: the investigation of the discursive construction of colonialism does not seek to replace or exclude other forms of analysis, whether they be historical, geographical, economic, military or political – and there are certainly plenty of studies of colonialism of those kinds. The contribution of colonial-discourse analysis is that it provides a significant framework for that other work by emphasizing that all perspectives on colonialism share and have to deal with a common discursive medium which was also that of colonialism itself: the language used to enact, enforce, describe or analyse colonialism is not transparent, innocent, ahistorical or simply instrumental. Colonial-discourse analysis can therefore look at the wide variety of texts of colonialism as something more than mere documentation or "evidence", and also emphasize the ways in which colonialism involved not just a military or economic activity, but permeated forms of knowledge which, if unchallenged, may continue to be the very ones through which we try to understand colonialism itself. Here we have the ultimate explanation for the "alienation effect" of much of the language of postcolonial criticism. It is for this reason also that a major task of postcolonialism must be the production of a "critical ethnography of the West", analysing the story of a West haunted by the excess of its own history.[11]

The underlying message of the increasing fervour of attacks on Said has probably less to do with his own work than with his influence, and the sense that from a theoretical rather than an archival perspective colonial-discourse analysis as a general method and practice has reached a stage where it is itself in danger of becoming oddly stagnated, and as reified in its approach – and therefore in what it can possibly produce at the level of investigation – as the colonial discourse that it studies. We have reached something of an impasse with regard to the theoretical questions raised in the study of colonial discourse, and this has meant a certain complacency about or neglect of the problems of the methodologies that have been developed. In other words, we have stopped asking questions about the limits and boundaries of our own assumptions. It is true that we now generally acknowledge the operation of conflictual structures within colonial discourse: but this very textual ambivalence prevents us from standing back to reconsider colonial discourse itself as an entity. Problems there are, certainly, that remain, and they are not hard to locate. To what extent is "colonial discourse" itself a legitimate general category? It is hard to avoid the accusation that there is a certain idealism involved in its use as a way of dealing with the totality of discourses of and about colonialism. If this has not been over-apparent it is because the dominance in recent years of India as object of attention among those working in the field – and therefore not surprisingly in the work done by them – has meant that there has been a noticeable geographical and historical homogenization of the history of colonialism. But does the fact that modern colonialism was effected by European or European-derived powers mean that the discourse of colonialism operated everywhere in a similar enough way for the theoretical paradigms of colonial-discourse analysis to work equally well for them all? Clearly the ideology and procedures of French colonialism, based on an egalitarian Enlightenment assumption of the fundamental sameness of all human beings and the unity of the human race, and therefore designed to assimilate colonial peoples to French civilization, differed very substantially from the indirect-rule policies of the British which were based on an assumption of difference and of inequality, or from those of the German or the Portuguese. (Even today, the weather report in *Le Monde* cites the temperature in Point-à-Pitre, capital of Guadeloupe, which, like Césaire's Martinique, is part of mainland France and thus of the European Union.) South America, where many states achieved independence in the early nineteenth century, would be only the most obvious example of a region where colonialism has a very different history from that of, say, India, which the British left only in 1947. Contemporary forms of colonialism, such as exist in Northern Ireland or Palestine, provide further complications. This heterogeneity points to the question of historical difference. Can we assume that colonial discourse operates identically not only across all space but also throughout time? In short, can there be a general theoretical matrix that is able to provide an all-encompassing framework for the analysis of each singular colonial instance?

In recent years there has also been a growing unease about the tendency of anti-Eurocentric writing to homogenize not just the "Third World" but also the category of "the West" as such – by writers who are, of course, very often themselves the product of that same "West". But in the face of such objections we need to remind ourselves that these increasingly troublesome general categories, such as "the West", or "colonialism" or "neocolonialism" – and even "colonial discourse" – are themselves in their current usage often the creation of Third World theorists, such as Fanon,

Nkrumah or Said, who needed to invent such categories precisely as general categories in order to constitute an object both for analysis and for resistance.[12] At a
certain level, most forms of colonialism are after all, in the final analysis, colonialism,
the rule by force of a people by an external power. In practical political terms, it was
necessary to construct a general object of attack in order to counter the divide-and-
rule policies of colonial administrations. During the independence struggles, it was
also imperative to form alliances with all those who were suffering from colonial
oppression from whatever source – particularly when the European, North American
and Asian colonial powers were themselves engaged in fierce struggles with each
other which were partly played out in colonial scenarios. Fanon points out how
colonialism itself was "separatist and regionalist", a technique designed to reinforce
separation and quietism.[13] Those who today emphasize its geographical and historical differences may in effect be only repeating uncritically colonialism's own parti-
tioning strategies. Yet at this point in the postcolonial era, as we seek to understand
the operation and effects of colonial history, the homogenization of colonialism does
also need to be set against its historical and geographical particularities. The question
for any theory of colonial discourse is whether it can maintain, and do justice to, both
levels.

It is also time to consider the extent to which certain Western assumptions,
evaluations and even institutional divisions operate within the emphases and priorities that we place through the selection of material for study. In Britain, work on
Latin America, for example, tends to function rather distinctly and in isolation from
much of the rest of colonial-discourse analysis, largely because it is not an area where
the English have played any great historical role, and therefore tends to remain the
preserve of Latin Americanists within Departments of Hispanic Studies. In comparison to the extensive work done on India, meanwhile, Africa remains comparatively
neglected.[14] In Britain the reasons for this doubtless begin with the greater number of
British Asians in higher education, as well as the difference in comparable numbers of
academics and graduate students from Africa and Asia. Nevertheless, the greater
attention accorded to India still seems to perpetuate the differing evaluations that the
British accorded to the various parts of their Empire. It was always India that received
the greatest economic, cultural and historical attention from the British. In the same
way, today India quite clearly retains that position of pride of place, the jewel in the
crown of colonial-discourse analysis.

ANTI-OEDIPUS: THE GEOPOLITICS OF CAPITALISM

From a theoretical point of view, this situation has occurred because the analytic
paradigms developed for other literatures or continents have not apparently been
strong enough to challenge the discursive model of *Orientalism*; indeed it is not
uncommon today to find cultural critics using the term 'Orientalism' as a synonym
for 'colonialism' itself. The problem with Said's book was that its historical and
theoretical argument was so persuasive that it seemed to allow no alternatives. As
the *New York Times* put it, "his case is not merely persuasive, but conclusive". After
his brilliant demonstration that Orientalism as a discourse constructed an all-

encompassing representation of, and form of knowledge about, the Orient, we have ever since been looking for chinks in its apparently hegemonic surface. The crucial point here is that it is not enough to produce individual instances that appear to contradict Said's thesis – for his thesis already includes that possibility. So I want to explore now a different tack, by taking instead Said's argument a bit further.

David Trotter has recently emphasized the way that the concept of colonial discourse implies an understanding of colonialism as "a text without an author": there will always be authors of individual texts, but colonial discourse as such makes up a signifying system without an author. Colonialism therefore becomes a kind of machine. At the same time, like Adam Smith's economic and historical machines, colonialism is also a determining, law-governed process; its workings, therefore, get attached to those of the historical and economic machines.[15] It was indeed as a machine that the colonialists themselves often envisaged the operations of colonial power. Said cites Lord Cromer's essay on "The Government of Subject Races" (1908), in which he

> envisions a seat of power in the West, and radiating out from it towards the East a great embracing machine, sustaining the central authority yet commanded by it. What the machine's branches feed into it in the East – human material, material wealth, knowledge, what have you – is processed by the machine, then converted into more power.[16]

Or, in a somewhat perverse but characteristic later reversal of the image, colonists argued that even resistance to the machine was a sign of its effectiveness. Lord Lugard, for example, cites approvingly a particularly interesting mixed metaphor from Lucas's "United Empire" (1919): "Nothing should appeal so strongly as the Empire to democracy, for it is the greatest engine of democracy the world has ever known. . . . It has infected the whole world with liberty and democracy."[17]

It is in the context of the widespread idea of the Empire as machine that I want to consider the work of Deleuze and Guattari; they offer, I suggest, not something that could be described as an alternative to Said's paradigm, but a related though different way of thinking about some of the operations of colonialism, particularly not just as a form of fantasy but also as a form of ambivalent desire. In the first place, the *Anti-Oedipus* has the advantage of decentring colonial analysis away from the East towards a more global surface.[18] It also redirects our attention towards two obvious but important points that tend to get lost in today's emphasis on discursive constructions – the role of capitalism as the determining motor of colonialism, and the material violence involved in the process of colonization. The attraction of Deleuze and Guattari's argument from a theoretical point of view is similarly the way in which philosophy, psychoanalysis, anthropology, geography, economics et al. are all brought together in one interactive economy and shown to be implicated in capitalism's colonizing operations.

The first thing to remark about Deleuze and Guattari's *Anti-Oedipus* is its virtual absence from discussions of postcolonial theory. Only their essay "What is Minor Literature?" has achieved any substantive impact in this area, though in recent years the formulations about minorities in *A Thousand Plateaus* have been increasingly cited in the context of discussions of new concepts of radical democracy.[19] Despite the very

real difficulty of the *Anti-Oedipus* which has doubtless been a major factor in preventing its widespread reception in this country (though why the difficulty of *this* book?),
its basic paradigm is relatively simple and is derived from Reich. The argument is that
the flow of desire, or as Deleuze and Guattari call it in their desubjectified version, the
desiring machine, has been repressed in our society through the mechanism of the
Oedipus complex. The Oedipal triad institutes a structure of authority and blockage
that operates not only in the family, but through the family at the level of society in
general. Freud's "discovery" of the Oedipus complex was therefore his most radical
insight, but one which he immediately suppressed by regarding it as the normal form
of development through which all individuals should go, rather than recognizing it as
the primary means of ideological repression in capitalist society. Psychoanalysis as a
therapeutic institution therefore operates, in this account, as a policing agent for
capitalism. While only those profiting from the analytic institution would probably
want to dispute this part of the argument, it is true that Deleuze and Guattari's
description of repression retains a Reichian or even a Lawrentian simplicity in its
nature / culture, natural / artificial opposition; the general panacea of "schizoculture"
as the preferred form for the production of desire and the curing of the ills imposed by
psychoanalysis and capitalism is no doubt a discouragement for many readers. But
despite this problem, I want to argue that there are good reasons for reconsidering the
Anti-Oedipus in the context of postcolonial critique.

What is important is the way in which Deleuze and Guattari produce a social
theory of desire which cuts through the problematic psychic–social opposition of
orthodox psychoanalysis. Central to Freud's repression of his own Oedipal insight
would be the way in which he failed to see the intimate connection between the
production of desire and social production in its widest sense – a schism that has
remained a defining feature of most psychoanalysis ever since. Deleuze and Guattari
retrieve this relation through their famous Spinozistic "body without organs" which
constitutes the (social) body to which desire attaches itself in a movement of coupling
and disjunction, as well as the unseen body of "capital as a proliferating body, money
that produces more money", and even the totality of the earth itself, a vast "surface
for the recording of the entire process of production of desire".[20] Desire flows laterally
according to points of disjunction and zones of intensity on the grids of this egg-like
surface. The "subject", instead of being at the centre, is "produced as a mere
residuum" of the processes of the desiring machines, the nomadic offshoot of striated
mental spaces and of the body defined as longitude and latitude: "Individual or group,
we are traversed by lines, meridians, geodesics, tropics, and zones marching to
different beats and differing in nature."[21]

Deleuze and Guattari are thus concerned to break down the conventional epistemological distinction between materiality and consciousness. The general thrust of
their work is to deny any differentiation between "the social production of reality on
the one hand, and a desiring production that is mere fantasy on the other": rather,
they maintain that "the social field is immediately invested by desire, that it is the
historically determined product of desire" (28–9). Desire is a social rather than an
individual product; it permeates the infrastructure of society – a position that Deleuze
and Guattari can hold because they have already separated desire from the subject by
defining sexuality as "the libidinal unconscious of political economy", a move that

opens up new possibilities for the analysis of the dynamics of desire in the social field.[22] Racism is perhaps the best example through which we can immediately grasp the form of desire, and its antithesis, repulsion, as a social production: "thus fantasy is never individual: it is *group fantasy*".[23]

Colonial discourse would provide another example of such a group fantasy, and we can see other ways in which the *Anti-Oedipus* impinges upon questions relating to colonialism. This is most pronounced in the theorization of capitalism according to a geospatial model of the inscription of the flows of desire upon the surface or body of the earth: the operations of global capitalism are here characterized as a form of "cartography".[24] Social production works, in Deleuze and Guattari's terms, as an inscription or writing machine:

> The prime function incumbent on the socius has always been to codify the flows of desire, to inscribe them, to record them, to see to it that no flow exists that is not properly dammed up, channeled, regulated. . . . But the *capitalist machine* . . . finds itself in a totally new situation: it is faced with the task of decoding and deterritorializing the flows. (33)

Where capitalism differs from earlier historical forms such as despotism is that it does not simply encode and therefore control desire: it has to operate through a double movement because it must first of all do away with the institutions and cultures that have already been developed. The basic need of capitalism is to engineer an encounter between the deterritorialized wealth of capital and the labour capacity of the deterritorialized worker.[25] The reduction of everything, including production and labour, to the abstract value of money enables it to decode flows and "deterritorialize" the socius. Having achieved a universal form of exchange, it then reterritorializes – "institutes or restores all sorts of residual and artificial, imaginary, or symbolic territorialities" such as states, nations or families:

> There is the twofold movement of decoding or deterritorializing flows on the one hand, and their violent and artificial reterritorialization on the other. The more the capitalist machine deterritorializes, decoding and axiomatizing flows in order to extract surplus values from them, the more its ancillary apparatuses, such as government bureaucracies and the forces of law and order, do their utmost to reterritorialize, absorbing in the process a larger and larger share of surplus value. (34–5)

This description of the operations of capitalism as a territorial writing machine seems not only especially suited to the historical development of industrialization, but also describes rather exactly the violent physical and ideological procedures of colonization, deculturation and acculturation, by which the territory and cultural space of an indigenous society must be disrupted, dissolved and then reinscribed according to the needs of the apparatus of the occupying power. These structures of decoding and recoding, of deterritorialization and reterritorialization, operate rather like the simultaneous antithetical categories of Roget's *Thesaurus*: their repetitive wave-like movements upon the territories and cultures of the earth provide a dynamic model for the processes of colonization, and also have the advantage of being able to describe both the historical material procedures of colonialism and its ideological operations, whether it be the severing of the body from the land, the destruction and reconstruction of cultures or the fabrication of knowledge according to the propriety of new disciplines. In this way it can be argued that Deleuze and Guattari have produced a theory of capitalism to which the operation of colonialism as a form of writing geography is central. It is not surprising, therefore, that the idea has been taken up most effectively, if briefly, by a geographer: in the *Condition of Postmodernity* (1989), David Harvey argues that

> the accumulation of capital is perpetually deconstructing ... social power by reshaping its geographical basis. Put the other way round, any struggle to reconstitute power relations is a struggle to reorganize their spatial basis. It is in this light that we can better understand "why capitalism is continuously reterritorializing with one hand what it was deterritorializing with the other".[26]

It is this link between capitalism, colonialism and spatiality that is so effectively articulated by Deleuze and Guattari. At the same time, Fanon provides a necessary complementary perspective of the historical and the actual, of the practices by means of which land and bodies are brought under colonial control, of the forms of violent inscription through which power relations are established. His account of "the enterprise of deculturation" no doubt inspired the theoretical paradigm of the *Anti-Oedipus* and its articulation of the mechanisms that the native population undergoes under colonial enslavement:

> For this its systems of reference have to be broken. Expropriation, spoliation, raids, objective murder, are matched by the sacking of cultural patterns, or at least condition such sacking. The social panorama is destructured; values are flaunted, crushed, emptied.[27]

At the same time, Fanon also emphasizes the dialectical effect of the violence of colonial imposition so that there is a complicity between the interventions of capitalism and colonialism and the reactive "violent forces that blaze up in colonial territory":

> The violence which has ruled over the ordering of the colonial world, which has ceaselessly drummed the rhythm for the destruction of native social forms and broken up without reserve the systems of reference of the economy, the customs of dress and external life, that same violence will be claimed and taken over by the native at the moment when, deciding to embody history in his own person, he surges into the forbidden quarters.[28]

The destruction of the colonizer's zone is fuelled by the way in which colonial violence has been enacted on the subjectivity of the native. In this articulation of the social with the subjective we find a further analogy between Fanon and Deleuze and Guattari. The latter link the geographical back to the psychical through what they call "the analytic imperialism of the Oedipus complex" (23). Once again they reverse the normal procedure whereby colonialism is seen as the aberrant offshoot of European civilization: according to them the link between the family and the state is achieved through a form of interior, ideological territorialization of the psyche that turns questions and dilemmas from the social realm into the problem of the individual. Freud participates in this transaction by using the Oedipus myth to interpret the neuroses of family life – "not as effects of the society which the family represents, but as the psychic production of the children who suffer them".[29] The foreign is thus made domestic in a movement of psychic recodification: "Oedipus is always colonization pursued by other means, it is the interior colony . . . it is our intimate colonial education." Oedipus is not simply the normal structure through which all humans travel on the path to mental, sexual and social maturity: it is the means through which the flow of desire is encoded, trapped, inscribed within the artificial reterritorializations of a repressive social structure – the family, the party, the nation, the law, the educational system, the hospital, psychoanalysis itself. The disruptive effect of the colonial space upon the claims of psychoanalysis, by demonstrating that the Oedipus complex is not universal outside the operations of capitalism, is a matter as much for the politics of psychoanalysis as of colonialism, but is significant for the theory in providing the basis of the proof that Oedipus consists of a limit-case and therefore a form of ideological reterritorialization.[30] The structure of the Oedipus complex may emerge in the colonial situation but only because the colonial subject is constructed through imposed cultural and political forms which are internalized as a condition of psychic reality, and then reproduced as the basis for normative social experience. In Deleuze and Guattari's argument, this procedure also operates equally for the subjects of the West: the metropolitan – colonial relation has thus once again been turned round so that global colonialism becomes the historical structure of capitalism, whether at home or abroad.[31]

Deleuze and Guattari's concept of territorialization is also particularly important in the context of colonialism and involves three further implications. The first serves as a reminder that colonialism above all involves the physical appropriation of land, its capture for the cultivation of another culture. It thus foregrounds the fact that cultural colonization was not simply a discursive operation but a seizure of cultural (in all senses of the word) space. Early examples of attempts at mapping the world show how colonialism was impelled by a global desire which fuelled its ever-increasing spatial expansion. This moved, inevitably, through different stages: in the first, space forms the basis of a trade which changed a self-sufficient feudal society into a city-culture based on trade between cultures absent to each other; the colonialism of "commerce and cultivation" sought land for the cultivation of hot-climate crops, while the colonialism derived from population surpluses required more temperate land for emigration; finally, there was imperial space – required because of a belief in the necessarily expansive nature of culture *per se*, a doctrine that fuelled the famous "scramble" for Africa from the 1880s onwards.[32] Each of these moments can be articulated with Deleuze and Guattari's definition of territorialization, deterritorialization and reterritorialization as the dynamics of the colonial or imperial propagation of economic, cultural and social spatialization.

The second implication of territorialization can be viewed in terms of the relation between the land and the state. The institution of the state is frequently regarded as the distinctive sign of the arrival of "civilization" over "primitivism". As Engels pointed out, the state is first and foremost a territorial concept.[33] In colonialism, therefore, we often have a conflict between societies that do and do not conceive of land as a form of private property: at one level indeed, colonialism involves the introduction of a new notion of land as property, and with it inevitably the appropriation and enclosure of land. This develops into a larger system of the imposition of economic roles and identities. Deleuze and Guattari's later concept of "nomadism", which appears in volume two of the *Anti-Oedipus*, *A Thousand Plateaus*, is important here. Nomadism works as a form of indirect opposition to the state; so Deleuze and Guattari challenge their readers to find "points of non-culture and underdevelopment, the zones of... third-worlds" in their own societies and knowledge systems.[34] Nomadism thus describes both the form of society that preceded feudalism and capitalism as well as a certain strategic manœuvring that can be employed in the terrain of the present. As the idea of movement across territories in its name suggests, nomadism involves forms of lateral resistance to any assertion of hegemonic control through strategies of multiplicity, forms of deterritorialization that cannot be reterritorialized because they frustrate interpretation and recording. Terrorism would be an extreme example of a political activity whose deeds are designed to resist interpretation as much as to assert power. But nomadism involves any activity that transgresses contemporary social codes through the dissolution of cultural and territorial boundaries.[35] At the same time, Deleuze and Guattari reach too quickly for such counter-strategies: if we recall the enforced dislocations of the peoples of the South, it means that we cannot concur with the idea that "nomadism" is a radically anti-capitalist strategy; nomadism is, rather, one brutal characteristic mode of capitalism itself.[36]

Territorialization in its third mode highlights that characteristic of colonialism so effectively emphasized, as we have already noted, by Fanon, *contra* Gandhi: violence. Colonization begins and perpetuates itself through acts of violence, and calls forth an answering violence from the colonized.[37] Here capitalism is the destroyer of signification, the reducer of everything to a Jakobsonian system of equivalences, to commodification through the power of money. This allows a certain degree of historical specificity: for colonialism operated through a forced symbiosis between territorialization as, quite literally, plantation, and the demands for labour which involved the commodification of bodies and their exchange through international trade. Commerce, by reducing everything in a society to a system of universal equivalency, to a value measured in terms of something else, thus performs an operation of cultural decoding that works according to the linguistic form of metaphor. At the same time, at a literal level, the goods provided in exchange for bodies were often articles like iron, copper or cloth that were already available locally. Such trade had the effect of destroying indigenous industries and thus deterritorializing and reterritorializing production through the creation of forms of dependency.

All this suggests the ways in which the *Anti-Oedipus* offers a means of thinking through not only the discourse, but also the repressive geopolitics of colonialism. The desiring machine provides a means of articulating the violent way in which colonial practices were inscribed both physically and psychically on the territories and peoples subject to colonial control. The problem with the *Anti-Oedipus* as it stands for any form of historical analysis, apart from its sheer difficulty, is that the processes of decoding, recoding and overcoding imply a form of cultural appropriation that does not do justice to the complexities of the way in which cultures interact, degenerate and develop over time in relation to each other. Decoding and recoding implies too simplistic a grafting of one culture on to another. We need to modify the model to a form of palimpsestual inscription and reinscription, an historical paradigm that will acknowledge the extent to which cultures were not simply destroyed but rather layered on top of each other, giving rise to struggles that themselves only increased the imbrication of each with the other and their translation into increasingly uncertain patchwork identities. In addition, contrary to the implication of deterritorialization and reterritorialization, it was often the case that colonial powers such as Britain did not erase or destroy a culture, but rather attempted to graft on to it a colonial superstructure that would allow the convenience of indirect rule, freezing the original indigenous culture by turning it into an object of academic analysis, while imposing the mould of a new imperial culture. This was not a simple process of the production of a new mimesis, however. Analysis of colonial discourse has shown that no form of cultural dissemination is ever a one-way process, whatever the power relation involved. A culture never repeats itself perfectly away from home. Any exported culture will in some way run amok, go phut or threaten to turn into mumbo-jumbo as it dissolves in the heterogeneity of the elsewhere.

Above all, however, what the *Anti-Oedipus* offers is a way of theorizing the material geopolitics of colonial history as, at the same time, an agonistic narrative of desire. While providing an overall theoretical paradigm, the desiring machine also allows for the specificity of incommensurable, competing histories forced together in unnatural unions by colonialism. Nothing catches this disavowed but obsessional tale of disjunctive connections between territories and bodies better than the pulsations of the desiring machines caught up in a continual process of breaks and flows, couplings and uncouplings, "crossing, mixing, overturning structures and orders...always pushing forward a process of deterritorialization".[38] The repressive legacy of the desiring machine of colonial history is marked in the aftermath of today's racial categories that speak of hybrid peoples, yoked together: Black British, British Asian, Kenyan Asian, Anglo-Indian, Indo-Anglian, Indo-Caribbean, African-Caribbean, African-American, Chinese-American.... The names of these diasporic doubles bear witness to a disavowal of any crossing between white and black. In today's political terms any product of white and black must always be classified as black. In the racial categories of the past, although the same general rule applied, it was not so simple. The traces of miscegenation were tracked with a furtive but obsessive interest and attention and marked with a taxonomic fervour through which we can glimpse an extraordinary ethnography of colonial desire.

COLONIAL DESIRE: RACIAL THEORY AND THE ABSENT OTHER

In the nineteenth century, for the most part the cultural relation between Britain and her colonies was thought through on the basis of what Foucault calls the sovereign model of power (the basic assumption of diffusionism). But we can also see in the endless discussions of questions of racial miscegenation the soft underbelly of that power relation, fuelled by the multifarious forms of colonial desire. So, for example, Frederick Marryat's Peter Simple differentiates between the participants at a fancy dress ball in Barbados before announcing his own sexual preference:

The progeny of a white and a negro is a mulatto, or half and half – of a white and mulatto, a *quadroon*, or one-quarter black, and of this class the company were chiefly composed. I believe a quadroon and white make the *mustee* or one-eighth black, and the mustee and white the mustafina, or one-sixteenth black. After that, they are *whitewashed*, and considered as Europeans.... The quadroons are certainly the handsomest race of the whole; some of the women are really beautiful.... I must acknowledge, at the risk of losing the good opinion of my fair country-women, that I never saw before so many pretty figures and faces.[39]

But as we have seen, such desire, constituted by a dialectic of attraction and repulsion, soon brings with it the threat of the fecund fertility of the colonial desiring machine, whereby a culture in its colonial operation becomes hybridized, alienated and potentially threatening to its European original through the production of polymorphously perverse people who are, in Bhabha's phrase, white, but not quite:[40] in the nineteenth century, this threatening phenomenon of being degraded from a civilized condition was discussed as the process of "decivilization". The obsessive detail with which the allegedly decivilizing activity of miscegenation was analysed can be seen at a glance in Table 1, originally published in the German Johann von Tschudi's *Travels in Peru*, and subsequently widely reproduced in anthropological accounts of race, for example in Nott and Gliddon's *Types of Mankind*, or, as here, Robert Brown's four-volume survey, *The Races of Mankind*.[41]

South America was always cited as the prime example of the degenerative results of racial hybridization ("Let any man turn his eyes to the Spanish American dominions, and behold what a vicious, brutal, and degenerate breed of mongrels has been there produced, between Spaniards, Blacks, Indians, and their mixed progeny", remarks Edward Long; "they are a disgrace to human nature", adds Knox, blaming the perpetual revolutions of South America on their degenerate racial mixture; observations that are dutifully repeated by Spencer and Hitler).[42] According to Alvar's *Lexico del mistiza en hispanoamérica*, published in 1987, there are 128 words in Spanish for different combinations of mixed races.[43] Such charting was important in all countries where there was slavery: in Latin America, where, since the *Real Pragmática* of 1776, the Imperial state had legislated rules governing marriage for Spanish subjects;[44] in the West Indies, where by law persons of mixed race could not vote or inherit property beyond £2,000; and of course in the United States, which shared the convention, recognized in law, that variously from one-eighth to one-thirty-second part African blood (i.e. three to five generations back) defined the boundary between being black and white.[45] But even for later generations who had become indistinguishably white, further tests were devised to track any furtive vestiges of secreted blackness. According to Sir William Lawrence:

Europeans and Tercerons produce Quarterons or Quadroons (ochavones, octavones, or alvinos), which are not to be distinguished from whites; but they are not entitled, in Jamaica at least, to the same legal privileges as the Europeans or the white Creoles, because there is still a contamination of dark blood, although no longer visible. It is said to betray itself sometimes in a relic of the peculiar strong smell of the great-grand-mother.[46]

Table 1 Tschudi's table of Peruvian "mongrelity", as reproduced in Brown's *The Races of Mankind* (1873–9)

Nothing could perhaps better illustrate the mongrel character of the Spanish-American population than by saying that twenty-three crosses can be determined, and have received names. They are as follows:

Parents	Children	Parents	Children
White father and negro mother	mulatto	Negro father and quintera mother	mulatto (rather dark)
White father and Indian mother	mestiza	Indian father and mulatto mother	chino-oscura
Indian father and negro mother	chino	Indian father and mestiza mother	mestizo-claro (frequently very beautiful)
White father and mulatto mother	cuarteron		
White father and mestiza mother	creole (pale-brownish complexion)	Indian father and chino mother	chino-cola
White father and chino mother	chino-blanco	Indian father and zamba mother	zambo-claro
White father and cuarterona mother	quintero	Indian father and chino-cola mother	Indian (with frizzly hair)
White father and quintera mother	white		
Negro father and Indian mother	zambo	Indian father and quintera mother	mestizo (rather brown)
Negro father and mulatto mother	zambo-negro	Mulatto father and zamba mother	zambo (a miserable race)
Negro father and mestiza mother	mulatto-oscura		
Negro father and chino mother	zambo-chino	Mulatto father and mestiza mother	chino (rather clear complexion)
Negro father and zamba mother	zambo-negro (perfectly black)	Mulatto father and chino mother	chino (rather dark)

In America the terms mulatto, quadroon and octoroon are commonly used to express the possession of a half, a fourth or an eighth of black blood, and the nomenclature goes no further, but experienced observers can detect much more minute quantities. A person with one half of Indian blood is usually styled a half-caste, or more commonly a half-breed. The term is used, however, very vaguely to denote the presence of a greater or less amount of white blood.

If the olfactory nerves were not sensitive enough for such mephitic clues, E. B. Tylor tells of a simpler visual test employed in the Southern United States where, as he puts it, "the traces of negro descent were noted with the utmost nicety":

> Not only were the mixed breeds regularly classed as mulattos, quadroons, and down to octoroons, but even where the mixture was so slight that the untrained eye noticed nothing but a brunette complexion, the intruder who had ventured to sit down at a public dinner-table was called upon to show his hands, and the African taint detected by the dark tinge at the root of the finger nails.[47]

Should that fail, the Anthropological Society President, James Hunt, cites a lady correspondent from the Confederate States of America, who informed him that:

> It is an attested fact, that if there is a drop of African blood in the system of a white person, it will show itself upon the scalp. The greater the proximity, the darker the hue, the larger the space: there may not be the slightest taint perceptible in any other part of the body, but this spot can never be wiped out, no intervening time will ever efface it; and it stands in the courts of law in the Southern Confederacy as a never-failing test, unimpeachable as a law of Nature.[48]

Such obsessive investigation was by no means confined to the Americas. In India, the government Census of 1901 was devised by Herbert H. Risley on the social Darwinist principle that "caste was the result of interactions between two racial types, a white and a black", and ended up by classifying the people of India into 2,378 main castes and tribes, competitively arranged according to social precedence.[49]

In the anthropological discussions of miscegenation, it is noticeable that reproductions of Tschudi's table unfailingly include his evaluative comments: the curious descriptions of the children of different proportions of mixed race that increasingly supplement the second column show the influence of the contemporary emphasis on the different mental and physical qualities of different races and the intermixtures between them. (It is no doubt symptomatic that despite its exhaustive categorizations, Tschudi never raises in the table the possibility of the coupling of any "Indian" or "negro" father with a white mother: the whole process is theoretically not reversible.) We can read this table of miscegenation or "mongrelity", as Brown describes it, as an obsessive tabulation of desire, as well as an analytic account of the intricate gradations of cultural fusion, regarded as a process of degeneration that mocked the nineteenth century's "diffusion" model of the spread of cultures with the confusion of fusion, subverted alike both evolutionist and polygenist schools of ethnography, and beyond these held out the threat of undoing the whole progressive paradigm of Western civilization. Here theories of racial difference as degeneration themselves fused with the increasing cultural pessimism of the late nineteenth century and the claim that not only the population of cities but the world itself, that is the West, was degenerating. Each new racial ramification of miscegenation traced an historical trajectory that betrayed a narrative of conquest, absorption and inevitable decline. For the Victorians, race and sex became history, and history spoke of race and sex.

It has often been suggested that the problem with Western historiography is that, generally speaking, only the West has been allowed a history. But in fact while this is in certain respects true, a different, covert history *was* assigned to the non-West in the nineteenth century, and that was the history produced by historical philology, which told of the development and diffusion of languages through a panoramic narrative of tribal migration and conquest, bringing in its wake the absorption of weak races by the strong. Aryan identity was also constituted through diaspora, through a history that equated migration with colonization. While this Darwinian, diasporic narrative of the Indo-European family was used as a way of giving European imperial expansion the status of natural law, its story of absorption, and therefore of linguistic and racial inmixing, at the same time also implicitly foretold the corruption, decadence and degeneration of European imperial civilization.

So much so, in fact, that it eventually gave rise to arguments for the necessity of decolonization. C. L. Temple, for example, in his *Native Races and Their Rulers* (published in 1918, just fifteen years after the British annexation of what was to become Nigeria), argued that history has showed that "one of three destinies awaits the conquered...race. It either fuses with, i.e. becomes absorbed in and absorbs the conquering race, and this is the usual result; or it re-captures its liberty; or, less often, it dies out." Temple reasons that Africans are unlikely to die out (far too fertile; it was, of course, precisely this third option that became part of Nazi ideology); but he also considers that "fusion between the European and the dark-skinned races of Africa is entirely out of the question". Temple therefore asks of the Africans: "What then is to be their future?" He answers: "Historical analogies lead us to one conclusion only, i.e., that they will some day recapture their liberty."[50] Fear of racial fusion, therefore, brings him to the extreme position of envisaging the necessity of the dismantling of the Empire itself. Forty years later, it was gone.

In recent years a whole range of disciplines has been concerned with the question of the exclusion and representation of "the Other", of inside / outside notions of otherness or of the difficulties, negotiated so painfully though not powerlessly by anthropologists, of self–other relations.[51] Our talk of Manichean allegories of colonizer and colonized, of self and Other, mirrors the ways in which today's racial politics work through a relative polarization between black and white. This remorseless Hegelian dialectalization is characteristic of twentieth-century accounts of race, racial difference and racial identity. I want to argue, however, that for an understanding of the historical specificity of the discourse of colonialism, we need to acknowledge that other forms of racial distinction have worked simultaneously alongside this model. Without any understanding of this, we run the risk of imposing our own categories and politics upon the past without noticing its difference, turning the otherness of the past into the sameness of the today. The loss that follows is not merely one for the knowledge of history: as with the case of hybridity, we can also remain unaware of how much that otherness both formed and still secretly informs our present.

Brown's finely gradated table suggests that Victorian racism, and therefore the colonialism with which it is associated, worked not only according to a paradigm of the Hegelian dialectic of the same and the Other but also according to the norm / deviance model of diversity and inequality.[52] Deleuze and Guattari get it right in their analysis of race and "faciality", where they argue that it is Christ's face that has come to be identified with the White Man himself:

> If the face is in fact Christ, in other words, your average ordinary White Man, then the first deviances, the first divergence-types are racial: yellow man, black man.... European racism as the white man's claim has never operated by exclusion, or by the designation of someone as Other.... Racism operates by the determination of degrees of deviance in relation to the White-Man face, which endeavours to integrate non-conforming traits into increasingly eccentric and backward waves.... From the view-point of racism, there is no exterior, there are no people on the outside. There are only people who should be like us and whose crime is not to be.[53]

Racial difference in the nineteenth century was constructed not only according to a fundamental binary division between black and white but also through evolutionary social anthropology's historicized version of the Chain of Being.[54] Thus racialism operated both according to the same–Other model and through the "computation of normalities" and "degrees of deviance" from the white norm, by means of which racial difference became identified with other forms of sexual and social perversity as degeneracy, deformation or arrested embryological development.[55] But none was so demonized as those of mixed race. A race, Deleuze and Guattari observe, "is defined not by its purity but rather by the impurity conferred upon it by a system of domination. Bastard and mixed-blood are the true names of race."[56] The uncontrollable expenditure of a "spermatic economy" was the real work of colonial dissemination. Paradoxically, it was the very desire of the white for the non-white, and the proliferating products of their unions, that "dislimned boundaries", in Gillian Beer's phrase, and undid the claim for permanent difference between the races while at the same time causing the boundary territories of the racial frontier to be policed ever more possessively.[57]

If it was through the category of race that colonialism itself was theoretically focused, represented and justified in the nineteenth century, it was also through racial relations that much cultural interaction was practised. The ideology of race, a semiotic system in the guise of ethnology, "the science of races", from the 1840s onwards necessarily worked according to a doubled logic, according to which it both enforced and policed the differences between the whites and the non-whites, but at the same time focused fetishistically upon the product of the contacts between them. Colonialism was always locked into the machine of desire: "the machine remains desire, an investment of desire whose history unfolds".[58] Folded within the scientific accounts of race, a central assumption and paranoid fantasy was endlessly repeated: the uncontrollable sexual drive of the non-white races and their limitless fertility. What was clearly so fascinating was not just the power of other sexuality as such, the "promiscuous", "illicit intercourse" and "excessive debauchery" of a licentious primitive sexuality, so salaciously imagined in the later editions of Malthus's *Principle of Population*, in the marriage-by-capture fantasies of McLennan's *Primitive Marriage* (1850), or in Spencer's chapters on "Primitive Relations of the Sexes" and "Promiscuity" in his *Principles of Sociology*.[59] As racial theories show in their unrelenting attempt to assert inalienable differences between races, this extraordinary vision of an

unbounded "delicious fecundity", in Virginia Woolf's phrase, only took on significance through its voyeuristic tableau of frenzied, interminable copulation, of couplings, fusing, coalescence, *between races*. At its core, such racial theory projected a
phantasmagoria of the desiring machine as a people factory: a Malthusian fantasy of
uncontrollable, frenetic fornication producing the countless motley varieties of inter-
breeding, with the miscegenated offspring themselves then generating an ever-
increasing *mélange*, "mongrelity", of self-propagating endlessly diversifying hybrid
progeny: half-blood, half-caste, half-breed, cross-breed, amalgamate, intermix, mis-
cegenate; alvino, cabre, cafuso, castizo, cholo, chino, cob, creole, dustee, fustee, griffe,
mamaluco, marabout, mestee, mestindo, mestizo, mestize, metifo, misterado, mongrel, morisco, mule, mulat, mulatto, mulatta, mulattress, mustafina, mustee, muste-
zoes, ochavon, octavon, octoroon, puchuelo, quadroon, quarteron, quatralvi,
quinteron, saltatro, terceron, zambaigo, zambo, zambo prieto. . . . Nineteenth-century
theories of race did not just consist of essentializing differentiations between self and
Other: they were also about a fascination with people having sex – interminable,
adulterating, aleatory, illicit, inter-racial sex.

But this steamy model of mixture was not a straightforward sexual or even cultural
matter: in many ways it preserved the older commercial discourse that it superseded.
For it is clear that the forms of sexual exchange brought about by colonialism were
themselves both mirrors and consequences of the modes of economic exchange that
constituted the basis of colonial relations; the extended exchange of property which
began with small trading-posts and the visiting slave ships originated, indeed, as
much an exchange of bodies as of goods, or rather of bodies as goods: as in that
paradigm of respectability, marriage, economic and sexual exchange were intimately
bound up, coupled with each other, from the very first. The history of the meanings of
the word "commerce" includes the exchange both of merchandise and of bodies in
sexual intercourse. It was therefore wholly appropriate that sexual exchange, and its
miscegenated product, which captures the violent, antagonistic power relations of
sexual and cultural diffusion, should become the dominant paradigm through
which the passionate economic and political trafficking of colonialism was conceived.
Perhaps this begins to explain why our own forms of racism remain so intimately
bound up with sexuality and desire. The fantasy of postcolonial cultural theory,
however, is that those in the Western academy at least have managed to free
themselves from this hybrid commerce of colonialism, as from every other aspect of
the colonial legacy.

NOTES

1 Said, *Orientalism*. Further references will be cited in the text. For an extended discussion of
   the work of Said, Bhabha and Spivak, see my *White Mythologies*, chapters 7–9.
2 Althusser, *Lenin and Philosophy*, 153.
3 Fanon, *The Wretched of the Earth*, and *Black Skin, White Masks*; Memmi, *The Coloniser and
   Colonised*; Nandy, *The Intimate Enemy*.
4 Bhabha, "Difference, Discrimination, and the Discourse of Colonialism", 200.
5 Bhabha, "Signs Taken for Wonders", 145–6.

6   Spivak, *In Other Worlds; The Post-Colonial Critic; Outside in the Teaching Machine*; "Can the Subaltern Speak?"; Guha, "On Some Aspects of the Historiography of Colonial India".

7   Holst-Peterson and Rutherford, *A Double Colonization*.

8   Cf. Said's comment in *Orientalism*: "Flaubert's encounter with an Egyptian courtesan produced a widely influential model of the Oriental woman; she never spoke of herself, she never represented her emotions, presence, or history. *He* spoke for and represented her" (6).

9   Spivak, "Theory in the Margin".

10 Mohanty, "Under Western Eyes"; Parry, "Problems in Current Theories of Colonial Discourse"; Ahmad, *In Theory*.

11 See Bhabha, "The Postcolonial Critic", 54.

12 Fanon, *The Wretched of the Earth*; Nkrumah, *Neo-Colonialism*.

13 Fanon, *The Wretched of the Earth*, 74.

14 In recent years, however, there has been some excellent work on Africa, which includes Appiah, *In My Father's House*, Boahen, *African Perspectives on Colonialism*, Curtin, *The Image of Africa*, Hobsbawm and Ranger, *The Invention of Tradition*, Mudimbe, *The Invention of Africa*, Ngugi, *Decolonizing the Mind*, Schipper, *Beyond the Boundaries*, Soyinka, *Myth, Literature and the African World*, Vaughan, *Curing Their Ills*.

15 Trotter, "Colonial Subjects"; Meek, *Social Science and the Ignoble Savage*, 220–1.

16 Said, *Orientalism*, 44, citing Cromer, *Political and Literary Essays, 1908–1913*, 35; cf. Inden, "Science's Imperial Metaphor – Society as a Mechanical Body", in *Imagining India*, 7–22.

17 Lugard, *The Dual Mandate*, 608.

18 Deleuze and Guattari, *Anti-Oedipus*. Further references will be cited in the text. For recent accounts of Deleuze and Guattari's work see Bogue, *Deleuze and Guattari*, and Massumi, *A User's Guide*.

19 Deleuze and Guattari, "What is Minor Literature?"; *A Thousand Plateaus*; JanMohamed and Lloyd, *Minority Discourse*. See also Spivak's judicious discussion of Deleuze's work in "Can the Subaltern Speak?", 272–6.

20 Deleuze and Guattari, "Balance Sheet – Program for Desiring Machines", 132; *Anti-Oedipus*, 11.

21 Deleuze and Guattari, *A Thousand Plateaus*, 260, 202.

22 Deleuze and Guattari, "Balance Sheet – Program for Desiring Machines", 133.

23 *Anti-Oedipus*, 30; cf. the attack on the traditional logic of desire as lack, and thus as an hallucinatory double of reality, 25.

24 For Deleuze and Guattari's account of maps and tracings, see especially *A Thousand Plateaus*, 12–15.

25 Deleuze and Guattari, "Balance Sheet – Program for Desiring Machines", 133.

26 Harvey, *The Condition of Postmodernity*, 238. This emphasizes the problem of the totalizing perspective of *Anti-Oedipus*: despite its emphasis on minorities, decentring etc., its very global pretensions as a theory continue to make a claim to a general status that will always be hard to sustain in the face of historical particularities. Harvey shows how the apparent absolutism of Deleuze and Guattari's account of the processes of capitalism can be modified to register the continual play of the power struggles of forms of regional resistance, but he ends with the observation that "the power of capital over the co-ordination of universal fragmented space and the march of capitalism's global historical time" will always achieve final victory (239).

27 Fanon, "Racism and Culture", in *Toward the African Revolution*, 41, 43.

28 Fanon, *The Wretched of the Earth*, 51, 31.

29 Deleuze and Guattari, "What is Minor Literature?", 28 n.3.

30　Deleuze and Guattari, *Anti-Oedipus*, 94, 169.

31　Cf. William Pietz, "The Phonograph in Africa", in Attridge, Bennington and Young, *Post-Structuralism and the Question of History*, 267–8.

32　See Kern, *The Culture of Time and Space*, 234–40, and cf. Noyes, *Colonial Space*.

33　Engels, *Origin of the Family, Private Property, and the State*, 208.

34　Deleuze and Guattari, *A Thousand Plateaus*, 27.

35　See Deleuze and Guattari, "What is Minor Literature?", 13–14.

36　Cf. Spivak's comments on the limitations of Deleuze's position in "Can the Subaltern Speak?", 272–4.

37　The role of violence in Fanon's *Wretched of the Earth* is consistently underestimated by commentators. Violence was, as Todorov points out, often quite openly proclaimed by the colonists themselves, by, for example, de Tocqueville (*Nous et les autres*, 231).

38　Deleuze and Guattari, "Balance Sheet – Program for Desiring Machines", 123.

39　Frederick Marryat, *Peter Simple* (1834), II, 195–7, partly cited by Brantlinger, *Rule of Darkness*, 59–60. The substance of Marryat's accompanying observations on how attentive everyone is to shades of lightness and darkness in skin colour can be found repeated by commentators again and again, and demonstrates graphically the way in which, as Dollimore observes, "discrimination is internalized psychically and perpetuated socially *between* subordinated groups, classes, and races" (*Sexual Dissidence*, 344).

40　Bhabha, "Of Mimicry and Man", 132.

41　Tschudi, *Travels in Peru*, 114; Nott and Gliddon, *Types of Mankind*, 455; Brown, *The Races of Mankind*, II, 6. Tschudi's table is a revision and correction of W. B. Stevenson's 1825 list, where there are no evaluative comments, which is reproduced in Pratt, *Imperial Eyes*, 152. Cf. W. Lawrence's discussion of human hybridity, also including a table, *Lectures*, 252–63.

42　Long, *History of Jamaica*, II, 327; Knox, *The Races of Men*, 505; Spencer, *Principles of Sociology*, I, 592; Hitler, *Mein Kampf*, 260.

43　Alvar, *Lexico del mistiza en hispanoamérica*. For further analysis see Mörner, *Le Métissage dans l'histoire de l'Amerique Latine*.

44　See Susan M. Socolow, "Acceptable Partners", in Lavrin, *Sexuality and Marriage in Colonial Latin America*, 210–13. Cf. François Bourricaud, "Indian, Mestizo and Cholo as Symbols in the Peruvian System of Stratification", in Glazer and Moynihan, *Ethnicity*, 350–87; and Stepan, *"The Hour of Eugenics"*.

45　In *The Classification of Mankind* (1852) P. A. Browne produced detailed tables and nomenclature for degrees of human hybridity based on a scientific analysis of hair (see Stanton, *The Leopard's Spots*, 152).

46　Lawrence, *Lectures*, 254.

47　Tylor, *Anthropology*, 3.

48　Hunt, *The Negro's Place in Nature*, viii.

49　See Inden, *Imagining India*, 58–66; cf. Ballhatchet, *Race, Sex and Class under the Raj*. I am grateful to Gauri Viswanathan for drawing my attention to the Census of India in this context.

50　Temple, *Native Races and Their Rulers*, 23.

51　For critical analyses of this paradigm, see Beer, "Speaking for the Others", and *Forging the Missing Link*, 8; Bhabha, "The Commitment to Theory", 16; Fabian, *Time and the Other*; Said, "Representing the Colonized"; Spivak, "Can the Subaltern Speak?", 280.

52　See Canguilhem's analysis of the ramifications of this model in *The Normal and the Pathological*.

53　Deleuze and Guattari, *A Thousand Plateaus*, 178.

54　Cf. Stepan, *The Idea of Race in Science*, 12 ff.

55   Cf. Stepan, "Biological Degeneration: Races and Proper Places", in Chamberlain and Gilman, *Degeneration*, 97–120.
56   Deleuze and Guattari, *A Thousand Plateaus*, 379. Stepan, *The Idea of Race in Science*, observes "that racial crosses were usually bad was an idea that was to endure very long in science. . . . It was not, in fact, until the 1930s that opinion changed and mulatto populations came to be considered as biologically fit as other populations" (105–6). Dover's *Half-Caste* (1937) constituted the most substantial attack on this powerful racial mythology. Franz Boas should also be given credit for his part in transforming attitudes: in 1911 he wrote: "It appears from this consideration that the most important practical questions relating to the negro problem have reference to the mulattoes and other mixed bloods – to their physical types, their mental and moral qualities, and their vitality. When the bulky literature of this subject is carefully sifted, little remains that will endure serious criticism" (*The Mind of Primitive Man*, 277).
57   For the "spermatic economy", see Barker-Benfield, "The Spermatic Economy: A Nineteenth-Century View of Sexuality", cited in Hyam, *Empire and Sexuality*, 57; Beer, *Arguing with the Past*, 74.
58   Deleuze and Guattari, *Anti-Oedipus*, 38.
59   Malthus, *Principle of Population*, 156, 195, 146; McLennan, *Primitive Marriage*; Spencer, *The Principles of Sociology*, I, 621–97.

Works cited

Ahmad, Aijaz. *In Theory: Classes, Nations, Literatures*. London: Verso, 1992.

Althusser, Louis. *Lenin and Philosophy, and Other Essays*. London: New Left Books, 1971.

Alvar, Manuel. *Lexico del Mistiza en hispanoamérica*. Madrid. Ediciones cultura hispánica, 1987.

Appiah, Kwame Anthony. *In My Father's House: Africa in the Philosophy of Culture*. London: Methuen, 1992.

Attridge, Derek, Geoff Bennington, and Robert Young, eds. *Post-Structuralism and the Question of History*. Cambridge: Cambridge University Press, 1987.

Ballhatchet, K. *Race, Sex and Class under the Raj: Imperial Attitudes and Policies and Their Critics, 1793–1905*. London: Weidenfeld and Nicolson, 1980.

Barker-Benfield, G. J. "The Spermatic Economy: A Nineteenth-Century View of Sexuality". In M. Gordon, ed., *The American Family in Social-Historical Perspective*. 2nd edition. New York: St. Martin's Press, 1978, pp. 374–402.

Beer, Gillian. *Arguing with the Past: Essays in Narrative from Woolf to Sydney*. London: Routledge, 1989.

——*Forging the Missing Link: Interdisciplinary Stories*. Cambridge: Cambridge University Press, 1992.

——"Speaking for the Others: Relativism and Authority in Victorian Anthropological Literature". In Robert Fraser, ed., *Sir James Frazer and the Literary Imagination: Essays in Affinity and Influence*. Basingstoke: Macmillan, 1990, pp. 38–60.

Bernal, Martin. *Black Athena: The Afroasiatic Roots of Classical Civilization*. 2 vols. New Brunswick, NJ: Rutgers University Press, 1987.

Bhabha, Homi K. "The Commitment to Theory". *New Formations* 5 (1988): 5–23.

——"Difference, Discrimination, and the Discourse of Colonialism". In Francis Barker, Peter Hulme, Margaret Iversen and Diana Loxley, eds, *The Politics of Theory*. Colchester: University of Essex, 1983, pp. 194–211.

—— "Of Mimicry and Man: The Ambivalence of Colonial Discourse", *October* 28 (1984): 125–33.

—— "The Postcolonial Critic", *Arena* 96 (1991): 47–63.

—— "Signs Taken for Wonders: Questions of Ambivalence and Authority under a Tree Outside Delhi, May 1817", *Critical Inquiry* 12.1 (1985): 144–65.

Boahen, A. Adu. *African Perspectives on Colonialism*. Baltimore: Johns Hopkins University Press, 1987.

Boas, Franz. *The Mind of Primitive Man*. New York: Macmillan, 1911.

Bogue, Ronald. *Deleuze and Guattari*. London: Routledge, 1989.

Brantlinger, Patrick. *Rule of Darkness: British Literature and Imperialism, 1830–1914*. Ithaca: Cornell University Press, 1988.

Brown, Robert. *The Races of Mankind: Being a Popular Description of the Characteristics, Manners and Customs of the Principle Varieties of the Human Family*. 4 vols. London: Cassell, Petter and Gilpin, 1873–9.

Browne, Peter A. *The Classification of Mankind, by the Hair and Wool of their Heads, with the Nomenclature of Human Hybrids*. Philadelphia: Jones, 1852.

Canguilhem, Georges. *The Normal and the Pathological*. Trans. C. Fawcett. New York: Zone Books, 1989.

Chamberlain, J. Edward and S. Gilman. *Degeneration: The Dark Side of Progress*. New York: Columbia University Press, 1985.

Cromer, Evelyn Baring. *Political and Literary Essays, 1908–1913*. London: Macmillan, 1913.

Curtin, Philip. *The Image of Africa: British Ideas and Action 1780–1850*. Madison: University of Wisconsin Press, 1964.

Deleuze, Gilles and Felix Guattari. *Anti-Oedipus: Capitalism and Schizophrenia*. Vol. I. 1972. Trans. Robert Hurley, Mark Seem and Helen Lane. New York: Viking, 1977.

—— "Balance Sheet – Program for Desiring Machines", *Semiotext(e)* 2.3 (1977): 117–35.

—— *A Thousand Plateaus: Capitalism and Schizophrenia*. Vol. II. 1980. Trans. Brian Massumi. London: Athlone, 1988.

—— "What is a Minor Literature?". In *Kafka: For a Minor Literature*. Trans. Dana Polan. Minneapolis: University of Minnesota Press, 1985, pp. 16–27.

Dover, Cedric. *Half-Caste*. London: Secker and Warburg, 1937.

Engels, Friedrich. *The Origin of the Family, Private Property, and the State*. 1884. Harmondsworth: Penguin, 1985.

Fabian, Johannes. *Time and Other: How Anthropology Makes its Object*. New York: Columbia University Press, 1982.

Fanon, Frantz. *Black Skin, White Masks*. 1952. Trans. Charles Lam Markmann. London: Pluto, 1986.

—— *Toward the African Revolution: Political Essays*. 1965. Trans. Haakon Chevalier. Harmondsworth: Penguin, 1970.

—— *The Wretched of the Earth*. 1961. Trans. Constance Farrington. Harmondsworth: Penguin, 1967.

Glazer, Nathan and Daniel P. Moynihan, eds. *Ethnicity: Theory and Experience*. Cambridge, MA: Harvard University Press, 1975.

Guha, Ranajit. "On Some Aspects of the Historiography of Colonial India", *Subaltern Studies: Writings on South Asian History and Society*. Vol. I. Ed. Ranajit Guha. Delhi: Oxford University Press, 1982, pp. 1–8.

Harvey, David. *The Condition of Postmodernity: An Enquiry into the Origins of Cultural Change*. Oxford: Basil Blackwell, 1989.

Hitler, Adolf. *Mein Kampf*. 1925–6. Trans. Ralph Manheim. London: Hutchinson, 1969.

Hobsbawm, E. J. and Terence Ranger, eds. *The Invention of Tradition*. Cambridge: Cambridge University Press, 1983.

Holst-Petersen, K. and A. Rutherford, eds. *A Double Construction: Colonial and Post-Colonial Women's Writing*. Aarhus: Dangaroo Press, 1985.

Hunt, James. *On the Negro's Place in Nature*. London: Anthropological Society, 1863.

Hyam, Ronald. *Britain's Imperial Century 1815–1914: A Study of Empire and Expansion*. London: Batsford, 1976.

Inden, Ronald. *Imagining India*. Oxford: Blackwell, 1990.

JanMohamed, Abdul R. and David Lloyd, eds. *The Nature and Context of Minority Discourse*. New York: Oxford University Press, 1990.

Kern, Stephen. *The Culture of Time and Space, 1880–1918*. London: Weidenfeld and Nicolson, 1983.

Knox, Robert. *The Races of Men: A Philosophical Enquiry into the Influence of Race over the Destinies of Nations*. 2nd edition. London: Renshaw, 1862.

Lavrin, Asuncion, ed. *Sexuality and Marriage in Colonial Latin America*. Lincoln: University of Nebraska Press, 1989.

Lawrence, William. *Lectures on Physiology, Zoology, and the Natural History of Man, Delivered to the Royal College of Surgeons*. 1819. 3rd edition. London: Smith, 1823.

Long, Edward. *The History of Jamaica. Or, General Survey of the Antient and Modern State of the Island; with Reflections on its Situation, Settlements, Inhabitants, Climate, Products, Commerce, Laws, and Government*. London: Lowndes, 1774.

Lugard, Frederick John D. *The Dual Mandate in British Tropical Africa*. Edinburgh: Blackwood, 1922.

Malthus, T. R. *An Essay on the Principle of Population; or, A View of its Past and Present Effects on Human Happiness; with an Inquiry into our Prospects respecting the Future Removal or Mitigation of the Evils which it Occasions*. 1786. 6th edition. 2 vols. London: Murray, 1826.

Marryat, Frederick. *Peter Simple*. 3 vols. London: Saunders and Otley, 1834.

Massumi, Brian. *A User's Guide to "Capitalism and Schizophrenia": Deviations from Deleuze and Guattari*. Cambridge, MA: MIT Press, 1992.

McLennan, J. F. *Primitive Marriage: An Inquiry into the Origin of the Form of Capture in Marriage Ceremonies*. Edinburgh: Black, 1865.

Meek, Ronald L. *Social Science and the Ignoble Savage*. Cambridge: Cambridge University Press, 1976.

Memmi, Albert. *The Colonizer and the Colonized*. London: Souvenir Press, 1974.

Mohanty, Chandra Talpade. "Under Western Eyes: Feminist Scholarship and Colonial Discourse", *boundary 2* (Spring/Fall 1984): 71–92.

Mörner, Magnus. *Le Métissage dans l'histoire de l'Amerique Latine*. Paris: Fayard, 1971.

Mudimbe, V. Y. *The Invention of Africa*. Bloomington: Indiana University Press, 1988.

Nandy, Ashis. *The Intimate Enemy: Loss and Recovery of Self under Colonialism*. Delhi: Oxford University Press, 1983.

Ngugi wa Thiong'o. *Decolonizing the Mind*. London: Currey, 1981.

Nkrumah, Kwame. *Neo-Colonialism: The Last Stage of Imperialism*. London: Heinemann, 1965.

Nott, Josiah C. and George R. Gliddon. *Types of Mankind; or, Ethnological Researches, Based upon the Ancient Monuments, Paintings, Sculptures, and Crania of Races, and upon their Natural, Geographical, Philological, and Biblical History: illustrated by Selections from the unedited papers of Samuel George Morton, M.D., and by additional contributions from Prof. L. Agassiz, LL.D., W. Usher, M.D.; and Proff. H. S. Patterson, M.D.* London: Trübner, 1854.

Noyes, John. *Colonial Space: Spatiality in the Discourse of German South West Africa 1884–1915*. Chur: Harwood, 1992.

Parry, Benita. "Problems in Current Theories of Colonial Discourse", *Oxford Literary Review* 9.1–2 (1987): 27–58.

Pratt, Mary Louise. *Imperial Eyes: Travel Writing and Transculturation*. London: Routledge, 1992.

Said, Edward W. *Orientalism: Western Representations of the Orient*. London: Routledge and Kegan Paul, 1978.

—— "Representing the Colonized: Anthropology's Interlocutors", *Critical Inquiry* 15 (1989): 205–25.

Schipper, Mineke. *Beyond the Boundaries: African Literature and Literary Theory*. London: Allison and Busby 1989.

Soyinka, Wole. *Myth, Literature and the African World*. Cambridge: Cambridge University Press, 1976.

Spencer, Herbert. *The Principles of Sociology*. Vol. I. London: Williams and Norgate, 1876.

Spivak, Gayatri Chakravorty. "Can the Subaltern Speak?". *Marxism and the Interpretation of Culture*. Ed. Cary Nelson and Lawrence Grossberg. Urbana: University of Illinois Press, 1988, pp. 271–313.

—— *In Other Worlds: Essays in Cultural Politics*. New York: Methuen, 1987.

—— *Outside in the Teaching Machine*. New York: Routledge, 1993.

—— *The Post-Colonial Critic: Interviews, Strategies, Dialogues*. Ed. Sarah Harasym. New York: Routledge, 1990.

—— "Theory in the Margin: Coetzee's *Foe* reading Defoe's *Crusoe* and *Roxana*". In Jonathan Arac and Barbara Johnson, eds, *Consequences of Theory: Selected Papers from the English Institute*. Baltimore: Johns Hopkins University Press, 1991, pp. 154–80.

Stanton, William. *The Leopard's Spots: Scientific Attitudes Toward Race in America 1815–59*. Chicago: University of Chicago Press, 1960.

Stepan, Nancy. *The Idea of Race in Science: Great Britain 1800–1960*. London: Macmillan, 1982.

Temple, C. L. *Native Races and Their Rulers: Sketches and Studies of Official Life and Administrative Problems in Nigeria*. Cape Town: Argus, 1918.

Todorov, Tzvetan. *Nous et les autres: La réflexion français sur la diversité humaine*. Paris: Seuil, 1989.

Trotter, David. "Colonial Subjects", *Critical Quarterly* 32.3 (1990): 3–20.

Tschudi, J. J. von. *Travels in Peru, During the Years 1838–1842 on the Coast, and in the Sierra, across the Cordilleras and the Andes, into the Primeval Forests*. Trans. Thomasina Ross. London: Bogue, 1847.

Tylor, Edward B. *Anthropology: An Introduction to the Study of Man and Civilization*. London: Macmillan, 1881.

Vaughan, Megan. *Curing Their Ills: Colonial Power and African Illness*. Oxford: Blackwell, 1991.

Young, Robert J.C. *White Mythologies: Writing History and the West*. London: Routledge, 1990.

Post-colonial Critical Theories

STEPHEN SLEMON

Stephen Slemon's essay might best be regarded as a species of "meta-critique" that attempts, like **Robert Young**'s, to further the student's understanding of the tradition of postcolonial studies. Its point of departure is what used to be called "Commonwealth literary studies," a movement that began in the 1960s and that reflected the desire of critics and theorists in former British colonies to contribute their voices to a dialogue dominated by an "Anglocentric" academy. Despite what might appear to be a narrow and even outdated frame of reference, Slemon advances a number of arguments that cut to the heart of ongoing debates within postcolonial studies. Of particular importance for the student of literature are his discussions of "anti-realist" writing and the concept of "writing for resistance." Like the essays of **Gayatri Chakravorty Spivak** and **Homi K. Bhabha**, Slemon's provides the student with a model for an engaged mode of interpretation that will enable her to understand the complex intersection of resistance and complicity that we find in postcolonial literature and criticism. Moreover, his discussion of history in postcolonial theory provides a framework for understanding the significance of theorists such as **Edward W. Said**, **Bhabha**, and **Spivak**; it will also help the student appreciate the historical points of view evident in so many of the other essays included in this *Anthology*.

Post-colonial Critical Theories

What is post-colonial theory? What are its foundational assumptions and its critical methods? And what does it have to say to a student of the "new", or "Commonwealth", or "post-colonial" literatures in English?

I begin with these perfectly reasonable questions because each one of them is just about impossible to answer. This is unsurprising – if we were to ask the same questions of "feminist theory", for example, or to seek solid definitions for concepts such as "allegory", or "modernism", or "multiculturalism" or "queer studies", we would find that whatever the field or object of study, scholarly discussion is rarely unified when it comes to the methods and goals of critical analysis, let alone the political outcomes such analysis attempts to bring about. The field of post-colonial theory is in this way no different from most critical fields in the humanities. Problems of definition, object, motive, ground, and constituency are, however, exacerbated within the field of post-colonial critical theory. Probably no term within literary and critical studies is so hotly contested at present as is the term "post-colonial"; probably no area of study is so thoroughly riven with disciplinary self-doubt and mutual suspicion.

For some commentators this lack of consensus and clarity is what is wrong with the field – listen to Russell Jacoby, a US-based academic Marxist, concluding his provocative article entitled "Marginal Returns":

> Post-colonial theory is all over the map. Of course, it is supposed to be.... The field is inchoate and can move in any number of directions. Nevertheless, the preliminary report is not positive. While post-colonial studies claims to be subversive and profound, the politics tends to be banal; the language jargonized; the radical one-upmanship infantile; the self-obsession tiresome; and the theory bloated.[1]

For others this lack of obvious clarity in post-colonial theory – the fluidity, the ambivalences, the theoretical anti-authoritarianism in the writing – is what is genuinely enabling about the field. Homi K. Bhabha, for example – whose remarkable contributions to post-colonial theory have been berated and celebrated in equal measure – argues that new forms of social collectivity have emerged in the contemporary post-colonial world, and these new forms require new ways of describing them. "The post-colonial perspective", he writes,

Taken from Bruce King (ed.), *New National and Post-Colonial Literatures: An Introduction* (Oxford: Clarendon Press, 1996).

forces us to rethink the profound limitations of a consensual and collusive "liberal" sense of cultural community. It insists that cultural and political identity are constructed through a process of alterity. Questions of race and cultural difference overlay issues of sexuality and gender and overdetermine the social alliances of class and democratic socialism. The time for "assimilating" minorities to holistic and organic notions of cultural value has dramatically passed. The very language of cultural community needs to be rethought from a post-colonial perspective.[2]

Regardless of where one stands on the question, there is no single post-colonial theory, and no one critic can possibly represent, or speak for, the post-colonial critical field. And so despite my pluralizing gesture in the title of this chapter, the following discussion of post-colonial critical theories is necessarily doomed at the level of comprehensiveness and coherence. What follows is about how I understand some aspects of some post-colonial critical and theoretical positions – for and against – in what is a complex and rapidly changing field of intellectual contestation and disciplinary debate.

Post-colonialism and Its Terms

One of the most vexed areas of debate within the field of post-colonial theory has to do with the term "post-colonial" itself. The debate lies in two parts: debates about the "post", and debates about "colonialism".

"Colonialism" comes under debate because the word is already predicated within a concept of "imperialism", a concept that is itself predicated within larger theories of global politics and which changes radically according to the specifics of those larger theories. Wolfgang Mommsen tells us that "the original meaning of 'imperialism' was not the direct or indirect domination of colonial or dependent territories by a modern industrial state, but rather the personal sovereignty of a powerful ruler over numerous territories, whether in Europe or overseas".[3] For Vladimir Lenin, on the other hand, imperialism meant a late stage in European capitalist expansion, a stage in which capital accumulates domestically, profit-taking slows, and so Europe seeks out foreign markets and foreign sources of labour.[4] Neither of these meanings lines up neatly with the general meaning of imperialism that predominates in literary critical discussions of the European empires – Edward Said, for example, uses imperialism to mean "the practice, the theory, and the attitudes of a dominating metropolitan centre ruling a distant territory".[5] Whatever they actually mean by the term, however, post-colonial theorists in the humanities – if not always their colleagues in the social and political sciences, for Marx did not use the word[6] – generally think of imperialism as constituting the larger political force that drives specific acts of colonialism (the direct rule of a nation or people by another nation or people) or colonization (the establishment of settler colonies in foreign lands). But without a specific theory of how imperialism drives these acts, it remains unclear how "colonialism" operates politically, economically, and culturally, and how "colonialism" and "colonization" are related.

This slippage in the concept of the "colonial" and its cognates becomes a problem when the "post" part of the "post-colonial" is brought into the equation. According to some theorists, after sustained anti-colonial struggle finally brings about national or "flag independence" in colonial locations through a process of political decolonization, a new kind of state formation comes into being. (Bill New's chapter in *New National and Post-Colonial Literatures* provides a useful chart of the moment of formal independence for Britain's former colonies.[7]) This new formation is the post-colonial state, or the "post-colony": a state thought to be at least institutionally free of foreign control, and one now possessing a greater measure of political autonomy than it did under colonialism.[8] Since most, but not all, of Europe's formal colonies have by now achieved political independence, the world itself, to some commentators, has shifted into a "post-colonial condition". Here, post-colonial nation-states develop new forms of international relations and self-constitution as they proceed. And the one-way traffic of imperial centre to colonial periphery is reformulated as a genuine circulation of peoples, so that members of various cultural and national backgrounds, ethnicities, religions, and languages move more freely across international borders than they used to, in the process developing new structures for group identification and collectivity.

The problem with the thesis of autonomous state "post-colonialism", however, is that the achievement of flag independence, or formal decolonization, may do nothing about the economic domination that continues after Empire: at the level of real politics in the "post-colonial" nation, some argue, nothing has really changed. To describe this political condition in which the old regulatory practices of direct colonialism are continued by new forms of foreign domination – the manipulation of national economies through the production and administration of "Third World debt", for example – Kwame Nkrumah, the first President of independent Ghana, coined the term "neo-colonialism". "The essence of neo-colonialism", wrote Nkrumah, "is that the State which is subject to it is, in theory, independent and has all the outward trappings of international sovereignty. In reality its economic system and thus its political policy is directed from the outside."[9]

The concept of a "post-colonial condition", then, is already a little different from the notion of a "post-colonial state" or nation, for the first describes a global situation (which may or may not be distributed equally across different nations and cultural groups) while the second refers to the political status of independent former-colonies of the European empires. This second term, however, begs the question of the difference between, on the one hand, "white" or "invader-settler" "post-colonial" nations like Australia, Canada, New Zealand, or South Africa and, on the other hand, "Third-World" "post-colonial" nations like Ghana, Pakistan, Vanuatu, or Barbados. On a crude scale that ranges from "oppressor" to "oppressed" within contemporary neo-colonial international relations, the political location of such nations may differ foundationally, and this raises a question as to whether both kinds of ex-colonial states ought to be thought of equally as "post-colonial nations". Further, the terms of nation and nationhood themselves are inherently monolithic ones, and they conceal important differences between constituent groups within the "post-colonial" nation. White settler "Canadians", to give one example, may be differently located within "post-colonialism" from the aboriginal or First Nations "Canadians" whose land they retain – the question of land-claims and "native" resistance is an enduring one, and many people in both communities consider

"Native Canadians" to remain under a condition of political colonialism in their own "post-colonial" country. To give another example: some "Melanesian" Fijian citizens understand their claim to political control in Fiji as constitutionally prior to the claims of those "Indian" Fijian peoples brought over by British colonizers as indentured plantation labourers in the nineteenth century. Both groups in Fiji have legitimate grounds for understanding themselves historically as "colonized" peoples under British colonialism, and for now thinking of themselves as post-colonial citizens of an independent Fiji, but the question of whether both groups have an equal constitutional claim to the category of Fijian citizenship was the subject of a political coup in 1989, and it remains unresolved. Of course, categories such as "native", "settler", "Melanesian", "white", "Canadian", and so on – as is always the case with the homogenizing nomenclature of race, class, gender, nation, sexual orientation, and the like – themselves conceal forms of division within groups, they conceal intersection lines and cross-over points between groups, they say nothing about the social processes that construct these groups in specific places at specific times, and they ignore the social forces that fuse different constituencies and individuals into social groups.

The term "post-colonial" or "post-colonialism", therefore, has to be seen as problematized at the outset by lack of consensus on what it is that makes the term "colonial" meaningful – that is, by a lack of consensus over how "colonialism" is structured within a concept of "imperialism" – and by a lack of consensus over what it might mean to be "post" the "colonial" moment. If neo-colonial relations still prevail between and within modern nations, if the "practices, theories and attitudes of dominating metropolitan centres" (to re-employ Said's words) remain in place after European colonialism has formally ended, then at some level contemporary "post-colonialisms", however they are conceived, must take place within a structure of contemporary and continuing imperial relations. For many commentators, this means that a critical practice that calls itself "post-colonial" must necessarily be confused about its political theory and compromised in its political aims. Here is how Anne McClintock puts the case:

> [T]he term post-colonial . . . is haunted by the very figure of linear development that it sets out to dismantle. Metaphorically, the term post-colonialism marks history as a series of stages along an epochal road from "the precolonial," to "the colonial", to "the post-colonial" – an unbidden, if disavowed, commitment to linear time and the idea of development. . . . Metaphorically poised on the border between old and new, end and beginning, the term heralds the end of a world era but by invoking the very same trope of linear progress which animates that era. . . . If post-colonial *theory* has sought to challenge the grand march of Western historicism and its entourage of binaries (self–other, metropolis–colony, centre–periphery, etc.), the *term* post-colonialism nonetheless reorients the globe once more around a single, binary opposition: colonial–post-colonial. . . . [I]t does not distinguish between the beneficiaries of colonialism (the ex-colonizers) and the casualties of colonialism (the ex-colonized). The post-colonial scene occurs in an entranced suspension of history, as if the definitive historical events have preceded our time and are not now in the making. . . . [T]he singularity of the term effects a recentering of global history around the single rubric of European time. Colonialism returns at the moment of its disappearance.[10]

A number of concepts from political and critical theory are being run together under the name of the "post-colonial" – if not by individual post-colonial theorists, then at least within the general field of post-colonial critical studies. One is a temporal concept about the decolonized nation-state, confused about its relation to neo-colonialism and imperialism. Another is a geopolitical concept of contemporary group identity, confused about what kinds of national or cultural groups deserve inclusion. A third is a sociological concept about global cultural conditions and experiences, confused about its constituency and about its relation to concepts of race, class, gender, ethnicity, and the like. At some point, therefore, most participants in the field of "post-colonial critical theory" find it necessary to position their own work in relation to some other critical theory, or methodology, or social object, or political goal. While "feminist theorists", for example, may generally understand themselves to be working in the interests of feminism (though not necessarily "for women"), few "post-colonial theorists" will understand their work as operating specifically in the interests of "post-colonialism" itself. "Post-colonialism" is a portmanteau word – an umbrella thrown up over many heads, against a great deal of rain. Confusion necessarily abounds in the area.

The result of this confusion is disciplinary anxiety, and one of the most salient features of post-colonial critical discussion is the ubiquity of debate over the extent to which any given post-colonial theory or critical practice really is opposed to colonialism. The passage I have just quoted from McClintock discusses how an unintended "colonialism" crops up in critical post-colonialism. The term "post-colonial", McClintock is arguing, is by definition intimately connected with the great progress myths that promulgated and sustained European empire-building, and with the assumptions about history, culture, and human development that underwrote those myths. Observations of this kind about the unintended political consequences of a great many critical positions that take place under the post-colonial umbrella are very common in contemporary critical debate – Vijay Mishra and Bob Hodge use the term "complicit postcolonialism"[11] to identify such compromised critical positions and social locations – and, as I have tried to suggest, the structure of disciplinary anxiety that produces such commentary comes about because the discipline of post-colonial studies houses so many different kinds of theoretical and critical work, and such a wide range of assumptions about what the terms of post-colonial criticism actually mean. And so: theorists who consider themselves part of the field of post-colonial studies may understand themselves to be working towards a description of imperial or colonizing cultures and their literatures at different moments, for example, or towards a description of specific colonized or "post-colony" cultures and their literatures, or towards a description of specific minority groups and individuals variously located within and across colonial or post-colonial cultures, or towards a description of what a comparative study of specific post-colonial conditions in specific locations should look like, or towards a description of a global condition of post-coloniality – the list goes on.

Obviously, these many "post-colonial" projects will assume no common object of description, let alone a common theoretical or critical methodology. And just as obviously, these descriptive enterprises will not be grounded in a common political goal – indeed, much post-colonial critical work carries no political commitment whatsoever. As for those post-colonial critics and theorists who do avow a political motive to their work, they may understand their scholarship to be aligned with a nationalist or pan-nationalist form of anti-colonialism, or with a group-based anti-nationalist form of post-colonialism, or with a decolonizing enterprise pitched at the level of cultural representations, or with a specific form of anti-imperialist social theory – again, the possibilities for understanding political goal and constituency within post-colonial studies are extremely multiple and diverse. Needless to say, a political commitment to social change in the contemporary world assumes no monadic theory of anti-imperialism or decolonization or "post-colonialism", and even if it did it would not necessarily find its way to a common critical methodology.

The noisy, and often remarkably angry, debates over the uses and abuses of "post-colonial critical theory", therefore, come about partly because of conceptual confluence in the discipline, partly because of confusion over the role of social and political theory in the field. But they also come about because many different social constituencies take up a position within post-colonial critical theory – and against it. In what follows, I want to identify just a few of the disciplinary roads that run into the post-colonial traffic jam, but again: these are only a few of the roads that interest me, and the commentary of a single traveller through a given landscape is never the same thing as a map.

A YELP AT THE ENGLISH FLAG

My title here is taken from the depressingly famous opening stanza to Rudyard Kipling's poem "The English Flag", which reads:

> Winds of the world, give answer! They are whimpering to and fro—
> And what should they know of England who only England know?—
> The poor little street-bred people that vapour and fume and brag,
> They are lifting their heads in the stillness to yelp at the English Flag!

One of the earliest, and still one of the most substantial, disciplinary "yelps" in the area of post-colonial studies took place under the mantle of "Commonwealth Literature Studies", a name now widely ridiculed within critical commentary but one which, as I read it, had much to do with bringing post-colonial studies into being as a discipline, and which continues to play a role in shaping theoretical debate within the field.

Commonwealth Literary Studies date formally from the mid-1960s though obviously there were a number of comparative studies between the various Commonwealth national literatures before this time.[12] Part of what brought this field into being was pure instrumentality: a number of young writers and critics from Commonwealth nations happened to be in England at this time, many of them on Commonwealth academic scholarships, and they came together at a conference for literary study (the first conference of the Association for Commonwealth Literature and Language Studies) at Leeds. Unsurprisingly, these diverse participants found much to talk about, and one of their common concerns was the maniacal

Anglocentrism that dominated English department curricula and canons in their home countries and throughout the English-speaking world. If they agreed on nothing else, they shared a desire to introduce creative works from the "Commonwealth" or "new" literatures onto English department syllabuses, and one of the strategies they employed for doing this involved a yoking together of the various Commonwealth literatures, whatever their differences, under terms that seemed to afford them a similarity and thus make them a coherent field. The reason for this was obvious: in a climate in which non-British and non-American literary texts could wilfully be ignored by departments of English in colonial and post-colonial universities, the collectivizing of those many literary texts under the banner of "Commonwealth Literary Studies" constituted a powerful argument against the dominant view that very little literary activity actually took place outside the USA and the UK, and that what few texts there were "out there" weren't very good.

In retrospect, this collectivizing strategy must be seen as a monumentally effective one. Courses in Commonwealth literature came into being, though of course not everywhere, and a series of scholarly books and articles appeared, each of them offering various ways of advancing the march of Commonwealth difference onto the unfeatured fields of literary Englishness. This strategy, needless to say, tended to shade much of the field construction of Commonwealth literary studies towards patterns of similarity across the various Commonwealth national literatures, sometimes at the expense of an articulation of the many differences between these literatures. "The search for identity", "a coming of age", "the absence of sentimentality" – these were just some of the early avowals of thematic and modal patterns of similarity across Commonwealth national literatures, but behind each of them was the idea that such a pattern could provide a useful location for comparing the Commonwealth national literatures with one another. Few critics within post-colonial studies would now employ these specific patterns as grounds for comparison – thematic criticism, generally, has shifted from the centre of literary critical methodology – but as Commonwealth studies has more recently moved into a "post-colonial" phase, new comparative principles have come forward in their place, and these principles for comparative analysis continue to excite debate within the field. I want to discuss two of them.

The first of these principles for reading post-colonial literatures has to do with the representational contract of "realism". Much can be said about how realism works contractually between text and reader, but one of the common arguments – possibly a prejudice, and certainly an argument that needs to be theorized – is that at some level at least, realist writing is tied to a naturalizing drive in language. This, if true, constitutes a problem for post-colonial writing, for one of the most insistent concerns of post-colonialism is the locating of English language-use in a history of imperial expansion. If language carries a naturalizing drive, one must remember where that language, that notion of the natural, is coming from, and question whose interests it is serving. As Derek Walcott puts it:

> This is my ocean, but it is speaking
> another language...
> I resist the return
> of this brightening noun.[13]

For some post-colonial thinkers, the imperial imposition of European language on non-European peoples binds post-colonial peoples to an uninterruptable condition of ironic relations with the world. Others assert that cultural continuities and exchanges consistently take place "under Western eyes", even if the imperial reader does not notice them. One of the most interesting post-colonial theorists to engage with the realist contract in language is the Guyanese novelist, poet, and critic Wilson Harris. For Harris, realism is nothing less than "a negation of the complexity of language" in post-colonial times, for it cultivates an addiction to "normality" in meaning – ethnographic positivism in the first world, protest realism in the third.[14] But Harris does not believe that post-colonial writing can simply step away from contractual realism, nor does he believe that a simple anti-realist approach to either reading or writing will lead anywhere but to cognitive scepticism – itself a kind of post-modern realism, in Harris's view, and one that cannot commit to principles of global change. The kind of literary practice Harris advocates, therefore, is one that fractures inherited representational conventions – the "block imprints" of imperial history – and thus activates a "ceaseless dialogue" between adversarial cultures and their orders of "meaning".[15]

At heart, those post-colonial critical theorists who attempt to ground the representational contract of literary realism to the modality of language diffusion under Empire are attempting to figure out how literary writing might contribute to a way out of the disempowering cognitive legacies of imperialism – to use the phrase of Ngugi wa Thiong'o, they are attempting to examine post-colonial writing at the level of literary mode in the hopes of making a contribution to the general project of "decolonizing the mind". This does not mean such critics believe that all genuinely useful post-colonial literary writing is somehow non-or anti-realist, but for many participants in post-colonial critical debates, an overarching attention to non-realist writing implicitly devalues realist post-colonial textual practice, and there is at present a great deal of debate in the field over which audiences prefer which kinds of literary texts, and why. One of the many counter-arguments to a post-colonial critical interest in non-realist literary writing is that First World reading tastes, fashioned as they are by the glitzy depthlessness of post-modernist performativity, actually programme the production of much post-colonial writing, and that "post-colonial" novels such as Salman Rushdie's *Midnight's Children* or Ben Okri's *The Famished Road*, for example, function far more as baubles for the bored infants of contemporary modernity than as epistemological interventions into the colonizing mind.

A second principle for theorizing post-colonial texts is the principle of reading for "resistance". Such a practice is so ubiquitous in post-colonial criticism as to make a general description of it impossible, but one of the most sustained engagements with the concept is advanced by Bill Ashcroft, Gareth Griffiths, and Helen Tiffin in their influential *The Empire Writes Back*. They begin with the proposition that "language is a medium of power":[16] this means, they argue, that post-colonial literary language has to "seize the language of the [imperial] centre and [re-place] it in a discourse fully adapted to the colonized place". This, they suggest, happens first by an "abrogation" or refusal of the normative standards of the imperial culture – the standards of "correct" grammar, syntax, and pronunciation, for example – and then by an "appropriation" of the colonizer's language, appropriately adapted, to the cultural and political ends of the colonized. They discuss many strategies by which they see this broad structure of literary resistance taking place in post-colonial writing: some-times it involves figuring literary silence (as in Lewis Nkosi's *Mating Birds*), for example; sometimes it involves the exorbitant rewriting of canonical literary texts from the other side of the colonial divide (as in the case of Timothy Findley's *Not Wanted on the Voyage*, Jean Rhys's *Wide Sargasso Sea*, or J. M. Coetzee's *Foe*); and sometimes it involves portraying the distortions that occur in colonized cultures when imperial languages have *not* successfully been abrogated and appropriated (as in V. S. Naipaul's *The Mimic Men*).[17]

Needless to say, this general tactic of reading for resistance comes in for much the same kind of debate within post-colonial criticism as does the tactic of reading against the contract of realism. Ashcroft, Griffiths, and Tiffin have a theory of literary resistance that has to do with an inevitable hybridization within, and "continuity of preoccupations" between, those cultures "affected by the imperial process" (p. 2) – a theory that is grounded in the Commonwealth studies strategy of collectivized literary intervention into the Anglocentric, English-department monologue. Since no text has been as influential as theirs has in advancing the claims of Commonwealth or post-colonial literary studies to a place at the table, *The Empire Writes Back* itself has to be seen as the primary factor in bringing about a disciplinary moment in which this specific part of its own argument is no longer as necessary as it once was, for the location of non-British, non-American literary writing in most departments of English has somewhat changed. Each of its three authors has subsequently refined his or her theory of post-colonial literary resistance in other published work. The question remains open, however, exactly how textual resistance ought to be theorized. Some critics have shifted to discourse-based models of power, grounded in the archaeolog-ical theories of Michel Foucault and mediated through Richard Terdiman's powerful thesis of literary textual repetition as a provisional and precarious "counter-discourse".[18] Other critics have turned to a culturalist model of resistance, where opposition to power is seen to be so thoroughly infused into the everyday experience of an oppressed people that resistance becomes an inherent aesthetic and finds its way into everything.[19] Still other critics have turned to psychoanalytic theory and the concept of "colonialist disavowal", with a view to identifying how colonial power itself enables forms of "native resistance" through differential repetitions (for ex-ample, in "mimicry") – repetitions that become resistances because they have the power to effect social transformations.[20]

History in the Wind

I began the previous section of this chapter with what I understand to be one of the foundational currents in the making of contemporary post-colonial critical theory. This section concerns another of those foundational currents, and to intro-duce it I will turn to the Uruguayan writer Eduardo Galeano's *Memory of Fire: Genesis*, a narrative that retells the Spanish conquest of South and Central America through a poetic, fragmented rewriting of original historical sources. Notice what Galeano focuses upon in telling of the slaughter of the people of Quetzaltenango in 1524:

The poet will speak of Pedro de Alvarado and of those who came with him to teach fear .... The children, seated in a circle around the poet, will ask: "And all this you saw? You heard?"

"Yes."

"You were here?" the children will ask.

"No. None of our people who were here have survived."

And he will teach them to smell history in the wind, to touch it in stones polished by the river, and to recognize its taste by chewing certain herbs, without hurry, as one chews on sadness.[21]

Why should Galeano figure the remembering of colonial history, at its most brutal and abject, in a language of smell, touch, and taste? There are many answers, but the one I want to develop here has to do with the problem of rethinking the category of history itself from the perspective of post-colonial critical theory.

Robert Young's important survey *White Mythologies: Writing History and the West* identifies the construction of history and historiography as the central problematic in the fashioning of a modern Eurocentric world-view. At the centre of this problematic, Young argues, is Hegelian historicism, which "articulates a philosophical structure of the appropriation of the other as a form of knowledge" and then presupposes a "dialectic of the same and the other" to posit a single, unifying "governing structure of self-realization in all historical process".[22] Such a description works when all forms of historical oppression can be subsumed under a centralizing category of oppression – gender and race as a subset of class, for example – but the problem with any single-motor theory of historical process, as Young sees it, is that "the dialectical structure of oppositional politics no longer works for the micro-politics of the post-war period in the West" (p. 5). Indeed, from the perspective of the colonized, any unitary notion of human "progress" or "development" may be seen to carry with it the appalling risk of justifying the "White Man's Burden" of globalizing enlightenment – a risk that as some see it Karl Marx himself gave substance to in his writings on English colonialism in India. "We must not forget", wrote Marx in 1853,

> that the idyllic village communities, inoffensive though they may appear, had always been the solid foundation of Oriental despotism, that they restrained the human mind within the smallest possible compass, making it the unresisting tool of superstition, enslaving it beneath traditional rules, depriving it of all grandeur and historical energies.... We must not forget that this undignified, stagnatory, and vegetative life, that this passive sort of existence evoked ... wild, aimless, unbounded forces of destruction, and rendered murder itself a religious rite in Hindustan. We must not forget ... [the] brutalizing worship of nature, exhibiting its degradation in the fact that man, the sovereign of nature, fell down on his knees in adoration of Hanuman, the monkey, and Sabbala, the cow.
>
> England, it is true, in causing a social revolution in Hindustan, was actuated only by the vilest interests, and was stupid in her manner of enforcing them. But that is not the question. The question is, can mankind fulfill its destiny without a fundamental revolution in the social state of Asia? If not, whatever may have been the crimes of England she was the unconscious tool of history in bringing about that revolution.[23]

What is post-colonial theory to do with such a statement, especially when it is made by the social theorist who stands at the headwaters of anti-capitalism and hence anti-colonialism? Aijaz Ahmad, in a spirited chapter on "Marx on India", argues that although Marx's writing is "contaminated in several places with the usual banalities of nineteenth-century Eurocentrism", Marx never argued that resistance to European colonialism was misdirected: his "systematic, universal history of all modes of production" may be "flawed", notes Ahmad, but nevertheless it is "brilliant" and empowering.[24]

Other theorists, however, have turned away from the central thesis of unitary historicism in order to come at the question of history – and histories – very differently, and this area of post-colonial theory has been at the centre of a great deal of contemporary critical debate. One branch of this turn from Eurocentric historicism is occupied by a coherent group of scholars who have come to be known as the "subaltern studies" collective. Taking their name from Antonio Gramsci's "subaltern" – as Robert Young explains, a name for subordinate individuals and groups "who do not possess a general 'class consciousness' " (p. 160) – the subaltern studies historians not only seek to identify the modes of domination that make subalterns subordinate to power, but also seek an understanding of subaltern peoples as "subjects of their own histories".[25] To do so, writes Veena Das, the subaltern historians focus on "the historical moment of rebellion" effected by subordinated, colonized people, with a view to discovering the specific nature of the "oppressive contract" those people were "compelled to make with the modern institutions of domination" (p. 314). "What is important", Das continues, "is that the subjects of this power are not treated as passive beings" – as they are, for example, in Marx's description, quoted above – "but are rather shown at the moments in which they try to defy this alienating power" (p. 314).

This sounds a little like "reading for resistance" as I described it in the preceding section, but the central difference here is that the documents the subaltern historians consider in arriving at their sense of the past are not those texts produced by oppressed figures – in most instances, such texts simply do not exist – but rather are the bureaucratic reports, the legal proceedings, the formal and informal administrative documentation produced by the colonizers. This already tells us something about what it must mean to have been subaltern, notes Das: it implies that "the moment of rebellion is also the moment of failure or defeat" (p. 315). This in turn produces the theory that subaltern peoples under colonialism are neither fully subjected to power nor fully agential, in the sense of having full self-knowledge, and will, and purpose – they somehow live out their lives between these two concepts of social subjectivity, and the historian's job is to describe that social location. The subaltern, notes Partha Chatterjee, "is a contradictory unity of two aspects: in one, the peasant is subordinate, where he accepts the immediate reality of power relations that dominate and exploit him; in the other, he denies those conditions of subordination and asserts his autonomy".[26]

The subaltern studies collective thus attempts to shift the project of history-writing away from a form of representation that unhesitatingly places Europe at the centre of theoretical knowledge. But needless to say, not all groups and individuals within colonized cultures are subalterns, and so subaltern historical studies – even if they avoid Eurocentric historicism – can never amount to a "complete" historical description. And, as the brilliant theorist Gayatri Chakravorty Spivak notes in a now-famous essay entitled "Can the Subaltern Speak?", subaltern historiography may not fully have considered the representational predication of the historical subject it seeks to retrieve from Eurocentrism. "The object of the group's investigation", writes Spivak,

> is itself defined as a difference from the elite. It is towards this structure that the research is oriented....What taxonomy can fix such a space? Whether or not they themselves perceive it [i.e. the subaltern historians]...their text articulates the difficult task of rewriting its own conditions of impossibility as the conditions of its possibility.[27]

Clearly, the project of understanding the colonized peoples as genuinely historical subjects, as subjects of their own histories, and not as passive figures in the burgeoning history of others, is of paramount importance to the field of post-colonial theory. But Spivak's argument raises a problem of seemingly insuperable difficulty: how do we retrieve a sense of colonized peoples as subjects of their own history when our understanding of those subjects and their histories depends upon colonial texts? Spivak's answer is that we cannot: "the subaltern cannot speak," she concludes. "Representation has not withered away" (p. 308). To act outside a knowledge of the impossibility of historical retrieval, she continues, is to encounter the "danger of appropriating the other by assimilation" (p. 308). And to do that would reinstall the Hegelian dialectic of Eurocentric historicism. And so Spivak counsels the critic to develop "a historical critique of our own position as the investigating person.... [T]hen you are indeed taking a risk... and can hope to be judged with respect."[28]

With a view to developing such a historical critique of the imperializing prerogatives of Western modernity itself, a very diverse group of "post-colonial" scholars has attempted to negotiate another way of challenging Eurocentric historicism – this is the branch of post-colonial critical theory known as "colonial discourse analysis". This group takes its cue from Michel Foucault's dismissal of a Marxist theory of ideology in favour of a notion of "discourse": at heart, a notion that considers social subjects, social consciousness, to be formed not through ideologies that have their base in economic or class relations but through a form of power that circulates in and around the social fabric, framing social subjects through strategies of regulation and exclusion, and constructing forms of "knowledge" which make possible that which can be said and that which cannot.[29] The problem with Western historicism, for Foucault, is that it overlooks these processes of social formation.

The ur-text of colonial discourse analysis is Edward Said's *Orientalism*, which provides a Foucauldian reading of those British and French scholarly treatises on, and fantastic projections onto, "the Orient" in the eighteenth and nineteenth centuries. In *Orientalism*, Said argues that although there indeed were and are peoples who actually live in a space Europe knows as "the Orient", this space was in fact never anything other than an "idea", "a creation with no corresponding reality".[30] What brought that purely conceptual space into being, argues Said, is a European "style of thought based on an ontological and epistemological distinction" made between "the Orient" and "the Occident" (p. 2). Said's name for that "style of thought" is Orientalism.

Orientalism, in short, is a Foucauldian "discourse", and by showing how such a discourse worked in a particular location and at a particular time, Said's book made possible the critical idea that colonial relations in general might be interwoven with – produced by and productive of – a "colonial discourse" that one could analyse through textuality. One of the most able practitioners of colonial discourse analysis is Peter Hulme, who defines "colonial discourse" as "an ensemble of linguistically based practices unified by their common deployment in the management of colonial relations".[31] Hulme's book *Colonial Encounters* locates the workings of colonial discourses in a variety of historical contexts – one of his chapters, for example, considers the extent to which one can employ a "symptomatic" reading to make a colonialist document disclose more than its writer himself knows about the rules and regulations that make possible European "knowledges" of itself and its others. Specifically, Hulme considers Columbus' journal of his voyage to the New World, and he meditates on the hidden discursive rules and regulations that might have been in effect when Columbus historically "mishears" an Arawak word for "Carib" as "caniba" or "cannibal" – a word Columbus understands to mean "a subject of the Great Khan", and thus a word that confirms his belief that he has found a sea-route to Asia. Interestingly, this discursively manufactured mishearing precipitates the noun "cannibal" into European language, but Hulme's greater point is that the discursive regulations that to some extent govern Columbus' understanding are productive of a specifically colonial discourse that regulates not only how Europe understands its Others but also, foundationally, how European "sovereign" subjects understand themselves. Instead of reinstalling a pure historicist notion of a single motor to human history, therefore, one that turns in Europe, Hulme's colonial discourse analysis presents the central argument that Western self-constitution is dependent, at least at a minimal level, on the actual historical acts and practices of its Others. Whereas for Said there is no necessary "other" figure in that style of European thought that constructs the "Orient" and thus the "Self", for Hulme some "other" at least has to speak – if only to be misheard. Such a formulation, of course, is a long way from a notion of full subaltern agency under colonial relations, but at least it begins to unsettle the historicist dialectic by asserting a minimal condition of contingency – if not actual negotiation – in the making of a historical European self.

Hulme's employment of the concept of "colonial discourse" is always highly specific to a particular moment and location in history, but not all practitioners of colonial discourse analysis have been as careful as Hulme has been, and several commentators have worried about the currency of the notion that a single "colonial discourse" regulates all colonial relations between European colonizers and non-European colonized peoples, in all places, and at all times. Other commentators have worried that the concept of colonial discourse, or Orientalism, although capable of describing specific Eurocentric formations, can actually become a "prisonhouse" for non-Western readers who seek a more enabling understanding of themselves within contemporary political relations, and a more enabling understanding of their culture under colonial management, than such a model of critical analysis can ever afford.[32] Colonial discourse analysis, despite its compelling recognition that colonial discourses circulate around both colonizing and colonized subjectivities, cannot substantially address the question of what a lived historical reality under colonialism might look like for non-European subjects, and the challenge remains for post-colonial critical theory to attempt to navigate between the Scylla of Eurocentric self-critique at the expense of a history of others, and the Charybdis of nativist historical recuperation at the expense of a theory of representation.

There are a number of remarkably promising responses to this challenge in theory, but the approach I want to conclude with is one taken by Homi K. Bhabha in an article entitled "In a Spirit of Calm Violence". Bhabha's essay addresses one of the most stereotypically charged narratives in British colonialism, the so-called "Indian Mutiny", and specifically, it focuses on British historical descriptions of how, at a moment of political panic before the sepoy rebellion began, Indian people "from village to village" and from hand to hand, "passed a mysterious token", a chapatti.[33] What interests Bhabha about this historical collective act of chapatti-passing is that it is simply not clear in the documents what self-knowledge and purpose – what social and historical agency – such an act posits for the colonial subjects who participated in it. The British seemed to believe that most of the participants understood the message of the chapatti to be "a signal of warning and preparation" – this is the form of "Orientalism" that claims the capacity to know the colonial Other, and the thesis of historical agency that individual subjects act with genuine self-knowledge and will. But the British also thought that some of the participants in the collective act of chapatti-passing acted out of "common superstition", and that others participated "in the belief that it would carry off...disease", and that others yet passed on the chapattis despite their horrified suspicions that the British had infiltrated "bone dust" into the chapattis as a way of violating Indian religious protocols and thus producing defiled colonial subjects more capable of being Christianized (p. 333). Clearly, Bhabha argues, a single, individualized notion of historical agency for either the British colonizers or the chapatti-passing colonized will not account for this collective and mystifying historical act.

Bhabha at once recognizes that the panic associated with the act of chapatti-passing, though projected squarely onto "native custom and ethnic particularity" by the British, had as much to do with panic among the British bureaucrats in 1857 as it did among the Indian peasants (p. 335). This means that the historical agency behind the act of chapatti-passing cannot purely be thought of as simple subaltern agency, even if a collective one – the episode of chapatti-passing must be seen to have taken place within "too much meaning and a certain meaninglessness" (p. 334). Whatever it is that produces this specific historical act, it cannot be conceptualized as any kind of a single motor. Having broadened the field of historical agency to include a remarkably wide range of disunified participants, conceptualized spatially – various forms of self-knowledge, kinship patterns, superstitions, various kinds of panics on the part of both British and Indian peoples – Bhabha then effects a form of theoretical "strong reading" on Foucault himself by pointing out that, in addition to all these spatial displacements of historical agency, a Foucauldian position also requires that one takes seriously the claim that historical moments are also temporally contingent: a point Foucault himself makes but then "massively" forgets (p. 327). This means for Bhabha that a theory of historical agency behind this act of chapatti-passing needs to be relocated into a "space for a new discursive temporality" (p. 327) – a space that includes subsequent meditations and panics on the part of colonized and colonizing peoples from every location, and that also includes the scholarly reconstructions of contemporary theorists and historians. It is this space, Bhabha argues – temporally discontinuous and spatially disunified – that provides a place for the contemporary theorist or historian to begin to formulate a critical understanding of the disparate and differential social processes "by which marginalized or insurgent subjects create a collective agency" under colonial relations.

This specific manoeuvre of Bhabha's represents a specific historical enactment of his general critical project, which he elsewhere describes as an attempt to pose the question of "solidarity and community from the interstitial perspective" of post-colonialism itself.[34] Bhabha attempts to shift our theoretical concern away from the monolithic building blocks of culture – nation, race, class, colonizer, colonized – towards a reading of the "in-between" spaces, the spaces in excess of the sum of the parts of social and cultural differences (p. 2). In doing so he can be seen to be aligning his critical method with the demand now being made by all kinds of "in-between" groups in the contemporary post-colonial world – diasporic and minority communities, migrant individuals and groups, aboriginal communities, disidentified social collectivities of all descriptions – that social and critical theory must discover new and articulate ways to come to terms with their experiences, past and present, that it must do so in a way that avoids appropriating those experiences into someone else's story, and that it must learn how to articulate a politics of cultural, or racial, or religious, or sexual differences without simply celebrating plurality at the expense of a cognizant description of social power and the differences it makes.

Few critical practices can actually accomplish what contemporary circumstances rightfully require, although they certainly need to try. As post-colonial theories attempt to come to terms with the massive complexifications of what Cornell West calls "the new cultural politics of difference",[35] they too become massively complexified, both in argument and in critical language. This complexification itself is the object of perhaps the most vociferous debate going on within the field. At their best, post-colonial theoretical complexities constitute exacting intellectual responses to heartfelt social demands. At their worst, they respond to the dismayingly insular and rarefied protocols of academic critical language itself. It is at least one measure of the precarious conditionality of post-colonial theory at this present moment that these necessary theoretical complexifications take place at a time when university-based scholarship slips further and further away from the notion of public intellectual engagement, and when more and more of those social citizens outside the university find themselves desperate for participation in social and public debate. The intellectual challenge for post-colonial critical theory is to attempt to come to know the story of colonial and neo-colonial engagements in all their complexity, and to find ways to represent those engagements in a language that can build cross-disciplinary, cross-community, cross-cultural alliances for the historical production of genuine social change. This is how I read Eduardo Galeano's message about the poet of the conquest, who seeks out history in the stones in the river, who teaches history in the smell of the wind.

NOTES

1 Russell Jacoby, "Marginal Returns: The Trouble with Post-colonial Theory", *Lingua Franca* (Sept–Oct 1995), 37.

2 Homi K. Bhabha, "Post-colonial Criticism", in Stephen Grenblatt and Giles Gunn (eds.), *Redrawing the Boundaries: The Transformation of English and American Literary Studies* (New York: MLA, 1992), 441.

3 Wolfgang J. Mommsen, *Theories of Imperialism*, trans. P. S. Falla (Chicago: University of Chicago Press, 1977), 3.

4 Anthony Brewer, *Marxist Theories of Imperialism: A Critical Survey* (2nd edn., New York: Routledge, 1987), 7 ff.; Kofi Buenor Hadjor, *The Penguin Dictionary of Third World Terms* (London: Penguin, 1992), 150.

5 Edward Said, *Culture and Imperialism* (London: Chatto & Windus, 1993), 9.

6 Brewer, *Marxist Theories*, 25.

7 W. L. New, "Colonial Literatures", in Bruce King (ed.), *New National and Post-Colonial Literatures: An Introduction* (Oxford: Clarendon Press, 1996), 102–19.

8 Hadjor, *Dictionary*, 250–1.

9 Ibid., 215.

10 Anne McClintock, *Imperial Leather: Race, Gender and Sexuality in the Colonial Contest* (New York: Routledge, 1995), 10–11.

11 Vijay Mishra and Bob Hodge, "What is Post(-)colonialism?" *Textual Practice*, 5/3 (Dec 1991), 407.

12 See Hena Maes-Jelinek, Kirsten Holst Petersen, and Anna Rutherford, *A Shaping of Connections* (Sydney: Dangaroo Press, 1989), 1–83.

13 Derek Walcott, "Midsummer", in *Collected Poems: 1948–1984* (New York: Farrar, Straus, & Giroux, 1986), 496.

14 Wilson Harris, "A Note on Zulfikar Ghose's 'Nature Strategies'", *Review of Contemporary Fiction*, 9/2 (Summer 1989), 181.

15 Wilson Harris, *The Womb of Space* (Westport, Conn.: Greenwood, 1983), 185; pp. xviii–xx.

16 Bill Ashcroft et al., *The Empire Writes Back* (London: Routledge, 1989), see 38–77.

17 Ibid.; see 83–8 for Nkosi, 88–91 for Naipaul, and 97–104 for Findley, Rhys, and Coetzee.

18 Helen Tiffin, "Post-colonial Literatures and Counter-discourse", *Kunapipi*, 9/3 (1987), 17–34.

19 Selwyn R. Cudjoe, *Resistance and Caribbean Literature* (Athens, Oh.: Ohio University Press, 1980); Barbara Harlow, *Resistance Literature* (New York: Methuen, 1987).

20 Homi K. Bhabha, "Signs Taken for Wonders: Questions of Ambivalence and Authority under a Tree outside Delhi, May 1817", *Critical Inquiry*, 12/1 (1985), 144–65.

21 Eduardo Galeano, *Memory of Fire: Genesis*, trans. Cedric Belfrage (New York: Pantheon, 1985), 77.

22 Robert Young, *White Mythologies: Writing History and the West* (New York: Routledge, 1990), 3–4.

23 *Marx/Engels: The First Indian War of Independence 1857–1859* (Moscow: Progress Publishers, 1959), 16–17.

24 Aijaz Ahmad, *In Theory* (London: Verso, 1992), 229.

25 Veena Das, "Subaltern as Perspective", in Ranajit Guha (ed.), *Subaltern Studies VI: Writings in South Asian History and Society* (New Delhi: Oxford University Press, 1989), 312.

26 Partha Chatterjee, *The Nation and its Fragments: Colonial and Post-colonial Histories* (Princeton: Princeton University Press, 1993), 167.

27 Gayatri Chakravorty Spivak, "Can the Subaltern Speak?" in Cary Nelson and Lawrence Grossbert (eds.), *Marxism and the Interpretation of Culture* (Urbana: University of Illinois Press, 1988), 286.

28 Gayatri Chakravorty Spivak, *The Post-colonial Critic: Interviews, Strategies, Dialogues*, ed. Sarah Harasym (New York: Routledge, 1990), 62–3.

29 Michel Foucault, *The Archaeology of Knowledge*, trans. A. M. Sheridan (London: Tavistock, 1972), 21–39.

30 Edward Said, *Orientalism* (New York: Pantheon, 1978), 5.

31 Peter Hulme, *Colonial Encounters: Europe and the Native Caribbean 1492–1797* (New York: Routledge, 1986), 2.

32 Zakia Pathak, Saswsati Sengupta, and Sharmila Purkayastha, "The Prisonhouse of Orientalism", *Textual Practice*, 5/2 (June 1991), 195–218.

33 Homi K. Bhabha, "In a Spirit of Calm Violence", in Gyan Prakash (ed.), *After Colonialism: Imperial and Post-colonial Displacements* (Princeton: Princeton University Press, 1995), 333.

34 Homi K. Bhabha, *The Location of Culture* (London: Routledge, 1994), 3.

35 Cornell West, *Keeping Faith: Philosophy and Race in America* (New York: Routledge, 1993), 3–32.

Part II
Indian Nations:
Conundrums of Difference

Ranajit Guha, "The Prose of Counter-Insurgency"
Partha Chatterjee, "The Nationalist Resolution of the Women's Question"
Rajeswari Sunder Rajan, "Representing Sati: Continuities and Discontinuities"
R. Radhakrishnan, "Nationalism, Gender, and the Narrative of Identity"

The Prose of Counter-Insurgency

Ranajit Guha

A founding member of the Subaltern Studies Group, Ranajit Guha takes as his subject-matter the hegemony of imperialist historiography. In this essay, Guha investigates official colonial documents pertaining to the problem of peasant spontaneity and insurgency and distinguishes between "primary" and "secondary" discourses. The former are always official by nature and are characterized by their immediacy with respect to a particular historical event; the latter are typically memoiristic in nature and reflect a temporal remove from the event in question. The student will find in Guha's essay a close textual examination of the hidden assumptions or messages contained in such documentary material – an examination which draws on the structuralist linguistics of Emile Benveniste and the semiotics of Roland Barthes. Like **Gayatri Chakravorty Spivak** and **Homi K. Bhabha**, Guha exemplifies the tendency in postcolonial theory to wed Western modes of critique to an indigenous practice of counter-discourse. His analysis reveals that even "liberal" forms of secondary discourse – those that attempt to critique colonialism – inevitably inscribe a form of "counter-insurgency" in their prose. The essay concludes with a consideration of what Guha calls "tertiary" discourse, that which emanates from indigenous or "radical" historians. However, he must conclude – as Spivak did in her famous essay – that the subaltern *cannot* speak within such a discourse. Guha's critique of colonialist and radical historiography with respect to their failure to represent adequately the phenomenon of peasant spontaneity ought to be read in light of **Frantz Fanon**'s essay in Part I.

The Prose of Counter-Insurgency

I

When a peasant rose in revolt at any time or place under the Raj, he did so necessarily and explicitly in violation of a series of codes which defined his very existence as a member of that colonial, and still largely semi-feudal society. For his subalternity was materialized by the structure of property, institutionalized by law, sanctified by religion and made tolerable – and even desirable – by tradition. To rebel was indeed to destroy many of those familiar signs which he had learned to read and manipulate in order to extract a meaning out of the harsh world around him and live with it. The risk in "turning things upside down" under these conditions was indeed so great that he could hardly afford to engage in such a project in a state of absent-mindedness.

There is nothing in the primary sources of historical evidence to suggest anything other than this. These give the lie to the myth, retailed so often by careless and impressionistic writing on the subject, of peasant insurrections being purely spontaneous and unpremeditated affairs. The truth is quite to the contrary. It would be difficult to cite an uprising on any significant scale that was not in fact preceded either by less militant types of mobilization when other means had been tried and found wanting or by parley among its principals seriously to weigh the pros and cons of any recourse to arms. In events so very different from each other in context, character and the composition of participants such as the Rangpur *dhing* against Debi Sinha (1783), the Barasat *bidroha* led by Titu Mir (1831), the Santal *hool* (1855) and the "blue mutiny" of 1860, the protagonists in each case had tried out petitions, deputations or other forms of supplication before actually declaring war on their oppressors.[1] Again, the revolts of the Kol (1832), the Santal and the Munda (1899–1900) as well as the Rangpur *dhing* and the jacqueries in Allahabad and Ghazipur districts during the Sepoy Rebellion of 1857–8 (to name only two out of many instances in that remarkable series) had all been inaugurated by planned and in some cases protracted consultation among the representatives of the local peasant masses.[2] Indeed there is hardly an instance of the peasantry, whether the cautious and earthy villagers of the plains or the supposedly more volatile *adivasis* of the upland tracts, stumbling or drifting into rebellion. They had far too much at stake and would not launch into it except as a deliberate, even if desperate, way out of an intolerable

Taken from Ranajit Guha and Gayatri Chakravorty Spivak (eds.), *Selected Subaltern Studies* (Delhi and New York: Oxford University Press, 1988).

condition of existence. Insurgency, in other words, was a motivated and conscious undertaking on the part of the rural masses.

Yet this consciousness seems to have received little notice in the literature on the subject. Historiography has been content to deal with the peasant rebel merely as an empirical person or member of a class, but not as an entity whose will and reason constituted the praxis called rebellion. The omission is indeed dyed into most narratives by metaphors assimilating peasant revolts to natural phenomena: they break out like thunder storms, heave like earthquakes, spread like wildfires, infect like epidemics. In other words, when the proverbial clod of earth turns, this is a matter to be explained in terms of natural history. Even when this historiography is pushed to the point of producing an explanation in rather more human terms it will do so by assuming an identity of nature and culture, a hall-mark, presumably, of a very low state of civilization and exemplified in "those periodical outbursts of crime and lawlessness to which all wild tribes are subject", as the first historian of the Chuar rebellion put it.[3]

Alternatively, an explanation will be sought in an enumeration of causes – of, say, factors of economic and political deprivation which do not relate at all to the peasant's consciousness or do so negatively – triggering off rebellion as a sort of reflex action, that is, as an instinctive and almost mindless response to physical suffering of one kind or another (e.g. hunger, torture, forced labour, etc.) or as a passive reaction to some initiative of his superordinate enemy. Either way insurgency is regarded as *external* to the peasant's consciousness and Cause is made to stand in as a phantom surrogate for Reason, the logic of that consciousness.

II

How did historiography come to acquire this particular blind spot and never find a cure? For an answer one could start by having a close look at its constituting elements and examine those cuts, seams and stitches – those cobbling marks – which tell us about the material it is made of and the manner of its absorption into the fabric of writing.

The corpus of historical writings on peasant insurgency in colonial India is made up of three types of discourse. These may be described as *primary*, *secondary* and *tertiary* according to the order of their appearance in time and their filiation. Each of these is differentiated from the other two by the degree of its formal and/or acknowledged (as opposed to real and/or tacit) identification with an official point of view, by the measure of its distance from the event to which it refers, and by the ratio of the distributive and integrative components in its narrative.

To begin with primary discourse, it is almost without exception official in character – official in a broad sense of the term. That is, it originated not only with bureaucrats, soldiers, sleuths and others directly employed by the government, but also with those in the non-official sector who were symbiotically related to the Raj, such as planters, missionaries, traders, technicians and so on among the whites and landlords, moneylenders, etc. among the natives. It was official also in so far as it was meant primarily for administrative use – for the information of government, for action on its part and for the determination of its policy. Even when it incorporated statements emanating from "the other side", from the insurgents or their allies for instance, as it often did by way of direct or indirect reporting in the body of official correspondence or even more characteristically as "enclosures" to the latter, this was done only as a part of an argument prompted by administrative concern. In other words, whatever its particular form – and there was indeed an amazing variety ranging from the exordial letter, telegram, despatch and communiqué to the terminal summary, report, judgement and proclamation – its production and circulation were both necessarily contingent on reasons of State.

Yet another of the distinctive features of this type of discourse is its immediacy. This derived from two conditions: first, that statements of this class were written either concurrently with or soon after the event, and secondly, that this was done by the participants concerned, a "participant" being defined for this purpose in the broad sense of a contemporary involved in the event either in action or indirectly as an onlooker. This would exclude of course that genre of retrospective writing in which, as in some memoirs, an event and its recall are separated by a considerable hiatus, but would still leave a massive documentation – "primary sources" as it is known in the trade – to speak to the historian with a sort of ancestral voice and make him feel close to his subject.

The two specimens quoted below are fairly representative of this type. One of these relates to the Barasat uprising of 1831 and the other to the Santal rebellion of 1855.

TEXT 1[4]

To the Deputy Adjutant General of the Army

Sir,

Authentic information having reached Government that a body of *Fanatic Insurgents* are now committing *the most daring and wanton atrocities on the Inhabitants* of the Country in the neighbourhood of Tippy in the Magistracy of Baraset and have set at defiance and repulsed the utmost force that the local Civil Authority could assemble for their apprehension, I am directed by the Hon'ble Vice President in Council to request that you will without delay Communicate to the General Officer Commanding the Presidency Division the orders of Government that one Complete Battalion of Native Infantry from Barrackpore and two Six Pounders manned with the necessary compliment [*sic*] of Golundaze from Dum Dum, the whole under the Command of a Field Officer of judgement and decision, be immediately directed to proceed and rendezvous at Baraset when they will be joined by 1 Havildar and 12 Troopers of the 3rd Regiment of Light Cavalry now forming the escort of the Hon'ble the Vice President.

2nd. The Magistrate will meet the Officer Commanding the Detachment at Barraset and will afford the necessary information for his guidance relative to the position of the Insurgents; but without having any authority to interfere in such Military operations as the Commanding Officer of the Detachments may deem expedient, for the purpose of routing or seizing or in the event of resistance destroying those who persevere in *defying the authority of the State* and *disturbing the public tranquil[l]ity*.

3rd. It is concluded that the service will not be of such a protracted nature as to require a larger supply of ammunition than may be carried in Pouch and in two Tumbrils for the Guns, and that no difficulties will occur respecting carriage. In the contrary event any aid needed will be furnished.

4th. The Magistrate will be directed to give every assistance regarding supplies and other requisites for the Troops.

Council Chamber   I am & ca

10th November 1831   (Sd.) Wm. Casement Coll.

                                                                              Secy. to Govt. Mily. Dept.

TEXT 2[5]

From W. C. Taylor Esqre.

To F. S. Mudge Esqre.

Dated 7th July 1855

My dear Mudge,

There is a great gathering of Sontals 4 or 5000 men at a place about 8 miles off and I understand that they are all well armed with Bows and arrows, Tulwars, Spears & ca. and that *it is their intention to attack all the Europeans round and plunder and murder them. The cause of all this is that one of their Gods is supposed to have taken the Flesh and to have made his appearance at some place near this, and that it is his intention to reign as a King over all this part of India, and has ordered the Sontals to collect and put to death all the Europeans and influential Natives round. As this is the nearest point to the gathering I suppose it will be first attacked* and think it would be best for you to send notice to the authorities at Berhampore and ask for military aid as *it is not at all a nice look out being murdered* and as far as I can make out this is a *rather serious affair.*

Sreecond   Yours & ca

7th July 1855   /Signed/W. C. Taylor

Nothing could be more immediate than these texts. Written as soon as these events were acknowledged as rebellion by those who had the most to fear from it, they are among the very first records we have on them in the collections of the India Office Library and the West Bengal State Archives. As the evidence on the 1831 *bidroha* shows,[6] it was not until 10 November that the Calcutta authorities came to recognize the violence reported from the Barasat region for what it was – a full-blooded insurrection led by Titu Mir and his men. Colonel Casement's letter identifies for us that moment when the hitherto unknown leader of a local peasantry entered the lists against the Raj and thereby made his way into history. The date of the other document too commemorates a beginning – that of the Santal *hool*. It was on that very day, 7 July 1855, that the assassination of Mahesh daroga following an encounter between his police and peasants gathered at Bhagnadihi detonated the uprising. The report was loud enough to register in that note scribbled in obvious alarm at Sreecond by an European employee of the East India Railway for the benefit of his colleague and the *sarkar*. Again, these are words that convey as directly as possible the impact of a peasant revolt on its enemies in its first sanguinary hours.

III

None of this instantaneousness percolates through to the next level – that of the secondary discourse. The latter draws on primary discourse as *matériel* but transforms it at the same time. To contrast the two types one could think of the first as historiography in a raw, primordial state or as an embryo yet to be articulated into an organism with discrete limbs, and the second as the processed product, however crude the processing, a duly constituted if infant discourse.

The difference is quite obviously a function of time. In the chronology of this particular corpus the secondary follows the primary at a distance and opens up a perspective to turn an event into history in the perception not only of those outside it but of the participants as well. It was thus that Mark Thornhill, Magistrate of Mathura during the summer of 1857 when a mutiny of the Treasury Guard sparked off jacqueries all over the district, was to reflect on the altered status of his own narrative in which he figured as a protagonist himself. Introducing his well-known memoirs, *The Personal Adventures And Experiences Of A Magistrate During The Rise, Progress, And Suppression Of The Indian Mutiny* (London, 1884) twenty-seven years after the event he wrote:

> After the suppression of the Indian Mutiny, I commenced to write an account of my adventures . . . by the time my narrative was completed, the then interest of the public in the subject was exhausted. Years have since passed, and an interest of another kind has arisen. The events of that time have become history, and to that history my story may prove a contribution . . . I have therefore resolved to publish my narrative.

Shorn of contemporaneity a discourse is thus recovered as an element of the past and classified as history. This change, aspectual as well as categorial, sites it at the very intersection of colonialism and historiography, endowing it with a duplex character linked at the same time to a system of power and the particular manner of its representation.

Its authorship is in itself witness to this intersection and Thornhill was by no means the only administrator turned historian. He was indeed one of many officials, civilian and military, who wrote retrospectively on popular disturbances in rural India under the Raj. Their statements, taken together, fall into two classes. First, there were those which were based on the writers' own experience as participants. Memoirs of one kind or another, these were written either at a considerable delay after the events narrated or almost concurrently with them but intended, unlike primary discourse, for a public readership. The latter, an important distinction, shows how the colonialist mind managed to serve Clio and counter-insurgency at the same time so that the presumed neutrality of one could have hardly been left unaffected by the passion of the other, a point to which we shall soon return. Reminiscences of both kinds abound in the literature on the Mutiny, which dealt with the violence of the peasantry (especially in the North Western Provinces and central India) no less than with that of the sepoys. Accounts such as Thornhill's, written long after the event, were matched by near contemporary ones such as Dunlop's *Service and Adventure with Khakee Ressallah; or Meerut Volunteer Horse during the Mutinies of 1857–58* (London, 1858) and Edwards' *Personal Adventures during the Indian Rebellion in Rohilcund, Futtehghur, and Oudh* (London 1858), to mention only two out of a vast outcrop intended to cater for a public who could not have enough of tales of horror and glory.

The other class of writings to qualify as secondary discourse is also the work of administrators. They too addressed themselves to a predominantly non-official readership but on themes not directly related to their own experience. Their work includes some of the most widely used and highly esteemed accounts of peasant uprisings written either as monographs on particular events, such as Jamini Mohan Ghosh's on the Sannyasi-and-Faqir disturbances and J. C. Price's on the Chuar Rebellion, or as statements included in more comprehensive histories like W. W. Hunter's story of the Santal *hool* in *The Annals of Rural Bengal*. Apart from these there were those distinguished contributions made by some of the best minds in the Civil Service to the historical chapters of the *District Gazetteers*. Altogether they constitute a substantial body of writing which enjoys much authority with all students of the subject and there is hardly any historiography at the next, that is, tertiary level of discourse that does not rely on these for sustenance.

The prestige of this genre is to no mean extent due to the aura of impartiality it has about it. By keeping their narrative firmly beyond the pale of personal involvement, these authors managed, if only by implication, to confer on it a semblance of truth. As officials, they were carriers of the will of the state no doubt. But since they wrote about a past in which they did not figure as functionaries themselves, their statements are taken to be more authentic and less biased than those of their opposite numbers, whose accounts, based on reminiscences, were necessarily contaminated by their intervention in rural disturbances as agents of the Raj. By contrast, the former are believed to have approached the narrated events from the outside. As observers separated clinically from the site and subject of diagnosis, they are supposed to have found for their discourse a niche in that realm of perfect neutrality – the realm of History – over which the Aorist and the Third Person preside.

IV

How valid is this claim to neutrality? For an answer we may not take any bias for granted in this class of historical work from the mere fact of its origin with authors committed to colonialism. To take that as self-evident would be to deny historiography the possibility of acknowledging its own inadequacies and thus defeat the purpose of the present exercise. As should be clear from what follows, it is precisely by refusing to *prove* what appears as obvious that historians of peasant insurgency remain trapped – in the obvious. Criticism must therefore start not by naming a bias but by examining the components of the discourse, vehicle of all ideology, for the manner in which these might have combined to describe any particular figure of the past.

The components of both types of discourse and their varieties discussed so far are what we shall call segments. Made up of the same linguistic material, that is strings of words of varying lengths, they are of two kinds which may be designated, according to their function, as indicative and interpretative. A gross differentiation, this is meant to assign to them, within a given text, the role respectively of reporting and explaining. This however does not imply their mutual segregation. On the contrary they are often found embedded in each other not merely as a matter of fact but of necessity.

One can see in Texts 1 and 2 how such imbrication works. In both of them the straight print stands for the indicative segments and the italics for the interpretative. Laid out according to no particular pattern in either of these letters, they interpenetrate and sustain each other in order to give the documents their meaning, and in the process endow some of the strings with an ambiguity that is inevitably lost in this particular manner of typographical representation. However, the rough outline of a division of functions between the two classes emerges even from this schema – the indicative stating (that is, reporting) the actual and anticipated actions of the rebels and their enemies, and the interpretative commenting on them in order to understand (that is, to explain) their significance.

The difference between them corresponds to that between the two basic components of any historical discourse which, following Roland Barthes' terminology, we shall call *functions* and *indices*.[7] The former are segments that make up the linear sequence of a narrative. Contiguous, they operate in a relation of solidarity in the sense of mutually implying each other and add up to increasingly larger strings which combine to produce the aggregative statement. The latter may thus be regarded as a sum of micro-sequences to each of which, however important or otherwise, it should be possible to assign names by a metalinguistic operation using terms that may or may not belong to the text under consideration. It is thus that the functions of a folktale have been named by Bremond, after Propp, as *Fraud*, *Betrayal*, *Struggle*, *Contract*, etc. and those of a triviality such as the offer of a cigarette in a James Bond story designated by Barthes as *offering*, *accepting*, *lighting*, and *smoking*. One may perhaps take a cue from this procedure to define a historical statement as a discourse with a name subsuming a given number of named sequences. Hence it should be possible to speak of a hypothetical narrative called "The Insurrection of Titu Mir" made up of a number of sequences including Text 1 quoted above.

Let us give this document a name and call it, say, "Calcutta Council Acts". (Alternatives such as "Outbreak of Violence" or "Army Called Up" should also do and be analysable in terms corresponding to, though not identical with, those which follow.) In broad terms the message "Calcutta Council Acts" (C) in our text can be read as a combination of two groups of sequences called *alarm* (a) and *intervention* (b), each of which is made up of a pair of segments – the former of *insurrection breaks out* (a') and *information received* (a") and the latter of *decision to call up army* (b') and *order issued* (b″), one of the constituents in each pair being represented in its turn by yet another linked series – (a′) by *atrocities committed* (a_1) and *authority defied* (a_2), and (b″) by *infantry to proceed* (b_1), *artillery to support* (b_2) and *magistrate to co-operate* (b_3). In other words, the narrative in this document can be written up in three equivalent steps so that

$$C \equiv (a + b) \dots\dots\dots\dots\dots\dots\dots\dots\dots \text{I}$$
$$\equiv (a' + a'') + (b' + b'') \dots\dots\dots\dots\dots \text{II}$$
$$\equiv (a_1 + a_2) + a'' + b' + (b_1 + b_2 + b_3) \dots\dots \text{III}$$

It should be clear from this arrangement that not all the elements of step II can be expressed in micro-sequences of the same order. Hence we are left at step III with a concatenation in which segments drawn from different levels of the discourse are imbricated to constitute a roughly hewn and uneven structure. In so far as functional units of the lowest denomination like these are what a narrative has as its syntagmatic *relata*, its course can never be smooth. The hiatus between the loosely cobbled segments is necessarily charged with uncertainty, with "moments of risk", and every micro-sequence terminates by opening up alternative possibilities only one of which is picked up by the next sequence as it carries on with the story. "Du Pont, Bond's future partner, offers him a light from his lighter but Bond refuses; the meaning of this bifurcation is that Bond instinctively fears a booby-trapped gadget."[8] What Barthes identifies thus as "bifurcation" in fiction, has its parallels in historical discourse as well. The alleged commitment of atrocities (a_1) in that official despatch of 1831 cancels out the belief in the peaceful propagation of Titu's new doctrine which had already been known to the authorities but ignored so far as inconsequential. The expression, *authority defied* (a_2), which refers to the rebels having "set at defiance and repulsed the utmost force that the local Civil Authority could assemble for their apprehension", has as its other if unstated term his efforts to persuade the Government by petition and deputation to offer redress for the grievances of his co-religionists. And so on. Each of these elementary functional units thus implies a node which has not quite materialized into an actual development, a sort of zero sign by means of which the narrative affirms its tension. And precisely because history as the verbal representation by man of his own past is by its very nature so full of hazard, so replete indeed with the verisimilitude of sharply differentiated choices, that it never ceases to excite. The historical discourse is the world's oldest thriller.

V

Sequential analysis thus shows a narrative to be a concatenation of not so closely aligned functional units. The latter are dissociative in their operation and emphasize the analytic rather than the synthetic aspect of a discourse. As such they are not what, by themselves, generate its meaning. Just as the sense of a word (e.g. "man") is not fractionally represented in each of the letters (e.g. M, A, N) which make up its graphic image, nor of a phrase (e.g. "once upon a time") in its constituting words taken separately, so also the individual segments of a discourse cannot on their own tell us what it signifies. Meaning in each instance is the work of a process of integration which complements that of sequential articulation. As Benveniste has put it, in any language "it is dissociation which divulges to us its formal constitution and integration its signifying units".[9]

This is true of the language of history as well. The integrative operation is carried out in its discourse by the other class of basic narrative units, that is, *indices*. A necessary and indispensable correlate of *functions* they are distinguished from the latter in some important respects:

> Indices, because of the vertical nature of their relations are truly semantic units: unlike "functions" ... they refer to a signified, not to an "operation". The ratification of indices is "higher up" ... a paradigmatic ratification. That of functions, by contrast, is always "further on", is a syntagmatic ratification. *Functions* and *indices* thus overlay another classic distinction: functions involve metonymic relata, indices metaphoric relata; the former correspond to a functionality of doing, the latter to a functionality of being.[10]

The vertical intervention of indices in a discourse is possible because of the disruption of its linearity by a process corresponding to dystaxia in the behaviour of many natural languages. Bally, who has studied this phenomenon in much detail, finds that one of several conditions of its occurrence in French is "when parts of the same sign are separated" so that the expression, "elle a pardonné", taken in the negative, is splintered and re-assembled as "elle *ne nous a jamais plus pardonné*".[11] Similarly, the simple predictive in Bengali "shé jābé" can be re-written by the insertion of an interrogative or a string of negative conditionals between the two words to produce respectively "shé *ki* jābé" and "shé *nā hoy nā* jābé".

In a historical narrative too it is a process of "distension and expansion" of its syntagm which helps paradigmatic elements to infiltrate and reconstitute its discrete segments into a meaningful whole. It is precisely thus that the co-ordination of the metonymic and metaphorical axes is brought about in a statement and the necessary interaction of its functions and indices actualized. However, these units are not distributed in equal proportions in all texts: some have a greater incidence of one kind than of the other. As a result a discourse could be either predominantly metonymic or metaphorical depending on whether a significantly larger number of its components are syntagmatically ratified or paradigmatically.[12] Our Text 1 is of the first type. One can see the formidable and apparently impenetrable array of its metonymic relata in step III of the sequential analysis given above. Here at last we have the perfect authentication of the idiot's view of history as one damn'd thing after another: *rising – information – decision – order*. However, a closer look at the text can detect chinks which have allowed "comment" to worm its way through the plate armour of "fact". The italicized expressions are witness to this paradigmatic intervention and indeed its measure. Indices, they play the role of *adjectives* or *epithets* as opposed to verbs which, to speak in terms of homology between sentence and narrative, is the role of functions.[13] Working intimately together with the latter they make the despatch into more than a mere register of happenings and help to inscribe into it a meaning, an interpretation so that the protagonists emerge from it not as peasants but as "*Insurgents*", not as Musalman but as "*fanatic*"; their action not as resistance to the tyranny of the rural elite but as *"the most daring and wanton atrocities on the inhabitants"*; their project not as a revolt against zamindari but as *"defying the authority of the State"*, not as a search for an alternative order in which the peace of the countryside would not be violated by the officially condoned anarchy of semi-feudal landlordism but as, *"disturbing the public tranquil[l]ity"*.

If the intervention of indices "substitutes meaning for the straight-forward copy of the events recounted,[14] in a text so charged with metonymy as the one discussed above, it may be trusted to do so to an even greater degree in discourses which are predominantly metaphorical. This should be evident from Text 2 where the element of comment, italicized by us, largely outweighs that of report. If the latter is represented as a concatenation of three functional sequences, namely, *armed Santals gathering, authorities to be alerted* and *military aid requested*, it can be seen how the first of these has been separated from the rest by the insertion of a large chunk of explanatory material and how the others too are enveloped and sealed off by comment. The latter is inspired by the fear that Sreecond being *"the nearest point to the gathering . . . will be first attacked"* and of course *"it is not at all a nice look out being murdered"*. Notice, however, that this fear justifies itself *politically*, that is, by imputing to the Santals an *"intention to attack . . . plunder . . . and put to death all the Europeans and influential Natives"* so that *"one of their Gods"* in human form may *"reign as a King over all this part of India"*. Thus, this document is not neutral in its attitude to the events witnessed, and put up as "evidence" before the court of history it can hardly be expected to testify with impartiality. On the contrary, it is the voice of committed colonialism. It has already made a choice between the prospect of Santal self-rule in Damin-i-Koh and the continuation of the British Raj and identifies what is allegedly good for the promotion of one as fearsome and catastrophic for the other – as *"a rather serious affair"*. In other words, the indices in this discourse – as well as in the one discussed above – introduce us to a particular code so constituted that for each of its signs we have an antonym, a counter-message, in another code. To borrow a binary representation made famous by Mao Tse-tung,[15] the reading, *"It's terrible!"* for any element in one must show up in the other as *"It's fine!"* for a corresponding element and vice versa. To put this clash of codes graphically one can arrange the indices italicized below of Texts 1 and 2 in a matrix called "TERRIBLE" (in conformity to the adjectival attribute of units of this class) in such a way as to indicate their mapping into the implied, though unstated terms (given in straight types) of a corresponding matrix "FINE" (see table 1).

Table 1

TERRIBLE	FINE
Insurgents	peasants
fanatic	Islamic puritan
daring and wanton atrocities on the Inhabitants	resistance to oppression
defying the authority of the State	revolt against zamindari
disturbing the public tranquil(l)ity	struggle for a better order
intention to attack, etc	intention to punish oppressors
one of their Gods to reign as a King	Santal self-rule

What comes out of the interplay of these mutually implied but opposed matrices is that our texts are not the record of observations uncontaminated by bias, judgement and opinion. On the contrary, they speak of a total complicity. For if the expressions in the right-hand column of table 1 taken together may be said to stand for insurgency, the code which contains all signifiers of the subaltern practice of "turning things upside down" and the consciousness that informs it, then the other column must stand for its opposite, that is, counter-insurgency. The antagonism between the two is irreducible and there is nothing in this to leave room for neutrality. Hence these documents make no sense except in terms of a code of pacification which, under the Raj, was a complex of coercive intervention by the State and its protégés, the native elite, with arms and words. Representatives of the primary type of discourse in the historiography of peasant revolts, these are specimens of the prose of counter-insurgency.

VI

How far does secondary discourse too share such commitment? Is it possible for it to speak any other prose than that of a counter-insurgency? Those narratives of this category in which their authors figure among the protagonists are of course suspect almost by definition, and the presence of the grammatical first person in these must be acknowledged as a sign of complicity. The question however is whether the loss of objectivity on this account is adequately made up by the consistent use of the aorist in such writings. For as Benveniste observes, the historical utterance admits of three variations of the past tense – that is, the aorist, the imperfect and the pluperfect, and of course the present is altogether excluded.[16] This condition is indeed satisfied by reminiscences separated by a long enough hiatus from the events concerned. What has to be found out therefore is the extent to which the force of the preterite corrects the bias caused by the absence of the third person.

Mark Thornhill's memoirs of the Mutiny provide us with a text in which the author looks back at a series of events he had experienced twenty-seven years ago. "The events of that time" had "turned into history", and he intends, as he says in the extract quoted above, to make a contribution "to that history", and thus produce what we have defined as a particular kind of secondary discourse. The difference inscribed in it by that interval is perhaps best grasped by comparing it with some samples of primary discourse we have on the same subject from the same author. Two of these[17] may be read together as a record of his perception of what happened at the Mathura sadar station and the surrounding countryside between 14 May and 3 June 1857. Written by him donning the district magistrate's topee and addressed to his superiors – one on 5 June 1857, that is, within forty-eight hours of the terminal date of the period under discussion, and the other on 10 August 1858 when the events were still within vivid recall as a very recent past – these letters coincide in scope with that of the narrative covering the same three weeks in the first ninety pages of his book written nearly three decades later donning the historian's hat.

The letters are both predominantly metonymic in character. Originating as they did almost from within the related experience itself, they are necessarily foreshortened and tell the reader in breathless sequences about some of the happenings of that extraordinary summer. The syntagm thus takes on a semblance of factuality with hardly any room in it for comment. Yet here again the welding of the functional units can be seen, on close inspection, to be less solid than at first sight. Embedded in them there are indices revealing the anxieties of the local custodian of law and order ("the state of the district generally is such as to *defy all control*"; "the *law* is at a *standstill*"), his fears ("*very alarming* rumours of the approach of the rebel army"), his moral disapprobation of the activities of the armed villagers ("the disturbances in the district . . . increasing . . . in . . . *enormity*"), his appreciation by contrast of the native collaborators hostile to the insurgents ("the Seths' house . . . *received us most kindly*"). Indices such as these are ideological birth-marks displayed prominently on much of this type of material relating to peasant revolts. Indeed, taken together with some other relevant textual features – e.g. the abrupt mode of address in these documents so revealing of the shock and terror generated by the *émeute* – they accuse all such allegedly "objective" evidence on the militancy of the rural masses to have been tainted at its source by the prejudice and partisan outlook of their enemies. If historians fail to take notice of these tell-tale signs branded on the staple of their trade, that is a fact which must be explained in terms of the optics of a colonialist historiography rather than construed in favour of the presumed objectivity of their "primary sources".

There is nothing immediate or abrupt about the corresponding secondary discourse. On the contrary, it has various perspectives built into it to give it a depth in time and following from this temporal determination, its meaning. Compare for instance the narration of events in the two versions for any particular day – for, say, 14 May 1857 at the very beginning of our three-week period. Written up in a very short paragraph of fifty-seven words in Thornhill's letter of 10 August 1858, this can be represented fully in four pithy segments without any significant loss of message: *mutineers approaching; information received from Gurgaon; confirmed by Europeans north of the district; women and non-combatants sent off to Agra*. Since the account starts, for all practical purposes, with this entry, there are no exordia to serve as its context, giving this instant take-off the sense, as we have noticed, of a total surprise. In the book, however, that same instant is provided with a background spread over four and a half months and three pages (pp. 1–3). All of this time and space is devoted to some carefully chosen details of the author's life and experience in the period preceding the Mutiny. These are truly *significant*. As indices they prepare the reader for what is to come and help him to *understand* the happenings of 14 May and after, when these enter into the narrative at staggered stages. Thus the mysterious circulation of chapatis in January and the silent but expressive concern of the narrator's brother, a high official, over a telegram received at Agra on 12 May conveying the still unconfirmed news of the Meerut uprising, portend the developments two days later at his own district headquarters. Again the trivia about his "large income and great authority", his house, horses, servants, "a chest full of silver plate, which stood in the hall and . . . a great store of Cashmere shawls, pearls, and diamonds" all help to index, by contrast, the holocaust which was soon to reduce his authority to nothing, and turn his servants into rebels, his house into a shambles, his property into booty for the plundering poor of town and country. By anticipating the narrated events thus, if only by implication, secondary discourse destroys the entropy of the first, its raw material. Henceforth there will be nothing in the story that can be said to be altogether unexpected.

This effect is the work of the so-called "organization shifters"[18] which help the author to superimpose a temporality of his own on that of his theme, that is "to 'dechronologize' the historical thread and restore, if only by way of reminiscence or nostalgia, a Time at once complex, parametric, and non-linear . . . braiding the chronology of the subject-matter with that of the language-act which reports it". In the present instance the "braiding" consists not only in fitting an evocative context to the bare sequence related in that short paragraph of his letter. The shifters disrupt the syntagm twice to insert in the breach, on both occasions, a moment of authorial time suspended between the two poles of "waiting", a figure ideally constituted to allow the play of digressions, asides and parentheses forming loops and zigzags in a story-line and adding thereby to its depth. Thus, waiting for news about the movements of the mutineers, he reflects on the peace of the early evening at the sadar station and strays from his account to tell us in violation of the historiographical canon of tense and person: "The scene was simple and full of the repose of Eastern life. In the times that followed it often recurred to my memory." And, again, waiting later on for transport to take away the evacuees gathered in his drawing room, he withdraws from that particular night for the duration of a few words to comment: "It was a beautiful room, brightly lighted, gay with flowers. It was the last time I thus saw it, and so it remains impressed on my memory."

How far does the operation of these shifters help to correct the bias resulting from the writer's intervention in the first person? Not much by this showing. For each of the indices wedged into the narrative represents a principled choice between the terms of a paradigmatic opposition. Between the authority of the head of the district and its defiance by the armed masses, between the habitual servility of his menials and their assertion of self-respect as rebels, between the insignia of his wealth and power (e.g. gold, horses, shawls, bungalow) and their appropriation or destruction by the subaltern crowds, the author, hardly differentiated from the administrator that he was twenty-seven years ago, consistently chooses the former. Nostalgia makes the choice all the more eloquent – a recall of what is thought to be "fine" such as a peaceful evening or an elegant room emphasizing by contrast the "terrible" aspects of popular violence directed against the Raj. Quite clearly there is a logic to this preference. It affirms itself by negating a series of inversions which, combined with other signs of the same order, constitute a code of insurgency. The pattern of the historian's choice, identical with the magistrate's, conforms thus to a counter-code, the code of counter-insurgency.

VII

If the neutralizing effect of the aorist fails thus to prevail over the subjectivity of the protagonist as narrator in this particular genre of secondary discourse, how does the balance of tense and person stand in the other kind of writing within the same category? One can see two distinct idioms at work here, both identified with the standpoint of colonialism but unlike each other in expressing it. The cruder variety is

well exemplified in *The Chuar Rebellion of 1799* by J. C. Price. Written long after the
event, in 1874, it was obviously meant by the author, Settlement Officer of Midnapur
at the time, to serve as a straightforward historical account with no particular
administrative end in view. He addressed it to "the casual reader" as well as to any
"future Collector of Midnapore", hoping to share with both "that keen interest which
I have felt as I have read the old Midnapore records".[19] But the author's "delight . . .
experienced in pouring over these papers" seems to have produced a text almost
indistinguishable from the primary discourse used as its source. The latter is, for one
thing, conspicuous by its sheer physical presence. Over a fifth of that half of the book
which deals specifically with the events of 1799 is made up of direct quotations from
those records and another large part of barely modified extracts. More important for
us, however, is the evidence we have of the author's identification of his own
sentiments with those of that small group of whites who were reaping the whirlwind
produced by the wind of a violently disruptive change the Company's Government
had sown in the south-western corner of Bengal. Only the fear of the beleaguered
officials at Midnapur station in 1799 turns seventy-five years later into that genocidal
hatred characteristic of a genre of post-Mutiny British writing. "The disinclination of
the authorities, civil or military, to proceed in person to help to quell the disturbances
is most striking", he writes, shaming his compatriots, and then goes on to brag:

> In these days of breech-loaders half a dozen Europeans would have been a match for
> twenty times their number of Chuars. Of course with the imperfect nature of the weapons
> of that day it could not be expected that Europeans would fruitlessly rush into danger,
> but I should have expected that the European officers of the station would have in some
> instances at least courted and met an attack in person and repulsed their assailants. I
> wonder that no one European officer, civilian or military, with the exception of perhaps
> Lieutenant Gill, owned to that sensation of joyous excitement most young men feel now-
> a-days in field sports, or in any pursuit where there is an element of danger. I think most
> of us, had we lived in 1799, would have counted it better sport had we bagged a
> marauding Chuar reeking with blood and spoils, than the largest bear that the Mid-
> napore jungles can produce.[20]

Quite clearly the author's separation from his subject-matter and the difference
between the time of the event and that of its narration here have done little to inspire
objectivity in him. His passion is apparently of the same order as that of the British
soldier who wrote on the eve of the sack of Delhi in 1857: "I most sincerely trust that
the order given when we attack Delhi will be . . . 'Kill every one; no quarter is to be
given'."[21] The historian's attitude to rebels is in this instance indistinguishable from
that of the State – the attitude of the hunter to his quarry. Regarded thus, an
insurgent is not a subject of understanding or interpretation but of extermination,
and the discourse of history, far from being neutral, serves directly to instigate official
violence.

There were however other writers working within the same genre who are known
to have expressed themselves in a less sanguinary idiom. They are perhaps best
represented by W. W. Hunter and his account of the Santal insurrection of 1855 in
The Annals of Rural Bengal. It is, in many respects, a remarkable text. Written within a
decade of the Mutiny and twelve years of the *hool*,[22] it has none of that revanchist and

racist overtone common to a good deal of Anglo-Indian literature of the period. Indeed, the author treats the enemies of the Raj not only with consideration but with respect, although they had wiped it off from three eastern districts in a matter of weeks and held out for five months against the combined power of the colonial army and its newly acquired auxiliaries – railways and the "electric telegraph". One of the first modern exercises in the historiography of Indian peasant revolts, it situates the uprising in a cultural and socio-economic context, analyses its causes, and draws on local records and contemporary accounts for evidence about its progress and eventual suppression. Here, to all appearances, we have that classic instance of the author's own bias and opinion dissolving under the operation of the past tense and the grammatical third person. Here, perhaps, historical discourse has come to its own and realized that ideal of an "apersonal . . . mode of narrative . . . designed to wipe out the presence of the speaker".[23]

This semblance of objectivity, of the want of any obviously demonstrable bias, has however nothing to do with "facts speaking for themselves" in a state of pure metonymy unsullied by comment. On the contrary the text is packed with comment. One has to compare it with something like the near contemporary article on this subject in *Calcutta Review* (1856) or even K. K. Datta's history of the *hool* written long after its suppression to realize how little there is in it of the details of what actually happened.[24] Indeed, the narration of the event occupies in the book only about 7 per cent of the chapter which builds up climatically towards it, and somewhat less than 50 per cent of the print devoted specifically to this topic within that chapter. The syntagm is broken up again and again by dystaxia, and interpretation filters through to assemble the segments into a meaningful whole of a primarily metaphorical character. The consequence of this operation that is most relevant for our purpose here is the way in which it distributes the paradigmatic relata along an axis of historical continuity between a "before" and an "after", forelengthening it with a context and extending it into a perspective. The representation of insurgency ends up thus by having its moment intercalated between its past and future so that the particular values of one and the other are rubbed into the event to give it the meaning specific to it.

VIII

To turn first to the context, two-thirds of the chapter which culminates in the history of the insurrection is taken up with an inaugural account of what may be called the natural history of its protagonists. An essay in ethnography, this deals with the physical traits, language, traditions, myths, religion, rituals, habitat, environment, hunting and agricultural practices, social organization and communal government of the Santals of the Birbhum region. There are many details here which index the coming conflict as one of contraries, as between the noble savage of the hills and mean exploiters from the plains – references to his personal dignity ("He does not abase himself to the ground like the rural Hindu"; the Santal woman is "ignorant of the shrinking squeamishness of the Hindu female", etc.) implying the contrast between his would-be reduction to servitude by Hindu moneylenders, his honesty ("Unlike the Hindu, he never thinks of making money by a stranger, scrupulously avoids all topics of business, and feels pained if payment is pressed upon him for the milk and fruit which his wife brings out"), the greed and fraud of the alien traders and landlords leading eventually to the insurrection, his aloofness ("The Santals live as much apart as possible from the Hindus"), the *diku*'s intrusion into his life and territory and the holocaust which inevitably followed.

These indices give the uprising not only a moral dimension and the values of a just war, but also a depth in time. The latter is realized by the operation of diachronic markers in the text – an imaginary past by creation myths (appropriate for an enterprise taken up on the Thakur's advice) and a real but remote past (befitting a revolt steeped in tradition) by the sherds of prehistory in ritual and speech with the Santals' ceremony of "Purifying for the Dead" mentioned, for instance, as the trace of "a faint remembrance of the far-off time when they dwelt beside great rivers" and their language as "that intangible record on which a nation's past is graven more deeply than on brass tablets or rock inscriptions".

Moving closer to the event the author provides it with a recent past covering roughly a period of sixty years of "direct administration" in the area. The moral and temporal aspects of the narrative merge here in the figure of an irreconcilable contradiction. On the one hand there were, according to Hunter, a series of beneficial measures introduced by the government – the Decennial Settlement helping to expand the area under cultivation and induce the Santals, since 1792, to hire themselves out as agricultural labourers; the setting up, in 1832, of an enclosure ringed off by masonry pillars where they could colonize virgin land and jungle without fear of harassment from hostile tribes; the development of "English enter- prise" in Bengal in the form of indigo factories for which "the Santal immigrants afforded a population of day-labourers"; and last but not the least of bonanzas, their absorption by thousands into labour gangs for the construction of railways across that region in 1854. But there were, on the other hand, two sets of factors which combined to undo all the good resulting from colonial rule, namely, the exploitation and oppression of the Santals by greedy and fraudulent Hindu landlords, money- lenders and traders, and the failure of the local administration, its police and the courts to protect them or redress the wrongs they suffered.

IX

This emphasis on contradiction serves an obviously interpretative purpose for the author. It makes it possible for him to locate the cause of the uprising in a failure of the Raj to make its ameliorative aspects prevail over the still lingering defects and shortcomings in its exercise of authority. The account of the event therefore fits directly into the objective stated at the beginning of the chapter, that is, to interest not only the scholar "in these lapsed races" but the statesman as well. "The Indian statesman will discover", he had written there referring euphemistically to the makers of British policy in India, "that these Children of the Forest are … amenable to the same reclaiming influences as other men, and that upon their capacity for civilisation the future extension of English enterprise in Bengal in a large measure depends". It is this concern for "reclamation" (shorthand for accelerating the transformation of the tribal peasantry into wage labour and harnessing them to charac-teristically colonialist projects for the exploitation of Indian resources) which explains the mixture of firmness and "understanding" in Hunter's attitude to the rebellion. A liberal-imperalist he regarded it both as a menace to the stability of the Raj and as a useful critique of its far from perfect administration. So while he censured the government of the day for not declaring Martial Law soon enough in order to cut down the *hool* at its inception, he was careful to differentiate himself from those of his compatriots who wanted to punish the entire Santal community for the crime of its rebels and deport overseas the population of the districts involved. A genuinely far-sighted imperialist, he looked forward to the day when the tribe, like many other aboriginal peoples of the subcontinent, would demonstrate its "capacity for civilisa-tion" by acting as an inexhaustible source of cheap labour power.

This vision is inscribed into the perspective with which the narration ends. Blaming the outbreak of the *hool* squarely on that "cheap and practical administration" which paid no heed to the Santals" complaints and concentrated on tax collection alone, it goes on to catalogue the somewhat illusory benefits of "the more exact system that was introduced after the revolt" to keep the power of the usurers over debtors within the limits of the law, check the use of false weights and measures in retail trade, and ensure the right of bonded labourers to choose freedom by desertion or change of employers. But more than administrative reform it was "English enterprise" again which radically contributed to the welfare of the tribe. The railways "completely changed the relation of labour to capital" and did away with that "natural reason for slavery – to wit, the absence of a wage-fund for free workmen". The demand for plantation labour in the Assam tea-districts "was destined still further to improve the position of the Santals" and so was the stimulus for indenturing coolies for the Mauritius and the Caribbeans. It was thus that the tribal peasant prospered thanks to the development of a vast sub-continental and overseas labour market within the British Empire. In the Assam tea gardens "his whole family gets employment, and every additional child, instead of being the means of increasing his poverty, becomes a source of wealth", while the coolies returned from Africa or the West Indies "at the expiry of their contracts with savings averaging £20 sterling, a sum sufficient to set up a Santal as a considerable proprietor in his own village".

Many of these so-called improvements were, as we know now looking back at them across a century, the result of sheer wishful thinking or so ephemeral as not to have mattered at all. The connection between usury and bonded labour continued all through British rule well into independent India. The freedom of the labour market was seriously restricted by the want of competition between British and indigenous capital. The employment of tribal families on tea plantations became a source of cynical exploitation of the labour of women and children. The advantages of mobility and contractuality were cancelled out by irregularities in the process of recruitment and the manipulation of the contrary factors of economic dependence and social differentiation by *arkatis*. The system of indenturing helped rather less to liberate servile labour than to develop a sort of second serfdom, and so on.

Yet this vision which never materialized offers an insight into the character of this type of discourse. The perspective it inspired amounted in effect to a testament of faith in colonialism. The *hool* was assimilated there to the career of the Raj and the militant enterprise of a tribal peasantry to free themselves from the triple yoke of *sarkari*, *sahukari* and *zamindari* to "English enterprise" – the infrastructure of Empire. Hence the objective stated at the beginning of the account could be reiterated towards the end with the author saying that he had written at least "partly for the instruction which their [the Santals'] recent history furnishes as to the proper method of dealing with the aboriginal races". The suppression of local peasant revolts was a part of this method, but it was incorporated now in a broader strategy designed to tackle the economic problems of the British Government in India as an element of the global problems of imperial politics. "These are the problems", says Hunter in concluding the chapter, "which Indian statesmen during the next fifty years will be called upon to solve. Their predecessors have given civilisation to India; it will be their duty to render that civilisation at once beneficial to the natives and safe for ourselves." In other words, this historiography was assigned a role in a political process that would ensure the security of the Raj by a combination of force to crush rebellion when it occurred and reform to pre-empt it by wrenching the tribal peasantry out of their rural bases and distributing them as cheap labour power for British capital to exploit in India and abroad. The overtly aggressive and nervous prose of counter-insurgency born of the worries of the early colonial days came thus to adopt in this genre of historical writing the firm but benign, authoritarian but understanding idiom of a mature and self-assured imperialism.

X

How is it that even the more liberal type of secondary discourse is unable thus to extricate itself from the code of counter-insurgency? With all the advantage he has of writing in the third person and addressing a distinct past, the official turned historian is still far from being impartial where official interests are concerned. His sympathies for the peasants' sufferings and his understanding of what goaded them to revolt do not, when the crunch comes, prevent him from siding with law and order and justifying the transfer of the campaign against the *hool* from civilian to military hands in order to crush it completely and quickly. And as discussed above, his partisanship over the outcome of the rebellion is matched by his commitment to the aims and interests of the regime. The discourse of history, hardly distinguished from policy, ends up by absorbing the concerns and objectives of the latter.

In this affinity with policy historiography reveals its character as a form of *colonialist knowledge*. That is, it derives directly from that knowledge which the bourgeoisie had used in the period of their ascendancy to interpret the world in order to master it and establish their hegemony over Western societies, but turned into an instrument of national oppression as they began to acquire for themselves "a place in the sun". It was thus that political science which had defined the ideal of citizenship for European nation-states was used in colonial India to set up institutions and frame laws designed specifically to generate a mitigated and second-class citizenship. Political economy which had developed in Europe as a critique of feudalism was made to promote a neo-feudal landlordism in India. Historiography too adapted itself to the relations of power under the Raj and was harnessed more and more to the service of the state.

It was thanks to this connection and a good deal of talent to back it up that historical writing on themes of the colonial period shaped up as a highly coded discourse. Operating within the framework of a many-sided affirmation of British rule in the subcontinent it assumed the function of representing the recent past of its people as "England's Work in India". A discourse of power in its own right, it had each of its moments displayed as a triumph, that is, as the most favourable upshot of a number of conflicting possibilities for the regime at any particular time. In its mature form, therefore, as in Hunter's *Annals*, continuity figures as one of its necessary and cardinal aspects. Unlike primary discourse it cannot afford to be foreshortened and without a sequel. The event does not constitute its sole content, but is the middle term between a beginning which serves as a context and an end which is at the same time a perspective linked to the next sequence. The only element that is constant in this ongoing series is the Empire and the policies needed to safeguard and perpetuate it.

Functioning as he does within this code, Hunter, with all the goodwill so solemnly announced in his dedicatory note ("These pages...have little to say touching the governing race. My business is with the people"), writes up the history of a popular struggle as one in which the real subject is not the people but, indeed, "the governing race" institutionalized as the Raj. Like any other narrative of this kind, his account of the *hool* too is there to celebrate a continuity – that of British power in India. The statement of causes and reforms is no more than a structural requirement for this continuum providing it respectively with context and perspective. These serve admirably to register the event as a datum in the life-story of the Empire, but do nothing to illuminate that consciousness which is called insurgency. The rebel has no place in this history as the subject of rebellion.

XI

There is nothing in tertiary discourse to make up for this absence. Farthest removed in time from the events which it has for its theme, it always looks at them in the third person. It is the work of non-official writers in most cases or of former officials no longer under any professional obligation or constraint to represent the standpoint of the government. If it happens to carry an official view at all this is only because the author has chosen it of his own will rather than because he has been conditioned to do so by any loyalty or allegiance based on administrative involvement. There are indeed some historical works which actually show such a preference and are unable to speak in a voice other than that of the custodians of law and order – an instance of tertiary discourse reverting to that state of crude identification with the regime so characteristic of primary discourse.

But there are other and very different idioms within this genre ranging from liberal to left. The latter is particularly important as perhaps the most influential and prolific of all the many varieties of tertiary discourse. We owe to it some of the best studies on Indian peasant insurgency and more and more of these are coming out all the time as evidence both of a growing academic interest in the subject and the relevance that the subaltern movements of the past have to contemporary tensions in our part of the world. This literature is distinguished by its effort to break away from the code of counter-insurgency. It adopts the insurgent's point of view and regards, with him, as "fine" what the other side calls "terrible", and vice versa. It leaves the reader in no doubt that it wants the rebels and not their enemies to win. Here, unlike in secondary discourse of the liberal-imperialist type, recognition of the wrongs done to the peasants leads directly to support for their struggle to seek redress by arms.

Yet these two types, so very different from and contrary to each other in ideological orientation, have much else that is common between them. Take for instance that remarkable contribution of radical scholarship, Suprakash Ray's *Bharater Krishak-bidroha O Ganatantrik Samgram*[25] and compare its account of the Santal uprising of 1855 with Hunter's. The texts echo each other as narratives. Ray's being the later work has all the advantage of drawing on more recent research such as Datta's, and thus being more informed. But much of what it has to say about the inauguration and development of the *hool* is taken – in fact, quoted directly – from Hunter's *Annals*.[26] And both the authors rely on the *Calcutta Review* (1856) article for much of their evidence. There is thus little in the description of this particular event which differs significantly between the secondary and the tertiary types of discourse.

Nor is there much to distinguish between the two in terms of their admiration for the courage of the rebels and their abhorrence of the genocidal operations mounted by the counter-insurgency forces. In fact, on both these points Ray reproduces *in extenso* Hunter's testimony, gathered first-hand from officers directly involved in the campaign, that the Santals "did not understand yielding", while for the army, "it was not war ... it was execution".[27] The sympathy expressed for the enemies of the Raj in the radical tertiary discourse is matched fully by that in the colonialist secondary discourse. Indeed, for both, the *hool* was an eminently just struggle – an evaluation derived from their mutual concurrence about the factors which had provoked it. Wicked landlords, extortionate usurers, dishonest traders, venal police, irresponsible officials and partisan processes of law – all figure with equal prominence in both the accounts. Both the historians draw on the evidence recorded on this subject in the *Calcutta Review* essay, and for much of his information about Santal indebtedness and bond slavery, about moneylenders' and landlords' oppression and administrative connivance at all this, Ray relies heavily again on Hunter, as witness the extracts quoted liberally from the latter's work.[28]

However, causality is used by the two writers to develop entirely different perspectives. The statement of causes has the same part to play in Hunter's account as in any other narrative of the secondary type – that is, as an essential aspect of the discourse of counter-insurgency. In this respect his *Annals* belongs to a tradition of colonialist historiography which, for this particular event, is typically exemplified by that racist and vindicative essay, "The Sonthal Rebellion". There, the obviously knowledgeable but tough-minded official ascribes the uprising, as Hunter does, to banias' fraud, mahajani transaction, zamindari despotism and sarkari inefficiency. In much the same vein Thornhill's *Personal Adventures* accounts for the rural uprisings of the period of the Mutiny in Uttar Pradesh quite clearly by the breakdown in traditional agrarian relations consequent on the advent of British rule. O'Malley identifies the root of the Pabna *bidroha* of 1873 in rack-renting by landlords, and the Deccan Riots Commission that of the disturbances of 1875 in the exploitation of the Kunbi peasantry by alien moneylenders in Poona and Ahmednagar districts.[29] One could go on adding many other events and texts to this list. The spirit of all these is well represented in the following extract from the *Judicial Department Resolutions* of 22 November 1831 on the subject of the insurrection led by Titu Mir:

> The serious nature of the late disturbances in the district of Baraset renders it an object of paramount importance that the *cause* which gave rise to them should be fully *investigated* in order that the motives which activated the insurgents may be rightly *understood* and such measures adopted as may be deemed expedient *to prevent a recurrence of similar disorders*.

That sums it up. To know the cause of a phenomenon is already a step taken in the direction of controlling it. To *investigate* and thereby *understand* the cause of rural disturbances is an aid to measures "deemed expedient *to prevent a recurrence of similar disorders*". To that end the correspondent of the *Calcutta Review* (1856) recommended "that condign retribution", namely, "that they [the Santals] should be surrounded and hunted up everywhere . . . that they should be compelled, by force, if need be, to return to the Damin-i-koh, and to the wasted country in Bhaugulpore and Beer-bhoom, to rebuild the ruined villages, restore the desolate fields to cultivation, open roads, and advance general public works; and do this under watch and guard . . . and that this state of things should be continued, until they are completely tranquillized, and reconciled to their allegiance".[31] The gentler alternative put forward by Hunter was, as we have seen, a combination of Martial Law to suppress an ongoing revolt and measures to follow it up by "English enterprise" in order (as his compatriot had suggested) to absorb the unruly peasantry as a cheap labour force in agriculture and public works for the benefit respectively of the same *dikus* and railway and roadwork engineers against whom they had taken up arms. With all their variation in tone, however, both the prescriptions to "make . . . rebellion impossible by the elevation of the Sonthals"[32] – indeed, all colonialist solutions arrived at by the casual explanation of our peasant uprisings – were grist to a historiography committed to assimilating them to the transcendental Destiny of the British Empire.

XII

Causality serves to hitch the *hool* to a rather different kind of Destiny in Ray's account. But the latter goes through the same steps as Hunter's – that is, *context–event–perspective* ranged along a historical continuum – to arrive there. There are some obvious parallelisms in the way the event acquires a context in the two works. Both start off with prehistory (treated more briefly by Ray than Hunter) and follow it up with a survey of the more recent past since 1790 when the tribe first came into contact with the regime. It is there that the cause of the insurrection lies for both – but with a difference. For Hunter the disturbances originated in a local malignance in an otherwise healthy body – the failure of a district administration to act up to the then emerging ideal of the Raj as the *ma-baap* of the peasantry and protect them from the tyranny of wicked elements within the native society itself. For Ray it was the very presence of British power in India which had goaded the Santals to revolt, for their enemies the landlords and moneylenders owed their authority and indeed their existence to the new arrangements in landed property introduced by the colonial government and the accelerated development of a money economy under its impact. The rising constituted, therefore, a critique not only of a local administration but of colonialism itself. Indeed, he uses Hunter's own evidence to arrive at that very different, indeed contrary, conclusion:

> It is clearly proved by Hunter's own statement that the responsibility for the extreme misery of the Santals lies with the English administrative system taken as a whole together with the zamindars and mahajans. For it was the English administrative system which had created zamindars and mahajans in order to satisfy its own need for exploitation and government, and helped them directly and indirectly by offering its protection and patronage.[33]

With colonialism, that is, the Raj as a system and in its entirety (rather than any of its local malfunctions), identified thus as the prime cause of rebellion, its outcome acquires radically different values in the two texts. While Hunter is explicit in his preference of a victory in favour of the regime, Ray is equally so in favour of the rebels. And corresponding to this each has a perspective which stands out in sharp contrast to that of the other. It is for Hunter the consolidation of British rule based on a reformed administration which no longer incites jacqueries by its failure to protect *adivasis* from native exploiters, but transforms them into an abundant and mobile labour force readily and profitably employed by Indian landlords and "English enterprise". For Ray the event is "the precursor of the great rebellion" of 1857 and a vital link in a protracted struggle of the Indian people in general and peasants and workers in particular against foreign as well as indigenous oppressors. The armed insurrection of the Santals, he says, has indicated a way to the Indian people. "That particular way has, thanks to the great rebellion of 1857, developed into the broad highway of India's struggle for freedom. That highway extends into the twentieth century. The Indian peasantry are on their march along that very highway."[34] In fitting the *hool* thus to a perspective of continuing struggle of the rural masses, the author draws on a well-established tradition of radical historiography as witness, for instance, the following extract from a pamphlet which had a wide readership in left political circles nearly thirty years ago:

> The din of the actual battles of the insurrection has died down. But its echoes have kept on vibrating through the years, growing louder and louder as more peasants joined in the fight. The clarion call that summoned the Santhals to battle...was to be heard in other parts of the country at the time of the Indigo Strike of 1860, the Pabna and Bogra Uprising of 1872, the Maratha Peasant Rising in Poona and Ahmednagar in 1875–76. It was finally to merge in the massive demand of the peasantry all over the country for an end to zamindari and moneylending oppression.... Glory to the immortal Santhals who... showed the path to battle! The banner of militant struggle has since then passed from hand to hand over the length and breadth of India.[35]

The power of such assimilative thinking about the history of peasant insurgency is further illustrated by the concluding words of an essay written by a veteran of the peasant movement and published by the Pashchimbanga Pradeshik Krishak Sabha on the eve of the centenary of the Santal revolt. Thus,

> The flames of the fire kindled by the peasant martyrs of the Santal insurrection a hundred years ago had spread to many regions all over India. Those flames could be seen burning in the indigo cultivators' rebellion in Bengal (1860), in the uprising of the raiyats of Pabna and Bogra (1872), in that of the Maratha peasantry of the Deccan (1875–76). The same fire was kindled again and again in the course of the Moplah peasant revolts of Malabar. That fire has not been extinguished yet, it is still burning in the hearts of the Indian peasants...[36]

The purpose of such tertiary discourse is quite clearly to try and retrieve the history of insurgency from that continuum which is designed to assimilate every jacquerie to "England's Work in India" and arrange it along the alternative axis of a protracted campaign for freedom and socialism. However, as with colonialist historiography this, too, amounts to an act of appropriation which excludes the rebel as the conscious subject of his own history and incorporates the latter as only a contingent element in another history with another subject. Just as it is not the rebel but the Raj which is the real subject of secondary discourse and the Indian bourgeoisie that of tertiary discourse of the History-of-the-Freedom-Struggle genre, so is an *abstraction* called Worker-and-Peasant, *an ideal rather than the real historical personality of the insurgent*, made to replace him in the type of literature discussed above.

To say this is of course not to deny the political importance of such appropriation. Since every struggle for power by the historically ascendant classes in any epoch involves a bid to acquire a tradition, it is entirely in the fitness of things that the revolutionary movements in India should lay a claim to, among others, the Santal rebellion of 1855 as a part of their heritage. But however noble the cause and instrument of such appropriation, it leads to the mediation of the insurgent's consciousness by the historian's – that is, of a past consciousness by one conditioned by the present. The distortion which follows necessarily and inevitably from this process is a function of that hiatus between event-time and discourse-time which makes the verbal representation of the past less than accurate in the best of cases. And since the discourse is, in this particular instance, one about properties of the mind – about attitudes, beliefs, ideas, etc. rather than about externalities which are easier to identify and describe, the task of representation is made even more complicated than usual.

There is nothing that historiography can do to eliminate such distortion altogether, for the latter is built into its optics. What it can do, however, is to acknowledge such distortion as parametric – as a datum which determines the form of the exercise itself, and to stop pretending that it can *fully* grasp a past consciousness and reconstitute it. Then and only then might the distance between the latter and the historian's perception of it be reduced significantly enough to amount to a close approximation which is the best one could hope for. The gap as it stands at the moment is indeed so wide that there is much more than an irreducible degree of error in the existing literature on this point. Even a brief look at some of the discourses on the 1855 insurrection should bear this out.

XIII

Religiosity was, by all accounts, central to the *hool*. The notion of power which inspired it was made up of such ideas and expressed in such words and acts as were explicitly religious in character. It was not that power was a content wrapped up in a form external to it called religion. It was a matter of both being inseparably collapsed as the signified and its signifier (*vāgarthāviva sampriktau*) in the language of that massive violence. Hence the attribution of the rising to a divine command rather than to any particular grievance; the enactment of rituals both before (e.g. propritiatory ceremonies to ward off the apocalypse of the Primeval Serpents – Lag and Lagini, the distribution of *tel-sindur*, etc.) and during the uprising (e.g. worshipping the goddess Durga, bathing in the Ganges, etc.); the generation and circulation of myth in its characteristic vehicle – rumour (e.g. about the advent of "the exterminating angel" incarnated as a buffalo, the birth of a prodigious hero to a virgin, etc.).[37] The evidence is both unequivocal and ample on this point. The statements we have from the leading protagonists and their followers are all emphatic and indeed insistent on this aspect of their struggle, as should be obvious even from the few extracts of source material reproduced below in the Appendix. In sum, it is not possible to speak of insurgency in this case except as a religious consciousness – except, that is, as a massive demonstration of self-estrangement (to borrow Marx's term for the very essence of religiosity) which made the rebels look upon their project as predicated on a will other than their own: "Kanoo and Seedoo Manjee are not fighting. The Thacoor himself will fight."[38]

How authentically has this been represented in historical discourse? It was identified in official correspondence at the time as a case of "fanaticism". The insurrection was three months old and still going strong when J. R. Ward, a Special Commissioner and one of the most important administrators in the Birbhum region, wrote in some desperation to his superiors in Calcutta, "I have been unable to trace the insurrection in Beerbhoom to any thing but *fanaticism*." The idiom he used to describe the phenomenon was typical of the shocked and culturally arrogant response of nineteenth-century colonialism to any radical movement inspired by a non-Christian doctrine among a subject population: "These Sonthals have been led to join in the rebellion under a persuasion which is clearly traceable to their brethren in Bhaugulpore, that an Almighty & inspired Being appeared as the redeemer of their Caste & their *ignorance & supersitition* was easily worked into a *religious frenzy* which has stopped at nothing."[39] That idiom occurs also in the *Calcutta Review* article. There the Santal is acknowledged as "an eminently religious man" and his revolt as a parallel of other historical occasions when "*the fanatical spirit of religious superstition*" had been "swayed to strengthen and help forward a quarrel already ready to burst and based on other grounds".[40] However, the author gives this identification a significantly different slant from that in the report quoted above. There an incomprehending Ward, caught in the blast of the *hool*, appears to have been impressed by the spontaneity of "a religious frenzy which ... stopped at nothing". By contrast, the article, written after the regime had recovered its self-confidence, thanks to the

search-and-burn campaign in the disturbed tracts, interprets religiosity as a propagandist ruse used by the leaders to sustain the morale of the rebels. Referring, for
instance, to the messianic rumours in circulation, it says, "All these absurdities were
no doubt *devised* to keep up the courage of the numerous rabble."[41] Nothing could be
more elitist. The insurgents are regarded here as a mindless "rabble" devoid of a will
of their own and easily manipulated by their chiefs.

But elitism such as this is not a feature of colonialist historiography alone. Tertiary
discourse of the radical variety, too, exhibits the same disdain for the political consciousness of the peasant masses when it is mediated by religiosity. For a sample let us
turn to Ray's account of the rising again. He quotes the following lines from the
Calcutta Review article in a somewhat inaccurate but still clearly recognizable translation:

> Seedoo and Kanoo were at night seated in their home, revolving many things . . . a bit of
> paper fell on Seedoo's head, and suddenly the Thakoor [god] appeared before the
> astonished gaze of Seedoo and Kanoo; he was like a white man though dressed in the
> native style; on each hand he had ten fingers; he held a white book, and wrote therein;
> the book and with it 20 pieces of paper . . . he presented to the brothers; ascended
> upwards, and disappeared. Another bit of paper fell on Seedoo's head, and then came
> two men . . . hinted to them the purport of Thakoor's order, and they likewise vanished.
> But there was not merely one apparition of the sublime Thakoor; each day in the week
> for some short period, did he make known his presence to his favourite apostles. . . . In the
> silvery pages of the book, and upon the white leaves of the single scraps of paper, were
> words written; these were afterwards deciphered by literate Sonthals, able to read and
> interpret; but their meaning had already been sufficiently indicated to the two leaders.[42]

With some minor changes of detail (inevitable in a living folklore) this is indeed a
fairly authentic account of the visions the two Santal leaders believed they had had.
Their statements, reproduced in part in the Appendix (Extracts 3 and 4), bear this out.
These, incidentally, were not public pronouncements meant to impress their followers.
Unlike "The Thacoor's Perwannah" (Appendix: Extract 2) intended to make their
views known to the authorities before the uprising, these were the words of captives
facing execution. Addressed to hostile interrogators in military encampments they
could have little use as propaganda. Uttered by men of a tribe which, according to all
accounts had not yet learnt to lie,[43] these represented the truth and nothing but the
truth for their speakers. But that is not what Ray would credit them with. What figures
as a mere insinuation in the *Calcutta Review* is raised to the status of an elaborate
propaganda device in his introductory remarks on the passage cited above. Thus:

> Both Sidu and Kanu knew that the slogan (*dhwani*) which would have the most effect
> among the *backward* Santals, was one that was religious. Therefore, *in order to inspire* the
> Santals to struggle they *spread* the word about God's directive in favour of launching
> such a struggle. The story *invented* (*kalpita*) by them is as follows.[44]

There is little that is different here from what the colonialist writer had to say about
the presumed backwardness of the Santal peasantry, the manipulative designs of their
leaders and the uses of religion as the means of such manipulation. Indeed, on each of

these points Ray does better and is by far the more explicit of the two authors in attributing a gross lie and downright deception to the rebel chiefs without any evidence at all. The invention is all his own and testifies to the failure of a shallow radicalism to conceptualize insurgent mentality except in terms of an unadulterated secularism. Unable to grasp religiosity as the central modality of peasant conscious-ness in colonial India he is shy to acknowledge its mediation of the peasant's idea of power and all the resultant contradictions. He is obliged therefore to rationalize the ambiguities of rebel politics by assigning a worldly consciousness to the leaders and an otherworldly one to their followers making of the latter innocent dupes of crafty men armed with all the tricks of a modern Indian politician out to solicit rural votes. Where this lands the historian can be seen even more clearly in the projection of this thesis to a study of the Birsaite *ulgulan* in Ray's subsequent work. He writes,

> In order to propagate this religious doctrine of his Birsa adopted *a new device (kaushal)* – just as Sidu, the Santal leader, had done on the eve of the Santal rebellion of 1885. Birsa knew that the Kol were a *very backward* people and were full of *religious superstition* as a result of Hindu-Brahmanical and Christian missionary propaganda amongst them over a long period. Therefore, it would not do to avoid the question of religion if the Kol people were to be liberated from those wicked religious influences and drawn into the path of rebellion. Rather, in order to overcome the evil influences of Hindu and Christian religions, it would be necessary to spread his new religious faith among them in the name of that very God of theirs, and to introduce new rules. *To this end, recourse had to be had to falsehood, if necessary, in the interests of the people.*
>
> Birsa *spread* the word that he had received this new religion of his from the chief deity of the Mundas, Sing Bonga, himself.[45]

Thus the radical historian is driven by the logic of his own incomprehension to attribute a deliberate falsehood to one of the greatest of our rebels. The ideology of that mighty *ulgulan* is nothing but pure fabrication for him. And he is not alone in his misreading of insurgent consciousness. Baskay echoes him almost word for word in describing the Santal leader's claim to divine support for the *hool* as propaganda meant "to inspire the Santals to rise in revolt".[46] Formulations such as these have their foil in other writings of the same genre which solve the riddle of religious thinking among the Santal rebels by ignoring it altogether. A reader who has Natarajan's and Rasul's once influential essays as his only source of information about the insurrection of 1855 would hardly suspect any religiosity at all in that great event. It is represented there *exclusively* in its secular aspects. This attitude is of course not confined to the authors discussed in this essay. The same mixture of myopia and downright refusal to look at the evidence that is there characterizes a great deal more of the existing literature on the subject.

XIV

Why is tertiary discourse, even of the radical variety, so reluctant to come to terms with the religious element in rebel consciousness? Because it is still trapped in the paradigm which inspired the ideologically contrary, because colonialist, discourse of the primary and secondary types. It follows, in each case, from a refusal to acknowledge the insurgent as the subject of his own history. For once a peasant rebellion has been assimilated to the career of the Raj, the Nation or the People, it becomes easy for the historian to abdicate the responsibility he has of exploring and describing the consciousness specific to that rebellion and be content to ascribe to it a transcendental consciousness. In operative terms, this means denying a will to the mass of the rebels themselves and representing them merely as instruments of some other will. It is thus that in colonialist historiography insurgency is seen as the articulation of a pure spontaneity pitted against the will of the State as embodied in the Raj. If any consciousness is attributed at all to the rebels, it is only a few of their leaders – more often than not some individual members or small groups of the gentry – who are credited with it. Again, in bourgeois-nationalist historiography it is an elite consciousness which is read into all peasant movements as their motive force. This had led to such grotesqueries as the characterization of the Indigo Rebellion of 1860 as "the first non-violent mass movement"[47] and generally of all the popular struggles in rural India during the first hundred and twenty-five years of British rule as the spiritual harbinger of the Indian National Congress.

In much the same way the specificity of rebel consciousness had eluded radical historiography as well. This has been so because it is impaled on a concept of peasant revolts as a succession of events ranged along a direct line of descent – as a heritage, as it is often called – in which all the constituents have the same pedigree and replicate each other in their commitment to the highest ideals of liberty, equality and fraternity. In this ahistorical view of the history of insurgency all moments of consciousness are assimilated to the ultimate and highest moment of the series – indeed to an Ideal Consciousness. A historiography devoted to its pursuit (even when that is done, regrettably, in the name of Marxism) is ill-equipped to cope with contradictions which are indeed the stuff history is made of. Since the Ideal is supposed to be one hundred per cent secular in character, the devotee tends to look away when confronted with the evidence of religiosity as if the latter did not exist or explain it away as a clever but well-intentioned fraud perpetrated by enlightened leaders on their moronic followers – all done, of course, "in the interests of the people"! Hence, the rich material of myths, rituals, rumours, hopes for a Golden Age and fears of an imminent End of the World, all of which speaks of the self-alienation of the rebel, is wasted on this abstract and sterile discourse. It can do little to illuminate that combination of sectarianism and militancy which is so important a feature of our rural history. The ambiquity of such phenomena, witnessed during the Tebhaga movement in Dinajpur, as Muslim peasants coming to the Kisan Sabha "sometimes inscribing a hammer or a sickle on the Muslim League flag" and young maulavis "reciting melodious verse from the Koran" at village meetings as "they condemned the jotedari system and the practice of charging high interest rates",[48] will be beyond its grasp. The swift transformation of class struggle into communal strife and vice versa in our countryside evokes from it either some well-contrived apology or a simple gesture of embarrassment, but no real explanation.

However, it is not only the religious element in rebel consciousness which this historiography fails to comprehend. The specificity of a rural insurrection is expressed in terms of many other contradictions as well. These too are missed out. Blinded by the glare of a perfect and immaculate consciousness, the historian sees nothing, for instance, but solidarity in rebel behaviour, and fails to notice its Other, namely, betrayal. Committed inflexibly to the notion of insurgency as a generalized movement, he underestimates the power of the brakes put on it by localism and territoriality. Convinced that mobilization for a rural uprising flows exclusively from an overall elite authority, he tends to disregard the operation of many other authorities within the primordial relations of a rural community. A prisoner of empty abstractions tertiary discourse, even of the radical kind, has thus distanced itself from the prose of counter-insurgency only by a declaration of sentiment so far. It has still to go a long way before it can prove that the insurgent can rely on its performance to recover his place in history.

NOTES

I am grateful to my colleagues of the editorial team for their comments on an initial draft of this essay.

1 The instances are far too numerous to cite. For some of these see *MDS*, pp. 46–7, 48–9 on the Rangpur *dhing*; *BC* 54222: Metcalfe & Blunt to Court of Directors (10 April 1832), paras 14–15 on the Barasat uprising; W. W. Hunter, *Annals of Rural Bengal* (7th edition; London, 1897), pp. 237–8 and *JP*, 4 Oct. 1855: "The Thacoor's Perwannah" for the Santal *hool*; C. E. Buckland, *Bengal Under the Lieutenant-Governors*, vol. I (Calcutta, 1901), p. 192 for the "blue mutiny". For a list of abbreviations used in the notes of this essay, see below.

2 See, for instance, *MDS*, pp. 579–80; *Freedom Struggle in Uttar Pradesh*, vol. IV (Lucknow, 1959), pp. 284–5, 549.

3 J. C. Price, *The Chuar Rebellion of 1799*, p. *cl*. The edition of the work used in this essay is the one printed in A. Mitra (ed.), *District Handbooks: Midnapur* (Alipore, 1953), Appendix IV.

4 *BC* 54222: *JC*, 22 Nov. 1831: "Extract from the Proceedings of the Honorable the Vice President in Council in the Military Department under date the 10th November 1831". Emphasis added.

5 *JP*, 19 July 1855: Enclosure to letter from the Magistrate of Murshidabad, dated 11 July 1855. Emphasis added.

6 Thus, *BC* 54222: *JC*, 3 Apr. 1832: Alexander to Barwell (28 Nov. 1831).

7 My debt to Roland Barthes for many of the analytic terms and procedures used in this section and generally throughout this essay should be far too obvious to all familiar with his "Structural Analysis of Narratives" and "The Struggle with the Angel" in Barthes, *Image-Music-Text* (Glasgow, 1977), pp. 79–141, and "Historical Discourse" in M. Lane (ed.), *Structuralism, A Reader* (London, 1970), pp. 145–55, to require detailed reference except where I quote directly from this literature.

8 Barthes, *Image-Music-Text*, p. 102.

9 Émile Benveniste, *Problèmes de linguistique générale, I* (Paris, 1966), p. 126. The original, "la dissociation nous livre la constitution formelle; l'intégration nous livre des unités signifiantes", has been rendered somewhat differently and I feel, less happily, in the English translation of the work, *Problems in General Linguistics* (Florida, 1971), p. 107.

10 Barthes, *Image-Music-Text*, p. 93.

11 Charles Bally, *Linguistique Générale et Linguistique Française* (Berne, 1965), p. 144.

12   Barthes, *Elements of Semiology* (London, 1967), p. 60.

13   Barthes, *Image-Music-Text*, p. 128.

14   Ibid., p. 119.

15   *Selected Works of Mao Tse-tung*, vol. I (Peking, 1967), pp. 26–7.

16   Benveniste, op. cit., p. 239.

17   *Freedom Struggle in Uttar Pradesh*, vol. V, pp. 685–92.

18   For Roman Jakobson's exposition of this key concept, see his *Selected Writings, 2: Word and Language* (The Hague and Paris, 1971), pp. 130–47. Barthes develops the notion of organization shifters in his essay "Historical Discourse", pp. 146–8. All extracts quoted in this paragraph are taken from that essay unless otherwise mentioned.

19   Price, op. cit., p. *clx*.

20   Ibid.

21   Reginald G. Wilberforce, *An Unrecorded Chapter of the Indian Mutiny* (2nd edition; London, 1894), pp. 76–7.

22   It appears from a note in this work that parts of it were written in 1866. The dedication bears the date 4 March 1868. All our references to this work in quotation or otherwise are to Chapter IV of the seventh edition (London, 1897) unless otherwise stated.

23   Barthes, *Image-Music-Text*, p. 112.

24   Anon., "The Sonthal Rebellion", *Calcutta Review* (1856), pp. 223–64; K. K. Datta, "The Santal Insurrection of 1855–57", in *Anti-British Plots and Movements before 1857* (Meerut, 1970), pp. 43–152.

25   Vol. I (Calcutta, 1966), Ch. 13.

26   For these see ibid., pp. 323, 325, 327, 328.

27   Ibid., p. 337; Hunter, op. cit., pp. 247–9.

28   Ray, op. cit., pp. 316–19.

29   Anon., op. cit., pp. 238–41; Thornhill, op. cit., pp. 33–5; L. S. S. O'Malley, *Bengal District Gazetteers: Pabna* (Calcutta, 1923), p. 25; *Report of the Commission Appointed in India to Inquire into the Causes of the Riots which took place in the year 1875 in the Poona and Ahmednagar Districts of the Bombay Presidency* (London, 1878), *passim*.

30   BC 54222: *JC*, 22 Nov. 1831 (no. 91). Emphasis added.

31   Anon., op. cit., pp. 263–4.

32   Ibid., p. 263.

33   Ray, op. cit., p. 318.

34   Ibid., p. 340.

35   L. Natarajan, *Peasant Uprisings in India, 1850–1900* (Bombay, 1953), pp. 31–2.

36   Abdulla Rasul, *Saontal Bidroher Amar Kahini* (Calcutta, 1954), p. 24.

37   The instances are far too numerous to cite in an essay of this size, but for some samples see *Mare Hapram Ko Reak Katha*, Ch. 79, in A. Mitra (ed.), *District Handbooks: Bankura* (Calcutta, 1953).

38   Appendix: Extract 2.

39   *JP*, 8 Nov. 1855: Ward to Government of Bengal (13 Oct. 1855). Emphasis added.

40   Anon., op. cit., p. 243. Emphasis added.

41   Ibid., p. 246. Emphasis added.

42   Ibid., pp. 243–4; Ray, op. cit., pp. 321–2.

43   This is generally accepted. See, for instance, Sherwill's observation about the truth being "sacred" to the Santals "offering in this respect a bright example to their lying neighbours, the Bengalis", *Geographical and Statistical Report of the District Bhaugulpoor* (Calcutta, 1854), p. 32.

44   Ray, op. cit., p. 321. Emphasis added.

45 Ray, *Bharater Baiplabik Samgramer Itihas*, vol. I (Calcutta, 1970), p. 95. Emphasis added.
    The sentence italicized by us in the quoted passage reads as follows in the Bengali original:
    "Eijanyo prayojan hoiley jatir svarthey mithyar asroy grahan karitey hoibey".

46 Dhirendranath Baskay, *Saontal Ganasamgramer Itihas* (Calcutta, 1976), p. 66.

47 Jogesh Chandra Bagal (ed.), *Peasant Revolution in Bengal* (Calcutta, 1953), p. 5.

48 Sunil Sen, *Agrarian Struggle in Bengal, 1946–47* (New Delhi, 1972), p. 49.

APPENDIX

Extract 1

I came to plunder ... Sidoo and Kaloo [Kanhu] declared themselves Rajas & [said] they would plunder the whole country and take possession of it – they said also, no one can stop us for it is the order of Takoor. On this account we have all come with them.

Source: JP, 19 July 1855: Balai Majhi's Statement (14 July 1855).

Extract 2

The Thacoor has descended in the house of Seedoo Manjee, Kanoo Manjee, Bhyrub and Chand, at Bhugnudihee in Pergunnah Kunjeala. The Thakoor in person is conversing with them, he has descended from Heaven, he is conversing with Kanoor and Seedoo, The Sahibs and the white Soldiers will fight. Kanoo and Seedoo Manjee are not fighting. The Thacoor himself will fight. Therefore you Sahibs and Soldiers fight with the Thacoor himself Mother Ganges will come to the Thacoor's (assistance) Fire will rain from Heaven. If you are satisfied with the Thacoor then you must go to the other side of the Ganges. The Thacoor has ordered the Sonthals that for a bulluck plough 1 anna is to be paid for revenue. Buffalo plough 2 annas The reign of Truth has begun True justice will be administered He who does not speak the truth will not be allowed to remain on the Earth. The Mahajuns have committed a great sin The Sahibs and the amlah have made everything bad, in this the Sahibs have sinned greatly.

Those who tell things to the Magistrate and those who investigate cases for him, take 70 or 80 R.s. with great oppression in this the Sahibs have sinned. On this account the Thacoor has ordered me saying that the country is not the Sahibs ...

P.S. If you Sahibs agree, then you must remain on the other side of the Ganges, and if you dont agree you cant remain on that side of the river, I will rain fire and all the Sahibs will be killed by the hand of God in person and Sahibs if you fight with muskets the Sonthal will not be hit by the bullets and the Thacoor will give your Elephants and horses of his own accord to the Sonthals ... if you fight with the Sonthals two days will be as one day and two nights as one night. This is the order of the Thacoor.

Source: JP, 4 October 1855: "The Thacoor's Perwannah" ("dated 10 Saon 1262").

Extract 3

Then the Manjees & Purgunnaits assembled in my Verandah, & we consulted for 2 months, "that Pontet & Mohesh Dutt don't listen to our complaints & no one acts as our Father & Mother" then a God descended from heaven in the form of a cartwheel & said to me "Kill Pontet & the Darogah & the Mahajuns & then you will have justice & a Father & Mother"; then the Thacoor went back to the heavens; after this 2 men like Bengallees came into my Verhandah; they each had six fingers half a piece of paper fell on my head before the Thacoor came & half fell afterwards. I could not read but Chand & Seheree & a Dhome read it, they said "The Thacoor has written to you to fight the Mahajens & then you will have justice"...

Source: JP, 8 November 1855: "Examination of Sedoo Sonthal late Thacoor".

Extract 4

In Bysack the God descended in my house I sent a perwannah to the Burra Sahib at Calcutta...I wrote that the Thacoor had come to my house & was conversing with me & had told all the Sonthals that they were to be under the charge of me & that I was to pay all the revenue to Government & was to oppress no one & the zamindars & Mahajans were committing great oppression taking 20 pice for one & that I was to place them at a distance from the sonthals & if they do not go away to fight with them.

...

Ishwar was a white man with only a dootee & chudder he sat on the ground like a Sahib he wrote on this bit of paper. He gave me 4 papers but afterwards presented 16 more. The thacoor had 5 fingers on each hand. I did not see him in the day I saw him only in the night. The sonthals then assembled at my house to see the thacoor.

...

[At Maheshpur] the troops came & we had a fight... afterwards seeing that men on our side were falling we both turned twice on them & once drove them away, then I made poojah ... & then a great many balls came & Seedoo & I were both wounded. The thacoor had said "water will come out of the muskets" but my troops committed some crime therefore the thacoors prediction[s] were not fulfilled about 80 sonthals were killed.

...

All the blank papers fell from heaven & the book in which all the pages are blank also fell from heaven.

Source: JP, 20 December 1855: "Examination of Kanoo Sonthal".

ABBREVIATIONS

BC: Board's Collections, India Office Records (London).
JC: Fort William Judicial Consultations in BC.
JP: Judicial Proceedings, West Bengal State Archives (Calcutta).
MDS: Maharaja Deby Sinha (Nashipur Raj Estate, 1914).

The Nationalist Resolution of the Women's Question

PARTHA CHATTERJEE

Partha Chatterjee joins many postcolonial theorists who have in recent years explored the importance of the "women's question" for nationalism. Nationalism itself has become a topic of considerable debate within postcolonial studies; it is of particular importance in the Indian context where modernization comes into contact with the conservatism of nationalism. Though this is a problem in other postcolonial countries, such as Ireland, in India it has taken on an urgency that is only partly alleviated by the desire to modernize the ambitions of nationalism itself. Chatterjee attempts to understand the problem of a conservative nationalism by critiquing the nationalist attitude toward women – an attitude that consigns women and women's concerns to a "spiritual" sphere linked to home, family, religion, and conservative Indian values, and one that comes into conflict with the progressive energies of modernization, which are linked to male-dominated spheres of politics, economics, business, and cultural production. Chatterjee uses the terms *ghar* and *bahir* (home and world) to differentiate between these two spheres. The "nationalist resolution" to the problem was to create a "new" woman who was superior to Westernized and "common" women – the "new *bhadramahila*" (respectable woman). But the social changes that created this "new woman" did not extend outside the home; the problem continues in the "national culture" of independent India. For further discussion of women's rights and the role of women in the construction of national culture and identity, see the essays by **Gayatri Chakravorty Spivak**, **Rajeswari Sunder Rajan**, and **Amina Mama**.

The Nationalist Resolution of the Women's Question

I

The "women's question" was a central issue in some of the most controversial debates over social reform in early and mid-nineteenth-century Bengal – the period of the so-called "renaissance." Rammohun Roy's historical fame is largely built around his campaign against *satidaha* (widow immolation), Vidyasagar's around his efforts to legalize widow remarriage and abolish Kulin polygamy; the Brahmo Samaj was split twice in the 1870s over questions of marriage laws and the "age of consent." What has perplexed historians is the rather sudden disappearance of such issues from the agenda of public debate towards the close of the century. From then onwards, questions regarding the position of women in society do not arouse the same degree of passion and acrimony as they did only a few decades before. The overwhelming issues now are directly political ones – concerning the politics of nationalism.

Was this because the women's question had been resolved in a way satisfactory to most sections of opinion in Bengal? Critical historians today find it difficult to accept this answer. Indeed, the hypothesis of critical social history today is that nationalism could not have resolved those issues; rather, the relation between nationalism and the women's question must have been problematical.

Ghulam Murshid states the problem in its most obvious, straight-forward, form.[1] If one takes seriously, i.e. in their liberal rationalist and egalitarian content, the mid-nineteenth century attempts in Bengal to "modernize" the condition of women, then what follows in the period of nationalism must be regarded as a clear retrogression. "Modernization" began in the first half of the nineteenth century because of the "penetration" of western ideas. After some limited success, there was a perceptible decline in the reform movements as "popular attitudes" towards them "hardened." The new politics of nationalism "glorified India's past and tended to defend everything traditional;" all attempts to change customs and life-styles began to be seen as the aping of western manners and thereby regarded with suspicion. Consequently, nationalism fostered a distinctly conservative attitude towards social beliefs and practices. The movement towards modernization was stalled by nationalist politics.

This critique of the social implications of nationalism follows from rather simple and linear historical assumptions. Murshid not only accepts that the early attempts at

Taken from Kumkum Sangari and Sudesh Vaid (eds.), *Recasting Women: Essays in Indian Colonial History* (New Brunswick, NJ: Rutgers University Press, 1990).

social reform were impelled by the new nationalist and progressive ideas imported from Europe, he also presumes that the necessary historical culmination of such reforms in India ought to have been, as in the West, the full articulation of liberal values in social institutions and practices. From these assumptions, a critique of nationalist ideology and practices is inevitable. It would be the same sort of critique as that of the so-called "neo-imperialist" historians who argue that Indian national-ism was nothing but a scramble for sharing political power with the colonial rulers, its mass following only the successful activization of traditional patron-client relationships, its internal debates the squabbles of parochial factions, its ideology a garb for xenophobia and racial exclusiveness. The point to note is that the problem lies in the original structure of assumptions. Murshid's study is a telling example of the fact, now increasingly evident, that if one only scrapes away the gloss, it is hard to defend many ideas and practices of nationalism in terms of rationalist and liberal values.

Of course, that original structure of assumptions has not gone unchallenged in recent critical history. The most important critique in our field is that of the Bengal renaissance.[2] Not only have questions been raised about the strictness and consist-ency of the liberal ideas propagated by the "renaissance" leaders of Bengal, it has also been asked whether the fruition of liberal reforms was at all possible under conditions of colonial rule. In other words, the incompleteness and contradictions of "renais-sance" ideology were shown to be the necessary result of the impossibility of thor-ough-going liberal reform under colonial conditions.

From that perspective, the problem of the diminished importance of the women's question in the period of nationalism deserves a different answer from the one given by Murshid. Sumit Sarkar has considered this problem in a recent article.[3] His argument is that the limitations of nationalist ideology in pushing forward a cam-paign for liberal and egalitarian social change cannot be seen as a retrogression from an earlier radical reformist phase. Those limitations were in fact present in the earlier phase as well. The "renaissance" reformers, he shows, were highly selective in their acceptance of liberal ideas from Europe. Fundamental elements of social conservatism such as the maintenance of caste distinctions and patriarchal forms of authority in the family, acceptance of the sanctity of the *shastra* (ancient scriptures), preference for symbolic rather than substantive change in social practices – all of them were conspicuous in the reform movements of the early and mid-nineteenth century. Specifically on the question of the social position of women, he shows the funda-mental absence in every phase of any significant autonomous struggle by women themselves to change relations within or outside the family. In fact, Sarkar throws doubt upon the very assumption that the early attempts at reform were principally guided by any ideological acceptance of liberal or rationalist values imported from the West. He suggests that the concern with the social condition of women was far less an indicator of such ideological preference for liberalism and more an expression of certain "acute problems of interpersonal adjustments within the family" on the part of the early generation of western educated males. Faced with "social ostracism and isolation," their attempts at "a limited and controlled emancipation of wives" were "a personal necessity for survival in a hostile social world." Whatever changes have come about since that time in the social and legal position of women have been "through objective socio-economic pressures, some post-independence legislation, rather than clear-cut ideology or really autonomous struggle. Mental attitudes and values have consequently changed very much less." The pattern, therefore, is not, as Murshid suggests, one of radical liberalism in the beginning followed by a conservative backlash in the period of nationalism; Sarkar argues that in fact the fault lies with the very inception of our modernity.

The curious thing, however, is that Sarkar too regards the social reform movements of the last century and a half as a failure – failure to match up to the liberal ideals of equality and reason. It is from this standpoint that he can show, quite legitimately, the falsity of any attempt to paint a picture of starry-eyed radicalism muzzled by a censorious nationalist ideology. But a new problem crops up. If we are to say that the nineteenth-century reform movements did not arise out of an ideological acceptance of western liberalism, it could fairly be asked: from what then did they originate? The answer that they stemmed from problems of personal adjustment within the family can hardly be adequate. After all, the nineteenth-century debates about social reform generally, and the women's question in particular, were intensely ideological. If the paradigm for those debates was not that of western liberalism, what was it? Moreover, if we cannot describe that paradigm in its own terms, can we legitimately apply once again the western standards of liberalism to proclaim the reform movements, pre-nationalist as well as nationalist, as historical failures? Surely the new critical historiography will be grossly one-sided if we are unable to represent the nineteenth-century ideology in its relation to itself, i.e. in its self-identity.

It seems to me that Sumit Sarkar's argument can be taken much further. We need not shy away from the fact that the nationalist ideology did indeed tackle the women's question in the nineteenth century. To expect the contrary would be surprising. It is inconceivable that an ideology which claimed to offer a total alternative to the "traditional" social order as well as to the western way of life should fail to have something distinctive to say about such a fundamental aspect of social institutions and practices as the position of women. We should direct our search within the nationalist ideology itself.

We might, for a start, pursue Sarkar's entirely valid observation that the nineteenth-century ideologues were highly selective in their adoption of liberal slogans. How did they select what they wanted? What, in other words, was the ideological sieve through which they put the newly imported ideas from Europe? Once we have reconstructed this framework of the nationalist ideology, we will be in a far better position to locate where exactly the women's question fitted in with the claims of nationalism. We will find, if I may anticipate my argument in the following sections of this paper, that nationalism did in fact face up to the new social and cultural problems concerning the position of women in "modern" society and that it did provide an answer to the problems in terms of its own ideological paradigm. I will claim, therefore, that the relative unimportance of the women's question in the last decades of the nineteenth century is not to be explained by the fact that it had been censored out of the reform agenda or overtaken by the more pressing and emotive issues of political struggle. It was because nationalism had in fact resolved "the women's question" in complete accordance with its preferred goals.

II

I have elaborated elsewhere[4] a framework for analysing the contradictory pulls on nationalist ideology in its struggle against the dominance of colonialism and the resolution it offered to these contradictions. In the main, this resolution was built around a separation of the domain of culture into two spheres – the material and the spiritual. It was in the material sphere that the claims of western civilization were the most powerful. Science, technology, rational forms of economic organization, modern methods of statecraft, these had given the European countries the strength to subjugate non-European peoples and to impose their dominance over the whole world. To overcome this domination, the colonized people must learn these superior techniques of organizing material life and incorporate them within their own cultures. This was one aspect of the nationalist project of rationalizing and reforming the "traditional" culture of their people. But this could not mean the imitation of the West in every aspect of life, for then the very distinction between the West and the East would vanish – the self-identity of national culture would itself be threatened. In fact, as Indian nationalists in the late nineteenth century argued, not only was it not desirable to imitate the West in anything other than the material aspects of life, it was not even necessary to do so, because in the spiritual domain the East was superior to the West. What was necessary was to cultivate the material techniques of modern western civilization while retaining and strengthening the distinctive spiritual essence of the national culture. This completed the formulation of the nationalist project, and as an ideological justification for the selective appropriation of western modernity it continues to hold sway to this day (*pace* Rajiv Gandhi's juvenile fascination for space-age technology).

We need not concern ourselves here with the details of how this ideological framework shaped the course of nationalist politics in India. What is important is to note that nationalism was not simply about a political struggle for power; it related the question of political independence of the nation to virtually every aspect of the material and spiritual life of the people. In every case, there was a problem of selecting what to take from the West and what to reject. And in every case, the questions were asked: is it desirable? is it necessary? The answers to these questions are the material of the debates about social reform in the nineteenth century. To understand the self-identity of nationalist ideology in concrete terms, we must look more closely at the way in which these questions were answered.

The discourse of nationalism shows that the material / spiritual distinction was condensed into an analogous, but ideologically far more powerful, dichotomy: that between the outer and the inner. The material domain lies outside us – a mere external, which influences us, conditions us, and to which we are forced to adjust. But ultimately it is unimportant. It is the spiritual which lies within, which is our true self; it is that which is genuinely essential. It follows that as long as we take care to retain the spiritual distinctiveness of our culture, we could make all the compromises and adjustments necessary to adapt ourselves to the requirements of a modern material world without losing our true identity. This was the key which nationalism supplied for resolving the ticklish problems posed by issues of social reform in the nineteenth century.

Now apply the inner / outer distinction to the matter of concrete day-to-day living and you get a separation of the social space into *ghar* and *bahir*, the home and the world. The world is the external, the domain of the material; the home represents our inner spiritual self, our true identity. The world is a treacherous terrain of the pursuit of material interests, where practical considerations reign supreme. It is also typically the domain of the male. The home in its essence must remain unaffected by the profane activities of the material world – and woman is its representation. And so we get an identification of social roles by gender to correspond with the separation of the social space into ghar and bahir.

Thus far we have not obtained anything that is different from the typical conception of gender roles in any "traditional" patriarchy. If we now find continuities in these social attitudes in the phase of social reforms in the nineteenth century, we are tempted to put this down as "conservatism," a mere defence of "traditional" norms. But this would be a mistake. The colonial situation, and the ideological response of nationalism, introduced an entirely new substance to these terms and effected their transformation. The material / spiritual dichotomy, to which the terms "world" and "home" corresponded, had acquired, as we have noted before, a very special significance in the nationalist mind. The world was where the European power had challenged the non-European peoples and, by virtue of its superior material culture, had subjugated them. But it had failed to colonize the inner, essential, identity of the East which lay in its distinctive, and superior, spiritual culture. That is where the East was undominated, sovereign, master of its own fate. For a colonized people, the world was a distressing constraint, forced upon it by the fact of its material weakness. It was a place of oppression and daily humiliation, a place where the norms of the colonizer had perforce to be accepted. It was also the place, as nationalists were soon to argue, where the battle would be waged for national independence. The requirement for this was for the subjugated to learn from the West the modern sciences and arts of the material world. Then their strengths would be matched and ultimately the colonizer overthrown. But in the entire phase of the national struggle, the crucial need was to protect, preserve and strengthen the inner core of the national culture, its spiritual essence. No encroachments by the colonizer must be allowed in that inner sanctum. In the world, imitation of and adaptation to western norms was a necessity; at home, they were tantamount to annihilation of one's very identity.

Once we match this new meaning of the home / world dichotomy with the identification of social roles by gender, we get the ideological framework within which nationalism answered the women's question. It would be a grave error to see in this, as we are apt to in our despair at the many marks of social conservatism in nationalist practice, a total rejection of the West. Quite the contrary. The nationalist paradigm in fact supplied an ideological principle of *selection*. It was not a dismissal of modernity; the attempt was rather to make modernity consistent with the nationalist project.

III

It is striking how much of the literature on women in the nineteenth century was concerned with the theme of the threatened westernization of Bengali women. It was taken up in virtually every form of written, oral and visual communication, from the ponderous essays of nineteenth-century moralists, to novels, farces, skits and jingles, to the paintings of the *patua* (scroll painter). Social parody was the most popular and effective medium of this ideological propagation. From Iswarchandra Gupta and the *kabiyal* (popular versifiers) of the early nineteenth century to the celebrated pioneers of modern Bengali theatre – Michael Madhusudan Dutt, Dinabandhu Mitra, Jyotirind-ranath Tagore, Upendranath Das, Amritalal Bose – everyone picked up the theme. To ridicule the idea of a Bengali woman trying to imitate the way of a European woman or *memsahib* (and it was very much an idea, for it is hard to find historical evidence that even in the most westernized families of Calcutta in the mid-nineteenth century there were actually any women who even remotely resembled these gross caricatures) was a sure recipe calculated to evoke raucous laughter and moral condemnation in both male and female audiences. It was, of course, a criticism of manners: of new items of clothing such as the blouse, the petticoat and shoes (all, curiously, considered vulgar, although they clothed the body far better than the single length of fabric or sari which was customary for Bengali women, irrespective of wealth and social status, until the middle of the nineteenth century), of the use of western cosmetics and jewellery, of the reading of novels (the educated Haimabati in Jyotirindranath's *Alikbabu* speaks, thinks and acts like the heroines of historical romances), of needlework (considered a useless and expensive pastime), of riding in open carriages. What made the ridicule stronger was the constant suggestion that the westernized woman was fond of useless luxury and cared little for the well-being of the home. One can hardly miss in all this a criticism – reproach mixed with envy – of the wealth and luxury of the new social elite emerging around the institutions of colonial administration and trade.

This literature of parody and satire in the first half of the nineteenth century clearly contained much that was prompted by a straightforward defence of "tradition" and outright rejection of the new. The nationalist paradigm had still not emerged in clear outline. On hindsight, this – the period from Rammohun to Vidyasagar – appears as one of great social turmoil and ideological confusion among the literati. And then, drawing from various sources, a new discourse began to be formed in the second half of the century – the discourse of nationalism. Now the attempt was made to define the social and moral principles for locating the position of women in the "modern" world of the nation.

Let us take as an example one of the most clearly formulated tracts on the subject: Bhudev Mukhopadhyay's *Paribarik Prabandha* (essays on the family) published in 1882. Bhudev states the problem in his characteristic matter-of-fact style:

> Because of our hankering for the external glitter and ostentation of the English way of life . . . an upheaval is under way within our homes. The men learn English and become sahibs. The women do not learn English but nevertheless try to become bibis. In house-holds which manage on an income of a hundred rupees, the women no longer cook, sweep or make the bed . . . everything is done by servants and maids; [the women] only read books, sew carpets and play cards. What is the result? The house and furniture get untidy, the meals poor, the health of every member of the family is ruined; children are born weak and rickety, constantly plagued by illness – they die early.

> Many reform movements are being conducted today; the education of women, in
> particular, is constantly talked about. But we rarely hear of those great arts in which
> women were once trained – a training which if it had still been in vogue would have
> enabled us to tide over this crisis caused by injudicious imitation. I suppose we will never
> hear of this training again.[5]

The problem is put here in the empirical terms of a positive sociology, a genre much
favoured by serious Bengali writers of Bhudev's time. But the sense of crisis which he
expresses was very much a reality. Bhudev is voicing the feelings of large sections of
the newly emergent middle class in Bengal when he says that the very institutions of
home and family were threatened under the peculiar conditions of colonial rule. A
quite unprecedented external condition had been thrust upon us; we were being
forced to adjust to those conditions, for which a certain degree of imitation of alien
ways was unavoidable. But could this wave of imitation be allowed to enter our
homes? Would that not destroy our inner identity? Yet it was clear that a mere
restatement of the old norms of family life would not suffice: they were breaking
down by the inexorable force of circumstance. New norms were needed, which would
be more appropriate to the external conditions of the modern world and yet not a
mere imitation of the West. What were the principles by which these new norms
could be constructed?

Bhudev supplies the characteristic nationalist answer. In an essay on modesty
entitled "Lajjasilata," he talks of the natural and social principles which provide the
basis for the "feminine" virtues.[6] Modesty, or decorum in manner and conduct, he
says, is a specifically human trait; it does not exist in animal nature. It is human
aversion to the purely animal traits which gives rise to virtues such as modesty. In
this aspect, human beings seek to cultivate in themselves, and in their civilization,
spiritual or god-like qualities wholly opposed to forms of behaviour which prevail in
animal nature. Further, within the human species, women cultivate and cherish
these god-like qualities far more than men. Protected to a certain extent from the
purely material pursuits of securing a livelihood in the external world, women express
in their appearance and behaviour the spiritual qualities which are characteristic of
civilized and refined human society.

The relevant dichotomies and analogues are all here. The material / spiritual
dichotomy corresponds to that between animal / god-like qualities, which in turn
corresponds to masculine / feminine virtues. Bhudev then invests this ideological
form with its specifically nationalist content:

> In a society where men and women meet together, converse together at all times, eat and
> drink together, travel together, the manners of women are likely to be somewhat coarse,
> devoid of spiritual qualities and relatively prominent in animal traits. For this reason, I do
> not think the customs of such a society are free from all defect. Some argue that because
> of such close association with women, the characters of men acquire certain tender and
> spiritual qualities. Let me concede the point. But can the loss caused by coarseness and
> degeneration in the female character be compensated by the acquisition of a certain
> degree of tenderness in the male?[7]

The point is then hammered home:

Those who laid down our religious codes discovered the inner spirituality which resides within even the most animal pursuits which humans must perform, and thus removed the animal qualities from those actions. This has not happened in Europe. Religion there is completely divorced from [material] life. Europeans do not feel inclined to regulate all aspects of their life by the norms of religion; they condemn it as clericalism. . . . In the Arya system there is a preponderance of spiritualism, in the European system a preponderance of material pleasure. In the Arya system, the wife is a goddess. In the European system, she is a partner and companion.[8]

The new norm for organizing family life and determining the right conduct for women in the conditions of the "modern" world could now be deduced with ease. Adjustments would have to be made in the external world of material activity, and men would bear the brunt of this task. To the extent that the family was itself entangled in wider social relations, it too could not be insulated from the influence of changes in the outside world. Consequently, the organization and ways of life at home would also have to be changed. But the crucial requirement was to retain the inner spirituality of indigenous social life. The home was the principal site for expressing the spiritual quality of the national culture, and women must take the main responsibility of protecting and nurturing this quality. No matter what the changes in the external conditions of life for women, they must not lose their essentially spiritual (i.e. feminine) virtues; they must not, in other words, become *essentially* westernized. It followed, as a simple criterion for judging the desirability of reform, that the essential distinction between the social roles of men and women in terms of material and spiritual virtues must at all times be maintained. There would have to be a marked *difference* in the degree and manner of westernization of women, as distinct from men, in the modern world of the nation.

IV

This was the central principle by which nationalism resolved the women's question in terms of its own historical project. The details were not, of course, worked out immediately. In fact, from the middle of the nineteenth century right up to the present day, there have been many controversies about the precise application of the home / world, spiritual / material, feminine / masculine dichotomies in various matters concerning the everyday life of the "modern" woman – her dress, food, manners, education, her role in organizing life at home, her role outside the home. The concrete problems arose out of the rapidly changing situation – both external and internal – in which the new middle-class family found itself; the specific solutions were drawn from a variety of sources – a reconstructed "classical" tradition, modernized folk forms, the utilitarian logic of bureaucratic and industrial practices, the legal idea of equality in a liberal democratic state. The content of the resolution was neither predetermined nor unchanging, but its form had to be consistent with the system of dichotomies which shaped and contained the nationalist project.

The "new" woman defined in this way was subjected to a *new* patriarchy. In fact, the social order connecting the home and the world in which nationalism placed the new woman was contrasted not only with that of modern western society; it was explicitly distinguished from the patriarchy of indigenous tradition. Sure enough, nationalism adopted several elements from "tradition" as marks of its native cultural identity, but this was a deliberately "classicized" tradition – reformed, reconstructed. Even Gandhi said of the patriarchal rules laid down by the scriptures:

> ... it is sad to think that the *Smritis* contain texts which can command no respect from men who cherish the liberty of woman as their own and who regard her as the mother of the race.... The question arises as to what to do with the *Smritis* that contain texts ... that are repugnant to the moral sense. I have already suggested ... that all that is printed in the name of scriptures need not be taken as the word of God or the inspired word.[9]

The new patriarchy was also sharply distinguished from the immediate social and cultural condition in which the majority of the people lived, for the "new" woman was quite the reverse of the "common" woman who was coarse, vulgar, loud, quarrelsome, devoid of superior moral sense, sexually promiscuous, subjected to brutal physical oppression by males. Alongside the parody of the westernized woman, this other construct is repeatedly emphasized in the literature of the nineteenth century through a host of lower-class female characters who make their appearance in the social milieu of the new middle class – maidservants, washerwomen, barbers, pedlars, procuresses, prostitutes. It was precisely this degenerate condition of women which nationalism claimed it would reform, and it was through these contrasts that the new woman of nationalist ideology was accorded a status of cultural superiority to the westernized women of the wealthy parvenu families spawned by the colonial connection as well as the common women of the lower classes. Attainment by her own efforts of a superior national culture was the mark of woman's newly acquired freedom. This was the central ideological strength of the nationalist resolution of the women's question.

We can follow the form of this resolution in several specific aspects in which the lives and conditions of middle-class women have changed over the last hundred years or so. Take the case of "female education", that contentious subject which engaged so much of the attention of social reformers in the nineteenth century.[10] Some of the early opposition to the opening of schools for women was backed by an appeal to "tradition" which supposedly prohibited women from being introduced to bookish learning, but this argument hardly gained much support. The threat was seen to lie in the fact that the early schools, and arrangements for teaching women at home, were organized by Christian missionaries; there was thus the fear of both proselytization and the exposure of women to harmful western influences. The threat was removed when from the 1850s Indians themselves began to open schools for girls. The spread of formal education among middle-class women in Bengal in the second half of the nineteenth century was remarkable. From 95 girls' schools with an attendance of 2,500 in 1863, the figures went up to 2,238 schools in 1890 with a total of more than 80,000 students.[11]

The quite general acceptance of formal education among middle-class women was undoubtedly made possible by the development of an educative literature and teaching materials in the Bengali language. The long debates of the nineteenth century on a proper "feminine curriculum" now seem to us somewhat quaint, but it is not difficult to identify the real point of concern. Much of the content of the modern school education was seen as important for the "new" woman, but to administer it in the English language was difficult in practical terms, irrelevant in view of the fact that the central place of the educated woman was still at home, and threatening because it might devalue and displace that central site where the social position of women was located. The problem was resolved through the efforts of the intelligentsia who made it a fundamental task of the nationalist project to create a modern language and literature suitable for a widening readership which would include newly educated women. Through text books, periodicals and creative works, an important force which shaped the new literature of Bengal was the urge to make it accessible to women who could read only one language – their mother-tongue.

Formal education became not only acceptable, but in fact a requirement for the new *bhadramahila* (respectable woman), when it was demonstrated that it was possible for a woman to acquire the cultural refinements afforded by modern education without jeopardizing her place at home. Indeed, the nationalist construct of the new woman derived its ideological strength from the fact that it was able to make the goal of cultural refinement through education a personal challenge for every woman, thus opening up a domain where woman was an autonomous subject. This explains to a large extent the remarkable degree of enthusiasm among middle-class women to acquire and use for themselves the benefits of formal learning. It was a purpose which they set for themselves in their personal lives as the object of their will; to achieve it was to achieve freedom. Indeed, the achievement was marked by claims of cultural superiority in several different aspects: superiority over the western woman for whom, it was believed, education meant only the acquisition of material skills in order to compete with men in the outside world and hence a loss of feminine (spiritual) virtues; superiority over the preceding generation of women in their own homes who had been denied the opportunity for freedom by an oppressive and degenerate social tradition; and superiority over women of the lower classes who were culturally incapable of appreciating the virtues of freedom.

It is this particular nationalist construction of reform as a project of both emancipation and self-emancipation of women (and hence a project in which both men and women must participate) which also explains why the early generation of educated women themselves so keenly propagated the nationalist idea of the "new woman." Recent historians of a liberal persuasion have often been somewhat embarrassed by the profuse evidence of women writers of the nineteenth century, including those at the forefront of the reform movements in middle-class homes, justifying the importance of the so-called "feminine virtues." Radharani Lahiri, for instance, wrote in 1875: "Of all the subjects that women might learn, housework is the most important ... whatever knowledge she may acquire, she cannot claim any reputation unless she is proficient in housework."[12] Others spoke of the need for an educated woman to "develop" such womanly virtues as chastity, self-sacrifice, submission, devotion, kindness, patience and the labours of love.[13] The ideological point of view from which such protestations of "femininity" (and hence the acceptance of a new patriarchal order) were made inevitable was given precisely by the *nationalist* resolution of the problem, and Kundamala Debi, writing in 1870, expressed this well when she advised other women:

> If you have acquired real knowledge, then give no place in your heart to *mem-sahib* like behaviour. That is not becoming in a Bengali housewife. See how an educated woman can do housework thoughtfully and systematically in a way unknown to an ignorant, uneducated woman. And see how if God had not appointed us to this place in the home, how unhappy a place the world would be![14]

Education then was meant to inculcate in women the virtues – the typically "bourgeois" virtues characteristic of the new social forms of "disciplining" – of orderliness, thrift, cleanliness, and a personal sense of responsibility, the practical skills of literacy, accounting and hygiene, and the ability to run the household according to the new physical and economic conditions set by the outside world. For this, she would also need to have some idea of the world outside the home into which she could even venture as long as it did not threaten her "femininity." It is this latter criterion, now invested with a characteristically nationalist content, which made possible the displacement of the boundaries of "the home" from the physical confines earlier defined by the rules of *purdah* (seclusion) to a more flexible, but culturally nonetheless determinate, domain set by the *differences* between socially approved male and female conduct. Once the essential "femininity" of women was fixed in terms of certain culturally visible "spiritual" qualities, they could go to schools, travel in public conveyances, watch public entertainment programmes, and in time even take up employment outside the home. But the "spiritual" signs of her femininity were now clearly marked: in her dress, her eating habits, her social demeanour, her religiosity. The specific markers were obtained from diverse sources, and in terms of their origins each had its specific history. The dress of the bhadramahila, for instance, went through a whole phase of experimentation before what was known as the *brahmika* sari (a form of wearing the sari in combination with blouse, petticoat and shoes made fashionable in Brahmo households) became accepted as standard for middle class women.[15] Here too the necessary differences were signified in terms of national identity, social emancipation and cultural refinement, differences, that is to say, with the memsahib, with women of earlier generations and with women of the lower classes. Further, in this as in other aspects of her life, the "spirituality" of her character had also to be stressed in contrast with the innumerable surrenders which men were having to make to the pressures of the material world. The need to adjust to the new conditions outside the home had forced upon men a whole series of changes in their dress, food habits, religious observances and social relations. Each of these capitulations now had to be compensated by an assertion of spiritual purity on the part of women. They must not eat, drink or smoke in the same way as men; they must continue the observance of religious rituals which men were finding it difficult to carry out; they must maintain the cohesiveness of family life and solidarity with the kin to which men could not now devote much attention. The new patriarchy advocated by nationalism conferred upon women the honour of a new social responsibility, and by associating the task of "female emancipation" with the historical goal of sovereign nationhood, bound them to a new, and yet entirely legitimate, subordination.

As with all hegemonic forms of exercise of dominance, this patriarchy combined coercive authority with the subtle force of persuasion. This was expressed most generally in an inverted ideological form of the relation of power between the sexes: the adulation of woman as goddess or as mother. Whatever be its sources in the classical religions of India or in medieval religious practices, it is undeniable that the specific ideological form in which we know the Sati-Savitri-Sita construct in the modern literature and arts of India today is wholly a product of the development of a dominant middle-class culture coeval with the era of nationalism. It served to emphasize with all the force of mythological inspiration what had in any case become a dominant characteristic of femininity in the new woman, viz. the "spiritual" qualities of self-sacrifice, benevolence, devotion, religiosity, etc. This spirituality did not, as we have seen, impede the chances of the woman moving out of the physical confines of the home; on the contrary, it facilitated it, making it possible for her to go out into the world under conditions that would not threaten her femininity. In fact, the image of woman as goddess or mother served to erase her sexuality in the world outside the home.

V

I conclude this essay by pointing out another significant feature of the way in which nationalism sought to resolve the women's question in accordance with its historical project. This has to do with the one aspect of the question which was directly political, concerning relations with the State. Nationalism, as I have said before, located its own subjectivity in the spiritual domain of culture, where it considered itself superior to the West and hence undominated and sovereign. It could not permit an encroachment by the colonial power into that domain. This determined the characteristically nationalist response to proposals for effecting social reform through the legislative enactments of the colonial state. Unlike the early reformers from Rammohun to Vidyasagar, nationalists of the late nineteenth century were in general opposed to such proposals, for such a method of reform seemed to deny the ability of the "nation" to act for itself even in a domain where it was sovereign. In the specific case of reforming the lives of women, consequently, the nationalist position was firmly based on the premise that this was an area where the nation was acting on its own, outside the purview of the guidance and intervention of the colonial state.

We now get the full answer to the historical problem I raised at the beginning of this essay. The reason why the issue of "female emancipation" seems to disappear from the public agenda of nationalist agitation in the late nineteenth century is not because it was overtaken by the more emotive issues concerning political power. Rather, the reason lies in the refusal of nationalism to make the women's question an issue of political negotiation with the colonial state. The simple historical fact is that the lives of middle-class women, coming from that demographic section which effectively constituted the "nation" in late colonial India, changed most rapidly precisely during the period of the nationalist movement – indeed, so rapidly that women from each generation in the last hundred years could say quite truthfully that their lives were strikingly different from those led by the preceding generation. These

changes took place in the colonial period mostly outside the arena of political agitation, in a domain where the nation thought of itself as already free. It was after
independence, when the nation had acquired political sovereignty, that it became
legitimate to embody the ideas of reform in legislative enactments about marriage
rules, property rights, suffrage, equal pay, equality of opportunity, etc.

Another problem on which we can now obtain a clearer perspective is that of the
seeming absence of any autonomous struggle by women themselves for equality and
freedom. We would be mistaken to look for evidence of such a struggle in the public
archives of political affairs, for unlike the women's movement in nineteenth- and
twentieth-century Europe, that is not where the battle was waged here in the era of
nationalism. The domain where the new idea of womanhood was sought to be
actualized was the home, and the real history of that change can be constructed
only out of evidence left behind in autobiographies, family histories, religious tracts,
literature, theatre, songs, paintings and such other cultural artefacts that depict life in
middle-class homes. It is impossible that in the considerable transformation of the
middle-class home in India in the last hundred years, women played a wholly passive
part, for even the most severe system of domination seeks the consent of the subordinate as an autonomous being.

The location of the State in the nationalist resolution of the women's question in
the colonial period has yet another implication. For sections of the middle class which
felt themselves culturally left out of the specific process of formation of the "nation,"
and which then organized themselves as politically distinct groups, the relative
exclusion from the new nation-state would act as a further means of displacement
of the legitimate agency of reform. In the case of Muslims in Bengal, for instance, the
formation of a middle class occurred with a lag, for reasons which we need not go into
here. Exactly the same sorts of ideological concerns typical of a nationalist response to
issues of social reform in a colonial situation can be seen to operate among Muslims as
well, with a difference in chronological time.[16] Nationalist reform does not, however,
reach political fruition in the case of Muslims in independent India, since to the extent
that the dominant cultural formation among them considers the community
excluded from the state, a new colonial relation is brought into being. The system
of dichotomies of inner / outer, home / world, feminine / masculine is once again
activated. Reforms which touch upon the "inner essence" of the identity of the
community can only be carried out by the community itself, not by the State. It is
instructive to note here how little institutional change has been allowed in the civil
life of Indian Muslims since independence and compare it with Muslim countries
where nationalist cultural reform was a part of the successful formation of an
independent nation-state. The contrast is striking if one compares the position of
middle-class Muslim women in West Bengal today with that in neighbouring Bangladesh.

The continuance of a distinct cultural "problem" of the minorities is an index of the
failure of the Indian nation to effectively include within its body the whole of the
demographic mass which it claimed to represent. The failure assumes massive proportions when we note, as I have tried to do throughout this discussion, that the
formation of a hegemonic "national culture" was *necessarily* built upon a system of
exclusions. Ideas of freedom, equality and cultural refinement went hand in hand

with a set of dichotomies which systematically excluded from the new life of the nation the vast masses of people whom the dominant elite would represent and lead, but who could never be culturally integrated with their leaders. Both colonial rulers and their nationalist opponents conspired to displace in the colonial world the original structure of meanings associated with western bourgeois notions of right, freedom, equality, etc. The inauguration of the national state in India could not mean a universalization of the bourgeois notion of "man."

The new patriarchy which nationalist discourse set up as a hegemonic construct culturally distinguished itself not only from the West but also from the mass of its own people. It has generalized itself among the new middle class, admittedly a widening class and large enough in absolute numbers to be self-reproducing, but is irrelevant to the large mass of subordinate classes. This raises important questions regarding the issue of women's rights today. We are all aware that the forms and demands of the women's movement in the West are not generally applicable in India. This often leads us to slip back into a nationalist framework for resolving such problems. A critical historical understanding will show that this path will only bring us to the dead end which the nationalist resolution of the women's question has already reached. The historical possibilities here have already been exhausted. A renewal of the struggle for the equality and freedom of women must, as with all democratic issues in countries like India, imply a struggle against the humanistic construct of "rights" set up in Europe in the post-enlightenment era and include within it a struggle against the false essentialisms of home / world, spiritual / material, feminine / masculine propagated by nationalist ideology.

NOTES

1   See Ghulam Murshid, *Reluctant Debutante: Response of Bengali Women to Modernization, 1849–1905* (Rajshahi: Rajshahi University Press, 1983).

2   See for example, Sumit Sarkar, "The Complexities of Young Bengal," *Nineteenth Century Studies*, 4 (1973), pp. 504–34, and "Rammohun Roy and the Break with the Past," in *Rammohun Roy and the Process of Modernization in India*, ed. V. C. Joshi (Delhi: Vikas, 1975); Ashok Sen, "The Bengal Economy and Rammohun Roy," in *Rammohun Roy*, ed. Joshi, and *Ishwar Chandra Vidyasagar and his Elusive Milestones* (Calcutta: Riddhi India, 1977); and Ranajit Guha, "Neel Darpan: The Image of the Peasant Revolt in a Liberal Mirror," *Journal of Peasant Studies*, 2, no. 1 (1974), pp. 1–46.

3   Sumit Sarkar, "The Women's Question in Nineteenth Century Bengal," in *Women and Culture*, eds. Kumkum Sangari and Sudesh Vaid (Bombay: SNDT Women's University, 1985), pp. 157–72.

4   See Partha Chatterjee, *Nationalist Thought and the Colonial World* (Delhi: Oxford University Press, 1986).

5   Bhudev Mukhopadhyay, "Grhakaryer vyavastha," in *Bhudevracanasambhar*, ed. Pramatha-nath Bisi (Calcutta: Mitra and Ghosh, 1969), p. 480.

6   "Lajjasilata" in ibid., pp. 445–8.

7   Ibid., p. 446.

8   Ibid., p. 447.

9   M. K. Gandhi, *Collected Works*, 64 (Delhi: Publications Division, 1970), p. 85.

10　See the survey of these debates in Murshid, *Reluctant Debutante*, pp. 19–62, and Meredith Borthwick, *The Changing Role of Women in Bengal, 1849–1905* (Princeton NJ: Princeton University Press, 1984).

11　Murshid, *Reluctant Debutante*, p. 43. In the area of higher education, Chandramukhi Bose and Kadambini Ganguli were celebrated as examples of what Bengali women could achieve in formal learning: they took their BA degrees from the University of Calcutta in 1883, before any British university agreed to accept women on their examination rolls. On Chandramukhi and Kadambini's application, the University of Calcutta granted full recognition to women candidates at the First of Arts examination in 1878. London University admitted women to its degrees later that year (Borthwick, *Changing Role of Women*, p. 94). Kadambini then went on to medical college and became the first professionally schooled woman doctor.

12　Cited in Murshid, *Reluctant Debutante*, p. 60.

13　See for instance, Kulabala Debi, *Hindu Mahilar Hinabastha*, cited in Murshid, *Reluctant Debutante*, p. 60.

14　Cited in Borthwick, *Changing Role of Women*, p. 105.

15　Ibid., pp. 245–56.

16　See Murshid, *Reluctant Debutante*.

Representing Sati: Continuities and Discontinuities

RAJESWARI SUNDER RAJAN

Rajeswari Sunder Rajan considers a subject of great importance in the Indian context – sati, the self-immolation of a Hindu widow – which remains a site of debate and ambivalence, primarily because of the conflicting attitudes toward the practice held by British colonialists, male Hindu leaders, and contemporary women. Rajan takes the problematic of *representation* as the central issue in her consideration. But for her, as for so many postcolonial critics, representation is meant to indicate something other than "the representation of reality": it is, rather, an autonomous structure of meaning, a code or system of signs that refers not to "reality" but to the materiality of codes, systems, and signs themselves. Rajan is thus engaged in a critique not of any particular historical occurrence of sati (that is, of a time when sati might have been voluntary and celebratory as opposed to a time when it was forced and punitive) but rather of the images of sati put forward by different writers in colonial and postcolonial India. Her readings of European texts are thus attempts at understanding a "fixed British attitude toward sati," which she then compares to attitudes found in Indian literary texts as well as in theoretical considerations by **Gayatri Chakravorty Spivak** and Lata Mani. The problematic relation between "tradition" and "reform" that animates the Indian attitudes toward sati can be usefully read alongside Chatterjee's discussion of women and nationalism as well as the discussions of ritualized violence toward women in essays by **Amina Mama**, **Kay Schaffer**, and **Angela Bourke**.

Representing Sati: Continuities and Discontinuities

I

As "the woman who dies," the sati eludes full representation.[1] The examination of some texts of sati that I undertake in this essay leads to the realization that it is, ironically, through death that the subject-constitutive "reality" of woman's being is created at certain historical junctures. The construction of the Hindu widow's subjectivity in terms of sati that these texts propose is a foreclosure of her existential choices; but to identify the woman as "widow" is already to have defined her proleptically. Around the subject position that is thus cleared for her in terms of death – her own, her husband's – various other positions, dictated by ideology and politics, irresistibly come to range themselves. I trace in this essay the intertwining of death, gender, and the politics of representation as it shapes the subject of sati.

My focus will be on some texts of colonial and contemporary (post-Independence) India that map out the discursive field of sati. They have in common, as I shall try to show, the following features: the identification of sati as a gendered issue; hence the definition of the widow as exclusively the *subject* of sati (conceptualized only as one who chooses to die or is forced to die); and finally, a pronounced ambivalence toward the practice.[2] It is necessary, nevertheless, to mark within this discursive field the gradual but significant *changes* from colonial history to the postcolonial present, especially as they relate to the question of female subjectivity, and to note the *divergences* between British (or, broadly, European) attitudes toward sati and the indigenous, mainly liberal / reformist adoption and adaptation of these.

In the concluding part of the essay I offer, by way of contrast, an analysis of the classical Tamil epic the *Shilappadikaram*, to point to what seems to me the entirely different ideological investments that are made in indigenous, precolonial representations of sati – so that it is possible to suggest that a major paradigm shift occurred at the point where a specifically colonial discourse on sati began to emerge and then gain ground.[3] The identification of sati as a woman's issue (as a practice that reflected women's status in society), and the consequent focus upon the sati's subjectivity only in terms of her willingness or reluctance to die, may be historicized as an aspect of the colonial and postcolonial discourses of sati. This occurs when we are able to recognize

Taken from Sarah Webster Goodwin and Elisabeth Bronfen (eds.), *Death and Representation* (Baltimore, MD: Johns Hopkins University Press, 1993).

that, by contrast, in precolonial periods and cultures (i.e., in ancient, medieval, or Islamic "India") sati, though always an act of suicide specific to women, subsumed gender within other social categories – of class, community, region, or nation – of which women were treated as representative members. In this construction of the widow's subjectivity, every act of sati is an expression of choice on the part of the woman (but such representations have also, invidiously, informed recent Hindu fundamentalist defenses of sati). More crucially, the woman who does *not* commit sati is equally, if often implicitly, expressing choice – an aspect of "choosing" that nowhere figures in later representations.

Since I have risked an oversimplified contrast in the interest of foregrounding a thesis, several clarifications and qualifications are in order. In the first place, the "precolonial past" of India is by no means a single, homogeneous period: it comprises several millennia of civilization, within which sati (which some scholars attribute to Dravidian cultures that predate the Aryan invasion of India) has had widely differing manifestations at different times and places. So any single notion of "sati in precolonial India" is only a broad generalization about a conceptual paradigm rather than an indication of invariable or prescriptive ritual.

In the second place, it is not my intention to read the various representations as unmediated reflections of different "realities": such a reading would lead one to the invidious distinction between "authentic" (voluntary) and "inauthentic" (forced) sati that nationalist and contemporary fundamentalist social scientists and religious leaders in India postulate, which corresponds to the distinction between sati in an early "golden age" of Hinduism and sati in "Kaliyuga," or the fallen age of the recent past. Such an idealized history is in danger of validating the concept of sati while condemning only its practice, and thereby reinforcing its ideological valorization. I must therefore repeat that by "representations" I mean not "representations of reality," but autonomous and paradigmatic conceptual structures.

Finally, I do not undertake here a history of sati. Such a history is yet to be written. The dialectical relation between "reality" and its representations, between history (itself a text but not reducible to it) and the "texts" of sati, remains unexplored here. Outside the circuit of ideology-narrative representations that I trace here lies (we cannot escape the reminder) the "reality" of a woman's death, which they both occlude and deploy in different ways. Colonial representations of sati, for instance, acquired force and materiality when they shaped colonial policy – precisely because they were offered as representations *of reality*. Therefore "history" is the always present subtext of my argument, and the readings of the handful of representative texts that I propose here are intended as a contribution to the historical enterprise.

My discussion in the following sections begins with an exposition of three exemplary ideological paradigms that structure the texts of sati in the nineteenth and twentieth centuries; I then offer a historical "placing" of contemporary feminist critiques of the colonial discourse on sati; and I conclude with some tentative observations on the representation of women in precolonial indigenous literatures, focusing on the *Shilappadikaram*.

II

The abolition of sati in 1829 was the first major legislation of the East India Company's administration in India. That it – like the series of laws that were subsequently enacted on behalf of women – served as the moral pretext for intervention and the major justification for colonial rule itself does not have to be argued further.[4] What is of concern here is how the colonial imagination seized upon and ordered the self-representation of such an administrative procedure: not merely, as Gayatri Spivak has succinctly formulated it, as a case of "white men...saving brown women from brown men" ("Can the Subaltern Speak?" 121), but as an actual narrative scenario of *a* white man saving *a* brown woman from a mob of brown men. In other words, it is the trope of *chivalry* that provides the contours of the scenario.

Whether the institution of chivalry in medieval and Renaissance Europe had an actual material basis or was nothing more than a literary invention, historians seem to agree that the ideology of knighthood was profoundly influential in constructing and sustaining actual structures of power based on class (ruler and vassal, as in feudal society), gender (lady and knight, as in the courtly love tradition), or religion (the church and its followers, as in the Crusades against Islamic "infidels"). It created reciprocal bonds of duty and obligation between the two parties that mediated relations of power and dependence. Further, chivalry, even while it formed and authorized the class, gender, and racial/religious superiority of the knight, also provided the young male of an aspiring lower aristocracy the means of upward social mobility at a historically transitional period; in other words, it was both a birthright and a career.[5] How eminently transferable such a concept is to the context of colonization is obvious. Large numbers of British young men, in the administrative, judicial, military, trading, and education services of colonial rule, or in missionary orders, found themselves unexpectedly authorized in the exercise of power. But they also discovered that they had to undergo rites of initiation into it. For the colonizer's racial superiority, however flagrant skin color or the appurtenances of power may have rendered it, had also to be demonstrated by acts of valor and authority.[6] It was this expectation that made intervention in the custom of sati both a test and a legitimation of British rule.[7]

The two texts I invoke here, Jules Verne's adventure tale *Around the World in Eighty Days* (1873) and M. M. Kaye's novel *The Far Pavilions* (1978), reproduce the ideological contours of the trope of chivalry in their representation of British India. Jules Verne's popular story is the account of an eccentric English clubman, Phineas Fogg; and in the portion of the narrative that covers his journey across India, from Bombay on the west coast to Calcutta on the east, Fogg manages to rescue a young princess from sati in the jungles of central India. In conformity with what had by then developed into a stereotype, the widow is young, beautiful, and a princess; the dead husband is old, ugly, and a king; the other villains are a bloodthirsty mob and a cabal of scheming Brahmans; and the rescue itself is an act of chivalry, combining daring adventure with the humanitarian gesture.

Sati, as one can see from the example of this late nineteenth-century French novel, continued to exercise the European imagination long after it was legally abolished by the 1829 act. It could continue to be regarded as one of the "realities" of "India" because the division of the country into "British" India and the princely "native" states meant that sati's legal abolition could be officially enforced only in the former. Hence the necessity for heroics in the 1872 escapade of Fogg and Company. With the growing dominion of British rule (India was taken over by the Crown in 1858), the native states were reduced to mere pockets that were regarded as backward ("medieval") and decadent, in contrast to the provinces of "enlightened" British rule.[8] The sati in *Around the World* is planned by the natives as a consciously transgressive act, a horrible ritual, to be performed in a clearing in the jungle of a native state; and the "heart of darkness" is penetrated by the band of adventures who then emerge from it into light, the railways, British-administered provinces, and safety, with the rescued Indian princess in tow.[9]

The same demarcation of two worlds is emphasized in *The Far Pavilions*, whose hero, Ashton Pelham-Martyn, is a conflict-ridden product of the two cultures. But these opposed worlds are not only those of "Britain" and "India," but also of "British" India (the North-West Frontier provinces), and "native" India (the kingdoms of Gulkote and Bhithor); and Pelham-Martyn's constant crossings over from one to the other are intended to emphasize the contrast between the two. One is the area of light, the other an area of darkness; the one is represented by the club and the army barracks, the other by labyrinthine palace interiors. Within the first world the hero is able to develop uncomplicated homoerotic relationships, with a British army fellow officer as well as a Pathan "subedar," whereas in the other he is caught up in a frustrated romantic affair with a half-caste Indian princess. His British life is the "open" life of war and heroism, his "native" experiences involve him in intrigue and treachery. And most strikingly, the position of women is marked differently in the two worlds: the English belle, Belinda, is a flirt, while the Indian princesses are forced into marriage and then sati.

The Far Pavilions describes two major historical events, the Indian Mutiny of 1857 and the second Afghan war of 1878, and spans the years between them. The "scene" of sati and the rescue is one of the climaxes of the book, the one that concludes the hero's involvement in native India with marriage to the princess Anjuli, whom he has rescued. The other climax is the storming of the Residency in Kabul, after which he makes his own "separate peace" and wanders off into the sunset in search of the no-man's-land of the "far pavilions." We must not forget that *The Far Pavilions* is a project of the late 1970s postempire, pre-Thatcher Britain, a book that has both marked and in a sense even inaugurated the whole complex cultural phenomenon now labeled "Raj nostalgia." Such a book would not have been complete without a scene of sati; but it would also have been expected to display a self-conscious liberal rectitude about the imperialist mission – which it does.

This is why the clear outlines of the scenario of "rescue" are somewhat blurred. The "rescue" is preceded by a brief history of sati, its origins and practices, provided by Ashton's Indian friend Sarji. With this friend Ashton also engages in a debate about sati, and Sarji's "native" views are allowed space: for the Indian nobleman death is a matter of little consequence, conjugal love is admirable, the women wish to die, faith is not to be mocked – and did not the West have its witch burnings? But the last word is allowed to Ashton: "Well if we have done nothing else, at least we can mark up one thing to our credit – that we put a stop to *that* particular horror" (618).

The rescue itself is in one sense not that: the princess Anjuli whom Ashton sets out to rescue is finally saved not from death but from blinding and incarceration (the rumor of her sati turns out to be false) while the queen, her half-sister Shushila, who actually wishes to die, is in fact not saved but only shot dead by Ashton at Anjuli's insistence so that she may be saved the horror of death by fire. Ashton's heroism is complicated by issues of morality and by considerations of the pragmatic costs of the enterprise. The moral issues include his guilt over the killing of Shushila (which is compared to the mercy killing of his wounded – and much loved – horse Dagobaz): "But then Shushila was not an animal: she was a human being, who had decided of her own free will to face death by fire and thereby achieve holiness: and he, Ash, had taken it upon himself to cheat her of that" (778). The pragmatic costs include his sorrow over the loss of his three loyal Indian friends, Sarji, Manilal, and Govind, who die while escaping.

The analogy with knight-errantry is explicitly drawn but is ironically repudiated immediately after (780). British officialdom, whose assistance Ashton first invokes to prevent the satis, is finally impotent and lacking in political will, so that the friends who finally help him effect the rescue are Indian. In spite of these complexities, the ideological core remains intact. *The Far Pavilions* retains the main structural aspects, and the ideologemes they encode, that we notice in *Around the World in Eighty Days*: the same actors; the discrediting of the woman's conjugal love as a possible motive for the sati; the suggestion of an actual or potential romance between the rescuer and the rescued; the representation of the rescue action as individual enterprise ("adventure") rather than official intervention; the establishment of a disinterested good through the act in a climate of benightedness. Ashton's scruples and his partisanship toward Indians therefore only embellish his knight-errantry, exemplifying both noblesse oblige and chivalric love.[10]

These texts record the progressive consolidation of what has come to be an essentially fixed British attitude to sati. By foregrounding Hindu women as passive and unresisting victims of Hindu patriarchy, as these texts do, it could be established beyond argument that the women were in need of saving.[11] However, the possibility that some widows might have *wished* to die as an act of conjugal love persisted as a doubt and gave rise to other views. This possibility is given some cursory credence in Ashton's self-questioning: "He had interfered in something that was a matter of faith and a very personal thing; and he could not even be sure that Shushila's convictions were wrong, for did not the Christian calendar contain the names of many men and women who had been burned at the stake for their beliefs, and acclaimed as saints and martyrs?" (778). It is no idle question. In the next section I examine how the conceptual paradigm of Christian martyrdom accommodated the unsettling possibility that the widow "chose" her death.

III

The positive view of sati – with its flip underside – had popular currency, as this mid-nineteenth century jingle advertising Maspero Egyptian cigarettes suggests:

Calm in the early morning
Solace in time of woes,
Peace of the hush of twilight,
Balm ere my eyelids close.
This will Masperos bring me,
Asking naught in return,
With only a Suttee's passion
To do their duty and burn.

The jingle is accompanied by an illustration of a burning cigarette in an ashtray: appearing in the swirls of smoke rising from the cigarette is the shrouded figure of the sati, suggestive simultaneously of a Christian martyr and of a genie from a magic lamp awaiting orders. The commodification of the sati's self-sacrifice effectively eclipses her subjectivity.

Even as the Indian widow's death with her husband was elevated to fit into the more recognizable paradigm of religious martyrdom, it was also, less admiringly, trivialized as a form of feudal – or "native" – subservience, an act of unthinking if not actually deluded loyalty. Therefore the two views of the sati – as a woman forced to die and as a woman who chooses to die – did not necessarily have to collide.[12] The perception that Hindu women were victims was the basis for the establishment of sati as a woman's issue, as I noted earlier; it provoked an implicit comparison of their devalued social position with the freedom and privileges of British women, thus offering further proof of the superiority of British civilization.

But the British women's movement was gaining ground at home even as British rule was being consolidated in the colonies, and its members were denying the superior advantages ascribed to their status in British society. It is in the face of this conflict that the powerful ideology of the family as the "woman's sphere" was assiduously developed on behalf of women (see Sangari). Within this ideological structure the Indian widow as *subject* of sati could be selectively admired as exemplifying chastity and fidelity – important components of the model of behavior that was being constructed for the Englishwoman at "home." Thus sati, whatever subject position was assigned to the Hindu widow, could be usefully fed into different ideological conjunctures.

These procedures of subjectification are less transparent in the literary text. A complex and suggestive ambivalence toward the sati can be located in the following passage from Charles Dickens's *Dombey and Son* (1848), which serves as my exemplary text in this section.

Susan Nipper, Florence Dombey's personal maid, is seen upbraiding Mr. Dombey for his ill-treatment of Florence; and she describes thus her own courage and determination in confronting the formidable man: "I may not be an Indian widow Sir and I am not and I would not so become but if I once made up my mind to burn myself alive, I'd do it! And I've made up my mind to go on!" (704). In this startling metaphor, Susan's simultaneous disavowal and embrace of the act of sati is characteristically ambivalent: however *like* an Indian widow Susan may be, she "would not ... become" one; but at the same time the qualities of determination and courage that motivate her are attributed to the Indian widow as well. Susan's allusion suggests that sati could be raised above its cultural and gender specificity to express, in popular usage, any kind of excessive zeal. Susan had earlier sought another analogy to convey her loyalty: "She's the blessedest and dearest angel is Miss Floy... the more that I was torn to pieces Sir the more I'd say it though I may not be a Fox's Martyr" (703). This conflation of sati with Christian martyrdom is a familiar cognitive procedure.

But the invocation has other implications in this narrative. For *Dombey and Son* is a profound study of marital discord, and one that is remarkably sympathetic to the wronged wife. Dickens's discomfort about the particular *form* that Edith Dombey's disloyalty toward her husband eventually takes – sexual infidelity – is well known (so much so that he does not permit actual adultery to take place: Edith defends her honor at knifepoint!). The allusion to sati, occurring at the precise juncture in the narrative when she is planning her elopement with Carker, is a brilliant irony. Susan's own blindness to this application of her metaphor – which she has displaced from conjugal love to feudal loyalty – is no less striking.[13] Between the actual English wife of the narrative (who plans to leave a living husband) and the figurative Indian widow, transiently evoked as a trope in its discourse (and who will burn with a dead husband) – between these two female subjects an implicit contest of conjugal loyalty is set up, and cultural relativism (racial otherness) is effectively elided.

Two feminist critics have recently carried further the analysis of the ideological uses to which are put the interracial "contests" between women around the subject of sati. Nancy Paxton has astutely diagnosed how, in Flora Annie Steel's *On the Face of the Waters* (1897), "the sexual politics of colonial life in India" drive the British heroine, Kate Erlton, into emulation of and rivalry with her Hindu maidservant, Tara. Ultimately, "Kate concedes the contest of purity to Tara, accepting her assertion of the absolute cultural differences that separate the English and the Indian woman." After her husband dies Kate marries again; it is Tara who "triumphs" by dying a sati-like death in the fires of war while helping Kate to escape.[14]

Steel's novel has a special significance because it is set in 1857, the year of the Indian Mutiny. This was an event in which the British women in India, because of the indignities and danger they publicly suffered at the hands of the native sepoys in the attack, became the objects of British men's protection. Thus they briefly came to occupy the same position as their Indian sisters, the women who committed sati, becoming, like them, both public spectacles and objects of salvation. Steel uses this historical irony to bring about a confrontation of the two women's worlds.

Such confrontations are of course stage-managed by an interested patriarchy. But an emergent feminist individualism could also deploy the "native" woman toward its own ends, as Gayatri Spivak has brilliantly demonstrated through her reading of three women's texts of the nineteenth century. She shows how another kind of struggle between the women of the two cultures may also have been the price paid for an "imperialist project cathected as civil-society-through-social-mission" ("Three Women's Texts" 244). In such a situation the emergence of the feminist individualist in the West cannot be an isolated development but is, instead, achieved through an imperialist project (that of "soul making") in which the "native female" must play a role. Spivak is talking of *Jane Eyre* (1848); and to counter the temptation to "see nothing there but the psychobiography of the militant female subject [Jane

Eyre]" (245), she invokes Jean Rhys's *Wide Sargasso Sea* (1966), whose "powerful suggestion" is that *"Jane Eyre* can be read as the orchestration and staging of the self-immolation of Bertha Mason as 'good wife'" (259). *Jane Eyre* must be read in conjunction also with the history of sati in British India for such a reading to carry conviction. Given such a perspective, we might also be able to see how Tara's death in Steel's *On the Face of the Waters* is directly the cost of Kate's escape and of the English-woman's eventual "liberation" of consciousness from the excesses of martyrdom.

To sum up: in the colonial encounter the Hindu "good wife" is constructed as patriarchy's feminine ideal; she is offered simultaneously as a model and as a signifier of absolute cultural otherness, both exemplary and inimitable. She is also, as Spivak points out, both indispensable (the justification for the imperialist project itself) and eminently dispensable (the sacrifice offered to an emergent Western feminist indi-vidualism). The colonial ambivalence toward sati was, in any case, productive for the achievement of the diverse goals of imperialism.

IV

The three Indian texts I identify in the following discussion – Henry Derozio's long poem *The Fakeer of Jungheera* (1826), Rabindranath Tagore's short story "Saved" (1918), and Gautam Ghosh's film (1987) based on Kamal Kumar Majumdar's novel of the same name, *Antarjali jatra* (1965) – are representative of what I shall call briefly, for convenience, the male indigenous reformist / liberal position on women's issues. The abolition of sati, as well as other colonial laws on behalf of women in nineteenth-century India, was considerably aided by the growing spirit of reform among the indigenous male, increasingly Western-educated elite. The reform move-ments on behalf of women tied in with other issues relating to caste, education, and later nationalism. In the texts listed above, therefore, while sati is undeniably viewed as a "women's issue," its abolition is also located within a matrix of broadly reformist ideals.

Within the constraints of narrative, what is retained in these texts is the paradigm of rescue, shorn no doubt of its trappings of European chivalry, but exploiting several of its other significant structural elements. As in the colonial texts of imperialism described earlier, the dramatis personae are stereotyped, and their triangular relation-ship persists.

The break with the past that we associate with "modernity" is never a clean one. Among the indigenous reformers, a sentimental affiliation with indigenous "tradi-tion," the early stirrings of nationalism, and an acute recognition of the resistance of social forces to change created a complex inheritance that considerably complicated the ideological stance toward issues relating to women. Thus, although sati could be condemned on both humanitarian and religious grounds, the prescribed alternative for widows, ascetic celibacy, was not so easily opposed. Therefore widow remarriage, long after it was made legally permissible, was a practically nonexistent practice.

It is this conflict of allegiances between "tradition" and "reform" that modifies the narrative paradigm of "rescue" that structures these texts. The crucial feature com-mon to all of them is that, in spite of not submitting to sati, *the woman dies.* The inhibition about representing the rescued widow with an afterlife of romantic / sexual fulfillment with her rescuer is striking. What her death also implies is the impotence of her rescuer, an inability to work out her salvation that accurately reflects the perceived difficulties of social change (as opposed to the ease of official intervention). The failure also reflects an internalization of the notion that the colonized male was not "man enough" to protect his womankind. Ashis Nandy has suggested that the sudden and major changes brought about by colonial rule produced effects of alienation in the Hindu male, and that the strong defense of sati advanced by some members of the indigenous male elite was an attempt to recover its identity by enforcing traditional patriarchal norms. Finally, what these texts also offer is a more complex construction of the subjectivity of the heroine than the polarities of "damsel in distress" / "martyr" (i.e., she was forced to die / she chose to die) scripted by the text of imperialism. Nevertheless these are texts that are historically divergent, and we must plot their interaction with the texts of imperialism differently.

Henry Derozio's *The Fakeer of Jungheera* (1826) runs to a thousand lines, but it has a simple enough plot: the young and beautiful widow Nuleeni is about to be burned with her dead husband, a rich old man whom she was forced to marry. She is rescued from the sati site by her former lover, an outlaw masquerading as a holy man (a *fakeer*), and his band of robbers. They enjoy a brief idyll on his solitary island-rock Jungheera. Meanwhile Nuleeni's distraught father approaches the Muslim ruler, Prince Soorjah, and with his help raises an army to fight the fakeer and avenge his daughter's "dishonor." The lovers are forced to part. The father kills the outlaw in a fierce battle. Nuleeni finds her slain lover on the battlefield and dies of heartbreak in his arms.

Henry Louis Vivian Derozio (1809–31) was the first Indian poet of any note to write in English. He was a precocious East Indian youth (of mixed Portuguese-Indian and English blood) who produced most of his poetry, including *The Fakeer*, before he was twenty. Derozio's role in what came to be called the Young Bengal movement has been recognized by historians to have had a significant impact on the later Bengal "Renaissance," itself a forerunner of nationalist struggles. Among the "superstitions" of religion that Derozio attacked was sati, which was in the 1820s, the decade preceding its abolition, an issue of intense debate and division among the indigenous elite as well as between its members and the colonial administration.

But if we expect *The Fakeer of Jungheera* to be an anti-sati tract we will be disappointed. There is little or no comment on the cruelty of sati or on the social debasement of women that it reflected. Instead, as the epigraph to the first canto makes clear, it is loveless marriage that Derozio condemns, and romantic love that he extols in its place. Romantic love as the only valid basis for marriage was, of course, a radically Westernized notion, and it is disconcerting to find an argument in its favor in the context of a widow's imminent death. Almost it seems that for Derozio sati would be tolerable if the wife had married the husband for love in the first place. And in fact to die of love is to die of a recognized Western disease. It is *this* death that Derozio devises for his heroine at the end of the poem.

Derozio is constructing a romantic tale, and it is the formal thrust of the genre that determines its message rather than a social critique of women's oppression. The poem is actually a pastiche of several English poetic forms, a medley of inset ballads, songs, and madrigals within a larger narrative made of rhymed couplets.[15] At the same time, Derozio exploits many of the features of self-conscious "exoticism": the set piece iconic sati scene (resembling the scene of religious martyrdom), the elaborate nature descriptions, and the fervent invocations to Vedic gods (Surya). But for all its formal derivativeness, the poem is still significant for our argument when we recognize that Nuleeni, the heroine, is granted a measure of selfhood: she submits to her sati not because she is coerced or deluded but because she is pining for her lost lover. And she is totally daring in expressing her love for a man other than the one she is married to and one who, further, belongs to a class and caste so different from her own (the outlaw is a Muslim, and Derozio makes a passing point about true love breaking caste barriers). The union of the lovers is of course frustrated. Nuleeni's death is sanctioned by the conventions of romantic poetry, and the social status quo is preserved by the cautionary deaths of both the lovers. However heroic the rescuer's death, it defeats the purpose of the rescue.

Rabindranath Tagore's short story "Saved" could not be more different. Whereas Derozio uses large contrasts of love and war, "nature" and "society" virtually to swamp the human characters, Tagore stages a small (five-page) domestic drama and tells the story of a frustrated wife, a jealous husband, and a *swami* (ascetic monk) to whom the wife turns for religious consolation. The swami begins to see himself in the role of rescuer and finally makes an assignation to meet Gouri and take her away: "I will with god's help rescue his handmaid for the holy service of his feet" (210). Gouri hides his letter in the loops of her hair, "as a halo of deliverance" (211), but it falls into the husband's hands. Gouri finds him struck down in his room, dead of apoplexy, the letter clenched in his fist. Gouri discovers that the swami's real intention was to seduce her: she then kills herself. The story ends: "All were lost in admiration of the wifely loyalty she had shown in her *sati*, a loyalty rare indeed in these degenerate days" (212). It is a laconic ending, the last line packed with a multitude of ironies. The authorial free indirect speech transcribes the nostalgia for and idealization of sati that is characteristic of large sections of orthodox Hindu society at the same time that it highlights the titillating sensationalism the double death provides. Does the irony lie in society's conclusion that Gouri committed sati, when she died perhaps for reasons quite other than conjugal loyalty? Or is there irony in the extent of Gouri's reformation, the transformation from her hatred of her husband to the guilt, remorse, and expiation of her death? Is she indeed "saved" by death – from her "savior"?

The notion of rescue is therefore itself framed for ironic examination. Gouri is beset and betrayed by both men, and when finally – trapped – she kills herself it is to be apotheosized as a sati. Her terseness in communication has been marked all through the story ("she was a woman of few words": "his wife treated it [his jealousy] with silent contempt"); and so the reticence about her final motive is appropriate.

Tagore's privatization of the bourgeois family drama, and his psychological subtlety in probing the woman's consciousness, parallels his ironic manipulation of the typical sati narrative. The figure of the "rescuer" as outlaw is here unequivocally reduced to that of would-be seducer; the *sanyasi* or ascetic monk is frequently a socially anomalous and displaced figure, treated either with veneration as a holy man or with suspicion as a charlatan. Gouri herself is given the responsibility for a number of the events of the story, and she acts decisively and even rebelliously at various crises. The jealous husband is treated with a measure of sympathy, as a financially insecure and perhaps sexually impotent failure. Tagore diagnoses this tragedy as the product of a certain "modernity" (characterized by skepticism, some mobility for women, the anomie experienced by the Bengal middle-class male under colonial administration) in conflict with residual orthodoxy (characterized by "faith," purdah for women, and traditional patriarchal authority). The status and meaning of the widow's death serve as the focus of this ironic inquiry.

My third text representing a male liberal / reformist view of sati, like the first two, is marked by a failure to imagine a viable way out for the widow; at the same time, it renders the "rescue" paradigm considerably more complex. *Antarjali jatra* ("Death by drowning"), directed by Gautam Ghosh, is a recent Bengali film. Set in 1832, immediately after the abolition of sati in Bengal, it narrates the story of Yashobati, a young girl hurriedly married off to a dying old man with her father's promise to the "pundits" and the family that she will commit sati. She is left with her dying husband at the burning ghats on the banks of the river Ganga, with only the *chandal* (the untouchable ghat-keeper, the burner of corpses) for company. The chandal urges her to escape; but she refuses, even though she dreads her death. Instead she tends her dying husband, who seems to revive under her care. The chandal pities her and reviles her fate. They are drawn together and become lovers. One night the river floods, and the old man's bier is swept away. Desperately, Yashobati swims out in search of her husband, finds the empty bier and clings to it, but is drowned. The sati prophecy appears to have been ironically fulfilled, but through death by drowning rather than fire. The chandal is full of rage and sorrow at her death.

Whereas Ghosh retains the features of the "rescue" paradigm, these are reworked to an almost unrecognizable degree. The characteristics of the chief dramatis personae – Brahmans, dying / dead husband, widow, rescuer – are intensified versions of the stereotypes. Thus the Brahmans, although they are identified as the chief "villains," are also seen close up: Ananta, the chief Brahman and astrologer, is at least partially motivated by the desire to defy the alien edict against an indigenous religious rite; the father of Yashobati, a poor Brahman, is tempted by the prospect of marrying off his daughter without having to provide a dowry; the doctor, an "enlightened" Brahman with some access to modern systems of medicine, does protest on legal and humanitarian grounds, but he is blackmailed into silence; the dying man, a *kulin* Brahman, and his grown sons welcome the glory and prestige of a sati in the family. This differentiated characterization makes it possible for Ghosh to probe the complex social phenomenon of sati. The husband, dying and comatose for most of the film, is a grotesque caricature whose resurrection is a parody of lust for a new and nubile wife.

The heroine too is shown as young and beautiful, but not merely to highlight her vulnerability sentimentally. The fact is an aspect of this film's insistence upon the female *body* as what is at stake in sati. The obsessive male gaze, directed by the husband, the lover, and the filmmaker himself at the female body, is inevitably sexual; but it is equally a reminder that the body will burn. A single episode makes the point. The chandal, prohibited by caste restrictions from touching a living Brahman, rakes Yashobati with his gaze in order to measure her for the pyre: a gaze that is necessarily enacted by the viewer as well, but with no such purpose to legitimize it. Yashobati's subjectivity includes the "objectification" that is cinema's characteristic endowment; but it is also given the more familiar novelistic dimension of "consciousness" through her "choosing" to die. Her acquiescence, however, is made more complex than a matter of faith. At one point she turns on the chandal for his incessant badgering; between him and those who wish her to die, she protests, she is made to feel a mere object. She seeks the realm of her true subjectivity outside the parameters of the question of her death – and her lovemaking with the chandal is one expression of this search.

The most complex rendering, finally, is that of the would-be rescuer, the chandal. His outsider status is not merely a romanticization of individualistic anti-establishment heroics: he is by class, caste, and occupation the most outcast of society's members, and his helplessness to save Yashobati is a function of this social marginality. By allying these two subaltern figures, the chandal and the woman fated to die, Ghosh tries to make the most telling point in his film. Further, the chandal does not intervene from the outside: his habitation is the cremation grounds, he is part of the hierarchical social structure, and he asserts his dharma (social/religious obligation) by refusing to burn a living body. By making him an articulate and fearless spokesman for the oppressed, Ghosh compensates for the speechlessness of the "victim." So we are forced to ask why, given this, as well as the desperation of the two characters, the frank sexuality of their relationship, and the pragmatic possibilities of escape (solitude, a moored boat), a different, happy ending was not envisaged for the film. Finally it seems to be only a grim naturalistic fatalism that forecloses it.

Antarjali jatra is a contemporary film, and its relation to its material is mediated by its historical distance from sati in Bengal 150 years ago. This distance makes possible a materialist analysis of sati based on contemporary historical and sociological research.[16] Paradoxically, it also proceeds from an understanding of the contemporary phenomenon of bride burning: the problem of providing dowry for unmarried daughters is so acute that their deaths may even be viewed as a "solution" by their parents. Further, *Antarjali jatra* reveals the attempt of the contemporary Left to explore the possibility of an alliance between women, the working class, and the lower castes based on the similarity of their oppression and the commonality of their oppressors.

Finally, female sexuality and its social control are allowed to appear as dominant rather than recessive aspects of the phenomenon of sati in this narrative. The imperialist text covered over sexuality by discrediting conjugal love and by sublimating chivalric love into disinterested justice or "romance"; or by elevating sati to an act of martyrdom, it represented it as transcending human, and merely sexual, affective bonds. In the indigenous liberal / reformist text the issue of female sexuality became a more overt factor in the social dynamics of marriage and widowhood, and consequently of sati. But although in *Antarjali jatra* the woman's body is blatantly foregrounded, the potency and the potential anarchy of her sexuality are not let loose; the metaphoric flood instead ravages the land, while she herself dies. In this sense Ghosh remains captive to his inheritance from the past.[17]

V

Though I conclude this part of my analysis with a brief consideration of the work on sati in the colonial period by two Indian feminist scholars, Lata Mani and Gayatri Spivak, it is not to offer it as the culmination of a progressive narrative.[18] Rather, I see their work, identified dialectically as *critique*, as being representative of the present historical moment of postcolonial feminism. Their own self-conscious adoption of the stance of the postcolonial woman intellectual whose politics – anti-imperialism and feminism – is overt, makes such a representation possible.

Mani and Spivak operate within the boundaries of the earlier discourse of sati, but with two major breaks. In the first place, they radically interrogate the "rescue" paradigm through fresh historical evidence (Mani), and through semiotic analysis (Spivak). Second, they reconceptualize and centralize the subjectivity of the sati as part of an explicitly feminist project.

In both cases, narrative intervenes significantly to structure their arguments. Though Mani, in fact, explicitly privileges synchronicity (discourse) over diachronicity (narrative), her "legislative history of sati" is nevertheless chronologically traced ("Production" 32–3). It emerges as a powerful counternarrative to the scenario of rescue that was the ideological translation of the colonial pretext for intervention. What Mani's researches restore is the long prehistory of abolition, a period of debate primarily concerning "the feasibility rather than the desirability" of abolition, so that "rather than arguing for the outlawing of *sati* as a cruel or barbarous act . . . officials in favour of abolition were at pains to illustrate that such a move was entirely consonant with the principle of upholding indigenous tradition" ("Production" 32). The settlement of this issue was sought through appeal to Brahman pundits who were to investigate the scriptural authority for sati. During this period (1789–1829) a number of circulars were issued to district officials based on official interpretation of the pundits' *vywasthas* (rulings), and a meticulous surveillance of all satis was undertaken to ensure that they were "legally" performed. In spite of this, the incidence of sati rose. The two were even connected in some analyses: "Government attention had given 'a sort of interest and celebrity to the sacrifice' . . . [The circulars] had a tendency 'to modify, systematise, or legalise the usage' and made it appear as though 'a legal sutte' was . . . better than an illegal one" ("Production" 34). This is a very different scenario from that of "rescue." At the same time, colonial reports on sati incidents assiduously circulated the stereotypes of cruel Brahmans, bloodthirsty mobs, and above all the widow as victim, which found their way into the narratives of rescue.[19]

It is not my intention to offer Mani's reading of the archives as the "correct," "historical" version in opposition to a "fabricated" colonial narrative construction. But neither do I subscribe to an extreme poststructuralist position that reduces history to narrative and makes all truth indeterminate or relative. The truth-value of Mani's reconstruction of the "production of an official discourse" seems to me inestimable. I merely refrain from positing these opposed versions as contests of truth. Instead, I emphasize Mani's historical location and the politics of postcolonial feminism as important constituents shaping the counternarrative that she (re)constructs.

Gayatri Spivak is also obliged to frame a narrative in order to keep the woman as signifier from disappearing into "a violent aporia" between (native patriarchy's) "subject-constitution" and (imperialism's) "object-formation." In responding to indigenous patriarchy's "constructed counter narrative of woman's consciousness" as "woman's desire [to die]," Spivak is led to "tabulate a psychobiographical norm" ("Can the Subaltern Speak?" 123). She concludes with an "example" to "illuminate the social text," the case of a young girl, Bhuvaneswari Devi, who hanged herself

(129). In another essay in "reading the archives," Spivak demonstrates that colonial intervention in the decision of the rani of Sirmur to commit sati had little to do with "saving" her: the rani had to continue to rule "because of the commercial/territorial interests of the East India Company" ("Rani of Simur" 263).

Since Mani and Spivak undertake a reconstructive project in history, motivated by a concern to "know" the subject of sati, both are frustrated by the unavailability of records of women's consciousness. "One never encounters the testimony of the women's voice-consciousness" (Spivak, "Can the Subaltern Speak?" 122); "precious little [is] heard from them; . . . one learns so little about them" (Mani, "Contentious Traditions" 152–3). It is, of course, this significant absence that engenders their powerful criticism of the British imperialist construction of the Indian woman as perennial victim (Mani) and of the native patriarchal endowment of her with a "dubious" free will (Spivak). Their historical analysis is clinched when they reveal how such constructions legitimated colonial intervention.

The force of their attacks upon the partial and interested representations of the woman who committed sati has significant implications in the area of female subject production. In Mani the reaction to "the discourses of salvation" is the privileging of what Spivak has called "the woman's unrepresentable willing subjectivity" ("Can the Subaltern Speak?" 122); in Spivak, on the other hand, the hegemonic repression of the woman's consciousness results in her stress upon the *abjectness* of women's subject constitution.[20]

The preoccupation with the sati as colonial female subject, which is a function of Mani's and Spivak's reiterated feminist concern with contemporary Indian women's issues in the postcolonial context, pushes them to further speculations that pounce upon absences in the text of history. For Mani, such partial and systematic subjectification "precludes the possibility of a complex female subjectivity" ("Contentious Traditions" 152); for Spivak, what is of "greater significance" than the debate on sati is that "there was no debate upon this exceptional fate of widows [i.e., celibacy] – either among Hindus or between Hindus and British," with the resultant "profound irony [of] locating the woman's free will in self-immolation" ("Can the Subaltern Speak?" (125–6). The role of the postcolonial woman intellectual is then clearly but variously indicated: there are suggestions that Mani's project would be the *restoration* of "full" subjectivity to the woman through more assiduous historical research. She counters, for instance, the "infantilising" of the Hindu woman by offering statistical proof that "a majority of *satis* were undertaken by women well past childhood" ("Contentious Traditions" 130). Spivak's lack of faith in such positivistic enterprises is well known. Noting that the archives have no records of the eventual fate of the rani of Sirmur (who had announced her intention to commit sati and whom British officials had sought to dissuade), Spivak responds, "I intend to look a little further, of course. . . . [But] to retrieve her as information will be no disciplinary triumph. . . . [T]here is no 'real Rani' to be found" ("Rani of Sirmur" 270–1). Since the subaltern "cannot speak," it is she herself, through an "exorbitation" of her self-assigned role as postcolonial critic, who must undertake to "plot a story, unravel a narrative and give the subaltern a voice in history."[21]

In attempting to locate both the gendering of sati and the subjectification of the woman who dies within a cognitive structure that is historically produced, it has not been my intention merely to subsume feminist critiques of imperialism and native patriarchy within the larger colonial / postcolonial discourse. These critiques advance the terms of the argument considerably and promise an alliance between the project of feminism and the female victim-as-subject that is entirely new and is both theoretically and politically challenging. At the same time it is important not to discredit the epistemological breakthrough achieved by the colonial establishment of sati as a "woman question" – however suspect its politics – that has fed into the contemporary feminist analyses of the issue. An examination of some texts of precolonial India that I will undertake in the next section – which produce a different focus on the issue of self-immolation, and consequently a different subjectivity for the widow – makes retrospectively clear where the "break" may be identified.

VI

The ancient epics and tales, the *Mahabharata*, the *Ramayana*, and the *Bhagavata Purana*, draw attention to the women who commit sati by celebrating their courage and devotion in panegyric verses. Such women are invariably the wives of warrior-heroes, kings, or *rishis* (sages) – "great men" of one kind or other – and their behavior is therefore intended to serve as a reflection of / on the status of the men on whose behalf they die rather than to be read as a gratuitous act of self-willed heroism. The failure of a woman to commit sati never seems to call for corresponding comment of any kind, whether of censure or surprise; the four wives of King Dasaratha (Rama's father, in the *Ramayana*), for instance, continue to live on after his death as revered dowager queens, leading the celibate life prescribed by the *shastras*. In the *Mahabharatha*, both wives of King Pandu (the father of the Pandavas) wish to commit sati at his death, and they argue about who should exercise the privilege. Finally Madri persuades Kunti, the senior queen, not to die since, because of her great love for her stepchildren as well as her own, she would be the better mother.

The three most famous of the legendary good wives – the eponymous "Sati" herself (the goddess Parvati), Sita (in the *Ramayana*), and Savitri (in the Puranas) – did not actually commit self-immolation as widows.[22] After the death of Savitri's husband Satyavan, she does battle with the god of death, Yama, himself and journeys to the underworld to reclaim her husband; because of her penances she is able to win back her husband's life as a boon from Yama. I do not argue that these women are not, in anything but a literal sense, satis: the word itself means only "good wife," and in all these cases the women must submit to trials of various kinds to establish good wifehood. But Savitri's "death," her journey to the netherworld, is a trial that is at least undertaken to some purpose: she not only reclaims her husband but herself comes back to the living. Although the widow's continuing concern (or obsession) is with the dead husband, her devotion may at least find expression in life rather than death.

The recourse to texts of the Indian past is of course a familiar move; it figured prominently in the debate on sati initiated in colonial India and has been resurrected – within a different political framework – in recent times. I have no wish to reproduce their dubious idealization of the past, or of Hindu women's status in earlier societies.[23]

My argument that the identity of the "good wife" (sati in the original sense) is a broader framework for female subjectification than that of the widow who burns (sati according to later usage) is based on the observation that good wifehood has different manifestations, and some of these included the option of life rather than death. The representation of the female subject as good wife in the *Shilappadikaram*, which I examine next, occupies this larger space cleared for the widow who "chooses" life over death.

The *Shilappadikaram* ("The ankle bracelet") is one of the three surviving "great poems" written in the third and last epoch of classical Tamil literature. Its author is the prince Ilanko Atikal, and the date attributed to the main body of the work is the second century AD. The story is summarized in a "preamble" to the book:

> In the ancient town of Puhar, immortal capital of the Chola kings...there lived a rich merchant named Kovalan. He dissipated his great wealth in the pleasure offered him by a dancing girl expert in her art. He had a wife named Kannaki. With her he went to Madurai, the capital of the celebrated Pandya kingdom. In need of funds, he wished to sell her beautiful ankle bracelet, and went into the main bazaar looking for a buyer. There he showed the ankle bracelet to a goldsmith, who said, "Only a queen can wear such jewelry." He suggested that Kovalan wait near his shop, and ran to the palace to inform the king that he had found the thief of the queen's gold bracelet. At that moment Kovalan's hour of destiny had come. The king ... did not bother to make an investigation, but simply ordered a guard to put the thief to death and bring back the queen's bracelet. The wife of Kovalan found herself abandoned and shed abundant tears. She tore away one of her breasts, adorned by a string of pearls. By the power of her virtue, she burned down the great city of Madurai and called down upon the Pandya king the anger of the gods.[24]

There are two major thematic aspects to this work, as the poet takes pains to point out: the domestic, or love (*aham*), and the political, or war (*puram*) (204). Its drama is also of two kinds, the "human tragedy" and the "mythological play" (144), and the precepts it illustrates deal with both justice and conjugal love (209). Thus Kannaki is at once an *instrument* (of political, as well as divine justice) and an *agent:* she therefore simultaneously asserts her righteousness in burning down the city and expresses sorrow and guilt at her crime; she must inflict punishment upon the king and queen and upon the entire polity, but also upon herself, as she tears out her left breast as a symbolic repudiation of her femininity.

These contradictions are resolved because Kannaki's virtue is conceptualized as a social trait, just as the Pandya King's injustice is a national shame. It is not individual motivation that prompts human action, but social roles. When Kannaki confronts the king it is as the representative of a city, a nation, a class, and her sex, and also as a subject. Kannaki claims she cannot act otherwise than she does because she comes from "Pukar, where these noble women with fragrant braids [whose stories she has narrated] live. If these stories are true, and if I am faithful, I cannot allow your city to survive" (131). Here it is the community that dictates women's behavior; the reverse of this, the invocation of the status or behavior of women to define a community as backward or "advanced," is a later argument, and one that has figured prominently in the debate on sati.

What is especially significant is that Kannaki is faced with a choice as soon as she confronts Kovalan's corpse, between abject, helpless widowhood and death. In an extended, fluently rhetorical passage, she repudiates the ways of widowhood (122). But the vision of Kovalan appears and advises her to stay: "Beloved! Stay there, stay! Remain peacefully in life!" (125). Kannaki takes this as an injunction to avenge his death: "I shall not search for my husband [follow him in death] before he is avenged. I shall meet this inhuman king and ask for his justice against himself" (126). After she has burned down the great city by the power of her curse, she leaves, wanders forlornly for fourteen days, and then dies "naturally," to ascend thereafter to heaven with her husband.

We cannot deny that Kannaki emerges as a complex and tragic figure if she is read from the familiar perspective of Western literary representation of character. But we must also recognize that within a different "worldview," that of the Tamil classical epoch, roles are prescribed for human beings by social expectation and divine arrangement (duty and fate). We see this in the comparison of Kannaki's action with that of another good wife's reaction to her husband's death. Kannaki's reproaches had shamed the king of Madurai so keenly that he died of heartbreak. His queen then, "unable to bear her sorrow . . . died, saying: 'I must follow my king.'" The question is posed: "A virtuous woman lost her life because her husband died. Another wandered in anger through our kingdom . . . [I]n your judgment, which one should we admire?" And the answer is that while both are great, the queen wins her rewards in heaven, but Kannaki has become "a new goddess of Faithfulness" who will be "forever honored" here, in this kingdom (158).[25]

The queen's death is a manifestation of sati, whereas Kannaki's curse is an expression of *shakti*, the powerful, ferocious, feminine cosmic principle. But it is the excess of sati, the ascetic virtue of good wifehood, that is converted into *shakti*.[26] These two generally opposed aspects of femininity in Hindu representations of the goddesses are linked in Kannaki, indicating that the source of feminine power lies in the virtue accumulated as a good wife.[27] And yet to envisage that such virtue can prove excessive – can overflow the domestic, conjugal relationship into the realms of history and polity – is to give another dimension to "good wifehood." In Kannaki's case "the woman who burns" has more than one meaning.

If we seek a more radical repudiation of the entire syndrome of "good wifehood" of which the act of sati is only an item, we shall find it in the lives and works of the women Bhakta poets of India.[28] These women – saints, mystics, poets – had to make life choices: their devotion to their god came into conflict with their sexuality and with the life of domesticity, both of which were normally regulated by the institution of marriage. They resolved this conflict either by bypassing marriage altogether or, once married, by opting out of marital commitment.[29] Here too we must be careful not to read their poems as feminist credos. The ideological structure of the man–woman relationship is not itself displaced; the god of these women poets is male, cast as lover, husband, father, or child, frequently indeed the first two, so that a highly eroticized idiom is brought into play (Ramanujan, "Talking to God" 14). Nevertheless, as Madhu Kishwar has pointed out, bhakti did make a "social space" available for women who "outrageously defied what are ordinarily considered the fundamental tenets of *stri dharma* [women's duty] – marriage and motherhood" (6).

The foregoing comparative exercise has not been substantial enough to prove absolute differences between two structures of representation, the one indigenous, the other characterized as colonial / postcolonial or British / European; still less does it seek to establish the superiority of one over the other.[30] The absence of any gendered perspective, and the ultimately deterministic framework of "choice" in precolonial representations of women, prevents any easy sentimentalization of the indigenous cultures. On the other hand, the colonial perception of a *collective* gendered identity for the women who die sharply contradicts a focus of the *individual* female subject, the sati, who is framed for scrutiny.

The identification of differences serves to indicate only the newness of the discursive terrain explored by colonial rulers in response to new ideological pressures. In this discourse death came to define women's behavior not descriptively – as male heroism, martyrdom, or suicide do – but absolutely; the subject of sati came into being as the absent (dead) subject. But of course, beyond the woman's death in life (burning alive) lay life-in-death, the (re)construction of her subjectivity: it is this paradox that I have tried to uncover.

NOTES

I am grateful to Tejaswini Niranjana, Uma Chakravarty, and Kamala Visweswaran for their attempts to save me from errors, ambiguities, and mistakes of fact and interpretation in this essay. Any that remain are my own responsibility. Grateful thanks also go to Sarah Goodwin and Elisabeth Bronfen for their editorial guidance.

A version of this essay is appearing simultaneously in my book *Real and Imagined Women: Postcolonialism and the Female Subject* (London: Routledge, 1993).

1   "Sati" is the self-immolation of a Hindu widow along with the corpse of her husband. The word is used here to refer both to the practice and to the widow who performs it.
2   The texts are for the most part narratives of various kinds – tales, long poems, short stories, novels, epics, and a film. I am interested in the way narrative structures encode ideologemes and, conversely, in the way ideological structures are accommodated within, and expressed through, narrative paradigms. See Jameson, 76, 87–8. There is an interesting argument here about the *differences* among the narrative genres in the production of specific ideological constructs, but I have allowed it to remain implicit.
3   Lata Mani ("Production" 32–40, esp. 32) has argued for the emergence of a specifically colonial discourse on sati.
4   Robert Southey's *The Curse of Kehama* (1810), a poem now little read but influential in its own day as the precorsor of the exotic "Eastern tale" made popular by the younger romantics (especially Byron and Moore), represents the clearing of the ground for such intervention, at a time when the East India Company was engaged in large-scale territorialization in India. It narrates the story of Kehama, a despotic Indian prince who represents the debasement of Hindu rule. Two vivid set pieces are provided to illustrate his unfitness to rule: the first, a scene where the victims are two young and beautiful Hindu princesses about to die with an old king, their husband; the second, a court scene where the king curses a peasant to a life of perpetual suffering. Thus a certain "Hinduism," with the spectacular inequities of its class, caste, and gender relations, provided the necessary pretext

for the overthrow of "native" rule; and Southey's poem creates the picturesque and narrative version of such cultural and civilizational decay.

5   See, for instance, Boase and Benson.

6   Often such acts involved big-game hunting. The most complex exposition of this "white man's burden" is found in George Orwell's "Shooting an Elephant."

7   My point will be clearer if I make a distinction between colonial self-representation and earlier interventions in the practice of sati in Islamic India. Muslim rulers had regarded sati as suicide and hence illegal according to the *Sharia* (the Muslim code), but they permitted it to Hindu women. The Mughal ruler Akbar took a strong stand against forcibly burning women and passed an ordinance to prevent such deaths. According to contemporary historians, Akbar personally intervened to rescue a Rajput princess, widow of his friend Jai Mall, who refused to die as a sati. But her son Udai Singh forced her onto the pyre; Akbar sent his agents, who saved her when the pile was already lighted and seized Udai Singh. See Thapar, I: 292; Malleson, 164–6. The point is that the prohibition of sati did not become a strategic political move, and hence did not feature in the Mughals' self and Other representation of the Islamic and Hindu communities. Sumit Sarkar has commented on the "secularism, rationalism and non-conformity . . . of pre-British Muslim ruled India" (53), within which the issue of sati could be raised.

8   Colonial historians like Edward Thompson could declare that after the abolition of sati in British India, "a practice which had caused the sacrifice of many hundreds of women annually was driven into the Native States." Henry Laurence, the British agent in Rajputana, boasted in 1854 of effective law enforcement even in the princely states, especially those under strong British supervision (Thompson, 26, 28–9).

9   In Conrad's *Heart of Darkness*, in contrast, Kurtz is unredeemable. Not only is he guilty of "unspeakable rites," he also has a native woman.

10 The afterlife of the rescued widow remains vague. However, in both books the heroines have some European blood/education, a great deal of predisposition to adapt to European ways, and sufficient Eastern acquiescence to ensure that the new partnership will work.

11 See Mani, "Production of an Official Discourse," for the establishment of such a view, esp. 32.

12 See Mani, "Contentious Traditions." Mani points out that in annual reports of sati, "women were cast as either pathetic or heroic victims." In the former instance they were seen to be "dominated by Hindu men," in the latter they were considered to be "victimized by religion" (129).

13 Susan makes the terms of her loyalty explicit: "I take no merit for my service of twelve years, for I love her . . . but true and faithful service gives me right to speak I hope" (703).

14 I am grateful to Nancy Paxton for making this paper available to me.

15 *The Fakeer* is closest in plot outline to Walter Scott's ballad "Lochinvar." In both, a dashing outlaw rescues his mistress dramatically in the nick of time. The differences – between death and marriage – are of course significant, but their elision is even more so.

16 Among these, Nandy's *At the Edge of Psychology* is important.

17 A slightly different version of this analysis of *Antarjali jatra* appears in my "Subject of Sati."

18 In addition to the works already cited, see also Spivak, "Rani of Sirmur."

19 This paragraph summarizes part of Mani's long and intricate argument in "Production of an Official Discourse."

20 These are only the implicit and perhaps merely logical corollaries of their theoretical positions. But they are given significant emphasis precisely through the disavowals they issue (such disavowals must surely be gratuitous given the transparency of their political commitments): "This criticism of the absence of women's subjectivity in colonial accounts is not to argue either that women died voluntarily or that I in any way endorse *sati*. From

my perspective, the practice was and remains indefensible" (Mani, "Contentious Traditions" 130); "it should therefore be understood that the example I discuss . . . is in no way
a plea for some violent Hindu sisterhood of self-destruction" (Spivak, "Can the Subaltern
Speak?" 129).

21 The observation is made by Parry, 27–58, esp. 35.

22 According to legend, Sati is so distressed by the exclusion of her husband, the god Shiva,
from her father's court that she dies. Shiva dances the *tandava* (the dance of destruction)
carrying Sati's corpse on his shoulder. In the *Ramayana* Sita, wife of Rama, has to undergo
an ordeal by fire in order to establish her chastity after she is rescued from Ravana, who
had abducted her.

23 Romila Thapar comments on the status of women at various periods. Their changing
features have to be understood within a specific historical context. For example, in the
early Aryan civilization, she argues, "the position of women was on the whole free" (40–
1). Sati was only a symbolic act, and the remarriage of widows was common. But in later
age, from about AD 300 to 700, women developed "a distinctly subordinate position"
(151). The practice of widow burning appears to have begun at this time. The only women
who had "a large measure of freedom" were those "who deliberately chose to opt out
of . . . the 'normal' activities of a woman" and became Buddhist nuns, or else actresses,
courtesans, or prostitutes (152). Feudalism in the Rajput states (from about AD 800 to
1200) led to the glorification of military virtues, so that "women . . . were taught to admire
men who fought well" and were themselves expected to commit sati when their husbands
died (247). During Muslim rule, from the thirteenth century to the sixteenth, the position
of both Hindu and Muslim women of all classes was an inferior one (301–2). Women's
seclusion (purdah) was the normal custom. There thus seems to be little ground for
celebrating the status of precolonial women – at least without careful qualification.

24 According to the translator's note (207–8), the preamble is considered by the ancient
commentators to be not part of the original text but a later addition.

25 The differences between the queen's passive behavior and Kannaki's active response are,
of course, functions of their class positions. The *Shilappadikaram* presents a vivid picture of
the wealth, power, and aspirations of the rising mercantile class, of which Kovalan and
Kannaki are members.

26 See Das, 28.

27 Kannaki has been shown to be a "good wife" in the first half of the book; she forgives
Kovalan for his desertion of her, makes him a gift of her gold anklet to be sold, and
uncomplainingly accepts the hardships of the journey to Madurai and of poverty with
him.

28 Bhakti is a religious devotion that signals a different, more personalized and intimate
relation between the devotee and his or her god; the members of the cult were often,
though not always, women, peasants, artisans, or untouchables. The movement began in
the fifth or sixth century AD in the Tamil kingdom and continued for well over a thousand
years, spreading from region to region throughout the country. I am indebted to a special
issue of *Manushi* on women Bhakta poets for information contained in this paragraph;
especially to articles by Madhu Kishwar, "Introduction" 3–8; A. K. Ramanujan, "Talking
to God in the Mother Tongue" 9–17; and Uma Chakravarty, "The World of the Bhaktin in
South Indian Traditions: The Body and Beyond" 18–29.

29 Chakravarty, 18–29. The Kannada poet Akka Mahadevi (twelfth century AD) writes:

     So my lord, white as jasmine, is my husband.
     Take these husbands who die, decay,

and feed them
to your kitchen fires!
                (Trans. Ramanujan, *Speaking of Siva*)

And Mira, the Rajput princess-poet (sixteenth century), asserts in a well-known prayer/
hymn:

I will sing of Girdhar [the lord Krishna]
I will not be a sati.

30   My omission of any texts of Islamic India from this analysis reflects only the constraints of
     length and the inadequacies of scholarship; it is not intended to exempt this period from
     colonial prehistory.

         Gauri Viswanathan has pointed out that in "the relativized domain of history," where
     differences are attributed to "the effect of historical change and movement," "concepts like
     absolute truth have no place" – instead "there is only formation, process, and flux" (97).
     This of course does not prevent the diagnosis of the political imperatives underlying
     ideological constructs. In other words, my method offers an explanatory model.

WORKS CITED

Benson, Larry D. *Malory's Morte d'Arthur: A Fifteenth-Century Chivalric Romance*. Cambridge:
    Harvard UP, 1976.
Boase, Roger. *The Origin and Meaning of Courtly Love*. Totowa, NJ: Rowman and Littlefield,
    1977.
Chakravarty, Uma. "The World of the Bhaktin in South Indian Traditions: The Body and
    Beyond." *Manushi* 50–52 (1989): 18–29.
Danielou, Alain, trans. *Shilappadikaram: The Ankle Bracelet*. New York: New Directions, 1967.
Das, Veena. "Shakti versus Sati: A Reading of the Santoshi Ma Cult." *Manushi* 49 (1988): 26–
    30.
Derozio, Henry Louis Vivian. *Poems*. Intro. F. B. Bradley-Birt. Foreword by R. K. Das Gupta.
    Delhi: Oxford UP, 1980.
Dickens, Charles. *Dombey and Son*. 1848. Harmondsworth, England: Penguin, 1970.
Jameson, Fredric. *The Political Unconscious*. Ithaca: Cornell UP, 1981.
Kaye, M. M. *The Far Pavilions*, 2 vols. New York: St. Martin's Press, 1978.
Kishwar, Madhu. "Introduction." *Manushi* 50–52 (1989): 3–8.
Malleson, G. B. *The Emperor Akbar and the Rise of the Mughal Empire*. Delhi: Sunita, 1986.
Mani, Lata. "Contentious Traditions: The Debate on *Sati* in Colonial India." *Cultural Critique* 7
    (1987): 119–56.
——. "Production of an Official Discourse on *Sati* in Early Nineteenth Century Bengal."
    Economic and Political Weekly 21.7, Review of Women Studies, April 26, 1986: 32–40.
Manushi 50–52 (1989). Special issue on women Bhakta poets.
Maspero advertisement. *Bombay Times and Journal of Commerce*, n.d. Rpt. in *Times Magazine*
    November–December 1988: 13.
Nandy, Ashis. *At the Edge of Psychology*. New Delhi: Oxford UP, 1982.
Orwell, George. "Shooting an Elephant." *"Shooting an Elephant" and Other Essays*. London:
    Secker and Warburg, 1945.
Parry, Benita. "Problems in Current Theories of Colonial Discourse." *Oxford Literary Review*
    9.1–2 (1987): 27–58.

Paxton, Nancy. "Unma(s)king the Colonial Subject: Subjectivity and the Female Body in the Novels of Flora Annie Steel and Anita Desai." Paper prepared for MLA Convention, December 1988.

Ramanujan, A. K. *Speaking of Siva*. Harmondsworth, England: Penguin, 1985.

——. "Talking to God in the Mother Tongue." *Manushi* 50–52 (1989): 9–17.

Sangari, Kumkum. "What Makes a Text Literary?" Paper prepared for Conference on English Studies in India, Miranda House, Delhi University, April 1988.

Sarkar, Sumit. "Rammohan Roy and the Break with the Past." *Rammohan Roy and the Process of Modernization in India*. Ed. V. C. Joshi. New Delhi: Vikas, 1975.

Spivak, Gayatri Chakravorty. "Can the Subaltern Speak? Speculations on Widow-Sacrifice." *Wedge* 7–8 (1985): 120–30. Reprinted in *Selected Subaltern Studies*. Ed. Ranajit Guha. Oxford: Oxford UP, 1988.

——. "The Rani of Sirmur: An Essay in Reading the Archives." *History and Theory* 24.3 (1987): 247–72.

——. "Three Women's Texts and a Critique of Imperialism." *Critical Inquiry* 12.1 (1985): 243–61.

Sunder Rajan, Rajeswari. "The Subject of Sati." *Yale Journal of Criticism* 3.2 (1990): 1–28.

Tagore, Rabindranath. "Saved." *"Mashi" and Other Stories*. Delhi: Macmillan, 1918.

Thapar, Romila. *History of India*. 2 vols. Harmondsworth, England: Penguin, 1966.

Thompson, Edward. *The Reconstruction of India*. Delphi: Kaushal Rakashan, 1985.

Viswanathan, Gauri. *Masks of Conquest: Literary Study and British Rule in India*. New York: Columbia UP, 1989.

Nationalism, Gender, and the Narrative of Identity

R. RADHAKRISHNAN

R. Radhakrishnan's essay is in part a response to **Partha Chatterjee**, and the two essays ought to be considered together. Like Chatterjee, he submits nationalism to a critique, one that seeks to deconstruct its political investments, especially insofar as these investments effect the "women's question." As with other postcolonial theorists (like those involved in the Subaltern Studies Group), Radhakrishnan advocates a new form of radical historiography; he draws on the work of Kumkum Sangari and Sudesh Vaid (see, for example, their *Recasting Women: Essays in Indian Colonial History*) who avoid some of the problems of postcolonial writers whose work is influenced by post-structuralism. Non-teleological and non-totalizing, the feminist historiography advocated by Radhakrishnan critiques the very notion of history itself. The same holds true for the notion of nationalism as well, for the author holds that, unlike the "monolithic" conception of nationalism rejected by many postcolonial critics, nationalism is historically specific, determined neither by a Western ideal of subjectivity nor by nativist essentialism. The place of women becomes, for Radhakrishnan, a kind of *displacement*, "the allegorical name for a specific historical failure": and that failure is the failure of a nationalism that remains indebted to Eurocentrism and Orientalism. The student of postcolonial nationalism will find in this essay an elaboration of the Fanonian idea of "national consciousness" and an incisive example of the idea of "continuance" (as **Frantz Fanon** and **Homi K. Bhabha** articulate it): the necessity to continue the critique not only of colonialism but also of the internal dynamics of nationalism itself.

Nationalism, Gender, and the Narrative of Identity

In a recent essay entitled "The Nationalist Resolution of the Women's Question," Partha Chatterjee elaborates the complex relationship between women's politics and the politics of Indian nationalism. His point is that while the women's question "was a central issue in some of the most controversial debates over social reform in early and mid-nineteenth-century Bengal," this very issue disappeared from the public agenda by the end of the century. "From then onwards," Chatterjee observes, "questions regarding the position of women in society do not arouse the same degree of passion as they did only a few decades before. The overwhelming issues now are directly political ones – concerning the politics of nationalism." Chatterjee concludes that "nationalism could not have resolved those issues; rather, the relation between nationalism and the women's question must have been problematical."[1] Although these critical comments are made in the highly specific context of Indian nationalism in the nineteenth century, they express a general truth concerning the relationship among different forms and contents of political struggle and the problems that emerge when any one politics (such as "the women's question") is taken over and spoken for by another politics (such as nationalism).[2]

The conjuncture wherein the women's question meets up with nationalism raises a number of fundamental questions about the very meaning of the term "politics." Why is it that the advent of the politics of nationalism signals the subordination if not the demise of women's politics? Why does the politics of the "one" typically overwhelm the politics of the "other"? Why could the two not be coordinated within an equal and dialogic relationship of mutual accountability? What factors constitute the normative criteria by which a question or issue is deemed "political"? Why is it that nationalism achieves the ideological effect of an inclusive and putatively macropolitical discourse, whereas the women's question – unable to achieve its own autonomous macropolitical identity – remains ghettoized within its specific and regional space? In other words, by what natural or ideological imperative or historical exigency does the politics of nationalism become the binding and overarching umbrella that subsumes other and different political temporalities?[3] For according to Chatterjee, the ideology of nationalist politics in its very specificity acts as the normative mode of *the political as such*, and "the imagined community" of nationalism is authorized as the most authentic unit or form of collectivity. Consequently, the women's question (or the *harijan* question, or the subaltern question...) is con-

Taken from *Diasporic Mediations: Between Home and Location* (Minneapolis: University of Minnesota Press, 1996).

strained to take on a nationalist expression as a prerequisite for being considered "political." Faced with its own repression, the women's question seems forced either to seek its own separatist political autonomy or to envision other ways of constituting a relational-integrative politics without at the same time resorting to another kind of totalizing umbrella.

The questions that I've already raised lead to still others, which will be posed here in all their political and epistemological generality: What does it mean to speak of "one" politics in terms of an "other"? How is a genuinely representative national consciousness (and here I have in mind the distinction that Frantz Fanon draws between the official ideology of nationalism and nationalist consciousness) to be spoken for by feminism and vice versa? Is it inevitable that one of these politics must form the horizon for the other, or is it possible that the very notion of a containing horizon is quite beside the point?[4] Can any horizon be "pregiven" in such an absolute and transcendent way? Isn't the very notion of the horizon open to perennial political negotiation? Since no one politics is totally representative of or completely coextensive with the horizon, should we not be talking about the ability of any subject-positional politics to inflect itself both regionally and totally? In other words, isn't the so-called horizon itself the shifting expression of equilibrium among the many forces that constitute and operate the horizon: gender, class, sexuality, ethnicity, and so on? If one specific politics is to achieve a general significance, it would seem that it has to possess a multiple valence, that is, enjoy political legitimacy as a specific constituency and simultaneously make a difference in the integrated political or cultural sphere. Without such access to an integrated cultural politics, any single subject-positional politics risks losing its interventionary power within that total field.

In their vigorously argued introduction to the volume *Recasting Women: Essays in Colonial History*, Kumkum Sangari and Sudesh Vaid advance the cause of feminist historiography toward "the integrated domain of cultural history." Claiming that "feminist historiography may be feminist without being, exclusively, women's history," they go on to say that "such a historiography acknowledges that each aspect of reality is gendered, and is thus involved in questioning all that we think we know, in a sustained examination of analytical and epistemological apparatus, and in a dismantling of the ideological presuppositions of so called gender-neutral methodologies." Carefully avoiding the pitfalls of both separatism and academicism that are only too ready to embody feminist historiography as a separate discipline based on a gender-coded division of labor, Sangari and Vaid contend that "feminist historiography rethinks historiography as a whole," and in this sense make feminist historiography "a choice open to all historians." Such a choice is understood, however, not "as one among competing perspectives" but rather "as a choice which cannot but undergrid *any* attempt at a historical reconstruction which undertakes to demonstrate our sociality in the *full* sense, and is ready to engage with its own presuppositions of an objective gender-neutral method of enquiry."[5]

There is so much being said in these passages that I wish to unpack some of it in detail before describing nationalism as a subject amenable to deconstructive investigation. In speaking for a particular feminist historiography, it would seem that Sangari and Vaid empower it in a double-coded way,[6] that is, feminist historiography is made to speak both representationally and post-representationally.[7] In other words, the articulation and the politicization of gender as an analytic category belong initially with feminism narrowly conceived as exclusively women's questions, but do not and cannot merely stop with that. If indeed gender is a necessary category in the context of cultural and historical and political analysis, how can its operations be circumscribed within the narrow confines of its origins? Just as the elaboration of "class" is in some sense intrinsic to the history of Marxism but is by no means exclusively Marxist, "gender" has a particular placement that is local and specific to "women's questions" but is by no means merely a regional concern.[8] Feminist historiography is representational in the sense that it speaks, by way of gender, for those questions and concerns that stem from women's issues initially, but in doing so it understands "gender" as a category that is much more comprehensive in its scope. In this sense, feminist historiography speaks post-representationally, activating the category of "gender" beyond its initial or originary commitment to merely one special or specific constituency. This point needs emphasis, for as we have already seen in the context of nationalism, it is precisely because the women's question was kept from achieving its own form of politicization that it was so easily and coercively spoken for by the discourse of nationalism, whereas with the arrival of gender as a fully blown historical-cultural-political-epistemic category, the women's question (which in and by itself was not yet a *politics*, but merely a constituency by description) is renamed and transformed as feminism. From this point on, feminist projects are interpellated by feminist ideology and not just covered under other and alien ideologies of patronage, amelioration, and redemption. But as has been observed already, this move in itself does not go far enough; true, it succeeds in politicizing the women's question in terms of its own ideology, but this very politics runs the danger of limiting itself as a form of "micropolitics."

Sangari and Vaid's formulation of the project of feminist historiography is refreshingly different from (and more far-reaching than) a number of current post-structuralist, radically subject-positional versions.[9] Unlike many of these versions that seem happy to accept their positional separateness and difference, Sangari and Vaid's elaboration of the project boldly and relevantly raises questions concerning the "full" and "total" rethinking of historiography as such. In opening up feminist historiography in a way that concerns all historians, it would appear that they are surrendering the specificity of the feminist project to other grand theories and ideologies. But a close reading of their text tells us something entirely different: the very openness of the "choice" is conceptualized as a form of historical and political inevitability. For the choice is not just any choice, or even one among many possible choices, but a choice that cannot but be made. In repudiating the very notion of gender neutrality, they integrate the category of gender into every aspect of reality; and in opening gender out to all historians, they make it impossible for other historians (who, for example, historicize along axes of nationality, class, race, and so on) not to integrate the feminist imperative within their respective projects. To put it differently, the field of historiography as such is made to acknowledge the reality of the feminist intervention as both micropolitical and macropolitical. In my reading, Sangari and Vaid forward the very strong claim that the feminist project cannot be considered complete or even sufficient unless it takes on the project of the "feminization" of the total field of historiography as such.[10] So much of post-structuralist feminism, rooted in epistemologies of relativism and difference, renounces global and macropolitical models on the basis of "epistemological purity," but Sangari and Vaid's analysis points out that such theories in themselves cannot be devoid of global projections and commitments. The category of "gender" in its particularity resonates with a general or universal potential for meaning (why else would it be a category?), and the task is not to eschew universality or globality in favor of pure difference or heterogeneity, but to read and interpret carefully the many tensions among the many forms of "particular-universal" categorical claims.

If we now put together the critical trajectories of Chatterjee's essay and Sangari and Vaid's historiographic agenda, we find ourselves confronting, with problematic urgency, the question we started out with: how is any one politics to be spoken in terms of another politics? If feminism or nationalism are expressions of "particular-universal" ideologies, and if, furthermore, each of these ideologies (from its own specificity) makes general claims on the entire social formation, how are we to adjudicate among these relativist discourses, none of which is legitimate enough to speak for the total reality? As I have suggested, the strategy of locating any one politics within another is as inappropriate as it is coercive. If that is the case, then from what space or within what domain does any historiography speak? Neither strategies of radical separateness nor those of hierarchic and organic containment do justice to the relational nature of the "absent totality" whose very reality, according to Ernesto Laclau and Chantal Mouffe, is "unsutured."[11] The task facing the many subject positions and their particular-universal ideologies is that of envisioning a totality that is not already there. Nationalist totality, we have seen, is an example of a "bad totality," and feminist historiography secedes from that structure *not to set up a different and oppositional form of totality, but to establish a different relationship to totality*. My objective here, as I loosely conflate Sangari and Vaid with Laclau and Mouffe, is to suggest both that no one discourse or historiography has the ethicopolitical legitimacy to represent the totality, and that the concept of "totality" should be understood not as a pregiven horizon but as the necessary and inevitable "effect" or function of the many relational dialogues, contestations, and asymmetries among the many positions (and their particular-universal ideologies) that constitute the total field.

A model that sees hegemony articulated among multiple determinations obviously poses serious representational problems. If the categories of gender, sexuality, nationality, or class can neither speak for the totality nor for one another but are yet implicated in one another relationally, how is the historical subject to produce a narrative from such a radical relationality, a relationality without recourse? For once we accept the notion of relational articulation, two consequences follow: (1) inside / outside distinctions become thoroughly problematized and displaced (for example, the idea of a feminist or an ethnic or a class-based historiography pursued entirely from within itself becomes highly questionable), and (2) the conception of relationality as a field-in-process undermines possibilities of establishing boundaries and limits to the relational field; in other words, relationality turns into a pure concept, an end in itself.

So when Sangari and Vaid make *their* transformative claims on behalf of feminist historiography it is not immediately clear if by "feminist historiography" they mean

Indian feminist historiography or postcolonial feminist historiography or subaltern feminist historiography or third world feminist historiography. There is a certain lack of situatedness, a certain rejection of the politics of location (in Adrienne Rich's sense of the term), in the manner in which "feminist historiography" resists being located in terms of Indianness, subalternity, postcoloniality, and so on. But clearly, judging from the general thrust of their essay, they do mean to situate feminist historiography in the specific context of colonial and nationalist history. So in this sense, feminist historiography cannot become its own pure signifier, nor can it avoid the project of interpreting itself in relation to other given discourses and ideologies. Thus, in seeking to recast women against the backdrop of colonial history, Sangari and Vaid enact an oppositional relationship between their discourse and colonial history and, by extension, nationalist history. In a similar vein, the entire school of South Asian subaltern historians intentionally revises colonialist and nationalist historiographies, seeking all along to expose patterns of "dominance without hegemony" in these discourses.[12] This sense of historical specificity bounds and gives determinate shape to a project that would otherwise remain a rarefied and contentless exploration of relationality as such. What helps these historians in negotiating the boundaries among feminism, colonialism, nationalism, capitalism, Eurocentrism, metropolitanism, and so on, is their commitment to the production of a critical history that has to acknowledge "realities" in the very act of challenging and discrediting them. In directing the revisionist deconstructive energies of gender and subalternity at colonialist and nationalist historiographies, these historians acknowledge the force of a prior placement, what we could term "the assigned nature" of their subject position. By thus taking a critical Gramscian inventory of their own historical positions, they deal with nationalism earnestly rather than dismissing it outright as a failed and flawed phenomenon: the history of nationalism is not easily bypassed just because it has been the history of a failure.[13]

But why study nationalism at all, especially at a time when avant-garde, metropolitan theory has passed the verdict that like "the voice," like "identity," like "representation," nationalism is or should be dead? There are several reasons why nationalism must continue to be studied:

1. Like all complex historical movements, nationalism is not a monolithic phenomenon to be deemed entirely good or entirely bad; nationalism is a contradictory discourse and its internal contradictions need to be unpacked in their historical specificity. The historical agency of nationalism has been sometimes hegemonic although often merely dominant, sometimes emancipatory although often repressive, and sometimes progressive although often traditional and reactionary.

2. While banished by certain theories, nationalism is back today with a vengeance all over the world. Western theorists cannot in good faith talk any more about the ugly and hysterical resurgence of nationalisms "out there and among them," as if "here and among us" nationalism is a thing of the past. The unification of the two Germanies in Europe, the breakup of the Soviet Union into fifteen national republics, and the current suppression of Chechnya by Russia have brought nationalism and the national question back into the very center of the historical stage. Neither the deracinating multinational or international spread of

capitalism nor the Marxist theoretical assimilation of the national question within an internationalist Communism has been able to do away with the urgencies of the imagined communities of nationalism. Right here in the United States (which would seem to have surpassed the nationalist threshold of universal history), we witnessed televisual images of jingoistic self-celebration during the US bombing of Libya. And all along, political commentators and media reporters were condemning the madman Qaddafi and the violent behavior of the Libyan zealots "out there."

3. The international community of nations continues to bear the shame and guilt of not yet acknowledging the Palestinian right to nationhood and self-determination. The Palestinians continue to be submitted to and brutalized by the duplicitous international consensus (spearheaded largely by the United States) that refuses to listen to the Palestinians because they are not yet a nation and at the same time frustrates their every attempt to become a nation.

4. And finally, stalemates such as the Salman Rushdie affair and the international impasse over Iraq's Saddam Hussein demonstrate yet again the poverty of a so-called international but in fact Western metropolitan framework when applied to other and different forms of collective identity.

It is with these polemical pointers that I would like to resume my analysis of the problems of nationalism; the particular structure that concerns me here is the dichotomy of the inside / outside that nationalist discourse deploys with telling effect. My point here is not to condemn or endorse in toto the politics of "inside / outside," but rather to observe the strategic and differentiated use of this dichotomous structure within nationalism. For instance, are we evaluating the Rushdie affair from within the spaces of Western secularism or from someplace else? Are we viewing the conduct of Arab politics from within the Arab nationalist umbrella, or from within an Arab but non-nationalist umbrella, or from yet another site? Our very mode of understanding is implicated in our mode of partisanship, and our mode of partisanship is an expression or function of our location – what that location includes and excludes. Inside / outside perceptions are indeed very much alive, and there is no transideological free space of arbitration to adjudicate among multiple nonsynchronous boundaries.

The particular instance of Indian nationalism makes use of the inner / outer distinction as a way of selectively coping with the West, and it is not coincidental that the women's question is very much a part of this dichotomous adjustment. Here again, by mobilizing the inner / outer distinction against the "outerness" of the West, nationalist rhetoric makes "woman" the pure and ahistorical signifier of "interiority."[14] In the fight against the enemy from the outside, something within gets even more repressed, and "woman" becomes the mute but necessary allegorical ground for the transactions of nationalist history. I turn again to Partha Chatterjee, who describes this effect in scrupulous detail. Chatterjee observes that nationalism could neither ignore the West completely nor capitulate to it entirely: the West and its ideals of material progress had to be assimilated selectively, without any fundamental damage to the native and "inner" Indian self. In other words, questions of change and progress posed in Western attire were conceived as an outer and epiphenomenal aspect of Indian identity, whereas the inner and inviolable sanctum of Indian identity had to do with home, spirituality, and the figure of Woman as representative of the true self. As Chatterjee puts it:

> Now apply the inner / outer distinction to the matter of concrete day-to-day living and you get a separation of the social space into *ghar* and *bahir*, the home and the world. The world is the external, the domain of the material; the home represents our inner spiritual self, our true identity. The world is a treacherous terrain of the pursuit of material interests, where practical considerations reign supreme. It is also typically the domain of the male. The home in its essence must remain unaffected by the profane activities of the material world – and woman is its representation. *And so we get an identification of social roles by gender to correspond with the separation of the social space into* ghar *and* bahir. (Emphasis added)

Chatterjee goes on to say that once "we match the new meaning of the home / world dichotomy with the identification of social roles by gender, we get the ideological framework within which nationalism answered the women's question."[15] The rhetoric of nationalism makes use of gender from its own ideological perspective and frames women narrowly in the way that feminist historiography, as articulated by Sangari and Vaid, soundly rejects. Like any framework whose finitude is the representation of its own limited and ideologically biased interests, the nationalist framework, too, thematizes its own priorities: the selective appropriation of the West and the safeguarding of one's essential identity. Unfortunately, in authorizing such a schizophrenic vision of itself, nationalism loses on both fronts: its external history remains hostage to the Enlightenment identity of the West while its inner self is effectively written out of history altogether in the name of a repressive and essentialist indigeny. And Woman takes on the name of a vast inner silence not to be broken into by the rough and external clamor of material history. Chatterjee's reading of the nationalist paradigm makes us acutely aware that the postcolonial project and its many narratives are still in search of a different political ethic or teleology (if that term is still permissible), one that is underwritten neither by the Western subject of Enlightenment nor by a reactionary and essentialist nativism. It is important to notice how nationalist ideology deploys the inner / outer split to achieve a false and repressive resolution of its identity. Forced by colonialism to negotiate with Western blueprints of reason, progress, and enlightenment, the nationalist subject straddles two regions or spaces, internalizing Western epistemological modes at the outer or the purely pragmatic level, and at the inner level maintaining a traditional identity that will not be influenced by the merely pragmatic nature of the outward changes. In other words, the place where the *true* nationalist subject *really is* and the place from which it produces historical-materialist knowledge about itself are mutually heterogeneous. The locus of the true self, the inner / traditional / spiritual sense of place, is exiled from processes of history while the locus of historical knowledge fails to speak for the true identity of the nationalist subject. The result is a fundamental rupture, a form of basic cognitive dissidence, a radical collapse of representation. Unable to produce its own history in response to its inner sense of identity, nationalist ideology sets up Woman as victim and goddess simultaneously. Woman becomes the allegorical name for a specific historical failure: the failure to coordinate the political or the ontological with the epistemological within an undivided agency.

In his book *Nationalist Thought and the Colonial World*, Partha Chatterjee addresses in great depth the political-epistemological predicament faced by nationalism. Nationalism, Chatterjee submits, should result in a double decolonization. Mere political decolonization and the resultant celebration of freedom, however momentous, does not by itself inaugurate a new history, a new subject, and a new and free sense of agency.[16] It is of vital importance that nationalist thought coordinate a new and different space that it can call *its* own: a space that is not complicit with the universal Subject of Eurocentric enlightenment, a space where nationalist politics could fashion its own epistemological, cognitive, and representational modalities. The break from colonialism has then to be both political and epistemological. The nationalist subject in its protagonistic phase of history (as against its antagonistic phase, when the primary aim was to overthrow the enemy) has to break away from the colonial past, achieve full and inclusive representational legitimacy with its own people – the many subspaces and the many other forms and thresholds of collective identity (such as the ethnic, the religious, the communal) – and fashion its own indigenous modes of cultural, social, and political production in response. Can nationalism as commonly understood fulfill these obligations?

The problem with nationalism, in Chatterjee's view, is that it sustains and continues the baleful legacies of Eurocentrism and Orientalism. The received history of nationalism argues for two kinds of nationalism: Eastern and Western.[17] By the logic of this Us – Them divide,[18] Western nationalisms are deemed capable of generating their own models of autonomy from within, whereas Eastern nationalisms have to assimilate something alien to their own cultures before they can become modern nations. Thus in the Western context, the ideals of Frenchness, Germanness, or Englishness – national essences rooted in a sense of autochthony – become the basis of a modernity that reroots and reconfirms a native sense of identity. On the other hand, Eastern nationalisms, and in particular "third world" nationalisms, are forced to choose between "being themselves" and "becoming modern nations," as though the universal standards of reason and progress were natural and intrinsic to the West. In this latter case, the universalizing mission is imbued with violence, coercion, deracination, and denaturalization. We can see how this divide perpetrates the ideology of a dominant common world where the West leads naturally and the East follows in an eternal game of catch-up in which its identity is always in dissonance with itself.

The real tragedy, however, is when postcolonial nationalisms internalize rather than problematize the Western blueprint in the name of progress, modernization, industrialization, and internationalism. This process seems difficult to avoid, since the immediate history of these nations happens to be Western and there are no easy ways available to reclaim a pure and uncontaminated history prior to the ravages of colonialism. Even if such recovery were possible, it would serve only to render the postcolonial nation hopelessly out of sync with the "international" present of modernity. How inevitable is this scenario? Is nationalism, then, "always already" corrupt and defective in its agency? Whatever the answer may be in the long run, Chatterjee reminds us that it is crucial for the postcolonial subject to produce a critical and deconstructive knowledge about nationalism. Only such a critical knowledge will help us identify and elaborate the complicity of the nationalist project with that of the enlightened European subject. It is on the basis of such knowledge that postcolonial subjects can produce a genuinely subaltern history about themselves and not merely replicate, in one form or another, the liberal-elitist narrative of the West. And it is in this context that Chatterjee makes a sharp distinction between what he calls the "problematic" of nationalism and the "thematic" of nationalism.

Drawing on the work of Edward Said and Anouar Abdel-Malek and routing it through the phenomenology of Sartre and Merleau-Ponty and the structural Marxism of Althusser, Chatterjee makes his unique contribution to our understanding of the two terms: thematic and problematic. His purpose is to "make a suitable distinction by which we can separate, for analytical purposes, that part of a social ideology ... which asserts the existence of certain historical possibilities from the part which seeks to *justify* those claims by an appeal to both epistemic and moral principles." The distinction takes the following form. The thematic "refers to an epistemological as well as ethical system which provides a framework of elements and rules for establishing relations between elements; the problematic, on the other hand, consists of concrete statements about possibilities justified by reference to the thematic." Applying this distinction to nationalist ideology, Chatterjee finds that "the problematic of nationalist thought is exactly the reverse of that of Orientalism." The only difference is that whereas in Orientalism the Oriental is a passive subject, in nationalism the object has become an active "subject," but one that remains captive to categories such as "progress," "reason," and "modernity," categories that are alien to him or her. Rather than being acted upon by these categories from the outside, this new subject internalizes them. Within such an ideological interpellation (which does not spring from the history of the postcolonial subject), the subject thinks that his or her subjectivity is "active, autonomous and sovereign." "At the level of the thematic, on the other hand," continues Chatterjee, "nationalist thought accepts the same essentialist conception based on the distinction between 'the East' and 'the West,' the same typology created by a transcendent studying subject, and hence the same 'objectifying' procedures of knowledge constructed in the post-Enlightenment age of Western science." The result is a constitutive contradictoriness in nationalist thought: its daring political agenda is always already depoliticized and recuperated by the very same representational structure that nationalist thought seeks to put in question. Hence, as Chatterjee concludes, the inappropriateness of posing the problem of "social transformation in a post-colonial country within a strictly nationalist framework."[19]

If we accept Chatterjee's analysis (I for one find it eminently persuasive), we have to conclude that the nationalist problematic pre-empts the nationalist thematic. The thematic of nationalism in a postcolonial country is constrained to remain a mere instantiation of a generalized nationalist problematic developed elsewhere. In other words, the processes and the procedures of the post-Enlightenment project are made to become the hallmark of the nation-building thematic in the postcolonial country. The post-Enlightenment telos begins to function as a free-floating signifier seeking universal confirmation. What remains concealed in such a false universalization is of course the fact that Western nationalism itself took shape under highly determinate and limited historical circumstances. In Chatterjee's terms, the thematic, justificatory rhetoric of Western nationalism is naturalized as an integral part of the very algebra of *nationalism as such*. In instantiating without historical relevance the second-order history of nationalism developed elsewhere, postcolonial nationalism forfeits its own thematic agenda. If in Western nationalism the thematic and the problematic are reciprocally and organically grounded, in the case of postcolonial nationalism the thematic and the problematic remain disjunct from each other.

What it all comes down to is the betrayal by nationalism of its own "inner" realities. Obsessively concerned with the West and other forms of local elitism, nationalism fails to speak for its own people; on the contrary, it suppresses the politics of subalternity. Paralyzed by the ideological view of its inner reality as merely a bulwark against excessive Westernization, nationalism fails to historicize this inner reality in its own multifarious forms. The very mode in which nationalism identifies its inner identity privileges the externality of the West, and the so-called inner or true identity of the nation takes the form of a mere strategic reaction formation to or against interpellation by Western ideologies. This inner self is not allowed to take on a positive and hegemonic role as the protagonist or agent of its own history. Nationalism as a mode of narration thus fails both to represent its own reality and to represent its own people.[20] The ideological disposition of nationalism toward its people or its masses is fraught with the same duplicity that characterizes its attitude to the women's question. To elaborate this thesis in the Indian context, I turn now to Chatterjee's critical analysis of the two great leaders of twentieth-century India, Mohandas Karamchand Gandhi and Jawaharlal Nehru and their very different orientations toward people's politics: Gandhi (the father of the nation), who is Indian and of the people, and Nehru (Gandhi's beloved protégé), the modern intellectual trying to bridge a nationalism of the people and a progressive interna-tionalism based on Western reason, science, technology, and industrial-economic progress.

One of the first moves Gandhi makes on his return to India from South Africa is to repudiate the urban politics practiced by the Indian National Congress. Gandhi locates his politics in the villages of India, where the majority of India's population resides (and this is basically true even today). He seeks an active common denomi-nator with the people of India, he changes his attire, his very mode of living, so that he can become one with the people. And this is not merely a vote-catching political stunt but Gandhi's vision of India: it is in the villages that India is to be experienced and discovered. It is in this context that the discovery of India becomes a major theme in nationalist history. Where and what is the real India? Sure enough, it exists, but how is it to be known? From what perspective is the real India to be represented so that the representation may be unified, inclusive, even total? How is national consciousness to be generated when it does not yet exist as such? The problem here is that the narrative cannot preknow its subject, which has itself to be the product of the narrative. The question that Gandhi raises is: Whose narrative is it going to be? The answer is certainly the "people's," but the term "people" covers a wide spectrum of positions, identities, and bases. How should nationalism forge from these many "subidentities" a unified identity to work for the common national cause?[21]

It is in this spirit that the discovery of India is undertaken, albeit differently, by Gandhi and Nehru. To dwell just a little longer on the semantics of the term "discovery," this theme presupposes that a certain India exists already waiting to be touched, known, and narrativized. In a narratological sense, the real India can only be the a posteriori effect of the narrative process, but ontologically, the reality of India is prior to the narrative. In other words, not any and every narrative can claim to be the signifier of the real India. Also, the criterion of reality serves two purposes: first, of demystifying the existing urban-elitist versions of India and second, of securing an ethicopolitical alignment between the knowledge produced about the real India and the sociopolitical transformations that are to follow on the basis of such knowledge. The Gandhian thesis is that no worthwhile plan of action can be based on a knowledge that is spurious and nonrepresentative. The people of India become the subject of the independence movement, and Gandhi's political ethic is to empower the people in a way that will enable them to lead themselves.

But a number of problems and contradictions arise here. Are the people the means or are they the end in the nationalist struggle? The contradiction lies in the fact that the unification of the people is going to be undertaken not in their own name, but in the name of the emerging nation and the nation-state that is to follow. The subaltern valence of the people has to be reformed as a prerequisite for their nationalization. The people thus become a necessary means to the superior ends of nationalism. The masses can neither be bypassed (for they are the real India) nor can they be legitimated qua people. And here, Gandhi's and Nehru's visions vary. Gandhi's advocacy of the people carries with it their full moral force. His model of independent India makes the people the teachers, and leaders such as himself become the pupils. Hence Gandhi's stern refusal of progress as an end in itself, and his rejection of all indices of growth and prosperity developed in the West. Hence, too, his insistence on decentralization, simple modes of production, and the ethic of self-sufficiency and his moral indictment of capital, accumulation, greed, and the systemic proliferation of want and desire. We must also remember that Gandhi was a rare leader who, in the name of the people, prescribed that the glorious Congress Party that had won India its independence should self-destruct once the aim of independence was achieved. But this of course was not to happen.

Jawaharlal Nehru's perspective on the masses of India is quite different. His discovery of India is much more ambivalent and doubt-ridden. He passionately admires the way in which Gandhi spontaneously establishes rapport with the people and becomes "one of them." But he often doubts whether he himself is capable of such organic identification with the masses.[22] Here then is Nehru in *The Discovery of India*:

India was in my blood and there was much in her that instinctively thrilled me. And yet, I approached her almost as an *alien critic*, full of dislike for the present as well as for many of the relics of the past I saw. To some extent I came to her via the West and looked at her as a friendly *Westerner* might have done. I was eager and anxious to change her outlook and appearance and give her the garb of modernity. And yet doubts rose within me. Did I know India, I who presumed to scrap much of her past heritage? (Emphasis added)[23]

A number of interesting tensions are played out here between India and her loving patriot. First, there are visceral references to "instinct" and "blood" whose strength has nothing whatsoever to do with Nehru's rational and theoretical understanding of India. Second, India figures both as a transcendent and marvelous identity awaiting ecstatic comprehension and as malleable raw material awaiting transformation by an act of production. A kind of mystical essentialism confronts a certain secular constructionism. While the present, the past, and the future of India are imperfectly aligned, the present through which India is being perceived is both the pure moment of nativism / indigeny and the contaminated perspective underwritten by the West. And finally, there is an aporetic tension between Nehru's strong visions on behalf of India and his uncertainties about his knowledge of India. Is it conceivable that Nehru, the architect of modern India, may in fact *not know* his country?

It is from such a divided consciousness that Nehru attempts to account for the "spellbinding" agency of Gandhi. It is somewhat surprising that Nehru's viewpoint comes very close to Marx's devaluation of the "idiocy of rural life." Yet Nehru is divided in his response, at once touched and disheartened if not intimidated by the Indian peasant. On the one hand, intimate exposure to the peasants and "their misery and overflowing gratitude" fills him "with shame and sorrow, shame at [his] own easy-going and comfortable life and [the] petty politics of the city which ignored this vast multitude of semi-naked sons and daughters of India."[24] But on the other hand, there is Nehru's strong and almost ruthless evaluation of the peasants as "dull certainly, uninteresting individually," and of their need "to be led properly, controlled, not by force or fear, but by 'gaining their trust,' by teaching them their true interests."[25] The vexing question is how to mobilize the masses in this nationalist-modernist cause. And the answer seems to be Gandhi.

In Partha Chatterjee's words: "On reading the many pages Nehru has written by way of explaining the phenomenon of Gandhi, what comes through most strongly is a feeling of total incomprehension." Gandhi becomes the voice of the people, a voice that is powerful, persuasive, legitimate, and yet inscrutable in its spellbinding effectivity. This voice intervenes successfully in the history of India precisely because it speaks for the masses, yet this very voice is considered misguided. Gandhian economics, Gandhian sociology, all of Gandhi's blueprints for independent India are all wrong, but Gandhi is the one who can inspire the masses; leaders like Nehru have the right facts, the right models for India's development, but are "powerless to intervene" in the history of the Indian masses. Gandhi thus becomes that mystical and incomprehensible genius exclusively responsible for India's independence, and yet Nehru has no hesitation in declaring that once *swaraj* is achieved, Gandhi's fads must not be encouraged. The affirmative project of building India finds itself thoroughly disconnected from the ethicopolitical modality of the independence movement. In a strange way, Nehru's understanding of Gandhi's historical agency lines it up with the "otherness" and the "unreason" of peasant consciousness, whereas the future of modern India becomes identified with the rationality of Western thought.

Nationalism is thus valorized as an inaugural moment precisely because it is also a project of deracination from an unreasonable prehistory. As Chatterjee sums it up:

And so the split between two domains of politics – one, a politics of the elite, and the other, a politics of subaltern classes – was replicated in the sphere of mature nationalist thought by an explicit recognition of the split between a domain of rationality and a domain of unreason, a domain of science and a domain of faith, a domain of organization and a domain of spontaneity. But it was a rational understanding which, by the very act of its recognition of the Other, also effaced the Other.[26]

In a real sense, then, the subject of nationalism does not exist. Conceived within this chronic duality, the nationalist subject is doomed to demonstrate the impossibility of its own claim to subjecthood. With the inner and the outer in mutual disarray, the nationalist subject marks the space of a constitutive representational debacle.[27]

The project that the subaltern historians are engaged in is the production of a subaltern critique of nationalism: a critique both to liberate those many spaces foreclosed within nationalism and to enable a nonreactive, nonparanoid mode of subjectivity and agency in touch with its own historically constituted interiority: a prey neither to the difference of the Western subject nor to the mystique of its own indigenous identity. In opening up new spaces, "the critique of nationalist discourse must find for itself the ideological means to connect the popular strength of the people's struggles with the consciousness of a new universality, to subvert the ideological sway of a state which falsely claims to speak on behalf of the nation and to challenge the presumed sovereignty of a science which puts itself at the service of capital."[28] Clearly, such a critique undertaken in the name of subalternity has to bear many different signatures within a universal and relational space, a space very much like the one invoked by Sangari and Vaid's feminist historiography.

NOTES

1 Partha Chatterjee, "The Nationalist Resolution of the Women's Question," in *Recasting Women: Essays in Colonial History*, ed. Kumkum Sangari and Sudesh Vaid (New Delhi: Kali for Women, 1989), 233 [p. 152 in this vol.]. This collection has since been reprinted as *Recasting Women: Essays in Indian Colonial History* (New Brunswick, NJ: Rutgers University Press, 1990).

2 For a spirited articulation of the need to realize the women's question as its own autonomous form of politics, *see* Shulamith Firestone, *The Dialectic of Sex* (New York: Bantam Books, 1970).

3 I am using the term "temporalities" here as developed by Chandra Talpade Mohanty in her essay, "Feminist Encounters: Locating the Politics of Experience," *Copyright* 1 (Fall 1987): 40.

4 Fredric Jameson argues in *The Political Unconscious: Narrative as a Socially Symbolic Act* (Ithaca, NY: Cornell University Press, 1981) that Marxism does and should continue to operate as the ultimate semantic horizon within which other political struggles are to be located. But the very notion of any single ideology operating as a containing horizon is deeply problematic. For a post-structuralist critique of Jameson's position, see my essay "Poststructuralist Politics: Towards a Theory of Coalition," in *Postmodernism/Jameson/Critique*, ed. Douglas Kellner (Washington, DC: Maisonneuve Press, 1989), 301–32.

5 Sangari and Vaid, "Recasting Women: An Introduction," in *Recasting Women*, 2–3.

6 For an insightful account of the double-coded nature of postcolonial narratives, see Kumkum Sangari, "The Politics of the Possible," *Cultural Critique* 7 (Fall 1987): 157–86.

7   For an in-depth discussion, in the context of Michel Foucault and Antonio Gramsci, of the implications of representational and post-representational politics, see chapter 2 of my *Diasporic Mediations: Between Home and Location* (Minneapolis: University of Minnesota Press, 1996).

8   I am referring here to a growing body of work by such feminist theorists as Gayatri Chakravorty Spivak, Teresa de Lauretis, Nancy Fraser, Linda Nicholson, Chandra Talpade Mohanty, Donna Haraway, and many others who elaborate gender both as a specific domain and as a general category of experience within the body politic.

9   My point here is that whereas postcolonial strategies of the politics of location are eager to take on macropolitical and global issues, Western conceptions of subject-positional politics (practiced in the manner of a Foucault or a Deleuze) tend to overlook global and macropolitical concerns. As Edward Said points out, there is a certain asymmetry that governs the relationship between discourses emanating from the world of former colonizers and those that rise from the world of the formerly colonized; see his essay "Intellectuals in the Post-Colonial World," *Salmagundi* 70–71 (Spring–Summer 1986): 44–81.

10 The tension between the local valence and the general or total valence of any constituency is illustrated powerfully in the American context, where "ethnicity" plays a constitutive role in the shaping of American identity. The concern of each ethnic group is both to legitimate its own form of ethnicity and to influence the general platform where different ethnic groups renegotiate the nature of American identity.

11 See Ernesto Laclau and Chantal Mouffe, *Hegemony and Socialist Strategy*, trans. Winston Moore and Paul Cammack (London: Verso, 1985).

12 See Ranajit Guha, "Dominance without Hegemony and Its Historiography," in *Subaltern Studies VI: Writings on South Asian History and Society*, ed. Ranajit Guha (Delhi, Oxford, and New York: Oxford University Press, 1989), 210–309.

13 For an important exchange about nationalism as a threshold in the development of a transnational and nonessentialist feminism, see the essays by Julie Stephens and Susie Tharu in *Subaltern Studies VI*.

14 In much the same way, Freudian psychoanalysis makes feminine sexuality "unknowable" without raising the question of knowledge itself as a gender-inflected category. French feminists such as Luce Irigaray, Hélène Cixous, Julia Kristeva, and Catherine Clément have raised the question of a feminine epistemics / *écriture* both within and without the economy of psychoanalysis.

15 Chatterjee, "The Nationalist Resolution," 238–9 [p. 156 in this vol.].

16 See Gayatri Chakravorty Spivak, "Reading *The Satanic Verses*," *Public Culture* 2, no. 1 (Fall 1989): 79–99, for a suggestive distinction between "subject formation" and "agency formation."

17 See John Plamenatz, "Two Types of Nationalism," in *Nationalism: The Nature and Evolution of an Idea*, ed. Eugene Kamenka (London: Edward Arnold, 1976), 23–36. The body of work on nationalism is too rich and complex to be fully represented, but here are a few significant (and of course, problematic) contributions: Benedict Anderson, *Imagined Communities: Reflections on the Origin and Spread of Nationalism* (London: Verso, 1983); John Breuilly, *Nationalism and the State* (Manchester: Manchester University Press, 1982); Horace B. Davis, *Toward a Marxist Theory of Nationalism* (New York: Monthly Review Press, 1978); Ernest Gellner, *Nations and Nationalism* (Oxford: Blackwell, 1983); Elie Kedourie, *Nationalism* (London: Hutchinson, 1960); Anthony D. Smith, *The Ethnic Origin of Nations* (Oxford: Blackwell, 1986); Kumari Jayawardena, *Feminism and Nationalism in the Third World* (London: Zed Press, 1986); E. J. Hobsbawm, *Nations and Nationalism since*

1780 (New York: Cambridge University Press, 1990); and Partha Chatterjee, *Nationalist Thought and the Colonial World* (Delhi: Oxford University Press, 1986).

18   See Satya Mohanty, "Us and Them: On the Philosophical Bases of Political Criticism," *Yale Journal of Criticism* 2, no. 2 (Spring 1989): 1–31.

19   Chatterjee, *Nationalist Thought and the Colonial World*, 38–9.

20   For a brilliant and varied discussion of the complicated relationship between nationalism and narration, see Homi K. Bhabha, ed., *Nation and Narration* (London and New York: Routledge, 1990), in particular the essays by Homi K. Bhabha, Tim Brennan, Doris Sommer, Sneja Gunew, and James Snead.

21   The rise of Hindu fundamentalism, the destruction of the Babri Masjid, violence against Muslims, and other related events point up the crisis of nationalism in India. The authority of the nation-state in itself does not guarantee the realization of an inclusive national consciousness.

22   Here I use the term "organic" as developed by Antonio Gramsci in his essay, "The Formation of Intellectuals," in *The Modern Prince and Other Writings*, trans. Louis Marks (New York: International, 1957), 118–25.

23   Jawaharlal Nehru, *The Discovery of India* (New York: John Day, 1946), 38.

24   Jawaharlal Nehru, *An Autobiography* (London: Bodley Head, 1936), 52.

25   Nehru as quoted in Chatterjee, *Nationalist Thought and the Colonial World*, 148.

26   Ibid., 150, 153.

27   For a complex reading of the nature of representation in the postcolonial context, see Homi K. Bhabha, "Signs Taken for Wonders: Questions of Ambivalence and Authority under a Tree outside Delhi, May 1817," *Critical Inquiry* 12, no. 1 (Autumn 1985): 144–65.

28   Chatterjee, *Nationalist Thought and the Colonial World*, 170.

Part III
African Identities:
Resistance and Race

An Image of Africa: Racism in Conrad's Heart of Darkness

CHINUA ACHEBE

Chinua Achebe is best known as a novelist, the author of *Things Fall Apart*, an account of life in a Nigerian village in the era of British colonialism that has often been read as a response to Conrad's *Heart of Darkness*. The essay here is a more explicitly critical response to Conrad's novel. Though published in the 1970s, this essay retains its relevance in large measure because its critique of Conrad's racism remains unsurpassed in its acuity and boldness. Calling Conrad a "bloody racist," Achebe proceeds to link his attitudes to the social world in which he lived and wrote. Like **Edward W. Said**, Achebe explores the essentially Orientalist relationship between European culture and the reality of Africa, a relationship in which Africa and Africans emerge as a mere backdrop, a "metaphysical battlefield devoid of all recognizable humanity." Anticipating some of the concerns of contemporary postcolonial theory, Achebe explores the peculiar absences and silences in Conrad's text: specifically the "non-presence" of African subjects who do nothing more than mark the space of a savage "Other." Reading Achebe's essay in tandem with Conrad's novel and his own *Things Fall Apart* will provide the student with a wealth of opportunities to explore issues of racism, identity, and colonial oppression as well as to consider the problem of a Western literary canon that can enshrine as great art "an offensive and totally deplorable book." These issues can be explored from another direction if Achebe's essay is read alongside **George Lamming**'s essay on the Caribbean novel and **Luke Gibbons**'s consideration of the concept of race in Irish history.

An Image of Africa:
Racism in Conrad's Heart of Darkness

It was a fine autumn morning at the beginning of this academic year such as encouraged friendliness to passing strangers. Brisk youngsters were hurrying in all directions, many of them obviously freshmen in their first flush of enthusiasm. An older man, going the same way as I, turned and remarked to me how very young they came these days. I agreed. Then he asked me if I was a student too. I said no, I was a teacher. What did I teach? African literature. Now that was funny, he said, because he never had thought of Africa as having that kind of stuff, you know. By this time I was walking much faster. "Oh well," I heard him say finally, behind me, "I guess I have to take your course to find out."

A few weeks later I received two very touching letters from high school children in Yonkers, New York, who – bless their teacher – had just read *Things Fall Apart*. One of them was particularly happy to learn about the customs and superstitions of an African tribe.

I propose to draw from these rather trivial encounters rather heavy conclusions which at first sight might seem somewhat out of proportion to them: But only at first sight.

The young fellow from Yonkers, perhaps partly on account of his age but I believe also for much deeper and more serious reasons, is obviously unaware that the life of his own tribesmen in Yonkers, New York, is full of odd customs and superstitions and, like everybody else in his culture, imagines that he needs a trip to Africa to encounter those things.

The other person being fully my own age could not be excused on the grounds of his years. Ignorance might be a more likely reason; but here again I believe that something more willful than a mere lack of information was at work. For did not that erudite British historian and Regius Professor at Oxford, Hugh Trevor Roper, pronounce a few years ago that African history did not exist?

If there is something in these utterances more than youthful experience, more than a lack of factual knowledge, what is it? Quite simply it is the desire – one might indeed say the need – in Western psychology to set Africa up as a foil in Europe, a place of negations at once remote and vaguely familiar in comparison with which Europe's own state of spiritual grace will be manifest.

This need is not new: which should relieve us of considerable responsibility and perhaps make us even willing to look at this phenomenon dispassionately. I have neither the desire nor, indeed, the competence to do so with the tools of the social and

Taken from *The Massachusetts Review* 18 (1977), pp. 782–94.

biological sciences. But, I can respond, as a novelist, to one famous book of European fiction, Joseph Conrad's *Heart of Darkness*, which better than any other work I know displays that Western desire and need which I have just spoken about. Of course, there are whole libraries of books devoted to the same purpose, but most of them are so obvious and so crude that few people worry about them today. Conrad, on the other hand, is undoubtedly one of the great stylists of modern fiction and a good storyteller into the bargain. His contribution therefore falls automatically into a different class – permanent literature – read and taught and constantly evaluated by serious academics. *Heart of Darkness* is indeed so secure today that a leading Conrad scholar has numbered it "among the half-dozen greatest short novels in the English language."[1] I will return to this critical option in due course because it may seriously modify my earlier suppositions about who may or may not be guilty in the things of which I will now speak.

Heart of Darkness projects the image of Africa as "the other world," the antithesis of Europe and therefore of civilization, a place where a man's vaunted intelligence and refinement are finally mocked by triumphant bestiality. The book opens on the River Thames, tranquil, resting peacefully "at the decline of day after ages of good service done to the race that peopled its banks." But the actual story takes place on the River Congo, the very antithesis of the Thames. The River Congo is quite decidely not a River Emeritus. It has rendered no service and enjoys no old-age pension. We are told that "going up that river was like travelling back to the earliest beginning of the world."

Is Conrad saying then that these two rivers are very different, one good, the other bad? Yes, but that is not the real point. What actually worries Conrad is the lurking hint of kinship, of common ancestry. For the Thames, too, "has been one of the dark places of the earth." It conquered its darkness, of course, and is now at peace. But if it were to visit its primordial relative, the Congo, it would run the terrible risk of hearing grotesque, suggestive echoes of its own forgotten darkness, and of falling victim to an avenging recrudescence of the mindless frenzy of the first beginnings.

I am not goint to waste your time with examples of Conrad's famed evocation of the African atmosphere. In the final consideration it amounts to no more than a steady, ponderous, fake-ritualistic repetition of two sentences, one about silence and the other about frenzy. An example of the former is "It was the stillness of an implacable force brooding over an inscrutable intention" and of the latter, "The steamer toiled along slowly on the edge of a black and incomprehensible frenzy." Of course, there is a judicious change of adjective from time to time so that instead of "inscrutable," for example, you might have "unspeakable," etc., etc.

The eagle-eyed English critic, F. R. Leavis, drew attention nearly thirty years ago to Conrad's "adjectival insistence upon inexpressible and incomprehensible mystery." That insistence must not be dismissed lightly, as many Conrad critics have tended to do, as a mere stylistic flaw. For it raises serious questions of artistic good faith. When a writer, while pretending to record scenes, incidents and their impact, is in reality engaged in inducing hypnotic stupor in his readers through a bombardment of emotive words and other forms of trickery much more has to be at stake than stylistic felicity. Generally, normal readers are well armed to detect and resist such underhand activity. But Conrad chose his subject well – one which was guaranteed not to put him in conflict with the psychological predisposition of his readers or raise the need for him to contend with their resistance. He chose the role of purveyor of comforting myths.

The most interesting and revealing passages in *Heart of Darkness* are, however, about people. I must quote a long passage from the middle of the story in which representatives of Europe in a steamer going down the Congo encounter the denizens of Africa:

> We were wanderers on a prehistoric earth, on an earth that wore the aspect of an unknown planet. We could have fancied ourselves the first of men taking possession of an accursed inheritance, to be subdued at the cost of profound anguish and of excessive toil. But suddenly, as we struggled round a bend, there would be a glimpse of rush walls, of peaked grass-roofs, a burst of yells, a whirl of black limbs, a mass of hands clapping, of feet stamping, of bodies swaying, of eyes rolling, under the droop of heavy and motionless foliage. The steamer toiled along slowly on the edge of a black and incomprehensible frenzy. The prehistoric man was cursing us, praying to us, welcoming us – who could tell? We were cut off from the comprehension of our surroundings; we glided past like phantoms, wondering and secretly appalled, as sane men would be before an enthusiastic outbreak in a madhouse. We could not remember because we were travelling in the night of first ages, of those ages that are gone, leaving hardly a sign – and no memories.
>
> The earth seemed unearthly. We are accustomed to look upon the shackled form of a conquered monster, but there – there you could look at a thing monstrous and free. It was unearthly, and the men were – No, they were not inhuman. Well, you know, that was the worst of it – this suspicion of their not being inhuman. It would come slowly to one. They howled and leaped, and spun, and made horrid faces; but what thrilled you was just the thought of your remote kinship with this wild and passionate uproar. Ugly. Yes, it was ugly enough; but if you were man enough you would admit to yourself that there was in you just the faintest trace of a response to the terrible frankness of that noise, a dim suspicion of there being a meaning in it which you – you so remote from the night of first ages – could comprehend.

Herein lies the meaning of *Heart of Darkness* and the fascination it holds over the Western mind: "What thrilled you was just the thought of their humanity – like yours. . . . Ugly."

Having shown us Africa in the mass, Conrad then zeros in on a specific example, giving us one of his rare descriptions of an African who is not just limbs or rolling eyes:

> And between whiles I had to look after the savage who was fireman. He was an improved specimen; he could fire up a vertical boiler. He was there below me, and, upon my word, to look at him was as edifying as seeing a dog in a parody of breeches and a feather hat, walking on his hind legs. A few months of training had done for that really fine chap. He squinted at the steam gauge and at the water gauge with an evident effort of intrepidity – and he had filed his teeth, too, the poor devil, and the wool of his pate shaved into queer patterns, and three ornamental scars on each of his cheeks. He ought to have been clapping his hands and stamping his feet on the bank, instead of which he has hard at work, a thrall to strange witchcraft, full of improving knowledge.

As everybody knows, Conrad is a romantic on the side. He might not exactly admire savages clapping their hands and stamping their feet but they have at least the merit of being in their place, unlike this dog in a parody of breeches. For Conrad, things (and persons) being in their place is of the utmost importance.

Towards the end of the story, Conrad lavishes great attention quite unexpectedly on an African woman who has obviously been some kind of mistress to Mr. Kurtz and now presides (if I may be permitted a little imitation of Conrad) like a formidable mystery over the inexorable imminence of his departure:

> She was savage and superb, wild-eyed and magnificent.... She stood looking at us without a stir and like the wilderness itself, with an air of brooding over an inscrutable purpose.

This Amazon is drawn in considerable detail, albeit of a predictable nature, for two reasons. First, she is in her place and so can win Conrad's special brand of approval; and second, she fulfills a structural requirement of the story; she is a savage counterpart to the refined, European woman with whom the story will end:

> She came forward, all in black with a pale head, floating towards me in the dusk. She was in mourning.... She took both my hands in hers and murmured, "I had heard you were coming"...She had a mature capacity for fidelity, for belief, for suffering.

The difference in the attitude of the novelist to these two women is conveyed in too many direct and subtle ways to need elaboration. But perhaps the most significant difference is the one implied in the author's bestowal of human expression to the one and the withholding of it from the other. It is clearly not part of Conrad's purpose to confer language on the "rudimentary souls" of Africa. They only "exchanged short grunting phrases" even among themselves but mostly they were too busy with their frenzy. There are two occasions in the book, however, when Conrad departs somewhat from his practice and confers speech, even English speech, on the savages. The first occurs when cannibalism gets the better of them:

> "Catch 'im," he snapped, with a bloodshot widening of his eyes and a flash of sharp white teeth – "catch 'im. Give 'im to us." "To you, eh?" I asked; "what would you do with them?" "Eat 'im!" he said curtly...

The other occasion is the famous announcement:

> Mistah Kurtz – he dead.

At first sight, these instances might be mistaken for unexpected acts of generosity from Conrad. In reality, they constitute some of his best assaults. In the case of the cannibals, the incomprehensible grunts that had thus far served them for speech suddenly proved inadequate for Conrad's purpose of letting the European glimpse the unspeakable craving in their hearts. Weighing the necessity for consistency in the portrayal of the dumb brutes against the sensational advantages of securing their conviction by clear, unambiguous evidence issuing out of their own mouth, Conrad chose the latter. As for the announcement of Mr. Kurtz's death by the "insolent black head of the doorway," what better or more appropriate *finis* could be written to the horror story of that wayward child of civilization who willfully had given his soul to the powers of darkness and "taken a high seat amongst the devils of the land" than the proclamation of his physical death by the forces he had joined?

It might be contended, of course, that the attitude to the African in *Heart of Darkness* is not Conrad's but that of his fictional narrator, Marlow, and that far from endorsing it Conrad might indeed be holding it up to irony and criticism. Certainly, Conrad appears to go to considerable pains to set up layers of insulation between himself and the moral universe of his story. He has, for example, a narrator behind a narrator. The primary narrator is Marlow but his account is given to us through the filter of a second, shadowy person. But if Conrad's intention is to draw a *cordon sanitaire* between himself and the moral and psychological malaise of his narrator, his care seems to me totally wasted because he neglects to hint however subtly or tentatively at an alternative frame of reference by which we may judge the actions and opinions of his characters. It would not have been beyond Conrad's power to make that provision if he had thought it necessary. Marlow seems to me to enjoy Conrad's complete confidence – a feeling reinforced by the close similarities between their careers.

Marlow comes through to us not only as a witness of truth, but one holding those advanced and humane views appropriate to the English liberal tradition which required all Englishmen of decency to be deeply shocked by atrocities in Bulgaria or the Congo of King Leopold of the Belgians or wherever. Thus Marlow is able to toss out such bleeding-heart sentiments as these:

> They were all dying slowly – it was very clear. They were not enemies, they were not criminals, they were nothing earthly now – nothing but black shadows of disease and starvation, lying confusedly in the greenish gloom. Brought from all the recesses of the coast in all the legality of time contracts, lost in uncongenial surroundings, fed on unfamiliar food, they sickened, became inefficient, and were then allowed to crawl away and rest.

The kind of liberalism espoused here by Marlow / Conrad touched all the best minds of the age in England, Europe, and America. It took different forms in the minds of different people but almost always managed to sidestep the ultimate question of equality between white people and black people. That extraordinary missionary, Albert Schweitzer, who sacrificed brilliant careers in music and theology in Europe for a life of service to Africans in much the same area as Conrad writes about, epitomizes the ambivalence. In a comment which I have often quoted but must quote one last time Schweitzer says: "The African is indeed my brother but my junior brother." And so he proceeded to build a hospital appropriate to the needs of junior brothers with standards of hygiene reminiscent of medical practice in the days before the germ theory of disease came into being. Naturally, he became a sensation in Europe and America. Pilgrims flocked, and I believe still flock even after he has passed on, to witness the prodigious miracle in Lamberene, on the edge of the primeval forest.

Conrad's liberalism would not take him quite as far as Schweitzer's, though. He would not use the word "brother" however qualified; the farthest he would go was "kinship." When Marlow's African helmsman falls down with a spear in his heart he gives his white master one final disquieting look.

> And the intimate profundity of that look he gave me when he received his hurt remains to this day in my memory – like a claim of distant kinship affirmed in a supreme moment.

It is important to note that Conrad, careful as ever with his words, is not talking so much about *distant kinship* as about someone *laying a claim* on it. The black man lays a claim on the white man which is well-nigh intolerable. It is the laying of this claim which frightens and at the same time fascinates Conrad, "...the thought of their humanity – like yours.... Ugly."

The point of my observations should be quite clear by now, namely, that Conrad was a bloody racist. That this simple truth is glossed over in criticism of his work is due to the fact that white racism against Africa is such a normal way of thinking that its manifestations go completely undetected. Students of *Heart of Darkness* will often tell you that Conrad is concerned not so much with Africa as with the deterioration of one European mind caused by solitude and sickness. They will point out to you that Conrad is, if anything, less charitable to the Europeans in the story than he is to the natives. A Conrad student told me in Scotland last year that Africa is merely a setting for the disintegration of the mind of Mr. Kurtz.

Which is partly the point: Africa as setting and backdrop which eliminates the African as human factor. Africa as a metaphysical battlefield devoid of all recognizable humanity, into which the wandering European enters at his peril. Of course, there is a preposterous and perverse kind of arrogance in thus reducing Africa to the role of props for the breakup of one petty European mind. But that is not even the point. The real question is the dehumanization of Africa and Africans which this age-long attitude has fostered and continues to foster in the world. And the question is whether a novel which celebrates this dehumanization, which depersonalizes a portion of the human race, can be called a great work of art. My answer is: No, it cannot. I would not call that man an artist, for example, who composes an eloquent instigation to one people to fall upon another and destroy them. No matter how striking his imagery or how beautiful his cadences, such a man is no more a great artist than another may be called a priest who reads the mass backwards or a physician who poisons his patients. All those men in Nazi Germany who lent their talent to the service of virulent racism whether in science, philosophy or the arts have generally and rightly been condemned for their perversions. The time is long overdue for taking a hard look at the work of creative artists who apply their talents, alas often considerable as in the case of Conrad, to set people against people. This, I take it, is what Yevtushenko is after when he tells us that a poet cannot be a slave trader at the same time, and gives the striking example of Arthur Rimbaud who was fortunately honest enough to give up any pretenses to poetry when he opted for slave trading. For poetry surely can only be on the side of man's deliverance and not his enslavement; for the brotherhood and unity of all mankind and against the doctrines of Hitler's master races or Conrad's "rudimentary souls."

Last year was the 50th anniversary of Conrad's death. He was born in 1857, the very year in which the first Anglican missionaries were arriving among my own people in Nigeria. It was certainly not his fault that he lived his life at a time when the reputation of the black man was at a particularly low level. But even after due allowances have been made for all the influences of contemporary prejudice on his sensibility, there remains still in Conrad's attitude a residue of antipathy to black people which his peculiar psychology alone can explain. His own account of his first encounter with a black man is very revealing:

> A certain enormous buck nigger encountered in Haiti fixed my conception of blind, furious, unreasoning rage, as manifested in the human animal to the end of my days. Of the nigger I used to dream for years afterwards.

Certainly, Conrad had a problem with niggers. His inordinate love of that word itself should be of interest to psychoanalysts. Sometimes his fixation on blackness is equally interesting as when he gives us this brief description:

> A black figure stood up, strode on long black legs, waving long black arms.[2]

as though we might expect a black figure striding along on black legs to have *white* arms! But so unrelenting is Conrad's obsession.

As a matter of interest Conrad gives us in *A Personal Record* what amounts to a companion piece to the buck nigger of Haiti. At the age of sixteen Conrad encountered his first Englishman in Europe. He calls him "my unforgettable Englishman" and describes him in the following manner:

> [his] calves exposed to the public gaze...dazzled the beholder by the splendor of their marble-like condition and their rich tone of young ivory...The light of a headlong, exalted satisfaction with the world of men...illumined his face...and triumphant eyes. In passing he cast a glance of kindly curiosity and a friendly gleam of big, sound, shiny teeth...his white calves twinkled sturdily.[3]

Irrational love and irrational hate jostling together in the heart of that tormented man. But whereas irrational love may at worst engender foolish acts of indiscretion, irrational hate can endanger the life of the community. Naturally, Conrad is a dream for psychoanalytic critics. Perhaps the most detailed study of him in this direction is by Bernard C. Meyer, MD. In this lengthy book, Dr. Meyer follows every conceivable lead (and sometimes inconceivable ones) to explain Conrad. As an example, he gives us long disquisitions on the significance of hair and hair-cutting in Conrad. And yet not even one word is spared for his attitude to black people. Not even the discussion of Conrad's antisemitism was enough to spark off in Dr. Meyer's mind those other dark and explosive thoughts. Which only leads one to surmise that Western psychoanalysts must regard the kind of racism displayed by Conrad as absolutely normal despite the profoundly important work done by Frantz Fanon in the psychiatric hospitals of French Algeria.

Whatever Conrad's problems were, you might say he is now safely dead. Quite true. Unfortunately, his heart of darkness plagues us still. Which is why an offensive and totally deplorable book can be described by a serious scholar as "among the half dozen greatest short novels in the English language," and why it is today perhaps the most commonly prescribed novel in the twentieth-century literature courses in our own English Department here. Indeed the time is long overdue for a hard look at things.

There are two probable grounds on which what I have said so far may be contested. The first is that it is no concern of fiction to please people about whom it is written. I will go along with that. But I am not talking about pleasing people. I am talking about a book which parades in the most vulgar fashion prejudices and insults from which a section of mankind has suffered untold agonies and atrocities in the past and continues to do so in many ways and many places today. I am talking about a story in which the very humanity of black people is called in question. It seems to me totally inconceivable that great art or even good art could possibly reside in such unwholesome surroundings.

Secondly, I may be challenged on the grounds of actuality. Conrad, after all, sailed down the Congo in 1890 when my own father was still a babe in arms, and recorded what he saw. How could I stand up in 1975, fifty years after his death and purport to contradict him? My answer is that as a sensible man I will not accept just any traveller's tales solely on the grounds that I have not made the journey myself. I will not trust the evidence even of a man's very eyes when I suspect them to be as jaundiced as Conrad's. And we also happen to know that Conrad was, in the words of his biographer, Bernard C. Meyer, "notoriously inaccurate in the rendering of his own history."[4]

But more important by far is the abundant testimony about Conrad's savages which we could gather if we were so inclined from other sources and which might lead us to think that these people must have had other occupations besides merging into the evil forest or materializing out of it simply to plague Marlow and his dispirited band. For as it happened, soon after Conrad had written his book an event of far greater consequence was taking place in the art world of Europe. This is how Frank Willett, a British art historian, describes it:

> Gaugin had gone to Tahiti, the most extravagant individual act of turning to a non-European culture in the decades immediately before and after 1900, when European artists were avid for new artistic experiences, but it was only about 1904–5 that African art began to make its distinctive impact. One piece is still identifiable; it is a mask that had been given to Maurice Vlaminck in 1905. He records that Derain was "speechless" and "stunned" when he saw it, bought it from Vlaminck and in turn showed it to Picasso and Matisse, who were also greatly affected by it. Ambroise Vollard then borrowed it and had it cast in bronze . . . The revolution of twentieth century art was under way![5]

The mask in question was made by other savages living just north of Conrad's River Congo. They have a name, the Fang people, and are without a doubt among the world's greatest masters of the sculptured form. As you might have guessed, the event to which Frank Willett refers marked the beginning of cubism and the infusion of new life into European art that had run completely out of strength.

The point of all this is to suggest that Conrad's picture of the people of the Congo seems grossly inadequate even at the height of their subjection to the ravages of King

Leopold's International Association for the Civilization of Central Africa. Travellers with closed minds can tell us little except about themselves. But even those not blinkered, like Conrad, with xenophobia, can be astonishingly blind.

Let me digress a little here. One of the greatest and most intrepid travellers of all time, Marco Polo, journeyed to the Far East from the Mediterranean in the thirteenth century and spent twenty years in the court of Kublai Khan in China. On his return to Venice he set down in his book entitled *Description of the World* his impressions of the peoples and places and customs he had seen. There are at least two extraordinary omissions in his account. He says nothing about the art of printing unknown as yet in Europe but in full flower in China. He either did not notice it at all or if he did, failed to see what use Europe could possibly have for it. Whatever reason, Europe had to wait another hundred years for Gutenberg. But even more spectacular was Marco Polo's omission of any reference to the Great Wall of China nearly 4,000 miles long and already more than 1,000 years old at the time of his visit. Again, he may not have seen it; but the Great Wall of China is the only structure built by man which is visible from the moon![6] Indeed, travellers can be blind.

As I said earlier, Conrad did not originate the image of Africa which we find in his book. It was and is the dominant image of Africa in the Western imagination and Conrad merely brought the peculiar gifts of his own mind to bear on it. For reasons which can certainly use close psychological inquiry, the West seems to suffer deep anxieties about the precariousness of its civilization and to have a need for constant reassurance by comparing it with Africa. If Europe, advancing in civilization, could cast a backward glance periodically at Africa trapped in primordial barbarity, it could say with faith and feeling: There go I but for the grace of God. Africa is to Europe as the picture is to Dorian Gray – a carrier onto whom the master unloads his physical and moral deformities so that he may go forward, erect and immaculate. Consequently, Africa is something to be avoided just as the picture has to be hidden away to safeguard the man's jeopardous integrity. Keep away from Africa, or else! Mr. Kurtz of *Heart of Darkness* should have heeded that warning and the prowling horror in his heart would have kept its place, chained to its lair. But he foolishly exposed himself to the wild irresistible allure of the jungle and lo! the darkness found him out.

In my original conception of this talk I had thought to conclude it nicely on an appropriately positive note in which I would suggest from my privileged position in African and Western culture some advantages the West might derive from Africa once it rid its mind of old prejudices and began to look at Africa not through a haze of distortions and cheap mystification but quite simply as a continent of people – not angels, but not rudimentary souls either – just people, often highly gifted people and often strikingly successful in their enterprise with life and society. But as I thought more about the stereotype image, about its grip and pervasiveness, about the willful tenacity with which the West holds it to its heart; when I thought of your television and the cinema and newspapers, about books read in schools and out of school, of churches preaching to empty pews about the need to send help to the heathen in Africa, I realized that no easy optimism was possible. And there is something totally wrong in offering bribes to the West in return for its good opinion of Africa. Ultimately, the abandonment of unwholesome thoughts must be its own and only reward. Although I have used the word *willful* a few times in this talk to characterize the West's view of Africa, it may well be that what is happening at this stage is more akin to reflex action than calculated malice. Which does not make the situation more, but less, hopeful. Let me give you one last and really minor example of what I mean.

Last November the *Christian Science Monitor* carried an interesting article written by its Education Editor on the serious psychological and learning problems faced by little children who speak one language at home and then go to school where something else is spoken. It was a wide-ranging article taking in Spanish-speaking children in this country, the children of migrant Italian workers in Germany, the quadrilingual phenomenon in Malaysia and so on. And all this while the article speaks unequivocally about *language*. But then out of the blue sky comes this:

> In London there is an enormous immigration of children who speak Indian or Nigerian dialects, or some other native language.[7]

I believe that the introduction of *dialects*, which is technically erroneous in the context, is almost a reflex action caused by an instinctive desire of the writer to downgrade the discussion to the level of Africa and India. And this is quite comparable to Conrad's withholding of language from his rudimentary souls. Language is too grand for these chaps; let's give them dialects. In all this business a lot of violence is inevitably done to words and their meaning. Look at the phrase "native language" in the above excerpt. Surely the only native language possible in London is Cockney English. But our writer obviously means something else – something Indians and Africans speak.

Perhaps a change will come. Perhaps this is the time when it can begin, when the high optimism engendered by the breathtaking achievements of Western science and industry is giving way to doubt and even confusion. There is just the possibility that Western man may begin to look seriously at the achievements of other people. I read in the papers the other day a suggestion that what America needs at this time is somehow to bring back the extended family. And I saw in my mind's eye future African Peace Corps Volunteers coming to help you set up the system.

Seriously, although the work which needs to be done may appear too daunting, I believe that it is not one day too soon to begin. And where better than at a University?

NOTES

This paper was given as a Chancellor's Lecture at the University of Massachusetts, Amherst, February 18, 1975.

1   Albert J. Guerard, Introduction to *Heart of Darkness* (New York: New American Library, 1950), p. 9.
2   Jonah Raskin, *The Mythology of Imperialism* (New York: Random House, 1971), p. 143.
3   Bernard C. Meyer, MD, *Joseph Conrad: A Psychoanalytic Biography* (Princeton, NJ: Princeton University Press, 1967), p. 30.
4   Ibid. p. 30.

5   Frank Willett, *African Art* (New York: Praeger, 1971), pp. 35–6.
6   About the omission of the Great Wall of China I am indebted to *The Journey of Marco Polo* as recreated by artist Michael Foreman, published by *Pegasus* Magazine, 1974.
7   *Christian Science Monitor*, Nov. 25, 1974, p. 11.

African Identities

KWAME ANTHONY APPIAH

Kwame Anthony Appiah has emerged as an important voice in postcolonial theory, in large part because of his desire to focus theoretical and philosophical attention on the "cultural life of black Africa." This essay concludes his influential book, *In My Father's House: Africa in the Philosophy of Culture*, in which the historical and "topological" specificities of African culture are analyzed within the larger context of international politics. As with so many of the essays in this *Anthology*, Appiah's is concerned with the problems of identity and agency and the need to find for both "securer foundations than race." Drawing on the ground-breaking work of **Chinua Achebe**, Appiah considers the problem of negotiating the various ethnic identities within African nations in a context of broader inter-national and postcolonial concerns. However, while biological theories of race are inadequate paradigms for constructing social and political consensus among com-peting identities in Africa, some form of consensus is need, some form of "Pan-Africanism" that will prevent the "divide and conquer" tactics that typify both colonialist and neocolonialist thinking. Like **Neil Lazarus** in his essay on "Afro-pop," Appiah calls for modes of unity and consensus that do not presuppose the common denominator of race or ethnicity. The student will find that for both it is precisely cultural practices – coalition-building, mutual interdependence, and cultural dialogue – that offer the best models of African unity. Reading Appiah alongside **Achebe**, **George Lamming**, **Stuart Hall**, and **Luke Gibbons** will afford the student an opportunity to study the role of race in colonialism from a number of different points of view.

African Identities

"It is, of course, true that the African identity is still in the making. There isn't a final identity that is African. But, at the same time, there *is* an identity coming into existence. And it has a certain context and a certain meaning. Because if somebody meets me, say, in a shop in Cambridge, he says, "Are you from Africa?" Which means that Africa means something to some people. Each of these tags has a meaning, and a penalty and a responsibility."[1]

Chinua Achebe

The cultural life of black Africa remained largely unaffected by European ideas until the last years of the nineteenth century; and most cultures began our own century with ways of life formed very little by direct contact with Europe. Direct trade with Europeans – and especially the slave trade – had structured the economies of many of the states of the West African coast and its hinterland from the mid-seventeenth century onwards, replacing the extensive gold trade which had existed at least since the Carthaginian empire in the second century BC. By the early nineteenth century, as the slave trade went into decline, palmnut and groundnut oils had become major exports to Europe, and these were followed later by cocoa and coffee. But the direct colonisation of the region began in earnest only in the later nineteenth century; and European administration of the whole of West Africa was only accomplished – after much resistance – when the Sokoto caliphate was conquered in 1903.

On the Indian ocean, the eastward trade, which sent gold and slaves to Arabia, and exchanged spices, incense, ivory, coconut oil, timber, grain and pig iron for Indian silk and fine textiles, and pottery and porcelain from Persia and China, had dominated the economies of the East African littoral until the coming of the Portuguese disrupted the trade in the late fifteenth century. From then on European trade became increasingly predominant, but in the mid-nineteenth century the major economic force in the region was the Arab Omanis who had captured Mombasa from the Portuguese more than a century earlier. Using slave labour from the African mainland, the Omanis developed the profitable clove trade of Zanzibar, making it, by the 1860s, the world's major producer. But in most of East Africa, as in the West, extended direct contact with Europeans was a late nineteenth-century phenomenon; and colonisation occurred essentially only after 1885.

Taken from *In My Father's House: Africa in the Philosophy of Culture* (London: Methuen, 1992).

In the South of the continent, in the areas where Bantu-speaking people predominate, few cultures had had any contact with Europeans before 1900: by the end of the century the region had adopted many new crops for the world economy, imports of fire-arms, manufactured in the newly industrialised West, had created a new political order, based often on force, and European missionaries and explorers – of whom David Livingstone was, for Westerners, the epitome – had travelled almost everywhere in the region. The administration of Southern Africa from Europe was established in law only by the ending, in 1902, of the Boer War.

Not surprisingly, then, European cultural influence in Africa before the twentieth century was extremely limited. Deliberate attempts at change – through missionary activity or the establishment of Western schools – and unintended influence – through contact with explorers and colonisers in the interior, and trading posts on the coasts – produced small enclaves of Europeanised Africans; but the major cultural impact of Europe is largely a product of the period since the First World War.

To understand the variety of Africa's contemporary cultures, therefore, we need, first, to recall the variety of the pre-colonial cultures. Differences in colonial experience have also played their part in shaping the continent's diversities; but even identical colonial policies identically implemented working on the very different cultural materials would surely have produced widely varying results.

No doubt we can find generalisations at a certain abstract level, which hold true of most of black Africa before European conquest. It is a familiar idea in African historiography that Africa was the last continent in the old world with an "uncaptured" peasantry, largely able to use land without the supervision of feudal overlords and able, if they chose, to market their products through a complex system of trading networks.[2] While European ruling classes were living off the surplus of peasants and the newly developing industrial working class, African rulers were essentially living off taxes on trade. But if we could have travelled through Africa's many cultures in those years – from the small groups of Bushman hunter-gatherers, with their stone-age materials, to the Hausa kingdoms, rich in worked metal – we should have felt in every place profoundly different impulses, ideas and forms of life. To speak of an African identity in the nineteenth century – if an identity is a coalescence of mutually responsive (if sometimes conflicting) modes of conduct, habits of thought, and patterns of evaluation; in short a coherent kind of human social psychology – would have been "to give to aery nothing a local habitation and a name".

Yet there is no doubt that now, a century later, an African identity is coming into being. I have argued throughout [*In My Father's House*] that this identity is a new thing; that it is the product of a history some of whose moments I have sketched; and that the bases through which it has largely so far been theorised – race, a common historical experience, a shared metaphysics – presuppose falsehoods too serious for us to ignore.

Every human identity is constructed, historical; every one has its share of false presuppositions, of the errors and inaccuracies that courtesy calls "myth", religion "heresy", and science "magic". Invented histories, invented biologies, invented cultural affinities come with every identity; each is a kind of role that has to be scripted, structured by conventions of narrative to which the world never quite manages to conform.

Often those who say this – who deny the biological reality of races or the literal truth of our national fictions – are treated by nationalists and "race-men" as if they are proposing genocide or the destruction of nations, as if in saying that there is literally no Negro race one was obliterating all those who claim to be Negroes, in doubting the story of Okomfo Anokye one is repudiating the Asante nation. This is an unhelpful hyperbole; but it is certainly true that there must be contexts in which a statement of these truths is politically inopportune. I am enough of a scholar to feel drawn to truth-telling, though the heavens fall; enough of a political animal to recognise that there are places where the truth does more harm than good.

But, so far as I can see, we do not have to choose between these impulses: there is no reason to believe that racism is always – or even usually – advanced by denying the existence of races; and, though there is some reason to suspect that those who resist legal remedies for the history of racism might use the non-existence of races to argue in the United States, for example, against affirmative action, that strategy is, as a matter of logic, easily opposed. For, as Tzvetan Todorov reminds us, the existence of racism does not require the existence of races; and, we can add, nations are real enough, however invented their traditions.[3]

To raise the issue of whether these truths are truths to be uttered is to be forced, however, to face squarely the real political question: the question, itself as old as political philosophy, of when we should endorse the ennobling lie. In the real world of practical politics, of everyday alliances and popular mobilisations, a rejection of races and nations in theory can be part of a programme for coherent political practice, only if we can show more than that the Black race – or the Shona tribe or any of the other modes of self-invention that Africa has inherited – fits the common pattern of relying on less than the literal truth. We would need to show not that race and national history are falsehoods, but that they are useless falsehoods at best or – at worst – dangerous ones: that another set of stories will build us identities through which we can make more productive alliances.

The problem, of course, is that group identity seems to work only – or, at least, to work best – when it is seen by its members as natural; as "real". Pan-Africanism, black solidarity, can be an important force with real political benefits; but it doesn't work without its attendant mystifications. (Nor, to turn to the other obvious example, is feminism without its occasional risks and mystifications either.) Recognising the constructedness of the history of identities has seemed to many incompatible with taking these new identities with the seriousness they have for those who invent – or, as they would no doubt rather say, discover – and possess them.[4] In sum, the demands of agency seem always – in the real world of politics – to *entail a misrecognition of its genesis*; you cannot build alliances without mystifications and mythologies. And this chapter is an exploration of ways in which what is productive in Pan-African solidarity can be fruitfully understood by those of us whose positions as intellectuals – as searchers after truth – make it impossible for us to live through the falsehoods of race and tribe and nation; and whose understanding of history makes us sceptical that nationalism and racial solidarity can do the good that they can do without the attendant evils of racism – and other particularisms; without the warring of nations.

Where are we to start? I have argued often in [*In My Father's House*] against the forms of racism implicit in much talk of Pan-Africanism. (And in other places, especially in "Racisms" and "Racism and Moral Pollution", I have offered further arguments against these racist presuppositions.) But these objections to a biologically-rooted conception of race may still seem all too theoretical: if Africans can get together around the idea of the Black Person, if they can create through this notion productive alliances with African-Americans and people of African descent in Europe and the Caribbean, surely these theoretical objections should pale in the light of the practical value of these alliances. But there is every reason to doubt that they can. Within Africa – in the OAU, in the Sudan, in Mauritania[5] – racialisation has produced arbitrary boundaries and exacerbated tensions; in the Diaspora alliances with other peoples of colour, *as* victims of racism – people of South Asian descent in England, Hispanics in the United States, "Arabs" in France, Turks in Germany – have proved essential.

In short, I think it is clear enough that a biologically-rooted conception of race is both dangerous in practice and misleading in theory: African unity, African identity, need securer foundations than race.

The passage from Achebe with which I began this essay continues in these words: "All these tags, unfortunately for the black man, are tags of disability." But it seems to me that they are not so much labels of disability as disabling labels; which is, in essence, my complaint against Africa as a racial mythology – the Africa of Crummell and Du Bois (from the New World) and of the *bolekaja* critics (from the Old); against Africa as a shared metaphysics – the Africa of Soyinka; against Africa as a fancied past of shared glories – the Africa of Diop and the "Egyptianists".

Each of these complaints can be summarised in a paragraph.

"Race" disables us because it proposes as a basis for common action the illusion that black (and white and yellow) people are fundamentally allied by nature and, thus, without effort; it leaves us unprepared, therefore, to handle the "intra-racial" conflicts that arise from the very different situations of black (and white and yellow) people in different parts of the economy and of the world.

The African metaphysics of Soyinka disables us because it founds our unity in gods who have not served us well in our dealings with the world – Soyinka never defends the African World against Wiredu's charge that since people die daily in Ghana because they prefer traditional herbal remedies to Western medicines, "any inclination to glorify the unanalytical [i.e. the traditional] cast of mind is not just retrograde; it is tragic". Soyinka has proved the Yoruba pantheon a powerful literary resource: but he cannot explain why Christianity and Islam have so widely displaced the old gods, or why an image of the West has so powerful a hold on the contemporary Yoruba imagination; nor can his myth-making offer us the resources for creating economies and polities adequate to our various places in the world.

And the Egyptianists – like all who have chosen to root Africa's modern identity in an imaginary history – require us to see the past as the moment of wholeness and unity; tie us to the values and beliefs of the past; and thus divert us (this critique is as old as Césaire's appraisal of Tempels) from the problems of the present and the hopes of the future.

If an African identity is to empower us, so it seems to me, what is required is not so much that we throw out falsehood but that we acknowledge first of all that race and history and metaphysics do not enforce an identity: that we can choose, within broad limits set by ecological, political and economic realities, what it will mean to be African in the coming years.

I do not want to be misunderstood. We are Africans already. And we can give numerous examples from multiple domains of what our being African means. We have, for example, in the Organisation of African Unity and the African Development Bank, and in such regional organisations as the Southern African Development Coordination Conference (SADCC) and the Economic Community of West African States (ECOWAS), as well as in the African caucuses of the agencies of the United Nations and the World Bank, African institutions. At the Olympics and the Commonwealth games, athletes from African countries are seen as Africans by the world – and, perhaps, more importantly, by each other. Being-African already has "a certain context and a certain meaning".

But, as Achebe suggests, that meaning is not always one we can be happy with; and that identity is one we must continue to reshape. And in thinking about how we are to reshape it, we would do well to remember that the African identity is, for its bearers, only one among many. Like all identities, institutionalised before anyone has permanently fixed a single meaning for them – like the German identity at the beginning of this century, or the American in the latter eighteenth century, or the Indian identity at independence so few years ago – being-African is, for its bearers, one among other salient models of being, all of which have to be constantly fought for and refought. And indeed, in Africa, it is another of these identities that provides one of the most useful models for such rethinking; it is a model that draws on other identities central to contemporary life in the sub-continent, namely, the constantly shifting redefinition of "tribal" identities to meet the economic and political exigencies of the modern world.

Once more, let me quote Achebe:

> The duration of awareness, of consciousness of an identity, has really very little to do with how deep it is. You can suddenly become aware of an identity which you have been suffering from for a long time without knowing. For instance, take the Igbo people. In my area, historically, they did not see themselves as Igbo. They saw themselves as people from this village or that village. In fact in some places "Igbo" was a word of abuse; they were the "other" people, down in the bush. And yet, after the experience of the Biafran War, during a period of two years, it became a very powerful consciousness. But it was *real* all the time. They all spoke the same language, called "Igbo", even though they were not using that identity in any way. But the moment came when this identity became very very powerful ... and over a very short period.

A short period it was; and also a tragic one. The Nigerian Civil War defined an Igbo identity: it did so in complex ways, which grew out of the development of a common Igbo identity in colonial Europe, an identity which created the Igbo traders in the cities of Northern Nigeria as an identifiable object of assault in the period that led up to the invention of Biafra.

Recognising Igbo identity as a new thing is not a way of privileging other Nigerian identities: each of the three central ethnic identities of modern political life – Hausa-

Fulani, Yoruba, Igbo – is a product of the rough-and-tumble of the transition through colonial to postcolonial status. David Laitin has pointed out that "[t]he idea that there was a single Hausa-Fulani tribe ... was largely a political claim of the NPC [Northern Peoples' Congress] in their battle against the South" while "[m]any elders intimately involved in rural Yoruba society today recall that, as late as the 1930s, 'Yoruba' was not a common form of political identification".[6] Nnamdi Azikiwe – one of the key figures in the construction of Nigerian nationalism – was extremely popular (as Laitin also points out) in Yoruba Lagos, where "he edited his nationalist newspaper, the *West African Pilot*. It was only subsequent events that led him to be defined in Nigeria as an *Igbo* leader."[7] Yet Nigerian politics – and the more everyday economy of ordinary personal relations – is oriented along such axes; and only very occasionally does the fact float into view that even these three problematic identities account for at most seven out of ten Nigerians.

And the story is repeated, even in places where it was not drawn in lines of blood. As Johannes Fabian has observed, the powerful Lingala and Swahili-speaking identities of modern Zaire exist "because spheres of political and economic interest were established before the Belgians took full control, and continued to inform relations between regions under colonial rule".[8] Modern Ghana witnesses the development of an Akan identity, as speakers of the three major regional dialects of Twi – Asante, Fante, Akuapem – organise themselves into a corporation against an (equally novel) Ewe unity.[9]

When it is not the "tribe" that is invested with new uses and meanings it is religion. Yet the idea that Nigeria is composed of a Muslim North, a Christian South and a mosaic of "pagan" holdovers is as inaccurate as the picture of three historic tribal identities. Two out of every five Southern Yoruba people are Muslim; and, as Laitin tells us: "[M]any northern groups, especially in what are today Benue, Plateau, Gongola, and Kwara states, are largely Christian. When the leaders of Biafra tried to convince the world that they were oppressed by northern Muslims, ignorant foreigners (including the pope) believed them. But the Nigerian army ... was led by a northern Christian."[10] It is as useless here as in the case of race to point out in each case that the tribe or the religion is, like all social identities, based on an idealising fiction, for life in Nigeria or in Zaire has come to be lived through that idealisation: the Igbo identity is real because Nigerians believe in it, the Shona identity because Zimbabweans have given it meaning. The rhetoric of a Muslim North and a Christian South structured political discussions in the period before Nigerian independence; but it was equally important in the debates about instituting a Muslim Court of Appeals in the Draft Constitution of 1976; and it could be found, for example, in many an article in the Nigerian press as electoral registration for a new civilian era began in July 1989.

There are, I think, three crucial lessons to be learned from these cases. First, that identities are complex and multiple and grow out of a history of changing responses to economic, political and cultural forces, almost always in opposition to other identities. Second, that they flourish despite what I earlier called our "misrecognition" of their origins; despite, that is, their roots in myths and in lies. And third, that there is, in consequence, no large place for reason in the construction – as opposed to the study and the management – of identities. One temptation, then, for those who see the centrality of these fictions in our lives is to leave reason behind: to celebrate and endorse those identities that seem at the moment to offer the best hope of advancing our other goals, and to keep silence about the lies and the myths. But, as I said earlier, intellectuals do not easily neglect the truth, and, all things considered, our societies profit, in my view, from the institutionalisation of this imperative in the academy. So it is important for us to continue trying to tell our truths. But the facts I have been rehearsing should imbue us all with a strong sense of the marginality of such work to the central issue of the resistance to racism and ethnic violence – and to sexism, and to the other structures of difference that shape the world of power; and they should force upon us the clear realisation that the real battle is not being fought in the academy. Every time I read another report in the newspapers of an African disaster – a famine in Ethiopia, a war in Namibia, ethnic conflict in Burundi – I wonder how much good it does to correct the theories with which these evils are bound up; the solution is food, or mediation, or some other more material, more practical step. And yet, as I have tried to argue in [*In My Father's House*], the shape of modern Africa (the shape of our world) is in large part the product, often the unintended and unanticipated product, of theories; even the most vulgar of Marxists will have to admit that economic interests operate *through* ideologies. We cannot change the world simply by evidence and reasoning, but we surely cannot change it without them either.

What we in the academy *can* contribute – even if only slowly and marginally – is a disruption of the discourse of "racial" and "tribal" differences. For, in my perfectly unoriginal opinion, the reality of these many competing identities in Africa today plays into the hands of the very exploiters whose shackles we are trying to escape. "Race" in Europe and "tribe" in Africa are central to the way in which the objective interests of the worst-off are distorted. The analogous point for African-Americans was recognised long ago by Du Bois.[11] Du Bois argued in *Black Reconstruction* that racist ideology had essentially blocked the formation of a significant labour movement in the US; for such a movement would have required the collaboration of the nine million ex-slave and white peasant workers of the South.[12] It is, in other words, because the categories of difference often cut across our economic interests that they operate to blind us to them. What binds the middle-class African-American to his dark-skinned fellow-citizens down-town is not economic interest but racism and the cultural products of resistance to it that are shared across (most of) African-American culture.

It seems to me that we learn from this case what John Thompson has argued recently, in a powerful but appreciative critique of Pierre Bourdieu: namely, that it may be a mistake to think that social reproduction – the processes by which societies maintain themselves over time – presupposes "some sort of consensus with regard to dominant values or norms". Rather, the stability of today's industrialised society may require "a pervasive *fragmentation* of the social order and a proliferation of divisions between its members". For it is precisely this fragmentation that prevents oppositional attitudes from generating "a coherent alternative view which would provide a basis for political action". "Divisions are ramified along the lines of gender, race, qualifications and so on, forming barriers which obstruct the development of movements which could threaten the *status quo*. The reproduction of the social order may depend less upon a consensus with regard to dominant values or norms than upon a *lack of consensus* at the very point where oppositional attitudes could be translated into political action."[13]

Thompson allows us to see that within contemporary industrial societies an identification of oneself as an African, above all else, allows the fact that one is, say, not an Asian, to be used against one; and in this setting – as we see in South Africa – a racialised conception of one's identity is retrogressive. To argue this way is to presuppose that the political meanings of identities are historically and geographically relative. So it is quite consistent with this claim to hold, as I do, that in constructing alliances *across* states – and especially in the Third World – a Pan-African identity – that allows African-Americans, Afro-Caribbeans and Afro-Latins to ally with continental Africans, drawing on the cultural resources of the Black Atlantic world – may serve useful purposes. Resistance to a self-isolating black nationalism *within* England or France or the United States is thus theoretically consistent with Pan-Africanism as an international project.

Because the value of identities is thus relative, we must argue for and against them case by case. And given the current situation in Africa, I think it remains clear that another Pan-Africanism – the project of a continental fraternity and sorority, *not* the project of a racialised Negro nationalism – however false or muddled its theoretical roots, can be a progressive force. It is as fellow Africans that Ghanaian diplomats (my father among them) interceded between the warring nationalist parties in Rhodesia under UDI; as fellow Africans that OAU teams can mediate regional conflicts; as fellow Africans that the human rights assessors organised under the OAU's Banjul Declaration can intercede for citizens of African states against the excesses of our governments. If there is, as I have suggested, hope, too, for the Pan-Africanism of an African Diaspora, once it, too, is released from bondage to racial ideologies (alongside the many bases of alliance available to Africa's peoples in their political and cultural struggles), it is crucial that we recognise the independence, once "Negro" nationalism is gone, of the Pan-Africanism of the Diaspora and the Pan-Africanism of the continent. It is, I believe, in the exploration of these issues, these possibilities, that the future of an intellectually reinvigorated Pan-Africanism lies.

Finally, I would like to suggest that it is really unsurprising that a continental identity is coming into cultural and institutional reality through regional and sub-regional organisations. We share a continent and its ecological problems; we share a relation of dependency to the world economy; we share the problem of racism in the way the industrialised world thinks of us (and let me include here, explicitly, both "Negro" Africa and the "Maghreb"); we share the possibilities of the development of regional markets and local circuits of production; and our intellectuals participate, through the shared contingencies of our various histories, in a discourse whose outlines I have tried to limn in [*In My Father's House*].

"Ɔdɛnkyɛm nwu nsuo-ase mma yɛmmɛfrɛ kwakuo sɛ ɔbɛyɛ no ayie," goes an Akan proverb: the crocodile does not die under the water so that we can call the monkey to celebrate its funeral. Each of us, the proverb can be used to say, belongs to a group with its own customs. To accept that Africa can be in these ways a usable identity is not to forget that all of us belong to multifarious communities with their local customs; it is not to dream of a single African state and to forget the complexly different trajectories of the continent's so many languages and cultures. "African" can surely be a vital and enabling badge; but in a world of genders, ethnicities, classes and languages, of ages, families, professions, religions and nations, it is hardly surprising that there are times when it is not the label we need.

NOTES

1 Interview with Anthony Appiah, D. A. N. Jones and John Ryle. In *Times Literary Supplement*. 26 February 1982. (Some passages cited in the text are from my own unpublished transcription of the full interview, which was edited for this briefer published version.)

2 See, for example, Robert Harms, *Times Literary Supplement* 29 November 1985, p. 1343.

3 Tzvetan Todorov, "'Race', Writing and Culture". In Henry Louis Gates, Jr., ed., *Race Writing and Difference*, Chicago: University of Chicago Press, 1986, pp. 370–80. You don't have to believe in witchcraft, after all, to believe that women were persecuted as witches in colonial Massachusetts.

4 Gayatri Spivak recognises these problems when she speaks of "strategic" essentialisms. See p. 205 of her *In Other Worlds: Essays in Cultural Politics*, New York: Methuen, 1987.

5 The violence between Senegalese and Mauritanians in the spring of 1989 can only be understood when we recall that the legal abolition of racial slavery of "Negroes", owned by "Moorish" masters, occurred in the early 1980s.

6 David Laitin, *Hegemony and Culture: Politics and Religious Change Among the Yoruba*, Chicago: University of Chicago Press, 1986, pp. 7–8.

7 Laitin, *Hegemony and Culture: Politics and Religious Change Among the Yoruba*, p. 8.

8 This passage continues: "Increasingly also Lingala and Swahili came to divide functions between them. Lingala served the military and much of the administration in the capital of the lower Congo; Swahili became the language of the workers in the mines of Katanga. This created cultural connotations which began to emerge very early and which remained prevalent in Mobutu's Zaire. From the point of view of Katanga / Shaba, Lingala has been the undignified jargon of unproductive soldiers, government clerks, entertainers, and, recently of a power clique, all of them designated as *batoka chini*, people from downriver, i.e. from Kinshasa. Swahili as spoken in Katanga was a symbol of regionalism, even for those colonials who spoke it badly." Johannes Fabian, *Language and Colonial Power*, Cambridge: Cambridge University Press, 1986, pp. 42–3. The dominance of Swahili in certain areas is already itself a colonial product. (*Language and Colonial Power*, p. 6.)

9 Similarly, Shona and Ndebele identities in modern Zimbabwe became associated with political parties at independence, even though Shona-speaking peoples had spent much of the late pre-colonial period in military confrontations with each other.

10 Laitin, *Hegemony and Culture: Politics and Religious Change Among the Yoruba*, p. 8. I need hardly add that religious identities are equally salient and equally mythological in Lebanon or in Ireland.

11 That "race" operates this way has been clear to many other African-Americans: so, for example, it shows up in a fictional context as a central theme of George Schuyler's *Black No More*, New York: Negro Universities Press, 1931; see, for example, p. 59. Du Bois (as usual) provides – in *Black Reconstruction*, New York: Harcourt, Brace and Co., 1935 – a body of evidence that remains relevant. As Cedric Robinson writes, "Once the industrial class emerged as dominant in the nation, it possessed not only its own basis of power and the social relations historically related to that power, but it also had available to it the instruments of repression created by the now subordinate Southern ruling class. In its

struggle with labour, it could activate racism to divide the labour movement into antagonistic forces. Moreover, the permutations of the instrument appeared endless: Black against white; Anglo-Saxon against southern and eastern European; domestic against immigrant; proletariat against share-cropper; white American against Asian, Black, Latin American, etc." Cedric Robinson, *Black Marxism: The Making of the Black Radical Tradition*, London: Zed Books, 1983, p. 286.

12   Robinson, *Black Marxism: The Making of the Black Radical Tradition*, p. 313.

13   John B. Thompson, *Studies in the Theory of Ideology*, Berkeley: University of California Press, 1984, pp. 62–3. Again and again, in American labour history, we can document the ways in which conflicts organised around a racial or ethnic group identity can be captured by the logic of the existing order. The financial support that Black Churches in Detroit received from the Ford Motor Company in the 1930s was only a particularly dramatic example of a widespread phenomenon: corporate manipulation of racial difference in an effort to defeat labour solidarity. See, for example, James S. Olson, "Race, Class and Progress: Black Leadership and Industrial Unionism, 1936–1945", in M. Cantor, ed., *Black Labor in America*, Westport, CT: Negro Universities Press, 1969, pp. 153–64; and David M. Gordon, Richard Edwards and Michael Reich, *Segmented Work, Divided Workers: The Historical Transformation of Labor in the United States*, Cambridge: Cambridge University Press, 1982, pp. 141–3; and Fredric Jameson, *The Political Unconscious*, Ithaca: Cornell University Press, 1981, p. 54.

"Unsystematic Fingers at the Conditions of the Times": "Afropop" and the Paradoxes of Imperialism

NEIL LAZARUS

Neil Lazarus is one of the most respected postcolonial critics writing about Africa. His *Resistance in Postcolonial African Fiction* was instrumental in bringing African fiction to the attention of Western readers. The essay reproduced here extends his interests in African culture to the realm of popular music and the revolutionary ideas of collectivity and indigenization that colonialism, inadvertently but inevitably, creates. Following **Frantz Fanon**'s warning in *The Wretched of the Earth*, Lazarus, like **Peter Hulme and Declan Kiberd**, resists the temptation to pit an "idealist" theory of indigenization against invidious concepts of an essentialized "native." The object, for him, is not to forget the abuses of imperialism (and neo-imperialism) in the celebration of a spurious unity of "tribal" voices. He urges the student to be aware of the "reach" of imperialism, while avoiding the defeatist tendency to see its reach as total. The student will find that Lazarus's discussion of popular African music affords a rich context in which to discuss the interventions of imperialism and neo-imperialism – interventions that at first glance appear to be gestures of solidarity. The example of Paul Simon's *Graceland* and the general phenomenon of "world music" point up not only the tremendous power of neo-imperialist strategies of cultural hegemony but also the equally tremendous power of local articulations of resistance to these strategies that serve at one and the same time to further the aims of "a progressive, internationalist politics." In this regard, Lazarus exemplifies the paradoxical formulation of continuance put forward by **Homi K. Bhabha** in which local action leads to ongoing international relevance in both the cultural and political spheres.

"Unsystematic Fingers at the Conditions of the Times": "Afropop" and the Paradoxes of Imperialism

I would like to begin by referring to a scene from *The Healers*, a novel by the Ghanaian writer Ayi Kwei Armah. Published in 1978, *The Healers* offers a perspective on the collapse of Ashanti power and the formal institution of British colonial rule in Ghana in the 1870s. The novel's final scene describes an official ceremony, as the ranks of the British forces against the Ashanti, composed overwhelmingly of African conscripts drawn from the entire region of West Africa, are marshaled to attend the departure for England of the victorious British general Wolseley. Here is how the novel ends:

> West Indian soldiers had come with [Wolseley] to the bay, with their guns and musical instruments.... [They] played solemn music to send the white general off. But once the ship had disappeared, their playing changed. The stiff, straight, graceless beats of white music vanished. Instead, there was a new, skilful, strangely happy interweaving of rhythms, and instead of marching back through the streets the soldiers danced. Others joined them.... All the groups gathered by the whites to come and fight for them were there and they all danced.... A grotesque, variegated crowd they made, snaking its way through the town....
>
> "It's the new dance," Ajoa said, shaking her head. She spoke sadly, and her sadness was merely a reflection of the sadness of [the other healers]...as they watched.
>
> But beside them they heard a long, low chuckle of infinite amusement. It came from Ama Nkroma.... "It's a new dance all right," she said, "and it's grotesque. But look at all the black people the whites have brought here. Here we healers have been wondering about ways to bring our people together again. And the whites want ways to drive us farther apart. Does it not amuse you, that in their wish to drive us apart the whites are actually bringing us work for the future? Look!"
>
> Together with Ama Nkroma's laughter, tears came to her eyes.[1]

In two respects this scene is exemplary of the line of argument I want to follow in this chapter. First, there is the recognition, familiar in its structure to any reader of Marx or Fanon or C. L. R. James, that colonialism creates the conditions of possibility of its own overthrow, since it brings the colonized into existence as a collectivity whose objective interests are not only diametrically opposed to those of the colonial

---

Taken from Jonathan White (ed.), *Recasting the World: Writing after Colonialism* (Baltimore: Johns Hopkins University Press, 1993).

state but also incapable of realization on the terrain of colonialism. Second, there is the identification of a latently resistive dynamic of cultural indigenization. The West Indian guard is spoken of as having appropriated "the white men's instruments." Instruments whose normative usage in this context is imperial and militaristic are domesticated and made over, refunctioned to bear the imprint of a different – and, indeed, opposing – cultural logic.

In what follows I would like to speculate further on this subject of indigenization, taking as my primary example the case of popular dance music from contemporary Zimbabwe. Before turning to this music, however, it is necessary to give some preliminary consideration to the concept of indigenization itself and to some of the theoretical and ideological implications of using it in cultural analysis.

Many ethnomusicologists and scholars of African culture would reject in principle the idea of taking as one's object of analysis a compound form such as African pop music. Their argument would be that the putative "Africanity" of this music has been wholly overdetermined and compromised by Western compositional grammars and styles of performance. As Deborah James has recently pointed out, the work of ethnomusicologists of this persuasion "is most often associated with an interest in 'pure' traditional music, and a scorn for hybrid styles or those which have evolved out of the experience of proletarianized communities."[2] James refers especially to Hugh Tracey and his assumptions that "urban African music lacks the formal integrity of its 'traditional' forebears, and that it has been bastardized by its assimilation of Western forms."[3] But similar assumptions are shared by other prominent scholars of African music: the Cameroonian musicologist Francis Bebey, for instance, opens his classic study *African Music: A People's Art* with the pointed definition of "authentic African music" as "the traditional music of the black peoples of Africa."[4] In terms of such a definition, obviously, the popular music of Africa today would be characterized as nontraditional and dismissed as inauthentic.

Several rejoinders to this kind of argument are possible. One can demonstrate, for instance, as David Coplan in the case of South Africa and John Storm Roberts and others in the general case of sub-Saharan Africa have done, that the so-called Western forms by which urban African music has allegedly been compromised are themselves strongly marked by the African forms on which they, in turn, were substantially predicated.[5] The extensive influence of Cuban and Brazilian music on playing styles in West Africa, Angola, and the Congo, for instance, is patently neither coincidental nor the result of any merely contingent factor. Rather, as Roberts notes, it is a function of the direct historical link between these cultures.[6]

Similarly, one can put pressure on the essentialist notion of tradition which ethnomusicologists such as Hugh Tracey and Bebey typically assume. Tracey's son, Andrew, who shares his father's general disapproval of popular and urban styles of African music, has lamented that "in traditional African music these days, you almost never hear the original harmony. There's always someone putting in that third note and you have this sickly-sounding Western harmony all the time."[7] The point here is that the Tracey's idea of a pure traditional African music is resolutely unhistorical. Like all cultural forms everywhere at all times, African music has been ceaselessly in the process of transformation, as it has moved to assimilate, and to accommodate itself to, new sounds, new instruments, new tongues, and new social imperatives. "The 'purity' of third world music" therefore, as Andrew Goodwin and Joe Gore have recently suggested, "must always be questioned not only for dangerous (we would say *racist*) ideological assumptions about the 'authenticity' of non-western cultures, but also for empirical flaws in the argument."[8] To listen – even as an "insider," which I am not – to a Mande song, sung in traditional style with *kora* accompaniment, is not and has never been to encounter unchanging tradition. Rather, it is to grapple, necessarily, with culture as a historical palimpsest: here the phrasing and intonation will be clearly Islamic; here the *kora's* lyrical range will have been influenced by flamenco guitar, or, in the case of a contemporary musician such as Toumani Diabate, by jazz and blues; here the references will be to a specific historical event in the days of the empire of Mali; and so on.

It is instructive, in this context, to listen to the most recent of Salif Keita's albums, *Soro* (Mango, 1987), *Ko-Yan* (Mango, 1989), and *Amen* (Mango, 1991). Keita is a Malian, born into the dynastic Keita family in 1949. Because of his royal birth, his road to musicianship was difficult. As he put it in 1985, in an interview with Chris Stapleton: "I come from a noble family. We are not supposed to become singers. If a noble had anything to say, he had to say it through a griot."[9] Keita's decision to leave school in the late 1960s to become a musician caused an uproar both in his family and in the wider Malian society. Yet, if he was setting his back against a caste system that had been upheld in Mali and elsewhere in West Africa for hundreds of years, he was emphatically not abandoning his cultural roots. The object of his antagonism was not the Mande cultural tradition but, instead, the rigid and uncritical positing of this tradition as a timeless social code: "At home, we are traditionalists. It's an attitude I disapprove of. It's we who make the history, and if we refer only to what has passed, there will be no history. I belong to a century that has little in common with the time of my ancestors. I want society to move."[10]

Keita's lyrics are addressed prescriptively to the arena of contemporary social existence, but they remain scrupulously attentive to Mande history. And the same nuanced and meditative reworking of traditional forms is evident in his musical arrangements, both with the band Les Ambassadeurs and, since 1985, as a solo artist. Built around his astonishingly expressive voice, in which the rhythms of the Bambara language are infused with Islamic and Arabic registers, Salif Keita's music is "powered by horns, keyboards and electric guitars which carry the inflections of kora and balafon music."[11] The total effects, as Nii Yamotei has written, is to provide a "powerful, seamless, and highly sensitive melting pot of influences; transplanting the traditional music of the griots into the present. He has blended in other West African influences from Guinea and Senegal, and influences from Cuba, Spain and Portugal, fusing his traditional vocal themes with modern instruments and style."[12] The album *Soro* was recorded at Studio Harry Son in Paris, on a 48-track digital machine. The title track, "Soro (Afriki)" is operatic in conception and features West African musicians on percussion (trap set drums, congas, *djembes*), guitars and vocals, and French session musicians on saxophone, trumpet, trombone, and keyboards. The call-and-response Bambara lyrics encourage Africans to seek happiness in unity, an appeal embedded in the traditional Mande concept of *djibe*:

If a wife is a true partner
In the home
We call her "djibe"

"Djibe" is the name we give
The white horse and honesty
Sincere and united neighbours
We call "djibe" too

Africans, let us be "djibe"
Let's try and find
Happiness in unity

The affirmative character of indigenization as a cultural dynamic should not be overstated, of course. In defining a position against essentialism, it is important to avoid an equally idealist theorization of indigenization as cultural "dialogue," a theorization that, in its hurry to celebrate the syncretic tendencies of contemporary African cultural practice, would "forget" about imperialism altogether, or bracket it as a "political" phenomenon, without implications for the putatively autonomous sphere of culture. Chinua Achebe has pointed out that one cannot talk about "cultural exchange in a spirit of partnership between North and South," because "no definition of partnership can evade the notion of equality" and because there is no equality in prevailing North–South relations.[13] The point here is that, if we wish to speak of contemporary African music in the light of anti-imperialist cultural struggle, it is necessary for us to begin by conceding the effectivity and reach of imperialism. This reach is not total; if it were, there would be no countering it. But, if it is not total, it is nevertheless extensive, both in material and in ideological terms. Billy Bergman, for instance, has drawn attention to the role played in the "Third World" by

the big five multinational record companies – CBS, EMI, Polygram, WEA, and RCA – with their complex system of subsidiaries and licensing arrangements.... They record local music and distribute it to local and, sometimes, international markets. Then they also promote and distribute Top Forties American and British hits with the same fervor that such music is promoted in the United States and Europe. The clout these multinationals have has been documented by musical economists Wallis and Malm: "Using hundreds of promotion men and over a thousand salesmen, [EMI, for example]... has the power to stimulate demand both in quantity and quality and to meet the demand when sales accelerate."[14]

The adverse ideological consequences of this general state of affairs have recently been demonstrated in South Africa in the aftermath of the release of Paul Simon's album *Graceland* in 1986. In *Graceland*, as South African musician Johnny Clegg has observed, Simon "basically presented to the world an image of South African music that [was]... sixteen, twenty years old. That music... you don't hear it any more.... There's a time warp. And young black musicians are being told by the record companies, 'Look, guys, you've got to go back twenty years, because that's where the market is now.' They feel quite resentful."[15] The crucial point here is that *Graceland* has been so successful internationally that, even though there has been little resurgence of interest in its style of music in South Africa itself, the big recording companies in the country have spent a considerable amount of energy in the intervening years pressuring sometimes reluctant local musicians to put out music in the *Graceland* idiom and making it difficult for them to get contracts otherwise. The net result has been a restrictive channeling of creative energies and a compounding of the already exploitative relations between black South African musicians and record producers in the country, the vast majority of whom are white.

The effect of *Graceland*, in short, has been to contribute to the *underdevelopment* of black South African music. The immanent trajectory of the development of this music has been put under threat of destabilization from without, since there are now powerful voices in the country calling for the production of music in accordance with the world system's dominant consuming interests, those in Europe and the United States. It is this fact, more than any other, that renders *Graceland* frankly imperialist.

There is in the work of Simon, David Byrne, Paul McCartney, Brian Eno, Lionel Richie, and many other influential musicians in the West a profound insensitivity to the politico-ethical implications of cultural appropriation across the international division of labor. Even in the best of the work of these musicians – I am thinking, for instance, of the brilliant and witty mock lament "Nothing but Flowers," on the 1988 Talking Heads album, *Naked* (Fly / Sire), or of any of the tracks on *Graceland* – there is a distressing unilateralism of influence. While "Nothing but Flowers" features Abdou M'Boup on congas, Yves N'Djock on guitars, and Brice Wassy on shaker and has a distinctly West African feel about it, it remains wholly and unrepentantly Euro-American in its lyric reference. The discrepancy between the self-conscious "One-Worldism" of the music and the unselfconscious "First-Worldism" of the lyrics is discomfiting, and not in a productive sense:

> Here we stand
> Like an Adam and an Eve
> Waterfalls
> The Garden of Eden
> *Two fools in love*
> So beautiful and strong
> The birds in the trees
> Are smiling upon them
> From the age of the dinosaurs
> Cars have run on gasoline
> Where, where have they gone?
> Now, it's nothing but flowers
> There was a factory
> Now there are mountains and rivers . . .
> We caught a rattlesnake
> Now we got something for dinner . . .
> There was a shopping mall
> Now it's all covered with flowers . . .
> If this is paradise
> I wish I had a lawnmower

It is hard to rid oneself of the suspicion that the organizing logic of this composition is that of advanced capitalist consumerism: as though from the center of the world system – his apartment in Manhattan – Byrne had selected diverse sounds, rhythms, and musical motifs from all over the world out of a catalog, and blended them into an exotic and hi-tech backdrop for his parodic, postmodern, but paradoxically *stabilizing* play on nature and culture.[16]

Similarly, while Simon draws his musical inspiration in *Graceland* not only from Sotho, Shangani, Zulu, and other South African musics but also from West Africa (Nigerian pedal steel guitarist Demola Adepoju plays on the title track and the popular Senegalese singer Youssou N'Dour is featured on "Diamonds on the Soles of Her Shoes"), Cajun Louisiana, and Chicano Los Angeles, his lyrics reveal a complete lack of cultural dialogism. Here, for instance, is the improbable opening verse from the *mbaqanga*-based track "Gumboots":

> I was having this discussion
> In a taxi heading downtown
> Rearranging my position
> On this friend of mine who had
> A little bit of a breakdown
> I said breakdowns come
> And breakdowns go
> So what are you going to do about it
> That's what I'd like to know
>
> You don't feel you could love me
> But I feel you could

There are even occasions in *Graceland* in which Simon's choice of lyrics seems actively to contribute to imperialist cultural assumptions about Africa and the "Third World." The album's opening track, "The Boy in the Bubble," begins as follows:

> It was a slow day
> And the sun was beating
> On the soldiers by the side of the road
> There was a bright light
> A shattering of shop windows
> The bomb in the baby carriage
> Was wired to the radio
>
> These are the days of miracle and wonder
> This is the long distance call
> The way the camera follows us in slo-mo
> The way we look to us all
> The way we look to a distant constellation
> That's dying in the corner of the sky
> These are the days of miracle and wonder
> And don't cry baby, don't cry

In the context of the "armed struggle" in South Africa, in which the African National Congress scrupulously attempted to avoid the kinds of attack on civilian targets which would enable the state to brand it unproblematically as a "terrorist" organization, these lyrics are ill-advised at best. And they are scarcely atypical. It is not for nothing, thus, that the hard-rock band Living Colour should have chosen to spoof Simon in the track "Elvis Is Dead" on their 1990 album, *Time's Up*. In the title track on *Graceland* Simon had sung of having

> a reason to believe
> We all will be received
> In Graceland.

In "Elvis Is Dead," by contrast, one finds what music critic Jon Pareles calls "a sly reversal" of these lines. Living Colour sing, "I got a reason to believe we all *won't* be received at Graceland," an apparent reference, as Pareles notes, "to Presley's racist public statements" and to Simon's wholesale neglect of the question of race in the lyrics of *Graceland*.[17]

Graceland was produced by Warner Brothers Records. *Naked* was produced by Sire Records Company but marketed by Warner Brothers. Until fairly recently multinational corporations were responsible for almost all of the recording that took place in Africa, and it was only the superstars in the African popular musical firmament – musicians such as Manu Dibango, Franco and Tabu Ley – who were able to exercise any creative control in the production, distribution, and marketing of their music. Today the situation is somewhat different: on the one hand, there has been a proliferation of small, predominantly privately owned recording companies in several African states; on the other hand, a number of European-based independent companies have emerged to challenge the dominance of the multinationals. It is these independents – labels such as Sterns, Earthworks, Globe-Style, Oval Records, Shanachie, WOMAD, and Discafrique – which have been largely responsible for the recent explosion of interest in African music among Euro-American listeners. To date, as Ronnie Graham has written, their contribution has been a positive one. Founded by individuals with "enthusiasm, imagination, a background in Africa and, most of all, access to 'progressive capital,'" they "have been able to make significant contributions to the promotion of African music while, in the main, correctly interpreting trends originating in Africa and throwing their meagre resources behind these innovations."[18]

Zimbabwe has been one of the African countries best served by the independent record labels. Doubtless, this is partly a matter of luck: the emergence of the independents, and of Euro-American interest in African music, happened to coincide with Zimbabwe's acquisition of political sovereignty in 1980 and the consequent burgeoning of the music industry in that country. But one should not underestimate the extent to which, reciprocally, Zimbabwe's widely publicized and internationally popular accession to sovereign statehood after years of struggle served as a catalyst, stimulating Westerners to listen to music from that country.

The recent history of music in Zimbabwe makes for a remarkable narrative. One can glean the centrality of the national liberation struggle merely from a casual recitation of the names of leading bands: Thomas Mapfumo and the Blacks Unlimited, the Bhundu Boys,[19] the Marxist Brothers, Ephat Mujuru and the Spirit of the People, the Fallen Heroes, Zexie Manatsa and the Green Arrows, Susan Mapfumo and the Black Salutarys, Robson Banda and the New Black Eagles, and many others. But before turning to the national liberation struggle it might be helpful to make a few prefatory historical remarks.

In the precolonial era the music of the Shona people in what would become Zimbabwe was founded on the mbira, a legendary instrument found in many parts of Africa and consisting of a set of between eight and fifty keys laid over a usually flat soundboard and typically placed in a box resonator or some other device for amplifying the sound.[20] Strongly associated with Shona religious and artistic practices, the mbira was ruthlessly disparaged, in the years following colonial conquest, by colonial officials and European missionaries. Performers often "found themselves subject to intense religious indoctrination as well as ridicule and abuse for being mbira players."[21] As a result of these pressures, Paul Berliner has written,

> Mbira music suffered a decline in popularity in certain parts of the country.... It would appear...that for a period of time the older generation of mbira players had difficulty finding members of the younger generation to whom they could impart their knowledge of mbira music. Young Shona students...had had a negative image of traditional African culture instilled in them and they therefore shunned identification with the ways of the elders. Those individuals who showed musical skill gravitated toward the guitar rather than the mbira.... In a sense, for a generation of Africans the guitar and the mbira came to symbolize a dichotomy of life-styles and values. Africans associated the mbira with the poverty of the reserves and with things "unChristian" and "old-fashioned," while the guitar represented the wealth and glamor of the cities and things "modern" and "Western."[22]

This dichotomy, characteristic of the years between 1920 and 1960, and so obviously convenient for the purposes of colonial rule, was challenged and eventually shattered by the rise of nationalism and the coming of the liberation struggle in Zimbabwe. Anticolonial nationalists began to pay attention to the mbira precisely *because* it was regarded with contempt by the colonial authorities, and when, during the struggle for liberation, the countryside became the resistance movement's center of gravity, the beauty and integrity of the mbira's sound was, however belatedly, once again recognized.

Remarkably, however, the return to the mbira was not in this case a mere nativist gesture. On the contrary, as the struggle intensified, an astonishing fusion of mbira sounds and conventions, Western instrumentation, and modern means of communication took the war to the remotest regions of the country. The fusion was called *chimurenga*, the Shona word for "struggle," and *chimurenga* came to refer both to the war of liberation and to the style of music which spread its message. From outside the country every evening at 8 p.m. Radio Mozambique broadcast the liberation movement's news program, "Voice of Zimbabwe," on shortwave and mediumwave. It was picked up throughout Zimbabwe, despite the efforts of the Rhodesian government to jam the signal, to restrict the ownership of transistor radios, and to market a new cheap transistor receiving only FM signals. The most popular feature of the "Voice of Zimbabwe" broadcasts was the "Chimurenga Requests" segment, in which listeners' written requests for *chimurenga* songs would be entertained. Most of these songs had been written by fighters in the various guerrilla bases in Mozambique and elsewhere. Usually traditional in structure and melody, they were sung in Shona, Sindebele, and other Zimbabwean languages and tended, as one might expect, to be explicit and lyrically direct:

> People of Zimbabwe
> Living under oppression
> The world is changing
> Arise! Arise![23]

Music from the "Chimurenga Requests" program was, of course, banned in Ian Smith's Rhodesia itself. In the mid-1970s, however, Thomas Mapfumo began to develop an "internal" variant of the form. At that time the dominant shaping influence on Zimbabwean pop music was Cuban-derived Congolese rumba. (Other major influences were American soul, funk, and rhythm and blues and South African township jive.) This Congolese sound, today called *soukous* (or, in much of East Africa, *sungura*), has been for the past two decades or so probably the most widely influential form of pop music in all of Africa. Its influence can be heard in Tanzania, Kenya, Mozambique, Angola, Cameroon, Senegal, the Ivory Coast, and elsewhere. Roberts has written of its "immense force and flexibility," adding that although *soukous* "at first sounds somewhat Latin American ... there is actually nothing like it in the New World. It seems to have grown partly from localizing techniques ... and partly from the playing on guitar of lines that, in Cuban music, were brass or sax lines."[24]

Yet, instead of basing himself on the sounds of *soukous*, Mapfumo predicated his music on the ancestral rhythms and cadences of the mbira, utilizing guitars that mimicked the mbira sound, producing driving guitar lines made up of discrete but cascading notes. Recording and performing in public in Zimbabwe, Mapfumo obviously could not duplicate the outspokenness of music from the Requests program. Here, too, however, confronted by the problem of censorship, he was able to formulate a tradition-based solution, for historically, as Paul Berliner has observed, ambiguity and innuendo have been central features in the performance of mbira music: "Since subtlety is an important element in the art of [mbira playing], performers strive to express themselves indirectly at times, and members of the audience must guess at the meaning of their words. It is not uncommon for individuals listening to a performance of mbira music to derive differing meanings from the singer's lines."[25]

This customary motif was tailor-made for incorporation into the underground *chimurenga* music pioneered by Mapfumo. Mapfumo himself attained enormous popularity in Zimbabwe in the late 1970s on the strength of a string of releases that alluded delicately or indirectly to the liberation struggle. These tracks were never played on the radio, but their indirection and apparent apoliticality was for the most part sufficient to ensure that they were not banned outright, and, despite the lack of radio play, and the total absence of publicity, several of them became best-sellers in Zimbabwe. One of these was "Pamuromo Chete" (These Are Mere Words), whose lyrics give some idea of the mode of address of Mapfumo's music in the 1970s:

> Some of our people, Lord,
> Live as squatters at the Market Square;
> Some of our people, Lord,
> Have no place to go;
> Some of our people, Lord,
> Are suffering;
> Some of our people, Lord,
> Are existing as strays.
>
> These are mere words.
> These are mere words.[26]

Mapfumo has said of this song that it "wasn't being sung directly": "I was telling Mr. Smith that there were people in such trouble that all his talking was mere words, talk without substance. He was saying that never in a thousand years would we have a majority government. And I was saying that people will fight for the freedom they want.... The people understood. They knew what I was talking about."[27]

Mapfumo was made to pay for his activism. He was continually harassed by the Rhodesian authorities. On one occasion he was detained for ninety days without trial. On another occasion he was kidnapped. He was forced to perform at political rallies for Bishop Abel Muzorewa, a conservative black political figure broadly aligned with the ruling white Rhodesian regime. And he was routinely summonsed to police stations and subjected to interrogation.

Since Zimbabwe's independence in April 1980 Mapfumo's career has gone from strength to strength. The independence period saw the release of several songs glorying in the success of the national liberation struggle and, in a more somber vein, attempting to weigh the continuing obstacles to prosperity. In "Ndamutswa Nengoma" (Drums Have Woken Me Up), for instance, Mapfumo sings:

> The sun has risen forever
> There will never be darkness again in Zimbabwe
> It has dawned forever
> Let's work together – let's have socialism...
> I have been asleep
> Drums have woken me up.[28]

Similar sentiments are voiced in tracks such as "Kwaedza Mu Zimbabwe" (It Has Dawned in Zimbabwe) and "Nyarai" (Be Ashamed), the former purely celebratory, the latter urging "reactionaries" to abandon their opposition to Robert Mugabe's new government.[29] Already by independence, however, Mapfumo was beginning to turn his commitment and political vision to the problems of postcolonialism in Zimbabwe. In "Chauya Chirizevha" (Rural Life is Back), composed before independence, for instance, he addressed the questions of reconstruction and of the return of citizens to their homes in the countryside:

> The Chief was really saddened
> Seeing all his people come back
> To rural life
>
> Some lost their legs
> Some died there (in the bush)
> Some died in their homes
> Some fled their homes because of the war
>
> Today the war is over
> For sure the war is over
> And finished, Chief.[30]

This extension in the reference of Mapfumo's music has continued throughout the 1980s and into the 1990s. The results can best be appreciated on *Corruption* and *Chamunorwa* (What Are We Fighting For?), two albums by Mapfumo and the Blacks Unlimited, released – to considerable fanfare – by Island Records' Mango subsidiary in 1989 and 1991, respectively. *Corruption*, in particular, offers a brilliant example of politically committed popular music making. Recorded at Shed Studios in Harare, the production values are extremely high. Mapfumo sings about the legacy of the liberation struggle in "Chigwindiri" (A Very Strong Person), but most of the tracks on the album are devoted to postcolonial issues of class division, political disunity, and public morality. Similarly, whereas some tracks, such as "Muchadura" (You Will Confess), are still instrumentally reminiscent of the electric mbira sound of *chimurenga* music, others sample freely from reggae, *kwela*, *mbaqanga*, funk, and *sungura* styles.

This tendency to reach out beyond the *chimurenga* sound to other musical styles, while retaining the political focus of *chimurenga*, typifies Zimbabwean pop music in the 1980s and early 1990s. One observes it, for instance, in the music of such outfits as the Four Brothers, Oliver Mutukudzi, the Jairos Jiri Sunrise Kwela Band, the Sungura Boys, Jonah Moyo and Devera Ngwena, and in the Bhundu Boys. Along with Stella Chiweshe, whose mbira-based sound has recently become very popular, the Bhundu Boys are, perhaps, the only Zimbabwean band whose fame and popularity, both within Zimbabwe and internationally, rivals Mapfumo's.

Like Mapfumo, they are committed to the political vision of a socialist Zimbabwe. Their superb third album, *True Jit* (Mango, 1988), for instance, is dedicated "to Robert Mugabe and the others who restored sanity to our country." Yet the Bhundu Boys sound nothing like Mapfumo. After all, the "jit" to which their album title refers is the name of a vibrant young people's music, heavily percussive and vocally melodic. The band's commitment to jit-jive, as Chris Stapleton has noted, puts them "at some distance from the elders of modern Zimbabwe pop, among them Thomas Mapfumo, who base their repertoire around the ancient mbira tradition."[31] Certainly, Mapfumo's mbira guitar style remains a heavy influence on a track such as "Chemedzevana" on *True Jit*, in which in counterpoint with the loping bass it provides the rhythmic anchor for the song's explorations into different musical domains. Yet the track is more noteworthy, perhaps, for its incorporation of elements from other southern and central African popular musics, a true case of "South-South dialogue." The jangling, bell-like guitar playing of the climax, for instance, is reminiscent of the guitar lines of Congolese *soukous*, as is the recognizably Latin-derived brass section.[32] By the same token the general pacing of the song recalls the temper of *marabi* music from South Africa.

Another track from *True Jit*, entitled "Vana" (The Children), is even more remarkable. Formally, like "Chemedzevana," the track is based not on the mbira sound but, instead, on *soukous*, although it employs in addition the call-and-response chorus of male voices which, in various modes, accompanied and unaccompanied, represents one of the distinctive features of southern African music in general. Yet, if the track therefore has a *transnational* feel to it, it is nevertheless clear that what is involved is not in any sense a postindependence dissipation of *chimurenga* music into a depoliticized "Afropop." On the contrary, "Vana" might not at first sound like *chimurenga* music, but lyrically it is entirely about *chimurenga*. It is composed in Shona but features one verse in English, declaimed over a solid rhythmic groove to the accompaniment of a tense, high-pitched, staccato guitar line, echoing like machine-gun fire:

> This song is dedicated to all our brothers and sisters
> Who were fighting for our liberation in Zimbabwe
> Who fought and died in the bushes of Zimbabwe
> The lions were eating the children
> They were left to be swollen by the sun
> When this song was sung, vana [the children]
> Of Zimbabwe were fighting for our liberation
> My friend Theo didn't come home
> But I knew we would overcome in the struggle.

The sustainedly melodic passages of this track are predicated on traditional melodies of the kind that were taken up and modified by fighters during the years of the liberation struggle. One notices also the characteristically indirect and metaphorical quality of the lyrics – "The lions were eating the children / They were left to be swollen by the sun" – and the self-conscious internationalism achieved not only through the use of English but also, more specifically, through the allusion to universally recognized progressive slogans such as "We shall overcome." Within the Zimbabwean context, in short, "Vana" – like the brilliant "Viva Chinhoyi" on *Pamberi!*, the fourth album by the Bhundu Boys (Mango, 1989) – might be said to represent an attempt to consolidate the gains of the revolution by extending the range of *chimurenga* music and broadening its musical vocabulary.

In Western media the mass marketing of Afropop and the recent incorporation of African, Caribbean, and Latin rhythms and styles into Euro-American rock music is often described as a welcome development, on the grounds that it has helped to breathe new life into an otherwise increasingly sterile cultural domain. Perhaps the claim that African pop music has helped to revitalize its Euro-American counterpart is true (although a glance at Top Forty charts or at radio playlists far from persuades one that this is so). But to argue thus is to assume an exclusively First-Worldist perspective. It is also preemptively to domesticate African pop music, to consign it in advance to secondary status, as an auxiliary phenomenon – paradoxically, indeed, *as a phenomenon within Euro-American pop music*. Ultimately, it seems to me, this kind of argument is incompatible with a progressive, internationalist politics.

Certainly, a good deal of the Afropop that is currently being recorded and marketed for Western consumption *can* appropriately be categorized under the rubric of Western pop music. What is true of the music of David Byrne or Paul Simon is true, too, of much contemporary Afropop. As Jane Kramer has written, with reference to France:

> There are English and American music critics who say that the African groups that Parisians like so much are really ordinary rock groups – guitar, bass guitar, keyboard, and drums – with the native instruments thrown in like spice, for flavor. Certainly there is not much harmonic complexity in most of the African music you are likely to hear on [the radio]...or find on cassettes [in music stores]....The international circuit that Parisians talk about can take the rhythmic – really the poly-rhythmic – complexity that African music does have and reduce it to French pop standards, to a kind of rock monotone. Unless a group is tough and confident...it can make that music as banal as elevator songs.[33]

A similar point has been made, with a nod toward Max Horkheimer and Theodor Adorno, by the South African musician Johnny Clegg. In an interview recorded in 1988 Clegg referred to the culture industry, or, as he called it, the "Western cultural monster which feeds off anything new, takes it, perverts it and reduces it to a common denominator, and then markets and sells it."[34]

Yet one needs to proceed carefully here, for many Western popular music critics, anxious to establish their credentials by voicing their opposition to the culture industry, have moved to take up a position that is disturbingly undialectical and even reactionary. Consider, for instance, the terms of Richard Gehr's recent critique of Clegg himself. Writing in the avant-gardist *New Trouser Press Record Guide*, Gehr trashes Clegg's music with the band Juluka, dismissing it as "a mush of sweet, laid-back California style harmonies over a loping backbeat, with mild anti-apartheid sentiments."[35] And Clegg's more recent music with his new band, Savuka, receives still harsher treatment. According to Gehr, it is "even more Western-oriented. The slicker production of *Third World Child* relieves it of the simple, unassuming emotionality of township music. The self-conscious, breast-beating lyrics of the title track and 'Berlin Wall' suggest that Clegg's gunning for the Nobel peace prize while attempting to forge a calculated commercial sound. Too bad Paul Simon beat him to the bank."[36] This is a deplorable piece of criticism, displaying a profound ignorance of Clegg's work and of South African culture and society generally. Against Gehr, it is perhaps worth repeating that Clegg has been among Paul Simon's firmest and most articulate critics in South Africa, and it is certainly worth insisting that there has been nothing remotely "mild" about the "anti-apartheid sentiments" of Clegg's music over the course of the past fifteen years. On the contrary, such tracks as "Asimbonanga (Mandela)" (We Have Not Seen [Mandela]), on Savuka's *Third World Child* album (EMI, 1986) – with its recitation of the names of Mandela, Steven Biko, Victoria Mxenga, and Neil Aggett, political activists silenced or murdered by the apartheid regime – or "One (Hu)Man One Vote," on *Cruel, Crazy, Beautiful World* (EMI, 1989), written in memory of the assassinated university lecturer David Webster, are as tough, politically committed, resourceful, and Afrocentric as any of Thomas Mapfumo's *chimurenga* releases.

Yet my purpose in quoting Gehr's broadside is not so much to protest its insufficiency as criticism, patent in any event, as to draw attention to the inadequacy of the way of thinking about African popular music which it exemplifies. For it is clear that what Gehr dislikes above all about Clegg's music is its fluent integration of "African" and "Western" musical idioms. Gehr does not complain about the fact that Savuka, a South African band, has added guitar techniques from Zimbabwe, Malawi, and elsewhere on the continent to its fundamentally South African mix. But he strongly objects to the "Western-orientation" that he sees as being the necessary consequence of Savuka's use of synthesizers, folk-rock harmonies, and multitrack recording facilities. It seems that there is a little bit of the ethnomusicological purist – and, indeed, of the orientalist – in Gehr. He likes his Afropop not only "simple" and "unassuming" but also uncontaminated by the commercialism of Western pop.

In its dogmatism this way of thinking is unhistorical and does violence to the essentially hybridic form of *all* African pop music today. Celebrating the African pop music that he *does* like for its alterity, its otherness from Western pop, Gehr paradoxically exoticizes it, thereby contributing to a situation in which African pop music is afforded only ghettoized airplay on specialty radio and television programs or written about only in isolated feature articles. The existence in music stores throughout the United States of shelves marked International testifies to the pervasiveness of this latently essentialist conception of African (or, for that matter, "world") music. To be labeled world music, it would seem, is to be categorized above all through reference to its *difference* from the prevailing Western forms; it is not rock, not rhythm "n" blues, not soul, not reggae (a rich irony here, of course, given the fact that most reggae music is still produced in Jamaica by Jamaicans), not punk, and not jazz.

Revealingly, Johnny Clegg himself has provided the appropriate response to this First-Worldist way of conceptualizing African pop music. In an interview recorded in 1988 Clegg described his musical "vision for the future" as being "to create and construct music which is based in the African experience. . . . My personal project is to define my African identity in the continent . . . and to communicate this with the world and my fellow Africans."[37] A skeptic could, of course, argue that, as a *white* South African – however radical and committed to a nonracial South Africa – Clegg's "African identity" is scarcely likely to be representative. The substantial validity of this objection should be conceded. Tracks by Savuka such as "Third World Child" (on the album by that name) and "African Shadow Man" and "Human Rainbow" (on the album *Shadow Man* [EMI, 1988]) clearly bespeak a restricted and, in the context of Africa at large, ungeneralizable subject position. Yet in another interview of 1988 Clegg insisted that the internationalization of "African experience" was a daily reality not only for himself but for all African musicians. Referring specifically to the South African scene – but to the South African scene *tout court*, not merely to the white South African scene – he argued: "What the new music is drawing on is not only, any more, the South African music experience, but the international one. People must understand and realise that we are exposed day and night to international music." Musicians in South Africa today, he continued – and one thinks of such figures as Ray

Phiri of the band Stimela or Condry Ziqubu or Ladysmith Black Mambazo, for example – tend to celebrate, rather than deplore, their internationalization, which they do not in the least regard as corresponding to their subordination to imperialist social imperatives or to the logic of consumer capitalism: "We do not want to be straight-jacketed politically by apartheid.... So there's been a reaction against this.... Young people now [are saying], we speak English, we sing in English, and we're part of that whole, international culture. And ... our music is reaching out to touch the soul and the spirit of that international music community, to be part of it."[38]

This formulation of the aspirations of *producers* of African pop music – echoed, incidentally, in the thinking of such musicians as Salif Keita of Mali and Ray Lema of Zaire – seems compelling, not least because it accords neatly with the views of many of the music's Western-based *consumers*, enthusiastic followers of Afropop. Most Western listeners, of course, tend to know little about social developments in Africa. They are initially attracted to African pop music because they find its sound exciting. What particularly stimulates them, I want to suggest, what enables them to find enjoyment in Afropop, is precisely its hybridity. Because it is a hybrid form, Afropop typically strikes Western listeners as simultaneously strange and familiar, accessible and inaccessible, opaque and immediately intelligible. This simultaneity – the relative alterity of Afropop, on the one hand, and the fact that it is "Euro-friendly" (to use the delightful term that one sees quite often today), on the other – is arguably the source of a pleasing intellectual challenge to Western enthusiasts, who endeavor, in exploring and sampling different Afropop sounds, to render these more and more comprehensible.

The music industry in the West attempts to exploit this passion on the part of Western consumers of Afropop – or, more generally, world music – by promoting world music as a new cultural resource waiting to be "discovered." It invites Western consumers to exoticize world music, to transform it into the musical equivalent of the "new" international cuisines, to which we in the West have been introduced as a direct consequence of our various imperial misadventures and which we like to sample once every now and then for a culinary change of pace. The code name for this strategy is "cultural pluralism," which, as Abdul JanMohamed and David Lloyd have recently argued, is "the great white hope of conservatives and liberals alike":

> The semblance of pluralism disguises the perpetuation of exclusion, in so far as it is enjoyed only by those who have already assimilated the values of the dominant culture. For this pluralism, ethnic or cultural difference is merely an exoticism, an indulgence which can be relished without in any significant way modifying the individual who is securely embedded in the protective body of dominant ideology. Such pluralism tolerates the existence of "salsa," it even enjoys Mexican restaurants, but it bans Spanish as a medium of instruction in American schools. Above all, it refuses to acknowledge the class basis of discrimination and the systematic economic exploitation of minorities that underlie postmodern culture.[39]

In light of this analysis the ideological implications of taking up the challenge posed by the hybridity of world music seem to me potentially considerable, for, ultimately, world music cannot be represented as a supplement to Euro-American music. Rather, it carries the potential to subvert the ideological parochialism of Euro-American music, not, of course, at the level of the music industry itself (this would be to claim far too much) but, instead, in the minds of a large audience of listeners and enthusiasts in the West. To those Western enthusiasts who, following the lead of British rock musician Peter Gabriel,[40] have heard enough to embrace the concept underlying it, world music is not to be thought of merely as a convenient name for a sprawling body of music deriving from Yemen or New Zealand or Brazil or Cameroon – in short, from anywhere but "here." It is, rather, the name of a movement that cannot be accommodated at all within the ideological universe of Western popular music. For what makes it *world* music is precisely its latent tendency to contribute to the dismantling of the subject of Western popular music, a subject whose identity rests squarely upon the political economy of empire. To listen to world music as a Western consumer is, in these dialogical terms, a distinctly subversive practice, for it is to allow oneself to take seriously the suggestion of a world free of imperial domination. Free of imperial domination, note – not "on the other side of the imperial divide." The proposal is not that we listen to world music for what it can tell us about life "over there" but rather, that we listen to it for what it can suggest to us about radically different ways of living *over here*, ways of living which are unimaginable under prevailing social conditions.

NOTES

I have taken the title of this chapter from a phrase in *Nervous Conditions*, the splendid first novel by the young Zimbabwean author, Tsitsi Dangarembga (Harare: Zimbabwe Publishing House, 1988). Near the beginning of the novel, Dangarembga has her central protagonist, Tambudzai, speak of "the new rumba that, as popular music will, pointed unsystematic fingers at the conditions of the times" (4).

1 Ayi Kwei Armah, *The Healers* (London: Heinemann Educational Books, 1979), 308–9.
2 Deborah James, "Musical Form and Social History: Research Perspectives on Black South African Music," *Radical History Review* 46, no. 7 (1990): 309.
3 Ibid., 313.
4 Francis Bebey, *African Music: A People's Art*, trans. Josephine Bennett (Westport: Lawrence Hill, 1975), I.
5 John Storm Roberts, *Black Music of Two Worlds* (New York: Praeger Publishers, 1972); David Coplan, *In Township Tonight! South Africa's Black City Music and Theatre* (London: Longman, 1986).
6 Roberts, *Black Music*, 259. See also John Collins and Paul Richards, "Popular Music in West Africa," in *World Music, Politics and Social Change*, ed. Simon Frith (Manchester: Manchester Univ. Press, 1989).
7 Andrew Tracey, quoted in Billy Bergman, *Goodtime Kings: Emerging African Pop* (New York: Quill, 1985), 32.
8 Andrew Goodwin and Joe Gore, "World Beat and the Cultural Imperialism Debate," *Socialist Review* 20, no. 3 (1990): 70.
9 Salif Keita, quoted in Chris Stapleton and Chris May, *African All-Stars: The Pop Music of a Continent* (London: Paladin, 1989), III. For a discussion of the social relationship between nobles and griots in Mande culture, see Christopher L. Miller, "Orality through Literacy: Mande Verbal Art after the Letter," *Theories of Africans: Francophone Literature and Anthropology in Africa* (Chicago: Univ. of Chicago Press, 1990), 68–113; see also 55, n. 51.

10 Stapleton and May, *African All-Stars*, 113.

11 Ibid., 112.

12 Nii Yamotei, liner notes to *Soro* (1987).

13 Chinua Achebe, "Impediments to Dialogue between North and South," in *Hopes and Impediments: Selected Essays 1965–1987* (Oxford: Heinemann, 1988), 15.

14 Bergman, *Goodtime Kings*, 19.

15 Johnny Clegg, interviewed on the television documentary production "The Sounds of Soweto," dir. Barry Coetzee (Picture Music International, 1988).

16 This play is overdetermined by the design of the album cover, which features a framed portrait of a chimpanzee (the frame presumably signifying "culture" and the chimp "nature"), and by the album's title, which gestures toward the distinction, made famous by John Berger, between nakedness and nudity (see *Ways of Seeing* [London: British Broadcasting Service and Penguin Books, 1986], 45–64).

17 Jon Pareles, "Righteous Rock; Issues You Can Dance To," *New York Times*, 26 August 1990, 23.

18 Ronnie Graham, *The Da Capo Guide to Contemporary African Music* (New York: Da Capo Press, 1988), 22, 20.

19 *Bhundu* is a slang term for *bush* in southern Africa.

20 See Paul Berliner, *The Soul of Mbira: Music and Traditions of the Shona People of Zimbabwe* (Berkeley: Univ. of California Press, 1981), 4, 10.

21 Ibid., 240.

22 Ibid., 240–1.

23 "Muka! Muka!" quoted in Julie Frederickse, *None but Ourselves: Masses versus Media in the Making of Zimbabwe* (Johannesburg: Ravan Press, 1982), 104. I have drawn extensively from Frederickse's indispensable study in my account of Zimbabwean music in the national liberation struggle.

24 Roberts, *Black Music*, 253.

25 Berliner, *Soul of Mbira*, 177.

26 "Pamuromo Chete," quoted in Frederickse, *None but Ourselves*, 107.

27 Thomas Mapfumo, quoted in ibid., 108.

28 Thomas Mapfumo and the Blacks Unlimited, "Ndamutswa Nengoma," on the compilation album, *Viva Zimbabwe!* (Carthage, 1983).

29 Both tracks are included on Thomas Mapfumo, *The Chimurenga Singles, 1976–1980* (Meadowlark, 1985).

30 Thomas Mapfumo, "Chauya Chirizevha," on *Chimurenga Singles*.

31 Stapleton and May, *African All-Stars*, 221.

32 In the context of a track like "Chemedzevana" Billy Bergman's observation of the similarities between *chimurenga* music and Congolese *soukous* is particularly interesting: "As in Congolese music," Bergman writes, *chimurenga* "harmonies are filled out by horn lines and the dance momentum is effected by a quasi-rumba bass. But the guitars are even faster and more twangy than in Zaire" (*Goodtime Kings*, 120).

33 Jane Kramer, "Letter from Europe," *New Yorker*, 19 May 1986, 112.

34 Clegg, interviewed in "Sounds of Soweto."

35 Richard Gehr, entry on Savuka / Juluka / Johnny Clegg, in *The New Trouser Press Record Guide*, ed. Ira A. Robbins (New York: Macmillan, 1989), 304.

36 Ibid., 305.

37 Johnny Clegg, interview on the television documentary production "Johnny Clegg," dir. Julian Caidan (Picture Music International, 1988).

38 Clegg, interviewed in "Sounds of Soweto."

39   Abdul JanMohamed and David Lloyd, "Introduction: Toward a Theory of Minority Discourse," *Cultural Critique* (Spring 1987): 9–10.

40   In "World Beat and the Cultural Imperialism Debate" Goodwin and Gore note the extent of Gabriel's commitment to the promotion of world music, citing, for instance, "his support for Britain's WOMAD organisation, and more recently ... his participation with the Real World record label and recording studio" (67).

Sheroes and Villains: Conceptualizing Colonial and Contemporary Violence Against Women in Africa

Amina Mama

Amina Mama's essay concerns itself with issues that are all too frequently ignored in postcolonial criticism and theory: the effects of violence against women. Mama's essay foregrounds the role of women in the construction of national identity and the ways in which violence against women is used in this construction – or ignored altogether. Rape, mutilation, unlawful detention, and other forms of violence are unveiled by Mama in an indictment against colonial, national, and postcolonial aggression. The student will find especially helpful the historical analysis that Mama presents. She begins by concentrating on the colonial period and the problem of patriarchal imperialism, especially the way in which "the contradictory sexuality of imperial masculinity" led to particularly pernicious forms of violence grounded in phantasmatic "privileges" of rape and despoilation. The legacy of this violence had profound effects on the nature of gender roles and gender relations in African nationalist movements. The links between imperialism and nationalism with respect to the violence toward women can be found to exert pressure on women in the context of postcolonial nationalism, primarily in the form of neo-colonialist economic policies that breed corruption and inequality across gender, class, ethnic, and racial lines. Mama's discussion of violence toward women and the role of women in nationalism can be illuminated by a comparison with essays by **Partha Chatterjee** and **R. Radhakrishnan**; more general considerations of gender and the representation of women, found in **Gayatri Chakravorty Spivak**, **Rajeswari Sunder Rajan**, **Moira Ferguson**, **Kay Schaffer**, **Helen Tiffin**, and **Angela Bourke**, will help the student situate Mama's argument in a broader theoretical context.

Sheroes and Villains: Conceptualizing Colonial and Contemporary Violence Against Women in Africa

Violence against women has been a central concern of the international women's movement over the last two decades. In many countries, violent abuse has been taken up as the most salient and immediate manifestation of women's oppression by men, and in Africa, in particular, widespread violence against women is now probably the most direct and unequivocal manifestation of women's oppressed status. In most societies, rape and domestic violence have on occasion provoked public outrage, but it has been left to women's organizations and movements to take more concerted action. Both the different manifestations of violence that can be considered as gendered and the diverse character of antiviolence praxis can be illustrated with examples from different areas of the developing world. For instance, the most dynamic campaigns in the Caribbean were initially provoked by the common occurrence of rape, the trivialization of which had led feminists to establish the first rape-crisis centers and, thereafter, to initiate campaigns and highly innovative cultural actions. On the Indian subcontinent, sati and dowry deaths have been responded to at least as vehemently as rape, and it has been rape by government officials that has most provoked the wrath of feminists. African women's campaigns, for their part, have been less movement-based, with individuals and welfare and health groups campaigning against genital mutilation, child marriages, and other indigenous practices.[1] Even so, Africans have been surprisingly reticent on wife-beating and sexual harassment, despite their prevalence and the negative effects of both on personal and public life. The widespread harassment and intimidation of women by power-crazed police and the overzealous implementation of antiwomen decrees and edicts by military forces also needs our serious attention.

A few incidents will illustrate both the severity of the situation and the range of forms that woman abuse takes:

- Piah Njoki was blinded in 1983 when her Kenyan husband, aided by two other men, gouged out both her eyes for bearing him daughters and not sons. In court, Mrs. Njoki implored the judge not to send her husband to prison, since she would then be left alone to fend for herself and her daughters in her state of blindness.

Taken from M. Jacqui Alexander and Chandra Talpade Mohanty (eds.), *Feminist Genealogies, Colonial Legacies, Democratic Futures* (New York: Routledge, 1997).

- On July 13, 1991, a group of male students attacked the girls' dormitories at St. Kizito secondary school in Kenya, raping seventy-one and killing nineteen.
- In 1987, twelve-year-old Hauwa Abubakar, from Nigeria, died after having both legs amputated. Her husband had attacked her with an axe after she had repeatedly run away from him.
- In 1983, several thousand women were detained by the Zimbabwean authorities, and many of them subjected to beating and other forms of abuse during "Operation Clean Up."

These examples raise a number of important questions about the social and cultural milieux in which abuse occurs, about the social and economic factors which oblige many women to tolerate life-threatening situations, and about the kind of political climate which empowers officials to perpetrate mass abuses against women on the streets of many African cities. All such situations have a history to them, and much of this essay is devoted to excavating this past, to tracing the genealogy of the conditions which foster violence against women, one of the most unpalatable facts of postcolonial life. It is my view that the prevalence of so many pernicious forms of gendered violence demands both historical and contemporary analysis. By deepening our understanding of violence against women during the epoch of imperialism, we will be better able to comprehend and so to counteract the multiple forms of violence meted out against women in postcolonial African states today. Imperialism is the major trope of this analysis because it is the common historical force that makes it possible to consider an area as large and diverse as the African continent as having general features that transcend the boundaries of nation, culture, and geography. This collective African experience – being conquered by the colonizing powers; being culturally and materially subjected to a nineteenth-century European racial hierarchy and its gender politics; being indoctrinated into all-male European administrative systems, and the insidious paternalism of the new religious and educational systems; and facing the continuous flow of material and human resources from Africa to Europe – has persistently affected all aspects of social, cultural, political, and economic life in postcolonial African states. The conditions of women's lives in Europe and Africa are also linked, since these two regions have been inextricably bound together in a dynamic of growing inequality since the dawn of colonialism. Imperialism, therefore, provides an important lens for studying the dynamics that have led to the present conditions, not to simplify or impose homogeneity on the diversities within either region but to lay out a foundation which may direct our investigation of the specificities of particular contexts.

I begin by examining the historical evidence which indicates that colonial penetration was both a violent and a gendered process, which exploited pre-existing social divisions within African culture. Paying particular attention to gender, I argue that the colonial period saw an increased vulnerability of African women to various forms of violence. Since the relationship between Europe and Africa entailed Africa's subjection by Europe, it may be worthwhile to take a look at gender relations and gender violence at the imperial source before addressing the genesis and perpetuation of gender violence in colonial and postcolonial Africa.

The final part of this essay examines the forms of resistance that women have spearheaded, indicating the strategies deployed by women in different parts of the African continent and comparing these to other Third-World and Western feminist antiviolence struggles.

THE COLONIAL PERIOD

Patriarchy at the imperial source

When imperialism is traced back to its roots in European history, the violent and male-dominated character of the civilization that set out to "civilize" the African continent emerges quite clearly. The history of gender violence in Europe raises many questions about European masculinity and about the gender ideologies that lay behind the emergence of today's European states. The misogynistic character of that nascent political culture can perhaps be most dramatically illustrated with reference to the witch-hunts and inquisitions of the Middle Ages. It is now common knowledge that over a four-hundred-year period (from the fourteenth to the seventeenth century), several million women were systematically dismembered, disfigured, and tortured before being drowned or burned alive (Chesler 1972, Mies 1986). Mies also cites the example of a lawyer in Leipzig, Germany, who personally sentenced 20,000 women to death in the course of his highly successful career.

More recently, during the last century, the lot of European women was so miserable that in 1853 a certain Mr. Fitzroy put it to the English House of Commons that the nation should treat married women "no worse than domestic animals" (Dobash and Dobash 1980). With the Industrial Revolution and the development of capitalist social relations, the European working classes, particularly women and children, were exploited in evil ways that would subsequently be perfected on African slaves and forced laborers in the colonies. Literature and public records indicate that physical violence characterized relations between men and women as well as between ruling and oppressed classes and between adults and children. Women from the oppressed classes were sexually as well as economically exploited and many of those who moved to the cities found themselves choosing between the brothel and the poorhouse. A great many were rounded up and deported in shiploads to the New World colonies where an even tougher existence awaited those who survived the passage. It is ironic that the Europeans, who came from such a patriarchal civilization, nevertheless had the audacity to pose as heroic protectors and uplifters of women when they arrived in the colonies (Mies 1986).

At the dawn of imperialism, Europe was also giving shape to and developing its racist ideologies and practices. As far back as the sixteenth century, Queen Elizabeth, the "Virgin Queen" who stood for purity, virtue, and whiteness, made several attempts to have black people removed from the kingdom; her 1601 proclamation called for the banishment of "blackamoores." In later centuries, the pedestalization of upper-class white womanhood was counterposed to an inferiorized construction of blackness. Black people were cast as hypersexual, corrupt, and pathogenic. Black women attracted sexual fascination, and by the nineteenth century had come to feature in the white male psyche as a metaphor for Africa, the dark and unknown continent, waiting to be penetrated, conquered, and despoiled. In the case of Saartjie Baartman, who, as "The Hottentot Venus," was displayed, catalogued, and had her genitals dissected, this dehumanization was rationalized, first, as harmless "entertainment," then, under the guise of "scientific interest."[2]

The oppression of women within Europe had a direct bearing on the treatment of women in the colonies. McClintock (1991b) argues that Britain's notorious Contagious Diseases Acts of 1864, 1866, and 1869 scapegoated women at a time when several key military defeats inflicted on the imperial armies had provoked a crisis in European masculinity. "Corrupt" women were blamed for weakening the troops, so attempts were made to regulate prostitution, both in Britain and in the colonies.[3] It hardly needs to be pointed out that legislation of this sort primarily affected women from the lower social strata, not upper-and middle-class women.

In eighteenth- and nineteenth-century Europe, class, race, and sexual inequalities acted in concert with one another, generating a repressive imperial ideology that was to be reflected in all aspects of colonial, legal, and administrative treatment of the subject peoples. This was to have particular implications for gender relations rendering African women more vulnerable to the violence emanating from both European and African sources.

Race and sex in the colonies

The development of legislative controls over relations between European men and African women indicates the contradictory sexuality of imperial masculinity, straddled as it was on the twin horns of the dilemma that resulted from simultaneous desire and contempt. It also indexes the steady degradation of African women's ascribed status under colonial regimes. In the early period, trading and other relations between European men and Africans followed the initial contact between their respective civilizations. The nineteenth-century institution of "signareship" and the significant numbers of interracial cohabitations and marriages found along the West Coast of Africa point to the existence of a great many relationships between French merchants and African women, although the racial politics of these liaisons have not been the subject of much discussion.[4]

The British appear to have had a more puritanical attitude toward interracial unions. This is reflected in the 1909 "concubinage circular," which imposed penalties on British men for having sex with African women. In 1914, Lord Lugard, the governor general of Nigeria, tactlessly issued "Secret Circular B," which equated miscegenation with bestiality.[5] Marriage to African women was made taboo in other parts of Africa, too. In 1905, the Germans, confronted with the so-called "bastard problem" in the territory that was to become Namibia, forbade marriage to African women, while, at the same time, encouraging prostitution and concubinage. In 1907, they declared marriages contracted before that date to be null and void, and in 1908, retroactivated this principle to dispossess all the offspring of such unions in order to exclude them from the possibility of claiming their German father's citizenship or inheriting property and land in the Fatherland (Mies 1986).

On the other hand, it was not uncommon for the colonizers to organize prostitution services for their troops, so that their desires for local women could be satiated in ways which did not undermine the racial status quo (Enloe 1989), with some even going so far as to reserve certain women "for white men only."

It would seem from this discussion that the legal status of African women was steadily degraded as imperialism advanced, consolidating patriarchal and racist gender values which commodified African women by encouraging prostitution but outlawing the contract of legitimate marriages between white men and black women. We shall see that these trends were continued by colonial states which cast all African women in urban areas as "prostitutes" and subjected them to periodic waves of victimization and harassment, while, at the same time, creating conditions that made the numerous services provided by women indispensable to the colonized male workforce.

The colonial state and violence toward women

Rape appears to have been a frequent accompaniment to military conquests, and was a favored means of ensuring the defeat and pacification of entire nations. Unfortunately, the historical record has been very scant on this subject. Even so, the limited evidence that is available suggests that sexual violence was an integral part of colonization.

Fanon (1980) notes the link between conquest of land and peoples and the violation of women, a link which has subsequently been identified as characterizing colonial literature of the Rider Haggard genre (Stott 1989). According to both, the colonized woman becomes associated in the mind of the European with fantasies of rape and despoliation. Such fantasies are fueled by the inaccessibility of local women (in Muslim areas), but more widely function as a metaphor for conquest of African lands and the humiliation of peoples.

The harsh reality of conquest in Africa included widespread violation and degradation of African women. Where there was resistance, rape and sexual abuse were inflicted on women and the same treatment was meted out to the wives, mothers, daughters, and sisters of men who were suspected of being members of the resistance movements simply to humiliate them.

The use of violent techniques in various European attempts to crush the nationalist movements in many parts of Africa also demonstrates the inadequacy of "gender-only" analysis. To simplify the nature of colonization and the violence that it deployed as just another instance of "male violence" is to obscure the full character of imperialism and the internal contradictions it has so successfully exploited.

In many parts of the continent, colonial regimes intent on the forcible introduction of waged- and migrant-labor systems, sought to restrict the movement of African women, who were expected to remain in the rural areas and continue to engage in subsistence production, while their menfolk were lured to the mines and towns. Nonetheless, women also migrated to the towns to earn money by providing support services; other women abandoned homesteads that were then in decline. Still others, as women have done throughout the ages, moved away to escape violent marriages or quite simply migrated in search of new ways of living. Whatever the case, women moved to the towns in large numbers and, as they were excluded from wage-work in the formal sector, found innovative ways of living on the margins of colonial society and its economy.[6]

Lacking any clear policy or any real knowledge, the colonial state demonstrated confused and contradictory attitudes toward African women. For example, Schmidt (1991) notes that in colonial Zimbabwe, official attitudes toward African women were even worse than those toward men, apparently because while men were "remarkably receptive of European ideas," women tended to "cling to old super-stitions, the old customs and the old methods." She further notes that African women were said to wield immense power over men, and that women's sexual demands were identified as obstructing the recruitment of men to work for the colonizers. Certainly, the presence of women in the colonial towns was viewed with immense suspicion. Measures taken to remove women from the urban areas included periodic round-ups and forcible deportations, often carried out with the connivance of elderly African men, who felt frustrated by what they saw as a loss of control over their homesteads. For example, in 1915, the British colonial officers attempted to restrict the number of "free women" in the Nigerian city of Katsina, proposing that those within the city walls be given seven days to marry, while those defined as prostitutes be driven away. Similarly, in Kenya, during the 1940s, local councils passed such oddly named measures as the "Lost Women Ordinance," which sought to limit the movement of women to the towns.

Women, for their part, waged intermittent struggles against the losses of power that they experienced. To cite only two examples out of a great many that occurred across the continent, in Eastern Nigeria women rose up periodically throughout the 1920s to resist the introduction of a range of measures which they saw as under-mining their rights (Van Allen 1972, Amadiume 1987). The colonial state responded to the Women's War with military action, killing at least fifty women. In Western Nigeria, women organized against colonially appointed chiefs and ousted some of the rulers who became too autocratic (Mba 1982).

So far, this discussion has mainly addressed the violent treatment meted out to African women by a colonial state which excluded women from all political and administrative structures and from the wage economy that was rapidly superseding precolonial modes of production. But it is also worth noting that overt violence, including widespread abuse of women and the reinforcement of the interests of male despots by the colonial regime, was not the whole picture. There was also the seemingly "benevolent" side of colonial patriarchy, a side which sought to "domes-ticate" and, so, to incorporate a small but significant number of African women. There is now a substantial literature addressing the ways in which the colonizers introduced a bourgeois Victorian ideology of domesticity into Africa. While the vast majority of African women gained no access to education at all, a minority was invited to acquire the graces of "civilized" femininity, namely, to be schooled in embroidery, cake decoration, and flower arranging. The purpose was to turn these women into suitable wives for those African men who performed administrative roles in the colonial state. Much of this indoctrination was undertaken by well-intentioned European women anthropologists, missionaries, and teachers, who set out for the African interior to educate and "uplift" the natives.[7] Hunt (1990) documents the activities of Le Foyer Sociale, a social institution specifically designed by the Belgians to create a small cadre of elite Congolese housewives. These colonially constructed "new women" were to stay at home and keep house for the small numbers of African men in the employ of the colonial regime.[8] Like other class ideologies, domesticity has affected even those who were not part of the elite that actually became European-style housewives. The dominance of the wife-and-mother ideal, an ideal which negated women's social and economic contribution, facilitated the devaluation of their work within the colonial economy.

In addition to perpetrating crude and overt acts of violence against African women, then, the colonization process also transformed African gender relations in complex, diverse, and contradictory ways that we have yet to fully understand. We now know that these transformations, and the dynamic between the colonial regime and the colonized society, varied across social classes. They must also have varied in part according to the character of gender relations in the pre-existing social and political systems, and the cultural, political, and economic powers that women had been able to mobilize in defense of their gender. Prevailing gender ideologies have much bearing on the types of violence that are manifested in a given context. The confinement of women to the economically dependent role of housewife is a condition that has made it difficult for many women to leave otherwise unbearably violent situations. In other words, the domestication of women is a precondition for the crime we define as domestic violence. Similarly, the power to coerce, intimidate, and harass that is wielded by officials and men in uniform in dictatorial societies is a condition for the widespread rape and abuse of women that occur under repressive regimes, since this power is sanctioned by military, religious, or other male-dominated authorities.

AFRICAN NATIONALIST MOVEMENTS AND THE GENDER QUESTION

If, as we have seen, colonialism brutalized, degraded, and domesticated African women, to what extent have the nationalist movements challenged the misogynistic and sexually contradictory legacies of the white masters? Have African women experienced greater liberation since the demise of colonial regimes, or have the nationalists merely continued the trajectories of contempt and disempowerment? What has been the role of women in anti-imperialist struggles, and how has this affected their position in post-colonial states?

Anne McClintock usefully reminds us of the gendered and continuously contested character of nations when she writes:

> All nationalisms are gendered, all are invented, and all are dangerous.... They represent relations to political power and to the technologies of violence ... legitimizing, or limiting, people's access to the rights and resources of the nation-state. (McClintock 1991a)

The foregoing discussion of rape and conquest indicates that colonialism also humiliated women, not only as colonial subjects but also in gender-specific ways. African nationalist discourses have often proclaimed the need to recover the damaged manhood of the African man. Cynthia Enloe (1989) points to the masculinity of many nationalist discourses and the exploitation of male humiliation by liberation movements; she identifies this as a source of male bias in emergent nations. But to what extent have African men been concerned with restoring the dignity of African women? It is now amply documented that women, who were completely excluded from the colonial administrative and political structures, actively participated in the nationalist movements as fighters and party activists. And on many occasions, they took independent action in defense of their own interests as women.

Still, today, women protest the betrayal of women's interests by the nation-states, citing Algeria and Zimbabwe as instances in which men have reneged on their promise to share the fruits of independence. But is there an empirical basis for this sense of betrayal? An examination of gender relations within nationalist discourses may deepen our understanding of the sources of present-day inequalities and enable more effective responses than angry polemics against the men who have monopolized power for themselves. What, then, were the terms on which women participated in these resistance struggles? Perhaps the poor status of the vast majority of women in postcolonial African countries can be traced to the terms of this participation!

The constructions of women in nationalist ideologies have been contradictory. On the one hand, nationalists have called for their own "new woman," while on the other hand, they have construed women as the bearers and upholders of traditions and customs, as reservoirs of culture.[9] In a great many contexts, the terms on which women participated in nationalist struggles have simply not been commensurate with fundamental changes in gender relations. The appearance of harem women on the streets of Egypt during the 1920s to protest against the British may have been welcomed by all supporters of national liberation, but it did not transform male attitudes towards women. Some time later, when the Wafdist Party disagreed with women on key political issues, Huda Sharaawi and other women broke away to form the Egyptian Feminist Union, which not only took more radical positions on a number of key political issues but also defended women's interests (Sharaawi 1986, Badran 1988).

National liberation movements such as the Nkrumah-led CPP, although radical when it came to establishing hegemony over traditional chiefs, cannot be described as propounding a radical gender politics, even though the movement derived enormous support from women's organizations. For all his revolutionary vision, Kwame Nkrumah was unable to view women beyond their reproductive and nurturing roles. He referred to women as: "Mothers of the nation, the beauty that graced the homes and the gentleness that soothed men's tempers" (Tsikata 1989). Many of the nationalists who inherited power from the colonial masters were overtly conservative when it came to matters of sexual politics. Jomo Kenyatta, for example, perhaps wishing to appear nationalistic in the face of missionary activity, asserted that "No Kikuyu worthy of the name would want to marry a girl who [had] not been excised, as this operation [was] a prerequisite for receiving a complete moral and religious education" (Kenyatta 1953).[10] Similar examples can be found in the writings of Sekou Touré, Julius Nyerere, and many other founding fathers of African nationalism. In 1955, Oliver Tambo made what must have been one of the most radical statements of his generation when he not only declared women's emancipation to be a national priority and a precondition for victory but also went so far as to deplore "outmoded customs" and call upon Congressmen to share in domestic work so that women could also be politically active. At the other extreme, one of the most retrograde examples was the Nigerian nationalist leader Tafawa Balewa, who opposed women being given the vote in the northern part of the country, despite the enfranchisement of women in the south.[11]

The African countries cited as most progressive on "the woman question" have tended to be those that have involved women in military action, and not uncoincidentally women across the globe have adopted posters of women carrying guns as icons of revolutionary feminism.[12] Urdang's (1989) study of women's place in the Mozambican war for independence reveals that most of the women fighters actually performed inglorious but necessary tasks (catering, porterage, etc). Others were dispatched to rural areas because as women in a sexually unequal society, they were able to shame men into volunteering. The participation of women in Namibia and in the ongoing liberation war in South Africa has also been studied, but this will require ongoing consideration if majority rule is to include more equal participation of women (not least of all because black women in South Africa have been so oppressed and excluded). It is now clear that even progressive statements from the leadership do not suffice to effect change in the gender relations of a society.

And what happened to women in those places where victory has been secured? Regrettably, the treatment of women in several of the independent states proves that participation in military activity does not necessarily translate into progressive gender politics. As revolutionary a hero as the late Samora Machel is on record reinforcing the sexual division of labor by calling on Mozambican women, but not men, to clean up the streets of Maputo. Reports from Zimbabwe inform us that many of the women who joined men in the bush to fight the white settler regime found themselves rejected in favor of more traditionally feminine women once the fighting was over. But if the gender relations amongst the fighters were as unequal in the field as Urdang's evidence suggests, what basis was there for assuming gender equality would be a necessary fruit of military victory?[13] Even if things were far more progressive on the field of battle, it is quite clear that it is necessary to wage a continuing struggle to deepen women's liberation, even after national independence has been granted or won by military action.

It seems clear that African women entered the postcolonial period at an immense disadvantage and under global conditions which, while increasingly unfavorable to Africa as a whole, nonetheless favored men, who arrogate to themselves the authority of articulating the nation's culture and politics. This background offers some insight into why postcolonial societies have continued to be so oppressive to women.

GENDER IDEOLOGIES AND VIOLENCE IN POSTCOLONIAL AFRICA

The gender politics of postcolonial African governments vary widely, but women continue to be underrepresented in positions of influence (Parpart and Staudt 1989). It often seems that those nations that opted for a socialist model of development have been more progressive than those that did not. In the nascent socialist states, strong women's organizations ensured women's participation in political life by waging campaigns for women's rights, and taking it upon themselves to challenge practices such as wife-beating and forced marriages. The existence of official women's organizations did much to raise the profile of women in the newly independent states. As a result, the legal and constitutional situation for women in Tanzania, Angola, Mozambique, or even Zimbabwe is ahead of many Western countries. Economic dependence continues to preclude fuller exercise of legal rights, however, and issues such as land ownership and the implementation of progressive marriage laws leave much to be desired.

On the other hand, states pursuing capitalist models of development show a different structure and practice of gender inequality. Wamalwa (1989) describes how male Kenyan Parliamentarians repeatedly opposed the replacement of old colonial laws and resisted the introduction of a Marriage Bill in 1968 which would have made wife-beating a criminal offense punishable by six months imprisonment; the Kenyan politicians claimed that wife-beating was "a normal customary practice." In West African states like Nigeria, bureaucratic, social, and cultural inequality prevail but, in practice, most women exercise a high degree of autonomy, a situation facilitated by their involvement in independent economic activities. The high public profile of the wives of the military elite gives the impression that at least these women are extremely powerful in contemporary Nigeria, but even a cursory examination of the empirical evidence indicates this to be far from the truth (WIN 1985).

Since the economic crisis gripped the continent in the 1970s, African women have faced some of the harshest living conditions and forms of oppression in the modern world. The decline of many African economies has been accompanied by political crises, and it is in this context that sexual and coercive controls over women have often been exercised with a vengeance, just as they were in the colonial period. This is exemplified by the "clean-up campaigns" that have taken place in a number of countries. The evidence from Zimbabwe (Jacobs and Howard 1987), Gabon, Zambia, Tanzania, and other nations reveals that these campaigns are frequently accompanied by widespread abuse of women. The women rounded up in Gabon in 1985, for example, were made available to soldiers for the latter's sexual pleasure (Tabet 1991).

Postcolonial national ideologies continue to call upon women to play a circumscribed role, this time as Mothers of the Nation. Mobutu's official doctrine involves the mass "promotion" of women to mere wives and mothers, in an economic climate that compels women to engage in all forms of work outside the home, and often to support entire households. In the postcolonial context, Mobutu's ideology of domesticity distorts the real production relations of the whole country by devaluing women's economic contributions, and thus facilitating greater exploitation of both women and men by international capitalism. Recent research conducted in Zimbabwe shows that since the end of the liberation war, the proportion of women gaining access to education has actually fallen, and that this is most pronounced in the field of higher education (Gaidzanwa 1991). In addition to the public victimization of women by postcolonial regimes, there is also a high tolerance of domestic violence. A Zimbabwean women's group informs us that between January and December 1990, in Harare alone, there were 576 reports of rape and 17,646 reports of assault, of which approximately 5,000 were defined as domestic assaults (Taylor and Stewart

1991). There is no reason to assume that Harare is different from any other post-colonial African capital.

There are a great many ways in which official ideologies interact with civil institutions to reinforce the subordination of women, both directly and indirectly. In Nigeria, we have seen a close interaction between the military governments' campaigns and rising religious fundamentalism, both of which target women directly but also promote violence against them. One of the most unpopular regimes mounted a "War Against Indiscipline" campaign, which attributed the country's worsening economic and political crisis to "moral decadence and laxity." Consequently dispossessed beggars, homeless people, street hawkers, and women were subjected to all manner of harassment. At the time, the media diffused negative images of women, blaming them for widespread immorality and corruption. In this context, in 1986, the military governor of Kano State issued an edict which outlawed single women and which included the ultimatum that women had three months to get married or "be dealt with."[14] A year later, an underground Muslim brotherhood known as "yan daukar amariya" was uncovered when several of its members were arrested for the rape and violent abuse of women.[15] The professed purpose of this fraternity was to molest and violate any woman found on the streets alone, on the basis that those women had no right to be there.

Wamalwa (1989) comments on the underreporting of violence, and draws our attention to the fact that 40 per cent of all cases of domestic violence identified by a preliminary survey in Kenya involved the murder or manslaughter of the woman. This suggests an extremely high tolerance for violence. More recently, during the public outcry over the massacre at St. Kizito school, the headmaster was reported to have remarked that the boys "meant no harm, they only wanted to rape." In any case, most of the press coverage focused on the killings rather than on the rapes.[16] As in many other contexts, woman abuse exists "beyond the law" since the existing legal provisions are not enforced by male police, magistrates, or courts. No man has ever been given the full sentence for rape in Kenya.

Reports by human-rights organizations reveal disturbing evidence of women being detained, sexually abused, and tortured by repressive regimes in Sudan, Mauritania, and Somalia.[17] In short, it seems that a tolerance for violence against women has continued to characterize African social and political life since independence; violence itself appears to be proliferating under the harsh and desperate economic and political conditions now prevailing in many parts of the continent. The final part of this essay considers what measures have been taken to curb this disturbing situation, and how these initiatives compare with those taken in other parts of the world.

ANTI-VIOLENCE STRUGGLES AND STRATEGIES

From the evidence presented above, it is clear that the coercive control of women, endemic in the colonial period, has gone unchallenged by postcolonial regimes. The evidence from women's studies in the West indicates that there, too, women are far from equal in most areas of social life. While a great many changes in women's positions and ways of living have occured in Africa as well as in Europe, violence against woman has continued to be widespread in both regions. Given the historical continuities and fractures in the structural relationships between black and white women in Europe and in the African colonies, it would be worthwhile to analyze the role violence plays in configuring these processes.

Feminist praxis on violence in the West

In the West, women have mobilized and campaigned both inside and outside state structures, with sometimes impressive results. In several European and North American countries, the laws and legal procedures affecting abused women have been changed. Policing practices have come under particularly heavy criticism (Edwards 1986), and this has led some police forces to introduce special training on how to respond better to domestic violence. Improved access to public housing and the provision of refuges for battered women are other concrete results of a long and committed struggle by women's movements. However, a recent study of responses to violence against black women in London indicated that these strategies have been less effective in ameliorating the situation of black and minority women who have been subjected to violence (Mama 1989b).

Mainstream Western feminist theorizations of violence often do not take into account the realities of black women's lives. This is partly because, in the West, it has been radical feminists who have been at the forefront of the organized campaigns aimed at eradicating male violence against women. Within radical feminist discourse, gender is regarded as the most fundamental social division, and men are viewed as being inherently and irredeemably aggressive. In keeping with this view, radical feminists treat women as if they were a single homogeneous group, devoid of class and racial inequalities, reduced to mere instances of male power. Socialist and liberal feminists have been less vocal in this area of feminist praxis, with the result that these particular radical views have dominated the antiviolence movement.

Feminist responses to violence against women in late-capitalist countries have also presumed a certain type of state structure, namely one that provides welfare support, such as housing, and a law-abiding, if recalcitrant, police force. It has been assumed that most women live in nuclear marriages with breadwinning husbands upon whom they are economically dependent. However, these assumptions do not hold for many black and working-class women. For one thing, public services have failed miserably in their attempts to offer appropriate support to black women, and welfare professionals (mostly from parochial middle-class backgrounds) have often demonstrated their class prejudices. For another, because of racism, black women face additional hardships in obtaining public housing, appropriate police protection, or legal support. On account of the increasingly discriminatory immigration laws many black women constantly confront the risk of being deported when and if they seek assistance, or of being racially harassed when and if they seek police or legal intervention.

Even within the so-called liberal democracies of Western Europe, women are subordinated in diverse ways, a fact which feminist theorists of violence have yet to fully address. But the transfer of European feminist theories and strategies to Africa cannot be easy. Not only are there historical biases which have not been purged, but these theories have also been developed in late-capitalist contexts under a specific set of conditions that are very different from those in African countries. Britain, for example, is a welfare state, and there are complex legal and public policy considerations which are preconditions for even the limited success of the women's movements there. Even within such contexts, black feminists have found it necessary to organize autonomously with a view to articulating a different antiviolence politics – drawing attention to acts of violence against both sexes, acts of aggression perpetrated by the state itself, the deaths of black men in police custody, and police assaults on black women. Also, they have had to highlight the vulnerability of black people to racial attacks on the streets and in housing estates. In short, black feminists in the so-called liberal democracies have concluded that it is inadequate to theorize violence as an inherently male characteristic with only women as victims.

To illustrate further the nontransferability of Western feminist strategies to the developing world, consider what happened when the British strategy of establishing refuges for women was adopted by some Indian women's groups. In the absence of long-term housing options for battered women in the Subcontinent, where there is not the same kind of public housing as in Britain, new problems of homelessness and destitution were created for the women survivors, who, having left their homes, had neither a home to return to nor any other alternative accommodation.

African antiviolence struggles

Only in very few countries has the state has been the main vehicle for antiviolence activism. In Uganda, women Parliamentarians have been extremely vocal. Perhaps because the rape and abuse of women had become so widespread during the years of dictatorship and war, after much heated debate, the controversial Immorality Act was passed in 1990.[18] This contains provisions for stringent sentences for rape (life imprisonment) and child rape (death sentence).[19] At the time of this writing, no one has yet been convicted or sentenced under these provisions but, at the local level, rape cases are being reported and dealt with by the local Resistance Councils.[20]

In other African countries, women's projects have been able to secure donor funding to conduct research and produce resource material and information packages for use in antiviolence work. The Tanzanian Women's Media Association in Dar Es Salaam and the Women and Law in Southern Africa research network are just two examples. In Nigeria, despite the huge amount of publicity surrounding the First Lady's "Better Life Programme," including the recent launching of a multimillion-dollar center for women's development, there has been no official action on woman abuse. Rather, it was left to an autonomons and relatively low-profile organization like Women in Nigeria to hold the first ever workshop on the subject as recently as March 1992.

It also needs to be said, on the basis of the ungathered evidence of millions of women all over the continent, that African women have not been passive recipients of abuse, as some authorities would have us believe. The evidence that is available suggests that they have found numerous ways of resisting the humiliations meted out to them, both individually and with the help of sympathetic friends and relatives. In the same way, African communities daily house and support millions of refugees locally, with none of the hostility that affluent nations now direct toward the few thousand who have been driven as far as Europe. Here, where there is no welfare-delivery system, it must be said that for every abused women who makes the headlines by being killed or maimed, or for each of those who suffer in clubbed-down silence, there must be many thousands who receive local support and who engage in a hidden struggle for their survival and dignity – a continuous struggle that neither receives nor demands acknowledgment.

CONCLUSION

From the historical record, we saw how, during the colonial period, new gender ideologies were introduced, ideologies regarding women's and men's status across the African continent. Colonial gender ideologies were the product of both internal and external factors, and were fed by cultural and material conditions which interacted in complex ways as we entered the postcolonial epoch. There is clearly a need for more detailed study of these developments in particular locales, even as we forge international links. We need to understand and theorize the diversity within different nations and across the African continent, and the ways in which Europe underdeveloped different parts of Africa differently, common legacies at the level of state structures and circumscribed constructions of womanhood notwithstanding.

This essay has sketched a general framework which highlights the ways in which the European chauvinistic constructions of femininity and a marginalizing ideology of domesticity decreased the legal and social status of African women in many spheres of life, in both rural and urban areas. As I have shown, when we consider the history of woman abuse, we must recognize that there have been pernicious continuites between colonial, nationalist, and postcolonial systems.

I have tried to argue that perhaps because of the pervasiveness and extreme character of woman abuse in the region, African women have had to rely on their own indigenous strategies; some have left violent situations while others embark upon completely different lifestyles, often with the covert support of other women or sympathetic members of their communities. No doubt, many of these heroic responses have been invisible because they have usually been individual reactions to horrendous conditions and have remained unsupported by the communities at large. In recent years, women have begun to resist violence in a more collective manner, both within and outside state structures. Women have deployed different strategies in different countries with varying degrees of success. It is high time that these bold initiatives won more definite support at the local, national, and international levels.

NOTES

The title of this essay is inspired by Angela Carter's postholocaust love story *Heroes and Villains*, published by Heinemann in 1969.

1   This essay does not address practices defined as cultural, medical, or cosmetic (for example, clitoridectomy, infibulation, scarification), but focuses on rape and other sexual

and physical assaults inflicted on women by men against their will, in both the private and public spheres.

2   The tragedy of Saarjie Baartman's life and the violence done to her even after her death indicate the perverse sexual fascination that an otherwise prudish society had for other races. The colonizers came from a Europe which fetishized Africans in displays and exhibitions, and relegated them to subhuman status (Mama, (1995) *Beyond the Masks: Race, Gender, and Subjectivity*, New York: Routledge.)

3   The Contagious Diseases Acts entitled the authorities to subject women suspected of "immoral" living to regular vaginal examinations and confinement for treatment (by force if necessary). In the colonies, the cost of treating African women identified as prostitutes was deemed prohibitive, so only the colonial forces were offered treatment.

    One cannot help but be reminded of the forced "virginity tests" and vaginal examinations to which Asian and African women were subjected at British ports-of-entry. While "virginity testing" was stopped after public outrage and black feminist campaigns in the early 1980s, vaginal examinations continue to be carried out, particularly on African women. Many African men are subjected to equally intrusive anal examinations. This practice also continues at African ports, enforced by regimes under pressure to counteract the flow of drug trafficking.

4   See Angela Carter's insightful reconstruction of the relationship between Baudelaire and his mistress, Jeanne Duval, in *Black Venus* (Picador, 1985).

5   This particular circular is reported to have been hastily withdrawn because of its "impracticality" (Callaway 1987, 49).

6   These services included catering, beer-brewing, laundry, and sex (White 1990; Naanen 1991).

7   It is a matter of historical record that a significant proportion of the early Western feminists were pro-imperialist (hooks 1984).

8   Similarly, the practice of purdah increased markedly during the colonial period in Northern Nigeria (Imam 1991).

9   Colonisers found the fact that African women were "more traditional" a negative trait, while many African men regard it as desirable. Both agree that urban women are "whores" and less "reputable" than the strangely simplified category of "rural women." According to the myth, rural women continue to live contentedly as beasts of burden, never challenging anyone's authority, least of all that of their menfolk.

10 "Kikuyu" here refers exclusively to men.

11 Gambo Sawaba, a leading woman activist, was repeatedly assaulted and harassed for her campaign to change this situation. Women in the North of independent Nigeria were finally allowed to vote in 1976, but regressive forces, continuing to protest during the current transition to civilian rule, have succeeded in their demands for separate arrangements for women voters in 1991.

12 Posters of Palestinian and Eritrean women fighters wearing "Arafat scarves" and the SWAPO poster of a woman with a gun over her shoulder and a baby on her back are found hanging in women's centers all over the West. I have yet to see a poster of a male fighter with a gun and a baby, or one simply carrying a baby, attract the same attention.

13 More recently, I observed the Eritrean celebration of the first anniversary of the end of the war with Ethiopia, referred to by many as the Eritrean Revolution. As many as 30 percent of the EPLF fighters were women, and a great deal has been said and written about the liberation of women on the battlefields. Consequently, I felt it almost sacrilegous that no Eritrean women were in evidence amongst the provisional government dignitaries on the parade ground or at the official reception celebrating the event. The very colorful and skilled cultural displays on that festive occasion were more about remembering the

martyred sons and recovering Eritrean "traditional cultures" than about forging new social relations between the genders or sustaining the equality that is reported to have been practiced behind the battlelines.

14 The 1986 edict is almost identical to that issued by the British in colonial Katsina in 1916 (referred to earlier in the text), except that it gave women three months instead of seven days in which to marry.

15 *West Africa* (March 1987). Other examples of religious fraternities perpetrating acts of violence against women in Sudan have been documented by Africa Watch (April 9, 1990).

16 Sources: Accounts of Nairobi residents are given in *Weekly Review*, Aug. 9, 1991. One women's magazine did take the opportunity to observe the extent to which ingrained male violence characterizes Kenyan women's lives. See *Presence* 7, no. 8 (1991).

17 See the Amnesty International 1991 report *Women in the Frontline*, and Africa Watch reports.

18 This rather strangely named legislation was featured in a community theater performance by an African women's group in Amsterdam that same year; it was humorously compared to the South African Immorality Act which made interracial sex illegal!

19 The widespread impact of AIDS on Ugandan society must be one of the reasons for such stringent measures being introduced. It remains to be seen how effectively they will be implemented and whether they will function as a deterrent.

20 Newspaper reports gleaned during October 1992.

WORKS CITED

Amadiume, I. 1987. *Male Daughters, Female Husbands: Gender and Sex in an African Society.* London: Zed Press.

Badran, M. 1988. "Dual Liberation: Feminism and Nationalism in Egypt, 1870–1925." *Feminist Issues* 8, no. 1 (1988).

Callaway, H. 1987. *Gender, Culture and Empire: European Women in Colonial Nigeria.* London: Macmillan.

Chelser, P. 1972. *Women and Madness.* New York: Doubleday.

Dobash, R. E. and Dobash, R. 1980. *Violence Against Wives.* London: Open Books.

Edwards, S. 1986. *The Police Responses to Domestic Violence in London.* Polytechnic of Central London.

Enloe, C. 1989. *Bananas, Beaches and Bases: Making Feminist Sense of International Politics.* London: Pandora.

Fanon, F. 1980. *A Dying Colonialism.* London: Writers and Readers.

Gaidzanwa, R. 1991. "Women and Education in Zimbabwe." Paper presented at CODESRIA workshop on "Gender Analysis and African Social Science," Dakar, Sept. 16–20, 1991.

Helie-Lucas, M. 1987. "Against Nationalism: The Betrayal of Algerian Women." *Trouble and Strife* 11 (Summer 1987).

hooks, b. 1984. *From Margin to Center.* Boston: South End Press.

Hunt, N. R. 1990. "Domesticity and Colonialism in Belgian Africa: Usumbura's Foyer Social, 1946–1960." *Signs* 15, no. 3 (1990): 447–74.

Imam, A. 1991. "Women Should Neither Be Seen Nor Heard? Identity Politics and Women's Mobilisation in Kano, Northern Nigeria." In Valentin Moghadan, ed. *Identity Politics and Women: Cultural Reassertions and Feminisms in International Perspective* (London: Oxford University Press).

Jacobs, S. and Howard, T. 1987. "Women in Zimbabwe: State Policy and State Action." In *Women, State and Ideology*, ed. H. Afshar. London: Macmillan.

Jayawardena, K. 1986. *Feminism and Nationalism in the Third World*. London: Zed Press.

Kenyatta, J. 1953. *Facing Mount Kenya: The Tribal Life of the Kikuyu*. London: Secker and Warburg.

Mama, A. 1989a. "Violence Against Black Women: Gender, Race and State Responses." *Feminist Review* no. 32 (1989): 30–48.

Mama, A. 1989b. *The Hidden Struggle: Voluntary and Statutory Responses to Violence Against Black Women*. London: Runnymede Trust.

Mba, N. 1982. *Nigerian Women Mobilised: Women's Political Activities in Southern Nigeria 1900–1965*. Berkeley: University of California Press.

McClintock, A. 1991a. " 'No Longer in a Future Heaven?': Women and Nationalism in South Africa." *Transition* no. 51 (1991): 104–23.

McClintock, A. 1991b. "The Scandal of the Whorearchy: Prostitution in Colonial Nairobi." *Transition* no. 52 (1991): 92–99.

Mies, M. 1986. *Patriarchy and Accumulation on a World Scale: Women in the International Division of Labour*. London: Zed Press.

Mohammed, P. 1991. "Reflections on the Women's Movement in Trinidad: Calypsoes, Changes and Sexual Violence." *Feminist Review*, no. 38 (1991): 33–47.

Naanen, B. 1991. " 'Itinerant Goldmines': Prostitution in the Cross River Basin in Nigeria 1930–1950." *African Studies Review* 34, no. 2 (1991): 57–9.

Okonjo, K. 1976. "The Dual Sex Political System in Operation: Igbo Women and Community Politics in Mid-Western Nigeria." in N. Hafkin and E. Bay. eds. *Women in Africa*. Palo Alto, Calif.: Stanford University Press.

Parpart, J. and Staudt, K. 1989. eds. *Women and the State in Africa*. London: Lynne Rienner Publishers.

Schmidt, E. 1991. "Patriarchy, Capitalism, and the Colonial State in Zimbabwe." *Signs* 16, 4 (Summer 1991): 732–56.

Sharaawi, H. 1986. *Harem Years: The Memoirs of an Egyptian Feminist*. London: Virago.

Stott, R. 1989. "The Dark Continent: Africa as Female Body in Haggard's Adventure Fiction." *Feminist Review*, no. 32 (1989): 69–89.

Tabet, P. 1991. " 'I'm the Meat, I'm the Knife': Sexual Service, Migration and Repression in Some African Societies." *Feminist Issues* (Spring 1991): 3–21.

Taylor, J. and Stewart, S. 1991. *Sexual and Domestic Violence: Help, Recovery and Action in Zimbabwe*. Women and Law in Southern Africa, PO Box VA 171, Union Avenue, Harare, Zimbabwe.

Tsikata, E. 1989. "Women's Organisation and the State in Ghana." *Women and History Series*. The Hague: Institute of Social Studies.

Urdang, S. 1989. *And Still They Dance: Women, War and the Struggle for Change in Mozambique*. New York/London: Monthly Review Press.

Van Allen, J. 1972. "Sitting on a Man: Colonialism and the Lost Political Institutions of Igbo Women." *Canadian Journal of African Studies* 6, no. 2 (1972): 165–82.

Wamalma, B.N. 1989. "Violence Against Wives and the Law in Kenya." in M. A. Mbeo and O. Ooko-Ombaka, eds. *Women and the Law in Kenya*, Nairobi, Public Law Institute.

White, L. 1990. *The Comforts of Home: Women and Prostitution in Colonial Nairobi*. Chicago: University of Chicago Press.

Part IV
Caribbean Encounters: Revolution, Hybridity, Diaspora

George Lamming, "Colonialism and the Caribbean Novel"
Stuart Hall, "Negotiating Caribbean Identities"
Peter Hulme, "Survival and Invention: Indigeneity in the Caribbean"
Moira Ferguson, "Sending the Younger Son Across the Wide Sargasso Sea: The New
  Colonizer Arrives"

Colonialism and the Caribbean Novel

George Lamming

George Lamming's *In the Castle of My Skin*, one of the first Caribbean novels, was revolutionary both in its experimentalism and in its willingness to confront the problems of racism and slavery. The essay reproduced here, which Lamming wrote as an introduction to his own novel over thirty years after its initial publication, addresses an array of concerns about the Caribbean novel. Like **Chinua Achebe**'s essay on Conrad, Lamming's essay engages the problem of race within a context of the silencing of subaltern experience that constitutes the history of imperialism and of the European novel, specifically Conrad's *Heart of Darkness* in which "demonic Europe" is "maliciously identified" with Africa. Lamming's discussion of Africa complements Achebe's in another sense, for Lamming is concerned both in this essay and in his novel with a quintessentially Caribbean problematic: that of migrancy and exile. Slavery is figured as the origin of this problematic, a European crime at the heart of Caribbean identity. Lamming's consideration of an Africa that "broods over the faces, the canefields, the broken huts and sugar fortunes" of the Caribbean can be usefully read alongside **Moira Ferguson**'s analysis of Jean Rhys's *Wide Sargasso Sea*. In this way, the student can get a sense of the complexity of the Caribbean novel, especially with regard to race. Reading Lamming's essay alongside **Stuart Hall**'s and **Peter Hulme**'s essays on Caribbean identity provides another critical nexus, one that can be broadened by considering other postcolonial experiences with identity-formation, like those described in essays by **R. Radhakrishnan, Kwame Anthony Appiah**, and **Helen Tiffin**.

Colonialism and the Caribbean Novel

The reading of fiction involves a certain conspiracy of feeling between the writer and his reader. They have both agreed to accord every act of the imagination the status of an absolute truth. And the world of fiction must work toward this end. It may be helpful, therefore, to alert readers to the kind of device which this writer has employed in the creation of that world; and especially since his methods denote a break from conventional practice.

In the Castle of My Skin introduces us to a world of poor and simple villagers; and the village functions both as place and symbol of an entire way of life.

> The village was a marvel of small, heaped houses raised jauntily on groundsels of limestone, and arranged in rows on either side of the multiplying marl roads. Sometimes the roads disintegrated, the limestone slid back and the houses advanced across their boundaries to meet those on the opposite side in an embrace of board and shingle and cactus fence. . . . There were days when the village was quiet: the shoemaker plied lazily at his trade and the washerwomen bent over the tubs droned away their complacency. At other times there were scenes of terror, and once there was a scene of murder.
>
> But the season of flood could change everything. The floods could level the stature and even conceal the identity of the village. With the turn of my ninth year it had happened again. From the window I looked at the uniform wreckage of a village at night in water. . . . I went away from the window over the dripping sacks and into a corner which the weather had forgotten. And what did I remember? My father who had only fathered the idea of me had left me the sole liability of my mother who really fathered me.

This world is not really the creation of individual wills. There is no privacy since the secret of each household can never escape communal scrutiny. I know your business and you know mine. The mother of the novel is given no name. She is simply G's mother, a woman of little or no importance in her neighborhood until the tropical season rains a calamity on every household; and she emerges, without warning, as a voice of nature itself.

> Then she broke into a soft repetitive tone which rose with every fresh surge of feeling until it became a scattering peal of solicitude that soared across the night and into the neighbour's house. And the answer came back louder, better organized and more communicative, so that another neighbour responded and yet another until the voices

Taken from *In the Castle of My Skin* (Ann Arbor: University of Michigan Press, 1991), pp. xxxv–xlvi.

seemed to be gathered up by a single effort and the whole village shook with song on its foundation of water.

I cite that passage in order to introduce readers to a characteristic of this type of fiction which has caused some difficulty for the conventional critic of the novel. And what I say now of *In the Castle of My Skin* is also true of other Caribbean writers. The book is crowded with names and people, and although each character is accorded a most vivid presence and force of personality, we are rarely concerned with the prolonged exploration of an individual consciousness. It is the collective human substance of the Village itself which commands our attention. The Village, you might say, is the central character. When we see the Village as collective character, we perceive another dimension to the individual wretchedness of daily living. It is the dimension of energy, force, a quickening capacity for survival. The Village sings, the Village dances; and since the word is their only rescue, all the resources of a vital oral folk tradition are summoned to bear witness to the essential humanity which rebukes the wretchedness of their predicament.

In this method of narration, where community, and not person, is the central character, things are never so tidy as critics would like. There is often no discernible plot, no coherent line of events with a clear, causal connection. Nor is there a central individual consciousness where we focus attention, and through which we can be guided reliably by a logical succession of events. Instead, there are several centers of attention which work simultaneously and acquire their coherence from the collective character of the Village.

The Novel has had a peculiar function in the Caribbean. The writer's preoccupation has been mainly with the poor; and fiction has served as a way of restoring these lives – this world of men and women from down below – to a proper order of attention; to make their reality the supreme concern of the total society. But along with this desire, there was also the writer's recognition that this world, in spite of its long history of deprivation, represented the womb from which he himself had sprung, and the richest collective reservoir of experience on which the creative imagination could draw.

This world of men and women from down below is not simply poor. This world is black, and it has a long history at once vital and complex. It is vital because it constitutes the base of labor on which the entire Caribbean society has rested; and it is complex because Plantation Slave Society (the point at which the modern Caribbean began) conspired to smash its ancestral African culture, and to bring about a total alienation of man the source of labor from man the human person.

The result was a fractured consciousness, a deep split in its sensibility which now raised difficult problems of language and values; the whole issue of cultural allegiance between the imposed norms of White Power, represented by a small numerical minority, and the fragmented memory of the African masses: between White instruction and Black imagination. The totalitarian demands of White supremacy, in a British colony, the psychological injury inflicted by the sacred rule that all forms of social status would be determined by the degrees of skin complexion; the ambiguities among Blacks themselves about the credibility of their own spiritual history.

All this would have to be incorporated into any imaginative record of the total society. Could the outlines of a national consciousness be charted and affirmed out of all this disparateness? And if that conciousness could be affirmed, what were its true ancestral roots, its most authentic cultural base? The numerical superiority of the black mass could forge a political authority of their own making, and provide an alternative direction for the society. This was certainly possible. But this possibility was also the measure of its temporary failures.

I was among those writers who took flight from that failure. In the desolate, frozen heart of London, at the age of twenty-three, I tried to reconstruct the world of my childhood and early adolescence. It was also the world of a whole Caribbean reality.

Migration was not a word I would have used to describe what I was doing when I sailed with other West Indians to England in 1950. We simply thought that we were going to an England which had been planted in our childhood consciousness as a heritage and a place of welcome. It is the measure of our innocence that neither the claim of heritage nor the expectation of welcome would have been seriously doubted. England was not for us a country with classes and conflicts of interest like the islands we had left. It was the name of a responsibility whose origin may have coincided with the beginning of time.

Today I shudder to think how a country, so foreign to our own instincts, could have achieved the miracle of being called Mother. It had made us pupils to its language and its institutions, baptized us in the same religion; schooled boys in the same game of cricket with its elaborate and meticulous etiquette of rivalry. Empire was not a very dirty word, and seemed to bear little relation to those forms of domination we now call imperialist.

The English themselves were not aware of the role they had played in the formation of these black strangers. The ruling class were serenely confident that any role of theirs must have been an act of supreme generosity. Like Prospero, they had given us language and a way of naming our own reality. The English working class were not aware they had played any role at all, and deeply resented our arrival. It had come about without any warning. No one had consulted them. Occasionally I was asked: "Do you belong to us or the French?" I had been dissolved in the common view of worker and aristocrat. English workers could also see themselves as architects of Empire. ·

Much of the substance of *In the Castle of My Skin* is an evocation of this tragic innocence. Nor was there, at the time of writing, any conscious effort, on my part, to emphasize the dimension of cruelty which had seduced, or driven by the force of need, an otherwise honorable black people into such lasting bonds of illusion. It was not a physical cruelty. Indeed, the colonial experience of my generation was almost wholly without violence. No torture, no concentration camp, no mysterious disappearance of hostile natives, no army encamped with orders to kill. The Caribbean endured a different kind of subjugation. It was a terror of the mind; a daily exercise in self-mutilation. Black versus black in a battle for self-improvement:

> Each represented for the other an image of the enemy. And the enemy was My People. My people are low-down nigger people. My people don't like to see their people get on. The language of the overseer. The language of the civil servant. . . . Not taking chances with you people, my people. They always let you down. Make others say we're not responsible, we've no sense of duty. Like children under the threat of hellfire they

accepted instinctively that the others, meaning the white, were superior, yet there was always the fear of realizing that it might be true. This world of the others' imagined perfection hung like a dead weight over their energy. If the low-down nigger people weren't what they are, the others couldn't say anything about us. Suspicion, distrust, hostility. These operated in every decision. You never can tell with my people. It was the language of the overseer, the language of the Government servant, and later the language of lawyers and doctors who had returned stamped like an envelope with what they called the culture of the Mother Country.

This was the breeding ground for every uncertainty of self. In the riot scene of the novel, a group of men armed with knives, and ready with stones, have ambushed the white landlord on his way home. There is a clear intention to kill him, but the act of political revenge is delayed by argument about its timing. Should we strike now or a little later? Their deliberations go on and on, and betray a latent ambivalence which is finally resolved by the arrival of their labor leader who pleads with them to withdraw. The landlord escapes, unharmed.

When I read this scene some twenty years after its publication, I was surprised by the mildness of its resolution. From the distant and more critical vantage point of London, the past now seemed more brutal. I wondered why I had allowed the landlord to go free. Was it the need to make the story conform to the most accurate portrayal of events as I had known them? No white man had been killed by rioters in Barbados in 1937. But I had taken greater liberty with other facts and done so in the interest of a more essential truth. Now I had begun to think that the most authentic response to the long history of shame and humiliation which had produced the riots demanded that the white landlord should have been killed.

The novelist does not only explore what had happened. At a deeper level of intention than literal accuracy, he seeks to construct a world that might have been; to show the possible as a felt and living reality. So for a long time I remained haunted by the feeling that the white landlord should have been killed; even if it were presented as the symbolic end of a social order that deserved to be destroyed.

The novel was completed within two years of my arrival in London. I still shared in that previous innocence which had socialized us into seeing our relations to empire as a commonwealth of mutual interests. The truth is there was never any such reciprocity of interests, and the various constitutional settlements which would gradually lead to the recent status of independence had a decisive influence in preserving much of the social legacy of the colonial period. Today the region is witnessing with alarm what is, in fact, an upheaval too long delayed. But the tactical withdrawal which the British now so proudly call decolonization simply made way for a new colonial orchestration. The Caribbean returns to its old role of an imperial frontier, now perceived as essential to the security interests of the United States.

It is interesting for me to reflect on the role which America was to play in shaping essential features of the novel. If England dominated our minds as the original idea of ultimate human achievement, the United States existed for us as a dream, a kingdom of material possibilities accessible to all. I had never visited the United States before writing *In the Castle of My Skin*; but America had often touched our lives with gifts that seemed spectacular at the time, and reminded us that this dream of unique luxury beyond our shores was true. This image of America has not changed. Almost everyone had some distant relation there who had done well. I had never heard of anyone being a failure in the United States. And Christmas was evidence of this when postal orders arrived with money and gifts of exotic clothes.

But the United States had also provided the character, Trumper, with a political experience which the subtle force of British imperialism had never allowed to flourish in the islands. After his sojourn in the United States as a migrant laborer, Trumper returned home with a new ideology, and the startling discovery that his black presence had a very special meaning in the world. He had learned the cultural and political significance of race.

Europe had trained black men to wear those white masks which Franz Fanon wrote so bitterly about, and which the racist culture of the United States would tear asunder. America was really the extreme example of Europe, stripped naked of all pretense about having a civilizing mission in the dark corners of the earth: a vast, energetic extension of that demonic Europe which the novelist Joseph Conrad had so maliciously identified as a Heart of Darkness in Africa.

> They were conquerors, and for that you want only brute force – nothing to boast of, when you have it, since your strength is just an accident arising from the weakness of others. They grabbed what they could get for the sake of what was to be got. It was just robbery with violence, aggravated murder on a great scale, and men going at it blind – as is very proper for those who tackle a darkness. The conquest of the earth, which mostly means the taking it away from those who have a different complexion or slightly flatter noses than ourselves, is not a pretty thing when you look into it too much.

Conrad, a child of Europe, understood the cultural racism of his own ancestry. Africa, a human continent to its own people, existed in Conrad's consciousness as a proper symbol of the demonic force which had driven his own white race to raid and vandalize every corner of the globe.

And so, in the United States, the black man was forced to recognize himself as a different kind of creature. Trumper embraced this new status, and on his return home offered it to the astonished villagers as the only foundation for a free human dignity among black people.

> You'll hear 'bout the Englishman, an' the Frenchman, and the American which mean man of America. An' each is call that 'cause he born in that particular place. But you'll become a Negro like me an' all the rest in the states an' all over the world, 'cause it ain't have nothin' to do with where you born. 'Tis what you is, a different kind o' creature. An' when you see what I tellin' you an' you become a Negro, act as you should, an' don't ask Hist'ry why you is what you then see yourself to be, 'cause Hist'ry ain't got no answers. You ain't a thing till you know it.

This stark and bitter message of Trumper, pan-African in character, is supported in argument by the recorded music of black people: "Let My People Go." The voice of Paul Robeson becomes his weapon.

It is difficult to write soberly about the persistent influence of race in the formation of human thought. It holds a unique place in the conciousness of black people wherever they may be; and this is unlikely to change until Africa becomes a black continent whose sovereignty is the product of her own institutions and is protected by an economic and military strength that can defy any intruder. The cordiality which exists between African countries and their former French imperialist masters, and the harrassment of Angola by apartheid South Africa are an odd and cruel sequel to the various declarations of African independence. It is as though nothing had changed except the flags and the expanding scale of western robbery.

There is a sense in which the Afro-American has acquired a critical awareness of this racial drama. He sees through the language of negotiation and diplomacy imposed upon African and West Indian leaders, and is often appalled by the terms of our accommodation to white privilege. But he doesn't often see with the same clarity how the process of colonization may have divided black majorities into conflicting social strata, pruning away from the main body or trunk of our human tree those elitist branches that are trained like termites to work corrosively on its roots. The overwhelming torment of race has made it difficult for Afro-Americans to perceive how central is the conflict of class in the ultimate liberation of black countries. On the other hand a false preoccupation with social status seduces the black West Indian into wishing the racial component away.

Africa broods over the faces, the canefields, the broken huts, and sugar fortunes of *In the Castle of My Skin*. But it is not recognized until the land is asleep, and the ocean threatens the island with the memories of that fatal crossing. An ancestral voice breaks through the dream of the village elder, Pa:

> And strange was the time that change my neighbour and me, the tribes with gods and the one tribe without. The silver of exchange sail cross the sea and my people scatter like clouds in the sky when the waters come. There was similar buying and selling 'mongst tribe and tribe, but this was the biggest of the bargains for tribes. Each sell his own.... A man walked out in the market square and one buyer watch his tooth and another his toe and the parts that was private for the coming of a creature in the intimate night. The silver sail from hand to hand and the purchase was shipped like a box of good fruit. The sale was the best of Africa's produce, and me and my neighbour made the same bargain. I make my peace with the Middle Passage to settle on that side of the sea and the white man call a world that was west of another world.... We were for a price that had no value; we were a value beyond any price....
>
> I see the purchase of tribes on the silver sailing vessels, some to Jamaica, Antigua, Grenada, some to Barbados and the island of oil and the mountain tops. And then as 'tis now, though the season change, some was trying to live and some trying to die, and some was too tired to worry about either. The families fall to pieces, and many a brother never see his sister nor father the son.

The ancestral spirit, speaking through the voice of an old man on the eve of his death, provides the kind of history which the village could not have learned from its official school. A different myth was planted there, interrupting and, in the view of some students, actually eliminating beyond recall the continuities of feeling and perception which linked Africa to her transplanted sons and daughters in the New World. It is this area of twilight which has attracted and teased the imagination of many Caribbean poets and novelists; and in more recent times has offered a promise of redemption for the cultural nationalist and the political activist.

In 1950 I could not have foreseen the drama that would launch Africa like a hurricane across the ocean and into the hearts of islands and cities of the black Americas. Many who were once afraid of Africa had now become afraid for Africa. The murder of Lumumba reminded us of an old conspiracy within our ranks. "There was a similar buying and selling 'mongst tribe and tribe." But these contradictions were not wholly negative. When the Kenyan novelist, Ngugi wa Thiong'o told me that *In the Castle of My Skin* was the signal which alerted him to what he had to do as a Kikuyu and a pan-Africanist writer, I too was assured that the continuities which united Africa and the Black Americas were at work.

This theme has been the main thrust of Edward Brathwaite's work as a poet and historian. But it is a difficult terrain. The demands of labor introduced a more complex world than either Europe or Africa could have bargained for.

> Now there's been new combinations and those that come after made quite a different collection. . . . Now not only black nor white, but all colours that give credit to the skin in these islands of the west.

Neither China nor India had then left any mark on Barbados. We had lived as a black majority under the fearful domination of a minority of white sugar planters and merchants. There was evidence of considerable miscegenation, but there was always a rigid code of separate development. Blacks divided along lines of complexion, and all were kept severely at a social distance from the white world. The island has never really overcome this barrier; and a concordat of silence descends on any crisis which appears to have its origins in race and color.

Africa existed in Barbados and throughout the Caribbean, and refuses to be buried by the institutions which sought to render it impotent and void of any spiritual force. School, church, the language and ritual of English courts of law, the mysteries of parliament: all these had to be learned in the interests of black survival and social advancement.

But Africa has remained a source of embarrassment here, although the actual nature of the embarrassment may have changed. Once we were truly nervous at any suggestion that we were part of a world that had not graduated to the status of human. We held this truth on the authority of the institutions which mediated our daily lives. We lived the purest racism without acknowledging that any such calamity had really touched our lives.

Today the embarrassment is more likely to be felt if there is a charge that we seek to deny Africa any part in our spiritual formation. The other response is a rhapsodic and uncritical embrace of Africa as a mother once stolen and now miraculously restored to our embrace. It was perhaps this fear the ancestral spirit tentatively warned against.

> So if you hear some young fool fretting about back to Africa, keep far from the invalid and don't force a passage to where you won't yet belong.

Sometimes the twilight startles with signs of recognition: an old woman who places bits of food under a tree and for no one in particular: the spontaneous libation of the run shop drinker, the hallucinatory form of worship that may suddenly strike a simple believer who can't explain what world she had been transported to. And always a reluctant faith in the supernatural force that heals, or intervenes in moments of domestic crisis. The politician is frequently in search of an obeah man.

Africa invades us like an invisible force we dare not acknowledge, fearing the journey may take us beyond the boundaries of our approved instruction. And all this subliminal life goes on in spite of the determined resistance of the official institutions. The white myths, firmly planted by conquest and enslavement, have been internalized, and continue to work like litmus on the black rock whose history we have not yet summoned to our rescue.

Sometimes the twilight darkens and threatens to obliterate all memory in the tidal wave of capitalist consumerism. America spreads itself like a plague everywhere, capturing the simplest appetite with the fastest foods and nameless fripperies the advertising industry instructs us are essential needs. It is this obstacle the world of the ancestral spirit may not survive. A new class of black housewife now flies from these islands to Los Angeles for some novel brand of underwear. This barbarism has become the style of a new ruling group: a new breed of professional nationalist who may be heard in international councils arguing the case for a new economic order. They are the adolescent offspring of that slave culture which has persisted through school and college, university and people's parliament.

In his introduction to the first American edition of the novel, Richard Wright made this observation:

> Notwithstanding the fact that Lamming's story, as such, is his own, it is, at the same time, a symbolic repetition of the story of millions of simple folk who, sprawled over half the world's surface and involving more than half of the human race, are today being catapulted out of their peaceful, indigenously earthy lives and into the turbulence and anxiety of the twentieth century.

Turbulence is at work everywhere, but anxiety does not adequately describe what has been happening with that half of mankind since Richard Wright wrote his introduction. The catapulted ones have become the subject of their own history, engaged in a global war to liberate their villages, rural and urban, from the old encirclement of poverty, ignorance, and fear.

This is the most fundamental battle of our time, and I am joyfully lucky to have been made, by my work, a soldier in their ranks.

Negotiating Caribbean Identities

STUART HALL

(Jamaican)

Stuart Hall is well known for his work in British cultural studies and has written extensively on politics in the age of Margaret Thatcher. Additionally, he has been instrumental in disseminating the idea of "diaspora" as a governing trope for Caribbean identities. In this essay, Hall addresses a number of issues connected to Caribbean identities – the plural is crucial in Hall's and other postcolonial critics' understanding of identity-formation in the wake of colonial rule – especially the problem of "essentialism" and the anti-essentialism of diaspora as a trope for multiple origins and thus multiple "essences." Drawing on his own experience, Hall underscores the ways in which migration, whether forced or freely entered into, bears "the stamp of historical violence and rupture." The student will find in Hall's remarks a rich resource of ideas about cultural assimilation and "cross-influence," the dynamic and dialogic processes by which the Caribbean is linked historically and psychically both to Africa and to the metropolitan centers of Britain and the United States. Hall's discussion of diasporic Caribbean identities within a context of modern Africa can be usefully paired with **Kwame Anthony Appiah**'s essay on the way in which African identity must aspire toward some form of pan-Africanism. The "cultural revolution" to which Hall refers is bound up with the recognition of what he calls an " 'imagined community' of Africa," which differs from the "real" Africa that so many Caribbean people look to as a lost origin. Like Appiah, Hall suggests that identity must be constructed in the interests of a liberating *self*-identity, one that takes Africa as the "real" sign of unity and belonging. Similar problems of identity formation are discussed in essays by **Declan Kiberd** and **R. Radhakrishnan**.

Negotiating Caribbean Identities

In this lecture I will address questions of Caribbean culture and identity. I want to suggest that such questions are not in any sense separate or removed from the problems of political mobilization, of cultural development, of economic development and so on. The more we know and see of the struggles of the societies of the periphery to make something of the slender resources available to them, the more important we understand the questions and problems of cultural identity to be in that process. I want to examine some of the themes of a topic which has been richly explored by Caribbean writers and artists – cultural identity presenting itself always as a problem to Caribbean people.

Why it should be a problem is not a mystery, but I want to probe this question of identity and why Caribbean writers, politicians, civic leaders, artists and others have been unable to leave worrying away at it. And in doing so, I want to problematize to some extent the way we think about identity. I want to explore the term "myth" itself – the English are not good at myth, always opposing it on the one hand to reality, on the other hand to truth, as if you have to choose between them. I specifically do not want to choose between myth and reality, but to talk about the very real contemporary and historical effects of myths of identity. And I want to do so with one other purpose which I hope will come through more clearly at the end. The issue of cultural identity as a political quest now constitutes one of the most serious global problems as we go into the twenty-first century. The re-emergence of questions of ethnicity, of nationalism – the obduracy, the dangers and the pleasures of the rediscovery of identity in the modern world, inside and outside of Europe – places the question of cultural identity at the very centre of the contemporary political agenda. What I want to suggest is that despite the dilemmas and vicissitudes of identity through which Caribbean people have passed and continue to pass, we have a tiny but important message for the world about how to negotiate identity.

THE SEARCH FOR ESSENCE

There is a very clear and powerful discourse about cultural identity, especially in the West. Indeed most of us have lived through, and are still living through an exercise in the definition and defence of a particular kind of British cultural identity. I was puzzled when Norman Tebbit asked which cricket team you would support, in

Taken from *New Left Review* (1 January 1995), pp. 3–14.

order to discover whether you were "one of us", "one of them" or maybe neither. My own response to that was, if you can tell me how many of the four hundred members of the British athletics team are properly British, I'd be ready to answer the question about the cricket team; otherwise not. But the discourse of identity suggests that the culture of a people is at root – and the question of roots is very much at issue – a question of its essence, a question of the fundamentals of a culture. Histories come and go, peoples come and go, situations change, but somewhere down there is throbbing the culture to which we all belong. It provides a kind of ground for our identities, something to which we can return, something solid, something fixed, something stabilized, around which we can organize our identities and our sense of belongingness. And there is a sense that modern nations and peoples cannot survive for long and succeed without the capacity to touch ground, as it were, in the name of their cultural identities.

Now the question of what a Caribbean cultural identity might be has been of extraordinary importance, before but especially in the twentieth century. Partly because of the dislocations of conquest, of colonization and slavery, partly because of the colonial relationship itself and the distortions of living in a world culturally dependent and dominated from some centre outside the place where the majority of people lived. But it has also been important for counter-identities, providing sources on which the important movements of decolonization, of independence, of nationalist consciousness in the region have been founded. In a sense, until it is possible to state who the subjects of independence movements are likely to be, and in whose name cultural decolonization is being conducted, it is not possible to complete the process. And that process involves the question of defining who the people are. In *Black Skin White Masks*, Fanon speaks of what he call "a passionate research directed to the secret hope of discovering beyond the misery of today, beyond self-contempt, resignation and abjuration, some beautiful and splendid area whose existence rehabilitates us both in regard to ourselves and others". And as I've said, that passionate research by Caribbean writers, artists and political leaders, that quest for identity, has been the very form in which much of our artistic endeavour in all the Caribbean languages has been conducted in this century.

CROSS-CURRENTS OF DIASPORA

Why, then, is the identity of the Caribbean so problematic? It is a very large question, but let me suggest some of the reasons. First of all, if the search for identity always involves a search for origins, it is impossible to locate in the Caribbean an origin for its peoples. The indigenous peoples of the area very largely no longer exist, and they ceased to exist very soon after the European encounter. This is indeed the first trauma of identity in the Caribbean. I don't know how many of you know what the coat of arms of Jamaica is. It has two Arawak Indian figures supporting a shield in the middle, which is crossed by pineapples surmounted by an alligator. Peter Hulme reports that in 1983 the then prime minister of Jamaica, Edward Seaga, wanted to change the coat of arms on the ground that he could not find represented in it a single recognizable Jamaican identity. "Can the crushed and extinct Arawaks," he asked, "represent the dauntless inhabitants of Jamaica? Does the low-slung near-extinct crocodile, a cold-blooded reptile, symbolize the warm soaring spirits of Jamaicans? Where does the pineapple, which was exported to Hawaii, appear prominently either in our history or in our folklore?" I read that quote simply to remind you that questions of identity are always questions about representation. They are always questions about the invention, not simply the discovery of tradition. They are always exercises in selective memory and they almost always involve the silencing of something in order to allow something else to speak.

Maurice Cargill, a famous commentator on Jamaican affairs in *The Gleaner*, responded to the prime minister, "What about a design containing entwined marijuana plants? Against a background of US dollar bills with tourists rampant and ladies couchant?" Silencing as well as remembering, identity is always a question of producing in the future an account of the past, that is to say it is always about narrative, the stories which cultures tell themselves about who they are and where they came from. The one way in which it is impossible to resolve the problem of identity in the Caribbean is to try looking at it, as if a good look will tell you who the people are. During the period in which I was preparing my BBC series on the Caribbean, I had the occasion in a relatively short space of time to visit a large number of Caribbean islands, several of which I had not seen before. I was absolutely staggered by the ethnic and cultural diversity I encountered. Not a single Caribbean island looks like any other in terms of its ethnic composition, including the different genetic and physical features and characteristics of the people. And that is before you start to touch the question of different languages, different cultural traditions, which reflect the different colonizing cultures.

It may be a surprise to some people in this room that there are several Caribbean islands, large ones, in which blacks are nowhere near a majority of the population. There are now two important ex-British Caribbean societies where Indians are in a majority. In Cuba, what you are struck by first of all is the long persistence of white Hispanic settlement and then of the mestizo population, only later of the black population. Haiti, which is in some ways the symbolic island of black culture, where one feels closer to the African inheritance than anywhere else, has a history in which the mulattos have played an absolutely vital and key historical role. Martinique is a bewildering place, it is in my experience more French than Paris, just slightly darker. The Dominican Republic is a place where it is possible to feel closer to Spain and to the Spanish tradition of Latin America than anywhere else I have been in the Caribbean. The melting-pot of the British islands produced everywhere you look a different combination of genetic features and factors, and in each island elements of other ethnic cultures – Chinese, Syrian, Lebanese, Portuguese, Jewish – are present. I know because I have a small proportion of practically all of them in my own inheritance. My background is African, also I'm told Scottish – of pretty low descent, probably convict – East Indian, Portuguese Jew. I can't summon up any more but if I searched hard I expect I could find them.

What is more, in another sense, everybody there comes from somewhere else, and it is not clear what has drawn them to it, certainly not whether the motives were ever of the highest level of aspiration. That is to say, their true cultures, the places they really come from, the traditions that really formed them, are somewhere else. The

Caribbean is the first, the original and the purest diaspora. These days blacks who have completed the triangular journey back to Britain sometimes speak of the emerging black British diaspora, but I have to tell them that they and I are twice diasporized. What is more, not therefore just a diaspora and living in a place where the centre is always somewhere else, but we are the break with those originating cultural sources as passed through the traumas of violent rupture. I don't want to speak about the nature of this rupture, with the majority of the populations wrenched from their own cultures and inserted into the cultures of the colonizing plantation relations of slavery. I don't want to talk about the trauma of transportation, of the breaking up of linguistic and tribal and familial groups. I don't want to talk about the brutal aftermath of Indian indenture. I simply want to say that in the histories of the migration, forced or free, of peoples who now compose the populations of these societies, whose cultural traces are everywhere intermingled with one another, there is always the stamp of historical violence and rupture.

Of course the peoples thus inserted into these old colonizing plantation societies instantly polarized. And if anyone is still under the illusion that questions of culture can ever be discussed free from and outside of questions of power, you have only to look at the Caribbean to understand how for centuries every cultural characteristic and trait had its class, colour and racial inscription. You could read off from the populations to the cultures, and from the cultures to the populations, and each was ranked in an order of cultural power. It is impossible to approach Caribbean culture without understanding the way it was continually inscribed by questions of power. Of course that inscription of culture in power relations did not remain polarized in Caribbean society, but I now understand that one of the things I was myself running away from when I came to England to study in 1951 was a society that was profoundly culturally graded, which is what the old post-colonial society I grew up in was like. Of course those cultural relations did not remain fixed, and the relative cultures were quickly open to integration, assimilation and cross-influence. They were almost never self-contained. They became subject at once to complex processes of assimilation, translation, adaptation, resistance, reselection and so on. That is to say, they became in a deep sense diasporic societies. For wherever one finds diasporas, one always finds precisely those complicated processes of negotiation and transculturation which characterize Caribbean culture. I don't want to try and sketch the cultural relations of that period, simply to identify three key processes which are at work creating the enormously refined and delicate tracery, the complexities of cultural identification, in Caribbean society in that time.

SURVIVAL AND ASSIMILATION

First, and especially with respect to the populations that had been enslaved, the retention of old customs, the retention of cultural traits from Africa; customs and traditions which were retained in and through slavery, in plantation, in religion, partly in language, in folk customs, in music, in dance, in all those forms of expressive culture which allowed men and women to survive the trauma of slavery. Not intact, never pure, never untouched by the culture of Victorian and pre-Victorian English society, never outside of Christianity or entirely outside the reach of the church, never without at least some small instruction in the Bible, always surrounded by the colonizing culture, but importantly – and to some extent today imperatively – retaining something of the connection. Often unrecognized, often only in practice, often unreflected, often not knowing that people were practising within a tradition. Nevertheless, in everyday life, in so far as it was possible, maintaining some kind of subterranean link with what was often called "the other Caribbean", the Caribbean that was not recognized, that could not speak, that had no official records, no official account of its own transportation, no official historians, but nevertheless that oral life which maintained an umbilical connection with the African homeland and culture.

But let us not forget that retention characterized the colonizing cultures as well as the colonized. For if you look at the Little Englands, the Little Spains and the Little Frances that were created by the colonizers, if you consider this kind of fossilized replica, with the usual colonial cultural lag – people are always more Victorian when they're taking tea in the Himalayas than when they're taking tea in Leamington – they were keeping alive the memory of their own homes and homelands and tradi- tions and customs. This very important double aspect of retention has marked Caribbean culture from the earliest colonial encounters.

Secondly, the profound process of assimilation, of dragging the whole society into some imitative relationship with this other culture which one could never quite reach. When one talks about assimilation in the Caribbean, one always feels Car- ibbean people constantly leaning forward, almost about to tip over, striving to reach somewhere else. My mother used to tell me that if she could only get hold of the right records, she would be able to stitch together a kind of genealogy for her household – not one that led to the West Coast of Africa, believe me, but a genealogy which would connect her, she wasn't quite sure, to the ruling house of the Austro-Hungarian empire or the lairds of Scotland, one way or the other. She probably thought that maybe in the quadrangle of Merton College Oxford, I might stumble across one of these secret stones that would somehow convert me into what clearly I was formed, brought up, reared, taught, educated, nursed and nurtured to be, a kind of black Englishman. When I first went home in the mid-1960s, my parents said to me, "I hope they don't take you to be one of those immigrants over there." And the funny thing is, I'd never called myself, or thought of myself as an immigrant before. But having once been hailed or interpellated, I owned up at once: that is what I am. In that moment I migrated. Again, the word "black" had never been uttered in my household or anywhere in Jamaica in my hearing, in my entire youth and adoles- cence – though there were all kinds of other ways of naming, and large numbers of people were very black indeed. So it was not until the mid-1960s, on another visit home, that my parents said to me, "There's all this black consciousness, black movement in the United States, I hope it's not having an influence over there", and I realized I had just changed identity again. I owned up once more and said, "Actually you know, I am exactly what in Britain we are starting to call black." Which is a sort of footnote to say, identity is not only a story, a narrative which we tell ourselves about ourselves, it is stories which change with historical circumstances. And identity shifts with the way in which we think and hear them and experience them. Far from only coming from the still small point of truth inside us, identities actually come from outside, they are the way in which we are recognized and then come to step into the place of the recognitions which others give us. Without the others there is no self, there is no self-recognition.

So given the skewed structures of growing up in such a society, of attempting whatever social rank or position in the racial colour structure you occupy, of trying to negotiate the complexities of who out of these complicated sets of stories you could possibly be, where you could find in the mirror of history a point of identification or recognition for yourself, it is not surprising that Caribbean people of all kinds, of all classes and positions, experience the question of positioning themselves in a cultural identity as an enigma, as a problem, as an open question. There are many writings about this question, but for me the overwhelmingly powerful statement is to be found in Fanon's *Black Skin White Masks*, for only in Fanon do you understand the internal traumas of identity which are the consequence of colonization and enslavement. That is to say, not just the external processes and pressures of exploitation, but the way that internally one comes to collude with an objectification of oneself which is a profound misrecognition of one's own identity. Consequently, against that background, in the New World and in the Caribbean, the attempts in the twentieth century to reach for independence, to decolonize, the movements in the nineteenth century in the Hispanic Caribbean societies for independence from Spain, the attempts to regenerate and ground the political and social life of the society, not in an absent picture or image which could never be fulfilled, not in the nostalgia for something outside the society, but in the complicated realities and negotiations of that society itself, is a question which had to entail the redefinition of identity. Without it there could have been no independence of any kind. And one of the complexities or perplexities of the independence movement – certainly in the British Caribbean islands – is that, in the early phases of those movements, so-called political independence from the colonial power occurred, but the cultural revolution of identity did not.

AFRICA AND MODERNITY

For the third process, which will form the rest of my talk, I want to start by looking at some of the other attempts to name the unnameable, to speak about the possibilities of cultural identification, of the different traditions of the peoples for whom on the whole there were no cultural models, the peoples at the bottom of the society. And as you can imagine, that always involved a renegotiation, a rediscovery of Africa. The political movements in the New World in the twentieth century have had to pass through the re-encounter with Africa. The African diasporas of the New World have been in one way or another incapable of finding a place in modern history without the symbolic return to Africa. It has taken many forms, it has been embodied in many movements both intellectual and popular. I want to say a word about two or three of them only. Perhaps best known in an intellectual sense is the movement around the notion of negritude, around the discovery of blackness, the affirmation of an African personality, very much associated with the name of Aimé Césaire, and of the group around Césaire in Paris and afterwards, coming out of Martinique, a tiny society which I described earlier on in a rather pejorative way, the most French place I have encountered in the Caribbean, certainly, but also the birthplace of both Fanon and of Aimé Césaire. Césaire's work lay in plucking out of that Caribbean culture with which he was most familiar the strands that related most profoundly back to the valorization of the African connection, the rediscovery of the African connection, of African consciousness, of African personality, of African cultural traditions.

I was fortunate enough in the programme on Martinique to be able to include an interview with Aimé Césaire, who must be nearly twice my age and looks about half of it, wonderfully fit and resilient at this moment. In that interview you can see the enormous pleasure with which he describes the story of having gone to Africa and rediscovered for the first time the source of the masks of the Martinique carnival which he had played in and helped to make when he was a boy. Suddenly the flash of recognition, the continuity of the broken and ruptured tradition. The enormously important work that flowed from his involvement in the negritude movement, not only the poems and the poetry and the writing which has come out of that inspiration, of the renegotiation of a Caribbean consciousness with the African past, but also the work which he has inspired in Martinique amongst poets and painters and sculptors, is a profound revelation of how creative this symbolic reconnection has been.

And yet of course the paradox is that when Aimé Césaire opens his mouth you hear the most exquisitely formed lycée French. I hardly know anyone who speaks a more perfect French, it is beautifully articulated. "I am," he says, "French, my mind is French." Looking for the right parallel, he says, "like if you went to Oxford you would be English. I went to a French school, I was taught the French language, I wasn't allowed to use *kréyole* at home, I learned only French classical culture. There's a strong tradition of assimilation, I went of course to Paris where all bright young Martiniquans went." And because of the tradition of political assimilation, he has in fact done what no black British Caribbean has ever done, which is to sit in the parliament of his own metropolitan society. Nevertheless, when Aimé Césaire started to write poetry, he wanted, because of his interest, alerted and alive to the subterranean sources of identity and cultural creativity in his own being, to break with the models of French classical poetry. And if you know his notebook on the *Return to My Native Land*, you will know how much that is a language which, in its open roaring brilliance, has broken free from those classical models. He becomes a surrealist poet. Aimé Césaire has never, as you perhaps know, argued for the independence of Martinique. Martinique has a very particular position, it is an internal department of France, and those of you who want to be crude and materialist about it had better go and see the kinds of facilities which that gives Martiniquan people, and compare them with the facilities available to most of the other peoples of the Caribbean islands, before you begin to say what a terrible thing this is. Nevertheless, my own feeling, though I have no enormous evidence for this, is that the reluctance of Césaire to break the French connection is not only a material one but also a spiritual one. He went to the Schoelcher lycée. Schoelcher was an important early Martiniquan figure, and in celebrating an anniversary of Schoelcher, Césaire said, "He associated in our minds the word France and the word liberty, and that bound us to France by every fibre of our hearts and every power of our minds." He said, "I know only one France, the

France of the revolution, the France of Toussaint L'Ouverture. So much for Gothic cathedrals."

Well, so much indeed for Gothic cathedrals. The France with which Césaire identifies, and it has played of course a most profound role in Caribbean history, is one France and not another, the France of the revolution, the France of liberté, égalité, fraternité, the France that Toussaint L'Ouverture heard, of course, the France that mobilized and touched the imagination of slaves and others in Haiti before the revolution. And yet in the actual accounts of the revolution that we have, one of the most difficult, one of the trickiest historical passages to negotiate is precisely how much, in the spark of the various things that went into the making of the Haitian revolution, can be attributed on the one hand to the ruptures sweeping out in the wake of the French revolution, and on the other hand to the long experience of a severe and brutal regime on the plantations themselves, what you might call the revolutionary school of life itself. There were also, of course, the traditions of Africa and of African resistance, and of marronage in the plantation villages themselves. We don't know. It is an impossible enigma to sort out, in one of the most momentous historical events of Caribbean history, to what the different elements that come together in that revolutionary conjuncture can be attributed.

Césaire was influenced in part by his contact at an early stage with an important movement in the United States which now goes under the title of the Harlem Renaissance. I don't know how much you know about the writers of the Harlem Renaissance, of Langston Hughes and Countee Cullen and Van Vechten, an important movement among writers, intellectuals and artists in New York in the early years of the twentieth century, that had an important influence on a variety of Caribbean writers, poets and artists. And one of the important things that the movement of the Harlem Renaissance did, was on the one hand to speak about the importance and the distinctiveness, the cultural and aesthetic distinctiveness, of the black American contribution to American culture. The other important thing that movement did was to stake a claim for American blacks in the centre and at the heart of modernism itself. The writers of the Harlem Renaissance did not wish to be located and ghettoized as ethnic artists only able to speak on behalf of a marginal experience confined and immured in the past, locked out of the claim to modern life. What they said was, the experience of blacks in the new world, their historical trajectory into and through the complex histories of colonization, conquest, and enslavement, is distinct and unique and it empowers people to speak in a distinctive voice. But it is not a voice outside of and excluded from the production of modernity in the twentieth century. It is another kind of modernity. It is a vernacular modernity, it is the modernity of the blues, the modernity of gospel music, it is the modernity of hybrid black music in its enormous variety throughout the New World. The sound of marginal peoples staking a claim to the New World. I say that as a kind of metaphor, just in case you misunderstood the point I was trying to make about Aimé Césaire. I am anxious that you don't suppose I see him as an assimilationist Frenchman, deeply in bad faith because he is invoking Africa. I am trying to do something else. I am talking about the only way in which Africa can be relived and rediscovered by New World blacks who are diasporized irrevocably, who cannot go back through the eye of the needle.

A CULTURAL REVOLUTION

Let me talk about finally going back through the eye of the needle. There was a very famous moment during the explosion of Rastafarianism in Jamaica in the sixties when a somewhat beleagured prime minister said, "Well perhaps you ought to go back to Africa. You've talked about it so much, you say you came from there, you say you're still in slavery here, you're not in a free land, the promised land is back there where somebody took you from, perhaps you ought to go back and see." Well of course, some people did go back and see, as you perhaps know. Of course they did not go back to where they came from; that was not the Africa they were talking about. Between the Africa that they came from and the Africa that they wanted to go back to, two absolutely critical things had intervened. One is, that Africa had moved on. Africa – one has to say it now and again to somewhat nostalgic and sentimental nationalists in the Caribbean – Africa is not waiting there in the fifteenth or seventeenth century, waiting for you to roll back across the Atlantic and rediscover it in its tribal purity, waiting there in its prelogical mentality, waiting to be a woken from inside by its returning sons and daughters. It is grappling with the problems of Aids and underdevelopment and mounting debt. It is trying to feed its people, it is trying to understand what democracy means against the background of a colonial regime which ruptured and broke and recut and reorganized peoples and tribes and societies in a horrendous shake-up of their entire cognitive and social world. That is what it's trying to do, twentieth-century Africa. There is no fifteenth-century Mother waiting there to succour her children. So in that literal sense, they wanted to go somewhere else, they wanted to go to the other place that had intervened, that other Africa which was constructed in the language and the rituals of Rastafarianism.

Now as you know, the language and rituals of Rastafarianism speak indeed of Africa, of Ethiopia, of Babylon, of the promised land, and of those who are still in suffering. But like every chiliastic language which has been snatched by the black people of the New World diasporas out of the jaws of Christianity, and then turned on its head, or read against the grain, or crossed by something else – and the New World is absolutely replete with them – it is impossible in my experience to understand black culture and black civilization in the New World without understanding the cultural role of religion, through the distorted languages of the one Book that anybody would teach them to read. What they felt was, I have no voice, I have no history, I have come from a place to which I cannot go back and which I have never seen. I used to speak a language which I can no longer speak. I had ancestors whom I cannot find, they worshipped gods whose names I do not know. Against this sense of profound rupture, the metaphors of a new kind of imposed religion can be reworked, can become a language in which a certain kind of history is retold, in which aspirations of liberation and freedom can be for the first time expressed, in which what I would call the "imagined community" of Africa can be symbolically reconstructed.

I said to you that when I left Jamaica in the 1950s it was a society which did not and could not have acknowledged itself to be largely black. When I went back to Jamaica at the end of the sixties and in the early seventies, it was a society even poorer than when I had left it, in material terms, but it had passed through the most profound cultural revolution. It had grounded itself where it existed. It was not any longer trying to be something else, trying to match up to some other image, trying to become something which it could not. It had all the problems in the world sticking together, finding the wherewithal to get to the next week, but in terms of trying to understand ordinary people – I'm not now talking about intellectuals, I'm talking about ordinary people – the important thing was the new realization that they could speak the language that they ordinarily spoke to one another anywhere. You know, the biggest shock for me was listening to Jamaican radio. I couldn't believe my ears that anybody would be quite so bold as to speak patois, to read the news in that accent. My entire education, my mother's whole career, had been specifically designed to prevent anybody at all, and me in particular, from reading anything of importance in that language. Of course, you could say all kinds of other things, in the small interchange of everyday life, but important things had to be said, good-ness knows, in another tongue. To encounter people who can speak with one another in exactly that transformation of standard English which is patois, which is creole – the hundreds of different creole and semi-creole languages which cover the face of the Caribbean in one place or another – that these have become as it were the languages in which important things can be said, in which important aspirations and hopes can be formulated, in which an important grasp of the histories that have made these places can be written down, in which artists are willing for the first time, the first generation, to practise and so on, that is what I call a cultural revolution.

And it was in my view made by the cultural revolution of Rastafarianism. What I mean by that is certainly not that everybody became Rasta, although there was a moment in the sixties there when it was pretty hard not to be. I once interviewed a very old Rastafarian figure about the large numbers of Kingston intellectuals and students who were growing their locks down to their ankles. And I asked him, as part of a long interview about the nature of Rastafarianism, how he'd got into it, and so on, "What do you think of these weekend Rastas, these middle-class Rastas? Do you think they're up to anything, do you think they can reason?" And he said, "You know, I don't say anything against them, I don't think anything against them, because in my church everybody reasons for themselves. So if they want to reason in that way, that's their business." Well I thought, that was a nice gentle remark, but I wanted to nail him, so I said, "Listen to me now, isn't Haile Selassie dead? So the bottom has just fallen out of this whole Rastafarian business? He's dead, how can the Son of God be dead?" And he said to me, "When last you hear the truth about the Son of God from the mass media?"

You see, it was not the literal Africa that people wanted to return to, it was the language, the symbolic language for describing what suffering was like, it was a metaphor for where they were, as the metaphors of Moses and the metaphors of the train to the North, and the metaphors of freedom, and the metaphors of passing across to the promised land, have always been metaphors, a language with a double register, a literal and a symbolic register. And the point was not that some people, a few, could only live with themselves and discover their identities by literally going back to Africa – though some did, not often with great success – but that a whole people symbolically re-engaged with an experience which enabled them to find a language in which they could re-tell and appropriate their own histories.

I want to close. I have said something about the intellectual movement of negritude. I've referred to another important movement, not in the Caribbean but with influence on the Caribbean, the Harlem Renaissance of the twenties, and I've talked about the cultural revolution in the wake of Rastafarianism. One of the most important things that people on this side of the Atlantic know about Rastafarianism is that it produced the greatest reggae artist in the world, Bob Marley. And I think many Europeans believe that reggae is a secret African music that we've had tucked in our slave knapsacks for three or four centuries, that we hid out in the bush, practised at night when nobody was looking; and gradually as things changed we brought it out and began to play it a little, feed it slowly across the airwaves. But as anybody from the Caribbean would know, reggae was born in the 1960s. Actually it was the answer to ska. When I returned to Jamaica I heard these two musical traditions. In *The Invention of Tradition*, the collection edited by Eric Hobsbawm and Terence Ranger, it's explained that many British traditions people believe have been around since Edward I were actually developed by Elgar or Disraeli, the day before yesterday. Well, reggae is a product of the invention of tradition. It is a sixties music, its impact on the rest of the world comes not just through preservation – though it is rooted in the long retained traditions of African drumming – but by being the fusion, the crossing, of that retained tradition with a number of other musics, and the most powerful instrument or agency of its world propagation was those deeply tribal instruments, the transistor set, the recording studio, the gigantic sound system. That is how this deeply profound spiritual music of Africa that we've been treasuring got here.

It's not part of my story to tell what it did here in Britain, but actually it not only provided a kind of black consciousness and identification for people in Jamaica, but it saved the second generation of young black people in this society. Is this an old identity or a new one? Is it an ancient culture preserved, treasured, to which it is possible to go back? Is it something produced out of nowhere? It is of course none of those things. No cultural identity is produced out of thin air. It is produced out of those historical experiences, those cultural traditions, those lost and marginal languages, those marginalized experiences, those peoples and histories which remain unwritten. Those are the specific roots of identity. On the other hand, identity itself is not the rediscovery of them, but what they as cultural resources allow a people to produce. Identity is not in the past to be found, but in the future to be constructed.

And I say that not because I think therefore that Caribbean people can ever give up the symbolic activity of trying to know more about the past from which they come, for only in that way can they discover and rediscover the resources through which identity can be constructed. But I remain profoundly convinced that their identities for the twenty-first century do not lie in taking old identities literally, but in using the enormously rich and complex cultural heritages to which history has made them heir, as the different musics out of which a Caribbean sound might one day be produced.

I want to end by quoting a passage from C. L. R. James. It's about a talk he had just heard by the Guyanese novelist Wilson Harris. This is what James has to say:

I went the other day to the West Indian students' hostel to hear Wilson Harris speak on the West Indian novel. Well, in the end, we decided we should print it. I was told I could write an introduction [a wonderfully C. L. R. James phrase, that!]; Larry Constantine had paid for it, and I have the proofs here. Harris is speaking about the West Indian novel, and I want to read one extract, because we can't have a talk about Wilson Harris without your hearing something that Harris says for himself. Harris says, "The special point I want to make in regard to the West Indies is that the pursuit of a strange and subtle goal, melting-pot, call it what you like, is the mainstream, though the unacknowledged tradition, of the Americas. And the significance of this is akin to the European preoccupation with alchemy, with the growth of experimental science, the poetry of science, as well as the explosive nature which is informed by a solution of images, agnostic humility, and essential beauty rather than vested in a fixed assumption and classification of things."

NOTE

This text was given as the 1993 Walter Rodney Memorial Lecture, at the kind invitation of Professor Alastair Hennessy, Centre for Caribbean Studies, University of Warwick.

Survival and Invention: Indigeneity in the Caribbean

PETER HULME

Peter Hulme is one of the most renowned practitioners of colonial discourse theory. His *Colonial Encounters: Europe and the Native Caribbean, 1492–1797* reveals his indebtedness to **Edward W. Said**'s *Orientalism* at the same time that it goes beyond that achievement by suggesting that the Other defined by Europe was equally responsible for Europe's self-definition. The essay included here considers the problem of determining precisely what constitutes an indigenous group, since "indigenous peoples" as they are defined by contemporary international organizations are not the same as those "colonized" groups fighting for independence. Hulme argues that Columbus's famous "discovery" of America is in fact the "the beginning of a set of original political and cultural *responses*" to Native American peoples, one that inaugurated a complex process of identification – both of those peoples by Europe and of Europeans *through* the experience of interacting with them. Within what Hulme calls "postcolonial ethnohistory," the concept of "invention," like that of "construction," emerges as an anti-essentialist mode of identity-formation that accounts for the unique ethnicity – determined as much by cultural contact as by miscegenation – of Caribbean peoples. "Ethnogenesis" is tied together with discursive interventions in which native Caribs seek to maintain some measure of control over their own survival as a people. Hulme's essay can be profitably read with **Said**'s discussion of "discrepant experience" and **Stuart Hall**'s discussion of negotiating identities in order to come to terms with one of the most dominant motifs in postcolonial studies: the "invention" of identity within the "continuance" of the struggle against the legacies of colonialism.

Survival and Invention: Indigeneity in the Caribbean

"Quel est ce pays?" demanda-t-il. Et il lui fut répondu: "Pèse d'abord chaque mot, connais chaque douleur."

Edouard Glissant, La Lézarde

I understood the invitation to contribute to [*Text and Nation*] as asking what happens when the term "text" is introduced into debates about ethnicity and nation. My response to the invitation involved the introduction of one other term – "indigenous" – and the location of the question within the Caribbean, implying an eventual focus on the surviving indigenous population of that area, the 3,000 or so Caribs or Karifuna on the island of Dominica. I approach the question of Carib ethnicity by contrasting two models of identity, referred to through the shorthand of the words "survival" and "invention" – though my interest is in the imbrication of these two models, rather than simply their difference.[1] I make no particular claims for the paradigmatic status of the Caribbean for these debates about nation, ethnicity and identity, however tempting it might be to go along with Edouard Glissant's suggestion that the Caribbean has become in some respects exemplary of the global cultural condition.[2]

I

The 1992 quincentenary attracted some attention to indigenous peoples in the Americas, but for the most part the development of postcolonial studies – to use that useful umbrella term – has paid little attention to indigenous issues, especially since what are now called "indigenous peoples" under accepted international definitions are rarely the same people who feature as the "colonized" groups fighting for political independence, either in the Americas in the eighteenth and nineteenth centuries, or in Africa and Asia in the twentieth. In particular, the continued colonial situation suffered by Native Americans throughout this continent is a topic all too often ignored in debates about "nationalism" or "postcolonialism," especially, it seems, in the United States, where the questions it poses are probably too close to home for comfort.

Taken from Laura Garcia Moreno and Peter C. Pfeiffer (eds.), *Text and Nation: Cross-Disciplinary Essays on Cultural and National Identities* (Columbia, SC: Camden House, 1996).

Some of those questions, relevant to matters of "Text and Nation," concern terminology. Consideration might be given, for example, to the word "native" as the adjective of "nation," if only to see whether it makes the "nation" of such a phrase look any different. Another fruitful area might be to consider the debates in international law about how to define adequately terms such as "tribal," "indigenous," "minority," and "people," debates which have often foundered on the so-called Blue Water thesis, which defines colonies as exclusively *overseas* possessions.[3] So for many years, according to their governments, the population of Bangladesh was *entirely* autochthonous; in India "tribal" groups were underdeveloped rather than colonized; in the Soviet Union, there were of course no oppressed indigenous populations, only "minorities"; and the term "colonialism" could not be applied to areas inside the borders of the sovereign USA. All these discussions reflect diacritically on the ways in which a term like "nation" might be used.

More particularly, in the last half century substantial discussions have taken place under the auspices of the United Nations and the International Labour Organization in which definitions of indigeneity and aboriginal rights have edged international law closer to accepting the usage "indigenous peoples," with the term "people" having the weight it is given in chapter XI of the UN Charter: indigenous *peoples* would have at least a claim to become self-determining nations in international law; and the constituent members of the World Council of Indigenous Peoples certainly make these kinds of *national* claims. At its strongest, indigeneity is an avowal of ethnic distinctiveness and national sovereignty based on the historical claim to be in some sense the descendants of the earliest inhabitants of a particular place. These are unfashionable claims, and their terms can all easily be put under erasure by cultural criticism; but they cannot – should not – be ignored.

I make these brief allusions to the large international context in part to suggest that questions of language and definition are not somehow "merely" discursive – and therefore alien to the realities of everyday political and economic life: they are the very coin of the political, at least in the realm of international law. Cultural identity can depend on formal as well as existential recognition, and formal recognition can depend in very particular ways on questions of language.

II

Moving to the Caribs, and the texts associated with them, I have in mind three stages which will structure this paper: firstly a process of ethnogenesis, which could be said to begin in 1492 and to end when the imperial guns fall silent – which in the case of the Lesser Antilles is the late eighteenth century; and then two subsequent moments: a "colonial" moment, for which I offer an incident from 1930 as indicative; and a "postcolonial" moment, for which 1995 can stand as exemplary. Both "process" and "moments" have their texts, and at the risk of considerable simplification, textual instances will be suggested for each of these three stages.

Only very slowly are postcolonial imperatives beginning to alter our picture of the native Caribbean and the part that it plays in Caribbean history. The conventional account of the native Caribbean is characterized by two features, both of which are dependent on an implicit theory of culture: this is the "survival" model. First, the indigenous population has certain innate characteristics that do not change over the colonial period and that were brought from original homelands in the Amazon and Orinoco basins; and second, the indigenous population is marked by a radical dichotomy between two groups, one naturally aggressive, one naturally peaceful, now usually called by the supposedly ethnic names "Taino" and "Carib."[4] The only point to be made here about this dichotomy is that during this early period there are actually examples of the use of the term "Carib nation" by Europeans to denote a political entity where none in fact at the time existed, with "nation" carrying – as it did in the sixteenth century – overtones of "race," or certainly of fixed identity. This happened with the Caribs because they were seen as a hostile and encroaching power putting into action the kind of well-laid plan that could not be imagined by Europeans except as the actions of a political state. As so often, what Europeans perceived in Native American actions was a distorted *self*-image projected onto their indigenous antagonists. Native Americans were usually seen as having *less* political organisation than they actually had, so it is worth pointing out that there were occasions, as with this Carib example, when they were imputed with *more*, precisely because that made them a more credible and dangerous enemy.

The underlying premise behind this "survival" model of cultural identity is that the initial contact in the Caribbean is between well-defined groups which got larger or smaller during the colonial period – and of course native Caribbean groups got smaller, African and European groups larger. This is an hydraulic notion of culture, in which cultures begin as full or plenary, and are drained of their essence until they disappear, and as that language suggests, this "survival" model ultimately depends on the notion of blood quantum as the measure of cultural identity. This conventional account of the indigenous Caribbean is based on sixteenth- and seventeenth-century sources, although it was articulated in its contemporary form in the aftermath of 1898. It is, in many ways, a US imperial view of the Caribbean, deeply marked in its assumptions by late nineteenth-century ideas of race and warfare, and therefore closely associated also with the growth of anthropology as a discipline, since it was precisely these cultural remnants – as the Caribs were always called – who provided the first material for anthropological study: "remnant" and "material" being appropriate words since under this model the "natives" are simply the débris left behind by the inexorable processes of modernization. The archetypal text here is the report on the "last man," the last survivor, the last speaker of the language, a text beautifully exemplified by the story of Alexander von Humboldt scribbling down a few words of a soon-to-be-extinct South American language from its last "speaker," a parrot.[5] The inadequacies of this "survival" model to deal with cultural change are by now apparent, even if in the Caribbean case they still tend to hold sway, but it should be remembered that this "survival" story tells a certain truth about the genocide of the native population that more processual models of identity risk obscuring, and it is also within this model that the few indigenous accounts we have of the Carib experience are found: it is the chosen textual model of the victims of genocide, and for that reason one to which we still need to pay attention.

This conventional picture is now being challenged by a postcolonial ethnohistory. The old picture was a snapshot, taken in October 1492, and which then gradually faded over the years as the native presence registered there became less and less easy to discern. The newer picture is more like a movie: at least it has a narrative and some character development. New scholarship, some of it based in the Caribbean itself, is now beginning to study 1492 not as the start of a genocide which the native population suffered passively, nor even as the start of a heroic but doomed defence of native strongholds, but rather as the beginning of a set of original political and cultural *responses* which was marked by small- and large-scale population movements throughout the islands. There were massive amounts of slave-raiding which moved huge contingents of Native Americans from various parts of the mainland onto the Caribbean islands in the early sixteenth century. New political and military alliances were formed. There was indigenous adaptation to peasant life under Spanish control, possibly within such forms as the *guajiro* and *jíbaro* traditions of Cuba and Puerto Rico. There was indigenous participation in unofficial Creole communities on the margins of authorized areas of settlement – sometimes involving guerrilla warfare, sometimes, especially in the eighteenth century, in conjunction with African maroons. Finally, and through these other processes, there was ethnic reconstruction and identity reformulation: indeed the Caribs themselves, one of the staple ingredients of the colonial picture of pre-Columbian America, may have been a *product* of what anthropologists are now calling the "tribal zone." What is beginning to emerge – in a word – is a wide-scale native Caribbean diaspora in the early colonial period: not a glorious story of survival and adaptation, but a desperate story of *trauma* and adaptation in which many hundreds of thousands died, but out of which emerged a recognizable Carib nation, forged in the crucible of colonial struggle.[6]

Carib ethnogenesis runs from 1492 at least until 1763 and "invention" is in many ways the appropriate word to describe how the resulting Carib ethnicity came into being: the product of forced but imaginative adaptation to vertiginous historical change. "Invention" has recently become something of a key term within cultural history, in part perhaps because of its ambivalence, since it can imply – as Benedict Anderson points out – either "fabrication" or "imagination" according to analytical preference: putting the emphasis on either the inauthentic or the postauthentic.[7] Recent discussion has focused on the ways in which communities have been imagined, putting the emphasis, rightly enough, on both nationalism and ethnicity as cultural processes. But it should also be emphasized that in the earlier "survival" model – which is sometimes seen as a bastion of "authenticity" against the supposed fabrications of postmodern theory – the conventional classifications are no less precisely inventions: the cultural units such as "Carib," defined by anthropology as existing at the moment of contact or earlier, are themselves fictions – not observations of fact, even if fictions of that peculiar colonial variety can call its inventions into being, so demonstrating the real power of the classificatory principle, still at work in national censuses, which often do the equivalent job for the 1990s.

One of the texts most famously, if indirectly, related to Carib ethnogenesis is Shakespeare's play *The Tempest*, which can be made to speak about the relationship between the two models of identity under discussion. In the middle part of the twentieth century much of what we can now see as Caribbean postcolonial theory clustered around readings of *The Tempest*, a work written at that crucial juncture just before the first major English settlements on the Caribbean islands. Particularly in

Aimé Césaire's powerful rewriting of the play, the dominant relationship in the play came to be seen as that between Prospero and Caliban, colonizer and colonized, a model taken from the Caribbean to Africa in the 1950s and grounded in anti-colonial struggle in the work of Frantz Fanon. In this reading, the key words of the play are "This island's mine by Sycorax my mother," spoken by Caliban: an assertion of his *native* rights to the land that has been taken from him by Prospero's usurpation. However much we might want to complicate the picture, and I shall try to complicate it myself, that claim to landrights articulated by Caliban has to be recognized as fundamental to indigenous peoples throughout the world, and nowhere more so than on the American continent.[8]

However, it is equally true that the conflict between Prospero and Caliban cannot be definitive of the colonial situation. Caliban is an overdetermined figure who can be read as either American or African, or both, but his compacted character obviously cannot suggest the triangular relationship – between white, red, and black – that defines so many parts of the continent during the colonial period. The real limitation of *The Tempest* for postcolonial work concerned with questions of ethnic identity comes from the very clarity with which it articulates one of the most powerful fears running at least through English America: here in the interdiction that Prospero puts on what might have been seen as the "inevitable" relationship between Caliban and Miranda on the island. One reading of the play would see Prospero's willingness to lose his beloved Milanese kingdom through Miranda's marriage to the heir of Naples as indicative of the high price he is willing to pay to avoid that relationship. Ultimately, *The Tempest* turns its back – deliberately if unconsciously – on what will become one of the defining factors of Caribbean and, indeed, American culture: what the nineteenth century would call miscegenation. Cultural *mestizaje* was not embraced as an American concept until the innovative work of José Martí, not accidentally at the very moment when the "survival" model of identity was becoming enshrined as the anthropological norm under the aegis of the newly expansionist United States. The unspeakable supplement to that model is, as always, what is perceived as the "mixed" race, beyond classification, and – to step beyond the world of *The Tempest* – beyond what that play could, as it were, imagine even in its unconscious: the truly unspeakable is the American Indian-African mix, the so-called red-black peoples that have, in the Caribbean as much as in the United States, been largely defined out of existence. Over the years the Caribs themselves have been defined out of that possible red-black identity.[9]

III

By the beginning of the twentieth century the Caribs were the relatively small groups descended from the indigenous population of the Caribbean and resident only on Dominica and St. Vincent, two of the islands of the Lesser Antilles in British possession. In one sense they were "merely" another of the indigenous peoples of the world sheltering as best they could in some corner of a European empire where they had been left to rot after their usefulness had been exhausted or their fight for survival overcome. But the Caribs had always been recognized as special, in part because their widespread reputation as cannibals earlier made them into the archetype of unregenerate savagery; in part because, as sole survivors of the native peoples who inhabited the Caribbean at the time of Columbus's arrival, they still stood as symbols of the first encounter of Europe with America, an encounter much discussed in the 1890s, as it has been again in the 1990s.

A hundred years ago Native Americans were still being killed in large numbers in many parts of the American continent. On the Caribbean islands, however, where the genocide had started earlier, a policy of aboriginal protection was put into place, following the general guidelines established at the 1884 Berlin Conference on Africa, however few "aboriginals" there were left to protect.[10] On Dominica, the key event at this time was, therefore, the establishment in 1903 of a Carib Reserve, still in existence. As recent Carib activists have pointed out, the gazetted notice which established the Reserve refers to the land which "the government of Dominica *desires* to reserve for the Caribs for their use": there is no reference to Carib landrights, no guidelines or procedures for entering into possession, no mention of title or treaty, no attempt to accommodate Carib participation in the proceedings. This was the doctrine of "benign guardianship." In addition, the Reserve was established out of the fiction of Crown Lands, one of the most powerful if least examined instruments for the dispossession of indigenous peoples, certainly in English America.[11] Just as the supposed solidity of empirical observation of native peoples turns out on skeptical inspection to consist of invented categories, so the colonial claim to sovereignty over land depends on historical fictions.

There has been only one occasion since the military defeat of the Caribs in St. Vincent in 1797 when the indigenous population of the Caribbean has made international news. That was in September 1930, when the London *Times* reported how starvation had hit the island following a violent hurricane in early September, leading to a riot on the Carib Reserve: "half-starving because of the loss of their crops . . . [the Caribs] advanced on Roseau, the capital of Dominica, looting food stores as they went. They were met by constabulary who were forced to use their firearms. A number of the rioters and four constables were wounded, the latter seriously." Hardly one word of this report was true: in fact an unprecedented dawn raid on the Reserve in search of smuggled liquor had led to a disturbance in which two Caribs were shot dead by policemen. The Caribs had not left their Reserve at all, let alone looted shops, but they were subsequently harassed there by a contingent of marines from HMS *Delhi*, which steamed over from Trinidad. Indeed, during the night the *Delhi* cruised down the coast shooting starshells over the Reserve in a bizarre echo of that scene in *Heart of Darkness* where the African coast is shelled by a French cruiser. The following day, local police with marines in attendance swept through the Reserve searching houses and making arrests. Eventually, seven Caribs were tried on charges of "Assaulting certain members of the Leeward Islands Police and Rescuing from them certain goods seized under the Trade and Revenue Act," but all the defendants were acquitted unanimously by the local jury.

This moment has a number of texts clustered around it, all narratives because the event marked a rupture in the fabric of imperial peace and native satisfaction – a rupture which needed explanation and repair. Chronologically these texts stretch from a telegram sent by the Administrator of Dominica to his Governor in Antigua:

"4 Police Constables on duty at the Carib Quarter have been attacked and danger-
ously injured by mob" (again no mention of dead Caribs here), to the narrator's dry
comment in Jean Rhys's story "Temps Perdi," set on Dominica six years later, when
told by a local policeman that nobody had been hurt in the incident, "only two or
three Caribs": "It might," she writes, "have been an Englishman talking."[12]

This was a "colonial" moment because the response was cast in disciplinary mode.
As so often in the Caribbean, *local* perceptions, even of those with enough wealth and
social status to sit on a jury, were ostentatiously at odds with metropolitan colonial
authority. Therefore, the Caribs, and especially their chief, needed to be *retried* and
found guilty; the policemen needed to be more or less exonerated – the question of
disciplining them in any way never arose, let alone charging them for unlawful
killing; and the Administrator had to be justified in his actions. These aims were all
achieved in classic fashion by a Commission of Enquiry, whose report constitutes
colonial discourse in its official register, producing a narrative that is closed and
definitive in its conclusions, although the seriousness with which the Colonial Office
took Carib claims to sovereignty demonstrates significant tensions within the hegemonic doctrine of benign guardianship.[13]

However, a different reason why this "moment" could be considered important is
that it provides one of the earliest examples in this area of a subaltern text, a text
written by a Carib. This text belongs to what I would argue was an important but
little-studied colonial genre, the petition, the indigenous text of national claim. The
1930 raid on the Carib Reserve was probably motivated by the island Administrator's
determination to break the authority of the Carib chief, who had been distinguishing
himself as an active advocate for the Caribs. The chief's weapon for this advocacy was
the petition to the monarch, by which subaltern groups could attempt to bypass the
local colonial administration and gain direct access to the king or queen in London
whose subjects they had been informed they were. This tactic rarely worked as
planned since the king or queen did not usually receive the petition addressed to
them, but the document would find its way to the Colonial Office which would
therefore become informed by a voice it did not normally hear from. For this to
happen at all usually depended on the services of an intermediary who was not
part of the local administration.

In June 1927 the Carib chief had drawn up a petition about the Carib situation,
stressing their poverty and lack of autonomy, and addressed it directly to King George
V. He enclosed this petition in a letter sent to a stamp-collector in Sheffield, along with
a request to put it into correct English and to forward it to the King. Instead, the
stamp collector sent the petition to the Colonial Office, who forwarded it to the
Administrator in Dominica so, eleven months after starting its long and eventually
circuitous journey the petition arrived in Roseau, twenty miles from its starting point,
having alerted the Colonial Office to native dissatisfaction it may otherwise have been
unaware of – but also confirming the local Administrator in his suspicions about the
chief.[14]

One final point about the Carib War. The landmark political settlement in the
Caribbean was the 1763 Treaty of Paris, after which British sugar planters were
supposed to complete the plantation of the Lesser Antilles, control of which had until
then been contested with France. Benedict Anderson notes this particular decade –

following the invention of an accurate chronometer – as marking the beginning of the squaring off of empty seas and unexplored regions in measured boxes, and Dominica was accordingly "boxed" and enthusiastically bought by lot all over England, with unfortunate disregard for the fact that the island consists entirely of steep and forested mountain sides: an early and devastating defeat for the geometrical grid.[15]

The 1763 "boxed" plan had given a minute section of 232 acres to the Caribs on the remote north windward coast; the 1903 Reserve of 3,700 acres was more carefully surveyed and a copy of the map kept by subsequent Carib chiefs. However, according to Carib oral tradition, this map was stolen by the police during the 1930 searches, and has since become a main bone of contention with both governments, British and then independent Dominican. One way of putting this would be to say that even today the story of the theft of the map functions as a metonym for the theft of Carib territory itself.[16]

IV

To move from 1930 to 1995 is to move from a "colonial" moment to a "postcolonial" moment, and it is important – not least for current debates about the term "postcolonial" – to gauge with some precision what has changed in those sixty-five years. In the Carib case, to focus on "text" is almost always to read what visitors have written, a record which now stretches for almost exactly five hundred years, and a reading of which would suggest extraordinary continuities in perceptions from the outside. Like many indigenous peoples over the last century, the Caribs have become known through being *visited*. If you take the entry in the *Oxford English Dictionary*, which serves to elucidate the verb, the Caribs have been "visitable" in two senses: "Liable to visitation by some competent authority" and "capable of being visited." What is common to both these senses of the word is that the party being visited has no choice in the matter. In other words the Caribs have never been "visitable" in the third – and now quaintly old-fashioned – *OED* sense: "having some social position in a neighbourhood," and therefore "capable of being visited on more or less equal terms by those of some standing in society"; they are very definitely "liable" or "capable" of being visited, passive recipients of the "visits" of those who deem them "visitable," in either a supervisory or a touristic capacity. The move from 1930 to 1995 is a move from supervision to tourism – which is not insignificant – but it is still a move within the sign of "the visit."

"Difference" may be a fashionable term for discussions of cultural or ethnic identity, but the indigenous people of the Caribbean have been seen as "different" ever since Columbus noted them in 1492 as "neither black nor white."[17] To a remarkable extent, that tripartite distinction has governed perceptions for five centuries, but in the last hundred years – in common with the experience of many Native Americans in the USA – the crucial distinction has been between "Indian" and black. One of the determinants of American Indian identity has been white racism in the Americas: some American Indian groups have only been able to survive at all by distinguishing themselves from black populations, distinctions made as sharply as they *had* to be made rather than as sharply as the Indians themselves necessarily *wanted* to make them. That would be true – to take an example close to Georgetown University itself – of the Powhatan Indians of Virginia, whose struggles in the middle part of this century to have themselves classified as Indian were struggles against the determination of white Virginian bureaucrats to classify them as "coloured."[18] This has been a factor in the Caribbean too, where, for example, one visiting writer can speak – very much in the language of survival – of the Caribs as a "doomed race lingering on the shores of extinction," awaiting the "black tide" that is going to sweep them away, genetically speaking.[19] Visitors – whether tourists or anthropologists – are still largely whites for whom the distinctiveness of the Caribs depends on their perceived difference from the surrounding African-descended population.

Let me give two brief textual examples. This is a US visitor in the 1960s on his first glimpse of a Carib woman washing clothes in a stream: "I had not really expected to find pure types. . . . But here I saw slanting eyes, high check bones, straight hair, and parchment-yellow skin. To me it was a scene from the Far East. She might have been Korean or Vietnamese" – not the most reassuring of comparisons to come out of the mouth of a visiting North American in the 1960s.

Then one of the most recent visitors' accounts: "One moment I was driving along a road where everyone was black, and then after an invisible barrier . . . many of the people look completely different. Although some were clearly of mixed race, many showed not the slightest sign of African descent. They had straight hair, pale skins and looked as if they could have come from some remote Indonesian island; often noticeable, too, was a Mongolian or Red Indian cast to their faces."[20] For visitors the *face* of the Carib – hair, cheekbones, eyes – is itself a text in which cultural difference can and must be read: that imperative – still the imperative of "blood" – has not changed in the postcolonial moment.

All that acknowledged, however, the shift from "colonial" to "postcolonial" is not insignificant. For one thing, the geography of power has changed substantially. In 1930 the Carib chief sought to bypass the outpost of British imperial authority in Roseau in order to speak directly to the sovereign political and economic power in London. Today there are many more axes to be considered. In 1995 the political power on the independent island lies in Roseau, and any Carib claims for self-determination would be asserted against a government of African descent which, unlike the colonial regime, bears no responsibility for taking Carib land, a fact that marks the Carib case as very different from those of their North American cousins.[21] Economic power still lies across the Atlantic, but it is wielded by the European Community rather than by Britain itself.

If there is in 1995 a paradigmatic text which goes beyond the continuities remarked in the visitors' accounts, then that text – imaginary as yet – would be the museum that the Caribs would like to build to display their own history and culture to visitors and tourists.[22] I offer this imaginary – and at least partially "postcolonial" – museum as a paradigm, not because it would necessarily solve any of the problems facing the Caribs, but because the very idea of self-presentation – even with the paradoxes involved in such self-presentation – would at least offer a partial break with the passive role that the Caribs have been locked into for the last two hundred years.

In the postcolonial period a Carib cultural revival has begun, with oral history and documentation projects under way, which could form the research base for such a museum.[23] Of course, the irony of the museum as postcolonial text is that whereas it allows for – and indeed encourages – the kind of cultural invention (or re-invention) that theorists such as Jim Clifford have applauded in similar contexts, the expectations that such a museum would have to meet are those that belong to the world of so-called "alternative tourism": expectations of "authenticity" and "purity" and "survival," expectations that are associated with the earlier and more obviously imperial model of cultural identity. To a degree – and especially if the museum took the form of a living village – the Caribs would be acting out for visitors a version of themselves and their own history which they would need to recognize and respond to, even if this version tried ultimately to contradict the expectations that tourists would bring with them: and these would continue to be, for the foreseeable future, expectations of indigenous difference.

The language of "invention" and "ethnogenesis" makes it clear that such a description of the imaginary museum should imply no betrayed essence. However, if ethnic identities are indeed negotiated and constructed through the interplay of self-knowledge and communal understandings, it is important to recognize that that process does not – to coin a phrase – occur under historical circumstances of the participants' own choosing, and those circumstances include the extreme economic and social pressures facing most indigenous communities in the Americas. On the one hand, this imaginary museum might provide the space in which the Caribs could tell their own version of their history. On the other hand, created in the context of tourism needing to be embraced as economic saviour, the museum would have to provide a "text" still legible to yet another set of visitors.[24]

V

What exactly then does it mean "to be Carib" in 1995, and what are the issues that confront the community today? The dialectic between self-identification and self-presentation is far from resolved. For visitors, the face is the text that counts, that bears the marks of cultural authenticity in the accidents of genetic survival; for the Caribs themselves, as for that Caliban to whom they gave their name, it is still land that matters: being born on the Carib Reserve itself is still the major index of Carib ethnicity.[25] The Caribs have successfully resisted attempts by both British and Dominican administrations to break up the Reserve and allot the land to individuals (despite the evident short-term financial benefits of such a scheme), and therefore still have some control over the vexed question of just who can call themselves "Carib" – a matter still of considerable tension in the North American Indian situation thanks to the continued deployment of degree-of-blood requirements imposed for access to federal services. Although not well-known enough to be referred to, Carib practice is close to the procedures recently adopted by the Oglala Lakota on Pine Ridge, where the crucial factors for Oglala identity are now residency on the reservation, affinity to, knowledge of, and service to the Oglala people.[26]

The deep historical irony here is that just at the moment when more sophisticated notions of identity seem to offer the prospect of a final break with the blood quantum obsession, there appears on the horizon, in the form of the Human Genome Diversity

Project, the "promise" of a supposedly conclusive and scientifically objective index of ethnic identity through genetic analysis. The Caribs – in common with many other indigenous groups – have refused to co-operate with this research, although much genetic material has already been obtained by fraud. It would seem that, not for the first time, our analytical tools are likely to lag behind our technological capabilities.[27]

One of the more recent of the "last man" stories has the last male Carib on Guadeloupe dying in the 1950s without being aware of the Carib community a handful of miles across the sea in Dominica.[28] That isolation was a feature of what I have called the "colonial" moment, what seemed to so many observers like the slow and lingering death of the scattered remnants of a culture. The most striking change in recent (postcolonial) years, and the one with the greatest potential impact on Carib ethnicity, is the growth in contact with groups outside the island: the roads that have brought more visitors have eventually enabled the international contacts that have allowed the Caribs to adopt additional Caribbean, Native American, and indigenous identities. If, in 1930, London was the centre of the imperial world for colonized peoples such as the Caribs, today the postcolonial map of significant places would include, apart from Roseau and London, say, Akwesasne or Regina as symbolic of Carib links with Native American organizations on the mainland, and Geneva as meeting place of the UN Working Group on Indigenous Peoples.

It would be wrong, however, to end with an exclusive emphasis on indigeneity, which tends always to put the indigenous group in potential conflict with its nation-state. A Caribbean writer pointed out in 1992 that the creation of the European single market in that year allows the European countries to do together and simultaneously to the Caribbean what for the previous five hundred years they had done separately and sequentially.[29] In this respect, the invented cultural identity to which most attention should be paid is the supra-national idea of "Europe," politically flexible enough to expand its internal market where necessary, but always presenting itself as culturally homogeneous, with its single classical origin and its newly impermeable frontiers. As banana-producers oppressed by this European wing of the New Economic World Order, the Caribs are no different from other Dominican (or indeed Caribbean) peasant farmers: they all face imminent financial ruin.[30] In this spirit, let me end with a few of Edouard Glissant's words, the apposite but typically elliptical epigraph from his novel La Lézarde: " 'What country is this?' he asked. And the answer was: 'First weigh each word, know every sorrow.' "[31]

NOTES

1   Cf. the distinction made by Les W. Field between what he identifies as the "cultural survival position" and the "resistance school" ("Who Are the Indians? Reconceptualizing Indigenous Identity, Resistance, and the Role of Social Science in Latin America," *Latin American Research Review* 29 (1994): 237–48; and that made by John H. Moore between "cladistic" and "rhizotic" theories of historical relationship to antecedent groups ("Putting Anthropology Back Together Again: The Ethnogenetic Critique of Cladistic Theory," *American Anthropologist* 96 (1994): 925–48). Moore discusses how to interpret the data from the

Human Genome Diversity Project, whose implications I come back to at the end of this paper.

2   See J. Michael Dash, *Edouard Glissant* (Cambridge: Cambridge University Press, 1994), 22–3.

3   For further discussion of these complex issues see, for example, Lee Swepston and Roger Plant, "International Standards and the Protection of the Land Rights of Indigenous and Tribal Populations," *International Labour Review* 124.1 (1985): 91–106; Russel Lawrence Barsh, "Indigenous Peoples: An Emerging Object of International Law," *American Journal of International Law* 80 (1986): 369–85; Julian Burger, *Report from the Frontier: The State of the World's Indigenous Peoples* (London, Atlantic Highlands, NJ: Zed Books, 1987); Lydia van de Fliert, ed., *Indigenous Peoples and International Organisations* (Nottingham: Spokesmen, 1994); John Howard Clinebell and Jim Thompson, "Sovereignty and Self-Determination: The Rights of Native Americans Under International Law," *Buffalo Law Review* 27 (1978): 669–714; Russel Lawrence Barsh, "Indigenous North America and Contemporary International Law," *Oregon Law Review* 62 (1983): 73–125; Vine Deloria, Jr. and Clifford M. Lytle, *The Nations Within: The Past and Future of American Indian Sovereignty* (New York: Partheon, 1984); Glenn T. Morris, "International Law and Politics: Toward a Right to Self-Determination for Indigenous Peoples," in M. Annette Jaimes, ed., *The State of Native America: Genocide, Colonization, and Resistance* (Boston, MA: South End Press, 1992), 55–86; Ward Churchill, *Struggle for the Land: Indigenous Resistance to Genocide, Ecocide, and Expropriation in Contemporary North America* (Monroe: Common Courage Press, 1993). The Caribs are often excluded from discussion, even within sympathetic accounts of indigenous peoples (see, for example, Burger, *Report from the Frontier*, 64).

4   See my discussion of this model in *Colonial Encounters: Europe and the Native Caribbean* (London, New York: Methuen, 1986), 45–88.

5   Referred to by Charles Darwin in the section called "On the Extinction of the Races of Man" in his *The Descent of Man, and Selection in Relation to Sex*, 2nd edn. (London, 1874), 281.

6   The significance of this emerging paradigm is not easy to gauge. Scholarship is never static, there are always reassessments, new models, each generation makes its subject anew, finds new materials, invents new methodologies. I am suggesting something more: that deeply embedded colonial assumptions about native passivity, lack of native polities, native military incompetence, allied with the unreflective reading of texts, and compounded by a conflation between archaeological and linguistic and ethnographic evidence, have prevented European and U.S.-American scholarship from understanding the history of the native Caribbean, a history which is still far from over.

    For the "tribal zone," see R. Brian Ferguson and Neil L. Whitehead, eds., *War in the Tribal Zone: Expanding States and Indigenous Warfare* (Santa Fe, NM: School of American Research Press, 1992). For new ethnohistorical work on the native Caribbean, see Jalil Sued Badillo, "Facing up to Caribbean History," *American Antiquity* 57 (1992): 599–607; Peter Hulme, "Making Sense of the Native Caribbean," *New West Indian Guide* 67, nos. 3 & 4 (1993): 189–220; and the papers collected in Neil L. Whitehead, ed. *Wolves from the Sea: Readings in the Anthropology of the Native Caribbean* (Leiden, 1995). For some of the texts through which the ethnogenetic process can be traced, see Peter Hulme and Neil L. Whitehead, eds. *Wild Majesty: Encounters with Caribs from Columbus to the Present Day* (Oxford: Clarendon Press, 1992).

7   Benedict Anderson, *Imagined Communities: Reflections on the Origin and Spread of Nationalism*, 2nd. edn. (London, New York: Verso, 1991), 6. Over the last twenty years there seems to have occurred such a paradigm shift that almost everything which was once taken as a set of facts, is now seen on closer inspection to be a social and imaginative construct. A small symptom of this consensus is the extraordinary number of recent books and essays that use

the words "invention" or "inventing" in their title. A brief and by no means comprehensive survey shows that over the last few years Scotland, Africa, Canada, Argentina and India have all been "invented," as have the French Revolution, progress, Leonardo da Vinci, the middle ages, the barbarian, the people, heterosexuality, national literature, the Indian, primitive society, and ethnicity. This recent trend in the use of "invention" as a title probably stems from the essays in Eric Hobsbawm and Terence Ranger's influential collection *The Invention of Tradition* (1983), though this book has several immediate predecessors, including Roy Wagner's *The Invention of Culture* (1980), Michel de Certeau's *L'Invention du quotidien* (1980), and Garry Wills's *Inventing America: Jefferson's Declaration of Independence* (1978). The ultimate progenitor, however, is of course Edmundo O'Gorman's classic *The Invention of America* (1961). For a study of this phenomenon, see Gaurav Desai, "The Invention of Invention," *Cultural Critique* 18 (1993): 119–41.

8   On mid-century re-readings of *The Tempest*, see Rob Nixon, "Caribbean and African appropriations of *The Tempest*," *Critical Inquiry* 13 (1987): 557–78.

9   Jack Forbes's work is the indispensable introduction to these questions: *Africans and Native Americans: The Language of Race and the Evolution of Red-Black Peoples*, 2nd edn. (Urbana, IL: University of Illinois Press, 1993). See also C. Matthew Snipp, "Who Are American Indians? Some Observations about the Perils and Pitfalls of Data for Race and Ethnicity," *Population Research and Policy Review* 5 (1986): 237–52.

10   See Barsh, "Indigenous North America and Contemporary International Law," *Oregon Law Review* 62 (1983): 73–125, at 74.

11   The *Official Gazette* (XXVI, 4 July 1903) is quoted from Hilary Frederick, *The Caribs and their Colonizers: The Problem of Land* (London: The International Organization for the Elimination of all Forms of Racism [EAFORD], 1983), 10 (italics added). On "Crown Lands," see Kent McNeil, *Common Law Aboriginal Title* (Oxford: Clarendon Press, 1989).

12   *The Times*, 2 October 1930, 11; Reginald St.-Johnston, *From a Colonial Governor's Note-Book* (London: Hutchinson, 1936), 154; Jean Rhys, "Temps Perdi," in *The Collected Short Stories* (New York, 1979), 272. A study of the so-called "Carib War" forms Chapter Four of my forthcoming *Remnants of Conquest: The Caribs and their Visitors, 1877–1992*.

13   J. Stanley Rae and Sydney A. Armitage-Smith, *Conditions in the Carib Reserve, and the Disturbance of 19th September, 1930* (London, 1931).

14   *Colonial Office* (London) 152/406 and 407.

15   Anderson, *Imagined Communities*, 173. On Byres' 1763 survey of Dominica, see Lennox Honychurch, *The Dominica Story: A History of the Island*, 2nd. edn. (Roseau: Dominica Institute, 1984), 45–6.

16   Frederick, *The Caribs*, 16–17.

17   See my "Tales of Distinction: European Ethnography and the Caribbean," in Stuart B. Schwartz, ed., *Implicit Understandings: Observing, Reporting, and Reflecting on the Encounters between Europeans and Other Peoples in the Early Modern Era* (New York, Cambridge: Cambridge University Press, 1994), 157–97.

18   See the superb study by Helen C. Rountree, *Pocahontas's People: The Powhatan Indians of Virginia Through Four Centuries* (Norman, OK: University of Oklahoma Press, 1990), 219–42.

19   Patrick Leigh Fermor, *The Traveller's Tree: A Journey Through the Caribbean Islands* [1950] (Harmondsworth: Penguin, 1984), 118. Cf. my "The Rhetoric of Description: The Amerindians of the Caribbean in Modern European Discourse," *Caribbean Studies* 23, nos. 3–4 (1990): 35–50.

20   Carleton Mitchell, *Isles of the Caribbees* (Washington: National Geographic Society, 1966), 95; John Hatt, "Dominica Done," *Harpers & Queen* (April 1993): 164–8, at 166.

21 Since independence the Roseau government has had an uneasy relationship with NGOs working with the Caribs: see Crispin Grégoire and Natalia Kanem, "The Caribs of Dominica: Land Rights and Ethnic Consciousness," *Cultural Survival Quarterly* 13.3 (1989): 52–5.

22 My invocation of the museum completes the trilogy discussed in Chapter 10 of Benedict Anderson's *Imagined Communities*. "Census, Map, Museum."

23 The oral history project contains an element on the 1930 "Carib War." The only monument raised by the Caribs themselves is a small one on the site of the 1930 killings, a monument that is not shown to tourists.

24 See James Clifford, *The Predicament of Culture: Twentieth-Century Ethnography, Literature, and Art* (Cambridge, MA: Harvard University Press, 1986). There are a number of "textual" models on offer in this area, such as Guillermo Gómez Peña posing as a caged Native American in the Smithsonian Museum of Natural History (see his own account, in John Kraniauskas, "Border Dialogue: Talking to Guillermo Gómez Peña," *Travesía: Journal of Latin American Cultural Studies* 3 (1995): 152–77, at 167–8). One of the most forthright visitors to the Carib Reserve, the French travel-writer Jean Raspail, gave his (perhaps prophetic) recommendations more than twenty years ago: "si j'étais roi des Caraïbes, je saurais très bien ce que je ferais: j'aurais une belle tunique drapée dessinée par un décorateur de théâtre, je construirais un village bidon de paillotes groupées autour d'un totem... je déshabillerais mon peuple et je lui collerais des plumes dans le derriére, j'organiserais des danses sacrées tous les jours à heure fixe, et je gagnerais beaucoup d'argent avec les touristes des croisières antillaises, ravis de découvrir enfin quelque chose de nouveau. Je ferais tout cela, car j'en sais le résultat. Je connais le grand sachem des Sioux du Niagara, un capitaliste qui règne sur un tribu de millionaires déguisées en sauvages: il vend des tomawaks qu'on lui livre par camion de dix tonnes, et campe sous la tente à la belle saison pour les besoins du bizenesse, en prenant soin de laiser sa Cadillac au vestiaire" (*Secouns le Cocotier*, edition revue et augmentée [Paris: R. Laffont, 1973], 149–50).

On tourism in Dominica, see David B. Weaver, "Alternative to Mass Tourism in Dominica," *Annals of Tourism Research* 18 (1991): 414–32. For an early proposal with respect to the Caribs, see Arthur Einhorn, *Proposal for Development of a Carib "Indian Village" and the Economic Development of the Carib Indian Reserve on the Island of Dominica, British West Indies* [1972] (Copy in the Public Library Roseau, Dominica). Cf. "Carib Council holds first-ever tourism consultation," *The New Chronicle* [Dominica], LXXXV (2 July 1993).

25 Under "The Carib Reserve, Act no. 22 of 1978" (in *Laws of Dominica* [Roseau, 1991], 51:2) "a person shall be deemed to have a right of residence in the Reserve if – (a) he was born in the Reserve; (b) at least one of his parents is a Carib; (c) he has lawfully resided in the Reserve for a period of 12 years or more."

For the reductive argument that the assertion of Carib ethnic identity is merely a stratagem to retain control of scarce resources, see Anthony Layng's two articles: "Ethnic Identity, Population Growth, and Economic Security on a West Indian Reservation," *Revista/Review Interamericana* 9, no. 4 (1979–80): 577–84; and "The Caribs of Dominica: Prospects for Structural Assimilation of a Territorial Minority," *Ethnic Groups* 6, nos. 2–3 (1985): 209–21. The theory is based on Leo A. Despres, *Ethnicity and Resource Competition in Plural Societies* (The Hague: Mouton, 1975). More sympathetic accounts of contemporary Carib ethnicity are Nancy H. Owen's two articles, "Land, Politics, and Ethnicity in a Carib Indian Community," *Ethnology* XIV (1975): 385–93, and "Conflict and Ethnic Boundaries: A Study of Carib/Black Relations," *Social and Economic Studies* 29, nos. 2–3, (1980): 264–74; Enrique Mayer, *The Carib Reserve in Dominica*, Integrated Rural

Development Project Supplementary Report (Washington DC, 1982), 16–31; and Grégoire and Kanem, "The Caribs of Dominica."

26 See M. Annette Jaimes, "Federal Indian Identification Policy: A Usurpation of Indigenous
Sovereignty in North America," in M. Annette James, ed., *The State of Native America:
Genocide, Colonization, and Resistance* (Boston, MA: South End Press, 1992), 123–38.

27 See Tom Wilkie, *Perilous Knowledge: The Human Genome Project and Its Implications* (Berkeley, CA: University of California Press, 1993); "Carib Council puts Genome programme on
hold," *The New Chronicle* [Dominica], LXXXV (23 July 1993); John H. Moore, "Putting
Anthropology Back Together Again." For two versions of the argument that our "newer"
cultural models are still haunted by "blood" identity, see Walter Benn Michaels, "The No-
Drop Rule," *Critical Inquiry* 20 (1994): 758–69; and Robert J. C. Young, *Colonial Desire:
Hybridity in Theory, Culture and Race* (London, New York: Routledge, 1995).

28 Jean Raspail, *Bleu Caraïbe et Citrons Verts: Mes Derniers Voyages aux Antilles* (Paris: R.
Laffont, 1980), 92.

29 Rex Nettleford, "Surviving Columbus: Caribbean Achievements in the Encounter of
Worlds 1492–1992," *Caribbean Quarterly* 38 (1992): 97–112; 97.

30 The Commission of the European Community claims that the basic prerequisite for
European union lies in "[t]he uniqueness of European culture." See the quote in Verena
Stolcke, "Talking Culture: New Boundaries, New Rhetorics of Exclusion in Europe,"
Current Anthropology 36 (1995): 1–24; 1.

31 Edouard Glissant, *The Ripening*, trans. Michael Dash (London: Heinemann, 1985). The
original French is quoted as the epigraph to this paper.

Sending the Younger Son Across the Wide Sargasso Sea: The New Colonizer Arrives

MOIRA FERGUSON

Moira Ferguson's essay, taken from her influential book, *Colonialism and Gender Relations from Mary Wollstonecraft to Jamaica Kincaid: East Caribbean Connections*, is a remarkable example not only of close, textual reading but also of theoretical reflection. Her reading of Jean Rhys's *Wide Sargasso Sea* explores the intertextual critique in which Rhys engages Charlotte Brontë's *Jane Eyre* and provides pertinent historical information that will allow the student to see just how Rhys's novel supplements Brontë's by "filling in" the gaps of Jane Eyre's story about her beloved Edward Rochester. Particularly important in this regard is Rochester's "historical complicity" with colonialism. By situating Rhys's and Brontë's fiction with respect to the Emancipation Bill of 1834, Ferguson underscores the dynamics of post-emancipation colonial rule which necessitated new modes of oppression and control on the part of the new breed of colonialists who take over from the pre-emancipation "plantocracy." Her reading draws out the complex relations between native Caribbeans, whose ancestry was African, and the white Creoles, whose social position was destabilized after emancipation. With the introduction of Rochester, Rhys complicates these relations by situating the white Creole woman between the poles of African Caribbeans and white Europeans. Ferguson's nuanced interpretation of the racial distinctions and interrelationships can be contextualized within the general project of Caribbean postcolonial theory as exemplified in the essays by **Peter Hulme** and **Stuart Hall**; moreover, it can be usefully paired with **George Lamming**'s considerations of the Caribbean novel and the problem of race. Students may also want to consider Ferguson's essay in light of feminist critiques of postcolonial identity by **Gayatri Chakravorty Spivak, Rajeswari Sunder Rajan, Kay Schaffer, Helen Tiffin**, and **Angela Bourke**.

Sending the Younger Son Across the Wide Sargasso Sea: The New Colonizer Arrives

> I do not like what I have seen of this honourable gentleman. Stiff. Hard as a board and stupid as a foot, in my opinion, except where his own interests are concerned.
>
> Jean Rhys, *Wide Sargasso Sea*, pp. 114–15

Wide Sargasso Sea affirms the idea that the colonial order was well advised to feel less secure as emancipation approached. And only disguised aggression, not overt violent aggression, worked as a temporary antidote, as the understated opening avows: "They say when trouble comes close ranks, and so the white people did." Set to the south of Antigua in Dominica, *Wide Sargasso Sea* extends the East Caribbean discussions to another British West Indian island. Written by Jean Rhys, a Dominican from the small white upper class, *Wide Sargasso Sea* (1966) narrates the post-emancipationist subversion by Jamaican and Dominican communities of gender and colonial relations.[1] Set in Jamaica, Dominica, and England in the 1830s, it explores that fluid historical era when black and white communities were adjusting to emancipation. Many-layered, *Wide Sargasso Sea* also comments obliquely on post-emancipation race relations in Jean Rhys's own period with the eruption of the Notting Hill Riots in London in 1958.[2] In that sense Jean Rhys directly and indirectly challenges two worlds of postcolonial emancipation. Although the novel overtly represents renegotiated colonial relations between the colonizer and the freed but still colonized, the text covertly intimates that the African-Caribbean communities drove out the English and the white creoles. In other words, freed slaves reject the new economic order of society based on capital accumulation by residual ex-plantocrats and their patriarchal allies.

Let me briefly recapitulate significant points. Jean Rhys is reconstructing *Jane Eyre* from the point of view of Antoinette, later Bertha Cosway Mason Rochester (part 1), then from the point of view of her husband, Edward Rochester (part 2), and last from the perspective of both Antoinette and Grace Poole, her keeper after Rochester has locked Antoinette in an attic on his English estate.[3] (For convenience I refer to the multiply named female protagonist as Antoinette.) Part 1 concerns Antoinette's childhood and marriage at the Coulibri estate near Spanish Town, Jamaica; her

Taken from *Colonialism and Gender Relations from Mary Wollstonecraft to Jamaica Kincaid: East Caribbean Connections* (New York: Columbia University Press, 1993).

special relationships with African-Caribbean friend Tia and housekeeper Christophine; her mother Annette's marriage to Richard Mason after the post-emancipation death of Antoinette's father, Mr. Cosway; the burning of Coulibri by freed slaves; and Annette Cosway Mason's psychic disintegration. Part 1 also intertextualizes some of Jean Rhys's experiences growing up, especially in Antoinette's awkward and eventually estranged relationship with her mother, her ambiguous, often ethnocentric descriptions of African-Caribbeans, and her eventual withdrawal and keen sense of alienation: "She was white but not English or European, West Indian but not black."[4] Part 2 narrates the honeymoon of Antoinette and Rochester in Granbois, Dominica, their interactions with the servants Amélie and Christophine as well as with Daniel Cosway, who controversially claims to be the son by a black woman of Antoinette's father. Part 3 sketches Antoinette's imprisonment in the attic of Rochester's English "Great House," her torching of that house, and her fatal jump. In contrast to this narrative of complex British-Caribbean interrelationships, Charlotte Brontë's text nearly silences Bertha Rochester – never naming her – and comments only briefly on Rochester's marriage to this white creole heiress. Put differently, it seems unlikely that Brontë could see Bertha at all except as the dangerous sign of Rochester's problematic youth. Rochester is traditionally configured as a tragic hero, victim of a trick marriage.

Precipitating the focal action in *Wide Sargasso Sea* are the Rochesters, a well-connected British family, contemptuous of a meretricious plantocracy but not above exploiting its vulnerable heiresses. (I call the family the Rochesters and the protagonist Edward Rochester, following Jean Rhys's notes for the novel and her transparent reinterpretation of *Jane Eyre*.) Capitalizing on their status, male family members are bent on usurping and administering estates and fortunes, if not restoring the political power of a vanquished and vanishing pre-emancipation planter class.

Duty bound to the law of the father, younger son Edward Rochester journeys to Spanish Town as a potential speculator in order to expropriate through marriage the inheritance of an unknown woman. In Kenneth Ramchand's words, Jean Rhys "is building upon a type situation in island history – the marrying of Creole heiresses for their dowry by indigent, but socially well-connected younger sons."[5]

This updated form of Caribbean predation had become common in the years following the passage of the Emancipation Bill in 1834 and is inscribed in the actions of Edward Rochester's predecessor, his economic forefather of sorts, the heiress's stepfather Mr. Mason. The community observes these white goings-on. A cynical black wedding guest sneers that Rochester came to "make money cheap as they all do. Some of the big estates are going cheap, and one unfortunate's loss is always a clever man's gain" (p. 30). With the encouragement of unscrupulous Richard Mason, stepbrother of his bride-to-be, Rochester has successfully drawn heiress Antoinette Cosway Mason into an economy that only can purport to be a market economy, given the precarious oppositions between freed slaves and former slaveowners within Jamaican and Dominican culture.

In a mental letter to his father, Edward acknowledges his role as an obedient son. He accedes to coercion but cannot entirely stifle his opposition, let alone his suppressed desires:

Dear Father.
The thirty thousand pounds have been paid to me without question or condition. No provision made for her (that must be seen to). I have a modest competence now. I will never be a disgrace to you or to my dear brother the son you love. No begging letters, no mean requests. None of the furtive shabby manoeuvers of a younger son. I have sold my soul or you have sold it, and after all is it such a bad bargain? The girl is thought to be beautiful, she is beautiful. And yet... (p. 70)

Less savory aspects of the transaction, absent in these ruminations, are supplied later in a conversation, which Antoinette overhears, between Richard Mason and her Aunt Cora, ironically a former slaveowner:

"It's disgraceful," she said. "It's shameful. You are handing over everything the child owns to a perfect stranger [Edward Rochester]. Your father would never have allowed it. She should be protected, legally. A settlement can be arranged and it should be arranged. That was his intention."
... He told her for God's sake shut up you old fool and banged the door when he left. So angry that he did not notice me [Antoinette] standing in the passage. She was sitting up in bed when I went into her room. "Halfwit that the boy is, or pretends to be. I do not like what I have seen of this honourable gentleman. Stiff. Hard as a board and stupid as a foot, in my opinion, except where his own interests are concerned." (pp. 114–15)

As an investor in women, Edward Rochester can think only in commercial terms that highlight his privileged Anglo-Saxon heritage; he cannot face, he even reverses, the implications of his own acts: "I have not bought her. She has bought me, or so she thinks" (p. 70). He thinks he hears a debased French patois when he hears a complex creole language. What he interprets as inexplicable "blanks in my mind" (p. 76) signify his ignorance, his immersion in the ethic of an imperial country, a steadfast denial of historical facts.

Antoinette is the site of negotiations of power between Rochester and Mason, foreclosing structures protested by herself and Aunt Cora. To her stepbrother she is dispensable property that can be bartered for a respectable lineage, something resident plantocrats rarely possessed but always craved. She is the site of a different version of slavery: a legally free woman is bought because she owns property. A handy commodity, she affords Edward Rochester's father an opportunity to get the younger son rich quick.[6] Male traders at the wedding are mute about the wedding's raison d'être though the groom discloses a sense of his function in an unself-conscious act of displacement when he speaks wryly of planters: "I remember little of the actual ceremony. Marble memorial tables on the walls commemorating the virtues of the last generation of planters. All benevolent. All slave-owners. All resting in peace" (p. 77).

Since Victorian proprieties demand that he stay a seemly amount of time to lend an air of respectability to the marriage, the ill-fitted pair travel with an African-Caribbean retinue to the bride's mother's small estate in Dominica. Yet Daniel Cosway interrupts their honeymoon with allegations about Antoinette's mad family and his own familial connections; discord implodes, then explodes, and never ceases: "I am your wife's brother by another lady, half-way house as we say.... They are white, I am coloured. They are rich, I am poor" (pp. 96–7).

In Dominica, Rochester's objectification of Antoinette as a marketable item is matched by his general attitude toward the black population. His insecurities are expressed in anxious body language, obvious to everyone but his unseeing self. "Sometimes a sidelong look or a sly knowing glance disturbed me" (p. 90), he confesses, with no cognizance of his own provocation, the bait of his very presence. He conducts himself as a latter-day Robinson Crusoe, forcibly shipwrecked at his family's instigation among diverse inferiors.[7] Even one of the songs the couple share features a character named Robin, evoking Crusoe-Rochester's imperial encounter, his quest for empire, his preternatural solitude – colonial beginnings that turn out catastrophically for Edward Rochester.

Fearful of losing control and oblivious to his pernicious and multiple interpellations vis-à-vis freed slaves and his newly acquired wife and family network, Rochester's only outlet is self-communion about felt hostility. He never acknowledges that he is married to the daughter of a former slave-owning family, even when he sarcastically notes her casual beneficence toward black servants. To permit any circulation of this history would amount to complicity in institutionalized colonialism. Ironically, of course – or is it symbolically? – his actions echo his father's and are scarcely distinguishable from traditional plantocratic conduct like Old Man Cosway's. Small wonder that Rochester ends up longing for the night and sex, since his only formulated plan, as he states in the opening lines of the novel, is to advance and retreat. Awaiting the right moment to retreat without losing face, he marks time while taking full advantage of his new status as husband.

When Daniel Cosway's letter disrupts their nightly sexual stupors, Rochester seizes upon it as the perfect excuse to sail away even more hastily than he had planned. The mirroring of his palpable greed in Cosway's own opportunistic ploy is quite beyond Rochester's perception. For Daniel Cosway has confirmed Rochester's most overt fears: he has married into a miscegenous family, his white colonial vision is a fraud, the source of his ill-gotten affluence is tainted. Consequently, the fact that he feels an uneasy attraction for the island and its way of life, as well as for his wife, somewhat unnerves him and wrestles his horror at Cosway's apparent revelations. He cannot think straight. (Even at the end, after he has abandoned the Caribbean for Britain and joined the absentee landlord class, aping old planters and betraying total alienation, he imagines that he is emotionally proffering Antoinette one last chance. Or he tells himself that he does. Colonial narcissism dictates that she should read his mind. Overseer Baptiste is left in Rochester's place at Granbois after Rochester's humiliating exodus.)

But a nagging question erupts here. Why does Jean Rhys choose the moment when Rochester is surrounded by black islanders – historically constituted as overground maroons – to kill off his father and brother? Is it simply a need of the plot to have Edward Rochester rich in his own right or does it presage his own future fall?

Contextualizing Daniel Cosway's letter explicates Rochester's dread of an oppositional environment. After 1834, when slaves were legally free, planter suicides were not uncommon. Legal compensation they received often had to be paid to insistent creditors, and sugar prices rocketed.[8] By 1847, 140 sugar estates had been abandoned, several of them "miserable worthless places thrown up in consequence of being plunged in debt long before the abolition of slavery."[9] Estate values collapsed:

> 64 petitions of insolvency have been filed; estate after estate thrown upon the market, and no purchaser found. Even where there has been no insolvency, many estates have been abandoned from the inability to raise money on the faith of the coming crop... Within the last few weeks Jordan Hill estate...with a crop of 450 to 500 hogsheads on the ground, and on which about £1,500 were expended last year, in laying down tram roads...has been sold for £4,000. This sale has taken place, not under an insolvency or bankruptcy, nor to meet the pressure of creditors, but by persons of wealth and respectability; and men here wonder, not at the sacrifice of the vendors so much as the rashness of the purchaser.[10]

Thomas McCormack, a well-known Jamaica estate owner for forty years, "cut his own throat in December 1848 after a period of severe mental depression and immediately following the destruction of his megass house at Stanton by the work of an incendiary. A year earlier sixteen Jamaica planters who owned nineteen estates free of debt or encumbrance and leased another thirteen declared themselves unable to cultivate for another year and incapable, without credit, of taking off the existing crop."[11]

Furthermore, estate owners in Dominica like Rochester fared even worse, another reason why Daniel Cosway's exposé bedevils Rochester. The number of actual Caribbean-based plantation owners diminished to virtual invisibility. As contemporary John Davy states, "In a recent communication from thence, it is stated that the number of resident proprietors (worthy of the name) does not exceed two."[12] Being outnumbered by angry slaves or freed individuals was a colonizer's nightmare.

Other estate owners were absentee landlords. Davy continues: "Of the other class, – the white inhabitants and the planters, I can give but little information, having, though twice in the island, but only a few hours, had no opportunity to become acquainted with them. Of the proprietors of estates, most of the English are, I believe, absentees" (p. 504). Demoralization among despised white property owners in Dominica makes Rochester's near paranoia and sociocultural paralysis a standard reaction for his class:

> Neither in the official reports on the state of the island, or in conversation with those connected with it, have I been able to find any proof of advancing intelligent exertion similar to that witnessed in Barbados, Antigua, and St. Kitt's. No attempt that I have heard of has been made to form an agricultural society, or to establish a library, or, in brief, to accomplish anything tending to promote the advancement of knowledge, the acquisition of science, without which, how is it possible at the present time that any people can be successful, even as regards the lowest, their worldly and material interests! I may perhaps, in making these statements, appear to those acquainted with the island, to express myself too strongly, inasmuch as an effort has been made within the last few years to institute in the town of Roseau, a higher school than the ordinary ones, an academy or grammar school, intended for the education of the children of the upper class; but even this, though aided by a proportionally large annual grant of money from the island treasury, does not appear to have been successful, and has been considered by

those who ought to be competent judges, the Lieut. Governor and Governor General, as ill-timed and injudicious.[13]

Burnt estates became familiar signifiers of historical resistance and revenge, of a celebratory, post-emancipation landscape. "Certainly," muses Edward Rochester, "many of the old estate houses were burned. You saw ruins all over the place" (p. 133). In point of fact Jamaica and Dominica, the only Caribbean locales named, had mounted severe, unprecedented opposition to the white plantocracy.

Constantly shifting colonial relations made for a traumatized childhood for Antoinette Cosway. They also evoke experiences Jean Rhys shares with Antoinette that further complicate the text. Antoinette grew up lonely and increasingly introspective – a double outsider – able to do little else than internalize the opprobrium of formerly colonized people on whose company and friendship she depended.[14] But realistically, as she sadly confesses, her childhood friend Tia and others "hated us. They called us white cockroaches...Nobody wants you" (p. 23).[15] At other times whites were disparaged as centipedes who had to be eliminated. One black witness to the fire on the Coulibri estate explains the need to demolish their presence this way: "You mash centipede, mash it, leave one little piece and it grow again" (p. 43). The population is acutely aware of imperial bonds and continuities. The *glacis* that Annette Cosway paces provides another negative plantocratic association: "The *glacis*, we know, was the wide stone platform for drying coffee. On Sundays and holidays it was here that the slaves would gather to play music and dance."[16] At one level the name of the home itself, *Coulibri*, quietly rebukes its plantocratic linkage. The word derives from a Dominican word – *cou* – for the Great House of the white plantation owner, melliflu-ously and ironically it is yoked to a version of *libre*, the French adjective for free. On the other hand, most Dominicans would have heard in *Coulibri* a variant of *Colibri*, the standard Carib loan-word meaning humming-bird.

By the time Edward Rochester appears, Antoinette has become so immune to her status as victim that she acquiesces to the marriage after one bold but short-lived refusal pressed by Aunt Cora. On their honeymoon Antoinette almost joyously acknowledges his power over her. After he has trampled the wedding wreath of frangipani, one of the multiple metonyms for the island's cryptic beauty, which eludes and confuses him, she somewhat coyly declares: "You look like a king, an em-peror...She knelt near me [continues Rochester] and wiped my face with her handkerchief" (pp. 73–4).

Antoinette has embraced one of the few spaces a powerless woman can occupy – that of the sexually desirable female – now that she has married and thereby relinquished her inheritance. Although she ostensibly is not forced, in this one respect her short, ardently sexual relationship to the "master" resembles a familiar aspect of the relationships many female slaves endured with white owners.

But this union, tenuous at best, needs very little to fracture it, at least from Rochester's point of view. The accusatory letter he receives from Daniel Cosway, claiming he is Antoinette's step-brother, does the trick. This stranger's claim to kinship means Rochester not only married into a family in which mother Annette and son Pierre are mentally unstable but also has (to his chagrin) married into a family of color. When his anger bursts, he experiences the historical complicity that he has vehemently suppressed. In that sense Cosway's exposé enables Rochester's self-confrontation.

At this point Rhys invites the reader (who is assumed to be white) to sympathize with Antoinette, her chance of a happy life disastrously thwarted once again. After the plural indignities already perpetrated on this naïve planter's daughter, Daniel Cosway's letter is the last straw. (Antoinette's status as a planter's daughter is metonymically linked to the painting of "The Miller's Daughter" on the wall at Coulibri that is destroyed in the fire. She is first framed and objectified, then burned unrecognizably in the final fire.) She is, after all, a white creole who sometimes empathizes with ex-slaves. Unlike unreconstructed Rochester, Antoinette nurtures a form of post-emancipationist self-knowledge: "No more slavery," she says at one point. "Why should *anybody* work? This never saddened me [that the Coulibri estate went wild]. I did not remember the place when it was prosperous" (p. 19). Elicited empathy for Antoinette as victim aside, the text also rationalizes her classic planto-cratic attitudes that wrestle her assimilative desires. In two minor, seemingly unre-lated incidents Antoinette's apparent conflict betrays some of Rhys's personal conflicts regarding white creole ideology. In the first instance an enraged Antoinette decries childhood friend Tia as a "cheating nigger," an outburst excused on the grounds of fatigue. More important, Rhys suggests that Antoinette's family bears a dual responsibility: they violate her emotional boundaries so cavalierly that she vents understandable anger on her young friend.

The next instance involves an exchange between Antoinette and the major Afri-can-Caribbean character in the text, Christophine, Antoinette's nurse and confidante. Antoinette finds Christophine waiting for her after she visits her troubled mother Antoinette: "'What you want to go up there for?' [Christophine] said, and I said, 'You shut up devil, damned black devil from Hell'" (pp. 134–5).[17]

Antoinette's desire for close friendship with Tia and Christophine, then, has to be juxtaposed against prejudicial remarks that pop out when Antoinette feels frustrated or agonized. Her status as a victimized creole, the silent argument seems to be, permits such indulgence. Its justice never becomes an issue for herself or other whites. Her conflicts, it almost seems, are supposed to speak for themselves and win sympathy. She shares a history with African-Dominicans, and she wants to be one of them but they reject her. Antoinette's largesse toward indigent blacks, scathingly disparaged by Rochester, her beautiful attire imported from the "Paris of the West Indies," while troped as evidence of a new self-respect, specify the indelible, colonizing mentality of a family that has extorted and appropriated Caribbean land, money, and labor over centuries.

Even her munificence is hollower than she realizes because, although Rochester bides his time and meditates about the time being "not yet" (meaning it is not yet time to control her), her money now legally belongs to him. Also unbeknown to naive Antoinette, the community pockets the "cockroach's" (Antoinette's) handouts with derision. And how could they not; she reaps what her family has sown, her inherit-ance of their attitudes in mediated form quite transparent. However, it is also true that her mother, Annette Cosway, chides second husband Richard Mason for his distorted views of black Antiguans and for racist language. By transversing such complex attitudes, Rhys disallows an easy decoding of Antoinette as an unreconstructed planter's daughter. Polyphony abounds as nuanced subtexts sidle into the overt text, author and characters at odds with each other.

Antoinette belongs to no one and belongs nowhere. Her self-alienation is unremitting, her subject position such that she can only grasp self-satisfaction moment by moment. A despised, unwilling wife, she feels a commonality with others whom Rochester directly and indirectly dominates. A victim of historical circumstance, she exists in the margins of everyone else's lives. Her dreams betray inner conflicts, mental debate about what lives she can and should live, their enactment an unconscious parody of Christophine's spiritual practices. Mostly they foretell Rochester's imminent menacing, his design to subsume her. But Antoinette never surrenders. She hails, after all, from stock that had hung on to the bitter end in slave colonies and had emancipation thrust upon them. In the last dream she means to rout him single-handedly, though it ends up as a pyrrhic victory for both. At her most dehumanized, incarcerated in perpetuity, she finally defines herself by leaping decisively toward Tia and life-in-death. She bridges the wide sargasso sea in an effort at black–white union and positive connection.

Wide Sargasso Sea, then, represents a struggle between old and new colonial enemies who act defensively toward African-Caribbeans and each other. Antoinette envies others' lives and feels excluded and by turns forlorn or arrogant; Rochester discerns that his wife, as well as the community, has rejected him and fluctuates between an aggrieved self-importance and desire for revenge. The couple negotiate their marital relationship almost as if the old colonizer awaits reconstitution by the heir apparent. In Rhys's formulation the old and now effete plantocracy is appropriately feminized while its usurpers are properly male. In the meantime the always aware and formerly colonized are bent on self-determination and exercising diverse psychological pressure on Edward Rochester and his wife, the daughter of a white plantation owner during slavery.

Daniel Cosway, the black servant Amélie, and Christophine – to take salient examples – mount mordant attacks on Rochester, whose Eurocentricity blinds him to their interconnections. His first move is to transform Daniel Cosway's damning letter, which explains family connections, into an accusation against Antoinette and his general situation; the letter becomes his rationale for enacting what his opening words in Dominica purport: to advance into the Caribbean, acquire a fortune, and retreat. Cosway's letter serves to dismantle Rochester's efforts to institute a new postcolonial order that privileges whites; it helps to reconfigure colonial and gender relations by precipitating a struggle to the death between the white pseudo-elite and the black communities. Rochester is forced to face the fact that he cannot construct his environment as he desires; he cannot refashion a pre-emancipation colonial scenario. Daniel Cosway confronts Rochester with ambiguous speculations as well as facts; he resites Rochester's position in the African-Caribbean community. The letter represents as-yet-unspoken versions of events hitherto told univocally by Rochester and Antoinette.

Rochester's Jamaican and Dominican environments now speak out from many sides with many voices and expose mythologies he has been nurturing about unilateral power. His anticipation that nighttime will bring sexual safety turns out to be just as unrealistic as Mr. Mason's false assurances that all will be well the night Coulibri burns to the ground. The new colonial order is so patently out of touch that its members have to be almost physically expelled before they will face facts; material relations have changed fundamentally. This new dispensation longs to live in a past they can control.

Staff members at Granbois, the Dominican estate, and in particular the African-Caribbean women, sabotage Rochester's planned appropriation of Cosway-Mason land and money. They resemble servants at Coulibri like Myra, who overheard and presumably acted upon Mason's talk of "import[ing] coolies ... from the East Indies" (p. 35). Their tactics range from poison, medicine, and spiritual practices to eaves-dropping, games of trickery, withdrawal of labor, psychological maneuvers, and sex.

From the first day of the honeymoon, obeah woman Christophine dissolves any hope Rochester might have cherished for a smooth life.[18] The night they arrive the honeymooners might toast "to our love and the day without end which would be tomorrow," but in that very tomorrow, Rochester discovers he cannot do as he chooses: he wanted to "take her in my arms ... [and] undo the careful plaits" (p. 84). Instead, Christophine serves them breakfast, even though Antoinette informs Rochester that she has sent her servant away twice (p. 84). When he comes out of the bathroom Christophine invites (taunts) him: "Taste my bull's blood, master" (p. 85). She challenges the primacy of his authority, reallocates it to herself. Internally he castigates "their lying talk" as she reprimands him about the mess he has created: "It bring cockroach in the house" (p. 85). Thus Christophine warns him that if he acts typically (like a cockroach, a troublesome nocturnal pest that hides in moist places during the day), he will reap a grim harvest.

Christophine's signifying name should have put Rochester on guard, but his insensitivity to the world around him occluded such insight. Certainly Jean Rhys alerts the reader, through nomenclature, of Christophine's power. A christophine, or choco, is a common Caribbean plant with a wholesome, succulent fruit. But its particularly striking feature is its growth of tendrils, which enable the fruit to spread and grow anywhere. A variant name for a christophine fruit is chayote, which mimes in reverse phonemes the name of neighboring St. Vincent's maroon revolutionary hero, Joseph Chatoyer. A famous letter found in Joseph Chatoyer's pocket after he was killed in battle by a British Major Leith in St. Vincent in 1795 exhorted: "We do swear that both fire and sword shall be employed against them [the white British], that we are going to burn their estates, and that we will murder their wives and children, in order to annihilate their race."[19]

In rage at one point Rochester refers to Christophine as "Josephine," a feminized designation of her revolutionary namesake, Joseph Chatoyer.[20] Raising the issue of power, Josephine is also the first wife of Napoleon and a woman from Martinique. Obviously, too, Christophine's name echoes that of Henri Christophe, first crowned king of independent Haiti. To augment these links with power, Christophine's last name, Dubois (literally translated, "of the wood") intertextualizes the celebrated resistance by maroons (living in rain forests) for which these two islands, Jamaica and Dominica, were especially renowned. As a practitioner of obeah, moreover, Christophine is a heavily ironic appellation: the first syllable evokes Christ in the context of a culture in which Christianity overlays and becomes syncretized with African belief systems. Christophine, in a sense, subsumes Rochester and his values and proclaims the power of Caribbean culture. Implicit in Christophine's name is the firm notion of struggle and revolution against colonial domination.

This metaphorical density of Christophine's name makes Rochester's remark, when he strides angrily through the forest, even more telling: "I knew how to avoid every creeper [tendril] and I never stumbled once" (p. 139). Rochester imagines he is above being interfered with or halted in his colonial tracks. He scarcely realizes that the interventions have already occurred, that the end of his life as a colonizer is more or less in sight. As the major representative of freed slaves Christophine can entangle him as no one else can, and shortly after Rochester's sojourn in the woods she proves his fears justified. In public she boldly challenges his abuse of Antoinette. In earshot of witnesses at Granbois, to his fury she harshly intones a litany of his duplicity and greed. A powerful member of the community denounces the political overlord; she exorcises his presence from the community.

At a further metaphorical level Christophine's name constitutes in the book another causeway – a bridge over marshy land – in that her name's link to maroons unpacks Annette Cosway's early lamentation: "Now we are marooned" (p. 18). Antoinette and Rochester later are always marooned – surrounded, that is, by insurgents whose opposition they neither acknowledge nor recognize.

After Christophine has taken Rochester to task for his treatment of Antoinette, he is reduced to a mimic, repeating her words and her questions; he becomes the Coulibri parrot with clipped wings, identified with Antoinette's mother, Annette, that tries hopelessly to identify intruders – Qui est là? Rochester cannot hear himself echoing the original colonial vanguard, a pathetic creature (like Annette) killed in combat. He threatens Christophine: "You'll go or I'll get the men to put you out." Her answer flaunts the fact that the community is, as its name embeds, a unity – people do their jobs, collect their salary, little more: "You think the men here touch me? They not damn fool like you to put their hand on me" (p. 159). Even when it is based on fear of obeah, the solidarity of the ex-slaves supersedes white authority.

Christophine destabilizes Rochester's power and empowers herself before his very eyes and in front of onlookers. She publicly humiliates him. That she is the one community member who manifestly makes a fool of him comes as no surprise, for her disrespect stands in inverse proportion to the treatment she received: she was presented to Antoinette as a wedding gift. In a superbly orchestrated display of poetic justice, an old slave-owning colonizer's gift becomes the prideful denouncer – almost the executioner – of the new colonizer. Revising Hélène Cixous's formulation, Christophine dares to make unheard-of intersections with Rochester, the other; she deracinates invisibility. Now, ironically, she wields more power through obeah practices than does Antoinette, the creole wife: "For once she blazes *her* trail.... And for good reason. There will have been the long history of gynocide. This is known by the colonized peoples of yesterday... those who are locked up know better than their jailers the taste of free air.... On the one hand she has constituted herself necessarily as that 'person' capable of losing a part of herself without losing her integrity. But secretly, silently, deep down inside, she grows and multiplies."[21] Christophine's challenge to white hegemony increases the chance of cultural autonomy. Rochester empowers her by treating her as a dire threat. Attempts to discipline her engender opposite results. By dogging Rochester's actions, goading him into further misadventure, and harassing Antoinette Cosway somewhat more subtly and protractedly, the African-Caribbeans inexorably negotiate their way toward new freedoms. Or to put it slightly differently, Frantz Fanon's analysis of mimicking locates Rochester as someone constructed in another's master discourse; freed slaves have become the masters, and his only recourse is to echo them deferentially. His mimicking constitutes a surrender of power to the other, an ultimate collaboration.[22]

In addition to Daniel Cosway and Christophine, Amélie is a third subaltern who operates as an insurgent double agent. From the start of his honeymoon Rochester is visibly affected by her presence and conventionally encodes her as a vamp-hussy. To devastate Antoinette he seduces Amélie, or so he thinks, but unbeknown to him, the servant has devised a protracted plan to outwit him. His arrogance, perhaps his expectation that women will be available and pliable, causes him to fall for it. As the deliverer of Daniel Cosway's letter, Amélie notes its impact on Rochester and prepares herself. The morning after their sexual encounter, which had been building up because of her calculated flirting, she is ready to leave for her sister's in Rio, her fear of Christophine another key factor. Amélie turns the main trope of the white couple's bonding – sex – against Rochester and Antoinette while respecting the black power-figure. Patiently waiting for the right opportunity while simultaneously mimicking the master's game and ridiculing him, Amélie avenges herself and the community for Antoinette's lineage and for her animosity and ill-concealed jealousy. She exploits Rochester's desire to teach Antoinette a lesson by using her black woman's body to her own end.

The fact that Christophine and Rochester in tandem, but for different reasons, compare and even confuse Antoinette and Amélie underpins personal interconnections that still remain between the community and vestigial white creoles. Rochester conflates them as sexual service stations and suspects miscegenous relationships everywhere. As Rochester states before his fierce argument with Antoinette: "She [Antoinette] raised her eyebrows and the corners of her mouth turned down in a questioning, mocking way. For a moment she looked very much like Amélie. Perhaps they are related, I thought. It's possible, it's even probable in this damned place" (p. 127). In speculating on Amélie's relation to Antoinette, he projects an incestuous desire. His implied guilt at daily indulged sexuality is partly assuaged when he engages with a black woman upon whose body such excesses are traditionally expected and condoned. He is oblivious to the rancor he radiates. The next morning the cook leaves, emblemizing the end of all nurturance.

Christophine, on the other hand, blends the unlikely pair together because she despises any human exploitation; she excoriates Amélie's antics toward Rochester and upbraids Antoinette for slave-owning connections. She wants to uphold standards of behavior for the community while assuming rapacious, self-serving conduct on the part of whites. Amélie is "worthless and good for nothing, she creep and crawl like centipede" (p. 102). On the other hand, when Rochester acts despotically, openly contemptuous of all others, she leaves. At a distance she can be detached and more in control. At this critical juncture opposed ideologies in the text clash. Christophine's departure from Granbois saps Antoinette of confidence. She can cope only as long as she has Christophine to lean on. Consequently, when Rochester baits Antoinette by having intercourse with Amélie within earshot, she heads for Christophine's home in the woods. Antoinette commandeers the narrative, wrests it from Rochester, as it were. Her alliance with Christophine silences the new colonizer, just as Daniel Cosway's letter makes him revert atavistically to the plantocratic ethic. Hence Christophine's strategy effectively causes the couple's separation, metonymic of the routing of white power from the Caribbean.

More happens besides. Not only does Rochester "lose" his narrative at this salient point, but in the course of Christophine's negotiations with Rochester, Antoinette also stops speaking. Mediated through Christophine, the representative of the white creole plantocracy is absorbed (assimilated) by the indigenous people. In the last section, when Rochester almost succeeds in transforming Antoinette into what he desires, a madwoman who will validate a neocolonizer's inhuman actions, African-Caribbeans – not even present – nullify his power over Antoinette. Antoinette conjures up Christophine and Tia as living presences before she leaps into the flames that destroy his property. They inspire her and provoke her victorious yet tragic decision. She dies as she lived, torn between old and new worlds, alienated from both on one hand and uniting them on the other, in an eternal posture of conflict.

In the course of interceding for Antoinette, Christophine reflects her plantocratic double, Aunt Cora; like Cora, Christophine forces Rochester to face his moral bankruptcy. Although he affects not to care if he and Antoinette separate, he cannot stomach the idea of her as another man's property. He may have had marriage forced upon him but personal and family mercenary values, patriarchal and colonial tendencies, ultimately coincide. Whether or not he covets her as a possession, Antoinette must belong to him exclusively. Unwilling to countenance his jealousy, he blames Christophine for the events; in classical reaction formation, he attributes to others his own self-serving aggressive act. He flees with Antoinette to England where she will be treated as his historical misfortune, a crazy wife whom he mercifully incarcerates in his own attic, not an institution; his retinue will pamper him for being a martyr. They will never know that he opted to degrade her in this way rather than manumit her, even symbolically.[23] His moods will not only be forgiven, they will be admired.

Despite multiple interventions from Daniel Cosway, Amélie, and Christophine, Rochester nonetheless still imagines he wields control, oblivious to the final realignment of oppositions against his status as an expropriated landowner. When he assaults Christophine, the most important African-Caribbean in the text and a purveyor of obeah, his only recourse is a plantocratic classic. He threatens her with his civil power, with jail. He reminds her that all whites, more or less, are in complicity. He will have her locked up just as he will lock up Antoinette. He uses the power of patriarchal, colonial institutions that affirm his class to stifle the people's culture and to further tyrannize marginalized African-Caribbean and white women. His collaborator is Mr. Fraser, a friend of the Cosways. Ironically, his in-laws' legal counsel enables him (he thinks) to get rid of Christophine, the one person who defends Antoinette and argues for justice. The moral world of the old and new colonizer has become a world turned upside down.

Despite Rochester's efforts to impose a Western scenario on the Caribbean, to treat African-Caribbeans as nonentities and deleted subjects, they never define him as anything besides the other. Rochester may represent the history of a European return, with all implied threats of mastery, but the community, despised objects of his observations, dissolve the rights he assumes to "take up...airs of superiority." Orientalizing, they assert, is at least a two-way street. Rochester learns the hard way that African-Caribbeans are representing themselves in an oblique cancelation of the white legal power that formerly controlled them.[24] Exerting constant pressure on the overlord is part of a collective will within subordinated communities to determine the destiny of the island, to nullify his threats of usurpation, to delete *him* as a subject.

Although Rochester remains vocal to the end, his agency has disintegrated. What counts for him is no longer his power but what other people are saying, how they are looking at him: He worries that Baptiste despises him; he notes that Hilda, the cook, has left without bidding him farewell; he parrots back to them admonitions by Daniel Cosway and Christophine. His authority has vaporized. The resistance script he hears all around him drowns out the colonizer's script. Even the gaze of the colonizer is denied him. His ostensible sign of control – the departure for Europe and a bankrupt "civilization" – also bespeaks his alterity; he is forced to retreat. The black community silently controls him, as his wild thoughts betray not only his inability to master the situation but his realization of impotence and the dual independent conspiracies of his family, as well as the island communities, to manipulate him. He is reduced to a fugitive status that necessitates taking an old colonizer – a form of himself – as prisoner. In a sense he becomes the community's ventriloquist, with Antoinette as a secondary dummy who can be voiced when memories of past life revivify her. The combined historical memory of the community and Antoinette undo him.

The African-Caribbean narrative mirrors his duplicities, its surplus meanings, the past and present oppositions it represents, like Christophine's final words, bespeaking the text's powerful unconscious. The stranger Rochester is a known and unfeared quantity:[25]

> "You think you fool me? You want her money but you don't want her. It is in your mind to pretend she is mad. I know it. The doctors say what you tell them to say. That man Richard he say what you want him to say – glad and willing too, I know. She will be like her mother. You do that for money? But you wicked like Satan self!"
> I said loudly and wildly, "And do you think that I wanted all this? I would give my life to undo it. I would give my eyes never to have seen this abominable place."
> She laughed. "And that's the first damn word of truth you speak. You choose what you give, eh? Then you choose. You meddle in something and perhaps you don't know what it is." She began to mutter to herself. Not in patois. I knew the sound of patois now.
> She's mad as the other, I thought, and turned to the window.
> The servants were standing in a group under the close tree. Baptiste, the boy who helped with the horses and the little girl Hilda.
> Christophine was right. They didn't intend to get mixed up in this business.
> When I looked at her there was a mask on her face and her eyes were undaunted. She was a fighter, I had to admit. Against my will I repeated, "Do you wish to say good-bye to Antoinette?"

"I give her something to sleep – nothing to hurt her. I don't wake her up to no misery. I leave that for you."

"You can write to her," I said stiffly.

"Read and write I don't know. Other things I know." She walked away without looking back.   (pp. 160–1)

In the end Christophine simultaneously disappears and disperses herself through the rest of the text; Rhys seems unable to choreograph a satisfactory position for the major African-Caribbean protagonist.[26] Perhaps Christophine's personal oppositional consciousness is beyond Rhys's imaginings.[27] The text is at an impasse and cannot respond to itself.

Nonetheless, despite Christophine's physical absence, the register of subaltern voices resonates. Not only does the community silently speak through and to Rochester but two of its members burn into Antoinette's imagination before the blaze. Rhys's choice of a fire does more than invoke estate burnings. In autobiographical terms she talks about associations growing up among England, fires, and deprivation: "I thought a great deal about England, not factually but what I had read about it. I pictured it in the winter, a country covered with snow and ice but also with millions upon millions of fires. Books, especially Dickens's, talked of hunger, starvation and poverty but very rarely of cold. So I concluded that either the English didn't feel the cold, which surely wasn't possible, or that everybody had a fire."[28] The community's unassailable power dominates despite the white creole author's transparent intention to heroinize the victimized Antoinette. Rochester is pressed into taking oppression that he transported to the islands back home to England. He abandons his pseudo-colonial fiefdom, a figure of contempt left with nothing more than an empty symbol – his alienated wife of a trick marriage. The days of richly laden vessels exporting sugar and coffee to England are gone, and their replacement pitifully reflects the colonial loss of power. Leaving the Caribbean Rochester has written himself out of the human community, an unwitting, unwilling vindicator of people's justice. The book's title, *Wide Sargasso Sea*, supplements the text's refusal to accede to any classic realist closure. The novel is named after a sea that is chockablock with sargassum seaweed and devoid of the plankton that supply basic food to fish. The particular type of sargassum that grows in the Sargasso Sea cannot reproduce sexually but only by fragmentation.[29] These colonizers, old and new, the title suggests, cannot reproduce themselves. They can only foster further distorted self-images.[30]

So the finale – Antoinette's jump to Tia – mocks the opening line and is every bit as elliptical: "They say when trouble comes close ranks, and so the white people did" (p. 17). Divided whites cannot close ranks, but one white can unite with Tia across the wide Sargasso Sea – provided Tia is willing – and start some intercultural bonding. More than that, the Caribbean cannot contain whites any more. They are people too divorced from life-affirming principles and from one another.

The last section, told principally by Grace Poole, Antoinette's keeper in the attic, and Antoinette herself recapitulates the lives of slaves who were locked up in cellars and barns, victims of systematic abuse. The attic of Thornfield Hall, Rochester's estate, provides an analogue to atrocious conditions of existence that continually punctuated the pages of pre-emancipation polemics and periodicals. To push the argument as far as it can go, Antoinette burns down the Great House, not just for atonement but as a representative insurrectionist who refuses the role of Sir Thomas Bertram's mute slaves. She will not be complicitous any longer in the "dead silence" of colonialism. In that sense Antoinette torches the Mansfield Park estate and symbolically avenges the colonized against the plantocratic class – both pre- and post-emancipation.[31]

Though immobilized, Antoinette strikes back with her only remaining weapon – a vivid memory. No matter how Rochester tries to deaden her with a protracted, bestial existence, she sporadically creates herself anew, resurrects parts of her old self. Like slaves of old she attempts to murder the owner of the Great House. Moreover and just as much to the point, instead of fleeing or resisting as many slaves did, she opts for that other time-honored alternative, long considered one of the quintessential revolutionary acts of slavery – suicide. Perhaps as a sign of identification, she wants to enter Jamaican-Dominican mythology. Any way she can, Antoinette becomes a different kind of Cosway: she tries to build a link with those earlier allies, Tia and Christophine, and with maroons too, with Rochester's designated others, in short.[32] Her suicide mimics the actions of slaves, of communities she could not join. Clinical or not, her madness derives from the anarchy of colonizers in a last ditch stand. She recognizes Rochester's inhumanity and in doing so, she acknowledges heinous past actions of her family toward slaves. In groping to avenge herself she vindicates the actions of insurrectionary slaves and attempts atonement.

Jean Rhys has recirculated a version of *Jane Eyre* in which she rewrites Charlotte Brontë's story of female identity. She refashions a female literary tradition, destabilizing its paradigmatic consciousness. Rochester is held accountable, and madness is problematized. His decision to lock a woman up for years more than justifies her attack on step-brother Richard Mason when he visits her in the attic and reminds her of her legal status and his original negotiations with Rochester; her "lowering look," attributed by the community to a condition derived from her mad family, is also encoded as a sign at the wedding that she knows what is destined to befall her. Her dreams signify the same way.

The narrative logic of the text upholds the author's planter-descendant politic only if we "believe" the closure of the original text, *Jane Eyre*. In *Wide Sargasso Sea*, instead, Rochester is the Coulibri parrot demanding to know who is there – Qui est là? – fighting him at the end; then he dies with his wings clipped in an act of symbolic justice. Even so, whether African-Caribbeans will celebrate or organize themselves after whites abandon the islands is left as an open question. On that question Jean Rhys also challenges the gender and colonial politics of her own exiled world in Britain.

Before Jean Rhys wrote *Wide Sargasso Sea* in the 1950s, two events occurred that were particularly relevant to her discussion in the novel: first, national, anticolonial independence movements erupted all over the world; second, African-Caribbean people emigrated to Britain in large numbers, a situation that culminated in ugly riots against black people in London and the provinces in 1958.[33] Thus only the suppressed of *Wide Sargasso Sea* hold out the possibility of a macrocosmic victory. Overtly readers witness Antoinette's and Rochester's doubled-edged triumphs: she "wins" because she leaps to Tia and life-in-death but dies anyway.[34] Excluded and unknown, she still terminates his family ties to the islands. He "wins" because, while he is left with her money unencumbered, he is wounded and socially displaced. He lives back home as an insider and outsider, a historical anachronism. If he dies in the fire – an optional reading not excluded in this text – then *Wide Sargasso Sea* is a different story. As it stands, the revised text of *Jane Eyre* offers no closure.

At the manifest level, then, the text favors Jean Rhys's class – the former white planter class to which Antoinette belongs. She is meant to be a tragic heroine, and although Rochester is represented as a villain, his family forced him and he was dutiful. Excuses have been concocted since the beginning for his abysmal conduct in locking a woman up *sine die*. At the same time Jean Rhys foregrounds African-Caribbean protagonists and the community as Charlotte Brontë never did. Christophine is a critical hero, although she and other members of the Jamaican and Dominican communities resist being shunted awkwardly out of the text to assert an oppositional agency. From a class, race, and gendered perspective, Jean Rhys cannot allow the implied victors of the text to be articulated as victors. That judgment lies in texts whose vested interest lies elsewhere. One such judgment resides in the texts of black Antiguan writer Jamaica Kincaid. In the past decade Kincaid's novel and polemical essay, *Annie John* and *A Small Place*, respectively, have documented a young woman's complex personal and political reaction to growing up in Antigua and have offered a searing vision of the island by a former resident now living abroad.

NOTES

1 Jean Rhys, *Wide Sargasso Sea* (1966; reprint New York: W. W. Norton, 1982), p. 17. All references will be to the Norton edition. For details of Jean Rhys's upbringing in Dominica, see particularly Jean Rhys, *Smile Please*, pp. 13–76. See also Dance, ed. *Fifty Caribbean Writers*, especially pp. 390–401.

2 See S. James, *The Ladies and the Mammies*. For details of Dominican emigration, see Myers, Dominica, pp. xvii–xxi.

3 Note also Jean Rhys's comments on *Jane Eyre* as she composes Wide *Sargasso Sea* and transforms Bertha: "Finally I got Jane Eyre to read and reread and hook on *my* Mrs Rochester to Charlotte Brontë's. I was a bit taken aback when I discovered what a fat (and improbable) monster she was. However I think I have seen how to do it though not without pain struggle curses and lamentation. (Whether I have any right to do it is a question which I'll face later. One thing at a time.)" (Wyndham and Melly, eds., *Jean Rhys Letters*, 1931–1966, p. 149).

4 Cudjoe, ed., *Caribbean Women Writers*, p. 113. For a compelling reading of the role of the mother in Rhys's "invention" of a "history for Bertha Mason," see Kloepfer, *The Unspeakable Mother*, especially pp. 142ff.

5 Ramchand, *The West Indian Novel*, p. 234.

6 Rubin, "The Traffic in Women," pp. 157–210. See also Nebeker, *Jean Rhys*, especially pp. 124–5.

7 For an inspired reading of Robinson Crusoe, see Hulme, *Colonial Encounters*, especially pp. 175–224.

8 Hall, *A Brief History of the West India Committee*, pp. 86–8.

9 Green, *British Slave Emancipation*, p. 221.

10 Ibid., p. 235.

11   Green, *British Slave Emancipation*, p. 238.

12   Davy, *The West Indies*, p. 504.

13   Ibid., pp. 504–5.

14   Jean Rhys's early autobiography is full of allusions to her gradual withdrawal from family and community as she came to terms with her society as she grew up. (*Smile Please*, pp. 46, 50, and passim.) At one point she talks of the "identification or annihilation I longed for" (p. 67).

15   Note that Jean Rhys discusses cockroaches at length in her autobiography. Growing up she hated them because of what she was told about them by Meta, a black servant. The metonymic transformation in *Wide Sargasso Sea* is very pointed. Now she is and symbolizes the cockroach in the African-Caribbean community. Rhys discusses mashed centipedes as part of the same scenario between her and Meta. See *Smile Please*, p. 23.

16   Honeychurch, *Dominica: A History of an Island*, p. 44.

17   Curiously enough, Jean Rhys explains in her autobiography that "we believed, or I believed, that Diablotin was eight thousand feet high and that it had never been climbed because the summit was rock. Round it flew large black birds called Diablotins (devil birds), found nowhere else in the West Indies or the world" (*Smile Please*, p. 15). In *Wide Sargasso Sea* her description of Christophine as a black devil intertextualizes not only an awe of Christophine but a sense of Christophine as a unique person.

18   Thomas Atwood describes the tradition and practices of obeah in Dominica, to which Christophine is heir, from an eighteenth-century ethnocentric historian's viewpoint (Atwood, *The History of the Island of Dominica*, pp. 268–74). For Rhys's ethnocentrisms, see also Plante, *Difficult Women*, p. 42.

19   Chatoyer, "The Declaration of Joseph Chatoyer, Chief of the Chariabs," in An *Account of the Black Chariabs*, pp. 117–18. See also Craton, *Testing the Chains*, pp. 149–53.

20   For an autoblographical dimension where Rhys discusses a maid called Josephine, see *Smile Please*, p. 38. See also Knapton, *Empress Josephine*.

21   Marks and de Courtivron, eds., *New French Feminisms: An Anthology*, pp. 258–9.

22   For an account of mimicking that pertains here, see Fanon, *Black Skin, White Masks*, ch. 1.

23   Sandler with Freud, *The Analysis of Defense*, p. 437. For Rochester's loathing of the idea she could be free, see Tiffin, "Mirror and Mask", pp. 328–41.

24   Said, *Orientalism*, pp. 21 and 31.

25   I am indebted here to Macherey's explication of this idea in *A Theory of Literary Production*, pp. 150, 194–9.

26   Spivak, "Three Women's Texts," p. 272.

27   Certainly even in retropect Rhys seems unable in *Smile Please* to compute Meta's actions as sabotage or perverse opposition to the dominant order.

28   Rhys, *Smile Please*, p. 51.

29   *The New Encyclopaedia Britannica* (Chicago! Encyclopaedia Britannica, 1991) 10: 452.

30   For elaborations on the sea, see also S. James, *The Ladies and the Mammies*, p. 62. Note also Rhys's description of the sea toward the end of the section on Dominica in her autobiography: "the blue, the treacherous tremendous sea" (*Smile Please*, p. 71).

31   S. James, *The Ladies and the Mammies*, pp. 68–72.

32   S. James usefully summarizes the controversy over the jump to Tia in *The Ladies and the Mammies*, pp. 90–2.

33   Ibid., pp. 72–3.

34   Spivak, "Three Women's Texts," p. 269.

WORKS CITED

Atwood, Thomas. *The History of the Island of Dominica*... 1791. London: Cass, 1971.

Chatoyer, Joseph. "The Declaration of Joseph Chatoyer, Chief of the Chariabs." In *An Account of the Black Chariabs in the Island of St. Vincents*... *Compiled from the Papers of the Late Sir William Young*. London: Sewell, 1795.

Craton, Michael. *Testing the Chains: Resistance to Slavery in the British West Indies*. Ithaca: Cornell University Press, 1982.

Cudjoe, Selwyn R., ed. *Caribbean Women Writers: Essays from the International Conference*. Wellesley, MA: Calaloux, 1990.

Dance, Daryl Cumber, ed. *Fifty Caribbean Writers: A Bio-Bibliographical Critical Sourcebook*. New York: Greenwood, 1986.

Davy, John. *The West Indies Before and Since Slave Emancipation*... 1854. London: Cass, 1971.

Fanon, Frantz. *Black Skin, White Masks*. 1952. Trans. Charles Lam Markmann. London: Pluto, 1986.

Green, William A. *British Slave Emancipation: The Sugar Colonies and the Great Experiment, 1830–1865*. Oxford: Clarendon Press, 1976.

Hall, Douglas. *A Brief History of the West India Committee*. Barbados: Caribbean Universities Press, 1971.

Honeychurch, Lennox. *The Dominica Story: A History of the Island*. Lennox Honeychurch, 1975.

Hulme, Peter. *Colonial Encounters: Europe and the Native Caribbean, 1492–1797*. London: Methuen, 1986.

James, Selma. *The Ladies and the Mammies: Jane Austen and Jean Rhys*. Bristol: British Falling Wall Press, 1983.

Kloepfer, Debora Kelly. *The Unspeakable Mother: Forbidden Discourse in Jean Rhys and H. D.* Ithaca: Cornell University Press, 1989.

Knapton, Ernest John. *Empress Josephine*. Cambridge, MA: Harvard University Press, 1964.

Macherey, Pierre. *A Theory of Literary Production*. Trans. Geoffrey Wall. London: Routledge and Kegan Paul, 1978.

Marks, Elaine and Isabelle de Courtivron, eds. *New French Feminisms: An Anthology*. New York: Schocken, 1981.

Myers, Robert A. *Dominica*. Oxford: Clio, 1987.

Nebeker, Helen. *Jean Rhys, Woman in Passage: A Critical Study of the Novels of Jean Rhys*. Montreal: Eden Press Women's Publications, 1981.

Plante, David. *Difficult Women: A Memoir of Three*. New York: Dutton, 1979.

Ramchand, Kenneth. *The West Indian Novel and Its Background*. New York: Barnes and Noble, 1970.

Rhys, Jean. *Smile Please: An Unfinished Autobiography*. New York: Harper and Row, 1979.

Rubin, Gayle. "The Traffic in Women: Notes on the 'Political Economy' of Sex." In Rayna R. Reitor, ed. *Toward an Anthropology of Women*. New York: Monthly Review Press, 1975, pp. 157–210.

Said, Edward W. *Orientalism*. New York: Vintage, 1979.

Sandler, Joseph, with Anna Freud. *The Analysis of Defense: The Ego and the Mechanisms of Defense Revisited*. New York: International Universities Press, 1985.

Spivak, Gayatri Chakravorty. "Three Women's Texts and a Critique of Imperialism." *Critical Inquiry* 12 (1985): 243–61.

Tiffin, Helen. "Mirror and Mask: Colonial Motifs in the Novels of Jean Rhys." *World Literature Written in English* 17 (1978): 328–41.

Wyndham, Francis and Diana Melley, eds. *Jean Rhys Letters, 1931–1966*. London: Andre Deutsch, 1984.

Part V
Rump Commonwealth: Settler Colonies and the "Second World"

Crimes and Punishments

Bob Hodge and Vijay Mishra

If we can speak of an "origin" of postcolonial theorizing about settler colonies, we might find it in Bob Hodge and Vijay Mishra's *Dark Side of the Dream: Australian Literature and the Postcolonial Mind* from which this essay is taken. As Hodge and Mishra demonstrate in this selection, the history of "crime and punishment" looms large in the "postcolonial mind" of Australia. This history is a legacy of the British practice of "transportation" in which criminals were removed from England and transported to penal colonies, the most famous of which were Botany Bay and Moreton Bay. The authors provide a useful summary of the history of transportation before moving on to consider the archetypal figures of the convict and the bushranger. Their exploration of the history of "convictism" takes the authors to a variety of historical and literary sources which, like the colonial documents analyzed by **Ranajit Guha**, reveal the ideological assumptions of the penal system and the imperial authority behind it. Of particular importance for understanding contemporary Australian culture and literature is the "bushranger myth," a tradition of narratives in which the "spectacle of resistance" to colonial authority is staged by escaped convicts whose criminal exploits point up the powerlessness of that authority. The authors conclude with a discussion of the concept of "deviancy," a phenomenon disseminated across all levels of Australian society that has its origins in convictism and the bushranger myth. Students might want to consider the way in which cultural texts are analyzed in this essay along with similar strategies in essays by **Neil Lazarus**, **Moira Ferguson**, **David Lloyd**, and **Kay Schaffer**.

Crimes and Punishments

Australia was founded on a double guilt: the dispossession of the Aboriginal people and the excessive punishment of large numbers of British and Irish people, mainly from the poorer classes, for crimes against the property of the ruling class. The last convicts were brought to Australia over 120 years ago, but Australia still has a legal system that constructs criminality and incarcerates deviants. It has now granted citizenship to Aborigines, but they take up a disproportionate share of space in Australian prisons. This juxtaposition of the two ends of White Australian history is of course simplistic, but it raises an important problem in a usefully stark form. How are we to link the historical reality of the convict era to the set of representations over time reaching up to the present? How should we read the patterns of similarity and difference in these representations against the background of developments in the construction and control of criminality and deviance? What is the social meaning and function of the theme of criminality in Australian mythology, in its double form, the virtuous convict and the heroic bushranger?

The Hartz thesis is again a useful starting point for grasping the dynamics of the foundation event. As purely as any instance of European colonisation, the colony at Botany Bay was constructed as a fragment, an intractable component of a much more complex metropolitan structure. With the loss of the American colonies the British penal system was in a state of crisis, unable to accommodate the prisoners who swelled the notorious hulks, who previously would have been sent to America. Transportation was only one option in a penal system that was only one part of an overall system of control. Over the period of the foundation event, that system itself was subjected to massive pressures for change. So the society that Governor Phillip presided over was a gross and unstable parody of the metropolitan situation. The legal system in Britain at the time was an instrument in a class war, but the alignments in that war were complex and shifting. The colony of Botany Bay, however, had an elemental simplicity. It was virtually a society of prisoners and warders, with a palpable opposition of interests between the two. It also had a contradictory double brief, as a penal colony and as a self-sufficient or even profitable component of Britain's maritime empire.

So from the outset the colony was not just a fragment seeking the completion of the metropolitan whole. It incorporated contradictions from the centre in a dynamic and unstable form. It is this fact which helps to explain the tenacity with which this early pattern has survived into the present. Ideological forms and patterns of behaviour

Taken from *Dark Side of the Dream: Australian Literature and the Postcolonial Mind* (North Sydney: Allen and Unwin, 1990).

that were laid down at this time were designed precisely to cope with the continuation of the penal system in another guise, so that the passing of convictism was in some respects just the operation of one tendency of the system, following transformational lines that were always implicit in it. The set of representations which is our particular concern in this chapter was therefore able to make the transition beyond the end of the convict period. However, the meaning and function of these forms, even when they apparently remained the same, were often transformed by the new place they occupied, in the new situation.

To understand how this worked we need to say a few words about the general relationship between the set of representations and the social conditions out of which they arose and which they ostensibly are about. We draw here on Althusser's (1971) distinction between what he calls ideological state apparatuses (ISAs) and repressive state apparatuses (RSAs). RSAs include the police and military and the penal system, physically coercing those who resist or defy the state. ISAs include religion, education and the media, systems that according to Althusser not only control systems of representation but also the construction of the subject. We will extend Althusser's scheme to theorise various important aspects of the history of representations of criminality in Australia. From the point of view of a ruling class, one of the functions of an ISA is to complement the operation of RSAs, legitimating the use of power and making it redundant. The direct exercise of power is expensive and divisive. The exercise of power through ISAs is naturalised and accepted, but needs the reality of state power as its sanction and support.

ISAs in this view are not simply sets of representations. They also incorporate rule systems of their own, which are part of their meaning. These rules, however, express not only the will of the rulers but also their recognition of the effective resistance of the ruled. The set of representations, in turn, incorporates a number of contradictions. Firstly we must note that they work with different media to construct radically different kinds of text. They construct various symbolic forms, images in words or pictures. They also inscribe meanings on bodies, coercing various individuals or groups to act out specific legitimating meanings. There are various categories of "deviant", whose existence, far from being an embarrassment to the system, is essential to its smooth operation. The deviants justify the repressive apparatus, aligning the "normal" majority with the rectitude of the state. The construction of deviance is carried out by a collaboration between RSAs and ISAs, and then confirmed by systems for the circulation of images.

But so far this account has given too much weight to the capacity of ruling classes to control all forms of representation. The degree of dominance of the dominant is variable, as is the cohesion of challenging groups and their capacity to achieve recognition of their competing interests and ideological forms. In the case of convictism in early Australia, the material and ideological control of the ruling group was never absolute, and there were profound divisions within the society that left its mark on the major ideological forms that it transmitted to succeeding ages. In this chapter we will outline some of the major fissures in the original construct, focused through the double figure of the convict and the bushranger, and trace the way in which later groups at later stages were able to make use of these forms for their own distinct but analogous purposes.

The Convict System

The system of transportation to Australia was not a unique phenomenon. It had well-recognised roots in developments in England and Europe at the time. We will use the important thesis of Foucault (1979) on the development of modern European carceral systems as a source of ideas to organise our sketch of the background and issues involved. Foucault argued that between 1760 and 1840 there was a profound change in the European system of punishment. In his view the previous regime worked through spectacles of punishment, dramatic displays of state power as in the grisly ritual of public executions. The later system emphasised surveillance, correction and reform. The spectacle of punishment was the inverse image of monarchical strategies for exercising control, which operated through spectacles of royal power as exercised through ceremony. The system of discipline, associated with bourgeois rationality, has now become the dominant force in modern society according to Foucault. We could expect, then, that insofar as the founding premises for Botany Bay were formed by the regime of the spectacle, then its ideological value today would be complex. A fierce attack on its brutal inefficiencies might even function as a kind of affirmation of the modern attitude to the carceral society.

We shall see that something like this was sometimes the case. But it is also important to recognise the contradictory and transitional nature of the system of transportation itself. Transportation was used as the opposite of a spectacle of punishment. The English legal system had proliferated so many capital offences over the 18th century that the spectacle of punishment could have solved the problem of carcerality at a stroke: but this was not a realistic possibility. Transportation was the transformation of the death sentence into another spectacle of punishment which was also useful behaviour (working in a distant part of the world). The sentence was intended to signify the meaning of royal mercy as well as royal power, a contradiction that was inherently unstable. No less than Jeremy Bentham attacked the whole Botany Bay scheme, and since Bentham's proposal for a "Panopticon" was taken by Foucault to be the exemplary instance of the new attitude we might suppose that transportation was linked to the old penal regime. The old system in practice had always needed some system of surveillance: its extravagant shows were only necessary because its means of surveillance were so ineffective. And the new system needed its own kinds of show, and its own forms of coercion of bodies and control through pain.

We can see both elements in the Australian penal colony as it evolved. Governor Phillip was a representative of the new attitudes to punishment, but others maintained the punitive practices that were also intrinsic to the system. The split that gave birth to the colony spawned analogous divisions within it, displacing fragments of penality from Botany Bay into such notorious settlements as Norfolk Island, Port Arthur and Moreton Bay. These acted as "spectacles of punishment" for the colony, as the hulks and Botany Bay did for England and Ireland. Tales of atrocities circulated about these which fed into the myth of convictism. They came from both above – from reformers of the kind whose enlightened views were to prevail – and below, from convict victims expressing their anger and opposition. They functioned as spectacles, to reinforce the image of the might of the state if not its justice. They also incorporated into the myth the radical premise that state justice can be not only excessive but even unjust, that criminality can be a social construction on behalf of a venal ruling class. But once they were located safely in the past, they served to confirm the legitimacy of a new ruling class by its contrast with the practices of the old.

Out of this contradictory situation came two characteristic forms of consciousness which are the legacies of this period, though as we have said they have been continually renewed by an endless supply of analogous contradictions. One is the construction of doublets, that is, images and values which appear simultaneously in two opposed and incompatible forms. The image of convicts and bushrangers alike as both heroes and scum is a case in point. The split image of women as "Damned whores and God's police", in Anne Summer's graphic phrase (1975), is another instance. But doublets are best seen as one way of resolving a more endemic quality of consciousness: double-think. The ambiguous coexistence of two systems of values leads to paranoia from above and from below, as each scans the texts of the other for their hidden content of hostility and opposition.

With these concepts in mind we are able to trace the shifts and contradictions in representations of crime and punishment from the foundation of the colony to the present, as they affect the reading of literary texts and cultural forms. In the 19th century convict and bushranger were sometimes constructed from above as romantic figures who were celebrated for their noble and convenient suffering and demise. Plot, character and setting were influenced by the conventions of Gothic, a genre that was far more prominent in Australian literature than in contemporary English fiction, one that was especially appropriate because of its obsession with guilt and its paranoid textual strategies. But at the same time from below came protest texts about injustice and cruelty against convicts, and popular celebrations of acts of resistance, especially the exploits of bushrangers. The two kinds of text circulated alongside each other, both of them available for various writers and artists to draw on in a complex and unstable tradition.

In the last quarter of the 20th century the theme is positioned against a different situation. The words "convict" and "bushranger" are archaic and no longer refer to contemporary prisoners, inmates or criminals, thus establishing a barrier against connections between past and present. But links can still be seen. It might seem fanciful to suggest that contemporary Australia is in some respects only a more complex and extensive disciplinary machine than Botany Bay was in 1800. But mechanisms for constructing deviance and maintaining surveillance still exist, in direct line of descent but more efficient and better resourced, with new objects of the disciplinary gaze to join the old. The connections between various sites and objects of discipline in the present and the past are not merely fanciful metaphors, in terms of a Foucauldian framework. On the contrary, they help us to understand how these texts and genres were interpreted in the past and how they can be read now, and with what functions and effects.

THE SPECTACLE OF PUNISHMENT

The history of convictism in Australia is complex and subject to theories and revisions by different historians. The process of interrogating the surviving texts, however, is continually crossed by another history, the history of the construction of the convict myth, which provides the momentum and agenda for the other histories. To give the terms of this second process in schematic terms, we can see its characteristic ambiguities and complexities as deriving from its double source from above and below, representing different experiences of different groups with different interests. For a variety of reasons, constructions from above have dominated in later versions of this piece of history. Amongst these, a decisive role has been played by Marcus Clarke's *His Natural Life* (1870–2) and its abridged "novel" version, *For The Term of His Natural Life* (1874) which we shall read as a single composite text. But in spite of its spectacular success as the definitive convict novel, this work and its meaning were dependent on other sources and traditions which it worked over and incorporated and helped to bury from view. These came from below, from popular traditions, often in oral form, which have now become barely accessible. To reconstruct something of the dialectic between the two sources of the convict myth, we need first to be able to go some way towards recovering the buried form.

The essential feature to recognise about the popular tradition was its closeness to traditional forms of oral culture. In early periods of the settlement it performed a community-sustaining role, contributing to the identity, cohesion and morale of a whole group. But the scope and richness and diversity of this cultural form has until recently been almost entirely neglected by historians and literary critics alike. The relevant texts have not survived in the prolific manner of written texts, and where they have, the reading practices of both disciplines have not been adequate to such texts and such cultural forms. Because they are now so scarce, given that they were once so widespread, a method more akin to archeology is needed, one which systematically over-reads the few surviving texts, to compensate for the asymmetrical action of time on their distribution. In the same way, archeologists reconstruct vases from fragments, and human beings and societies from bits of bone and pottery.

Texts from the early period survive in collections of ballads and unreliable scraps of prose and song, whose provenance is often worryingly uncertain. One way of dealing with this uncertainty comes from an understanding of the dynamics of oral cultures. In oral cultures, individual texts are not tied so closely to a single author, nor to a single version. As versions circulate, they accumulate differences that are themselves significant, establishing a meaning which is irreducibly social. But the opposition between oral and literary cultural practices should not be pushed to an extreme. In ancient Greece, Homer worked with a rich set of oral sources in ways that were characteristic for oral cultures, but at the same time he produced a definitive text, as an individual, highly valued performer. In the same way, the anonymous oral convict tradition produced a single major figure, who became known as "Frank the Poet". Only a few poems can be attributed to Frank the Poet, none of them in a text that can be relied on. None is on the scale of a Homer. These are not unrecognised "masterpieces" of western culture. But Frank the Poet's importance is part of his meaning within his own culture. The connections between different versions of the works that can be included in his oeuvre give a social resonance that goes beyond the meaning of individual texts, in a way that is impossible to reconstruct from any other kind of source.

Frank the Poet has only recently begun to exist as a possible object of knowledge as the result of the effort of two historians, John Meredith and Rex Whalan (1979), who have painstakingly established a corpus of poems (sixteen only, some in several versions) and a historical identity. Their book is cheaply produced and leaves many questions unanswered, but it provides an indispensable starting point for future scholars to build on. They identify Frank the Poet as Francis MacNamara, born 1811, transported for seven years in 1832 for larceny (stealing a plaid). His biography illustrates one of the archetypal patterns of convict life. First there is his Irish nationality, which established him as part of that potent subclass of convicts. His crime is typically trivial compared to his sentence, and Meredith and Whalan cite evidence to suggest that there were political overtones to his case. On reaching the colony his fate showed one of the two outcomes of convictism: not reform and incorporation into useful membership of the new community but stubborn opposition and consistent punishment. His original seven-year sentence grew to seventeen years. He was flogged on fourteen occasions, receiving a total of 650 strokes of the lash. He did three and a half years hard labour in irons, and three months on the treadmill. Meredith and Whalan comment on this history: "He became hardened and more abandoned after each punishment" (1979: 4). The main "crimes" that led to this savage increase in his sentence were running away and "insubordinate conduct" or "refusing to work". To a rational observer from another time it is a minor mystery why he was so foolish as to accumulate such severe penalties for so little cause. Clearly his body was used as a spectacle of punishment, and his mind remained uncorrected and unreformed.

The other aspect of his history was less typical. This is the importance of his role as "the Poet", a function that was evidently of the utmost importance to him and to his community. It had roots in Celtic tradition, in the role of the Bard in social life. Frank fulfilled this function in the new situation in Australia, where the Irish population needed cohesion and identity. Frank's poems include commemoration of heroes and great victories: his version (or versions) of the lives of the bushrangers Jack Donohoe and Martin Cash contributed to the construction of the bushranger myth. His celebration of the mutiny that led to the capture of the *Cyprus* helped to establish this as a symbolic triumph, an Antipodean *Battleship Potemkin*. The Reverend West writing in Tasmania in 1850 is quoted as acknowledging the effectiveness of this form of protest: "The prisoners who waged war with society regarded the event with exultation; and long after, a song, composed by a sympathizing poet, was propagated by oral tradition, and sung in chorus around the fires in the interior" (Meredith and Whalan 1979: 56).

Marcus Clarke adapted the *Cyprus* incident (and neutralised it, as we will see) in his novel. Ned Kelly incorporated an adaptation of some of Frank's most famous lines in the successful propaganda of his "Jerilderie letter" of 1879, and Dan Kelly sang a song by Frank the Poet to inspire the beleaguered gang during the siege at Glenrowan. Frank was not a participant in most of the events that he chose to celebrate.

His role was more public and almost official: to draw together and shape an alternative mythology, an alternative version of history which was not, however, his own individual creation and which was transmitted and recreated much more actively by his community than would have been the case with written texts in the dominant culture. The scale of their influence is now impossible to determine with any precision, but it clearly had an important role in constructing the images of the convict and the bushranger as potent organising principles for the Irish community, carrying this alternative version of events into the wider community. This oral tradition undoubtedly played its part in preparing the roles of both Ned Kelly and the community which sustained his act of rebellion. More importantly, its reading of those events had a powerful impact on the aftermath of the Kelly trial, and the construction of the Kelly legend itself.

Given the unreliability of the texts that have survived and the impossibility of assigning every word to the conscious hand of the individual poet, traditional literary criticism would find it hard to pronounce on the literary qualities of Frank the Poet. Nonetheless there are many qualities shared by the texts in the corpus, even between different versions of the same text, which give unity to the construction of "Frank the Poet" as a social fact, irrespective of the mechanics of authorship of individual texts. We will take as an instance one of his most famous poems, called variously "The Convict's Arrival/Lament" or "Moreton Bay".

Moreton Bay was one of the notorious penal settlements, part of the spectacle of punishment that was invoked to control the convict population. The poem includes mention of savage and unjust punishment:

> For three long years I've been beastly treated,
> Heavy irons each day I wore,
> My poor back from flogging has been lacerated,
> And oft times painted with crimson gore.

This is a description of a spectacle of punishment which had no intent to reform. But the terms of it seem slightly disappointing, if this was to be a denunciation of the brutality of a convict's life. Frank the Poet was not sent to Moreton Bay, but he did endure three and a half years (not three) on a chain gang, and his back was indeed "oft times painted with crimson gore". But there are far more vivid descriptions of floggings elsewhere: "I was to leeward of the floggers . . . I was two perches from them. The flesh and skin blew in my face as it shook off the cats" wrote Joseph Holt in his journal in 1800, of a savage flogging administered to two Irish convicts suspected of treason, quoted by Hughes (1987: 189).

Frank the Poet is deliberately understating the reality of brutality, and from the point of view of a convict bard it is easy to see why. A melodramatic description of flogging would do the work of the enemy, constructing and endorsing the spectacle of punishment. The quaintly colloquial "beastly treated" (complete with Irish accent) undercuts the force of the image in one way, while the poetic diction of "oft times painted" neutralises it in another. Physical suffering is thus acknowledged but not made central. The poem goes on to emphasise the "excessive tyranny" of everyday life, and the demands of "daily labour" made by these tyrants. Forced labour is presented as a major injustice, and refusal to work (under these conditions) as one of the most significant acts of resistance. And in practice, this was the cause of most of Frank's own floggings. So the poem carries the anti-ideology of convicts, in a situation that explains and legitimates it.

The poem not only records daily life in Moreton Bay, it also recounts the death of a notorious "tyrant", Captain Logan, who was killed in an ambush by "a native black". This act of liberation is attributed to "kind Providence" not to any convict initiative, and the unproven contemporary assumption that the killer was an Aborigine is kept intact. Again we see that the poet avoids specious consolations, establishing instead a nexus of connections (between convicts, Aborigines and Providence) that is comprehensive and positive but still sufficiently loose so as not to contradict the reality of convict life.

This structure of positive and negative aspects of convict life is set in a complex frame. It begins with the singer:

> I am a native of the land of Erin,
> And lately banished from that lovely shore,

and traces his journey from Ireland to Sydney Harbour, "in transient storms". But on his arrival he receives a further sentence, to Moreton Bay. The singer there meets another prisoner:

> Early one morning as I carelessly wandered,
> By the Brisbane waters I chanced to stray,
> I saw a prisoner sadly bewailing,
> Whilst on the sunlit banks he lay.

After this moment of lyricism, with its echo of the Babylonian exile, the rest of the poem contains the inserted narrative of this other prisoner, who as it emerges has done his time and is about to leave Moreton Bay. The two narratives intersect, the arrival and the departure, the prospect of suffering and the fact of survival. The poem concludes on an optimistic note:

> Fellow prisoners be exhilarated,
> Your former sufferings you will not mind,
> For it's when from bondage you are extricated,
> You'll leave those tyrants far behind.

Another version has the more interesting "We'll leave" in the last line, a complex relationship of identity and difference between new and old prisoners, but both versions construct solidarity and affirmation ("exhilarated") out of the normal conditions of convict existence. The simple diction masks a complex rhetorical strategy, whose reassurance stays close to the problematic reality that it has to work over. We can see why the ballad proved so durable and inspiring.

Marcus Clarke's treatment of convict life has a very different quality to Frank's restraint. His passionate indictment of the system reads like a clarion call on behalf of the convict oppressed, but it was produced after the end of transportation, from a different point of view, Clarke did work with popular traditions, perhaps including texts produced by or derived from Frank the Poet. Meredith and Whalan speculate that he and Frank once met, as recorded in a description by Clarke of a trip through back-alleys of Melbourne in 1868: "One of the men around the table, a little Irishman, with a face that would make his fortune on the stage, is a well-known character in the low public houses. He is termed the 'Poet', and gains his living by singing his own compositions" (Meredith and Whalan 1979: 24). Clarke seems to have been quite impressed by the "Poet's" skill at improvising ditties (he calls him "really clever") but he dismisses him as "an unconscionable drunkard", and Clarke's party, "having made him temporarily grateful by the bestowal of largesse", continue their tour of this delectable low life. Whether or not this "poet" was Frank, the passage shows Clarke's ambiguous relationship to the popular tradition, his Bohemian fascination with "low life" along with his patronising sense of superiority.

The ambiguity of Clarke's position is crucial to his role as the gateway for the convict experience, the mediator of this part of the past into the official Australian consciousness. Clarke's origins were in the legal system not the criminal underworld. His father was a barrister, and the uncle who was in Australia when he emigrated there was a Country Court judge. When Clarke arrived in Australia in 1863, transportation had ceased in the eastern colonies of Australia for over a decade, and the abolitionists were mounting their successful assault on the last bastion of the system, Western Australia, which was to end transportation in 1868. So Clarke's work has the passion of a reformer, after the evil had ceased to exist. It celebrates the triumph of the reformers, writing the history that legitimates their victory. At the core of its rewriting is the representation of the essence of transportation as a spectacle of punishment that was lurid, seductive and inadequate. Its subtext, then, is the superiority of bourgeois discipline and bourgeois rationality over the irrationalities of the previous system. This ignores the extent to which transportation itself was a hybrid form that incorporated many of the tendencies of the newer ideology of penal reform.

The novel on which Clarke's fame rests was in fact the end product of a process which itself was significant and revealing. Clarke worked at first with records and first hand reporting, producing journalistic accounts of convictism and its remains. He then drew on this body of materials to write a lengthy serial, which was published without great acclaim between 1870 and 1872. Finally in 1874 he compressed the serial down into the novel itself for which he is now best known. This transformational chain is not simply the record of a creative process. Since the novel was valued so much more highly than the other two texts, we can use the sequence diagnostically, to pinpoint the social functions the novel served, and the forces that it expressed.

As a sample of Clarke's journalism, here is a piece from one of a series on Port Arthur in Tasmania, published in the Melbourne *Argus* of July 1873, describing his visit to the prison there, now converted to an asylum. They are conducted around by a guide, "Mr Dale", and see the human degradation of the inmates, many of them convicts. Mr Dale gives them a list:

...and with a bow (and a touch of rum) he departed.

The list was as follows:-

Convicts	301	
Do., invalids	13	
Do., insane	8	
		322
Paupers not under sentence	166	
Lunatics do.	86	
		252
26th Jan., 1870.		574.

How shorn of its glories was Babylon! How ill had the world wagged with it since the days of the settlement of Port Phillip in 1835, when the prison owned 911 men and 270 boys, their labour for the year being valued at £16000! (Clarke 1976: 525)

Clarke's target here is the convict system at a moment of transition into the system that succeeded it. The collection of inmates, convicts, lunatics and paupers neatly encapsulates the major categories of deviant that the new system would control (only Aborigines are not represented here). In repeating the list, with a gesture of contempt at the official who is so totally satisfied with this as a strategy of control, Clarke satirises the new mentality, whose bureaucratic indifference to common humanity is as reprehensible as the overt brutality and injustice of the old.

If we turn from this piece of journalism to the narrative of the serial and the novel, we can see a progressive elimination of history and its connections with practices and problems of the present. The serial begins with the evening of May 3, 1827, but flashbacks in the first book take the story back to the earlier story of the main protagonist, Richard Devine. The serial takes events up to the 1850s, the period of the goldrush and the end of transportation in the eastern colonies. The novel slices off the beginning and end, compressing the earlier narrative into a brief prologue, and eliminating the last section, so that nothing can distract from the pathos of its hero's unjust death, clinging in death as he could not in life to the beautiful woman who in all innocence was responsible for much of his suffering. The openness of the journalism is transformed into the elegant closure of the novel, which intensifies the past in order to colonise it.

The central character of the serial and the novel does not come from any records or observations of Clarke's. Richard Devine is a figure from Gothic literature superimposed upon William Godwin's Caleb Williams. Of wealthy or aristocratic birth, he is sentenced for a crime that he did not commit, and is transported under the name of Rufus Dawes. By putting him at the centre of the novel, Clarke effectively displaced the problematic reality of the experience and ideology of convictism as represented by Frank the Poet. Instead of a vindictive system of justice that discriminates against the poor and the Irish, conflating political and social crimes, Devine/Dawes is the innocent victim of a series of malign coincidences, so extraordinary that no system of justice could be expected to circumvent them, culminating in the heroine, Sylvia, being overcome with amnesia when her story could have saved Rufus before the novel was half-way through. The problem, clearly, is not with the system of justice but the conventions of a genre that legitimates such implausible plots.

The obsessive theme of the genre that attracted Clarke and his audience was legitimacy. He shared the concern of romance with genealogies, and genealogies drive the action of both serial and novel, though he made some significant changes between the two. In the serial, Richard Devine is the reprobate son but rightful heir of Sir Richard Devine, a wealthy merchant. The son is about to be disinherited on behalf of his cousin, Maurice Frere (cf. the French *frère*, brother), when he is accused of a murder that he did not commit. He assumes the name of Rufus Dawes in order to serve his time in Australia without disgracing the family name. Frere also goes out to Australia, as lieutenant, warder, and implacable foe of Dawes / Devine. In this scheme, Devine and Dawes are a doublet, reprobate heir and innocent criminal. This double character also forms a doublet with Frere, as usurping and usurped brother and warder and prisoner. The serial first establishes Australia as the site where values are inverted (so that the criminal is innocent and the warder is illegitimate) but Dawes finally triumphs over adversity, proving his innate worth which shines through even in such adverse conditions. His career thus parallels that of his father, Sir Richard, who likewise rose by sheer ability to a position of great wealth. In this sense the serial can be seen as a romance of high capitalism, and a vindication of the innate abilities of the ascendant bourgeoisie.

The novel shifts these alignments in some important ways. Devine finds out that he is the illegitimate son of an aristocrat, Lord Bellasis, and it is Lord Bellasis that he is now falsely accused of murdering. Frere, still the nephew of Sir Richard, is now a more legitimate heir to Sir Richard's wealth, and his role as nemesis of Dawes is now complicated by the earlier pattern of similarities. The contradictions are now concentrated in Dawes / Devine, who contains in his two personas the extremes of nobility (compromised by illegitimacy) and criminality (and innocence). The action of the novel then eliminates this contradictory structure, since Dawes dies heroically but without inheritance or issue. His vindication is purely symbolic, his life a proof that blood and breeding do matter after all, in even the hell-hole of a penal settlement.

The novel has other doublets. One is the opposition between Rufus Dawes and John Rex, the imitation and the real convict. Rex (some of whose exploits are based on historical incidents, including the *Cyprus* affair) is an unscrupulous survivor. Clarke's narrative gives a realistic portrait of Rex's role, but shifts the centre of attention from the mutiny organized by Rex (the core of Frank the Poet's narrative) to Dawes' selfless act of rescue of Frere and the beautiful Sylvia. In the historical incident on which this was based, the convict Popjoy received a free pardon. Clarke's Frere pleaded successfully on behalf of Rex, and denigrated Dawes. So in this indirect way, Clarke affirms the "real" convict against Dawes, though Dawes' superior virtue is not in doubt. The alliance / opposition between Frere, Dawes and Rex is also played out in the double construction of woman. The heroine, Sylvia, is loved by both Frere and Dawes, but marries Frere. Golden-haired, virtuous, infantilised, she is opposed to Sarah Purfroy, who is introduced as her mother's maid, with "black hair, coiled around a narrow and flat head" (a criminal skull) and "scarlet lips". The pair represent a form of the Madonna–Whore double, with class affiliations. On the voyage out, Sarah seduces both Rex and Frere (and others), but her primary alliance is with Rex. Clarke's characterisation of both women is two-dimensional but they are structural in his scheme, making a direct connection between the social structures of the class system under conditions of a penal settlement, and this recurring construction of women and sexuality.

In his fiction, Clarke yoked together a European literary tradition – more specifically Victor Hugo's *Les Misérables* (1862) – with a serious historical concern to produce a powerful but contradictory hybrid. It was primarily with the historical background that Clarke made use of his research into convict conditions, and this gave considerable authority to what otherwise would have seemed an attractive but familiar and implausible generic text. The generic elements clearly made the convict experience more palatable, leaving it comfortably on the margins of a pleasurable reading experience. But there was also a significant interaction between historical case and novelistic conventions that further subverted the effects of the historical case.

To show how this worked in practice we will consider the following passage, a reflection on Rufus Dawes' despair after six years in the colony:

> Is it possible to imagine, even for a moment, what an innocent man, gifted with ambition, endowed with power to love and to respect, must have suffered during one week of such punishment?...We know that were we chained and degraded, fed like dogs, employed as beasts of burden, driven to our daily toil with threats and blows, and herded with wretches among whom all that savours of decency and manliness is held in an open scorn, we should die, perhaps, or go mad...No human creature could describe to what depth of personal abasement and self-loathing one week of such a life would plunge him...Imagine such torment endured for six years! (Clarke 1969: 116)

We have compressed the exposition somewhat, because the passion of Clarke's denunciation is not in question. His plea for compassion for such as Rufus Dawes includes some of the grievances mentioned by Frank the Poet. But there are other grievances, the climax of his litany, that had no place in Frank's poem. The contempt for the "wretches" with whom one must be herded would include Frank and all his companions, who did not see that as part of their degradation at all. This victim is totally helpless, entirely passive, without dignity but at last without guilt because of the sheer scale of his sufferings. Frank and his convict fellows retained lyricism and wit and self-respect, the capacity to endure and even to resist. If Dawes were typical, then Clarke's compassion would be safe, because such a convict could represent no threat. But of course, he is not typical. He is innocent (the term accepts that there is a single moral system which normally underpins the legal system, except in aberrant cases like the present). He is also like "us", the comfortable, secure middle-class readers who are only tentatively asked to "imagine" this situation, not to see it or enter into it. Clarke carefully constructs the reading position from which the whole novel is viewed, entirely on one side of the class divide. The focus on the middle-class Devine / Dawes, then, gives the *frisson* of engaging in an imaginary experience which gains its power precisely from the strength of its repudiation of real convicts, provoking a reaffirmation of the solid certainties of bourgeois existence.

As is to be expected with so successful a work, Clarke's novel performed a number of distinct functions with elegant simultaneity. At a single stroke it put Australia's convict origins on the agenda while constructing a melodramatic substitute for historical understanding. Readers relied on Clarke's genuine if partial research into the history of convictism to trust his novelistic account and inquire no further. The reassuring lesson from the ghastly past was that the present was now much better. The complex meaning of transportation as a penal strategy was simplified and encoded as a pure symbol of the past, obscuring its real connections with carceral regimes in Clarke's present, precisely at the time when those regimes were beginning to enlarge their scope.

But this strategy of displacement is also Clarke's strength since melodrama and sentimentalism rendered through essentially Gothic categories of genre becomes, for the Australian, a means of bypassing the tyranny of history. In reconstructing history through melodrama the legend of brutalisation, hitherto rendered in realist texts through an excessive deferral towards historical truth, is transformed into the text of the colonised. If history can be legitimated only by the guardians of its "truth-conditions", the English aristocracy, then it is only through explicitly anti-historical forms that the merit of the colonised could be given expression.

In addition to this complex ideological work, Clarke was able to restate the long-standing Australian concern with legitimacy. Dawes represented in a dramatic form the experience of the early settlers, their sense of dispossession from the old land and alienation in the new. His real innocence was as important in constructing this effect as his savage punishment. His acceptance of a guilt that was not his meant that he could expiate the guilt of others who could feel equally innocent yet still be in need of expiation. The serial allowed him to live and prosper after his expiation was complete, merging in with those he had justified. But that personal benefit detracted from his capacity to act as a scapegoat for the whole society. As Clarke came to realise when he revised his text, middle-class Australia had more need of a purified Dawes locked safely in the past than a reformed Dawes living on into the present. And if injustice has to be acknowledged in the foundation event of Australia's history, better that it be done by a Marcus Clarke than by such as Frank the Poet.

THE BUSHRANGER MYTH

As a social phenomenon the Australian bushranger was an instance of what Hobsbawn (1969) called the "social bandit", a figure who rose from an oppressed and subordinated group and whose "criminal" career had political overtones and a large measure of popular support. Ned Kelly has entered into Australian mythology as the archetypal bushranger, but it is a fact with its own significance that Kelly was the last of the bushrangers, the end as well as the symbol of the tradition.

In doing justice to the meaning of the bushranger it is especially important to both recognize and go beyond any simplistic dichotomy between "fact" and "myth". Throughout the eight decades when bushrangers flourished it is always possible to question the purity of their "real" motives, and discover desperate or brutal acts that would tarnish the romantic image that has been constructed on their behalf. It is also the case that never in this period were bushrangers a numerically large group, able on their own to constitute a serious threat to existing authorities, though some of the outbreaks, that of the Kellys included, did give rise to considerable anxieties. They were neither entirely noble, nor really effective in immediate terms.

But an analysis in these terms misrepresents the nature of the phenomenon itself, and uses inappropriate means to analyse it. At its core the bushranger phenomenon was always important primarily as a symbolic mode of action, a set of texts enacted with actual bodies and actual bullets, a hyper-real form of political theatre. The key events themselves were performance texts, the site where prior texts intersected and around which subsequent texts wove their further acts of meaning-construction. Things would not have happened as they did (whatever that was) but for these prior texts, and the performance-text was neither stable nor powerful enough to control the meanings that came to be assigned to it. What we have, then, is not a gap between truth and fiction, but complex processes in the social construction of meaning, processes which had material agents and conditions and effects at every point, and a history that is not without significance.

The bushranger was a spectacle of resistance constructed from below, and it is with this point of origination that we must begin. As an example of the phenomenon we will take the short career of "Bold Jack Donohoe", an Irishman who was transported at the age of 18, convicted of "intending a felony" according to Meredith, who suspects that it was of a political nature (Meredith 1960: 1). In 1828, aged 21, he was indited on a charge of highway robbery but managed to escape. He remained free for the next two years, but was shot dead on September 1, 1830. During this period he achieved no spectacular successes as a robber to match the Kelly gang's exploits, but the powerlessness of the authorities to capture him was reported enthusiastically, as evidence of their incompetence and the depth of popular support. With his death the interest in him did not die. On the contrary, he became the central figure in a series of popular ballads that became associated with the name of Frank the Poet, part of a broader complex that included perhaps the most famous of all Australian ballads, "The Wild Colonial Boy" in its many versions. At precisely the same time, his fate was the subject of the first important dramatic work written by an Australian, Charles Harpur's *The Tragedy of Donohoe* of 1835, later revised over a 30-year period to become *Stalwart the Bushranger* of 1867. This set of texts (including the life of Donohoe as itself a text) makes up an exemplary as well as a historically important instance, and we will look at the interrelations from both points of view.

With the ballad tradition we face again the seeming problem of deciding which text we look at, and perhaps which text did Frank the Poet really write. But the need to suppose that Frank was responsible for only one of them (as assumed by Meredith and Whalan in their otherwise excellent edition) is as unjustified as the supposition that Clarke or Harpur could have written only one of the versions of their text that survive. There are many differences in the surviving ballads of Donohoe, but there are two levels where we find recurring patterns. One is the overall structure. Some versions include some of Donohoe's early triumphs, but all focus primarily on his death and his defiant last words. And weaving through the Donohoe and Wild Colonial Boy texts there are recurring phrases, nomadic formulae wandering from poem to poem almost disregarding their context, with every fresh recurrence signifying their truth and their immortality.

As an example of such formulaic phrases, here is one line in the version that Meredith and Whalan attribute to Frank the Poet:

> He'd scorn to live in slavery or be humbled to the crown.

This phrase recurs in versions of "The Wild Colonial Boy", like a defining property rather than an incidental description. This gives it a much greater salience in the construction of the narrative and its social meaning, along with another such phrase, "We'll fight but not surrender, our freedom to maintain". The narrative becomes a fluid setting for the repetition of these phrases, rather than the phrases relying on the narrative to prove them true.

This quality, a typical resource of oral narrative, accounts for the paradoxical effect of these texts, which seem to dwell on the moment of failure of the act of rebellion but communicate instead the opposite feeling, a sense of optimistic celebration. It's no coincidence that the death or capture of notorious bushrangers, whether Donohoe or Kelly, by no means cast their admirers into a state of passivity or despair. This kind of text, in its verbal and enacted forms, could incorporate defeat and death effortlessly and endlessly, because the repetitive form of the celebration guaranteed that the defiance likewise would always recur. By foregrounding the moment of apparent defeat it was able to negate it, using it to carry on the message of freedom. In this way it constructed a spectacle that was designed in advance to negate the official spectacle of punishment, by refusing the official spectacle the right to end the show.

Harpur's version of the myth came from a complex point in the social structure. Harpur was a literate and educated free citizen of radical views, but he was also the illegitimate son of a former Irish convict, an emancipist who for a while made good in the new colony, proof of the ability of the system to deliver reformation. We would expect a profound ambivalence in his treatment of the Donohoe story, and this is indeed what we find, within each text and between them over time. The first text is called *The Tragedy of Donohoe*, the last one *Stalwart the Bushranger*. We see even in the title the transformation of the historical Donohoe to the abstract type "Stalwart", an ever greater distance from the originating Irish performance text. But even in the first version the term "Tragedy" distances the form from the popular ballad tradition of a Frank the Poet. This text included a mixture of blank verse and prose. Harpur was advised to increase the amount of prose, but instead he turned it all into blank verse. English classic literary texts overwhelmed traces of the Irish popular tradition in Stalwart, in particular Marlowe's *Dr Faustus* and Milton's *Paradise Lost*, which between them provided the inspiration for the central character as well as much of the diction.

In this and many other ways, Harpur constructed a fissured text. Where the achievement of the traditional ballad was to link activity and passivity, success and failure into a single persuasive unity, Harpur wrote along the lines of cleavage in the myth. His working-class Irish hero has the mental baggage of a member of the English middle-class, and the cast-list is full of split or doubled forms. In the earlier version Donohoe is opposed to the virtuous William, a respectable settler and the lover of

Mary. Donohoe falls in love with this Mary, and out of envy at William's good fortune he kills him. But Donohoe is himself loved by another Mary, the daughter of Mrs O'Brien, a small-time criminal. The opposition between the two men corresponds to the two responses to convictism (though William is not specified as an emancipist). The sense that these two are alternatives is reinforced by Harpur's renaming of William as Abel, in the later version, thus constructing Donohoe / Stalwart as Cain. The two women are both identical (both named Mary) yet opposed, as a mirror image of the opposition between the men. But although in these terms this seems a repetition of the classic opposition between citizen and criminal, damned whore and virtuous woman, Donohoe / Stalwart is not debased or evil, only desperate, and Mary O'Brien (later Fence) is by no means a whore. On the contrary, Donohoe feels that she also is too good for him in his present state.

Harpur's radicalism emerges in the critical stance that he takes towards the forces of the law. In the *Tragedy*, these are represented by the venal constable Bomebard, the hypocritical Canterbury and the implacable chief officer Dreadnought. In the later *Stalwart*, Canterbury becomes ''Cant'', and the cast also includes Roger Tunbelly, JP and Wealthiman Woolsack Esq, JP, whose qualities are clear enough from their names. *Stalwart* contains vigorous satire at the expense of all these except for Dreadnought, who is competent and effective in spite of the quality of his troops. So the forces of the law are split along the same lines as Donohoe / Stalwart and his women: three sets of parallel contradictions locked into a symmetrical pattern. Instead of the monolithic unity of Donohoe in the ballad tradition, every entity in Harpur's text carries its self-cancelling shadow wherever it goes. In the ballad tradition, defiance and defeat alternate in an eternal dance. In Harpur, the ambiguity of agents is so acute that every action carries contradictory meanings. Donohoe's resistance is both justified and criminal, and his crimes are also punishments. It is a very different kind of moral universe from the world of the ballads. Since it works over the raw materials of the bushranger legend, in some respects it is an attack on it, demolishing it from the inside as well as from the outside. So it is interesting to note that at the time it was written, no one wanted it. It was not performed as a play, and it made no inroads at all on the thriving oral tradition. It was without influence and effect in its time. But it also laid down patterns which can be seen in works in the subsequent tradition.

Here the crucial date is 1880, when Ned Kelly was captured and executed. The remaining years saw the final political accommodation with bushrangerism, with trials of police, promotions and demotions, and new policies towards the disaffected supporters of the Kellys. Ned Kelly's superb performance was the spectacle that ended the possibility of a repeat, just as Marcus Clarke's novel only a few years earlier marked the end of the spectacle of convictism by constructing its definitive form. Boldrewood / Thomas Alexander Browne's extremely successful *Robbery Under Arms* of 1888 played a role in relation to bushrangers similar to the relation between Clarke's novel and the convict system. Because it was so positive about bushrangers (while not allowing them to be seen to escape capture and punishment) it acquired the same authority as Clarke did with his negative image of the penal system. In both cases, this was only possible, and greeted with such relief, because the community believed that the problem was now resolved. Thus their relation to the performance texts to which they referred differed from that of earlier works. The ballads and even Harpur were part of a single textual complex that included performance texts, i.e. "reality" itself, where literature could affect the meaning of "reality" and vice versa, in a dialectic process. After 1880 the definitive images of the bushranger and the convict could be endorsed from above, undisturbed by the threat of revolt from below.

Boldrewood worked with the romantic image of the bushranger, appropriating it on behalf of a progressive politics. But the figure itself had other possible structures of meaning, which allowed it to be used as Harpur had done, as a way of exploring major fissures in Australian social life. One example of this strategy is *Outlaw and Lawmaker*, written by Rosa Praed and published in 1893. Praed's novel deals with a character who is totally split: Morres Blake, Baron Coola, member of the Legislative Council and Colonial Secretary, is also Captain Moonlight, a bushranger whose illegal gains go towards the Irish cause to which he is fanatically faithful. But Praed's concern is with women rather than men, and Blake / Moonlight is only one counter that she uses to explore the contradictions of women's position in 19th-century Australian society. Her central character is not Blake but Elsie, who is in love with Blake but is pursued by a large collection of other men, virtually every male who meets her, as it seems. The attractions of Blake compete with the attractions of other "lawmakers", Frank Hallett, virtuous and without a stain on his past, and Trant, who is also Captain Moonlight's less idealistic offsider. Hallett proposes honourable marriage, while Trant abducts her.

Blake is implausibly ideal in both roles, as lover and as romantic outlaw with a dark past, but he plays a part in Praed's exploration of the possibilities facing a young woman of marriageable age. The sexual excitement he represents is cancelled out by the dark secret. Hallett's worthy love is without passion. Blake contrasts the two as a "shortlived rapture (which) might be worth more than a long married life of decorous commonplace conventional happiness – a Frank Hallett kind of happiness" (Praed, 1988: 114). Trant's passion is more urgent than Blake's noble selflessness; aggressive, acquisitive and dangerous. Elsie's life, during the period covered by the novel, is a frenetic whirl of seduction and resistance, as the males circle like sharks in a feeding frenzy. She is not exactly a whore, though she is rather unchaperoned much of the time. But after the death of Blake, her only love, the novel summarises the rest of her life in one page, as a celibate existence lived out in faithful devotion to the dead Blake.

There is some parallel here with Rosa Praed's own life. Praed too had a period of hectic gaiety between 1867 and 1872, as the daughter of a widowed member of parliament with duties to entertain. In 1872, aged 21, she finally acquiesced in her father's pressure on her to marry, and found that marriage to the wealthy Campbell Praed was an oppressive form of existence. There was a stark contrast between the courtship stage, where she was expected to be attractive to all males, and the marriage stage, when she must be faithful and subordinate to one (who felt himself to be under no such obligation). It was this opposition between the roles that women were socialised into that underlay the polarisation into madonna / whore. Praed's novel has the merit that it explores this opposition from the point of view of a woman's experience, instead of seeing it as purely a construct of male attitudes. It is the corresponding split in male identity that is projected in the characterisation in her work. And here the image of the bushranger lay ready to hand, ambivalent and yoked to his double the lawmaker, allowing her to externalise and express her own sense of self-division and ambivalence as woman.

By the 1890s, then, the myth of the bushranger was no longer an active part of the social and political struggle of a distinct group of oppressed people. No longer anchored in that struggle, it was available as a metaphoric resource, to express a contradictory relationship to contradictions of power throughout society. In plays such as Stewart's *Ned Kelly* of 1943, in paintings such as Nolan's famous Kelly series, in films dealing with Ned Kelly or in successful TV series such as *Ben Hall*, the bushranger myth poses general problems of justice and the role of the individual caught up in an unjust society. The specific themes that can be thought through this figure are various: Nolan's concerns are very different from Rosa Praed's. But there is one dimension that is almost always necessarily lacking from later uses of the myth: the political dimension that in many obvious and less obvious forms was always part of the early traditional use. There is only one exception to this, but a significant one. The Aboriginal oral tradition celebrated its trickster figures, its unsuccessful heroes of resistance, in similar ways and with similar strategies to the Irish bards, and that resistance was a fact of experience within recent memory. Colin Johnson / Mudrooroo Narogin's *Long Live Sandawara* of 1978 engaged in a task similar to that faced by Harpur over 100 years before, coming to terms with the oral culture and political struggles of his people using the dominant literary modes of the day.

THE USES OF DEVIANCY

Historians dispute the value of the convict heritage, and the extent to which it has come down to the present. Russel Ward (1958) is at one extreme, with his influential claim that the convict experience contributed its brand of anti-authoritarianism to the Australian ethos, what he called "The Australian Legend". Humphrey McQueen (1970) at the other extreme is contemptuous of actual convicts and unimpressed by claims that they have any continuing influence. Robert Hughes, in his massive study of the convict era, is seemingly more confused in his assessment. On the one hand he talks of "the defensive, static, levelling, two-class hatred that came out of convictry", but he also doubts the influence of the "convict past" today. "Thus, it made Australians cynical about Authority; or else it made them conformists." Then he has further thoughts: "Perhaps there are roots of social conduct that wind obscurely back to the convict era, and the familiar Australian habit of cursing authority behind the hand while truckling to its face may well be one of them" (Hughes 1987: 596). There is only one legacy that he is sure of: that the stain of convictism helped Australians to forget the past and replace it with images of "grand guignol", epitomised by the work of Marcus Clarke.

Hughes's uncertainty in fact reflects the contradictions in the nature of convictism and its representation over time, better than either of the extreme positions on its own. The continuing relevance of the image of the convict / criminal comes from the issues of carcerality as outlined by Foucault as they play on the present. In Foucault's account, the disciplinary system has not only triumphed in the restricted realm of the penal system, it has now become ubiquitous. "Is it surprising that prisons resemble factories, schools, barracks, hospitals, which all resemble prisons?" he asks (1979: 228). Secondly he suggests that the apparent failure of the prison system to eliminate crime in fact should be seen as a systemic success, producing "delinquency . . . a politically or economically less dangerous – and, on occasion, usable – form of illegality . . . producing the delinquent as a pathologised subject" (1979: 277). David Ireland in *The Unknown Industrial Prisoner* of 1971 portrayed Australia in these terms, as a single continuous penal colony, an Australian dystopia in the tradition of Orwell's *1984*.

This is a system which could produce docile delinquency in all Australians, viewed as the inhabitants now of an open prison that covers the whole continent. We can see why Hughes very properly doubts whether the characteristic Australian double-think towards authority should be blamed entirely on the convict past. But the continuity also allows the forms from that past to function powerfully into the present, both as the instruments of control and as the focus of resistance. And part of the tradition is an effective strategy for appropriating history, replacing the surveillance of the past by various spectacles, a kind of screen memory to use the Freudian term. But none of these devices is new, or irresistible. Throughout its history the construction of deviance has always been contested, and this history of effective resistance has also left its traces on the tradition.

The double messages of this open prison produce the classic symptoms of paranoia as described by Gregory Bateson (1973). In a lighter vein, the first chapter in *How to Survive in Australia*, a popular satire of the Australian character by Robert Treborlang, is entitled "For a Start . . . Don't Ask Questions". Treborlang illustrates his proposition, that "asking questions is the one thing a true Australian never does", with the following anecdote:

> Let's say you are having lunch with some new friends at the factory cafeteria or at the office where you have found employment. Excited and curious, you decide to get things going by making what you believe to be innocuous conversation.
>
> YOU: What do you folks do on weekends?
> THEM: (An embarrassed silence and interchange of looks followed by an outbreak of mysterious unease).
> Without knowing it, you have just made the following thoughtless allegations:
> 1   What gay bars do you frequent?
> 2   Don't your Alcoholics Anonymous meetings interfere with your weekend social life?
> 3   Do you happen to own a truck that could help me move my things on Sunday?
>   (Treborlang 1985: 9–10)

Treborlang's satire represents the typical Australian as a rampant paranoiac, mis-interpreting the most innocent of questions. What he himself seems not to notice (like other anthropologists collecting data on other exotic tribes) is that his question and manner are not entirely simple. There is some contradiction between being "excited and curious" and trying to ask an "innocuous question". Then there is the curious word "folks" (in the plural, too) implying that his hearers have the quaintly primitive status of proper objects for the anthropological gaze. The general present of "do", along with the plural "weekends", in Treborlang's mind removes the question from the dangers of particularity, but instead they suggest the greater intrusion of a sociological survey. These people are being asked, by an obviously over-educated factory worker, to summarise the pattern of their lives for some act of surveillance that has not been declared. Treborlang is right to notice the paranoiac overinterpretation, but he fails to recognise his own double messages, of power and pseudo-friendliness, that have provoked it.

This text comes from a satire on Australian life in general. The same prohibition on asking questions is emphasised in a text about prison life, Gabrielle Carey's *Just Us* of 1984. Gabrielle Carey fell in love with Terry Haley, a long-term prisoner in Parramatta jail, when she was visiting the prison. *Just Us* was an autobiographical account of the relationship. For a long time Terry totally refused to answer any questions even from his lover. In a text included in the book he describes the double message system in a modern jail that gives rise to such paranoia: "You'd think if they really believed in all this crime and punishment shit that they would tell you – so you'd know when you'd been bad (by their books) and you wouldn't do it again – so the whole system would be put to work the way they reckon it works. But that's far too rational for them. Far too fucking rational" (Carey 1984: 17).

The result of this contradiction in the very aims of the system, as it is perceived by the prisoner in the modern penal system, is what he calls paranoia: "In gaol you get to develop this sort of sixth sense because everyone's so paranoid, you can't find things out through the normal channels. No one trusts anyone else enough to talk about stuff truthfully. So you have to feel everything. And you get pretty good" (Carey 1984: 18).

Haley here describes the radical distrust that generates paranoia, emanating from above, in the double messages that express the double ideology of the modern penal system, and also affect communication from below. He also illustrates the kind of pared-down language which evolves to meet the need to communicate in these conditions: apparent vagueness, behind which multiple meanings lurk, and a rigid, formulaic repetitiveness, in which whole clauses reappear unchanged in new contexts. Along with this seeming rigidity and simplicity goes an extraordinary sensitivity to under-messages and a dangerous trust in the ability to read them. If Treborlang had read this text, he might have understood the aberrant response of his almost-mates.

Haley as described in this book had been constructed as a classic "delinquent". First institutionalised at the age of nine for "illegal use of a bicycle", he had spent only one year outside surveillance up to the age of 35, when the book was published. The pattern seems hardly changed from the days of Frank the Poet. But if Haley seems to be a typical "delinquent", Carey his biographer and lover is much less typical. In 1979 she co-authored the very popular novel *Puberty Blues* with Kathy Lette, and she met Terry for the first time in that year. The novel describes the encounter of two girls with the surfing subculture of a Sydney beach. The rules and rituals of this antiworld are implacable and sexist, a persuasive and cohesive alternative to school discipline, a mirror image of the dominant hierarchical structures. The narrative follows the initiation of the two girls into this world, and their progress to an autonomous existence as women, outside the oppressive and ultimately suicidal world of the surfies.

Surfies are one of the modern faces of the Australian legend, carrying on the long tradition of defying authority and the values of the work ethic. But Carey and Lette deconstruct this group's claims to dissidence by adopting a stance as outsiders in this world of outsiders: as females who are oppressed by the traditional sexism of the Australian male. In the book they frame the narrative with another form of discourse: academic social theory. The novel begins with a description of the surfie rule system governing the beaches of Sydney, in the tone of a "participant observer" as anthropologists would put it. It ends with an appendix listing the fates of the members of the surfie group, mostly a sorry tale of drug abuse and delinquency, like a social worker's case file being brought up to date. The film of the book dropped this alienating conclusion. It showed the two girls walking off together, two free individuals, after they have learned to surf and just demonstrated their skill to the amazed surfies and their chicks. This jaunty feminist conclusion was made for a popular film in the 1980s, but in spite of such differences there is the same fluid pattern of contradictions in the stance of Carey (as author or co-author of both *Puberty Blues* and *Just Us*) and in *Puberty Blues* (as book and film). The three texts have an intertextual relationship that is analogous to the oral tradition of Frank the Poet. In their different ways they all show the ambivalent fascination felt by 'straight' outsiders for the frighteningly recognisable inverted world of the officially delinquent.

The fascination can be seen in the success of two TV series of the 1970s and '80s, *Prisoner* and *A Country Practice*. *Prisoner* attracted huge ratings and equally intense opposition from anti-television lobbyists for its subversive construction of the anti-world of a woman's prison. The women prisoners were sympathetic characters, totally opposed to the 'screws' though in a more gentle way than in male prison or convict drama since 1788. The locale allowed an audience including many children to make the Foucauldian connection between prison and school, and explore issues of power and authority in a stark and demystified form: precisely the legacy of the convict tradition. And for that reason lobbyists committed to the ideal of benign discipline were hostile to it. *A Country Practice*, however, has had no problems of acceptability. It is set in an idealised country town, where its stable, loveable and caring characters deal with one social problem after another, each carried by a single representative guest "delinquent". The challenge to the Wandin Valley community and to the audience is to expand its sympathies to recognise the humanity and the pain of each kind of delinquent, so that they can all be reincorporated into a caring community. Although *Prisoner* was the earlier of the two programs and is no longer a competitor for top ratings against *A Country Practice*, it would be unwise to see a definitive change as having occurred. The two programs represent two alternative attitudes to the image of the "delinquent" which have coexisted for 200 years already, and are likely to last longer yet.

There is, then, not a single image of the criminal or the delinquent that defines Australian culture. On the contrary what the culture contains is a rich and complex meaning-resource, one that allows a range of different issues of power and authority to be explored or mystified or both. And certain dimensions of the experience of incarceration offer in a usefully heightened or extreme form some of the most problematic elements of the Australian consciousness, elements that are not of course unique to Australians. It is in this respect that the experience of Aboriginal people comes to have an unacknowledged function for other Australians. Rowley (1970) and others have documented the ravages of forced institutionalisation on Aboriginal society, when the term "Aboriginal Protection" was enshrined into the very Acts of Parliament which legitimated a whole range of punitive actions towards Aboriginal people "for their own good". Hardly an Aborigine today is not scarred in some way by this still recent history. The carceral mind is one of the central themes of Australian culture today, and Aborigines as a group are Australia's experts on carcerality.

It is undoubtedly an overwhelming theme, directly or indirectly, in contemporary Aboriginal writing. Many works deal with life on Aboriginal reserves. Jack Davis in *No Sugar* reconstructed a traumatic but typical incident on the Moore River reserve in Western Australia in the 1930s. But his more recent *Barungin* of 1989 takes his exploration of the theme one step further. The play was written as a reaction to the death of John Pat, victim of police brutality and one of the triggers to the Commonwealth Government Royal Commission into Black Deaths in Custody. That commission had a brief that was similar to those of many inquiries that have been held since 1788, all investigating spectacular instances when the penal system has lapsed from its professed ideals and standards of custodial concern.

Most of Davis's play, however, seems to ignore the basic issues of law and justice that such a commission must address. He depicts a typical Aboriginal family, with a typical dependence on the welfare system, and a typical number of its members in trouble with the law for minor offences. The play seems a realist text, characterised by humour and insight into aspirations and tensions of such a group. Then towards the end of the play Peter, a young Aborigine, is released from gaol, and he goes off with a group to a party. His younger brother, meanwhile, has engaged in some petty theft, accumulating an excessive stock of electronic equipment. His uncle, meaning to protect him, puts the stolen gear into the boot of a car – the car that Peter takes. The uncle's well-intentioned if slightly criminal act then has catastrophic consequences. The police find the gear and presume Peter's guilt, and in the process of their pursuing their enquiries, Peter is killed. The play changes dramatically from social realism to tragedy. It closes with the mother of Peter intoning the list of black deaths in custody that were matters of public record at the time of writing, but she goes back to Yagan, the Black resistance leader who was executed in Perth in 1831.

The reading of the list is clearly an overt political statement, reinforcing Jack Davis's message about black deaths in custody. But the form of his play at first seems curiously indirect to support this theme and the final speech. What he shows is a connection between crime and punishment as oblique as in Clarke's novel, yet inexorable. There is a crime – Peter's brother's theft, and his uncle's complicity – and there is a punishment, the catastrophically excessive death of Peter, the wrong punishment for the wrong person. But the real "crime" is different: the whole family are being punished for their Aboriginality, for the whole complex of ways of coping that this group has had to evolve to survive in White society. The play constructs the experience of this mentality, where there is an inexhaustible requirement to expiate a crime which has been in fact committed against, not by, these people, and a threat of punishment hangs over every unassimilated head that is Aboriginal, as the price of its Aboriginality.

The shattering force with which the cataclysm descends on the very ordinary household recreates this experience for the non-Aboriginal audience as well. In a White family this would be a paranoid view. In Aboriginal society it is an instance of the contradictory logic of the system under which they have lived for so long. It is also tinged with paranoia, however, just as the world of the Irish convicts and modern prisoners was and is both true to its conditions and yet self-destructive in its excess. That is why the form of Jack Davis's conclusion is so effective. The list is the product of another discourse, the discourse of the dominant legal system announcing its own inadequacies, and it is spoken by an Aboriginal woman with full knowledge and control. Not only does it have polemical force through its acknowledged "truth": it is also the kind of non-equivocating discourse that is the only safeguard for Aborigines and nonAborigines alike, against the endemic Australian condition of paranoia and double-think.

Davis's play allows us to see the curious irrelevance as well as the importance of history for understanding how images of crime and punishment function in Australian literature and culture. The Australian "criminal past" for Australians today is an abstract but potent metaphor for a kind of legal double-think, a crime that is not a crime, committed by society on criminals, by warders on prisoners and by the system on warders, threatening the destruction and purification of society itself. The events that happened and the repressive apparatus that was constructed in the early days of the colony had repercussions at the time, as confused and contradictory as the system itself, with structural consequences that have continued till now. But the force of the metaphor in the present comes from the schizogenic processes by which delinquency is still constructed and managed, in terms of which social life is organised by the double message of the disciplinary regime. Australia demands its images of convicts and bushrangers, criminals and victims, if only for the sake of its collective sanity.

Bibliographical Note

In addition to Robert Hughes' popular and substantial history of convictism, J. Hirst, *Convict Society and its Enemies* (1983) is a useful study of the phenomenon. Humphrey McQueen makes a fierce case against romanticising convicts (1970). Paul Wilson and J. Braithwaite, *Two Faces of Deviance* (1978) contains some important essays on the construction of criminality in Australia. Elizabeth Egglestone, *Fear, Favour and Affection* (1976) is an authoritative study of the treatment of Aborigines in the legal system.

Foucault makes a very effective use of Bentham's Panopticon in *Discipline and Punish* (1975). "Panopticism", for Foucault, was the mode of dissociating the seer from the seen. In the design of the Panopticon, which is formed around a central tower overlooking a semi-circle with cubicles which extend the whole breadth of the building, Foucault discovers an architectural form capable of sustaining domination and power by its mere design. Given such a design, he writes, "in the peripheric ring, one is totally seen, without ever seeing; in the control tower, one sees everything without ever being seen" (p. 202).

Marcus Clarke's *His Natural Life* was first published in serial form in the *Australian Journal* between March 1870 and June 1872. The novel "version" was published in 1874, having lost about one third of the original. For detailed examination of the two versions see Joan Poole, "Maurice Frere's Wife: Marcus Clarke's Revision of *His Natural Life*" (1970). The title by which the novel is best known, *For the Term of His Natural Life*, was introduced in 1884, three years after the author's death. The complete serial version was not reissued until 1970 when Stephen Murray-Smith edited it for Penguin Books. See Michael Wilding, *Marcus Clarke* (1977), for a lucid essay on Marcus Clarke. In Marcus Clarke there is considerable equivocation between the laws of genre (romance) and social realism (the portrayal of the establishment of a penal colony). For an account of the literary uses of history in Clarke see L. E. Robson, "The Historical Basis of *For the Term of His Natural Life*" (1963).

A more considerable equivocation with a correspondingly greater textual "chaos" is to be found in James Tucker's *Ralph Rashleigh* (1845/1952), which is something of a literary curiosity. The manuscript surfaced in 1920 and appears to have been in the possession of the family of Mrs Margaret Baxter née Burnett. A garbled version of *Ralph Rashleigh* or *The Life of an Exile, by Giacomo de Rosenberg* appeared in 1929 as a literary memoir. Though historically it is not possible to give *Ralph Rashleigh* a "precursor" status, nevertheless, Tucker's hero traversed the three major ingredients of early fiction: convictism, bushranging and Aboriginalism. Two more recent works should also be mentioned. The first is Thomas Keneally's *Bring Larks and Heroes* (1967) which reads the brutal history of convictism through a metaphysical mix of Melville's *Billy Budd* and Patrick White's *Voss*. The second is David Ireland's *The Unknown Industrial Prisoner* (1971) which is basically an allegorical rendition of industrial capitalism through the generic constraints of the Australian convict novel.

Rolf Boldrewood/Thomas Alexander Browne's *Robbery Under Arms* (1888) was originally published as a serial in the *Sydney Mail*, 1882–3. Earlier, the bushranging theme had entered Henry Kingsley's *The Recollections of Geoffrey Hamlyn* (1859) through the character of George Hawker who turns bushranger. The "genteel" pretensions of Kingsley's style and his colonial preferences (he spent no more than four years in Australia) are parodied in Joseph Furphy/Tom Collins's *Such is Life* (1903).

In art, Sydney Nolan's *Ned Kelly* series established a dominant iconography of the Bushranger. He also painted a number of "escaped convict" paintings. Convictism has proved a reliable staple in both film (e.g. *For the Term of His Natural Life* in 1927 (Dawn)) and TV (e.g. the televised version of *For the Term of His Natural Life* (1983) and the historical series *Against the Wind* (1983)). In the popular but controversial TV series *Prisoner* (1979–86) prison functioned as a complex metaphor which viewers used to explore the role of institutions (including school and the work place) in everyday life; see Hodge & Tripp (1986). Graeme Turner (1986) analyses the connections between convictism and constructions of the self in Australian society in similar terms to ours, including an excellent discussion of Stephen Wallace's film *Stir* (1980).

WORKS CITED

Althusser, Louis. *Essays on Ideology*. London: New Left Books, 1971.

Bateson, Gregory. *Steps to an Ecology of Mind*. Frogmore: Paladin, 1973.

Boldrewood, Rolf [Thomas Alexander Browne]. *Robbery Under Arms*. 1888. Hawthorn, Victoria: Lloyd O'Neil, 1970.

Carey, Gabrielle. *Just Us*. Ringwood: Penguin, 1984.

Carey, Gabrielle and Kathy Lette. *Puberty Blues*. Ringwood: Penguin, 1979.

Clarke, Marcus. *For the Term of His Natural Life*. 1874. Sydney: Pacific Books, 1969.

——*His Natural Life*. 1929. Ringwood and Harmondsworth: Penguin, 1970.

——*Marcus Clarke*. Portable Australian Authors. Ed. Michael Wilding. St. Lucia: University of Queensland Press, 1976.

Foucault, Michel. *Discipline and Punish: The Birth of the Prison*. Trans. Alan Sheridan. Harmondsworth: Penguin, 1979.

Furphy, Joseph [Tom Collins]. *Such is Life*. 1903. Hawthorn, Victoria: Lloyd O'Neil, 1970.

Hirst, J. *Convict Society and Its Enemies*. Sydney: Allen and Unwin, 1983.

Hobsbawm, Eric. *Bandits*. London: Weidenfeld and Nicolson, 1969.

Hodge, B. and D. Tripp. *Children and Television*. Cambridge: Polity Press, 1986.

Hughes, R. *The Fatal Shore: A History of the Transportation of Convicts to Australia 1787–1868*. London: Collins Harvill, 1987.

Ireland, David. *The Unknown Industrial Prisoner*. Sydney: Angus and Robertson, 1971.

Keneally, Thomas. *Bring Larks and Heroes*. Melbourne: Sun Books, 1967.

Kingsley, Henry. *The Recollections of Geoffrey Hamlyn*. 1859. Hawthorn, Victoria: Lloyd O'Neil, 1970.

McQueen, Humphrey. *A New Britannia*. 1970. Ringwood: Penguin, 1975.

Meredith, John. *The Wild Colonial Boy: The Life and Times of Jack Donohoe*. Sydney: Wentworth Press, 1960.

Meredith, John and Rex Whalan. *Frank the Poet*. Melbourne: Red Rooster, 1979.

Praed, Rosa. *Outlaw and Lawmaker*. 1893. London: Pandora, 1988.

Rowley, C. D. *The Destruction of Aboriginal Society*. Canberra: Australian National University Press, 1970.

Summers, Anne. *Damned Whores and God's Police*. Ringwood and Harmondsworth: Penguin, 1975.

Treborlang, Robert. *How to Survive in Australia*. Sydney: Major Mitchell Press, 1985.

Tucker, James. *Ralph Rashleigh*. 1845. Sydney: Angus and Robertson, 1952.

Turner, Graeme. *National Fictions*. Sydney: Angus and Robertson, 1986.

Ward, Russel. *The Australian Legend*. Melbourne: Oxford University Press, 1958.

Wilding, Michael. *Marcus Clarke*. Melbourne: Oxford University Press, 1977.

Wilson, P. and J. Braithwaite. *Two Faces of Deviance*. St. Lucia: Queensland University Press, 1978.

Colonizing Gender in Colonial Australia: The Eliza Fraser Story

KAY SCHAFFER

Kay Schaffer's essay provides the student with an example of colonial discourse analysis that considers the ways in which Eliza Fraser, a white Englishwoman shipwrecked in Australia in 1836, becomes a "colonial and postcolonial object of power/knowledge." The Foucauldian orientation of her analysis unveils the gap between the "real" Eliza Fraser and the representations of her that constitute the legend of her survival. The student will find here an incisive analysis of the genre of the captivity narrative and how such narratives were transformed in the colonialist press and how they served to regulate and police racial, gender, and class divisions. The legendary figure of Eliza Fraser emerges as part of a Manichean discourse that draws sharp distinctions between civilized Europeans and savage Others; her experience, distorted and falsified – often by Fraser herself – foregrounds the way in which the figure of woman comes to signify the precarious nature of colonial authority. She is a discourse rather than a real human being, and as such she is both victim and agent of Empire. Schaffer's essay is particularly valuable in that it considers the problem of ambivalence in the representation of women caught within a discourse that both furthers colonial rule and treats them as colonial victims. If Eliza Fraser has a voice, "it is a voice made present through the masculine constructions of 'woman.'" In this context, Schaffer joins **Gayatri Chakravorty Spivak, Rajeswari Sunder Rajan**, and **Angela Bourke** in investigating the problem of women and their ability to attain genuine historical agency. Like **Bob Hodge and Vijay Mishra**, Schaffer explores the ramifications of this historical dilemma for Australian cultural politics and national identity in general.

Colonizing Gender in Colonial Australia: The Eliza Fraser Story

Anyone who knows anything about Australia will tell you that it's a "man-zone" country.[1] It is not, of course, except by a facile but enduring reputation. A myriad of white masculine images of Australian national identity pervade popular film and the media as well as the literary and historical representations of the academy. This is one reason why Eliza Fraser is remarkable within an Australian frame. In 1836 Mrs. Fraser was shipwrecked off the northeastern coast of Australia, thus becoming the first white woman to encounter Aborigines and to tell her (less-than-sympathetic) tale. Although of some local interest in the 1830s, her story receives scant attention in mainstream historical texts. But as a 20th-century figure of legend – represented as a captive victim who seduced and then betrayed her convict rescuer – Mrs. Fraser has taken on nearly mythical status in Australia, as anyone who has read Patrick White's novel *A Fringe of Leaves* (1976), or seen any of Sidney Nolan's paintings from his *Mrs. Fraser* series (1947–1964), or viewed the David Williamson and Tim Burstall film *Eliza Fraser* (1976) could attest.[2]

Her story is legendary today: but the legend has little to do with the actual woman or the historical event in which she figured. I suggest, however, that what is known of the woman as a historical agent pales in significance next to the textual production of "Eliza Fraser" as a colonial and postcolonial object of power / knowledge.[3] What is known of the event is less significant than its representation in the various discourses in which it is situated. In the 19th century, the significance of the Eliza Fraser story was understood with reference to imperialism, Christianity, the natural science of evolutionism, and Victorian sexual politics. Controversy surrounding the event contributed to the evolution of Australia as a nation, beyond its status and identity as an outpost of empire. In the 20th century, the legend surrounding Eliza Fraser became enmeshed within the aesthetic, ideological, and political networks supporting Australian nationalism. Throughout the time in which the story has circulated within so-called high and popular culture, it has operated as a means of regulating racial, class, and gender divisions, the effects of which can be traced within Australian cultural politics today.

This chapter, then, will examine the Eliza Fraser story not as a historical event but as a foundational fiction aligned to the maintenance of a colonial empire and to the making of the Australian nation. Focusing on the 19th century, it will attend to a variety of texts that reproduce her story in various ways: government documents,

Taken from Alison Blunt and Gillian Rose (eds.), *Writing Women and Space: Colonial and Post-Colonial Geographies* (New York: Guilford Publications, 1994).

histories, ballads, hand-bills, and newspaper reports. The analysis aims not to get at the "truth of the thing," but to examine Mrs. Fraser's position(s) in the narratives and that of other speakers, writers, and commentators; to examine her construction as a victim of native savagery; and to explore the ways in which different forms of narrative contribute differently to colonial constructions of race, gender, and class divisions and hierarchies. The chapter will also examine the ways in which the texts have been read and received as representations that uphold or resist conflicting notions of imperial, colonial, or national authority. The approach assumes that there is no guarantee of knowledge beyond the textual representations of the event. The event, through narration, becomes placed in a number of fields of meaning, themselves embedded in Western, rationalist, imperial discourses of history.[4] There is no way to recover the real, no "real" outside of representation to recover.

First, a brief account of the story, offered here in order to construct a ground from which it will be possible to speak, and to give my readers a point of reference / departure. In 1836 Eliza Fraser, the English wife of an ailing Scottish ship captain, James Fraser, accompanied her husband on what was to prove to be a fatal voyage to the antipodes. The couple left their three children behind at the Orkney Islands off the north coast of Scotland in the care of the Presbyterian minister. Their brig, the *Stirling Castle*, was a merchant ship that carried goods and emigrant passengers from England to the colonies. On the return voyage the vessel was wrecked on a reef 500 miles off the present Queensland coast. The crew spent six treacherous weeks at sea in two leaky lifeboats, one of which abandoned the captain's party. Members of the longboat that included Captain and Mrs. Fraser eventually landed on what is now called (after the captain) Fraser Island, but only after the crew threatened to "draw lots" if the captain, who was mortally afraid of native violence, did not pull ashore. Mrs. Fraser and seven men eventually survived the ordeal.

The survivors spent six weeks on the island. While "in captivity" among "natives"[5] Mrs. Fraser experienced severe personal hardship, as well as witnessing the spearing and death of her husband and the sufferings of several other crew members before being rescued "from a fate worse than death" during a corroboree (an Aboriginal dance festival held at night) by the convict John Graham, who had volunteered his services as part of an official government rescue party that set out from the penal settlement at Moreton Bay. Years later, runaway convict David Bracefell claimed that he had rescued Eliza and walked her some 100 miles back to Moreton Bay before she turned on him, threatening to report him for his abuse of her person. This has been the version favored by some Queenslanders and built into the legend of Eliza Fraser, but it appears to be without historical foundation. After the rescue, Mrs. Fraser was returned to Moreton Bay, where local residents nursed her back to health before she departed for Sydney. In Sydney she gave several interviews to the press about her experiences before meeting Captain Alexander Greene of the *Mediterranean Packet*, marrying him, and accompanying him back to England. On arrival in England, she appealed to the authorities (first in Liverpool and then in London) for funds, representing herself as "Mrs. Fraser," a poor widow woman without a farthing, despite the fact that she had received £400 and two trunks full of clothing donated by the citizens of Sydney. She also gave further interviews to the press which by now had taken on a wildly exaggerated air. A subscription fund was set up by the lord mayor of London which attracted some £500 before news reached the city from Liverpool that her claims were somewhat inflated. She was accused of being an ingenious imposter and of perpetrating fraud. A Commission of Inquiry followed, and resulted in the lord mayor transferring the money to a trust fund for Mrs. Fraser's children under guardianship of the Protestant minister at Stromness. Details of the inquiry were reported daily in the press and later resulted in the publication of the first "official" history of the event, *The Shipwreck of the Stirling Castle* (1838), written by John Curtis, a court reporter for the *Times*. The last reference to Mrs. Fraser concerns a woman (who may have been an actress) who appeared as a sideshow attraction in Hyde Park, admission 6d.

One can map Mrs. Fraser's journey from the isolation of the Orkney Islands, through a treacherous voyage to the new Australian colony, through shipwreck, captivity, and rescue on Fraser Island, followed by recovery at Moreton Bay and Sydney, and finally to notoriety in Liverpool and London. At each point in her journey different interests were brought to bear on her story: those of the colonial government and the British naval authorities, the mutinous crew, her convict rescuers, the colonial settlers in Australia, and the public in Britain. At each point along the way, what identity(ies) it was possible for her to assume, what she meant to others, and how she was able to represent herself and be represented were all dependent on her geographic locations, their political contexts, and the network of power relations in which she and her story were embedded.

NARRATIVE CONSTRUCTIONS

Mrs. Fraser gave three different reports of her ordeal to a number of different audiences: she filed an official report with the commandant at Moreton Bay, gave interviews to the local press in Sydney, and prepared an extended sensationalized account that was released to the popular press upon her arrival in Liverpool. The later account was published as a classic captivity narrative in the United States, appeared in ballad form on handbills and as a penny dreadful in London, and was picked up and circulated by the colonial press throughout the English-speaking world. She also gave testimony at the London Inquiry, along with Baxter, the second officer, and seaman Darge, one of the mutinous crew, and was interviewed further by John Curtis in the preparation of his book-length defense of Mrs. Fraser-Greene against charges of fraud. The plethora of materials the event generated contributed to an expanding discursive network supporting new knowledges and sustaining the imperialist impulse of the West.

At Moreton Bay all survivors were interviewed by the commandant and official statements were taken. Eliza's report is about 1,500 words in length. Two-thirds of the narrative details the shipwreck and performance of the captain and crew, while the final third summarizes events that occurred on the island and describes her treatment by the "natives." In the main the document attends to the mutinous behavior of the crew. This involved their refusal to rescue food and valuables from the *Stirling Castle* and led to the parting of the pinnace from the longboat with Mrs. Fraser's twelve-year-old nephew on board. Later, on the island, the remaining crew abandoned Eliza, the captain, the first mate, the second mate, and the steward to their fate after taking possession of firearms, ammunition, and navigational instruments. The report is clearly addressed to an official government audience for which Mrs. Fraser speaks not only for herself but also for her dead husband. It attempts to relieve the captain of responsibility for mismanagement or wrongdoing. The report success-fully led to the punishment of the surviving crew members, all of whom had pre-viously received a hero's welcome. In this narrative, although the "natives" are accused of treating the party "with the greatest cruelty," there is no mention of the "savagery" and "barbarism" that creeps into subsequent accounts.

The second account of Mrs. Fraser's ordeal resulted from interviews by local journalists in Sydney who reported her story to the public via the local press. These accounts, which pay considerably more attention to her encounters with the natives on the island, are more sensational. They detail the spearing and death of the captain; the death of the first mate, Brown, after he was tortured and burnt; and the stripping and intense privations of Eliza prior to her rescue by the convict John Graham under the guidance of Lieutenant Otter. For the first time a clear delineation of "us" and "them" categories emerges. The terms "cannibals" and "savages" are employed to describe the natives and Mrs. Fraser is represented as an innocent victim of fate's outrageous fortune, miraculously rescued by Divine Providence. These press reports tell the local public what it wants to hear. They titillate the colonial imagination with a depiction of the horrible sufferings of a vulnerable woman and incite fear of the savage "others" at the fringes of the new society, fear that would lead later to bloodshed and the near-extinction of the indigenous population of Fraser Island. A subscription campaign was launched by the bishop of Sydney for Mrs. Fraser and other members of the surviving crew, although only she would benefit from it. An outpouring of sympathy, hospitality, and generosity for Mrs. Fraser followed, as the citizens of the new colony attempted to rescue not only the woman but their own reputation for maintaining a civilized and ordered bourgeois life in the antipodes. As news filtered through to Sydney about the crew's mutiny and possible cannibalism among them, sympathy began to shift from the party of eight survivors to Eliza alone.

Although Mrs. Fraser gave three official reports of her ordeal, it is the third one, first published in the London *Courier* on August 19, 1837, and later adapted (with lurid illustrations) as a penny dreadful and advertised on handbills similar to those that announced her sideshow performance in Hyde Park, which reached the English-speaking colonial world in the form of a classic captivity narrative. Other London, provincial, and colonial papers were quick to reprint this account. Its preface draws the readers' attention to

> the deplorable case of Mrs. Fraser and others, who have miraculously survived an awful shipwreck, and the cruelties practiced on them by the savages of New South Wales, amongst whom they were thrown, and by whom the majority of the ship's crew have been enslaved in lowest bondage, and in short tortured to death, by means at which the old Inquisition of Spain might blush.[6]

It contains tales of warfare between native tribes and refers to their savagery and cannibalism in ways that had not been reported to the official government administrators after the event and could not be corroborated by other crew members. It includes fantastic descriptions of events, including reports of grotesque, blue-haired natives and a gruesome tale of the torture and beheading of one James Major whose body was said to have been eaten by natives and his head preserved for use as a figure bust for one of their canoes. It was this sensational and melodramatic version of the story that appeared in *Alexander's East India and Colonial Magazine* and the *Army and Navy Chronicle* (Washington, DC) in September and October 1837, followed by publication in the tabloid magazine *Tales of Travellers* (London, 1837), and was later repeated in an editorial in the *Sydney Gazette* (January 1838). In the words of a recent historian, "This one article set black/white relations in the Wide Bay area [of Queensland] back at least a hundred years."[7]

Within months the Americans had published an "Americanized" version of the captivity narrative, complete with tepees, squaws, Indian chiefs, tomahawks, bows and arrows, and crude illustrations. The illustrations detail Captain Fraser's death and Eliza's conveyance to the chief's "hut or wigwam," which suggests to the reader that "fate worse than death" (miscegenation) that the American captivity genre made famous. The narrative contains all the elements of the genre, albeit laced with the melodramatic elements associated with the sentimental novel. Some indications of its tone can be detected in the introduction, which appeared on the title page along with two suggestive illustrations. It reads:

> [After the wreck the crew] were driven to and thrown on an unknown island, inhabited by Savages, by whom Captain Fraser and his first mate were barbarously murdered, and Mrs. Fraser . . . [was] for several weeks held in bondage, and after having been compelled to take up her abode in a wigwam and to become the adopted wife of one of the Chiefs, Mrs. F. was providently rescued from her perilous situation.[8]

Here the crew, which is quickly reduced to a woman, is plunged into a perilous ordeal, from which it (but textually only "she") is miraculously rescued. The lone woman is the classic victim of the captivity narrative. It is her vulnerability that excites sympathy and incites the instincts of revenge against the barbarous enemy within colonial discourse. This sensational text proceeds to establish Mrs. Fraser's credentials as a reluctant narrator, unprepared for her performance, having had an "indifferent education" and deprived of the aid of her husband. But this constructed autobiographical author promises a "plain, unvarnished tale; exaggerating nothing, but recording truly and faithfully the particulars" of her ordeal, an ordeal in which she moves from "a state of content and enviable happiness, to that of inconceivable wretchedness" before being "miraculously rescued" from her "bondage." The natives appear in the text as types, marked by their violence, their physicality, and their orality. The husbands are "lazy" or "naturally very indolent," the squaws are "savage monsters" who nonetheless "perform the most laborious duties . . . cheerfully . . . without complaint or murmur." All the natives yell, whoop, and howl. Unlike the classic captivity narrative, however, this one revolves around the death of Captain Fraser (or his "savage/brutal murder" at the hands of "remorseless demons," to be true to the text). This moment produces a climax in the text that plunges Eliza into chaos. Threats of sexual violation are signaled by a crisis of narrative address: "Alas, it is impossible to reflect on what I endured . . . to imagine the shock of horrors to come. . . . The reader cannot have any idea of the horrors I suffered." More horrors follow, until, finally, Eliza is rescued "not from the devouring jaws of a ravenous lion, but from the hands of a savage ruffian, far more to be dreaded!"

The American version differs only in minor details from those published in England and in the colonial magazines. American commentators have suggested that its interest may have been motivated by the outbreak of the Seminole Wars between the colonists and the Indians of Florida, Nat Turner's slave rebellion, and, beyond the local interest, America's Manifest Destiny: "Inevitably, these patterns included the notion that the Pacific was yet another American frontier."[9] With these publications Mrs. Fraser becomes a figure of display for an imperial/colonial audience and her story a myth by which the popular imagination understood the civilized world by means of its difference from the savage "others" at its margins. In terms of the construction of social space, Mrs. Fraser's captivity narrative provided for a widespread Western colonial audience the justification for control by the West over the rest of the world.

HISTORICAL ACCOUNTS

At the same time, other historical records appeared. John Curtis's book-length defense of Eliza, *The Shipwreck of the Stirling Castle*, was published in England in 1838 and reprinted in 1841. In Australia, a mild local interest in the story was revived with the rescue of the escaped convict David Bracefell, who in 1842 was brought back to Moreton Bay by a party of explorers intent on land settlement. He reported that he (not John Graham) had rescued the said Eliza and had walked her back to Moreton Bay (some 100 miles away) in the hope of a pardon and possibly a reward but that the ungrateful lady had turned on him at the edge of civilization, threatening to complain of him to the authorities. One of the explorer party, Henry Stuart Russell, includes this reminiscence in his memoirs, *The Genesis of Queensland*, published to commemorate the centenary of Queensland in 1888.[10] Here, within an Australian colonial context, Eliza becomes a foil to Bracefell, her British duplicity standing out against his convict heroism. These historical texts of Curtis and Russell provide a reference point for 20th-century postcolonial constructions of Eliza Fraser in Australia that turn the tale into a romance, with David Bracefell as her rescuer. They present Eliza as an unreliable narrator, a seductress, and a betrayer of men – repetitions of which have won her near mythical status on an international scale in the 20th century.[11]

In the 19th century, however, Curtis's history became the official account of the event and a reference point for future commentators. Curtis's book is a polysemic text of empire. Throughout the text he engages in a spirited defense of Eliza Fraser that serves to disguise the wider social, political, and ideological implications of this first engagement between the innocent, saintly, white, female victim and her encounter with a savage "otherness" at the margins of the British Empire.[12] The main text attempts to reconstruct events that occurred on Fraser Island by telling Eliza's story through a series of divergent voices. At the same time, extensive footnotes create for the reader a subtext through which Curtis addresses the fields of navigation, emigration, and the legal system, as well as presents a wealth of anthropological, geological, and scientific information. Within these two textual spaces there is a negotiation between doubt and certainty, between Eliza's dubious story of captivity and the verities of scientific truth. The text utilizes a number of narrative modes including direct address, debate, description, exhortation, the scientific treatise, the diary, and the epistolary novel. It also succumbs to a series of narrative crises. The promise of new disclosures and proofs concerning Mrs. Fraser's veracity and innocence of wrongdoing is constantly subverted by tangential textual delays that occur in the footnotes and all-but take over the page. These diversions occur particularly before the disclosure of possible evidence of rape or cannibalism, hinted at but never quite proven.

An irony here is that the scientific verities are wildly inaccurate. Curtis's description of Fraser Island Aborigines, for example, was lifted from an 1827 ethnography of Port Jackson Aborigines in New South Wales; his descriptions and illustrations of ritual cannibalism and other burial practices are derived from sailor's tales of the South Pacific possibly brought back by Captain Greene, Eliza's new husband, who captained whaling vessels around the coast of New Zealand and wrote sensational traveler's tales for the colonial magazines. The text is connected to empire in diverse ways. Curtis relates in the preface that his aims are to justify Mrs. Fraser's cause; to tell the story of the wreck, captivity and rescue; to encourage missionary work among the natives; to promote emigration; and to enhance anthropological and geographical knowledge.[13]

It has been argued that this text contributed to the emigration and settlement of Australia's northeastern seaboard, to the extension of racial colonization, and to the imposition of Christianity through the mission movement in Australia, which later in the century virtually wiped out the native population of Fraser Island. The text was published in 1838, a year after the founding of the British and Foreign Aboriginal Protection Society and in the same year as the Sydney-based Aboriginal Protection Society came into existence, a society that established the term by which native peoples would be uniformly categorized as "Aborigines" and through which their affairs would be managed.[14] The calls that Curtis made to the builders of empire would be heeded, in part, in Mrs. Fraser's name. Indeed, the first official expedition to Fraser Island and surrounding coastal areas in 1842 was mounted ostensibly to bring back the runaway convicts whom Mrs. Fraser had encountered. It resulted in the first official survey of the land for white settlement, the European naming of land-marks (including Fraser Island), and the demarcation of possible sites for capital expansion of the pastoral and timber industries. What followed brought about the settlement wars of the 1850s, white colonization, and the disruption and dispersal of traditional Aboriginal culture in the area.

MRS. FRASER AS A HISTORICAL AGENT

To what degree can Eliza Fraser be considered a historical agent? To what degree is "she" here at all? What the foregoing discussion has demonstrated is the degree to which the woman and the historical event collapse into a number of discontinuous fields of meaning into which they are placed. Mrs. Fraser's stories to the press, her sensational trial in London, her side-show performances, and the popular literature they invoke all serve to provide the British people as well as the citizens of colonial Australia with a foundational fiction that marks the boundaries between civilization and the wilderness. Not Mrs. Fraser, but her story in its various guises provides the white, male Western hero of progress the space in which to perform a "rescue" operation through which he marks the boundaries between colonizer and colonized, man and his "others" – an operation that protects the idea of "a people" through the exclusion of native inhabitants on an alien, yet-to-be-claimed, physical, psychic, and mythically constructed landscape. Mrs. Fraser has a voice, but it is a voice made present through the masculine constructions of "woman." The natives have no voice and can only be present in the form of representations of their difference from their "civilized" observers, a difference that marks the boundaries of civilization. Imaginary projections of the ideas of woman, race, and sexuality motivate the circulation of her tale. "Woman" and her "others" function to guarantee the constructed status, identity, and authority of the British peoples, and later of the Australian nation. Mrs. Fraser is there, but only in the spaces allowed her by her commentators and constructed through categories of femininity already available to her for self-representation, and to her popularizers for the edification / titillation of her various audiences.

What can be said of "Mrs. Fraser" in the narratives that bear her name? They require us to locate her in a number of positions. It is not enough to view Eliza Fraser only and essentially as a woman. If we locate Eliza Fraser within the various discourses of power, we can see that she was complicit with the politics of domination. She became a conduit of the Empire, regardless of what her personal motivations may have been. Additionally, the meaning of "Eliza Fraser" differs depending on the contexts of her narratives and their intended audiences. From the moment she entered history, she was already situated within the discourses of power – patriarchy, imperialism, Christianity, and capitalism – but in a number of contradictory ways. From the outset, gender, but also class, relations dominate. She was the captain's wife, traveling on a trading ship that also took emigrant families from Imperial Britain to colonial Australia. But there were no emigrants on board at the time of the wreck, no passengers who could have helped her uphold the captain's rank, authority, and position. Given the power vested in ship's captains in the 19th century, and given the condition of her particular husband, her insistence on his authority in her first official report should not be surprising. During the wreck and its aftermath the captain was ill. Mrs. Fraser attempted to act as his representative. But the crew would have none of it. Despite her superior class position and the ailing condition of her husband, whose rank she attempted to uphold, the crew would not obey her. They called her the "She Captain" and threatened to drown her.[15] When she attempted to collect water for her husband, the water vessel was forcibly taken from her hands. What power was not available to her at the time through social practice, however, was supplied textually in her official report after the event, and concretized by the punitive actions of the colonial administrators at Moreton Bay.[16] In addition, the Caribbean steward from the brig remained faithful to her throughout the voyage.[17] If the crew would not rescue her trunks of clothing and the special food she had prepared for the captain, he would and did, thereby alienating himself from the crew, denying his own limited space of freedom, and upholding relations of dominance and submission marked by race and class.

Once on the island, her race takes on significance, for she was a white woman among the natives. But she was no conqueror. Placed in the care of the women without the company or protection of her husband or any of the crew, without language or knowledge of their customs, she was quickly subjected to their authority. In this situation, her race (a white woman among Aborigines); her class status (one of assumed middle-class authority amid a working-class crew); her patriarchal position (wife of an ailing captain and aunt to the ship's second mate) were to no avail. But race, class, and gender hierarchies are restored in the historical constructions of the event. Indeed, her identity as constituted through these hierarchies of race, class, and gender impels the necessity of History itself.

There are other complications, recorded by the histories but for which no evidence exists, which influence the ways it has been possible to read and thus place the historical Eliza. Michael Alexander, her 20th-century historian of note, reports that although descended from Derbyshire tenant farmers, she was born and raised in Ceylon.[18] She thus would have been an early daughter of the British Raj. No archival evidence has been found to support Alexander's claims, but that is inconsequential. His claims influence the reading of Eliza by subsequent commentators, which in turn feeds the discourses of colonialism with regard to race and class. In addition, they supply a historical interpretation that she herself (like the other white women of the Raj?) was sensual and indulgent, thus providing a motive for the crew's hostility to her. Then there are the biological contingencies of her situation. Mrs. Fraser's third sensational account maintains that she was pregnant when she left Liverpool and gave birth five days after the wreck to a child who drowned shortly after birth. If this is so, she would then have been in a postpartum condition during the time of her so-called captivity, a condition that could be used to explain her treatment by the natives, her position among the women, and her availability to the men of the group.[19] These factors also have bearing on and interact with her gender position as read by future commentators, sometimes in contradictory ways.

SPATIAL DELINEATIONS OF POWER

These race, class, and gender distinctions also have relevance when we consider the spatial dynamics of power. An emigrant ship was a microcosm of class and power relations in England. Its space was assumed to be a unitary social space promoted as a community but divided, policed, and regulated along the boundaries of power. The captain, although he may have come from a lowly class background at home, was by rank the supreme authority on board his vessel. Vested with the judicial powers of arrest and punishment, he also possessed religious and secular power to baptize, marry, and bury while at sea.[20] His authority was mapped out in the spatial arrangements on board – in the distance between the captain, first- and second-class passengers, and the (lowly) crew. These spatial arrangements confer an illusive power, one that must be constantly policed and enforced by social practice. The captain's quarters occupied the poop deck, at the apex and at the rear of the ship, mirroring his position at the apex of its command structure, his gaze directed out and down upon his empire. The crew, on the other hand, were billeted in the worst accommodation, in the forecastle before the mast, and denied access to space allocated (albeit differentially) to the passengers. According to Hassam, "The division of space on board ship work[ed] primarily on the basis of exclusion, of excluding different groups from certain areas of the ship, and this in turn [led] to contestations of space which provide both the focus for the bringing into being of the captain's power and a focus for the affirmation and maintenance of social identity."[21] In the case of the *Stirling Castle*, even though incapacitated by ill health, it was possible for Captain Fraser to maintain his control, status, and class position while the ship was at sea prior to the wreck, despite the absence of passengers whose place might have further enhanced his authority. But the wreck initiated a disintegration of the social order and a breakdown of borders and boundaries, both physical and ideological. Try as she might, Eliza could not step into her husband's shoes. Her good health and her desire to command the vessel on behalf of the captain were no substitute for masculinity. She was no match for a mutinous crew.

After the wreck, the shift in power relations becomes clear with the division of crew into the two lifeboats. Although larger, the longboat, into which the captain was put with his wife, was less seaworthy. He attempted to enforce his command by placing the first mate in charge of the longboat and his second mate in charge of the pinnace. Clearly, his command of these spaces was as important as his naval command. His personal authority broke down, however, when the second mate became ill and was transferred to the longboat, his twelve-year-old nephew was pressed into the service of the mutineers, and a seaman took command of the pinnace, which abandoned the party. On another level, Mrs. Fraser attempted to demand respect for her own and the captain's status by insisting that her / their possessions be brought on board. The crew refused but the faithful mulatto steward rescued them for her from the brig. She thus extended the space occupied by the couple through the presence of two large trunks in the longboat. This act also established a domestic woman's space on board the vessel: the trunks were all that she had to represent "home," although they were mightily resented by the crew. She was afforded no privileges, however, as the crew demanded that she bail water for both herself and her ailing husband. This is the space in which she was said to have given birth, knee-deep in water, attended by the first mate who eventually wrapped the drowned child in his shirt and commended it to the deep.

On the island another configuration of spatial relations evolved, designed in this instance to separate the survivors from the natives. To the survivors the island was wholly alien space, roughly mapped only as coastline on navigational charts and never before inhabited (or known to be inhabited) by white Europeans. Here the shipwreck victims stayed together, interacting tentatively with the natives, bartering clothing for food, knowing themselves and their identity as Britons primarily through their group identity, their proximity to one another. They clung to the shoreline, making their way south, until surrounded by natives and divided among several small groups. Mrs. Fraser was left alone until taken up by a party of women. This was a new social space, totally outside the boundaries of European knowledge, beyond the gaze of the Father's Law. If it can be said that Mrs. Fraser was "in captivity" with the natives, her captivity was as much related to the alterity of this space as it was to the physical controls and constraints placed upon her. Socially and symbolically she was "nowhere" and that spatial positioning robbed her of an identity. What is captivity outside the symbolic order and the rule of the Father's Law? Where there is no Law, there can be no identity.[22] Mrs. Fraser's subjection was effected through her location and absorption in the space of "otherness."

But not completely. When she was found, her rescuer John Graham reported that the only article of clothing on her person was a tangle of vines around her waist which "her dead and most lamented husband had put on" in which she had hidden her wedding ring and earrings.[23] These become emblematic words for Patrick White and his novel, *A Fringe of Leaves*. Thus, readers of the history are reminded at the point of her rescue of the symbolic presence of her husband through the fringe of leaves that inscribes her body within patriarchy and calls attention to her status as female, protecting herself and her "femininity" from total dissolution.

FOUNDATIONAL FICTIONS

I want to return to the 19th-century origins of the story and to study it as a liminal narrative, that is, a narrative arising from first contact between Europeans and the indigenous people, Europeans and the foreign land occurring in an alien situation that has no predetermined meaning. These liminal stories of first contact, which in Australia would include tales of shipwreck, captivity, and convict escape, could be said to have several important, although discontinuous, effects. Through newspaper articles, oral histories, and local legends they incite the popular imagination and provide initial constructions of racial, class, and gender differences in and for the colony. Through rescue expeditions, they make possible the first mappings of the land, producing a new Western geography, a social production of space. At least two types of official governmental and academic interest follow in the wake of these historical events. The governmental interest concerns colonial policies and practices. Knowledge of the shipwreck and captivity led to further geographic expeditions, observations of Aboriginal life, missionary work, penal surveillance and punishments, as well as the institution of social, ethical, and moral values – all of which change the character of colonial life. The other academic, historical, and ethnographical interest in Mrs. Fraser's ordeal feeds information into broader Western academic classification systems and taxonomies (natural history, philology, ethnography, cartography). These create, maintain, and / or reinforce race and gender hierarchies, legitimize the "natural superiority" of Western rule in colonial empires, *and* provide the structures, ideologies, and institutions of power utilized to constitute the new nation-state.

FORMATIONS OF THE NATION-STATE

My conclusions are informed by a number of relevant postcolonial and feminist writers whose critiques open up a new set of questions concerning the construction of the postcolonial nation-state. Postcolonial theoretical perspectives suggest that the basis for a contemporary politics of both global and national power relationships can be found in the complex web of 19th-century power relations embedded in the discourses of colonialism. In *Nation and Narration*, for example, Homi Bhabha argues that discourses establish the cultural boundaries of a nation, containing the thresholds of meaning that must be crossed, erased, and translated in the processes of cultural production. He and other contributors to the anthology analyze the concept of nation *as* narration, exploring ways by which strategies invoked within poststructuralist theories of narrative knowledge – textuality, discourse, enunciation, *écriture*, "the unconscious as a language" – might be evoked to open up the ambivalent margins of nation-space.[24] Feminist postcolonial writers suggest further that through an analysis of colonial discourse it is possible to trace the dynamics of contemporary Western knowledge through an analysis of its categories and assumptions that marginalize women, natives, and others.[25] In the main, these theoretical perspectives concern colonial discourses that emerge in so-called Third World countries previously under the control of imperialist forces. My examination of the Eliza Fraser story and the recent cultural critiques of a number of other Australian postcolonial commentators indicate that, at least in part, they provide appropriate frameworks for analysis of settler societies like Australia as well.[26]

AUSTRALIAN NATIONAL IDENTITY AND THE ELIZA FRASER STORY

The idea of nation, as I argued in *Women and the Bush*, emerges out of social and cultural constructions that posit identity through difference.[27] If the nation is an imagined community, as Anderson maintains,[28] the maintenance of a coherent identity relies on historical narratives that posit and secure its continuance. In the case of Australia, the dominant mythical structure out of which concepts of national identity arise is figured with reference to the white, native-born, Australian male and his battle with the land / Aborigines / "others," framed against the English parent culture. Although women are said to be absent from the annals of Australian history, the idea of the feminine figures metaphorically as the category of difference from the masculine, in a play of masculine sameness and of feminine difference. The white Australian native son battles against a hostile feminine environment, an "enemy to be fought." Sometimes actual women are the enemy, but more often the category is filled in by fire, flood, and drought, and by the presence of Aborigines, the Chinese, and other migrants. Man posits his identity as "Australian" in opposition to his "others" – women, natives, the land – that which "he" is not.

Although it is generally assumed that Australian national identity emerged in the decade of the 1890s, it could be argued that that decade fused elements already nascent in the underlying imaginings of the colonial state. My analysis of the Eliza Fraser story leads in this direction. As a character in a 19th-century drama of empire she can be figured as masculine and given status and authority. In 20th-century Australian versions of the story she is located within the despised British parent culture as a betrayer of her underdog rescuer. In both the 19th- and 20th-century accounts, however, whether directed toward mass culture or a high-minded academic audience, "Eliza Fraser" marks the territory of a superior white civilization. Her story polices the borders of difference within colonial, neocolonial, and postcolonial frameworks of meaning. Her story provides an instance of the nation's representational work: how it understands racial and gender differences, what happens on their sites of contestation, and what are their changing political effects. Analyzing her story in this way significantly alters present dominant understandings of Australian nationalism and the rise of the nation-state. In addition, such a reading challenges the historical assumptions that geography is simply the ground on which historical events take place. Finally, the Eliza Fraser story provides a specifically Australian context for the wider exploration of postcolonial perspectives that mark the field of cultural studies in an intranational arena.

NOTES

1   This is the title of a chapter and the name that Anne Summers coins for Australia as an object of analysis in her pioneering feminist history, *Damned Whores and God's Police* (Ringwood, Australia: Penguin, 1975).

2   The 20th-century representations of the legend have been critically examined by Jim Davidson in "Beyond the Fatal Shore: The Mythologization of Mrs Fraser," *Meanjin* 3 (1990): 449–61, and by me in "Australian Mythologies: The Eliza Fraser Story and Constructions of the Feminine in Patrick White's 'A Fringe of Leaves' and Sidney Nolan's 'Eliza Fraser' Paintings," *Kunapipi 11*, no. 2 (1989): 1–15. In addition to these studies, a historical biography of Eliza Fraser is being prepared by Yolanda Drummond, a New Zealand writer, and promises to include the New Zealand connection (Eliza reputedly migrates to New Zealand with her second husband in the 1840s). A master's thesis on the history of the Cooloola area, which includes Fraser Island, is in preparation by Elaine Brown through the History Department, University of Queensland.

3   See Michel Foucault, *The Order of Things: An Archaeology of the Human Sciences*, Alan Sheridan, trans. (London: Tavistock, 1970) and *Power/Knowledge: Selected Interviews and Other Writings, 1972–1977*, Colin Gordon, ed., and Colin Gordon, Leo Marshall, John Mepham, and Kate Sopor, trans. (New York: Pantheon, 1980).

4   For an insightful explication of this perspective, see Robert Young, *White Mythologies: Writing History and the West* (London: Routledge, 1990), 1–19.

5   I use the term within quotation marks in the first instance to indicate an ironic distance from its 19th-century significations. Although Eliza and subsequent narrators viewed the event as a captivity, from another perspective it could be seen as her salvation. She was not held captive. Her life, although harsh from her perspective, nonetheless paralleled that of other female members of the group. The term "native" was employed in 19th-century British accounts as a racist expression of inferiority to refer to what were in this instance members of three different clans of the Kabi language group. The term "native" is in the process of being rescued to some degree in the 20th century by indigenous peoples, as the debates in Australia over native title legislation demonstrate. The term "Aboriginal" (another totalizing racist signifier) did not come into existence until 1838 when, with the foundation of the Aboriginal Protection Society, it was introduced to designate indigenous peoples of colonized territories throughout the British Empire.

6   Anon., "Disastrous Wreck of the Ship 'Stirling Castle,' Bound from Sydney, New South Wales, to Singapore," *Alexander's East India Colonial Magazine 14*, part 82 (1837): 258.

7   Neil Buchanan and Barry Dwyer, *The Rescue of Eliza Fraser* (Noosa, Queensland: Noosa Graphica, 1986), 42.

8   Anon., *Narrative of the Capture, Suffering, and Miraculous Escape of Mrs. Eliza Fraser* (New York: Charles Webb and Sons, 1837), 1.

9   See James Levernier and Hennig Cohen, eds. comps., *The Indians and Their Captives* (Westport, CN: Greenwood Press, 1977), 267.

10 Henry Stuart Russell, *The Genesis of Queensland* (London: Vintage Books, 1888; reprint, Toowoomba, Queensland, Australia: Vintage Books, 1989). 257–8.

11 The legend both in Australia and overseas took shape as a result of Sidney Nolan's first international exhibition in London in which a series of "Mrs Fraser" paintings were included. Colin MacInnes's introduction to the catalogue *Sydney Nolan: Catalogue of an Exhibition of Paintings from 1947 to 1957 Held at the Whitechapel Art Gallery, London, June to July, 1957* (London: Whitechapel Gallery, 1957) summarizes the story in the following way:

> Mrs Fraser was a Scottish lady who was shipwrecked on what is now Fraser Island off the Queensland coast. She lived for 6 months among the aborigines, rapidly losing her clothes, until she was discovered by one Bracefell, a deserting convict who himself had hidden for 10 years among the primitive Australians. The lady asked the criminal to restore her to civilisation, which he agreed to do if she would promise to intercede for his free pardon from the Governor. The bargain was sealed and the couple set off inland.
>
> At first sight of European settlement, Mrs Fraser rounded on her benefactor and threatened to deliver him to justice if he did not immediately decamp. Bracefell returned disillusioned to the hospitable bush, and Mrs Fraser's adventures aroused such admiring interest that on her return to Europe she was able to exhibit herself at 6d a showing in Hyde Park.

This is the legend surrounding the event to which both Michael Ondaatje and Andre Brink had reference. It forms the basis for Andre Brink's South African novel, *An Instant in the Wind* (London: Minerva, 1976) and for Michael Ondaatje's long poem, *The Man with Seven Toes* (Toronto: Coach House Press, 1969).

12 For more extensive treatment of the London media coverage of the shipwreck, see Kay Schaffer, "Eliza Fraser's Trial by Media," *Antipodes (US)*, (December 1991): 114–19, and Kay Schaffer, "Captivity Narratives and the Idea of Nation," in Kay Schaffer, Kate Darian-Smith, and Roslyn Poignant, *Captured Lives: Australian Captivity Narratives* (London: Sir Robert Menzies Centre for Australian Studies, University of London, 1993), 1–17.

13 John Curtis, *The Wreck of the Stirling Castle* (London: George Virtue, 1838), preface.

14 John Stratton, "A Question of Origins," *Arena 89* (1989): 134.

15 In the official report Mrs. Fraser singles out one member of the defiant crew by name, a Henry Youlden, who "curses" Eliza and takes rainwater from her which she had collected for her ailing husband. His words are the only ones to appear in direct quotation: "Damn you, you She-Captain, if you say much more I'll drown you." Youlden's side of the story would emerge a decade later, in an article published in the New York *Knickerbocker Magazine*, ostensibly written to warn would-be gold prospectors about the dangers of a voyage to Australia, but also no doubt to vindicate himself from the charges brought against him by Mrs. Fraser. See Henry Youlden, "Shipwreck in Australia," *Knickerbocker 41*, no. 4 (1853): 291–300.

16 Within a 20th-century Australian nationalist context, of course, these behaviors of the recalcitrant crew toward Mrs. Fraser (as a representative of English colonial authority) would be read as heroic. Youlden's article to an American public also details to his mind the unjust punishments meted out to the crew whom he represents as able, sober, and

responsible actors caught in an irrational power struggle with the captain's party and a hostile public.

17 Various survivors including Mrs. Fraser, Baxter, and seamen Hodge and Darge commented on Corallis's devotion to Mrs. Fraser; see Curtis, *Wreck of the Stirling Castle*, 30, 49, 174.

18 Michael Alexander, *Mrs Fraser on the Fatal Shore* (London: Michael Joseph, 1971), 8. Yolanda Drummond, a New Zealand researcher who is preparing a biography of Eliza Fraser, has located a copy of the book by Robert Gibbings, *John Graham, Convict, 1824*, in the possession of one of Eliza Fraser's descendants in New Zealand which contains a marginal note, written by a great-grandson. In response to Gibbing's contention that Mrs. Fraser had lived all her life in the Orkney Islands, he responds: "Wrong. She came from Ceylon where her parents lived." Drummond suggests that this is the source for Alexander's claim. See "Progress of Eliza," *Royal Historical Society of Queensland Journal 15*, no. 1 (February 1993): 16.

19 These considerations are taken up in Elaine Brown, "History of the Cooloola Region" (MA thesis [in progress], History Department, University of Queensland). Drummond casts doubt on the whole story, see "Progress," 17, 20–1.

20 See Andrew Hassam, " 'Our Floating Home': Social Space and Group Identity on Board the Emigrant Ship," *Working Papers in Australian Studies*, no. 76 (London: Sir Robert Menzies Centre for Australian Studies, University of London, 1992), 3.

21 Ibid., 7.

22 This discussion assumes a Lacanian psychoanalytic understanding of the subject. According to Lacan, and also to psychoanalytic French feminist thought, each of us takes on our personal, social, and cultural identity within a network of social and symbolic meanings organized by and through language. In a phallocentric culture, masculinity (or what Lacan calls "the Father's Law") is the overriding signifier of status, power, and authority for the Self (whether one is born biologically male or female). What this means is that identity is constituted through language that takes masculinity as its norm. Both men and women can occupy the cultural position of a masculine subject, that is, one who has power, status, and authority, but women will also be marked as different, and inferior. The feminine position (a category that can include the lower class, Aborigines, convicts, and other "deviant" types) is designated as inferior, lacking, "other". If subjectivity is constituted through one's position(s) within the symbolic order of culture, then finding oneself in a totally alien environment would constitute a site of non-meaning/nonidentity. See Jacques Lacan, "The Mirror Phase," *New Left Review 51* (1968): 71–7, and Helene Cixous, "Laugh of the Medusa," *Signs 4*, no. 4 (Summer 1976): 879.

23 From John Graham's log, quoted in Robert Gibbings, *John Graham, Convict* (London: J. M. Dent, 1956), 98.

24 Homi Bhabha, "Introduction: Narrating the Nation," in *Nation and Narration*, Homi Bhabha, ed. (London: Routledge, 1990), 4.

25 See, for example, Mary Louise Pratt, *Imperial Eyes: Travel Writing and Transculturation* (London: Routledge, 1992); Gayatri Chakravorty Spivak, "Can the Subaltern Speak? Speculations on Widow Sacrifice," in *Marxism and the Interpretation of Culture*, Cary Nelson and Lawrence Grossberg, eds. (London: Macmillan, 1988), 271–313. Gayatri Chakravorty Spivak, "Subaltern Studies: Deconstructing Historiography," 197–221, and "A Literary Representation of the Subaltern: A Woman's Text from the Third World," in *In Other Worlds: Essays in Cultural Politics*, 241–68 (New York: Routledge, 1988); Marianna Torgovnick, *Gone Primitive* (Chicago: Chicago University Press, 1990); and Trinh T. Minh-ha, *Woman, Native, Other* (Bloomington: Indiana University Press, 1989).

26 Relevant here is the work of Bill Ashcroft, Gareth Griffiths, and Helen Tiffin, eds., *The Empire Writes Back: Theory and Practice in Post-Colonial Literatures* (New York: Routledge, 1989); Gareth Griffiths, "Imitation, Abrogation and Appropriation: The Production of the Post-Colonial Text," *Kunapipi* 9, no. 1 (1987): 13–20; Sneja Gunew, "Denaturalizing Cultural Nationalisms: Multicultural Readings of 'Australia,' " in *Nation and Narration*, Homi Bhabha, ed. (London: Routledge, 1990), 99–120; Sneja Gunew, "PMT (Post Modernist Tensions): Reading for (Multi)cultural Difference," in *Striking Chords: Multicultural Literary Interpretations*, Sneja Gunew and Kateryna Longley, eds. (Sydney: Allen and Unwin, 1992): 36–46; and Stephen Meucke, *Textual Spaces: Aboriginality and Cultural Studies* (Sydney: University of New South Wales Press, 1992).

27 Kay Schaffer, *Women and the Bush: Forces of Desire and the Australian Cultural Tradition* (Sydney: Cambridge University Press, 1988), 8–15.

28 Benedict Anderson, *Imagined Communities: Reflections on the Origin and Spread of Nationalism* (London: Verso, 1983, 1991), 16, 145.

The Body in the Library: Identity, Opposition and the Settler-Invader Woman

HELEN TIFFIN

Helen Tiffin, one of the authors of the landmark work, *The Empire Writes Back: Theory and Practice in Postcolonial Literatures*, belongs to a generation of critics and theorists who have redefined the concerns of "Commonwealth studies" in terms of a more global postcolonial condition. The essay included here concerns the ambivalent figure of the "settler-invader woman," whose social position, like that of the Anglo-Irish and the white Creole, is somewhere between colonizer and colonized. It focuses on the problem of a colonial or postcolonial subjectivity invented or constructed by what Tiffin calls the "European archive." The settler-invader woman's contradictory implication in "both colonialist and patriarchal systems of oppression" underscores a number of instabilities in these systems, exposing their monolithic character and authority. Tiffin's analysis of contemporary women writers from Australia and Canada underscores the ambiguity of their positions in settler-invader colonies by calling attention to the strategy of "dispersive citation," a form of "intertextuality" that serves to link their texts in subversive ways to the canon of English literature. Exploring the ways in which these authors "cite" Mary Shelley's *Frankenstein* and Joseph Conrad's *Heart of Darkness*, Tiffin argues that women writers from settler-invader colonies must come to terms with "the monstrousness that might lurk (reproductively) within the European heart but whose existence and origin must be projected 'out there.'" The student can usefully read Tiffin's essay alongside those of **Chinua Achebe**, **George Lamming**, and **Moira Ferguson** for a fuller sense of citational strategies employed by postcolonial writers whose subjectivity (whose very bodies) are products of the "European archive."

The Body in the Library: Identity, Opposition and the Settler-Invader Woman

I have deliberately invoked the formulation of the traditional British murder mystery in the title of this paper. But the problem to be addressed in this context is both "who dunnit?" and "who is it?" – or to borrow the title of a collection of critical articles on Australian women writers, "who is she?"[1] Who is this settler-invader Jane Doe in her over-inscribed post-colonial room? For Australian and Canadian women writers, notions of identity and opposition are inevitably connected, and it is this complex I wish to address through a consideration of Jessica Anderson's *Tirra Lirra by the River* and Daphne Marlatt's *Ana Historic*. My more general area of address is the ways in which opposition and identity work in these novels – and in other post-colonial texts – through inscription and reinscription.

For those peoples annihilated, enslaved, decimated and marginalized by the post-Renaissance European drive of conquest and colonization, the roles within that "murder plot" seem clear. The culprits are the Europeans; the victims are those peoples whose territories were conquered and / or colonized. But the murder weapons are not always immediately as obvious. As well as military technologies (and later bureaucracy), it was texts, those "invisible bullets" to use Greenblatt's term, which facilitated, energized, and consolidated the conquest and colonization of other peoples by Europeans. The Africans who insist that Stanley burns the journal in which he has been taking notes about their cultures;[2] Caliban in *The Tempest* who advises Stephano and Trinculo to seize Prospero's "book"; all know what Gauri Viswanathan would later demonstrate from the 1852–1853 British Parliamentary Papers:[3] that adventitiously and often quite deliberately, "the European book," which had facilitated exploration and conquest, could be actively used as a means of colonialist control.[4]

Education throughout the Empire was an essential part of this "plot." Where peoples had not already been murdered, their cultural identities were erased by colonialist education systems. The famous *Irish* and *Royal Readers* (and their local versions) used in both the settler-invader colonies and in India, Africa and the Caribbean, fostered Empire loyalty; lauded the superiority of the mother country in

Taken from Marc Delrez and Bénédicte Ledent (eds.), *The Contact and the Culmination* (Liège, Belgium: L3-Liège Language and Literature, 1997).

terms of everything from military might to artistic taste; and as well as being actively colonialist, these *Readers* (used for over 60 years in virtually unchanged form in, for instance, Queensland) were deeply gendered. Teaching methodologies were extremely efficient in ensuring that the values enshrined therein were "learned by heart."[5] In all these ways we have throughout the colonies examples of the metaphor of the "body in the library" – a colonial or post-colonial subjectivity which is a product of the European archive – a local body apparently "lost" to foreign textual construction and interpellation.

The contemporary Antiguan writer Jamaica Kincaid uses this metaphor to structure her wonderful indictment of European and American colonialists (the contemporary ones are the white tourists) in *A Small Place*. Acutely conscious of the (dis)placement of the Antiguan body within a British library, she addresses her murderers directly, in the second person, and deftly places their bodies under the scrutiny / erasure of the Antiguan gaze by forcing them to look at themselves through Antiguan eyes disguised as their own:

> You see a beautiful boy skimming the water, godlike, on a Windsurfer. You see an incredibly unattractive, fat, pastrylike-fleshed woman enjoying a walk on the beautiful sand, with a man, an incredibly unattractive, fat, pastrylike-fleshed man [...]. Still standing, looking out the window, you see yourself lying on the beach enjoying the amazing sun [...]. You see yourself taking a walk on that beach, you see yourself meeting new people (only they are new in a very limited way, for they are people just like you).[6]

This resistance to the contemporary tourist gaze (and historically that of the invader / colonialist) is made possible through a retrieval of a Black Antiguan perspective, which, though necessarily deeply interpellated by a European subjectivity, is distinguishable for *strategic* purposes of resistance from that of the white exploiters, both historical and contemporary. The second-person address, the clear notion of foreign imperial audience ("You did this to us" etc), facilitates the establishment of this necessary distance, and enacts a counter-colonial reversal of the textual interpellation of the colonized subject which Kincaid describes in the portrait of the black Antiguan girl reader in the library:

> You loved knowledge, and wherever you went you made sure to build a school, a library (yes, and in both of these places you distorted or erased my history and glorified your own). (p. 36).

And:

> If you saw the old library [...] the beauty of us sitting there like communicants at an altar, taking in, again and again, the fairy tale of how we met you, your right to do the things you did, how beautiful you were, are, and always will be. (p. 42).

Kincaid addresses the foreign reader not from a position of an essentialist local identity, but from one deliberately, i.e. narratively, adopted to enable her to accuse the murderers clearly and directly. In resisting the textual history of Empire she is thus able to invoke an *apparently* stable "self–other" binary. The deed was committed on the kidnapped and enslaved Afro-Antiguans by the British, in the library, with the European textual archive, the twentieth-century textbook, and the tourist brochure as continuing agents of oppression.

But the Jane Doe I began with – the overdetermined yet unidentifiable settler-invader woman – cannot so neatly classify murderer, victim and murder weapon. Nor is *she* easily identified. For in this imperial murder story she is both killer and victim; writer, reader, pupil and teacher; accessory to murder, yet often a (complicit) victim herself. Consequently settler-colony contestation of imperial textual interpellation proceeds from a deeply compromised and ambiguous position.

In one of the most important post-colonial theoretical statements of the last five years, Stephen Slemon describes "a genuine difference" in contestatory activity between second- and third-world post-colonial writing. This difference, Slemon argues, is that

> the *illusion* of a stable self / other here / there binary division has *never* been available to second world writers, and [...] as a result the sites of figural contestation between oppressor and oppressed, colonizer and colonized have been taken *inward* and *internalised* in second-world post-colonial textual practice. [...] The ambivalence of literary resistance is the "always already" condition of second-world settler and post-colonial literary writing, for in the white literatures of Australia, or New Zealand, or Canada, or Southern Africa, anti-colonialist resistance has *never* been directed at an object as a discursive structure which can be clearly seen as purely external to the self.[7]

The settler-invader "Jane Doe," the woman difficult to identify, the nature of her "crime" complex and ambiguous, has too many identities. It is the overinscription that produces the "blank" of what is often referred to as settler-invader "space" – though by "space" is meant a highly overinscribed, textually overdetermined arena. Like Caribbean or African writers such as Kincaid, Selvon, Lamming, or Achebe, settler-invader colony writers, and particularly women writers, have been conscious of the imperial and patriarchal production of their subjectivity, and of the necessity to somehow escape from or at least unmask, dismantle, and oppose it; to re-enter those texts and re-write their terms. But hampered – or perhaps energized – by their ambivalent positions within their own systems of colonialist oppression, they have found difficulty in constructing a stable – or even unstable – identity from which to re-consider the murder plot and their roles as perpetrator-victims.

Feminist criticism, too, has become increasingly aware of what Martin and Mohanty term "the instability of positions within systems of oppression."[8] For as they argue, only a conception of power that "refuses totalisations" can account for the possibility of resistance:

> The system is revealed to be not one but multiple, overlapping, intersecting systems or relations that are historically constructed and recreated through everyday practices and interaction, and that implicates the individual in contradictory ways. All that without denying the operations of actual power differences, overdetermined though they may be. Reconceptualising power without giving up the possibility of conceiving power.[9]

"Reconceptualising power without giving up the possibility of conceiving power" echoes the project of many post-colonial writers who offer various forms of literary resistance to power structures through a reconceptualization of that power. The particular kind of textual opposition I wish to explore here works in a way more closely aligned with "opposition" and "reconceptualization" than with revolution. Ross Chambers argues that

> oppositional behaviour consists of individual or group survival tactics that do not challenge the power in place, but make use of circumstances set up by that power for purposes the power may ignore or deny. It contrasts then, with revolution, which is a mode of resistance to forms of power it regards as illegitimate, that is, as a force that needs to be opposed by a counterforce.[10]

Moreover, revolutionary materialism tends to "undervalue the power of words," and in "correctly diagnosing" oppositional behaviour as "ultimately conservative" (p. 1) it fails to see that "oppositional behaviour has a particular potential to change states of affairs" by changing "people's mentalities" by altering "desire." Bakhtinian and Gramscian formulations of the counter-hegemonic ultimately "exclude the possibility of anything but either repression or cooption"; but the *oppositional* within narrative, "has characteristics that enable it, in an important sense, to elude both repression and recuperation, or more accurately, to 'maneuver' within the room that opens up between the two" (p. 3).

It is into this room – the "room for maneuver" – that I wish to drag the body of the settler-invader Jane Doe, and examine the ways in which the charting of her identity within a framework of this kind of textual oppositionality might shed new light on the old colonialist murder plot. The settler-invader woman is Martin and Mohanty's classic subject "implicated in contradictory ways" within both colonialist and patriarchal systems of oppression, "systems" which themselves are coming to seem increasingly less monolithic. And correspondingly, strategies which seek effectively to oppose and interrogate them, become increasingly protean and ambiguous.

The oppositional intertextual strategy I wish to examine here is one that might be termed "dispersive citation." Jessica Anderson's novel *Tirra Lirra by the River* has a complex intertextual relationship with Tennyson's poem "The Lady of Shalott." Although most post-colonial writing is inevitably involved in intertextual relations of one sort or another with the European archive, post-colonial textual strategies of resistance or opposition differ radically depending on the particular circumstances of their origin, production and consumption. Where George Lamming in *Water With Berries*, Jean Rhys in *Wide Sargasso Sea*, or J. M. Coetzee in *Foe* address particular European texts (and through these, of course, the whole of that discursive field within which *The Tempest*, *Jane Eyre*, or *Robinson Crusoe* were and are enmeshed in colonial and post-colonial societies) Jessica Anderson in *Tirra Lirra by the River* uses Tennyson's poem as a source of a series of linked metaphors which allow her to explore the life of an Australian woman deeply interpellated by a sense of her own (colonial) artistic inferiority and belief in the "backwardness" of her local place, but who comes at the end of her life to re-read the imperial script which constructed her and to alter her attitude to herself and her identity.

The particular dispersive citation I wish to consider in *Tirra Lirra by the River* and in Daphne Marlatt's *Ana Historic* is that of Mary Shelley's *Frankenstein*. In using the term "dispersive citation" I wish to describe a specific kind of post-colonial oppositional practice, one that is not restricted to settler-colony writing or to writing by women, but one particularly appropriate to the complex site where these positions intersect. In dispersive citation, aspects of a "canonical" text energize oppositionality and ambivalence within the *post-colonial* text, though the latter is no sense a comprehensive re-writing of the former. Instead, it seeks to use a text shared (known / imposed) throughout the empire, first to act as a reminder of the textual subjectivity of the post-colonial woman within an imperial / patriarchal framework, and secondly to offer specific narrative / metaphoric clusters that, re-cited in the post-colonial context, help designate / delimit a specifically post-colonial (and in this case settler-invader) female identity.

Mary Shelley's *Frankenstein* has been traditionally interpreted as a cataclysm caused by man's usurpation of God's role, a warning against the malignant effects of rampant (Western) technology and / or what can happen when the mothering role is taken away from women. But equally *Frankenstein*, product of a nineteenth-century imagination, can be read as a locus of imperial / colonial, and specifically settler-invader colony tropes. *Frankenstein* also is about reproduction, reproduction of the self that produces unexpectedly abhorrent "others"; as the monster himself says, "more horrid even from the very resemblance."[11] *Frankenstein* thus both destabilizes that self / other binary (which Lamming or Kincaid could mobilize) and makes self-reproduction itself a site of deep ambivalence. Moreover, the monster is created by Frankenstein out of the archive of Western technology – from books – "re-membered scientific knowledge" and from dismembered bodies. His construction takes place in the laboratory but the latter is dependent on and energized by the library – the monster is made by men's books. His own education, the way he learns language is by watching – through a glass darkly (like the Lady of Shalott, except she is incarcerated in the tower, and he is locked out of it) – the behaviour of a small family group: father, son, and daughter. His attempts to become part of this "family" always meet with disaster.

Frankenstein returns us to the image of a body in the library; to a textual subjectivity and to the ambivalence of the relations between self and other, here and there, and the problem of the settler-invader; and to the idea of the unleashing of the combined destructive technologies of books and living creatures on the rest of the world. Interestingly too, we have a patterns of persisting identification (and recoiling separation) between the monster and his creator, and a complex of family, not-family, home, and exile. Contemporary popular usage (like the patterns of analogy in Mary Shelley's novel) still conflates the monster and the scientist. In Marlatt's formulation,

> that's the trouble with Frankenstein – you have to kill him before he kills you. – Actually Frankenstein was the man who created him. Did you ever read the book? And now we call the monster by his name [...].[12]

Reproduction of the self, whether of bodies or ideas was / is the crucial technology of imperialism. Central to the idea of self-reproduction is the extension of control, whether of individual, species, or ideology. Thus notions of reproduction are focal in colonization, and related to the trope of "parenting" – the literal or metaphorical raising of "children."

Quoting a nineteenth-century manual of obstetrics cited by Mary Poovey, Gillian Whitlock has referred to the specific deployment of women's bodies for childbearing in the production of (white) settler-invader populations: "The uterus is to the Race what the heart is to the Individual: it is the organ of circulation to the species."[13] Colonization and the settler colonies in particular are thus the crucial locus of the intersection of two powerful imperial and patriarchal technologies. The very *production* of (white) children and their education within the framework of imperial ideology signal the destruction of the indigenous peoples whose capture and "naturalization" within a European textual archive, itself complicit in their conquest and colonization (or the source of their enslavement and transportation), are also effected. Bodies and libraries again.

A positive presentation of parenting and parenthood lay at the heart of the rhetoric of empire, even if, like Frankenstein, the mother country was sometimes appalled by the settler-colony monster children she had produced. "I am your mother and your father" was the missionary rhetoric whose standard slippage in India, Africa, and the Caribbean was from God to Queen Victoria and the British government. The white children of empire, the settler-invader populations, looked to the mother country for protection, guidance, sustenance and for the memory of a cultural / ancestral past. (A parent, in Margaret Mead's definition, is someone who remembers what you did yesterday.) All the countries of the Empire were part of one great "family," sisters and brothers of the same mother who "remembered" yesterday, even if, as in most families, some children were definitely preferred to others. This sentimental, powerful, and persisting figuration and rhetoric of Empire and the family – mothers and fathers, parents and children – masked the destructiveness of conquest and the continuing colonization of indigenous peoples – the literal destruction of their cultural groupings and familial arrangements; and in the settler colonies it masked a continuing geno-cide that was the inevitable result of the spread of European-descent populations and their usurpation of indigenous lands. As far as the white settlers were concerned, the rhetoric fostered infantilism, encouraged dependence, and inculcated a deep sense of inferiority – the so-called "cultural cringe." Within empire and colonization, then, parenthood and family are the loci of deep ambivalence.

On the one hand we are as a species, though to varying degrees in different cultures, educated / conditioned to believe that reproducing ourselves, producing human babies is a good thing – a source of joy, promise, possibility, life against death, a future. As we put band-aids on world pollution and destruction of the planet we prefer not to think or at least talk about its root cause – too many people. It is easier, and definitely more acceptable, to blame local corruption in the Water Board, industrial emissions, capitalism, or communism. But slowly, in the modern world, the idea of choosing to produce children is becoming less axiomatically a positive one. Within the discourse of Empire, which produces a positive rhetoric of identity, home and safety through tropes of parents and family (while sponsoring genocide and / or cultural and social inferiority) re-production is also associated with re-production of culture through the deployment and fetishization of the British book.[14] Using the trope of parenting / production of the text *and* of bodies and their ambivalent position in *Frankenstein* and colonialist discourse generally, I wish to move now to a consideration of the dispersive citation of *Frankenstein* in Jessica Anderson's *Tirra Lirra by the River* and Daphne Marlatt's *Ana Historic*.

Like *Frankenstein* and *Ana Historic*, Anderson's novel interrogates notions of family and home in terms of both patriarchy and imperialism, and the pervasive tropes which connect it to *Frankenstein* and the "body in the library" are those of re / membering and dis / membering.

In Nora Porteous's re-reading of her life, which is a process of remembering (one which, significantly, is not presented chronologically, but is instead related to degrees of emotional intensity and the "free spin" of her "globe of memory,"[15]) there are two particularly important revelations. These memories have, however, been rendered cryptic for much of her life. The first is Nora's re-membering of her father and her grief at his death; the second is Dorothy Rainbow's dis-membering of her husband and children and her subsequent suicide.

Throughout her life Nora has been disturbed by the memory of a helmet and a plume, one that evokes mixed emotions of promise, excitement, romance, but which also provokes inexplicable grief. She has always associated this image / memory with her infatuation with the idea of Sir Lancelot in Tennyson's poem "The Lady of Shalott," a poem, and Lancelot in particular, associated with the romantic promise of the ideal male, and for the colonial reader, with the romance of the motherland, England. The internalization of these dreams / ideals, i.e. the Anglo-written world of patriarchy and imperialism, have emotionally and imaginatively severed Nora from her childhood place in the Australian city of Brisbane, and from her own body. This dissociation from her body through the colonial idealization of the Anglo-written, and her quest for "romance" in the "motherland" culminate ironically in the abortion performed by the deranged misogynist English doctor in London, and in the later coda of the failed facelift. After the abortion Nora never has sex again, and the facelift is a testament to the vacating of a body which becomes something to be seen, something constructed and reconstructed from the outside; not something to be or be in.

It is on her return to Brisbane that her body is to some extent re-membered, and it is significant that it should be a sudden and painful memory of her father's legs, just the legs, as they climb the stairs, which begins the recuperation of the repressed memory of his funeral and the extent of her own wild grief. The plumes of Lancelot are re-membered as those on the curbed horses at her father's funeral, and the ideal male promise, and the colonial's ideal world of England, the motherland, are associatively remembered now as death. But the re-reading of this persistent memory is a prelude to reconciliation, not just with the lost body of the father and her own, but with the Australian landscape and culture. The re-membering of the death of the father signals for Nora the culmination of a process of coming to terms with the prior construction of her home city, Brisbane, within settler colonialist discourse as "a backward, unworldly place." When she finds what she refers to as "the real river" at last, she has not literally *seen* it. What she means is that she has re-read (revised) her former Anglo-dictated reading of the colonial landscape as inferior.

On the way back from her attempt to find Mrs Partridge's house, Nora is "attacked" by a *Monsterio*. "In my day," she tells the Custs, "plants weren't so tropical."

"Everybody grows those things now," Jack Cust tells her, and he contrasts this with those earlier years when "the old people fought the place" (p. 139) by importing and growing English flowers and trees. Nora may still construct herself here as having been "attacked" by the tropical *Monsterio*, but she too now re-reads the landscape not through Tennyson and a "flaw in the cheap glass" but through a palimpsestic discourse of the local.[16] And like the body of the father and the memory of his death, the recuperation of local possibility is associated with re-membering, dis-membering, and the ambiguity of "monsterdom." The full species name of the plant is *Monsterio deliciosa* – a delicious tropical "monster" recuperated from the Anglo-written and from settler-invader horticultural practice.

But the direct reference to *Frankenstein* in *Tirra Lirra by the River* occurs not in the context of the re-membering of the body of the father or the retrieval of the local landscape and its "monstrous" vegetation, but in relation to Dorothy Rainbow, whose dismembering of her husband and children with an axe has left only one child alive, Dr Gordon Rainbow who attends Nora when she has pneumonia. Gordon is described by Nora to her friends at "Number 6" early in the novel as "*an enormous glum doctor on the model of Frankenstein's monster*" (p. 31). In this representation of Gordon Rainbow, she is still deeply influenced by the tone and mode of conversation (and self-representation) at "Number 6," and this Anglo-construction of the colonial self and society for an English audience is one from which Nora on her return to Brisbane progressively withdraws. But at this point I want to consider not this idea of an English audience, but the context within which the further dispersive citation of *Frankenstein* occurs in the novel, in connection with the "monsterdom" of Dorothy Rainbow, whose murders and suicide are not known to Nora when Dr Rainbow first attends her.

Dorothy Rainbow is the figure who erupts into the text, threatening the symmetry of the Australia / Britain, settler-invader colony / imperial power relations that the rest of the text explores. She is said to have Polynesian blood, and anyone of that particular ancestry settled in Brisbane invokes the brutal history of "blackbirding," the kidnapping and enslavement during the nineteenth and early twentieth century of Pacific Island peoples to provide labour for Queensland sugar plantations. Like the Squamish in Marlatt's text, Dorothy Rainbow serves as a striking reminder of that other face of settler-invasion: the monstrousness of its destruction of indigenous peoples, and in this particular case, the enslavement and transportation of "native" labour in the cause of colonial settlement and eventual cultural / economic independence from the imperial motherland.

But although Dorothy Rainbow is thus a marker of radical "difference" in *Tirra Lirra by the River*, she is also persistently *associated* with Nora, most notably through their habit of walking the streets, and their criss-crossing paths around the suburb are suggestive of a palimpsest. In terms of this analogue the novel thus invites a palimpsestic reading (and later re-reading) of the text of locality on which another story is told, a story or indeed stories similar to those explored in Minnie Bruce Pratt's paradigmatic description of "home" in "Identity: Skin, Blood, Heart" as the conscious retrieval of a variety of occluded oppressions.[17]

In *Tirra Lirra by the River*, Dorothy Rainbow is reported by Nora's sister Grace to be thoroughly assimilated within the white suburban middle-class community. She marries "a good solid man" who works at the bank, and has a number of children. Mother, not Other. It is some time after she returns to Brisbane that Nora learns of Dorothy Rainbow's "monstrous" murder of her husband and family and her subsequent killing of herself. Significantly, Grace had written to Nora in London about this, but within the complex patterns of similarity and difference drawn between Nora and Dorothy, Nora destroys this particular letter without reading it because she too is planning to commit suicide after the failed facelift. In London, the motherland, the centre of empire, she burns Dorothy's "story" without reading it, subconsciously rejecting the disruption of "mother" by the "monstrousness" of "other." Nora is however forced to confront this on her return to Brisbane, when, erupting into her remembering process, it disturbs the idea of an unproblematic transfer of English middle-class values and mores to Australian territory. The settler-invader child of the imperial family in the "new" world is revealed / re-read not as the locus of safety, but as the heartland of destruction and disruption, the volcanic site of intersecting oppressions.

Moreover, to the extent that Dorothy is both Nora's "other" and yet her double, her "alter / native," she situates the settler-invader woman on that ambiguous terrain between mother and other. *Tirra Lirra by the River* explores the ambivalent nature of monstrousness with which Marlatt's text also engages. The murders Dorothy Rainbow commits may be monstrous, but like Shelley's monster's killings, they are the inevitable result of the monstrous crimes of their creators. Empire and patriarchy wield the axe which kills all but one of the Rainbow children, while the survivor, Gordon, *Dr* Gordon Rainbow, is associated in the text with both Dr Frankenstein, and with the monster through Nora's description of him. He remains the surviving product of a scientific, imperial and patriarchical dialectics in which, like settler-colony women, he is both perpetrator and victim, doctor and patient.

Dorothy's name "Rainbow," like that of the *Monsterio deliciosa*, suggests the protean and ambivalent role of monstrousness in the settler-invader and female contexts. Nora's re-reading of the text of her own life, her remembering, is also a drift away from what now appears as the constraints of an English (and in the case of Fred, misogynist) audience at Number 6. The rather arch and deliberately literary reference to Gordon Rainbow as Frankenstein's monster, gives place in the text to a re-reading of "monstrousness" in the very different post-colonial context, and Mary Shelley's novel is much more ambivalently (and less self-consciously) and automatically invoked, as Nora now reconstructs herself for herself, and not for an English audience.

For Marlatt in *Ana Historic* women have been captured within the patriarchal text, overinscribed, yet "blank." Preoccupied – in the male view – with things of the flesh, women are (ironically) deprived of their bodies within patriarchal discourse.

> "(Her body) is a burden: worn away in service to the species, bleeding each month, proliferating passively, it is not for her a pure instrument for getting a grip on the world but an opaque physical presence; it is no certain source of pleasure and it creates lacerating pains; it contains menaces; woman feels endangered by her 'insides'."

a woman of your generation wrote that, Ina, in a country where birth control was illegal, but i think it was true for you too, to some extent for all of us, perhaps that explains why our writing, which we also live inside of, is different from men's and not a tool, not a "pure instrument for getting a grip on the world." "it contains menaces," traps, pitfalls – i stop at the word "our" and think of yours, how it hurts to think of your "scribblings" under the bed (the bed!) in a language which was not yours. (p. 133)

Marlatt links body and text throughout *Ana Historic*, and her purpose is the revival of the "dead" female body in the patriarchal library, a body with its *own* script, its own active and sacred text; and its ability to produce a child as part of this revival / reinscription is crucial. But Marlatt is aware not only of the implications of white birthing in settler colonies – first white child born . . . last indigenous child born – but of the destructive potential of all writing / reproduction including that by women, whether with the body or through hand to pen. The Woods, the great woods are felled to produce settler family homes, and timber, and the paper on which Mrs Richards writes. And even if women's writing is, in Marlatt's important distinction, less "instrumental" than that of men, there is still a problem of (re)producing white bodies and (white) writing. One retrieval, that of women's bodies from patriarchal script, threatens to erase the indigenous text.

As in *Tirra Lirra by the River* the problems of the intersection of women and the oppression of the indigenes only briefly surfaces in *Ana Historic* – in neither text is it focal. But what each novel does do, and Marlatt's in particular, is to re-read the imperial and patriarchal scripts to unlock the conflation / confusion of creator and creation, of Frankenstein and the monster; to see "text" and producer of "text" as separate if always / already interconnected. This allows "the monster" (and the notion of monstrousness) much greater "room for maneuver" – the monster can be separated from her / his mode of imperial / patriarchal construction and re-cited within her / his own narrative and under her / his terms.

Frankenstein appears first in Marlatt's text in relation to Anne's (f)actual recreation of Mrs Richards:

When she turned she could see the mountains behind her hanging close, close and yet aloof. Beautiful, she thought, or perilous, but not pretty. Well-versed in the Romantics, she had arrived with images of the Alps inside her eyes. Yet she knew this was not Europe and Mary Shelley's monster would never speak his loneliness here. (pp. 15–16)

This environment is thus different; what is "inside her eyes" – the European text of foreign woods, of "other" worlds inhabited by monsters (monsters of its own creation / fear) – will not provide the key to read / write this landscape. Annie's mother Ina, and Annie's husband Richard still, however, have that text "inside their eyes" and they read the "new" world culture and landscape by it. And it is new ways of seeing as well as ways of reading and writing that *Ana Historic* investigates.

Imperial technologies – the book, and child production – depend for both their conception and their colonialist effectivity on a series of interconnected and powerful binaries: self/other; domestic/wild; child/parent; mind/body; writer/reader; author/ audience. Together these plot the trajectory of imperialist domination, and these are the binaries *Ana Historic* destabilizes. In Marlatt's novel, the passage "A man's name for man's fear of the wild" continues, "That's where *she* lives." Monster – a man's name for man's fear of the wild, the other, the undomesticated; that which has not been contained or captured, like Annie's mother Ina to the confinement of children and family. (In the case of Annie's mother, this "confinement" leads to institutional incarceration and electric shock treatment, an obscene attempt at re-animation of the dis/membered woman within patriarchy and medical "science" that is both parodic of and paralleled by Shelley's monster's electrification.) But as Shelley's *Frankenstein* demonstrates, this fear of the wild is the fear of one's own creation – of something, then, within oneself – "more horrid from the very resemblance," or as Marlow expresses his fear of the Africans in Conrad's *Heart of Darkness*, "what thrilled you was just the thought of their humanity – like yours – [...]. Ugly."[18] Empire and colonization, a series of confrontations between Euro-domesticity and its own construction of the wild, what was "inside its (own) eyes" became "the horror, the horror" of Conrad's widely-travelled classic, the monstrousness that might lurk (reproductively) within the European heart but whose existence and origin must be projected "out there."

In writing this monstrousness for their *European* audiences, however, both Shelley and Conrad domesticate that horror through a series of frames which filter the adventure / narrative of their protagonists, Marlow and Frankenstein. In the linear trajectories of their journeys, the troubling encounter is with the near-self, even though the binaries of self–other have to remain axiomatic (or the resemblance would not be disturbing). That potential boundary dislocation is at least partially "domesticated" through the device of a series of sterilizing chambers or narrative frames which act to facilitate its presentation to solid, middle-class European citizens, in particular to women – Walton's sister, Kurtz's intended – who thus also serve as filtering framing devices. These are the women who stayed at "home," and they provide an analogy for the "domestic" audience to whom the men tell their stories of "wilderness" and adventure which lie beyond the realm of the Euro-domestic. For Marlow women were "out of it, and rightly so"; Walton's sister is simply the audience for his narrative, and they provide safe familiar contexts through which, in Marlatt's words, "man's fear of the wild" might be domesticated, the brush with the terrible possibility of the collapse of the self / other binary apparently contained – "self and other" safely transposed into "home and mother." But if "the wild" is where, as *Ana Historic* claims, "*she* lives," the recuperation of women's bodies, the writing by women "out of the blank" in the settler colony situation involves a removal of the "safety net" of such frames and an embracing of the "monstrous" possibilities of wildness in a world *potentially* outside Euro-patriarchy. Both Anderson and Marlatt invoke that potential through strategies which erode the distinctions between European settler-invaders and their racial "Others" (Mrs Richards's mis-reading of the Squamish; the analogical patterns established between Nora Porteous and Dorothy Rainbow) but for Marlatt this embracing of otherness is largely played out in textual terms, with the annihilation of the distance between writer and reader; text and body; one body writing/reading another. And the instrumental linear trajectory of the male/imperial/textual adventure is deliberately fragmented. The author/ity of his/tory is re-placed by the cyclical interplay of fictional shapes and cycles. Thus the once passive female recipient "frame" of male history/adventure becomes the active *re/* reader and writer.

> When she let herself out of the house it was night – it was moonlight and briars, it was the fascination of desire for what lay out of bounds. not Frankenstein but the touch of the terrible, what she had only imagined her sister saw. God there in the burnt out orchard in the woods. to come back and say she had seen them, this scarred face with the scary eyes, His inhuman head, to touch and run back home-free. it wasn't even the game (or that she was) – it was knowing where the real began under the words that pretended something else. (p. 77)

The text of and by the female body is the identity / place found "under the words that pretended something else" in an active re-reading of those earlier scripts. But again the writing, like the parenting, is not presented as an unqualified positive. Mrs Richards:

> I try again – It seems no foot, or none other than mine, disturbs the living intimacy of these Ferns and small Bushes, the roots of enormous Trees going down into – its brackish waters erode the eye – "Tis a nameless colour as if stained by the Trees themselves darker than tea. [...] those enormous Trees with their capital letter. a colour no word can convey. i lean over her shoulder as she tries, as she doubts: why write at all? why not leave the place as wordless as she finds it? because there is 'into –'? what? frightening proposition. into the unspoken urge of a body insisting itself in the words. (p. 46)

When Zoe suggests the possibility of a lesbian relationship between Mrs Richards and Birdie Stewart, it seems to Annie a "monstrous leap of the imagination" (p. 135). "So be monstrous, then," Zoe says. In the last pages of the novel it is the relationship between Annie and Zoe which embodies the rebirth of a textual possibility that collapses rather than depends on binary distinctions of self/other, body/mind, writer/reader. And the non-linear, but fragmented nature of the text not only devolves fiction into history (or herstory) and his/story into fiction, but rejects that instrumental trajectory of the European text. Though the female body, including its amazing capability to produce children, is celebrated, the sites of parenting, whether of texts or of children, do not go uninterrogated. Marlatt negotiates in a complex and humane novel some of the difficulties of the intersecting, overlapping and contradictory oppressions involved in imperialism, patriarchy and the settler-invader experience.

If *Frankenstein* in Barbara Johnson's formulation was a novel which anatomized the "monstrousness" of the production of the female text, Marlatt's *Ana Historic* dispersively recites *Frankenstein* to recuperate the dismembered female body from its incarceration and/or erasure in male textuality and its implication in imperialist technologies. But although there are seven or eight references to Frankenstein in the text, "he" (the conflated male creator and his creation; God; the patriarchal text) is always somewhat elusive, absent: "Frankenstein would not speak his loneliness here"; "this was not Frankenstein [...]"; "it isn't even Frankenstein but a nameless part I know" and so on. While, then, a positive monsterdom is recuperated *from* "a man's name for man's fear of the wild" for an assertive female corporeality, Marlatt avoids the charge of reinscribing (teaching) and thus recuperating a European text in a post-colonial context. Instead, Euro-patriarchal narrative is dis/mantled by the female body/text, and writing becomes a practice of re-reading and of dispersive citation. "We give the place, giving words, giving birth, to each other – she and me [...] the reach of your desire, reading us into the page ahead" (p. 153). Out of the library/archive into the female settler-wild, into the life of the body.

NOTES

1 *Who is She?*, ed. by Shirley Walker (St Lucia: University of Queensland Press, 1983).
2 H. M. Stanley, *The Congo and the Founding of its Free State* (New York: Harper, 1885), p. 162.
3 Gauri Viswanathan, "The Beginnings of English Literary Study in British India," *Oxford Literary Review*, 9.1 & 2 (1987), 27–58.
4 Viswanathan has examined the ways in which not just texts in general – histories, explorers' diaries, anthropologies, government records – but focally, literature and literary criticism were deliberately put to service by the British Government in India to produce, in Macaulay's now infamous terms, "a class of persons Indian in blood and colour; but English in taste, in opinions, in morals and in intellect." Thomas B. Macaulay, "Indian Education Minute of 2nd February, 1835," in *Macaulay Prose and Poetry*, ed. by G. M. Young (London: Rupert Hart-Davis, 1952), p. 729.
5 See Harold Coward, *Sacred Word, Sacred Text: Scripture in World Religions* (New York: Orbis, 1988) for further discussion of the significance of "learning by heart."
6 Jamaica Kincaid, *A Small Place* (London: Virago, 1988), p. 13. Further references to this edition are given in the text.
7 Stephen Slemon, "Unsettling the Empire: Resistance Theory for the Second World," *World Literature Written in English*, 30.2 (1990), 38.
8 Biddy Martin and Chandra Talpade Mohanty, "Feminist Politics: What's Home Got to Do With It?," in *Feminist Studies / Critical Studies*, ed. by Teresa de Lauretis (Bloomington: Indiana, 1986), pp. 191–212 (p. 209).
9 "Feminist Politics," p. 209.
10 Ross Chambers, *Room for Maneuver: Reading the Oppositional in Narrative* (Chicago: University of Chicago Press, 1990), p. 1. Further references to this edition are given in the text.
11 Mary W. Shelley, *Frankenstein* (London: Dent, Everyman's Library, 1963), p. 136.
12 Daphne Marlatt, *Ana Historic* (Toronto: Coach House, 1988), p. 142. Further references to this edition are given in the text.
13 The quotation is from W. Tyler Smith's *Manual of Obstetrics* cited in Mary Poovey, *Uneven Development: The Ideological Work of Gender in Mid-Victorian England* (London: Virago, 1989), p. 35.
14 In Barbara Johnson's intricate argument about Mary Shelley's text, *Frankenstein* becomes a critique of the reproduction of the self – and the "monstrousness" of woman's production of text. Barbara Johnson, "My Monster / My Self," *Diacritics*, 12 (1982), 2–10.
15 Jessica Anderson, *Tirra Lirra by the River* (Ringwood, Vic: Penguin, 1984), p. 140. Further references to this edition are given in the text.
16 See Elizabeth Ferrier, "Mapping the Space of the Other: Transformations of Space in Post-colonial Fiction and Postmodern Theory" (unpublished dissertation, University of Queensland, 1990), pp. 115–36, for an extended discussion of "the discourse of the local."

17   See Minnie Bruce Pratt, "Identity: Skin, Blood, Heart," in *Yours in Struggle: Three Feminist Perspectives on Anti-Semitism and Racism*, ed. by Elly Bulkin, Minnie Bruce Pratt, and Barbara Smith (Brooklyn, NY: Long Haul Press, 1984), pp. 11–63.

18   Joseph Conrad, *Heart of Darkness* (1902; Harmondsworth: Penguin, 1973), p. 51.

Out of the Center: Thoughts on the Post-colonial Literatures of Australia and New Zealand

Ralph J. Crane

Ralph J. Crane has written on Indian and Irish writers and in this essay he reflects on the characteristics of postcolonial literatures in Australia and New Zealand. Like **Simon Slemon**, Crane is concerned with the position of such literatures with respect to the metropolitan tradition in England. Crane notes that much of the early literature in Australia and New Zealand was written by European colonizers, and fears that because of this tradition of privileging the metropolitan center over the periphery a literature of "homogenized 'cosmopolitan Anglocentrism' " is likely to evolve. Of particular importance is Crane's discussion of the periods of nationalism during which an indigeneous literature begins to arise. But this literature does not address the issues of postcolonialism that we see in other regions, in large measure because Australia and New Zealand, though accepted as postcolonial countries, are not postcolonial in the sense that the colonial rulers have left or relinquished power. Crane's analysis might be read alongside **Slemon**'s in order to gain a fuller understanding of the problem of postcolonialism, particularly with respect to the role of indigenous peoples in constituting an "authentic" postcolonial literature. The student might then compare Crane's and **Slemon**'s analyses of settler-colony (or "Commonwealth") experiences with the kind of Caribbean experiences described by **Stuart Hall** and **Peter Hulme**.

Out of the Center: Thoughts on the Post-colonial Literatures of Australia and New Zealand

INTRODUCTION

"Post-colonial literature" is now the accepted designation for what has in the past been referred to as "commonwealth literature" and the "new literatures in English." But while this term may be politically correct, it is not without its problems: the inclusiveness of the term has left it vulnerably vague and imprecise. The national identities of the various literatures gathered under the all-embracing post-colonial banner seem to emphasize diversity rather than homogeneity. Yet there is enough commonality to allow the myriad national literatures to be fruitfully considered alongside one another. That commonality is, of course, tied to the shared experience of colonization and the emergent interest in the effects of colonialism, an interest in the experience of the post-colonial condition itself. This is mediated in the various uses of the language of the colonial power, and language is the ultimate tool of colonialism, which has in turn been successfully colonized by the margins – as even a cursory glance in the direction of West Indian poetry shows. Or as Ian Wedde pleads in his introduction to *The Penguin Book of New Zealand Verse*. "The History of a literature with colonial origins is involuntarily written *by* the language into its location, to the point where English as an international language can be felt to be original *where it is*" (23). Alan Riach suggests that the converse may be as true, too – that as the international language of domination and exploitation English is the ultimate symbol of the colonial process, and that it is a perpetual foreigner (70).

The literatures of Australia and New Zealand are both distinct in themselves, yet indistinct enough from each other to make the homogenizing term "Australasian Literature" a useful if not always a desirable one. Whether or not one wishes to accept the notion of a federated literature, the literatures of the two countries share enough in common to warrant their parallel consideration in this essay. I'm thinking here of their common settler culture, their shared language question, and their similar relationship to the two major literary movements, Romanticism and Modernism.

What follows is a brief and inevitably incomplete historical survey of the gradual shift from a colonial to post-colonial consciousness in the literatures of Australia and New Zealand.

Taken from Radhika Mohanram and Gita Rajan (eds.), *English Postcoloniality: Literatures from around the World* (Westport, CT: Greenwood Publishing, 1996).

ABSENT SIGNIFIERS AND SIGNIFICANT ABSENCES: THE COLONIAL CONDITION

Early Australian and New Zealand literature (leaving aside the oral literatures of the aboriginal peoples of Australia and the Maori in New Zealand for the moment) inevitably came from the pens of the colonizers. As elsewhere, the writers whose hands directed those pens frequently sought to explain their new environments through references to the homes they had left behind. In New Zealand Edward Tregear's poem "Te Whetu Plains" is an example of this:

> All still, all silent, 'tis a songless land,
>   That hears no music of the nightingale,
> No sound of waters falling lone and grand
>   Through sighing forests to the lower vale,
>   No whisper in the grass, so wan, and grey, and pale. (O'Sullivan, 1)

This stanza illustrates the way the poem laments an absent landscape instead of celebrating the present one; the land, of course, would not have been silent, but it would have been without the familiar birdsong of the center, which for the poet effectively renders the land songless. Similarly, in Australia there was much nostalgia and sentimental longing for the center evident in the poetry of the mid-nineteenth century, and even though the subjects of the poems were often inspired by the Australian landscape, the form and style of the poetry were distinctly English – as is the case, for example, with Henry Kendall's "The Rain Comes Sobbing to the Door." Poets like Kendall and his contemporary Adam Lindsay Gordon failed to find a distinctly Australian voice in their verse, and instead succeeded only in mimicking the narrative and lyrical poetry of the center. In other words, in the early colonial poetry of Australia and New Zealand the center was privileged over the periphery to the extent that Australia and New Zealand are effectively absent, while Britain is omnipresent. Or at least discrete parts of it are. While the literatures of Australia and New Zealand are not yet post-colonial literatures, they are already the literatures of dispossessed people, but rapidly evolving into the literature of a homogenized "cosmopolitan Anglocentrism."

In much of the early convict prose fiction of Australia, like James Tucker's *Ralph Rashleigh* (probably written 1844–5, first published in 1929), in which the convict system is described in all its horrific detail, there is none of the explicit criticism of the center, which is such a common trait of revisionist historical fiction and post-colonial literatures in general today. Tucker, a privileged convict at the Port Macquarie penal settlement when he wrote the novel, was in some respects writing as the "plaything" of the colonial power. But there is explicit criticism of the convict system, and by extension the center, in what is perhaps the best-known Australian convict novel, Marcus Clarke's *For the Term of His Natural Life* (revised and first published in book form in 1874). Meanwhile, across the Tasman, what Lawrence Jones labels "Pioneer" or "Early Colonial" literature (107) – which includes the first novel published in New Zealand, Henry Butler Stoney's *Taranaki: A Tale of the War* (1861) – for the most part set out to celebrate the pioneer experience, and was often heavy with pro-colonial values.

In short fiction of this period the pioneer spirit was likewise celebrated, and much of merit to be found in Australia and New Zealand had British origins. But this colonial myopia, while apparent in a great many novels and short stories of the time, was by no means universal. In his convict tales William Astley (who wrote under the name Price Warung) set out to expose the evil and injustice of the convict system. In the satiric story "Parson Ford's Confessional" (1892), to cite just one example, it is clear that the colony of Tasmania is populated by rogues, and that the greatest rogues are not the convicts, but those who govern the colony.

Also noticeable in the poetry and prose of the early colonial period is the manner in which the indigenous peoples are frequently represented as savage, and entirely lacking in the work ethic so prized by the colonists. Although their customs are sometimes described, as in Tucker's *Ralph Rashleigh* or the New Zealand novel *Te Rou; or, The Maori at Home* (1874) by John White, Aborigines and Maori are often portrayed as Other in a way which was designed to highlight (by contrast) the noble qualities of the invaders.

The literature of this period, in European terms, was entirely the product of the settler culture. In Australia and New Zealand there had been a tradition of oral literature dating back to well before the arrival of the European invaders; but unlike some of the other colonies, notably India, there had been no tradition of written literature. Consequently, whereas in countries like India the educated upper classes began at an early stage to write in the language of the colonizers, and to contribute to the body of colonial and post-colonial literatures, this stage only took place much later in Australia and New Zealand, and as a result Aboriginal and Maori literatures in English are largely without that early body of work which sought to mimic the center at the expense of its own identity.

Nationalist Traditions and Beyond: Breaking Away From the Center

Periods of nationalism, in the 1890s in Australia and four decades later in the 1930s in New Zealand, marked the beginning of a rejection of the predominantly Anglo-centric perceptions of the two countries that had previously characterized Australian literature. Instead the focus was shifted to the internal (but not necessarily indigenous) cultures of the two antipodean countries. In Australia this frequently manifested itself in celebrations of the land and its people without recourse to the previously defining Anglo- or Eurocentrism, while in New Zealand it began the slow process of reinterpreting the country as a Pacific island. The earlier move toward a national identity in Australian literature probably has much to do with the considerable percentage of convicts and otherwise dispossessed people who inhabited the country and bore little love for the English center, while in New Zealand the free settlers who made up the majority of New Zealand's early European population had less cause to reject the Anglocentric hegemony that had fed rather than starved them.

In Australia the Sydney *Bulletin* under the guidance of J. F. Archibald and A. G. Stephens was instrumental in taking the first faltering steps towards the creation of a distinctly national Australian literature and the hand-in-hand rejection of the center. Other important early steps on the path toward what we now refer to as post-colonial literature can be seen in the poetry of Henry Lawson, in the stories of Barbara Baynton, and in novels like Louis Stone's *Jonah* (1911), in which an authentic Australian urban landscape is inhabited by characters like the larrikin Jonah who are convincing Australian, rather than colonial, types. Baynton's stories are particularly interesting in the context of this essay. A story like "Billy Skywonkie," in which the bush itself appears to bring out the brutal racial and sexual discrimination which confront the unnamed female protagonist when she journeys to the "Never-Never," anticipates some essential post-colonial concerns.

This move away from the center toward an identifiable Australian (post-colonial) literature was continued in, for example, the work of the poet Mary Gilmore, and later in the work of the "Jindyworobaks," the group of poets who are frequently associated with a second phase of Australian nationalism which began in the 1930s. In the work of these poets an interest in Aboriginal culture and the environment came to the fore, and perhaps paved the way for an understanding of the grim realities of white settlement in Australia which was to come in later Australian literature.

In the 1930s, across the Tasman Sea in New Zealand the Auckland University College student literary magazine *Phoenix* and the writers associated with it – including the poets Allen Curnow, A. R. D. Fairburn, and Denis Glover, who became known as the *Phoenix* generation – set out to foster a recognizable *New Zealand* literature. The same motivation was also behind the journal *Landfall*, launched fifteen years later, in 1947, under the editorship of Charles Brasch. Though nationalist in intent, the New Zealand writers of this generation were nevertheless essentially Anglocentric in their outlook, borrowing many of their ideas from the center they were supposedly rejecting, as their identification with the poets of the Pylon School – principally W. H. Auden, Cecil Day-Lewis, Louis MacNeice, and Stephen Spender – illustrates. Another writer who did not seem to be interested in subscribing to a national literary tradition was John Mulgan. Nevertheless, his novel *Man Alone* (1939) is widely regarded as a founding novel in the New Zealand canon, one which set out to show the country as it really was, and one which deliberately challenged the cozy romanticism of Anglophile New Zealand writers of the previous generation like his own father, Alan Mulgan. The stories of Frank Sargeson, taken together, also present a remarkable picture of New Zealand, inhabited by distinctly New Zealand characters.

Although Australia and New Zealand are generally accepted as post-colonial countries (despite the fact that in neither country has the colonizing power left or in any real fashion relinquished the power acquired by invasion), much of the fiction produced by Australian and New Zealand writers does not address post-colonial issues. There is a well-nourished body of fiction in both countries which deals with universal themes such as human relationships (the novels of Elizabeth Jolley or Maurice Gee, for example), and other various aspects of contemporary society – the drug culture, as in Helen Garner's *Monkey Grip* (1977), French nuclear testing in the Pacific, which is the subject of Maurice Shadbolt's *Danger Zone* (1975), and so on. These books are only to be considered as post-colonial in the sense that they are written *out of* this condition. In fact much contemporary Australian and New Zealand fiction has more in common with contemporary American fiction than South American or West African fiction. The New Zealand poet and novelist Ian Wedde, for example, has as much in common with, say, the American writer William Gaddis as he does with the Nigerian writer Ben Okri. Nevertheless, there is also an equally well-nurtured body of fiction in each country that *does* confront the post-colonial condition, that does challenge the beast.

The Nature of Post-coloniality in Australia and New Zealand

In post-colonial discourses the center-periphery model has provided a useful framework for exploring the relationship between the ex-colonial power and an ex-colony. In the "settler colonies" like Australia and New Zealand the challenge to the center has often manifested itself in the form of revisionist historical fiction, which, in reinterpreting history, either by taking the perspective of the periphery or by including the perspective of the periphery, effectively challenges or subverts the hegemonical center. In Australia writers like Thomas Keneally in novels such as *The Chant of Jimmie Blacksmith* (1972) and *The Playmaker* (1987), Mudrooroo Narogin (formerly Colin Johnson) in *Doctor Wooreddy's Perscription for Enduring the Ending of the World* (1983), and Kate Grenville in *Joan Makes History* (1988) – which challenges the patriarchal perspective of history – to choose some diverse examples, have successfully used historical fiction to write back to the center. Similarly in New Zealand, writers like Maurice Shadbolt, in his trilogy of the New Zealand Wars, *Season of the Jew* (1986), *Monday's Warriors* (1990), and *The House of Strife* (1993), and Witi Ihimaera in *The Matriarch* (1986) have used historical fiction to challenge the hegemony of the center. But in both countries historical fiction which has challenged the center and given voice to the previously silenced periphery has constructed a further periphery-center dichotomy in itself, and in this context, it has often failed to give adequate voice to the other. Indeed, as Joanne Tompkins explains, white literature in Australia and New Zealand has often only included indigenous versions of history for the purpose of humor (485). In some respects the historical situation in the settler colonies has meant that the center, rather than becoming the ex-colonial power, has been absorbed into the periphery, pushing the indigenous peoples, the Aborigines and the Maori, into what is effectively an outer periphery.

Central to the literature of this outer periphery is the desire to reclaim the histories of the indigenous peoples, and to educate non-indigenous readers about Aboriginal and Maori cultures. And herein lies the major difference between the post-colonial literatures of the "settler colonies," (including South Africa) and the post-colonial literatures of the "non-settler colonies." While it may be convincingly argued that white Australian writers and Pakeha writers in New Zealand do write back to the center, they do so from the privileged position of the settler, whereas indigenous writers are frequently not writing back to the absent (British) center so much as writing back to this present and dominant "settler cultures," which have maintained a Eurocentric perspective at the expense of a deliberately muted indigenous one.

Recovering silenced indigenous histories is a central concern of much Aboriginal literature in Australia and Maori literature in New Zealand. Traditionally history has been told from the perspective of the colonizers, deliberately denying colonized or indigenous peoples their place as a consequence. In *Doctor Wooreddy's Perscription for*

Enduring the Ending of the World and *The Matriarch* (to continue with the same examples) Mudrooroo Narogin and Witi Ihimaera deliberately set out to "recapture our history and culture," as Mudrooroo Narogin explains in the essay "White Forms, Aboriginal Content" (29). They also set out to expose the lies of history sanctified by the center, as a telling passage from *The Matriarch* illustrates:

> All New Zealand schoolchildren were taught about Captain James Cook's discovery of New Zealand and his historic landfall at Poverty Bay in the *Endeavour* in October 1769. They are told that the event was quite glorious – that a lad at the masthead shouted "Land Ahoy!" at 2 p.m. on 7 October 1769, a curly-headed youth after whom the landform that he had sighted, Young Nick's Head, was named. They are asked to imagine the sight as the *Endeavour* anchored off the mouth of the Turanganui River. They are told, to some amusement, that the reaction of the Maori people on shore was one of awe for the huge white bird, the floating island, and the multicoloured gods who had come on the bird. Ah yes, the stuff of romance indeed!
>
> But what the schoolchildren are not told is that Cook's first landing was marked by the killing of a Maori called Te Maro, shot through the heart by a musket bullet, Monday 9 October, 1769. Then on the morning of Tuesday 10 October, 1769, another Maori called Te Rakau was shot and killed, and three others were wounded. During the afternoon of that same day a further four Maoris were murdered in the bay merely because they had showed fight when molested, and three of their companions were taken captive.
>
> Captain James Cook claimed New Zealand for Britain. The *Endeavour* finally left Poverty Bay on Thursday 12 October, 1769. The glorious birth of the nation has the taste of bitter almonds when one remembers that six Maoris died so that a flag could be raised and that the *Endeavour* had lain in Poverty Bay for only two days and fourteen hours. (36–7)

Here, as elsewhere in the novel, the "accepted" Eurocentric / Pakeha version of history is recounted, only to be challenged and rejected in favor of a revised version which retells the story from a Maori perspective. Thus Ihimaera (and Narogin in Australia, too) reverse the past trend of black (hi)stories being rejected in favor of white ones.

Moreover, white histories have tended to be told in a linear fashion which does not necessarily reflect Aboriginal or Maori views of time. To counter this, in *Tangi* (1973), the first Maori novel in English, and again in *The Matriarch* Witi Ihimaera rejects the linear narrative in favor of a circular structure or pattern which is distinctly Maori in order to wrest the past from the strangling grip of the center; throughout the novel stories of the past wash over and rearrange our perceptions of the present in much the same way as waves, continually advancing and retreating, rearrange the sand on a beach. Thus the past is seen literally to shape the present; it continues to be a tangible presence in the present, just as ancestors are a tangible presence in Maori life. And here we glimpse what has been called the educative purpose of indigenous literatures which seek to show what it is like to be Aboriginal / Maori in Australia / New Zealand (see for example, Arvidson, 117). As Patricia Grace explained in an interview: "I hope [my] stories show aspects of a way of life that is essentially Maori and they give some insight into what it is to be a Maori" (Arvidson, 117–18). And in the post-colonial context this educative function helps Maori and Aborigines to promote a visible sense of identity within the larger New Zealand and Australian societies.

Many Maori and Aboriginal writers, like Ihimaera or Narogin, whose *Doctor Wooreddy's Perscription for Enduring the Ending of the World* is set in Tasmania in the early part of the nineteenth century and deals with the historical figures of Wooreddy, the last male Aborigine from Bruny Island, and George Augustus Robinson, use history to challenge the discourse of the center and / or the periphery. Other indigenous writers focus more on recent historical events, as Patricia Grace does in her novel *Potiki* (1986), which is partly based on a dispute over Maori land at Ragland on the west coast of New Zealand's North Island.

But indigenous writers do not by any means only focus on the past in their fiction. Narogin's *Wild Cat Falling* (1965), the first novel to be published by an Aboriginal writer, tells the story of an Aboriginal youth who is denied the privileges of the white-dominated society he is forced to live in because of his racial background. His fight against that society is seen as futile, but it does lead him into the company of an old Noongar, from whom he learns a new sense of pride in his cultural identity. Similarly, in her most powerful short stories, which focus on Maori identity in contemporary New Zealand society, Patricia Grace, like Mudrooroo Narogin, combines an educative purpose with a political one, and clearly challenges the dominant periphery. In "The Hills," for example, Grace begins by reminding the reader of the colonial connotations of the word "boy," which effectively marginalizes the boy in this story, confirms him as other in a still white-dominated "settler culture":

> "Boy" means little kid, "boy" means dirty with a filthy mind. It means "smart arse". A "boy" is a servant and a slave.... Anyway, I'm not a slave or a servant. I'm just myself. One day I'll call myself a man, and I won't just be an old "boy" like my father. (65)

But outside the marginalized framework, the word "boy" also has an apolitical meaning that signifies youth and innocence:

> When the mist comes down to cover the hills I don't think grey. I think of parcels and coloured wrapping, and clothes and tits and bums. Then I have a good laugh at myself and think that I'm only a boy after all. I don't mean a servant or a slave or a smart brat. I just mean "boy" in a different, youngish way.
> 　　Then something can happen to you that's too much for a boy. You can't be a boy any more afterwards. (66)

What happens to the Maori youth shows that in a society born of imperial aggression, in which many of the prejudices of the center linger, those two different meanings of the word "boy" are linked after all, as Grace emphasizes as she draws the story to a close:

> Later that day I went outside and walked up the street, and when I got to the top of the road I wouldn't look out at the hills. The hills could've been clear, or the mist could've been down or it could've been just lifting off. I turned and went back home. I remember wondering if I would ever look there again. (69)

It is because of this prejudice, the legacy of a colonial past, that the narrator will never again be able to call himself a "boy" in a youngish way, nor, ironically, will he ever be prepared to accept the role of "boy" as servant or slave, which is the role that the dominant white culture is trying to impose on him.

In my introduction I referred briefly to the power of language and commented on the way the English language has in turn been successfully colonized by post-colonial writers, in the West Indies and elsewhere. In Australia and New Zealand the pattern is somewhat different: the language of the center has never been as successfully colonized because the cultures of the antipodean countries are essentially born of the center, and much of what we now refer to as Australian English or New Zealand English has its origins in the various shires of England, or the various regions of Scotland, Wales, and Ireland. Indigenous writers, however, have used language for clear political ends. (It is worth remembering that in New Zealand most Maori writers are bicultural and make serious attempts to bridge the two cultures, whereas most Pakeha writers are monocultural and subsume the cultural differences they have inherited as white New Zealanders.) In Witi Ihimaera's early works like *Tangi* we find the English language being molded by the rhythms of the Maori language, and the spiraling patterns of the oral narrative as performed by storytellers. More significantly, perhaps, Maori writers, like Ihimaera, Grace, Hone Tuwhare, Keri Hulme, Apirana Taylor and others, and also some Pakeha writers, notably the poet James K. Baxter (in poems like "He Waiata me Te Kare" and "Te Whiore o te Kuri"), have increasingly used untranslated Maori words in their fiction, which inscribes difference by suggesting that certain cultural experiences can't be reproduced in the language of the center or white periphery (see Ashcroft et al., 53). And this use of Maori words also challenges the cultural hegemony of English itself, as well as making deliberately muted voices heard. Similarly, Aboriginal writers like the poet Kevin Gilbert (whose play *The Cherry Pickers* was, in 1971, the first play by an Aboriginal playwright to be performed in Australia) regularly use words from their own indigenous languages in their work, though in Australia the situation has been complicated by the often all-too-thorough genocide carried out against Aboriginal tribes and languages by the colonizers. Thus in the work of a poet like Lionel Fogerty, the only Aboriginal words the reader encounters tend to be place names or tribal names as in the poem "Nyarki's Place." As Narogin explains, to understand Fogerty's poetry one must leave behind the safety of language and explore the Aboriginality that is inherent in a poem like "Free Our Dreams" (*Writing from the Fringe*, 54–9).

CONCLUSION

In Australia and New Zealand white writers have begun to write back to the center in an attempt to exorcise some of the Eurocentrism that has fashioned so much of the literature of the dominant culture in the two countries. In turning away from the center white writers in Australia and Pakeha writers in New Zealand are beginning instead to redefine themselves in relation to the indigenous cultures of their countries.

Post-coloniality in Australia and New Zealand thus involves not only writing back to the center, but also recognizing and accepting the cultural heterogeneity which defines the post-colonial national identity of each country.

The work of the Australian poet Les Murray brings out this sense of a post-colonial national identity. His poetry, which is often very local, antimodern, is also attentive to the cultural differences in his own makeup. His poetry pays attention to Scotland, thus recognizing his European ancestry, and also to Aboriginal culture, which is part of his identity as an Australian. Writing from the periphery, Murray includes both the center and the outer periphery in his work, providing a synthesis of what at times have appeared to be the disparate elements of the post-colonial condition in Australia and New Zealand.

WORKS CITED

Arvidson, Ken. "Aspects of Contemporary Maori Writing in English." In *Dirty Silence: Aspects of Language and Literature in New Zealand*. Ed. Graham McGregor and Mark Williams. Auckland: Oxford University Press, 1991. 117–28.

Ashcroft, Bill, Gareth Griffiths, and Helen Tiffin. *The Empire Writes Back: Theory and Practise in Post-Colonial Literatures*. London and New York: Routledge, 1989.

Grace, Patricia. *Electric City and Other Stories*. Auckland: Penguin, 1987.

Ihimaera, Witi. *The Matriarch*. 1986. Auckland: Picador, 1987.

Jones, Lawrence. "The Novel." *The Oxford History of New Zealand Literature*. Ed. Terry Sturm. Auckland: Oxford University Press, 1991. 105–99.

Narogin, Mudrooroo [Colin Johnson]. "White Forms, Aboriginal Content." *Aboriginal Writing Today*. Ed. Jack Davis and Bob Hodge. Canberra: Australian Institute of Aboriginal Studies, 1985. 21–33.

Narogin, Mudrooroo. *Writing from the Fringe*. Melbourne: Hyland House, 1990.

O'Sullivan, Vincent, ed. *An Anthology of Twentieth Century New Zealand Poetry*, 3rd edn. Auckland: Oxford University Press, 1987.

Riach, Alan. "Stranger Eyes: Charles Olson, 'Pacific Man' and Some Aspects of New Zealand Poetry." *Landfall* 43.1 (1989): 57–73.

Tompkins, Joanne. " 'It All Depends on What Story You Hear': Historiographic Metafiction and Colin Johnson's *Doctor Wooreddy's Perscription for Enduring the Ending of the World* and Witi Ihimaera's *The Matriarch*." *Modern Fiction Studies* 36.4 (1990): 483–98.

Wedde, Ian. "Introduction" In *The Penguin Book of New Zealand Verse*. Ed. Ian Wedde and Harvey McQueen. Auckland and Harmondsworth, England: Penguin, 1985. 23–52.

Part VI
The Case of Ireland: Inventing Nations

Adulteration and the Nation

DAVID LLOYD

David Lloyd has emerged in recent years as one of the most influential theorists of postcolonialism, especially as it manifests itself in the Irish context. His *Anomalous States: Irish Writing and the Post-Colonial Moment*, from which this essay is taken, has proven instrumental in introducing important concepts – particularly the idea of "adulteration" – in an attempt to define more precisely the kinds of strategies that Irish writers have taken in responding to colonialism. Lloyd's argument here begins with the problem of nationalism and the role literature plays in constituting it. Of crucial relevance in the Irish context is the ballad literature which, for Lloyd, functions in the absence of an epic tradition. The problem of "hybridization," which for Irish nationalists suggested both disintegration of an authentic Irish tradition and homogenization within a British tradition, necessitates what Lloyd calls a "translational aesthetic": "what must be constantly carried over is the essential spirit rather than the superficial forms of Irish poetry" in Gaelic and English. In his discussion of James Joyce's *Ulysses*, Lloyd suggests that the mid-nineteenth-century debates about nationalism and the role of ballad literature in representing national aspirations were repeated in the Irish Literary Revival, which Joyce both represents and critiques. Joyce's text posits a "citational" strategy that maintains the subversive heterogeneity or "adulteration" of Irish cultural texts and which stands in contradistinction to the "translational aesthetic" of Irish nationalism. The student interested in the problem of nationalism and postcolonialism might read Lloyd's essay together with essays by **Partha Chatterjee** and **R. Radhakrishnan**; for further discussion of "citational" strategies, see **Helen Tiffin**. The question of language in nationalist and anti-colonial discourse is treated also in **Declan Kiberd**.

Adulteration and the Nation

Irish cultural nationalism has been preoccupied throughout its history with the possibility of producing a national genius who would at once speak for and forge a national identity. The national genius is to represent the nation in the double sense of depicting and embodying its spirit – or genius – as it is manifested in the changing forms of national life and history. The idea could be reformulated quite accurately in terms derived from Kantian aesthetics: the national genius is credited with "exemplary originality".[1] That is to say, the national genius not only presents examples to a people not yet fully formed by or conscious of their national identity, but does so by exemplifying in himself the individual's ideal continuity with the nation's spiritual origins. True originality derives from the faithful reproduction of one's origins. Thus far, Irish nationalism represents, as indeed does Kant, merely another variant on the Enlightenment and Romantic critical tradition for which the originality of genius is understood as the capacity to reproduce the historical or individual sources of creativity itself. The Irish nationalist merely insists on a different notion of what is to be formed in the encounter with genius: not so much the intermediate subject of taste as, directly, the political subject, the citizen-subject, itself.

Unlike Kant, however, the Irish nationalist is confronted with a peculiar dilemma, succinctly expressed by Young Ireland's most influential aesthetician, D. F. Mac-Carthy, as the great national poet's being "either the creation or the creator of a great people".[2] The expression points to an unavoidable aporia for the doubly representational aesthetics of nationalism, since the poet must either be created by the nation which it is his (always his) function to create, or create it by virtue of representing the nation he lacks. Neither a continuous national history, which could connect the individual to the national genius, nor even nature, on whose invocation in the form of *Naturgabe* the category of genius has traditionally been grounded, are easily available to the Irish nationalist.[3] For the nationalism of a colonized people requires that its history be seen as a series of unnatural ruptures and discontinuities imposed by an alien power while its reconstruction must necessarily pass by way of deliberate artifice. Almost by definition, this anti-colonial nationalism lacks the basis for its representative claims and is forced to invent them.[4] In this respect, nationalism can be said to require an aesthetic politics quite as much as a political aesthetics.

Historically, this constitutive paradox of Irish nationalism has not been practically disabling, though in cultural terms it leaves the problem that Ireland's principal

Taken from *Anomalous States: Irish Writing and the Post-Colonial Moment* (Durham, NC: Duke University Press, 1993).

writers have almost all been remarkably recalcitrant to the nationalist project. I have discussed this more extensively elsewhere in relation to the extreme demand for identification with the nation that nationalism imposes upon the Irish writer.[5] Here, I wish to explore more fully how not only the anti-representational tendency in Irish literature but also the hybrid quality of popular forms constantly exceed the monologic desire of cultural nationalism, a desire which centres on the lack of an Irish epic. Both the popular and the literary forms map a colonial culture for which the forms of representational politics and aesthetics required by nationalism begin to seem entirely inadequate, obliging us to conceive of a cultural politics which must work outside the terms of representation. Incidentally, this colonial situation may also suggest the limits of the Bakhtinian formulations on which this analysis will in the first place be based.

I

At several points in *The Dialogic Imagination*, Mikhail Bakhtin isolates as a definitive characteristic of the novel its capacity to represent the heteroglossia internal to an apparently unified but nonetheless stratified national language.[6] Requiring the depiction of the conflictual, dialogic nature of social relations, this characteristic underlies the generic mobility and, at given historical moments, subversiveness of the novel, opposing it to the epic, as well as to other stabilized and "monologic" genres. The epic belongs to a closed and completed world, and characteristically represents the unity of that world and the integration of its exemplary heroes (p. 35). Typically, the epic casts backwards to "an absolute past of national beginnings and peak times" (p. 15), correlative to which is its stylistic closure: unlike the novel, the epic is a genre closed to development and therefore insusceptible to the representation of historical development (pp. 16–17). Intrinsic to Bakhtin's discussion of epic and novel is, accordingly, an historical periodization which derives the novel from the disintegration of the epic and its culture.[7] In the long term, the dialectic of the novel form leads to the disintegration of the myth of "a unitary, canonic language, of a national myth bolstered by a yet-unshaken unity" (p. 370), and a concomitant displacement of the ideological by the human speaking subject.

Bakhtin, as that last citation serves to recall, posits the moment of unitary national culture in the past. The instance of a decolonizing nationalism, such as Ireland's throughout the nineteenth and early twentieth centuries, leads us to pose the question in slightly different terms. What if the epic of a nation has yet to be written and if the unity of the nation is desired as a prerequisite to the anti-colonial struggle? In such a case, exactly what seems to be required is the monologic form of the epic as a means to rather than a mere legitimating record of national unity, while the function of the epic may be seen not only as the unification of a culture but also, in a quite specific sense, as the production of a dialogic subversion of the colonizing power. For these purposes, which are integral to the politically mobilizing project of cultural nationalism, the *heteroglossic* mode of the novel could be seen as distinctly counter-productive. Precisely that which, according to Bakhtin, the novel is constantly adapted to represent, the multiplicity of contending social voices, is what Irish nationalism must, for entirely coherent political reasons, seek to supersede in the form of a unified national identity. For the cultural nationalists of the nineteenth and early twentieth centuries, believing "that Irishmen were enslaved because they were divided",[8] the principal task of nationalism was to overcome the sectarian, class and ethnic divisions that split Ireland. The task of producing representations of a common identity was accordingly entrusted to literature, and to a literature whose very rationale was monologic insofar as it was intended to produce exactly the "national myth" that Bakhtin envisages as having collapsed when the novel supplanted the epic.[9]

As I have argued elsewhere, the literary project of Irish nationalism, stemming from the Young Ireland movement of the 1840s, involves a quite sophisticated theory of generic development linked to a universal history of cultural developments. In this argument, fully developed cultures such as England's can rely on a political constitution which expresses the underlying unity of their conflicting social forces, whereas underdeveloped cultures such as Ireland's must turn to literary institutions for the same unificatory effects. Due, however, to the apparently fragmentary and strife-ridden course of Irish history and to the divided society of its present, that literature has yet to be created. If, "rightly understood, the history of Ireland . . . had the unity and purpose of an epic poem", that epic had yet to be written and could not be prematurely forged. Before it could be written, the prior stages of literary development had to be passed through, permitting, as if at accelerated tempo, the recomposition of all those ballads and folk-songs on which it was believed such epics as Homer's were founded.[10] Hence the enormous quantity of ballads produced and collected in nineteenth-century Ireland was not merely a question of propaganda but directly concerned the constitution of an idea of Irishness which could "contain and represent the races of Ireland".[11]

But this project of presenting to the Irish a single "spirit of the nation" (to cite the title of one enormously popular collection) is confronted with peculiar problems as soon as it turns to extant ballads as examples of that spirit. Collectors of Irish ballads classify them generally into three subdivisions: Gaelic or peasant songs, street ballads, and literary or Anglo-Irish ballads.[12] To the latter class we will return, since it is the problematic status of the first two that most acutely confronts the cultural nationalist.

By the mid-nineteenth century, the study of Gaelic language and culture had proceeded little beyond the scarcely systematic amassing of materials, while distinctions between "high" and "low" literary productions remained relatively fluid and uncertain.[13] Collections were recognized to be provisional and incomplete. Yet despite the objective grounds for the fragmentary corpus of Gaelic literature, nationalists who review it in order to distinguish and define Irish identity time and again trace in that corpus a fragmentariness lodged in the artefacts themselves. Thus when Davis remarks that "There are great gaps in Irish song to be filled up," he refers not to the state of research but to the nature of the object, a nature that is for him historical and absolutely not essential. The "bulk of the songs", he asserts, "are very defective":

> Most of those hitherto in use were composed during the last century, and therefore their structure is irregular, their grief slavish and despairing, their joy reckless and bombastic, their religion bitter and sectarian, their politics Jacobite and concealed by extravagant and tiresome allegory. Ignorance, disorder and every kind of oppression weakened and darkened the lyric genius of Ireland.[14]

The historical oppression of the Irish has contaminated both the structure and the content of the Gaelic poetry, so that if it appears gapped, that gapping is internal to it, consisting in its "defective" or "extravagant" deviation from the essential "genius" of the Irish nation. There is something alien in the poetry, and the job of the popular editor is accordingly one of condensation: "cut them so as exactly to suit the airs, preserve the local and broad historical allusions, but remove the clumsy ornaments and exaggerations" (pp. 225–6). The *perfection* of the defective native Irish poetic tradition requires a process of refinement which is, in principle at least, the antithesis of supplementation, involving instead the purging of extraneous materials and the unfolding of an obscured essence. Davis's formulation is characteristic of nationalist reception of Gaelic songs, which are similarly perceived by D. F. MacCarthy as "snatches and fragments of old songs and ballads, which are chapters of a nation's autobiography".[15] In every case, the fragmentary autobiography is to be completed in the formation of a national identity properly represented in a national literature imbued with its spirit rather than with the accidental traces and accretions of its colonial history. Consistent with this is an implicit rejection of the allegorical in favour of the symbolic: in quite traditional Romantic terms, the extravagance of allegory is eschewed while historical and local allusion is promoted as "participating in that which it represents".[16] The aesthetic of nationalism accords with its political ends, subordinated at every level to the demand for unity.

It is on the same grounds that the second class of street ballads is criticized by nationalists, but with more vehemence. Condemnation of the ballads, purchased widely by the already substantial portion of the people whose principal language was English, was virtually universal among Young Ireland critics, who argued for their supplanting by ballads imbued with the national spirit, such as those published in *The Spirit of the Nation* or in Duffy's and MacCarthy's collections of Irish ballads. Though their dismissals are fairly summary, one can decipher the basis for the antagonism. Most importantly, the ballads are urban: "The mass of the street songs", remarks Duffy, "make no pretence to being true to Ireland; but only to being true to the *purlieus* of Cork and Dublin."[17] Nationalist antagonism to urban Ireland, which continues by and large to structure the nation's ideological self-representation, is by no means as simple and self-evident a phenomenon as its constancy has made it seem. It belongs to the constitutive contradiction of a modernizing ideology forced to seek its authenticating difference from the imperial culture on which it remains dependent by way of an appeal to a rural and Gaelic culture already in decay. Indeed, it is not to that culture in itself that appeal is made, but rather to a "refinement" or "translation" of its essence, traced among the fragmentary survivals of an already decimated past life. The antagonism to the urban is, accordingly, an antagonism to the inauthenticity legible in its cultural forms. Cork and Dublin, along with Belfast, represent in mid-nineteenth-century Ireland, as already for several centuries in the case of Dublin, sites of cultural hybridization as well as centres of imperial authority and capital domination. Garrison as well as industrial or port cities, they represent concentrations of an English domination which penetrates every level of Irish social life. They are both nodes for the flows of English capital and imperial authority, and conduits for the contrary flows of a dislocated population, the points to which a dislocated rural population gravitates in search of employment or prior to emigration. The Pale area around Dublin had always seemed, to English eyes, under constant threat of contamination by Gaelic culture and by the transformation of old or new English into a settler population "more Irish than the Irish". But a rapid acceleration of the process of cultural hybridization, now more threatening to the nationalist than to the English, would appear to have taken place in the late eighteenth and early nineteenth centuries as an overdetermined set of effects of the English Industrial Revolution, the serial crises in Irish agriculture after the Napoleonic Wars and the gradual lifting of the Penal Laws in the decades preceding the Union of Great Britain and Ireland in 1801. Simultaneously, the Irish language was perceived to be in decline.[18]

Even a quite casual collection of eighteenth- and nineteenth-century street ballads like Colm Ó Lochlainn's *Irish Street Ballads* indicates the extent to which such works register, both thematically and stylistically, these processes as they are apprehended by the Irish population.[19] A very high incidence of the songs is devoted to migration or emigration, to conscription or enlistment in the British army, as well as to the celebration of the 1798 uprising and a range of rebel heroes. Even the many love songs are coursed through more by laments for grinding poverty, imprisonment under English law, or the necessity of emigration or vagrancy than by complaints of fickleness and inconstancy, a characteristic considerably at odds with their frequent use, by colonizer and nationalist alike, to ground the stereotype of pure Irish sentimentality. At the stylistic level, the street ballads at moments provide an even more intimate register of the processes of cultural hybridization. They are, most often, adaptations of traditional airs to English words, enforcing frequently a distortion of standard English pronunciation or syntax to fit Gaelic musical and speech rhythms, a trait frequently celebrated in the more refined literary productions of translators and adapters like Moore, Ferguson and Callanan.[20] This primary hybridization is matched by varying degrees of incorporation of Irish-language fragments into the predominantly English texts of the ballads. Usually phonetically transcribed by writers illiterate in Irish, these fragments can be whole refrains, as in "The Barrymore Tithe Victory" (1831), which keeps as part of its refrain the words of the Gaelic ballad "A Dhruimfhionn Donn Dílis", whose tune it appropriates, but which it transcribes as "A Drimon down deelish a heeda na moe" and turns to a celebration of the popular hero and political leader Daniel O'Connell. Others, by far the majority, seem little more than tags from the Gaelic, placenames or mythological and legendary figures, which from the dominant perspective would appear as recalcitrant recollections of a culture in transformation but still politically and culturally resistant. From another perspective, however, that of the balladeers and many in their audiences, such tags would resonate with familiar and quite complex allusions to allegorical and historical figures from Gaelic culture, adding a richer, if occluded, dimension to the ballads' reception. Thus the refrain of "A New Song in Praise of Fergus O'Connor and Independence", celebrating the election of Chartist O'Connor as MP for Cork, runs "So vote for brave Fergus and Sheela na Guira", the Gaelic tag being again the original ballad, "Sighile Ní Ghadhra" from which the tune is borrowed. Even less political street ballads, such as the later "Kerry Recruit", which relates the story of a young peasant enlisted for the Crimean War, used fragments of Irish as well as of Anglo-Irish dialect as a means of linguistically dramatizing the

experience of dislocation and the role of such institutions as the army in the transformation of the colonized population:

> So I buttered my brogues and shook hands with my spade,
> And I went to the fair like a dashing young blade,
> When up comes a sergeant and asks me to 'list,
> "Arra, sergeant a grá, put the bob in my fist."
>
> "O! then here is the shilling, as we've got no more,
> When you get to head-quarters you'll get half a score."
> "Arra, quit your kimeens," ses I, "sergeant, good-bye,
> You'd not wish to be quartered, and neither would I."[21]

This last example, though somewhat later than the Young Ireland writings
instanced above, features a further element of the street ballads which drew nationalist criticism: their frequently burlesque tone. Precisely because of the heterogeneity
of the ballads, whether taken as collections or as individual specimens, it would be
impossible to establish a "typical character" for the street ballads or to fix their tone.
In "The Kerry Recruit", for example, it becomes exceedingly difficult to specify the
object of the mockery, the country gosthoon or the sergeant, peasant ignorance or
British institutions. Tonal instability of this kind is common, as is a similarly vertiginous mixture of realism and burlesque, "high language" and slang. Two further
examples will suffice: one, "Father Murphy", being an anonymous rebel ballad on
the 1798 rebellion; the other, "Billy's Downfall", attributed to the most celebrated of
Dublin street balladers, "Zozimus" (Michael Moran), being a satirical commemoration
of the blowing up of a unionist monument to William III on College Green in 1836:

> The issue of it was a close engagement,
> While on the soldiers we played warlike pranks;
> Thro' sheepwalks, hedgerows and shady thickets,
> There were mangled bodies and broken ranks,
> The shuddering cavalry I can't forget them;
> We raised the brushes on their helmets straight –
> They turned about and they bid for Dublin,
> As if they ran for a ten-pound plate.
>
> By brave Coriolanus and wiggy McManus
>   By dirty King Shamus, that ran from the Boyne,
> I never was willing dead men to be killing,
>   Their scurry blood spilling, with traitors to join.
> For true-heart allegiance, without much persuadience,
>   Myself and all Paddies we're still at a call,
> But to burke a poor king, 'tis a horrible thing,
>   Granu's sons never heard it in Tara's old hall.[22]

As both indicate, the processes of hybridization registered in the street ballads go far
beyond the integration of Gaelic into English-language forms. To the ambiguities
resulting from the refusal to differentiate the burlesque from the serious corresponds a

similar indifference to cultural registers. Military language can cohabit with that of
the racecourse, or classical references give way to citations of ancient and modern
history, folk heroes and contemporary slang. Much of the pleasure of the street ballad,
as with so many "popular" forms, derives from precisely this indifference to cultural
hierarchies.[23] It may even be that the very adaptability of the ballad, as a kind of
template transformable to fit any given locality or momentary reference, subserves
not only the continual demand for the "new song" as instant commodity, but also a
more discrete function. Beyond the cultural resistance they articulate, such ballads as
"Father Murphy" in their very descriptions of combat conceivably acted to preserve
and transmit not merely the historical memory of insurrections but also the repertoire
of means to resist, the tactical knowledge of how and where to conduct armed
struggle. For a rural audience, "Father Murphy" may serve exactly the same function
in terms of tactical knowledge as John Mitchel's regular military lessons in the *United
Irishman* of 1848, themselves adapted from a British military handbook.[24]

Such speculations aside, the stylistic elements of the street ballads throw into
greater relief the grounds for cultural nationalist criticisms of them. The cultural
nationalism developed within the Young Ireland movement was quite strictly a
Romantic nationalism and, like its unionist counterparts, derived much from English
and German high Romanticism. But the forces that a poet like Wordsworth seeks to
counteract, the spectacle of the city as a "perpetual whirl / Of trivial objects, melted
and reduced / To one identity, by differences / That have no law, no meaning, and no
end",[25] are accentuated in the Irish case by the colonial encounter that both accel-
erates the processes of cultural disintegration and gives a specific political name,
anglicization, to the phenomenon of "reduction to identity". What we have described,
in the wider sphere of the Irish political economy as well as in that of the street
ballads, as "hybridization" is necessarily grasped by nationalists as the paradoxically
simultaneous process of multiplication or disintegration and homogenization. The
flooding of the market with English commodities both disintegrates what is retrospectively constructed as a unified Irish identity and absorbs its residues into the
single field of the British industrial and imperial empire. And since the only means to
resist this process, in the absence of autonomous national political institutions,
appears to be the formation of nationalist subjects through literary institutions, the
field of popular literature becomes peculiarly fraught. For if the ultimate desire of the
nationalist must be for the state (in every sense of the word "for"), that desire must in
fact be not first of all for the state itself, as a body of specific institutions to be
controlled, but for what the state in turn is held to represent, namely, the unity or
reconciliation of the people. Hence the necessity for a cultural nationalism, not merely
as a supplement to, but as a prerequisite for, a military nationalism, and hence the
requirement that that nationalist culture be monologic in its modes of expression. The
representation as a desired end of an homogeneous Irish nation is a necessary
preliminary to the political struggle in any form.

Accordingly, the aesthetic choices that oppose the nationalists' literary recreations
of Irish ballad poetry to both the street ballads and to the Gaelic songs are also at
every level political choices. Their collections are designed to give law, meaning and
end to a specific difference which would constitute an Ireland independent of England
and in opposition to the heterogeneous image of Irish social life and culture borne in

the street ballad or in extant translations of Gaelic poetry. A national poetry must speak with one voice and, unlike those street ballads in which it is often difficult to tell if the hero is subject or object of the burlesque, must represent the Irish people as the agent of its own history, of a history which has "the unity and purpose of an epic poem". This demands a "translational" aesthetic, in the sense that what must be constantly carried over is the essential spirit rather than the superficial forms of Irish poetry in each language.[26]

As Denis Florence MacCarthy puts it in his *Book of Irish Ballads*:

> This peculiar character of our poetry is, however, not easily imparted. An Irish word or an Irish phrase, even appositely introduced, will not be sufficient; it must pervade the entire poem, and must be seen and felt in the construction, the sentiment, and the expression.[27]

In the examples cited above, "Sheela na Guira" or the "Granu's sons" are juxtaposed in contiguity to Fergus O'Connor or Coriolanus, achieving an expansion – and complication – of referential range without requiring the subordination of the elements to one another. MacCarthy's aesthetic programme, on the contrary, requires the subordination of the Gaelic element as a representative instance consubstantial with the homogeneous totality of Irish identity. In keeping with an antagonism to the allegorical tendency of Gaelic poetry and the street ballads in favour of a generally symbolist aesthetic, nationalist writing must perform a transfer from the metonymic axis of contiguity to that of metaphor. Where the metonymic disposition of popular forms lends itself to the indiscriminate citation of insubordinate cultural elements, the fundamentally narrative structure of metaphoric language seeks to reorganize such cultural elements as representative moments in a continuous epic of the nation's self-formation.[28]

MacCarthy himself provides us with an exemplary instance in his ballad "The Pillar Towers of Ireland", which, though by no means the most celebrated of Young Ireland productions, almost self-consciously enacts the appropriation of historical Irish elements to a seamless representation of Irish destiny. The pillar towers become symbols of the continuing spirit of Ireland, both its products and its organizing representatives, giving shape and relationship to the several races which have passed through or settled the land in the course of its history:

> Around these walls have wandered the Briton and the Dane –
> The captives of Armorica, the cavaliers of Spain –
> Phoenician and Milesian, and the plundering Norman Peers –
> And the swords men of brave Brian, and the chiefs of later years![29]

A persistent and resistant element of the Irish landscape, the round or pillar tower stands as itself a metaphor for the metaphoric process by which an initial perception of difference can be brought over time into a superior recognition of identity:

> There may it stand for ever, while this symbol doth impart
> To the mind one glorious vision, or one proud throb to the heart;

While the breast needeth rest may these grey old temples last,
Bright prophets of the future, as preachers of the past!
                                    (*Book of Irish Ballads*, p. 128)

It is not necessary to be aware of the continuing exploitation of the round tower by the Irish Tourist Board and other such institutions to sense how rapidly this representation of an authentic Irish identity veers towards kitsch. Indeed, the constant gravitation of cultural nationalism towards kitsch is a virtually inevitable consequence of its aesthetic programme, if not, indeed, to some extent a mark of its success. The commodification of style and the mechanical reproduction of standardized forms of affect that define kitsch have their close counterpart in cultural nationalism.[30] Here, the incessant injunction to produce representative ballads which will reproduce Gaelic styles known to the producers only by way of representations is directed towards the homogenization of a political rather than an economic sphere. It similarly requires, nonetheless, the production of novelties which are always interchangeable, a condition partly of the journalistic sphere in which most nationalist ballads first appeared, and the immediate evocation of an affect which is the sign of identification with the nation. Congruent in most respects with Romantic aesthetics generally, the subordination of the nationalist ballad to a conscious political end denies it the auratic distance usually held, if often erroneously, to guarantee the critical moment of the modern artwork.

Ironically, what is properly, in Brechtian terms, an *epic* distance belongs more frequently to the street ballad than to the nationalist ballads intended to replace them. Self-consciously produced as commodities, and with the ephemeral aptness to momentary need or desire that is the property of the commodity, the street ballads often achieve an effect akin to montage in which the contours of an heterogeneous and hybridized culture can become apparent without necessarily losing political force. Indeed, a large part of the pleasure of the street ballad is political and lies in its use of "extravagant allegories": what it exploits is precisely the unevenness of knowledge that characterizes the colonized society. The variegated texture of colonized society permits an exploitation by the colonized of those elements that are unfamiliar to the colonizer, and therefore appear encoded, like the Gaelic tags cited above, as a means of at once disguising and communicating subversion, as message to the colonized and as uncertainty to the colonizer. The very inauthenticity of the colonized culture enables an unpredictable process of masking. Where the colonizer, whose proper slogan should be that "Ignorance is Power", seeks to reduce the colonized to a surveyable surface whose meaning is always the same, and where the nationalist responds with an ideal of the total translucence of national spirit in the people, the hybridized culture of the colonized offers only surfaces pitted or mined with uncertainty, depths and shallows whose contours vary depending on the "familiarity" of each observer. On this surface, demarcations of the borderline between damage and creative strategies for resistance are hard to fix. As we shall see, neither the damage nor the resistance lend themselves easily to assimilation.

Captured in the contradiction between its modernizing effects and its conservative appeal, nationalist culture on the other hand is drawn into a process of stylization, the representation of a style, which constantly returns it to an inauthenticity akin to, though not identical with, that of the street ballad it seeks to supplant. This effect of stylization is probably inseparable from the fundamental dislocation which colonization effects in any culture and which is the necessary prior condition for the emergence of any specifically *nationalist* resistance. In proceeding, it is necessary only to insist again that the dislocation of the colonized culture should not be thought of in terms of a loss of a prior and recoverable authenticity. Rather, authenticity must be seen as the projective desire of a nationalism programmatically concerned with the homogenization of the people as a national political entity.

II

Unsurprisingly, given the virtually aporetic status of its contradictions, the terms of mid-nineteenth-century nationalist cultural discussions are reproduced half a century later in the Irish Literary Revival. James Joyce presents them prominently in *Ulysses* as a prelude to Stephen Dedalus's development of his own conception of genius out of Saxon Shakespeare:

> —Our young Irish bards, John Eglinton censured, have yet to create a figure which the world will set beside Saxon Shakespeare's Hamlet though I admire him, as old Ben did, on this side idolatry.
> . . .
> Mr Best came forward, amiable, towards his colleague.
> —Haines is gone, he said.
> —Is he?
> —I was showing him Jubainville's book. He's quite enthusiastic, don't you know, about Hyde's *Love Songs of Connacht*. I couldn't bring him in to hear the discussion. He's gone to Gill's to buy it.
>
> > *Bound thee forth, my booklet, quick*
> > *To greet the callous public,*
> > *Writ, I ween, 'twas not my wish*
> > *In lean unlovely English.*
>
> —The peatsmoke is going to his head, John Eglinton opined.
> . . .
> —People do not know how dangerous lovesongs can be, the auric egg of Russell warned occultly. The movements which work revolutions in the world are born out of the dreams and visions in a peasant's heart on the hillside. For them the earth is not an exploitable ground but the living mother. The rarefied air of the academy and the arena produce the sixshilling novel, the musichall song. France produces the finest flower of corruption in Mallarmé but the desirable life is revealed only to the poor of heart, the life of Homer's Phaeacians.[31]

It is not merely that Joyce alludes here, in compressed fashion, to the principal concerns that continue to play through Irish cultural nationalism: the desire for the masterwork; the opposition between the spirit of peasant song, "racy of the soil", and the hybrid "flowers of corruption"; the turn to Homer as the figure representing the unification of the work of genius with the "genius of place". Furthermore, he indicates the complexity of the cultural transactions that take place in the thoroughly hybridized culture of "West Britain", where Irishmen discourse on English, German and Greek culture while an Englishman, Haines, studies the Celtic element in literature and Hyde regrets the necessity that forces him to exemplify a Gaelic metre in lean, unlovely English.

Joyce's evocation of Hyde at this juncture allows us to grasp both the extent to which turn-of-the-century cultural nationalism recapitulates its earlier forms and the extent to which its terms had become at once more sophisticated and more problematic. Douglas Hyde, founder-president of the Gaelic League, was a principal advocate of the Irish-language revival, a scholar, poet-translator and folklorist. His most famous single essay, "The Necessity for De-Anglicising Ireland" (1892), resumes Young Ireland's attacks on the penetration of Ireland by English culture as well as capital, and on the consequent emergence of an entirely "anomalous position" for the Irish race, "imitating England and yet apparently hating it".[32] In large part, this essay presents a dismal catalogue of hybridization which ranges through place and family names to musical forms and clothing. Its conclusion, that de-anglicization of Ireland is the necessary prelude to and guarantee of eventual Irish autonomy, is prescriptive for efforts like Hyde's own laborious collection and translation of Irish folk-songs and poetry. In these, as he had already argued in his essay "Gaelic Folk Songs" (1890), the Irish genius was properly to be deciphered:

> We shall find that, though in their origin and diffusion they are purely local, yet in their essence they are wholly national, and, perhaps, more purely redolent of the race and soil than any of the real *literary* productions of the last few centuries.[33]

When it comes to deciphering that essence, nonetheless, Hyde is confronted with the dilemma that led to Young Ireland's translational aesthetic: there remain "great gaps in Irish song". For Hyde, however, as a scholar whose intimacy with the Gaelic material was far greater than Davis's or MacCarthy's, the question as to whether the "gapped" nature of Irish folk-song was of its essence or an accident based upon the contingent, historical determinants of an oral culture, remains correspondingly more difficult to resolve. After giving a number of instances from Gaelic love songs, he pauses to remark on the necessity to cite examples in order to represent the nature of these songs in general. The ensuing reflections lead him to an unusually complex rendering of the "nature" of the Gaelic spirit, leaving him unable to decide between the historical and the essential:

> It may appear strange, however, that I have only given stray verses instead of translating entire songs. But the fact is that the inconsequentness of these songs, as I have taken them down from the lips of the peasantry, is startling.
> Many adjectives have been applied by many writers to the Gaelic genius, but to my mind nothing about it is so noticeable as its inconsequentness, if I may use such a word – a peculiarity which, as far as I know, no one has yet noticed. The thought of the Irish peasant takes the most surprising and capricious leaps. Its movement is like the career of his own goblin, the Pooka; it clears the most formidable obstacles at a bound and carries

across astonishing distances in a moment. The folk-song is the very incarnation of this
spirit. It is nearly impossible to find three verses in which there is anything like an
ordinary sequence of thought. They are full up of charms that the mind must leap, elipses
[sic] that it must fill up, and detours of movement which only the most vivid imagination
can make straight. This is the reason why I have found no popular ballads amongst the
peasantry, for to tell a story in verse requires an orderly, progressive, and somewhat slow
sequence of ideas, and this is the very faculty which the Gael has not got – his mind is too
quick and passionate . . .

    But even this characteristic of Gaelic thought is insufficient to account for the perfectly
extraordinary inconsequentness and abruptness of the folk-songs, as I have found them. I
imagine that the cause of this peculiarity is not to be ascribed wholly to the authors of the
songs, but also in great part to the medium which the songs passed through before they
came to us – that medium, of course, being the various generations of local singers who
have perpetuated them. These singers often forgot, as was natural, the real words of the
song, and then they invented others, but more frequently they borrowed verses from any
other piece that came into their head, provided it could be sung to the same tune, and
hence the songs as we have them now are a curious mixture indeed. What between the
"unsequacious" mind of the original makers, the alterations made by generations of
singers who forgot the words, and the extraneous verses borrowed from completely
different productions, two out of three of the folksongs which I have collected, resemble
those children's toys of paper where when you pull a string you get a different pair of legs
or a different head, joined to a different body. The most beautiful sentiments will be
followed by the most grotesque bathos, and the tenderest and most exquisite verses will
end in the absurdest nonsense. This has been done by the singers who have transmitted
them. (pp. 113–14)

The folk-songs appear here as at once the representation of an essence, the Gaelic
spirit, and the products of the specific and contingent conditions of their transmission.
But if we take these representations as those of an essence, then the essence itself
makes it impossible to define any essential character of the race, since a character, to
have any identity at all, must be consistent, as Young Ireland and their followers in
the Literary Revival consistently argued. On the other hand, the historical argument
in its turn, recognizing the sheer contingency that has conditioned the forms and
peculiarities of the folk-songs, would make it impossible to derive a national character
from them.

    Despite his momentary hesitation at this acknowledgment of the overdetermined
grounds for the "great gaps in Irish song", Hyde rapidly recuperates the Irish identity
by offering, after citing a thoroughly adulterated verse, "one specimen of a comparatively perfect folk-song which has not been interfered with" (p. 115). The song, "Mo
bhrón ar an bhfarraige" ("Oh, my grief on the sea!"), which concludes with the lines,

> And my love came behind me –
> He came from the south –
> With his breast to my bosom,
> His mouth to my mouth,

appears as a perfect because consistent expression of "genuine passion", lacking any
of the marks, "the alliteration, adjectives, assonance, and tricks of the professional

poet" (p. 117). Hyde's "restoration" of the essential folk-song requires, in other words, not only its purification from hybridization internal to the culture or resulting from external influence, but even the representation of the work of the Gaelic bards as a deviation from the true passion of the people. Irish folk culture is transformed into an ahistorical ground on which the defining difference of "Irishness" can be established over against the homogenizing/hybridizing influence of "Anglicization". Ironically, the values by which the genuine item is identified and canonized themselves derive, perhaps by way of earlier translators, like the unionist Samuel Ferguson, from the "common language" of British Romanticism.

It is more than probable that Joyce knew Hyde's essays, and certain that he knew this particular song, if only from the slightly revised version in *The Love Songs of Connacht*, since it appears transformed early in *Ulysses*. It reappears, however, not in the context of "genuine passion", but in the course of Stephen's "morose delectation" on Sandymount Strand as his thoughts shift back and forth between the cockle picker's woman passing him and the memory of his dead mother:

> She trudges, schlepps, trains, drags, trascines her load. A tide westering, moondrawn, in her wake. Tides, myriadislanded, within her, blood not mine, *oinopa ponton*, a wine-dark sea. Behold the handmaid of the moon. In sleep the wet sign calls her hour, bids her rise. Bridebed, childbed, bed of death, ghostcandled. *Omnis caro ad te veniet*. He comes pale vampire, through storm his eyes, his bat sails bloodying the sea, mouth to her mouth's kiss. (*Ulysses*, p. 40)

The verses emerging here recur somewhat later, in the "Aeolus" section, in a form closer to that given by Hyde:

> On swift sail flaming
> From storm and south
> He comes, pale vampire,
> Mouth to my mouth.
> (*Ulysses*, p. 109)

We may read in the gradual transformation of the folk-song a representation at several levels of the processes of hybridization as they construct the individual consciousness. Many of the elements of that hybridization are superficially evident: the chain of foreign, or rather "anglicized", words used to describe the cockle picker's woman, the phrases from Homer and from the Latin of Catholic ritual, or the parody of biblical invocations. The *effect* of hybridization, however, needs more careful analysis, both at the formal literary level and at that of the representation of an individual subjectivity which it entails. The most familiar stylistic term in Joyce criticism used to describe the representation of subjective interiority is "stream of consciousness", which implies a certain consistency within the representation as well as a relative transparency and evenness among the elements. As such, the term is largely inadequate, even in the earlier sections of the novel, to describe the staccato or interrupted rhythms, the varying accessibility of the allusions, whether to different readers or to the represented subject (Stephen or Bloom), or to the several levels of implicit "consciousness" that these stylistic effects constitute.

Equally inadequate would be any description of these effects as instances of "assim-ilation" or "appropriation", terms employed by Bakhtin in his description of the normative dialogical formation of the subject:

> As a living, socio-ideological concrete thing, as heteroglot opinion, language, for the individual consciousness, lies on the borderline between oneself and the other. The word in language is half someone else's. It becomes "one's own" only when the speaker populates it with his own intention, his own accent, when he appropriates the word, adapting it to his own semantic and expressive intention. (p. 293)...One's own dis-course is gradually and slowly wrought out of others' words that have been acknowl-edged and assimilated, and the boundaries between the two are at first scarcely perceptible. (p. 345n)

Despite the difficulties he recognizes as afflicting these processes, Bakhtin is clearly operating here with an at least residually Kantian subject, one existent as potential prior to any engagement with word or object, and, perhaps more importantly, on its way to conformity with those maxims of enlightenment that for Kant define the autonomous subject: independence, consistency, and formal, universal identity.[34]

It is, of course, towards the production of such a subject, capable, for example, of assimilating the alien English language to Irish identity or the equally alien Gaelic language to the English "mother-tongue", that Irish nationalism is directed. What it constantly diagnoses, however, is a subject-people always the *object* of imperfect assimilation to either culture, in a state, that is, of continuing *dependence*. It is for this reason that Joyce's "citational" aesthetic in *Ulysses* cuts so strongly against both Bakhtin's description of the subjective processes which the novel typifies, and the translational aesthetic of Irish nationalism. One could, indeed, argue that Bakhtin's assimilation is itself a version of a generally translational aesthetic for which the subject is formed in a continual appropriation of the alien to itself, just as translation, as opposed, for example, to interpretation or paraphrase, is seen as essentially a recreation of the foreign text in one's own language.[35] Joyce's, or Stephen's, version of this love song of Connacht rather insists on its heterogeneity in the course of an essentially "inconsequential" meditation or miscegenates it with an entirely different – but no less "Irish" – tradition of Gothic vampire tales.[36]

Accordingly, where the principal organizing metaphor of Irish nationalism is that of a proper paternity, of restoring the lineage of the fathers in order to repossess the motherland, Joyce's procedures are dictated by adulteration. Joyce's personal obses-sion with adultery is well documented and it is a commonplace that the plot of *Ulysses* itself turns around Molly Bloom's adulterous relationship with Blazes Boylan.[37] That the figure of the nineteenth-century leader of the Home Rule party, Charles Stewart Parnell, recurs from Joyce's earliest works as a victim of betrayal consequent on his adulterous relationship with Kitty O'Shea underlines the extent to which adultery is also an historical and political issue for Irish nationalism. The common tracing of the first Anglo-Norman conquest of Ireland in 1169 to the adulterous relationship between Diarmaid MacMurchadha, King of Leinster, and Dearbhghiolla, the High King's wife, establishes adulteration as a popular myth of origins for Irish nationalist sentiment. As the Citizen puts it, in the "Cyclops" chapter of *Ulysses*: "The adultress and her paramour brought the Saxon robbers here...A dishonoured wife...that's what's the cause of all our misfortunes" (*Ulysses*, p. 266).

For the nationalist citizen, the identity of the race is adulterated by "la belle infidèle" and, as in the old expression, the restoration of that identity by translation (*traditore*) is haunted by the anxiety of a betrayal (*traduttore*). This chapter, that in *Ulysses* in which issues of nationalist politics and culture are played out most intensely and in which the various elements of Irish culture are most thoroughly deployed, circulates not only thematically but also stylistically around adulteration as the constitutive anxiety of nationalism. For while the citizen is militant against the hybridization of Irish culture, the chapter itself dramatizes adulteration as the condition of colonial Ireland at virtually every level. Barney Kiernan's pub is at the heart of Dublin, but also located in Little Britain Street, in the vicinity of the Linenhall, the law courts and the Barracks, and across the river from Dublin Castle, the centre of British administration. Most of the characters who pass through the bar (already a parodic form of the legal bar, both being sites of censure and debate) are connected in one or other way with these institutions, while the legal cases cited continually associate the influence of British institutions with economic dependency in the form of debt, and that in turn with the stereotype of financial and cultural instability, the Jew.[38] The slippage among institutional, cultural, racial and political elements is a function of a stylistic hybridization that refuses to offer any normative mode of representation from which other modes can be said to deviate.

These features of the "Cyclops" chapter have been noted in different ways by many commentators. What needs to be stressed, however, is that by and large the mingling of stylistic elements is rendered by critics in terms which reduce the process of hybridization to the juxtaposition of a set of equivalent representational modes, a reduction which, even where it refuses to posit the register of colloquial speech as an "original" of which all other modes are "translations", implies the essential coherence or integrity of each mode in itself. To do so is to leave fundamentally unchallenged the principle of equivalence on which the translational aesthetic is based. This is the case even in one of the most astute accounts of the chapter. After rewriting a passage from "Cyclops" in what is effectively parallel text, Colin MacCabe comments:

> Ignoring for the moment that part of the second text which has no parallel in the first, what is important in this passage is not the truth or falsity of what is being said, but how the same event articulated in two different discourses produces different representations (different truths). Behind "an elder of noble gait and countenance" and "that bloody old pantaloon Denis Breen in his bath slippers" we can discern no definite object. Rather each object can only be identified in a discourse which already exists and that identification is dependent on the possible distinctions available in the discourse.[39]

MacCabe's description of Joyce's procedures at this juncture is comparable to Bakhtin's general description of the novel as a genre:

> The novel can be defined as a diversity of social speech types (sometimes even diversity of languages) and a diversity of individual voices, artistically organized. The internal stratification of any single national language into social dialects, characteristic group behaviour, professional jargons, generic languages, languages of generations and age

groups, tendentious languages, languages of the authorities, of various circles and of passing fashions, languages that serve the specific sociopolitical purposes of the day, even of the hour (each day has its own slogan, its own vocabulary, its own emphases) – this internal stratification present in any given language at any given moment of its historical existence is the indispensable prerequisite for the novel as a genre. (pp. 262–3)

Adequate so far as they go, neither description is capable of grasping the internal heterogeneities, the adulteration of discourses as Joyce constructs them in "Cyclops" and throughout *Ulysses*. This process of adulteration ranges from a phenomenon of colloquial Irish speech to which Oscar Wilde gave the name of "malapropism" to the ceaseless interpenetration of different discourses. Malapropism varies from casual misspeaking, sometimes intentional, sometimes based on mishearings of an improperly mastered English ("Don't cast your nasturtiums on my character" [p. 263]), to deliberate and creative polemical wordplay (as in English "syphilisa-tion").[40] As a larger stylistic principle, the adulteration of interpenetrating discourse is unremitting, blending, among other things, pastiches of biblical / liturgical, medie-val, epic (based in large part on Standish O'Grady's already highly stylized versions of old Irish heroic cycles), legal, scientific and journalistic modes. Frequently, the legal and journalistic discourses at once contain and disseminate adulteration, represent-ing as institutional formations material sites for the clash of heterogeneous languages and interests. The following example instantiates the possible modulations among different registers:

And whereas on the sixteenth day of the month of the oxeyed goddess and in the third week after the feastday of the Holy and Undivided Trinity, the daughter of the skies, the virgin moon being then in her first quarter, it came to pass that those learned judges repaired them to the halls of law. There master Courtenay, sitting in his own chamber, gave his rede and master Justice Andrew, sitting without a jury in probate court, weighed well and pondered the claim of the first chargeant upon the property in the matter of the will propounded and final testamentary disposition *in re* the real and personal estate of the late lamented Jacob Halliday, vintner, deceased, versus Livingstone, an infant, of unsound mind, and another. And to the solemn court of Green street there came sir Frederick the Falconer. And he sat him there about the hour of five o'clock to administer the law of the brehons at the commission for all that and those parts to be holden in and for the county of the city of Dublin. And there sat with him the high sinhedrim of the twelve tribes of Iar, for every tribe one man, of the tribe of Patrick and of the tribe of Hugh and of the tribe of Owen and of the tribe of Conn and of the tribe of Oscar and of the tribe of Fergus and of the tribe of Finn and of the tribe of Dermot and of the tribe of Cormac and of the tribe of Kevin and of the tribe of Caolte and of the tribe of Ossian, there being in all twelve good men and true . . . And straightway the minions of the law led forth from their donjon keep one whom the sleuthhounds of justice had apprehended in consequence of evidence received. (p. 265)

Categorization of this and similar passages as "dialogic" would be limited insofar as what occurs here is not an opposition, conversational or polemical, between coherent "voices", but their entire intercontamination. Indeed, precisely what is lacking or erased here is *voice*, which, as Bakhtin remarks, is a category fundamental "in the realm of ethical and legal thought and discourse . . . An independent, responsible and active discourse is *the* fundamental indicator of an ethical, legal and political human being" (pp. 349–50).

It is through the question of voice and its dismantling that we can begin to grasp the complex ramifications of Joyce's deployment of adulteration as both motif and stylistic principle in *Ulysses*. Where nationalism is devoted to the production, in stylistic terms, of a singular voice, and to the purification of the dialect of street ballads or Gaelic songs, it produces equally what we might envisage as a matrix of articulated concepts which provide the parameters of its political aesthetic or aesthetic politics. Thus this singular voice correlates with the formation of the Irish subject as autonomous citizen at one level and with a collective Irish identity at another. That analogical relation between the individual and the national moments is permitted by a concept of representation which requires a narrative movement between the exemplary instance and the totality that it prefigures. The identification of each representative individual with the nation constitutes the people which is to claim legitimate rights to independence as an "original", that is, essential, entity. Consistent representation of that essence underwrites simultaneously the aesthetic originality, or autonomy, of the literary work that takes its place as an instance of the national culture. Such a self-sustaining and self-reinforcing matrix of concepts furnishes the ideological versimilitude of cultural nationalism, permitting its apparent self-evidence.

Joyce's work, on the contrary, deliberately dismantles voice and verisimilitude in the same moment. Even if, as MacCabe has suggested, particular discourses attain dominance at given points in the text, the continual modulations that course through "Cyclops", as indeed through the work as a whole, preclude any discursive mode from occupying a position from which the order of probability that structures mimetic verisimilitude could be stabilized. But even beyond this, the constantly parodic mode in which given discourses are replayed prevents their being understood as internally coherent, if rival, systems of verisimilitude. The double face of parody, at once dependent on and antagonistic to its models, constantly undercuts both the production of an autonomous voice and the stabilization of a discourse in its "faithful" reproduction.[41] Adulteration as a stylistic principle institutes a multiplication of possibility in place of an order of probability and as such appears as the exact aesthetic correlative of adultery in the social sphere. For if adultery is forbidden under patriarchal law, it is precisely because of the potential multiplication of possibilities for identity that it implies as against the paternal fiction, which is based on no more than legal verisimilitude. If the spectre of adultery must be exorcized by nationalism, it is in turn because adulteration undermines the stable formation of legitimate and authentic identities. It is not difficult to trace here the basis for nationalism's consistent policing of female sexuality by the ideological and legal confinement of women to the domestic sphere.[42] Nor is there any need to rehearse here the anxieties that Bloom raises for the Citizen on racial as well as sexual grounds, or the extent to which the narrative as a whole occupies aesthetic, cultural and sexual terrains in a manner that continually runs counter to nationalist ideology.[43] What must be noted, however, is the extent to which its anti-representational mode of writing clashes with nationalist orders of verisimilitude precisely by allowing the writing out of the effects of colonialism that nationalism seeks to eradicate socially and psychically. This is not merely a matter of the content of a representation but also inseparably an issue of stylistics.

Thus, for instance, Bloom cannot be the exemplary hero of what might be an Irish epic, not only because of his status as "neither fish nor fowl", to quote the Citizen, but because *Ulysses* as a whole refuses the narrative verisimilitude within which the formation of representative man could be conceived. The aesthetic formation of the exemplary citizen requires not alone the selection of an individual sociologically or statistically "normative", but the representation of that individual's progress from unsubordinated contingency to socially significant integration with the totality. This requires in turn what Bakhtin describes as "a combining of languages and styles into a higher unity", the novel's capacity to "orchestrate all its themes" into a totality (p. 263). *Ulysses'* most radical movement is in its refusal to fulfil either of these demands and its correspondent refusal to subordinate itself to the socializing functions of identity formation.[44] It insists instead on a deliberate stylization of dependence and inauthenticity, a stylization of the hybrid status of the colonized subject as of the colonized culture, their internal adulteration and the strictly parodic modes that they produce in every sphere.

III

We will become, what, I fear, we are largely at present, a nation of imitators, the Japanese of Western Europe, lost to the power of native initiative and alive only to second-hand assimilation. (Douglas Hyde)

Everywhere in the mentality of the Irish people are flux and uncertainty. Our national consciousness may be described, in a native phrase, as a quaking sod. It gives no footing. It is not English, nor Irish, nor Anglo-Irish.... (Daniel Corkery)

[The *pachuco's*] dangerousness lies in his singularity. Everyone agrees in finding something hybrid about him, something disturbing and fascinating. He is surrounded by an aura of ambivalent notions: his singularity seems to be nourished by powers that are alternately evil and beneficent. (Octavio Paz)

We Brazilians and other Latin-Americans constantly experience the artificial, inauthentic and imitative nature of our cultural life. An essential element in our critical thought since independence, it has been variously interpreted from romantic, naturalist, modernist, right-wing, left-wing, cosmopolitan and nationalist points of view, so we may suppose that the problem is enduring and deeply rooted. (Roberto Schwarz)

A European journalist, and moreover a leftist, asked me a few days ago. "Does a Latin-American culture exist?"...The question...could also be expressed another way: "Do you exist?" For to question our culture is to question our very existence, our human reality itself, and thus to be willing to take a stand in favor of our irremediable colonial condition, since it suggests that we would be but a distorted echo of what occurs elsewhere. (Roberto Fernandez Retamar)

The danger is in the neatness of identifications. (Samuel Beckett)

Riding on the train with another friend, I ramble on about the difficulty of finishing this
book, feeling like I am being asked by all sides to be a "representative" of the race, the
sex, the sexuality – or at all costs to avoid that.   (Cherrié Moraga)[45]

Since there is insufficient space for a more exhaustive account, the above citations
must serve as indicators of a recurrent and problematic set of issues that course
through numerous colonial situations, perhaps especially in those where an "original" language has been displaced by that of the colonizing power.[46] This problematic
can be described as a confrontation with a cultural hybridization which, unlike the
process of assimilation described by Bakhtin and others, issues in *inauthenticity* rather
than authentic identity. To describe this confrontation as problematic is to insist that
the experience of inauthenticity intended here is not to be confused with that of the
celebrated post-modern subject, though clearly the overlapping geographical and
historical terrain of each ultimately requires that they be elaborated together. For
the aesthetic freedom of the post-modern subject is the end-product of a global
assimilation of subordinated cultures to the flows of multinational capital in the
post-colonial world, and to fail to specify that subject is to ignore equally the powerful
dissymmetry between the subject who tastes and the indifferent, that is, interchangeable objects of his / her nomadic experience.[47] It should be recalled that the experience of colonized cultures such as Ireland's, with differing but increasing degrees of
intensity, is to be subjected to an uneven process of assimilation. What is produced,
accordingly, is not a self-sustaining and autonomous organism capable of appropriating other cultures to itself, as imperial and post-modern cultures alike conceive
themselves to be, but rather, at the individual and national-cultural level, a hybridization radically different from Bakhtin's in which antagonism mixes with dependence and autonomy is constantly undermined by the perceived influence of alien
powers.

A complex web of specular judgments constructs this problematic. On the side of
the colonizer, it is the inauthenticity of the colonized culture, its falling short of the
concept of the human, that legitimates the colonial project. At the other end of
the developmental spectrum, the hybridization of the colonized culture remains an
index of its continuing inadequacy to this concept and of its perpetually "imitative"
status. The colonizer's gaze thus overlooks the recalcitrant sites of resistance that are
at work in hybrid formations such as those we have been analysing. From the
nationalist perspective, hybridity is no less devalued; the perceived inauthenticity of
the colonized culture is recast as the contamination of an original essence, the
recovery of which is the crucial prerequisite to the culture's healthy and normative
development. The absence of an authentic culture is the death of the nation, its
restoration its resurrection. In this sense, nationalist monologism is a dialogic inver-
sion of imperial ideology, caught willy-nilly in the position of a parody, antagonistic
but dependent.[48]

These remarks need to be qualified, however, by reiterated stress upon the dissymmetry of the specular relation. Nationalism is generated as an oppositional discourse
by intellectuals who appear, by virtue of their formation in imperial state institutions,
as in the first place subjected to rather than the subjects of assimilation. Their
assimilation is, furthermore, inevitably an uneven process: by the very logic of

assimilation, either the assimilated must entirely abandon their culture of origins, supposing it to have existed in anything like a pure form, or persist in a perpetually split consciousness, perceiving the original cultural elements as a residue resistant to the subject formed as a citizen of the empire. Simultaneously, the logic of assimilation resists its own ideal model: since the process is legitimated by the judgment of the essential inferiority of the colonized, its very rationale would be negated in the case of a perfect assimilation of colonized subjects without remainder. Therefore, it is at once the power and the weakness of assimilation as the cultural arm of hegemonic imperialism that a total integration of the colonized into the imperial state is necessarily foreclosed. Recognition of this inescapable relegation to hybrid status among "native" intellectuals formed by the promise of an ever-withheld subjecthood is a principal impulse to nationalism at the same time as it determines the monologic mode of nationalist ideology.[49]

We should recall, however, that the desire for the nation is not merely to be formative of an authentic and integral subjecthood, but also the means to capture the state which is the nation's material representation. This fact has crucial theoretical and practical consequences. The formation of nationalist intellectuals takes place through both the repressive and the ideological state apparatuses of the empire, the army and police forces being as instrumental as the schools or recreationary spaces. This entails the space of the nation itself being constituted through these apparatuses which quite literally map it and give it its unity in the form of the state. Accordingly, just as the state form survives the moment of independence, the formation of the citizen-subject through these apparatuses continues to be a founding requirement of the new nation state.[50] What is time and again remarked of the post-colonial world, that "independent" states put in place institutions entirely analogous to those of the colonial states that dominated them, is not merely to be explained as a ploy by which the defeated empires continue their domination in renovated guise. For the state form is a requirement of anti-colonial nationalism as it was its condition. By the same token, post-colonial nationalism is actively engaged in the formation of citizen-subjects through those institutions and thereby on the analogy of the metropolitan subject. This is an instance of the "modernizing" effect of the state as the ensemble of institutions which ensures the continuing integration of the post-colonial state in the networks of multinational capital. But it is no less an instance of the modernizing effect of nationalism itself.

The terrain of colonial hybridization here analysed in the Irish context but with specific counterparts virtually everywhere in the colonial world falls in a double and, for the new nation, contradictory sense under the shadow of the state. Even where its most immediate instruments seem to be economic or cultural forces remote from the purview of the state, hybridization is impelled and sustained by the intervention of the imperial state – by its commercial and criminal laws, its institutions, its language, its cultural displays. Against this process reacts a monologic nationalism which, though already marked by hybridization, seeks to counter it with its own authentic institutions. In the post-independence state, these very institutions continue to be the locus of a process of hybridization despite the separation out of a more or less reified sphere of "national culture" whose functions, disconnected from oppositional struggle, become the formal and repetitive interpellation of national subjects and the residual demarcation of difference from the metropolitan power. In this respect also, the post-independence state reproduces the processes of metropolitan culture, the very formality of the "difference" of the national culture ensuring that the interpellation of its citizens always takes the "same form" as that of the metropolitan citizen.

Consequently, the apparatuses of the state remain crucial objects for a resistance which cannot easily be divided into theoretical and practical modes, not least because what determines both is an aesthetic narrative through which the theoretical is articulated upon the practical and vice versa. What begins as a Kantian precept finds specific material instantiation in post-colonial politics. For though the mode of formation of the citizen-subject may appear as a merely theoretical issue, the narrative of representation on which it depends for the principle by which individual and nation can be sutured determines equally the forms of schooling and of political institutions adopted. These in turn demarcate the limits of what can properly, in any given state, be termed a political practice. For, like any other social practice, politics is an effect of an ideological formation obedient to specific laws of verisimilitude. To have a voice in the sphere of the political, to be capable either of self-representation or of allowing oneself to be represented, depends on one's formation as a subject with a voice exactly in the Bakhtinian sense.

I have been arguing throughout that the processes of hybridization active in the Irish street ballads or in *Ulysses* are at every level recalcitrant to the aesthetic politics of nationalism and, as we can now see, to those of imperialism. Hybridization or adulteration resist identification both in the sense that they cannot be subordinated to a narrative of representation and in the sense that they play out the unevenness of knowledge which, against assimilation, foregrounds the political and cultural positioning of the audience or reader. To each recipient, different elements in the work will seem self-evident or estranging. That this argument does not involve a celebration of the irreducible singularity of the artistic work, which would merely be to take the detour of idealist aesthetics, is evident when one considers the extent to which *Ulysses* has been as much the object of refinement and assimilation in the academy as were the street ballads before. This is, after all, the function of cultural institutions, metropolitan or post-colonial, which seek to reappropriate hybridization to monology. By the same token, such works are continually reconstituted as objects in a persistent struggle over verisimilitude.

It is precisely their hybrid and hybridizing location that makes such works the possible objects of such contestations, contestations that can be conducted oppositionally only by reconnecting them with the political desire of the aesthetic from which they are continually being separated. The same could be said for the multiple locations that make up the terrain of a post-colonial culture: it is precisely their hybrid formation between the imperial and the national state that constitutes their political significance. If, as post-colonial intellectuals, we are constantly taunted – and haunted – by the potentially disabling question, "Can the subaltern speak?", it is necessary to recall that to speak politically within present formations one must have a voice and that the burden of the question here cited is to deprive two subjects of voices: the subaltern, who cannot speak for herself, and the intellectual, who, by speaking for him or herself, is deprived of the voice that would speak for others. The post-colonial intellectual, by virtue of a cultural and political formation which is for the state, is inevitably formed away from the people that the state claims to constitute and represent and whose malformation is its *raison d'être*. What this entails, however, is not occasion for despair and self-negation but rather that the intellectual's own hybrid formation become the ground for a continuing critique of the narrative of representation that legitimates the state and the double disenfranchisement of sub-altern and citizen alike. Within this project, the critique of nationalism is inseparable from the critique of post-colonial domination.[51]

NOTES

1 See Immanuel Kant, *The Critique of Judgement*, James Creed Meredith (trans.) (Oxford 1952), p. 181. I have discussed the ramifications of the concept of exemplarity for politics and pedagogy in "Kant's Examples", *Representations*, 28 (Autumn 1989), pp. 34–54.

2 D. F. MacCarthy, cited in Charles Gavan Duffy, *Four Years of Irish History, 1845–1849* (London 1883), p. 72.

3 On the concept of *Naturgabe* as grounding the economy of genius, see Jacques Derrida, "Economimesis", Richard Klein (ed.), *Diacritics*, 11.2 (Summer 1981), pp. 10–11.

4 Jacques Derrida explores the logical paradoxes involved in the founding of the state in the name of the people in "Déclarations d'indépendance" in *Otobiographies: l'enseignement de Nietzsche et la politique du nom propre* (Paris 1984), pp. 13–32. The consequences of these logical paradoxes are worked out later in Ireland's own declaration of independence in 1916, as I have tried to show in "The Poetics of Politics", *Anomalous States: Irish Writing and the Post-Colonial Moment* (Durham DC 1993).

5 See especially chapter 2 of my *Nationalism and Minor Literature* (Berkeley and Los Angeles 1987), and "Writing in the Shit", in *Anomalous States*.

6 See Mikhail Bakhtin, *The Dialogic Imagination: Four Essays*, Michael Holoquist (ed.), Caryl Emerson and Michael Holquist (trans.) (Austin 1981), pp. 67, 262–3, and *passim*.

7 To this extent, Bakhtin is still in accord with Erwin Rohde, whose history of the Greek novel he cites critically: both see the condition of emergence of the novel as being the collapse or disintegration of "a unitary and totalizing national myth" (p. 65).

8 See Charles Gavan Duffy, *Young Ireland: A Fragment of Irish History, 1840–1850* (London 1880), p. 155.

9 As Thomas Flanagan has argued in his *The Irish Novelists, 1800–1850* (New York 1959), especially chapter 3, the problem for Irish novelists was precisely to overcome the polemical heteroglossia of "race, creed and nationality" (p. 35). In a society in which identity is defined by opposition to others, the conventional form of the novel, which concentrates on individual development set over against social conventions, what Lukács describes as "second nature", is unavailable. I have discussed some of the crises of representation faced by Irish novelists and constitutional thinkers in the early nineteenth century in "Violence and the Constitution of the Novel", in *Anomalous States*. The tendency of Bakhtin's analysis of the novel and its social determinants makes it impossible for him to grasp the normative socializing function of the novel and therefore to explore fully the implications of Hegel's remark, which he cites (p. 234), that "the novel must educate man for life in bourgeois society". Bakhtin's representation of the novel as a largely progressive and subversive genre stands in need of considerable correction by other theorists who have more fully grasped its ideological and socializing functions. See for example Franco Moretti,

The Way of the World: The Bildungsroman in European Culture (London 1987) and D. A. Miller, *The Novel and the Police* (Berkeley/Los Angeles 1988), as well as Georg Lukács, *The Theory of the Novel*, Anna Bostock (trans.) (Cambridge 1971).

10 See Lloyd, *Nationalism and Minor Literature*, chapter 2. Citation from Duffy, *Four Years*, p. 153.

11 See Thomas Osborne Davis, "The Ballad Poetry of Ireland", in *Selections from his Prose and Poetry*, T. W. Rolleston (intro.) (Dublin n.d), p. 210.

12 It should be remarked that these classifications are constitutive more than analytic, inventing both demographic and aesthetic categories which, as this essay will suggest, subserve distinct political ends. All of them are, in different ways, highly problematic.

13 Daniel Corkery's *The Hidden Ireland: A Study of Gaelic Munster in the Eighteenth Century* (1924; Dublin 1967) is one of the first texts to decipher in Gaelic poetry of the eighteenth century the remnants of the traditions forged in a high or aristocratic tradition rather than the effusions of illiterate peasants.

14 Davis, "The Songs of Ireland", *Prose and Poetry*, p. 225.

15 Denis Florence MacCarthy, *The Book of Irish Ballads*, new edition (Dublin 1869), p. 24.

16 Samuel Taylor Coleridge, "The Statesman's Manual" (1816), in R. J. White (ed.), *Lay Sermons*, Bollingen Edition (Princeton 1972), p. 29. For the symbolist tradition in Irish nationalism's aesthetic politics, see my "The Poetics of Politics", in *Anomalous States*.

17 Charles Gavan Duffy (ed.), *The Ballad Poetry of Ireland* (Dublin 1845), p. xv.

18 On the anxiety concerning English miscegenation with the Gaels, see David Cairns and Shaun Richards, *Writing Ireland: Colonialism, Nationalism and Culture* (Manchester 1988), pp. 5–7. On the economic and social currents in nineteenth-century Ireland that affected the emergence of Irish cultural nationalism, see Lloyd, *Nationalism and Minor Literature*, chapter 2. The question of the decline of the Irish language is more vexed, since recent research gives us reason to doubt the inexorability and rapidity of the decline of the language. Akenson, *Irish Educational Experiment*, pp. 378–80, uses census data to corroborate the notion, current since at least Davis's 1843 essay, "Our National Language", that the language was in use only in the western half of the country and among less than 50 per cent of the population. (See "Writing in the Shit", in *Anomalous States*, for the consequences of this view.) Yet it may be that such statistics reflect only the predominant language of literacy, and that for a far greater proportion of the population than was formerly acknowledged, oral proficiency in Irish went along with literacy in English. The ballads often seem to assume a considerable degree of passive competence in Irish, at the least, and certainly an awareness of Gaelic cultural referents. Kevin Whelan remarks:

> I would argue that in 1841 the absolute number speaking Irish was at an all-time high. Remember the population of Ireland in 1600 was ca. 1.5 million. By 1841, it was up to 8.5 million. 100% of 1.5 million is still 1.5 million, 50% of 8.5 million is 4.25 million. Thus, the decline model of 18th and 19th century Irish is misleading in absolute terms – and remember population was increasing rapidly in the west and south west – the Irish-speaking areas. The vitality and flexibility of pre-famine Gaelic-speaking culture has been severely underestimated. (Private correspondence)

See also Niall Ó Cíosáin, "Printed Popular Literature in Irish 1750–1850: Presence and Absence" and Garrett FitzGerald, "The Decline of the Irish Language 1771–1871" in Mary Daly and David Dickson (eds), *The Origins of Popular Literacy in Ireland: Language Change and Educational Development 1700–1920* (Dublin 1990), pp. 45–57 and 59–72 respectively, and Tom Dunne, "Popular Ballads, Revolutionary Rhetoric and Politicisation", in David Dickson and Hugh Gough (eds), *Ireland and the French Revolution* (Dublin 1990), p. 142.

19 Colm Ó Lochlainn (ed.), *Irish Street Ballads* (1939; revised edn., Dublin 1946).

20 See for example Robert Welch, *Irish Poetry from Moore to Yeats*, Irish Literary Studies, 5 (Gerrards Cross 1980), pp. 43–5, 71 and 131.

21 For "The Barrymore Tithe Victory" and "A New Song", see Georges-Denis Zimmermann, "Irish Political Street Ballads and Rebel Songs, 1780–1900", doctoral thesis presented to University of Geneva (Geneva 1966), pp. 204–5 and 208–9; for "The Kerry Recruit", see Ó Lochlainn, *Street Ballads*, pp. 2–3. I am grateful to Brendán Ó Buachalla for alerting me to the wider significance of such allusions.

22 "Father Murphy" in Ó Lochlainn, *Street Ballads*, pp. 54–5; "Billy's Downfall" in Zimmermann, "Irish Rebel Songs", pp. 220–1. Dunne, "Popular Ballads", pp. 149–50, discusses six recorded versions of "Father Murphy", and comments on the extent to which different versions may indicate either popular adaptations of bourgeois songs or, contrarily, bourgeois refinements of popular ballads.

23 An excellent account of the confusion of high and low in popular forms and of its pleasures is Peter Stallybrass and Allon White, *The Politics and Poetics of Transgression* (Ithaca, New York 1986). Zozimus's own defence at his trial for causing an obstruction in the Dublin streets is itself a magnificent example of the mixing of genres with exuberant disrespect for the canons:

> Your Worship, I love me countbry. She's dear to me heart, an' am I to be prevented from writin' songs in her honour, like Tommy Moore, Walter Scott an' Horace done for theirs, or from singin' them like the an-shent bards, on'y I haven't got me harp like them to accompany me aspirations! ... An' as a portion ov the poetic janius ov me country has descended upon me showlders, ragged an' wretched as the garmint that covers them, yet the cloth ov the prophet has not aroused more prophetic sintiments than I entertain, that me countbry shall *be* a free countbry! ... Homer sung the praises ov his countbry on the public highways; an' we are informed that dramatic performances wor performed in the streets, with nothing else for a stage but a dust cart. (Laughter.)

Quoted in the Dublin publican and antiquarian P. J. McCall's pamphlet, *In the Shadow of St Patrick's* (1893; Blackrock 1976), pp. 32–3, this account is clearly refracted through oral history. Yet even in its own parodic fashion, it stands as an interesting index of the unstable tone of the popular discourse on cultural politics, which reproduces serio-comic-ally all the terms of nationalist aesthetics but with an indeterminacy of address calculated to pull the wool over the authorities' eyes.

24 See John Mitchel, "Our War Department", *United Irishman*, I. ii (22 April 1848), p. 171.

25 See William Wordsworth, *The Prelude*, in *Poetical Works*, Thomas Hutchinson (ed.) (Oxford 1973), Book VII, p. 546, ll. 701–4.

26 I have developed these arguments in *Nationalism and Minor Literature*, chapters 2 and 3.

27 MacCarthy, *Irish Ballads*, p. 26.

28 Paul Ricoeur has noted the relation between the minimal element of metaphor and the maximal element of plot in Aristotle's *Poetics*, both narrating a coming to identity of disparate elements. See Paul Ricoeur, "Metaphor and the Main Problem of Hermeneutics", *New Literary History*, 6, no. 1 (Autumn 1974), pp. 108–10. I have argued that the transfer from the metonymic to the metaphoric axis is the fundamental rhetorical structure of cultural assimilation and racist judgments in "Race under Representation", *Oxford*

Literary Review, 13 (Spring 1991), pp. 71–3. See also my "Violence and the Constitution of the Novel" in *Anomalous States* for further reflections on the political meaning of this distinction.

29 MacCarthy, *Irish Ballads*, p. 127. In his symbol-making, MacCarthy ignores recent discoveries by George Petrie, who showed that the round towers which are so prominent a feature of Irish landscapes were of relatively recent Christian origin, thus dispelling numerous myths of origin which had gathered around them. See my *Nationalism and Minor Literature*, chapter 3.

30 On the proliferation of kitsch, nationalist and otherwise, see Kevin Rockett, "Disguising Dependence: Separatism and Foreign Mass Culture", *Circa*, 49 (January/February 1990), pp. 20–5. Nationalist artefacts work precisely, and not without calculated political effect, as kitsch in the sense that Franco Moretti defines it: "kitsch literally 'domesticates' aesthetic experience. It brings it into the home, where most of everyday life takes place." See *The Way of the World*, p. 36.

31 James Joyce, *Ulysses* (New York 1986), pp. 152–3.

32 Douglas Hyde, "The Necessity for De-Anglicising Ireland" in Breandán Ó Conaire (ed.), *Language, Lore and Lyrics: Essays and Lectures* (Blackrock 1986), p. 154.

33 Douglas Hyde, "Gaelic Folk Songs", in *Language, Lore and Lyrics*, p. 107.

34 In both *Anthropology from a Pragmatic Point of View*, pp. 96–7, and *The Critique of Judgement*, pp. 152–3, Kant describes the enlightened subject as adhering to three precepts: to think for oneself; to think consistently; and to think from the standpoint of all mankind. Though Bakhtin's formulation apparently abandons the final maxim, it is formally and therefore universally prescriptive in exactly the same manner as Kant's. Samuel Beckett's terse formulation, "I'm in words, made of words, others' words," is perhaps the most succinct deconstruction of both. See *The Unnamable* (London 1959), p. 390.

35 I have discussed the complexities, largely resistant to nationalist aesthetics, of the process of translation in chapter 4 of *Nationalism and Minor Literature*.

36 Robert Tracy, in his essay "Loving You All Ways: Vamps, Vampires, Necrophiles and Necrofilles in Nineteenth Century Fiction", in Regina Barreca (ed.), *Sex and Death in Victorian Literature* (London 1990), pp. 32–59, gives an excellent account of the social and political background to the vampire tales of Irish writers like Sheridan Le Fanu and Bram Stoker, creator of Dracula. Alan Titley, *Dublin and Dubliners*, derives the name Dracula itself from the Gaelic Droch-Fhola, or bad blood, confirming its Irish origins. I am indebted to Kevin Whelan for this reference.

37 On Joyce's personal obsession with adultery and betrayal, see for example Richard Ellmann, *James Joyce* (Oxford 1959), pp. 255, 288–93. This obsession was written out not only in *Ulysses*, but also in "The Dead", the last story of *Dubliners*, and *Exiles*, Joyce's only play.

38 On the question of the hybridization of Irish culture, the most useful study is Cheryl Herr's *Joyce's Anatomy of Culture* (Urbana/Chicago 1986), which analyses in detail the various institutions which compose and interact within colonial Ireland. As she remarks, "The distortions of reality which one institution imposes on a semantic field operate endlessly in a culture composed of many competing institutions" (p. 14). The chapter pivots around Leopold Bloom's scapegoating as an alien Jew, and opens with the figure of the Jewish money-lender, Moses Herzog, whose name connects directly with the identically named Zionist leader. Since in this chapter Bloom is also given credit for Sinn Féin leader Arthur Griffith's adaptation of Hungarian nationalist strategies, it is clear that Joyce is deliberately playing up the paradox that lies at the heart of nationalism, namely, its dependence on the dislocatory forces of modernization for its "local" appeal. If Leopold Bloom be considered

Everyman, that is, in Odysseus's own formulation to the Cyclops, "Noman", then he is so only in the sense that he fulfils Karl Marx's prediction in "On the Jewish Question", that the principle of exchange for which anti-Semitism castigates the Jew will be most fully realized in "Christian" civil society. See especially the second essay in *Early Writings*, Rodney Livingstone and Gregor Benton (trans.) (New York 1975). Morton P. Leavitt, in "A Hero for our Time: Leopold Bloom and the Myth of Ulysses", in Thomas F. Staley (ed.), *Fifty Years Ulysses* (Bloomington, Indiana 1974), p. 142, makes a representative claim for the notion that "In the urban world in which we all live, no man could be more representative." For J. H. Raleigh, "he is modern, secular man, an international phenomenon produced in the Western world at large in fairly sizable numbers by the secular currents of the eighteenth, nineteenth and twentieth centuries, a type often both homeless in any specific locale and at home in any of the diverse middle-class worlds in the Europe and America of those centuries." See "Ulysses: Trinitarian and Catholic" in Robert D. Newman and Weldon Thornton (eds), *Joyce's Ulysses, The Larger Perspective* (Newark 1988), pp. 111–12.

39 See Colin MacCabe, *James Joyce and the Revolution of the Word* (London 1979), p. 92. See also Karen Lawrence, *The Odyssey of Style in Ulysses* (Princeton 1981), whose excellent analysis of the "Cyclops" chapter recognizes its hybrid or uneven character stylistically (especially pp. 106–7), but confines its implications to a modernist problematic of style and to "Joyce's skepticism about the ordering of experience in language *and* a personal desire to be above the constraints that writing usually imposes" (p. 119). The nature of this chapter has best been described, in terms that would be quite critical of MacCabe's rendering of it, by Eckhard Lobsien, *Der Alltag des Ulysses: Die Vermittlung von ästhetischer und lebensweltlicher Erfahrung* (Stuttgart 1978), p. 106: "Die zunächst so selbstverständlich anmutende Perspektive des Ich-Erzählers zeigt sich alsbald ebenso verformt und von undurchshauten Spielregeln eingeschränkt wie die Interpolationen" ("The at first apparently self-evident perspective of the first person narrator reveals itself directly to be just as deformed and restricted by inscrutable rules as the interpolations"); and p. 110: "Die verschiedenen, in sich geschlossenen Versionen von Alltagswelten werden derart in Interferenz gebracht, daß die Leseraktivität auf die Aufdeckung der geltenden Spielregeln und damit eine Desintegration des Textes abzielt" ("The various, self-enclosed versions of everyday worlds are thus brought into interference with one another so that the reader's activity aims at discovering the appropriate rules and thereby a distintegration of the text"). Lobsien emphasizes throughout the "interference" that takes place at all discursive levels in "Cyclops" and its effect of relativizing the "Repräsentation-sanspruch jeder einzelnen Sprachform" ("representational claims of every individual form of language") (p. 108). In the present essay, I seek to give back to that "claim to representation" its full political purview.

40 Joyce's fascination with malapropism is evident from as early as the first story of *Dubliners*, "The Sisters", in which Eliza speaks of the new carriages' "rheumatic wheels", to *Finnegans Wake*, for which it might be held to be a stylistic principle. Unlike the pun, which generally is more likely to be "forced", i.e. the product of an eager intention to subvert, malapropism (as the name nicely implies) evokes a subject not entirely in control of the metonymic productivity of language. If puns condense, malapropisms displace. *Finnegans Wake* clearly plays on the borderline between the two, generating more displacements than an individual subject can master. The Citizen's pun on "civilisation" and "syphilisation" is especially interesting insofar as it invokes standard nationalist attacks on the corrupting effects of English civilization on a morally pure Irish culture in the form of a verbal corruption. The movements of displacement or dislocation that construct colonized

society are grasped in the displaced language of the colonized. Both are at once indices of damage and impetuses to the dismantling of the appropriative autonomous speaking subject.

41 See Lloyd, *Nationalism and Minor Literature*, pp. 113–15, for a fuller discussion of the oscillation between antagonism and dependence in parody. An excellent study of the dynamics of parodic forms is Margaret A. Rose, *Parody/Metafiction: An Analysis of Parody as a Critical Mirror to the Writing and Reception of Fiction* (London 1979).

42 In first writing this essay for a publication on Chicano culture, I was forcibly reminded of the figure of La Malinche in Mexican/Chicano culture, who, as Cortez's mistress and interpreter, condenses with exceptional clarity the complex of racial betrayal, translation and adultery that Joyce equally seeks to mobilize in "Cyclops". On La Malinche, see Octavio Paz, "The Sons of La Malinche" in *Labyrinths of Solitude* (New York 1961), pp. 65–88; Norma Alarcón, "Chicana Feminist Literature: Re-vision through Malintzin/or Malintzin: Putting Flesh Back on the Object" in Cherríe Moraga and Gloria Anzaldua (eds), *This Bridge Called My Back: Writings by Radical Women of Color* (New York 1983), pp. 182–90; and Cherríe Moraga, "A Long Line of Vendidas" in *Loving in the War Years: lo que nunca paso por sus labios* (Boston 1983), especially pp. 113–14 and 117. In his essay "Myth and Comparative Cultural Nationalism: the Ideological Uses of Aztlan", in Rudolfo A. Anaya and Francisco Lomeli (eds), *Aztlan: Essays on the Chicano Homeland* (Albuquerque 1989), Genaro Padilla provides a valuable critical history of such recourses to mythic figures in Chicano cultural politics and indicates the similarities in political tendency and value of such tendencies across several cultural nationalisms, including Ireland's. In the Chicano as in the Irish context, what is politically decisive is the appropriative or mala-propian displacing effect of the mythic gesture with regard to dominant culture.

43 Colin MacCabe explores all these issues in Joyce's writings throughout *James Joyce and the Revolution of the Word*. See also Bonnie Kime Scott, *Joyce and Feminism* (Bloomington, Indiana 1984), especially chapter 2, "Mythical, Historical and Cultural Contexts for Women in Joyce", pp. 9–28; Dominic Manganiello, *Joyce's Politics* (London 1980); Hélène Cixous, *L'Exil de James Joyce ou l'art du remplacement* (Paris 1968), especially II. 1, "Le reseau des dépendances", is a valuable exploration of the linkages between family, church and nation, which perhaps surprisingly takes the father's rather than the mother's part.

44 On the socializing function of the novel, see especially Moretti, *The Way of the World*, pp. 15–16. Even where he lays claim to Irish identity ("I'm Irish; I was born here"), or where he seeks to define a nation ("The same people living in the same place"), Bloom appeals to the contingencies of merely contiguous relationships as opposed to the nationalist concern with a lineage of spirit and blood which must be kept pure. Bloom's insistence on contiguity underwrites his own figuration as a locus of contamination or hybridization as against the assimilative principles of nationalist ideology.

45 See respectively: Hyde, "The Necessity for De-Anglicising Ireland", p. 169; Daniel Corkery, *Synge and Anglo-Irish Literature* (Cork 1931), p. 14; Paz, "The Pachuco and Other Extremes" in *Labyrinths of Solitude*, p. 16; Roberto Schwarz, "Brazilian Culture: National-ism by Elimination", *New Left Review*, 167 (January/February 1988), p. 77; Roberto Fernandez Retamar, "Caliban" in *Caliban and Other Essays*, Edward Baker (trans.) (Min-neapolis 1988), p. 3; Samuel Beckett, "Dante . . . Bruno. Vico . . . Joyce" in Ruby Cohn (ed.), *Disjecta: Miscellaneous Writings and a Dramatic Fragment* (New York 1984), p. 19; Cherríe Moraga, *Loving in the War Years*, p. vi.

46 Retamar writes in "Caliban" (p. 5) of the singularity of Latin American post-colonial culture in terms of its having always to pass through metropolitan languages, those of the colonizer. In this, as in many other respects, there are evidently close affinities between the

Irish and the Latin American experience. But this appeal to specificity may in fact be spurious. As Ngugi wa Thiong'o has pointed out, African literature has also by and large been written in the colonizer's languages despite the ubiquitous survival of African vernacular languages. See *Decolonising the Mind: The Politics of Language in African Literature* (London, 1986), pp. 4–9. What this indicates, as I shall argue in what follows, is that the crucial issue is the space constituted for the citizen-subject in the post-colonial nation not only by the languages but also by the institutional and cultural forms bequeathed by the departing colonizer. As Thiong'o grasps, these are the sites and the subjects in which colonialism continues to reproduce itself.

47 See for example Jean-François Lyotard, *The Postmodern Condition: A Report on Knowledge*, Geoff Bennington and Brian Massumi (trans.) (Minneapolis 1984), p. 76:

> When power is that of capital and not that of a party, the "transavantgardist" or "postmodern" (in Jenck's sense) solution proves to be better adapted than the anti-modern solution. Eclecticism is the degree zero of contemporary general culture: one listens to reggae, watches a western, eats McDonald's food for lunch and local cuisine for dinner, wears Paris perfume in Tokyo and "retro" clothes in Hong Kong; knowledge is a matter for T. V. games. It is easy to find a public for eclectic works... But this realism of anything goes is in fact that of money; in the absence of aesthetic criteria, it remains possible and useful to assess the value of works of art according to the profits they yield. Such realism accommodates all tendencies, just as capitalism accommodates all "needs", provided that the tendencies and needs have purchasing power. As for taste, there is no need to be delicate when one speculates or entertains oneself.

Perceptive as this critique is of a vulgar post-modernism's "cosmopolitanism", we might note that the "one" of "general culture" is restored at a higher level only by the invocation of "taste" and "aesthetic criteria", that is, at the level of the cosmopolitan point of view of the Subject.

For an excellent critique of the confusion between post-colonial and post-modern forms, see KumKum Sangari, "The Politics of the Possible", *Cultural Critique*, 7 (Autumn 1987), pp. 157–86. Both she and Julio Ramos, in his "Uneven Modernities: Literature and Politics in Latin America", forthcoming in *Boundary*, 2, have pointed out that many of the distinguishing characteristics of Latin American literature, which often appear as post-modern effects, can in fact better be derived from the uneven processes of modernization that have occurred there. This is not, of course, to suggest a single developmental model for all societies but, on the contrary, to suggest the radical variability of modes as well as rates of change. Given the contemporary allure of the "nomadic subject" or of "nomadic theory", it is perhaps cautionary to recall that the legitimating capacity of the imperial subject is his ability to be everywhere (and therefore nowhere) "at home". For some exploration of this notion as it structures imperialist and racist representations, see Satya Mohanty, "Kipling's Children and the Colour Line", in *Race and Class*, special issue, "Literature: Colonial Lines of Descent", 31, no. 1 (July/September 1989), especially pp. 36–8.

48 Early twentieth-century nationalist appeals to Celticism are an excellent instance of this process, reversing the value but retaining the terms of stereotypes of the Celt first promulgated systematically by Samuel Ferguson and then extended by Matthew Arnold. I have discussed the formation of this stereotype in Ferguson's writings of the 1830s and Arnold's in the 1860s in "Arnold, Ferguson, Schiller: Aesthetic Culture and the Politics of Aesthetics", *Cultural Critique*, 2 (Winter 1986), pp. 137–69.

49 Homi Bhabha has explored the hybrid status of the colonized subject in "Of Mimicry and Man: The Ambivalence of Colonial Discourse", *October*, 28 (Spring 1984), pp. 125–33. On the foreclosure of the native intellectual's assimilation to the imperial state, see Benedict Anderson, *Imagined Communities* (London 1983), p. 105. I owe the distinction between the dominant and hegemonic phases of colonialism to Abdul JanMohamed's powerful essay, "The Economy of Manichean Allegory: The Function of Racial Difference in Colonial Literature", in Henry Louis Gates, Jr (ed.), *"Race", Writing and Difference* (Chicago 1985), pp. 78–107. JanMohamed criticizes Bhabha in this essay for failing to respect the dissymmetry between the colonizing and colonized subject in the Manichean social relations of colonialism. I try to show here that the two positions are intervolved, insofar as any nationalist opposition to colonialism is first articulated through the transvaluation of forms furnished by the colonial power. The moment of dependence in the relationship in no way diminishes the force of the antagonism in the national struggle for independence, but it does determine the forms taken by the post-colonial state and the necessity for a continuing critique of nationalism as a mimicry of imperial forms. On these aspects of nationalism, see Partha Chatterjee's *Nationalism and the Colonial World, A Derivative Discourse?* (London 1986), especially chapters 1 and 2. With regard to the logic of assimilation and its perpetual production of residues, I am greatly indebted to Zita Nunes' analysis of the formation of Brazilian national identity in literary modernism and anthropology of the 1920s and 1930s. Her work lucidly shows how the Manichean construction of otherness and the hybrid forms produced by colonialism are logically interdependent moments in the process of assimilation. It thus provides a means to repoliticizing Bhabha's understanding of "hybridization", since that process is shown to be captured in the hierarchic movement of assimilation which necessarily produces a residue that resists. Hybridization must accordingly be seen as an unevenness of incorporation within a developmental structure rather than an oscillation between or among identities. Nunes also demonstrates clearly the necessarily racist constructions implicit in cultural solutions to problems of national identity, thus introducing an invaluable corrective to concepts such as *mestizaje* which continue to be uncritically espoused even by thinkers such as Retamar. See Nunes, "Os Males do Brasil: Antropofagia e Modernismo", Papeis Avulsos do CIEC (Rio de Janeiro), no. 22.

50 My terms here are indebted to Louis Althusser's essay "Ideology and Ideological State Apparatuses (Notes towards an Investigation)" in *Lenin and Philosophy and Other Essays*, Ben Brewster (trans.) (New York 1971), pp. 127–86. Anderson, *Imagined Communities*, pp. 108–9, indicates the extent to which nationalist intellectuals are formed within the colonial state apparatus, a perception borne out in the case of Young Ireland by Jacqueline Hill's analysis of the social composition of the movement in "The Intelligentsia and Irish Nationalism in the 1840s", *Studia Hibernica*, 20 (1980), pp. 73–109. See also Frantz Fanon's essays "The Pitfalls of National Consciousness" and "On National Culture" in *The Wretched of the Earth* (New York, 1963), pp. 148–205 and 206–48 respectively. These essays analyse the dialectical process by which a bourgeois anti-colonial nationalism may give way to a popular nationalism in the post-independence state which is not subordinated to a fetishized "national culture". As such, they provide the ground for a critique of intellectual tendencies such as Irish revisionist history which criticize the anti-modernist and Manichean tendencies of nationalism only to valorize British imperialism as an essentially modernizing force.

51 I allude of course to Gayatri Chakravorty Spivak's seminal essay "Can the Subaltern Speak?" in *Marxism and the Interpretation of Culture*, Cary Nelson and Lawrence Grossberg (eds) (Urbana and Chicago 1988), pp. 271–313. I make no attempt to paraphrase this

essay here, wishing only to suggest that the opposition it establishes between *Darstellung* and *Vertreten* requires to be transformed dialectically through the concept of the state in which both are subsumed into a unity of being and of being capable of being represented. That the subaltern cannot speak in our voice is a problem only insofar as the post-colonial intellectual retains the nostalgia for the universal position occupied by the intellectual in the narrative of representation. Similarly, the inevitability of employing Western modes of knowledge is a critical condition of the intellectual's formation and inseparable from his/her occupation of a national space. The logical inverse of these propositions is that the contradictory existence of the post-colonial intellectual equally affects the coherence of Western modes of knowledge which are necessarily reformed and hybridized in other locations. The most interesting discussion of these issues is Homi Bhabha's "The Commitment to Theory", *New Formations*, 5 (1988), pp. 5–24. In all this, as in the composition of this essay as a whole, I am indebted to conversations with Dipesh Chakrabarty.

Reading a Woman's Death: Colonial Text and Oral Tradition in Nineteenth-Century Ireland

ANGELA BOURKE

Angela Bourke has emerged in recent years as the most influential woman writing about Ireland's colonial and postcolonial traditions. Her essay is concerned with the opposition between oral and written discourse, the former tending to be the province of women, especially in the countryside, the latter tending to express the concerns of men and colonial and nationalist authority. Her analysis of the accounts of an Irishwoman's death and the role folklore played in it underscores the deep division between an oral folk tradition in which women find a "counter-discourse" of identity that offers freedom from sexual and economic oppression and an official written tradition in which "a repressive social morality . . . worked hand in hand with the institutions of the state." Bourke considers the role of imperialist Celticism, the colonialist press and the Irish Literary Revival, all of which tended to foster a view of the colonized Irish as feminine. Against this pervasive feminization, Bourke argues that Irish women in the late nineteenth and early twentieth centuries constructed "narratives of passage" derived from folklore and fairy legends, taking on the identity of the fairies or *sidhe* in order to escape social and sexual oppression. The specific case of Bridget Cleary offers Bourke an example of how marriage as an economic institution both traps Irish women and encourages them to develop "a coded form of speech" out of the tradition of folklore. The student interested in feminist strategies to attain genuine historical agency in colonial and postcolonial contexts should read Bourke's essay alongside essays by **Gayatri Chakravorty Spivak**, **Rajeswari Sunder Rajan**, **Kay Schaffer**, and **Helen Tiffin**.

Reading a Woman's Death:
Colonial Text and Oral Tradition in Nineteenth-Century Ireland

In March 1895, when a twenty-six-year-old woman called Bridget Cleary was burned to death in her own kitchen in rural Tipperary, her body was hastily buried and a story concocted to account for her disappearance. Her family and neighbors, using the idiom of oral legend, said she had been taken away by the fairies of nearby Kylenagranagh Hill and a changeling – a non-human substitute – left in her place. Some of them claimed that it was this changeling and not the real Bridget which had been burned.

Over the previous days as Bridget lay ill in bed the story of fairy abduction had been taking shape. Her husband, Michael Cleary, assisted by several male neighbors, had touched her with a hot poker, drenched her with urine, forced her to drink concoctions of herbs in milk, and held her over the kitchen fire – asking insistently whether she was in fact Bridget Cleary or a fairy changeling. A magisterial inquiry held ten days later was told that this treatment was part of a traditional "cure" for fairy abduction and that it had proceeded in so orderly a manner that, although some people present had found it distressing, they had done nothing to stop it. The treatment was believed to have succeeded, but sometime after midnight on Friday, 15 March, Michael flung his wife on the floor before the fire, brandished a piece of burning wood before her mouth and demanded that she say her name three times. When she failed to answer to his satisfaction he doused her with lamp oil and set her ablaze.

According to one witness, Bridget's cousin, Johanna Burke, "the house was full of smoke and smell" and all of those present were terrified.[1] At about 2:00 a.m. Cleary asked Johanna Burke's brother, Patrick Kennedy, to help bury the body. They wrapped it in a sheet and carried it some quarter of a mile from the house. On 22 March, following a week of rumor, speculation, and extensive search, the body was discovered by members of the Royal Irish Constabulary, buried in swampy ground. In the meantime Michael Cleary had spent three nights at the nearby "fairy fort" or "rath" of Kylenagranagh, apparently in the expectation of seeing his wife ride out on a white horse, cutting her free, and so rescuing her from the fairies.

By the time the body was discovered, thirty-three-year-old Michael Cleary and nine of his neighbors were in police custody. Reporters from various newspapers covered both the magisterial inquiry and the summer assizes of the following July, where sentences ranging from six months' imprisonment to twenty years' penal servitude

Taken from *Feminist Studies* 21 (1995), pp. 553–86.

were handed down. Had Cleary been found guilty of murder as charged, he would have been hanged, but the evidence given in court was so extraordinary that with the judge's approval, the jury brought in a verdict of manslaughter instead.

How, one hundred years later, are we to read Bridget Cleary's death? Her life has not been written. Her story is known today because it was elicited in a court of law and extensively covered by journalists. It provided sensational copy for the local, the Dublin, and the London newspapers, and although nationalist editors in Ireland were at pains to distance themselves and their readers from the events they described, the anti-Irish press seized on them as propaganda. Representing a young woman as innocent victim and her tormentors – the men of her own community – as benighted and dull-witted peasants, these newspapers constructed a narrative which juxtaposed the incomprehensible, primitive supersitions of a colonized people with the rationality and enlightenment of Victorian British justice. Nationalist papers protested, but newspapers of all persuasions, in an apparent attempt to disentangle the paradoxes and reduce the anxiety of a society undergoing rapid modernization, polarized the forces at work: tradition against law; country against town; men against women. In the process, the gender opposition which was clearly central to the woman's torture and death was subordinated to and read as a metaphor for the relation between colonizer and colonized.[2]

But the newspaper narratives of Bridget Cleary's death were not the only accounts available. The story of her abduction by fairies, regarded by the British press as superstitious and incomprehensible, was not totally without authority. Produced by a system quite independent of Victorian expectations, and subtly different in its representation of social relations including questions of gender, this narrative was bound by different rules of credibility and was capable of interpretation simply as metaphor. Oral tradition, as the product of a subaltern class, served a different agenda from that of the courts and newspapers. Decentralized, discontinuous, and unstandardized, its discourse was available in 1895 to women as well as to men, both as tellers and as listeners. Attempting to tell the story of Bridget Cleary, however, oral tradition was drowned out by a version propounded in print culture, so that a narrative which might have made sense in some contexts came to be regarded as madness, a cause of embarrassment. In its place was constructed an account having a beginning, middle, and end, which showed Irish men as misguided savages and women as victims or innocent bystanders, with guilt assigned and punishment imposed.

The oral narrative that grew up about the death of Bridget Cleary emerges from a discourse on gender relations which, like the fictional fairy communities through whose activities it is expressed, has long been driven underground. Reading Bridget Cleary's death in all its complexity therefore requires that we decipher several layers of discourse. The newspaper accounts, the most easily available, are heavily influenced by colonialism, and secondarily by romantic Celticism, its offshoot. These written discourses in turn collude in presenting oral tradition as anterior: archaic and unchanging. In local reaction to Bridget Cleary's death, however, we find legend makers actively at work. We can observe the construction of a narrative designed to contain and comprehend violent events while holding at bay the forces of the intrusive and inquisitive centralized state. In the very moment of her death a narrative seems to have been at work whose terms may become more comprehensible to modern readers if they are understood as metaphors for jealousy, conflict, and rage.

One hundred years later, the account arrived at by the law courts and newspapers remains the basis of several renderings of Bridget Cleary's story,[3] but new questions emerge. On the one hand, a series of disclosures in Ireland, some of them involving trusted public figures, others revealing appalling mistreatment of women and children, have led to a radical shifting of social paradigms.[4] At the same time, postcolonial and feminist scholarship has re-examined received narratives, asking by whom they have been constructed and to what end and what is revealed by their logic and their silences. Bridging the space between these phenomena is a movement among creative writers and scholars in Ireland to reread the discourse of oral tradition, particularly as it reflects women's and children's lives, with the transitions, gaps, and contradictions they contain.[5] Such a rereading of the oral narrative of Bridget Cleary's death, based on an acceptance of fairy legend as a subtle and many-layered art form, can illuminate the issues which were at stake in 1895, both in the Cleary home and in the wider world of Anglo-Irish relations.

Newspaper Reports: The Colonial Context

The first reports of Bridget Cleary's death were carried in local newspapers. Differences emerged immediately between unionist and nationalist treatments, and when Dublin and London papers took up the story a colonialist rhetoric of "savagery" and "barbarism" began to be employed. I shall discuss later the elements of fairy belief tradition contained in the reports but for the present will concentrate on their reception in ever-widening circles at greater and greater distances from the parts of Ireland where oral legend could be understood on its own terms.

On Wednesday, 20 March 1895, the *Clonmel Chronicle* carried the following short item:

> "Gone with the Fairies"
> A good deal of excitement has been caused in the district about Drangan and Cloneen by the "mysterious disappearance" of a labourer's wife, who lived with her husband, a farm labourer, in that part of the country. The poor woman had been ill for some time, and a few days ago she told her husband that if he did not do something for her by a certain time "she would have to be going." An old woman who had been nursing the sick woman was sitting up with her as usual one night last week, and as she puts it, the invalid was "drawn" away. Search has been made everywhere and the police have been communicated with, but up to this afternoon no trace of the missing woman has been discovered. The country people entertain the opinion that she has "gone with the fairies!"

The *Clonmel Chronicle* was one of the two newspapers published each Wednesday and Saturday in Clonmel, county town of the South Riding of Tipperary, and a municipal borough with a population of about ten thousand. Unionist in sympathy, it supported the policies of the Tory government in London which had taken office the previous year. Its rival, the *Nationalist and Tipperary Advertiser*, presented the other side, appealing more to the Catholic than the Protestant population of County Tipperary and enthusiastically supporting the cause of home rule for Ireland.[6]

The *Nationalist and Tipperary Advertiser* for 20 March carried two reports of the woman's strange disappearance. As befitted a newspaper aimed at the Catholic population, it adopted a less distancing tone than the *Clonmel Chronicle* in commenting on rural affairs. Nevertheless, its readers and potential readers would have been drawn more from the class of town merchants and prosperous tenant farmers than from among the laborers, so although it assumes a certain acquaintance with popular tradition about "fairies" or "good people," it places itself firmly on the side of "rational belief," against "fairy quackery," and looks to the "authorities" and the law courts for the elucidation of the mystery:

> Mysterious Disappearance of a Young Woman
> The Land of the Banshee and the Fairy
>
> What would read as a kin to the fairy romances of ancient times in Erin, is now the topic of all lips in the neighbourhood of Drangan and Cloneen. It appears that a young woman named Cleary, wife of a cooper, living with her father and husband in a labourer's cottage in the townland of Ballyvadlea, took ill a few days ago, was attended by priest and doctor, and believed to have been suffering from some form of nervous malady, she suddenly disappeared on last Friday night, and has not since been heard of. Her friends who were present assert that she had been taken away on a white horse before their eyes, and that she told them when leaving, that on Sunday night they would meet her at a fort on Kylenagranagh hill, where they could, if they had the courage, rescue her. Accordingly, they assembled at the appointed time and place to fight the fairies, but, needless to say, no white horse appeared. It has transpired that her friends discarded the doctor's medicine, and treated her to some fairy quackery. However the woman is missing, and the rational belief is that in the law courts the mystery shall be elucidated. I need not say that the authorities have their own notions of the matter, but I shall reserve further comments until events more clearly develop themselves.

On the following Saturday, 23 March, both newspapers reported that following "informations" sworn before a local magistrate by Bridget's cousin Johanna Burke and William Simpson, caretaker of a nearby farm, a number of men and one woman had been arrested and charged with ill-treating Bridget Cleary. Meanwhile the search for the missing woman continued, and the *Nationalist and Tipperary Advertiser* carried in its second edition a stop press, "The Body Found," with a description of its condition and a report on the inquest.

During the following weeks, while witnesses were examined and suspects arrested and remanded in custody, newspapers in other parts of Ireland, in Britain, and in the United States took up the story. Tory papers followed the line taken by the *Clonmel Chronicle* but with less inhibition, interpreting Bridget Cleary's death as evidence of general barbarism and savagery in rural Ireland. Nationalist and liberal opinion constructed a more sympathetic view, wavering between condemnation and repudiation of the few people responsible for the crime and, in London, wistful attempts to understand it in terms of what has come to be called "Celticism" – a romantic view of

Irish (and Scottish, Welsh, Breton, and Cornish) people as driven by emotion, sometimes to extremes.[7] The London correspondent of the *New York Times* noted on Sunday, 31 March, that "as might be expected, the barbarous episode near Fethard, in Tipperary, of a woman being tortured to death by her husband and her male relatives in the process of expelling a witch that had taken possession of her body is being gravely cited by the anti-Irish papers here as evidence of the mental degradation and savagery of the Irish peasant population."

Home rule for Ireland was a question still hotly debated in 1895, when its achievement seemed to depend on Irish people's ability to prove themselves worthy of it in the eyes of Britain. Tory propaganda, concerned with justifying the contemporary "scramble" for Africa, characterized all colonized peoples as children, whose wise schoolmasters would decide when they were ready to govern themselves. This view was reflected in the cartoons of *Punch* and other periodicals which had long depicted the Irish as ignorant, superstitious, and simian. But after the Irish famine of the 1840s, a prosperous Catholic middle class of grazier-farmers and traders had emerged who were at pains to distance themselves from such images, pushing them off instead, when they could not be completely dispelled, on to the rural laborers – the class which had suffered most in the famine.

In the years following the famine the propertied middle class accumulated land and commercial assets and dictated a repressive social morality based on a newly centralized, authoritarian, and misogynist Catholicism which worked hand in hand with the institutions of the state. Social problems were increasingly brought under state and church control, and the Irish landscape still displays the hospitals, orphanages, workhouses, jails, asylums, and Magdalen homes (for "fallen" women), through which Victorian society regulated those people who could not easily be contained within its categories or who deviated from its norms of respectability. Many of these institutions were staffed by religious sisters, whose numbers increased enormously during the nineteenth century, as did the number of convents built.

The values of the middle class were those of literacy, rather than orality; English rather than the Irish language; shop-bought rather than homespun clothing; "devotions" and novenas in the recently built, imposing Catholic churches rather than "stations" in private homes or outdoor "patterns" in honor of local saints. Their daughters were educated in convent schools, learning French, fine needlework, deportment, and etiquette.[8] The middle class's response to colonization was not unusual: they were appropriating the culture of the colonizer, although their version was not Protestant but Catholic. For "respectable" Catholics, who were readers of the *Nationalist and Tipperary Advertiser*, stories of fairies, the banshee, or the pooka were a thing of the past – quaint relics of an earlier, less civilized time.[9]

The story that Bridget Cleary had gone away with the fairies corresponded to a model familiar to the Catholic middle class in the verbal art of their servants, and perhaps of their old people, but when it was used as propaganda against them, they needed urgently to repudiate it. The *Nationalist and Tipperary Advertiser* expressed their reaction in no uncertain manner. Under the heading "The Ballyvadlea Murder Inquiry – Public Horror and Indignation – Tory Slander Again," the editorial writer protests at the treatment of the story in a Dublin paper:

> [W]e found yesterday that the dreadful occurrence has been utilized editorially by the Tory-Unionist *Dublin Evening Mail* for purposes of political capital and as a suitable occasion to pour forth slander, odium, and abuse on Irish people generally; to stir up racial and religious passion and prejudice, and if possible to damage the cause of Home Rule. Had the editor of the Dublin Orange paper been in Clonmel he would have seen with his own eyes the storm of spontaneous popular indignation and horror recorded in our report today and which in the most forcible manner give the lie direct to his atrocious impeachment. Had he been in or near the local Catholic Church last Sunday, he could have witnessed how emphatically and how speedily the priest and the people there marked their reprobation of the horrible crime that has darkened the district.[10]

"Dark" was of course a favorite adjective of colonial discourse, simultaneously suggesting ignorance, superstition, crime, and the skin color of African and Asian peoples, as well as the growing contrast between town and country as streets were lighted first by gaslight and then by electricity.

The *Nationalist and Tipperary Advertiser*'s editorial continues, contrasting the "spartan" and "intelligent" conduct of the Crown witnesses, Johanna Burke and her eleven-year-old daughter Katie, with the savagery and barbarism imputed to the local people by the *Dublin Evening Mail*. It places the *Nationalist and Tipperary Advertiser* and its readers firmly on the side of law and order, repudiating the "dark" and "druidical" elements which have led the Tory paper to compare the moral and intellectual conditions of South Tipperary with those of Dahomey, and the coroner at the inquest on Bridget Cleary to say that "amongst Hottentots one would not expect to hear of such an occurrence."

> Ignorance and superstition may have gathered and no doubt did gather, darkly and dreadfully, around the Druidical or Danish rath at Ballyvadlea, but politics have nothing whatever to do with the abominable business. Let the guilty be tried and judged without fear, favour or affection; and let justice be done according to the truth, the whole truth, and nothing but the truth.[11]

In insisting on the unique horror of what happened to Bridget Cleary and rejecting an interpretation based on widespread superstition, this editorial anticipates the use of *sati* by British commentators as an index of the need for colonial administration in India and the repudiation of the practice by progressive natives. Gayatri Chakravorty Spivak has argued that before colonization, *sati*, far from being the barbarous norm by which brown men ill-treated brown women – necessitating their rescue by white men – was practiced only exceptionally and always from pressing economic motives. She points out that "what the British see as poor victimized women going to the slaughter is in fact an ideological battle-ground" and notes that discussion of *sati* entered the political domain at a time when the British in India were moving from a mercantile and commercial role to a territorial and administrative one.[12] In Ireland, British administration was at the peak of its centralized efficiency in 1895; any suggestion that Bridget Cleary's treatment was "normal" in the colonized culture would have been profoundly damaging to native middle-class interests. It followed that the oral discourse which surrounded her death was so thoroughly repudiated as to preclude its thoughtful appraisal.

Tory newspapers in Ireland and England had seized on the case of Bridget Cleary as an illustration of the brutality of rural Irish men, deploying a rhetoric established in the 1860s to condemn the activities of the oath-bound Irish Republican Brotherhood known as the Fenians. They presented Irish women – Bridget, the victim; her cousin Johanna, chief witness for the Crown; Johanna's daughter Katie, and her elderly mother, Mary Kennedy (tried and found guilty along with the men but then released by the judge) – as innocent, pure, and / or in need of protection by agents of the state. Journalists' construction of this picture recalls a Tenniel cartoon entitled "The Fenian-Pest," published in *Punch* on 3 March 1866, which shows, in the words of L. P. Curtis, Jr., "the virago Britannia defending the chaste Hibernia from the clutches of Irish-American Fenians with huge jaws and low facial angles" (see illustration).[13]

PUNCH, OR THE LONDON CHARIVARI.—March 3, 1866.

THE FENIAN-PEST.

Hibernia. "O MY DEAR SISTER, WHAT *ARE* WE TO DO WITH THESE TROUBLESOME PEOPLE?"
Britannia. "TRY ISOLATION FIRST, MY DEAR, AND THEN——"

Hibernia wears a shamrock garland in her hair. Her appearance suggests softness, movement, and fluidity, in striking (and appealing) contrast to the stern military bearing of Britannia: nineteenth-century discourse eroticizing the colonized female while brutalizing and dehumanizing the colonized male.

The *Nationalist and Tipperary Advertiser* reports approvingly on the words spoken by Johanna Burke and her daughter Katie in evidence, but it is clear that their permission to be heard is contingent on their submission to the court's authority and to its ways of structuring narrative. Subsequent accounts have continued to confer approval on them for coherence and conscientiousness, contrasting their evidence either implicitly or explicitly with that given by their neighbors, most of whom were male.[14] Among their own community, however, their position was more problematic.

Early accounts reported that Johanna Burke was arrested along with others who had been present in the house while Bridget was carried to and from the kitchen fire, but she seems to have made a choice that was not available to her male relatives. In the heavily gendered environment of colonization a woman could escape punishment by allying herself with the colonizer: in this case by turning Queen's evidence. Johanna's testimony was extensive and implicated three of her own brothers in the killing. All four brothers received prison sentences, including Michael Kennedy, who was in the house only briefly but was deemed guilty by virtue of his presence. But the price Johanna paid for acceptance by the wider world of print and the forces of the state was the loss of her place in her community: she later needed police protection and moved away from the area. When the census was taken six years later in 1901, her daughter Katie was working as a domestic servant in a Protestant household several miles away. Both women had been media stars for a brief period before sinking once more into obscurity. It was left to their dead cousin, Bridget, to symbolize the colonized female as tragic heroine.

CELTIC TWILIGHT AND THE COLONIZED FEMININE

The same paradigm of colonial femininity which could more easily imagine Johanna Burke as helpless witness than as engaged participant or complacent accessory influenced the media view of Bridget Cleary as victim. Here, however, another set of discourses comes into play, for it was not enough that the colonized female should be helpless. She must also, in order to be marked positive, be erotically appealing and exotically mysterious.

The *Nationalist and Tipperary Advertiser*'s first report of Bridget Cleary's disappearance compared it with "the fairy romances of ancient times in Erin." Use of the archaic and poetic "Erin" in preference to the more usual "Ireland" signals the influence of Celticism: "Erin" is a misty far away and long ago, an image personified as female and sustained by the contemporary popularity of both medieval Irish literature in translation and verbal art from contemporary oral tradition.

The nineteenth century had seen a huge growth in the investigation and publication of folk traditions, and the places where folklore was collected and studied were, not by coincidence, the same wild, remote, and picturesque landscapes so beloved of the romantic gaze: Sicily, Tuscany, the Highlands of Scotland, the Welsh mountains, the west of Ireland. This process had begun with the publication in 1760 of James Mac-Pherson's poems attributed to Ossian; the fact that they were largely spurious did nothing to diminish their popularity. The four volumes of J. F. Campbell's *Popular Tales of the West Highlands* were published in 1860–2, and by the time of Bridget Cleary's death fairies were highly fashionable among the reading public of London and Dublin.

As the nineteenth century ended, scientific advances and a long period without major war gave reason for optimism about the future, but publication of oral narratives as texts betrayed nostalgia for older ways. Jeremiah Curtin's *Myths and Folklore of Ireland* appeared in 1890 and his *Tales of the Fairies and of the Ghost World* in 1895. W. B. Yeats, the self-styled "last romantic," published *Fairy and Folk Tales of the Irish Peasantry in London* in 1888, *Representative Irish Tales* in 1891, *Irish Fairy Tales* in 1892, and *The Celtic Twilight* in 1893. Andrew Lang's *Blue Fairy Book* was published in London in 1889; and the *Yellow, Green,* and *Pink Fairy Books* had followed by 1897. Folklore studies were also deeply indebted to the new discipline of anthropology. In 1883 the Folk-Lore Society, founded five years earlier, began publishing its *Folk-Lore Journal.* In 1890 that publication merged with the *Archaeological Review* to form *Folk-Lore,* which in December 1895 published a sober, unsigned account of the burning of Bridget Cleary by direction of the society's council, "so as to preserve the relevant facts in a form accessible to scientific students."[15]

Both pseudoscientific and romantic approaches to folklore depended on a view of colonized and marginalized people as feminine. As this discourse developed in the work of Matthew Arnold and others, the Celt appeared as somehow all flesh, while the hard and rational Teuton was all bones. Not surprisingly, the balanced English temperament incorporated the best of both. It was in the interest of members of the "Celtic" races, particularly the more privileged among them, to accept part of this model. Irish writers could reasonably collude in fostering an image of their essential nature as ethereal and fey when the media alternative was the apelike image propounded in *Punch* and other periodicals. Opposed to the characterization of the Irish as apes was a nationalist convention that portrayed them as images of integrity and beauty. "Pat" was the idealized Irish man – handsome, thoughtful, and responsible. But "Erin" was simply the "Hibernia" of *Punch* appropriated from the colonizer's iconography; an abstraction more than a person; perhaps marginally less helpless, but still a victim. Curtis describes her:

> Erin was a stately as well as sad and wise woman, usually drawn in flowing robes, embroidered with shamrocks. Her hair was long and dark, falling well down her back; her eyes were round and melancholy, set in a face of flawless symmetry. Occasionally she wore a garland of shamrocks and appeared with a harp and an Irish wolfhound in the foreground. Erin suggested all that was feminine, courageous, and chaste about Irish womanhood, and she made an ideal Andromeda waiting to be rescued by a suitable Perseus.... [T]his figure of Erin, which was far more feminine than the virago known as Britannia, was the one symbol on which the cartoonists of London, Dublin and New York were in more or less complete agreement.[16]

Such a representation of the Irish feminine was more prescriptive than descriptive. Carol Coulter has argued that under colonization in Ireland, indigenous patterns of gender relations were progressively devalued and driven out of public sight to emerge much later in forms of women's resistance that might appear novel to metropolitan feminists. Quoting Ashis Nandy's observation that in India, "Western sexual stereotypes produced a cultural consensus in which political and socio-economic dominance symbolized the dominance of men and masculinity over women and feminity" – so that the feminine was allowed no place in the public sphere – she points out that these stereotypes were equally foreign in much of Ireland.[17] In fact married women above the poorest class had a high degree of decision-making power and financial independence in rural Ireland.

The stately, sad figure of Erin, large-eyed and dark-haired, although drawn from earlier Irish tropes about land and sovereignty as female, was an invention of the

PUNCH, OR THE LONDON CHARIVARI.—October 29, 1881.

TWO FORCES.

colonial process. It was particularly beloved of Yeats, one of the chief proponents of romantic Celticism.[18] In 1893, two years before Bridget Cleary's death, he published a poem called "The Stolen Bride" (later titled "The Host of the Air"), which remarkably anticipates the story told in rural Tipperary about Bridget and Michael Cleary. The central figure of this poem is a pre-Raphaelite Bridget: a bride with "long, dim hair," whom the fairies sweep away before her husband's eyes. It may well have influenced the treatment of the Cleary case by the newspapers, which described it as "kin to the fairy romances of ancient times in Erin."

Readers of the reports of Bridget Cleary's death would have learned from Yeats and other writers to equate Irishness, and oral tradition in particular, with mystery and breathless emotion. This expectation seems also to have influenced the progress of the trial, leading to a verdict of manslaughter rather than murder.[19] Mr. Justice O'Brien, who presided, addressed the jury in terms that recall another *Punch* cartoon, this time from 29 October 1881, which shows Britannia consoling a willowy and weeping Hibernia and protecting her from a simian, stone-throwing Irish man. Calmly, without brandishing it, she holds an unsheathed sword marked The Law (see illustration opposite).[20] Justice O'Brien's address left no doubt that the law would chivalrously intervene to defend a helpless woman and avenge her on the inadequate males of her own community:

> A young woman in the opening of her life was put to death – a young married woman, who suspecting no harm, guilty of no offence, virtuous and respectable in all her conduct and all her proceedings – from those of all others who were bound to protect her, from the hands of her own husband, who swore at the altar to cherish and protect her, and from her own father, has met her death under circumstances which remind us of the lines –
> > Pleading like angels, trumpet-tongued,
> > Against the deep damnation of her taking off.[21]

The Celtic mystery which underlay this colonial model of gender relations was the concern of poets. In creating the erotically mysterious personae of "The Host of the Air" and other work later collected in *The Wind among the Reeds* (1899), Yeats had drawn on both of Celticism's major sources: contemporary translations of medieval sagas from Irish manuscripts in the libraries of London, Paris, and Dublin, and oral legends, which Yeats heard around his uncle's home in County Sligo. He had not simply left them as he found them, however. Both medieval sagas and oral legends are highly laconic in tone, legends in particular being designed for informal public performance, not private consumption. The emotionalism of Yeats's "Caoilte tossing his burning hair and Niamh calling 'Away! Come away!'" in "The Hosting of the Sidhe," was a nineteenth-century innovation, but it had become part of London's idea of what "Celtic" meant.

FAIRY LEGENDS AS DISCOURSE ON GENDER

Local people told journalists that Bridget Cleary had been taken away by the fairies of Kylenagranagh and would emerge from the fairy fort riding a white horse. Yeatsian though the image may be, it was hardly intended for consumption by the literati of Dublin or London. Rather, it was an articulation of recent painful events in the terms of a metaphorical or euphemistic discourse which had long been used in the close-knit communities of rural Ireland as a way of dealing with the marginal and the transitional. Oral rather than written, it had the advantage of ephemerality, of allowing opinions to be expressed and information to be conveyed in a highly coded and unattributable way.

Fairies, also called "little people" or "good people," are well known in the oral tradition of Ireland and Scotland and in the Maritime Provinces of Canada, where Scottish and Irish immigrants found a landscape not unlike the ones they had left.[22] In Ireland people still tell stories about a race of beings supposed to live alongside humans and occasionally encountered by them. These tellings are sometimes short and offhand, at other times longer and more circumstantial, sometimes serious, sometimes frankly ridiculous. They are never written down, except by scholars or other outsiders to the groups for which they are a medium of exchange. Legends arise apparently artlessly from conversation and deal with the actions of real people in real places and real time.[23] Tellers may insist that the events they recount really happened, or they may disclaim all responsibility, explaining that "the old people used to believe such things." Barbara Rieti suggests that because such stories are often told to impress or discipline children, perhaps every generation thinks its parents or grandparents "really believed."[24]

Fairy legends are intimately linked to the features of a known landscape, particularly to dangerous, marginal, or conspicuous places within it. Slievenamon, the mountain in sight of which Bridget Cleary lived, rises approximately 2,000 feet from a plain of rich agricultural land, dominating the landscape for many miles around. It has been described as "one of the three or four most famous of Irish hills,"[25] and certainly its name occurs often in stories and songs. Literary and oral traditions preserve the idea that Slievenamon, like other conspicuous hills, is an outpost of the otherworld. Its name – "The Women's Mountain" – probably derives from a persistent idea that that world is ruled by women.

Michael Cleary told his neighbors he expected to find his wife in a "fairy fort" at Kylenagranagh, a much smaller hill near Ballyvadlea, just north of the mountain. Fairy forts – circular earthworks known to archaeology as early medieval dwelling places – are also known as "forths" or "raths."[26] They are sites of avoidance, overgrown and undisturbed, metaphors for areas of silence and circumvention in the social life of the communities which tell stories about them. They are places out of place; their time is out of time.

Central to the repertoire of fairy-legend tellers is the idea that the fairies take people away into these forts, that they abduct healthy, happy members of the community and leave sickly, withered, cantankerous changelings in their place. Sometimes men are taken, sometimes even cows; but the vast majority of changeling legends concern women and children. Anyone who enters a fairy fort will emerge changed, if at all, and here gender differences are underlined: men who return to ordinary life possess new musical or medical abilities, while, with the exception of midwives, women who return or are rescued are usually mute, injured, or mutilated.

In the compendious *Fairy Legends from Donegal*, stories collected in Irish between 1935 and 1955 and published with English translation in 1977, are examples of women swept away by the fairies as they gave birth, midwives called to attend such women inside fairy hills, and women restored to their husbands after fairy abductions had been foiled. Michael and Bridget Cleary and their neighbors would have heard such legends often, for the same stories were current all over rural Ireland. In one of them a shoemaker rides to town to fetch a midwife, leaving his wife in labor. He buys some nails for his work and returns with the midwife riding pillion:

> It was a cloudy moonlit night and as they were going through a place called Alt an Tairbh he heard a sound as if a flock of birds was coming towards them in the air. It came directly in their way and as it was passing overhead he threw the paperful of nails up in the air. He was full of anger and spoke out from his heart: "May the devil take you with him!" No sooner were the words out of his mouth than he heard the sound of something falling at the horse's feet. He turned around and dismounted, and when he looked at the thing that had fallen, what did he find but a woman! He looked sharply at her and what did he find her to be but his own wife whom he had left lying at home. He took her up and put her on the horse with the midwife who held her while he led the horse home by its head.
>
> Well. As they were approaching the house there was a hullabaloo there that they were too late, that his wife had died since he left, and there was great crying and clamour. The man led the two women he had with him into the stable with the horse and asked them to stay until he returned. He himself went into the house as if nothing had happened, and went over to the bed where the supposed corpse was lying.
>
> Everyone was astonished that he was not crying nor the least distraught as men usually are when their wives die. He turned on his heel and out with him and in again in a moment with the pitch-fork from the byre. He went up to the bed and made a swipe at the thing that was lying there, but, well for her, when she saw him drawing at her she rose and went out of the window like a flash of lightning.
>
> He went out then and brought his wife and the midwife. Everything went well then and in due time the child was born. He and his wife spent a long life after that at Gortalia and neither the wee folk nor the big people gave them any more trouble![27]

The many fairy legends which tell of women in childbirth being swept through the air are vividly metaphorical: narratives of passage – analogous to rites of passage.[28] Stories like this one reflect the dangers and anxieties of childbirth and the fact that women do sometimes die or almost die. They also reflect the anxiety surrounding the whole question of human fertility, already compromised by late and selective marriage.

It is hard not to see in such stories a coded aggression against women: attacking the changeling-corpse with a pitch-fork is justified by the terms of the narrative, but even the innocent wife is dropped from a horse in mid-air, while in the last stages of pregnancy, and is then left in the stable with the horse.[29] Extreme violence – by fire or metal implements – is one of the most conspicuous features of changeling legends, always connected to the reported abhorrence by fairies of both fire and iron. Bridget Cleary's is the only case I know in which an adult woman has been treated as a changeling in fact rather than in fiction, but there are several factual accounts of child-changelings being placed on red-hot fire shovels, one of them in South Tipperary only eleven years earlier.[30] Folklore scholars have observed the functional power of fairy abduction stories: sudden infant death, failure to thrive, birth defects, and a variety of congenital disabilities correspond to the descriptions of babies taken away, or "swept," and replaced by mute, wizened, hairy creatures, or lifeless images.[31] Many societies practice infanticide in such cases, often with some sort of belief narrative to absolve adults from guilt.

Adult women taken by the fairies were usually said to be brides, or pregnant, or lactating, and again it is not difficult to imagine the variety of physical and mental illnesses, from anorexia to tuberculosis to postnatal and other depression, for which the discourse of fairy abduction might be found appropriate.[32] Even if changeling belief did not usually lead to attacks on adult women, they would have encountered its verbal sanctions and imaginative possibilities at every point of stress in their lives. The anxieties of social life might find expression in changeling accusations[33] but might also give rise to claims of changeling status. Some fairy legends may certainly be read as expressions of the loneliness and alienation of young women married by the decisions of older men.[34]

A woman had a certain amount to gain, in terms of privacy, prestige, and sanction for subversions of her social role, if she admitted or claimed to have been "away with the fairies." It was suggested at the time of her death that Bridget Cleary herself had said she was going with the fairies, and the court was told of a conversation in which she told Michael that his own mother had been in the habit of "going away" with them. This may have been a way of taunting him, of demanding privacy, or of claiming some esoteric knowledge shared by women but not by men. A woman "away with the fairies" might be spared some of the inconveniences of her social role, as a Mrs. Sheridan suggested when she told Yeats's friend, Augusta Gregory:

> I know that I used to be away among them myself, but how they brought me I don't know, but when I'd come back, I'd be cross with the husband and with all. I believe when I was with them I was cross that they wouldn't let me go, and that's why they didn't keep me altogether, they didn't like cross people to be with them. The husband would ask me where I was and why I stopped so long away, but I think he knew I was taken and it fretted him, but he never spoke much about it. But my mother knew it well, but she'd try to hide it. The neighbours would come in and ask were was I, and she'd say I was sick in the bed – for whatever was put there in place of me would have the head in under the bedclothes. And when a neighbour would bring me in a drink of milk, my mother would put it by and say "Leave her now, maybe she'll drink it tomorrow." And maybe in a day or two I'd meet someone and he'd say, "Why wouldn't you speak to me when I went into the house to see you?" And I was a fresh young woman at that time.[35]

Stories of fairy abduction take on a very different coloring when told in the first person. Such first-person narratives (called "memorates" by folklorists) are less hardy than the "fabulates" which tend to take over from them and which tell the individual's experiences in the third person. The number of people by whom a story may be told as personal experience is necessarily limited: other tellers recounting the first individual's experience will use the third person. In the process, they round and smooth the narrative, assimilating it to a body of previously existing legend. The result is that although women characters are found prominently in fairy legends, and many legends are told by women, women's voices as subjects within them are relatively scarce. Restoring a first-person voicing to such legends, as poet Nuala Ní

Dhomhnaill does frequently, shows their potential for subversion. Her poem "Fua-dach," which I translate "Swept Away," expresses in terms of fairy abduction a woman's depression and sexual alienation in a twentieth-century marriage. The speaking voice tells how a strange woman arrived in her house, supplanting her in household tasks like a Stepford Wife:

> ...When my husband came
> home for his tea,
> he didn't notice she wasn't me.
>
> But I'm in the fairy field
> in everlasting dark.
> I'm freezing, with only
> the mist to cover me.
> And if he wants me back,
> here's what he must do:
> get a fine big ploughshare
> and butter it well,
> then make it red-hot in the fire.
> Then go to the bed
> were that bitch lies,
> and let her have it!
> "Push it into her face,
> burn her and scorch her,
> and all the time she's going,
> I'll be coming.
> All the time she's going,
> I'll be coming."[36]

A first-person voicing like this one, or like Mrs. Sheridan's as reported by Lady Gregory, is a form of resistance. For an initiated audience, it might also be understood to underlie a third-person narrative of the same events and be heard either as a coded expression of the same resistance or as a warning.

A PARTICULAR CASE: BRIDGET AND MICHAEL CLEARY

To see how the narrative of fairy abduction may have empowered Bridget Cleary for a while but then become a rationale for her torture and killing, it will be necessary to consider how she and Michael were situated in the socioeconomic environment of rural Ireland at the end of the nineteenth century. From the point of view of contemporary metropolitan commentators – unionists in particular – they belonged to Catholic rural Ireland, that great reservoir of superstition and credulity, not to mention sinister "Fenianism." Commentators with a more intimate knowledge of Irish society distinguished sharply among classes and identified them as landless laborers. As we shall see, however, that description is less than adequate. In con-sidering the dynamics of fairy abduction, it is important to consider to what extent

Bridget and Michael Cleary were turning their backs on an older way of life and what may have been the price exacted for that by others whose choices were more limited.

To begin with generalizations, the social position of young married and marriage-able women in late nineteenth- and early twentieth-century Ireland could be extremely vulnerable. A mass of historical and sociological research shows a society intensely focused on the economic needs of the stem family – the male line – to the exclusion of all considerations of compatibility or emotional fulfillment. Only one son on a farm could marry, and he had to marry for dowry. Land was fixed wealth, while cattle were movable, so in marriage sons stayed and daughters moved. Legends of fairy abduction express metaphorically what Richard Breen has called the "floating" position of women in the status hierarchy: like the cows which accompanied them as dowry, women were regularly bartered and exchanged in marriage contracts.[37] Unmarried, they were placeless. Fertility was all-important: it was essential to "keep the name on the land," and a woman might be returned to her family if she failed to produce an heir. "Children are the curse of the country," one woman in County Clare said to anthropologist Conrad Arensberg in the 1930s, "especially if you haven't any."[38] Another informant told him that the husband of a woman without children might feel entitled to "bounce a boot off her" now and then.

Bridget and Michael Cleary had no children, although they had been married for about six years and both were relatively young. Had they been landed farmers this would have been an economic and social as well as a personal disaster. In most cases they would have been living in his family's house, hoping to "keep the name on the land," and Bridget would have brought a dowry or "fortune" of cows to "buy" her place.[39] In such circumstances, it might well be in the interest of a husband, perhaps under pressure from his family, to decide that the woman who shared his bed but had produced no heir was not his wife and to use the excuse of a fairy changeling to repudiate her, maybe even allowing another son to marry and inherit the land.[40]

It might be tempting to read Bridget Cleary's death as a tragically inevitable work-ing out of the social paradigm of marriage as economic bargain, as indeed most commentators have done in one way or another, but her individual circumstances must be considered too. Bridget was not an outsider marrying in: she lived where she had grown up, surrounded by father, aunt, and cousins, and her father told the court that far from being an economic liability, she had been his only support. Most socio-logical research has focused on farmers and shop-keepers, but the Clearys were neither. They had come from the class of landless farm laborers for whom life was changing faster than perhaps for any other group in Irish society. The spread of literacy, the change from the Irish to the English language, and the increased influence of state agencies in the countryside all made them less dependent than their ancestors on agricultural subsistence work. Some, but by no means all of their generation and background, had been to school, learned to read, become proficient in trades, familiar with consumer products, and comfortable handling money.

All indications are that the Clearys were a modern couple, much more upwardly mobile in socioeconomic terms than their neighbors or Bridget's relatives. Michael was a cooper, and unlike almost all his elderly neighbors and many of his contem-poraries about whom information was gathered at the time of the trial, he was literate. The *Irish Times* reporter at the magisterial inquiry described him as a "respectable and good-looking man," although with "a rather wild look about the eyes." Witnesses described Bridget as a very nice-looking young woman. Evidently too, even in illness she took care of her appearance. During most of the two days before her death she wore a nightdress and a "chemise" (the nightdress, made of striped flannelette, was produced in court), but on the night of her death she got up and, with help from Mary Kennedy and Johanna Burke, dressed in clothes her husband handed her: "two petticoats...a navy blue jacket and a white knitted shawl, shoes and stockings," according to Mary Kennedy; "a red petticoat and navy-blue flannel dress, green stays and navy blue cashmere jacket," according to Johanna Burke.[41] Black stockings were found on the body, and one gold earring, suggesting that her ears were pierced.[42] Her bed had sheets, one of which was used to wrap her body for burial. Ten or fifteen years earlier it had been commonplace to describe the Irish rural laborer as living in squalor, dressed in rags: clearly this description did not apply to the Clearys.

Bridget had trained as a milliner and dressmaker and also kept hens and sold eggs.[43] She seems to have been in charge of the household budget, for Johanna Burke stated that as she lay in bed on the night of her death Michael handed her a coffee canister, saying there was twenty pounds in it (about eighteen hundred dollars in today's terms): "She tied it up and told her husband to take care of it, that he would not know the difference until he was without it. 'She handed it to me and told me to put it in a box under the bed, which I did.'"[44]

The Clearys' house alone would have been enough to mark them as different: it was a new "laborer's cottage," a slated, two-bedroom dwelling of a type built only after the passing of the Labourers (Ireland) Act of 1883 and a vast improvement on the earlier housing of the rural working class. Significantly, one of the early accounts of the case reported that the house was on the site of a "rath" or fairy fort.[45] This may well have been the case; the modernizing forces of Victorian colonial power were notoriously indifferent to traditional pieties. But such a label would suggest that the Clearys did not subscribe to the same values as their neighbors and that they paid little heed to fairy belief. If Bridget did claim to have a special relationship with fairies as the newspapers suggested, she may have been either attempting to placate a hostile mob of neighbors by submitting to sanctions they invoked or using their uneasiness about the site of her house (perhaps itself a coded expression of resentment) to increase her own prestige.

If anyone appears marginal and therefore vulnerable in the community depicted in the court depositions, it is Michael Cleary. He had come into the area from Killenaule, about eleven miles to the north, and had been living childless among his wife's people for about six years. Their neighbors told the court, and Michael insisted, that he and Bridget had an excellent relationship, but the fact remains that she died through his violent action.[46] It is difficult at this remove to speculate with confidence about the reasons behind that action, but several possibilities present themselves.

On the evening of her death, 15 March, Bridget was up and dressed and sitting in the kitchen with her husband. Several neighbors were present, and to Tom Smyth, who asked how she was, Bridget replied "that she was middling, that he was making a fairy of her now." Mary Kennedy said, according to her own testimony, "Don't mind him, Bridgie; don't be that way." Johanna Burke gave the following description:

> They were talking about the fairies and Mrs. Cleary [Bridget] said to her husband, "your mother used to go with the fairies, and that is why you think I am going with them."
>
> Then he asked her, "Did my mother tell you that?" She said she did, adding that she gave two nights with them. I made tea, and offered Bridget Cleary a cup of it. Her husband got three bits of bread and jam and said his wife should eat them before he would take a sup. He asked her three times, "Are you Bridget Cleary, my wife, in the name of God?" She answered twice, and ate two pieces of bread and jam. When she did not answer the third time he forced her to eat the third bit of bread saying "If you don't take it you will go." He flung her on the ground, put his knee on her chest and one hand on her throat and forced the bread and jam down her throat, saying "Swallow it. Is it down, is it down?"[47]

According to her own testimony, Burke tried to reason with him, but he stripped Bridget's clothes off, "except her chemise," and began her final torture with fire.

Is it possible that Bridget was taunting her husband with talk about fairy abduction and that this was the last straw which made him finally act with such violence? Her suggestion that his mother "used to go with the fairies" must be read as provocative. A coded form of speech, it may have meant that she suffered periods of depression or mental illness, that she was a liar, that she neglected her children or her household duties, or was unfaithful to her husband. Several interpretations are available, but the idea of stigma is common to all of them. While Bridget was ill, news had been brought to Michael of his own father's death in Killenaule, but he had not gone to the wake; his connection with his family of origin evidently had its own complications.

According to the first newspaper reports of Bridget Cleary's disappearance, she herself had said that she was going with the fairies to Kylenagranagh, where Michael waited to see her ride by on horseback. Witnesses told the court that she had said she would stay with him then "if he was able to keep her."[48] They may have been lying, or Bridget may have been using the idiom of fairy legend to assert her independence and autonomy or perhaps to protect herself from a violent and impulsive man. At one point during her torture, witnesses said she sat on the side of her bed and said "The Peelers are at the window. Mind me now," in answer to which Michael took up "a certain utensil" and threw what was probably urine on her and on the window. The Peelers, called after Sir Robert Peel, were the Royal Irish Constabulary, a nineteenth-century innovation. Bridget may have attempted to keep her husband in line by appealing, if only in imagination, to the forces of the state as well as to the unseen power of local oral tradition.

Hubert Butler has suggested that jealousy about a possible affair between Bridget and an egg merchant, mentioned once in testimony, may have been what drove Michael to such a pitch that he convinced himself of her fairy possession and killed her.[49] She may indeed have had a lover; she may even have been pregnant by a lover at the time of her death. As the poem cited earlier by Nuala Ní Dhomhnaill shows, fairy legend is rich in resources for the oblique discussion of sexuality. Michael's mother's being "away with the fairies" could have meant that he was conceived outside his parents' marriage. He may have been impotent. In any event Bridget used to go walking alone on the low road near the fairy fort of Kylenagranagh, and although that seems innocuous enough, it was thought worth mentioning at the trial, perhaps as an indication of disaffection with her marriage. It would certainly have been enough to mark Bridget as somehow more independent or headstrong than some of her neighbors could accept.

But there may have been another factor at work. Dr. Crean, the local physician, told the inquest he had visited Bridget during her last illness and diagnosed "slight bronchial catarrh and nervous excitement," but local tradition in Tipperary asserts that Bridget Cleary was suffering from tuberculosis.[50] Raging out of control, particularly in poor areas, tuberculosis was a highly stigmatizing disease in the late nineteenth century, much as AIDS has been in our time. Sufferers and their families risked being shunned and resorted to euphemism and prevarication rather than admit the nature of the ailment. The paradox of tuberculosis – the disease most associated with poverty and squalor – infecting someone whose life was as relatively glamorous as Bridget Cleary's, whose bed had sheets and whose ears were pierced, may have been too much to deal with for a community whose worldview was already severely under pressure.

If blame had to be assigned and a scapegoat elected, Michael Clearly was the obvious candidate. Already perhaps the focus of envy in the area because of his relative prosperity, he was without relatives there once Bridget was dead. When the statements of Bridget's father, Patrick Boland, and her aunt, Mary Kennedy, were read out in court, Michael cried out in protest:

> I would make an objection to that statement. There is not one word of truth in it, and, if I am to get justice between them, they are all one. If I will not get justice here I will get it in heaven. They are all one there, and no one of them has told the truth. They are all a lot. They are after doing their best, and their father is the worst to do the like of that on me. If I am going to get justice – I don't care whether I will or not – I will get it in another place. It is their badness and dirt, I did not do it, but they did it, and burned her.[51]

"They are all one," he says – meaning apparently that the Kennedys, mother and sons, with their sister Johanna Burke, his dead wife, her father, and John Dunne, another neighbor, were all related. Already alienated in some way from his own family, he seems to feel himself excluded by his wife's relatives, several of whom even walked the eleven miles to his father's wake while he did not.

Contemporary and later commentators have read Bridget Cleary's death as a story about categories of people, about beliefs held or not held as though controlled by a two-way switch. But belief in the supernatural works much more like a sliding switch than one with on / off settings: credulity is increased by stress, and social pressure can produce behavior (such as churchgoing) whose whole social message is ostensibly about inner conviction. Bridget and Michael Cleary were members of a class and a local community, but they were also individuals in a society which increasingly rewarded individuality. Poised between the modernizing forces of the centralized state and demands for conformity from traditionalist members of their own community, they were knocked off balance by Bridget's illness. Dependent on neighbors for such simple necessities as milk and laundry, they seem to have lost control of the symbolic world in which they lived.

CONCLUSION

The telling of fairy-belief legend is, among other things, a way of handling social deviance and stigma, a vocabulary and a system of metaphor through which to contain the sort of tensions that Victorian administrators preferred to house in grim four-story buildings. It is not surprising, given what we know about responses to colonization, that those who embraced a town-centered respectability with its promise of access to the modern world should have preferred not to be reminded of the rural and the oral by the case of Bridget Cleary. In 1895, newspapers reported that during the trial of Michael Cleary and his fellow defendants in Clonmel, "on each visit to the Court during the taking of the depositions the prisoners were 'groaned and hooted at vigorously' by large crowds which followed them on their way back to gaol." This rejection by their town neighbors was in strong contrast with the sympathy extended to the defendants by some of the London papers. For individuals in Clonmel, however, with its two convents, its breweries, flour mills, and tanneries, its barges on the River Suir and its important railway junction, Ballyvadlea, less than fifteen miles away beyond the mountain of Slievenamon, must have seemed at once far away and uncomfortably near. It was too close to be exotic, too distant to be relevant.

During Bridget's illness, Michael summoned both Dr. Crean, the physician from Fethard, a small town four or five miles to the southwest on the road to Clonmel, and a man described as an "herb-doctor," Denis Ganey, who lived in Kylatlea – about the same distance in the opposite direction, on the slope of Slievenamon.[52] These two practitioners represent the conflicts at work at the time of Bridget Cleary's death: between the scientific, middle-class optimism of the modernizing nineteenth century, with its roads, railways, and newspapers; and the increasing isolation and marginalization of those still invested in an older, oral culture, who lived generally far from main roads.

Michael's trade and education would have predisposed him to consult the physician, but evidence given in court suggests that he felt himself under pressure to seek a traditional remedy as well: John Dunne, a fifty-five-year-old neighbor and cousin of Patrick Boland, seems to have been particularly insistent on the rituals of changeling banishment. Ashis Nandy has remarked in writing about *sati* in the context of colonization that in India "groups rendered psychologically marginal by their exposure to Western impact . . . had come under pressure to demonstrate to others as well as themselves, their ritual purity and allegiance to traditional high culture. To many of them *sati* became an important proof of their conformity to older norms at a time when these norms had become shaky within."[53]

If we substitute "oral culture" for "high culture," Michael Cleary's action becomes more understandable, as does the dilemma in which he found himself. Most modern commentators have seen him as the most "superstitious" of the people involved in his wife's death, the most credulous about the existence and agency of fairies. In fact, he was the one person involved in her torture who had not grown up in the vicinity of the fort at Kylenagranagh; he seems rather to have come from the town of Killenaule. He had worked for several years in the much larger town of Clonmel and might well have been psychologically marginal to his wife's community by virtue of his exposure to Clonmel's more urban culture and money-based economy. Faced with his wife's troubling illness, he was apparently not strong enough to hold out against his older neighbor, John Dunne, who insisted that its causes were not natural. He went to the herb doctor and brought back the prescribed remedy – quite possibly against his own better judgment – and, having so far invested in "fairy quackery," did not know how to withdraw.

Stories about women taken away by fairies and perhaps rescued by violence were told all over rural Ireland about the time of Bridget Cleary's death, but the implementation of the actions they described would have been a last resort, a way of keeping troublesome women down. Even then, contained within a fictional framework, those actions would have something of the nature of ritual or play and could stop before visible damage was done. Michael's outburst in court accuses Bridget's relatives of conspiracy against him. In fact, they seem to have aided and abetted him in all but the final murder of his wife. They accompanied him along the road of credulity paved by fairy legends, but instead of leading him to the neat conclusion of fiction, and an honorable exit, they abandoned him to the consequences of his anger and frustration.

Bridget was thought on the night of her death to have recovered – in fact to have been recovered. Then something made Michael, acting alone, commit his last act of violence. I have already suggested that this "something" was her reference to his mother's having been "away with the fairies." It was after Bridget had been burned – in what I read as an act of blind rage and frustration – that Michael took refuge in the elaborate narrative of the white horse and her expected reappearance. He told Johanna Burke that he would pretend to be crazy, and in fact a form of insanity defense did work for him. However, his waiting for three nights at Kylenagranagh was probably not so much a cynical pretense as a performance, expressing his isolation and his horror – to the point of insanity – at the consequence of his acts.

Like most stories, the one told at the time of Bridget Cleary's death drew on narratives already known and perhaps partly believed. Under other circumstances, it might have served as euphemism or as a coded discussion of the issues and personalities involved in Bridget Cleary's fate. But the seriousness of the crime and the efficiency of Victorian state agencies and means of communication meant that it was told far beyond the community where it had been composed. A narrative developed as commentary on gender relations in domestic contexts was suddenly freighted with the politics of the wider society, and in the process, its finely woven web of observations on marriage and women's lives was lost.

Had Bridget Cleary not died of her burns, there might still have been an oral narrative about her. With time, however, it would have become more fictional and less factual. Had Michael and Bridget continued to live in the area, the narrative might have explained why they were set apart and perhaps why they had no children, for women abducted by fairies were often said to be infertile afterwards. Had Bridget's body not been discovered it could have provided a reason why Michael was avoided or an inducement to him to leave the area. The story would have joined other narratives in marking Kylenagranagh Hill as a significant place, and at that point the names of the protagonists might have dropped out. Later it might have been told in other communities and assigned to other families, other "fairy forts."

But Bridget Cleary did die, and at least one of her neighbors – significantly the tenant of an evicted, farm and therefore an outsider in the community – was sufficiently disturbed to inform the police. So the forces of the state became involved and instead of oral narratives which ascribed agency only to supernatural forces, which could be revised with every telling, and which would dissipate with time, written reports were prepared whose contents continue to be perused one hundred years later. Instead of a story, the public was given a report on a story – a written metanarrative not only about Bridget Cleary's death but also about the desired death of fairy legend as a way of thinking and speaking: an uncentralized, anti-authoritarian discourse whose elements and structures were anathema to the linear accounts of cause and effect favored by both newspapers and courts of law.

The story of Bridget Cleary's abduction by fairies itself became a shibboleth, revealing a cultural outlook which by the late nineteenth century in Ireland had become deeply unfashionable. Many households in South Tipperary still possess copies of the newspapers published in 1895 which carried reports of the death of Bridget Cleary and its investigation, but until recently few people have been willing to talk about it. The oral legend aborted in the making did have the effect of preserving Michael Cleary from the gallows, but in general, rather than protecting those present from responsibility for Bridget Cleary's death, it made them figures of repudiation and ridicule, guilty not just of one crime but of a worldview that threatened to taint a whole country.

NOTES

In thinking about the story of Bridget Cleary I have been greatly helped by discussions with Beth Parkhurst, Ruth-Ann Harris, and other members of the Boston Irish Colloquium; with Vera, Ivan, and Jacob Kreilkamp, Jo Radner, Lucy MacDiarmid, Liz Cullingford, Philip O'Leary, Kevin O'Neill, Nuala Ní Dhomhnaill, Tommy McArdle, Dóirín Saurus, and John Cooney. I thank them and all the other friends and colleagues with whom discussions continue. The paper on which this essay is based was presented at American University, in Washington, DC, in March 1994. For hospitality and stimulating questions I am most grateful to the organizers and audience. For tracking down references, thanks to Stuart Murray and George Bornstein.

1 Where not otherwise stated, information on the Bridget Cleary incident is based on contemporary reports in the *Irish Times* and other newspapers. See *Irish Times*, 27 Mar. 1895.

2 For discussion of gender in the context of colonialism, see Ashis Nandy, *The Intimate Enemy: Loss and Recovery of Self under Colonialism* (Delhi: Oxford University Press, 1983); for the relevance of this argument to Ireland, see David Cairns and Shaun Richards, *Writing Ireland: Colonialism, Nationalism, and Culture* (Manchester: Manchester University Press, 1988), chap. 3; and Carol Coulter, *The Hidden Tradition: Feminism, Women, and Nationalism in Ireland* (Cork: Cork University Press, 1993).

3 See Hubert Butler, "The Eggman and the Fairies," in his *Escape from the Anthill* (Mullingar: Lilliput Press, 1986), 63–74; Richard Jenkins, "Witches and Fairies: Supernatural

Aggression and Deviance among the Irish Peasantry," *Ulster Folklife* 23 (1977): 33–56, rev. in Peter Narváez, ed., *The Good People: New Fairylore Essays* (New York/London: Garland, 1991); Diarmuid Ó Giolláin, "The Fairy Belief and Official Religion in Ireland," in *The Good People*, 199–214; Thomas McGrath, "Fairy Faith and Changelings: The Burning of Bridget Cleary in 1895," *Studies* 71 (summer 1982): 178–84; Carlo Gébler's novel *The Cure* (London: Hamish Hamilton, 1994); Pat Feeley, "The Burning of Bridget Cleary," RTE Radio 1 Documentary, 10 Apr. 1995; Tony Butler, "The Burning of Bridget Cleary: The 100th Anniversary," *The Nationalist*, 25 Mar. 1995, 21.

4   In January 1984, fifteen-year-old Ann Lovett died giving birth outdoors before a statue of the Virgin Mary. Later that year the discovery of the body of a newborn infant with stab wounds led to the inquiry known as the "Kerry Babies" case (see Nell McCafferty, *A Woman to Blame: The Kerry Babies Case* [Dublin: Attic Press, 1985]). Numerous cases of child sex abuse by clergy came to light during the late 1980s and the 1990s; the bishop of Galway admitted being the father of a seventeen-year-old son in Connecticut. In 1992 a fourteen-year-old pregnant schoolgirl was prevented from traveling to England for an abortion (illegal in Ireland; see Ailbhe Smyth, *The Abortion Papers: Ireland* [Dublin: Attic Press, 1992]). In the same year a young woman in County Kilkenny brought charges of incest and severe physical abuse against her father. In 1994 the Irish government fell when delays in processing child sex-abuse charges against a Catholic priest were brought to light.

5   See, for instance, the poetry of Nuala Ní Dhomhnaill, *Pharaoh's Daughter* (Wake Forest, NC: Wake Forest University Press, 1990), and *The Astrakhan Cloak* (Wake Forest, NC: Wake Forest University Press, 1992); Eilís Ní Dhuibhne's short story "Midwife to the Fairies," in her *Blood and Water* (Dublin: Attic Press, 1993), and her play *Dún na mBan trí Thine* [The (Fairy) Women's Fort is on Fire], performed by Amharclann de hÍde at the Peacock Theater, Dublin, 1994; Angela Bourke, "Bean an Leasa: ón bPiseogaíocht go dtí Filíocht Nuala Ní Dhomhnaill," in *Leath na Spéire*, ed. Eoghan Ó hAnluain (Dublin: An Clóchomhar, 1992): 74–90, and "Fairies and Anorexia: Nuala Ní Dhomhnaill's Amazing Grass," in *Proceedings of the Harvard Celtic Colloquium* 13 (1993): 25–38.

6   Gladstone's second Home Rule Bill had been defeated in 1894.

7   See L. P. Curtis Jr., *Apes and Angels: The Irishman in Victorian Caricature* (Washington, D.C.: Smithsonian Institution Press, 1971), chap. 9; and Cairns and Richards, 47–8.

8   See Mary Carbery, *The Farm by Lough Gur* (1937; rpt., Cork and Dublin: Mercier, 1973), 98 passim; Caitriona Clear, *Nuns in Nineteenth-Century Ireland* (Dublin: Gill & Macmillan; Washington, DC: Catholic University of America Press, 1987); Margaret MacCurtain, "Fullness of Life: Defining Female Spirituality in Twentieth-Century Ireland," in *Women Surviving*, ed. Maria Luddy and Cliona Murphy (Dublin: Poolbeg, 1990), 233–63.

9   See Carbery, 157–66, and compare S. J. Connolly, *Priests and People in Pre-Famine Ireland, 1780–1845* (New York: St. Martin's Press, 1982), 100–20.

10 *Nationalist*, 27 Mar. 1895.

11 Ibid., 23 Mar. and 27 Mar. 1895.

12 Gayatri Chakravorty Spivak, "Can the Subaltern Speak?" in *Colonial Discourse and Post-Colonial Theory: A Reader*, ed. Patrick Williams and Laura Chrisman (New York and London: Harvester, 1994), 94, 96.

13 Curtis, 25.

14 See "The 'Witch-Burning' at Clonmel," *Folk-Lore: Transactions of the Folk-Lore Society* 6 (December 1895): 374 ff; and Hubert Butler, 66–7.

15 See "'Witch-Burning' at Clonmel." The romantic approach reflected the continuing influence of James MacPherson's spurious and widely translated *Poems of Ossian*, while

the scientific owed much to Darwinism and to the studies in comparative philology undertaken by the Grimm brothers in Germany. For the work of the eighteenth-century theologian Johann Gottfried von Herder, with its emphasis on "das Volk" and on the concept of national character, see Jennifer Fox, "The Creator Gods: Romantic Nationalism and the En-Genderment of Women in Folklore," *Journal of American Folklore* 100 (October–December 1987): 563–72. Cities, of course, have folklore too, but this was not studied until much later.

16   Curtis, 75.

17   Ashis Nandy, quoted in Coulter, 23; see also Cairns and Richards, 49.

18   See Elizabeth Butler Cullingford, *Gender and History in Yeats's Love Poetry* (Cambridge: Cambridge University Press, 1993), chap. 4.

19   *Irish Times*, 6 Jul. 1895.

20   Curtis, 41.

21   *Irish Times*, 5 Jul. 1895.

22   See Barbara Rieti, *Strange Terrain: The Fairy World in Newfoundland* (St. John's: ISER Books, 1991); and *The Good People*. Similar traditions have been recorded across most of Northern Europe.

23   Folktales or fairy tales, on the other hand, begin and end with formulaic flourishes like "Once upon a time" and concern themselves with an escapist, fictional world of wonders and magic.

24   Rieti, chap. 4. See also Patricia Lysaght, "Fairylore from the Midlands of Ireland," in *The Good People*, 22–46.

25   Butler, 63.

26   Forth, or rath, in Irish (sing.) is *lios*, or *si*, or some variant of those names. Lysaght quotes Jenny McGlynn describing the "Rusheen," where many fairy encounters occur in her stories as "a bit of a hill with a rath on top of it, covered with bushes" (p. 30).

27   Seán Ó hEochaidh, Séamus Ó Catháin, and Máire Mac Neill, *Fairy Legends from Donegal* (Dublin: Comhairle Bhéaloideas Éireann, 1977), 56–61. The narrator, a man, makes clear in his introduction that he learned this story from a woman: "When I was a boy about thirty years ago I was hired in a townland called Rualach in the parish of Kilcar. Here is a little story I heard from the woman of the house tell one night."

28   Angela Bourke, "The Woman Who Flew Though the Air" (paper delivered at the American Folklore Society Annual Meeting, St. John's, Newfoundland, 1991).

29   On coding, see Joan N. Radner and Susan S. Lanser, "Strategies of Coding in Women's Cultures," in *Feminist Messages: Coding in Women's Folk Culture*, ed. Joan N. Radner (Urbana: University of Illinois Press, 1993), 1–29.

30   See *Daily Telegraph*, 19 May 1884, and E. S. Hartland, *The Science of Fairy Tales, an Inquiry into Fairy Mythology* (1890). In a seminar I taught at Harvard University in 1993, Karin Lewicki remarked that we read no stories in which a woman must resort to violence to banish a changeling and restore her husband. As in real life, it is women and children, not men, who are subjected to family violence "for their own good."

31   See Joyce Underwood Munro, "The Invisible Made Visible: The Fairy Changeling as a Folk Articulation of Failure to Thrive in Infants and Children," in *The Good People*, 251–83.

32   See Bourke, "Bean an Leasa," and "Fairies and Anorexia."

33   See Jenkins, "Witches and Fairies."

34   See Bourke, "Bean an Leasa."

35   Lady Gregory, *Visions and Beliefs in the West of Ireland* (1920; rpt. Gerrard's Gross [U.K.]: Colin Smythe, 1970), 56. "Mrs Sheridan . . . was old, for she had once met Raftery, the Gaelic poet, at a dance, and he died before the famine of '47" (p. 50).

36   Nuala Ní Dhomhnaill, *Féar Suaithinseach* (Maynooth, Ireland: An Sagart, 1984), 65–66, my translation. "Fuadach" is published with Michael Hartnett's translation, titled "Abduction," in Nuala Ní Dhomhnaill's *Selected Poems* (Dublin: Raven Arts Press, 1988).

37   Richard Breen, "Dowry Payments and the Irish Case," *Comparative Studies in Society and History* 26, no. 2 (1984): 292.

38   Conrad Arensberg, *The Irish Countryman* (1937; rpt., New York: American Museum Science Books, 1968), 91.

39   Breen, 292.

40   Arensberg, 92.

41   Butler, 66.

42   Johanna Burke testified that on the day after Bridget's death Michael found the second earring. Raking through the ashes of the fire he called to her, "Hannah, I have got one of poor Bridget's earrings." *Irish Times*, 29 Mar. 1895.

43   McGrath, 178.

44   *Irish Times*, 27 Mar. 1895.

45   *Nationalist*, 23 Mar. 1895.

46   This is a common perception of husbands in cases of domestic violence.

47   *Irish Times*, 27 Mar. 1895.

48   The idea that a person taken by the fairies could be rescued by being pulled from the back of a white horse is common in Irish folklore and has entered literature in English through the ballad "Tam Lin"; see E. B. Lyle, "The Ballad *Tam Lin* and Traditional Tales of Recovery from the Fairy Troop," *Studies in Scottish Literature* 6 (July 1968): 175–85. Compare Alice Munro's story, "Hold Me Fast, Don't Let Me Pass," in her *Friend of My Youth* (New York: Knopf, 1990).

49   Butler, 63–74.

50   Tony Butler, "The Burning of Bridget Cleary: The 100th, Anniversary," *Nationalist*, 25 Mar. 1995.

51   *Irish Times*, 8 Apr. 1895.

52   Kylatlea is probably derived from *Coill an tSléibhe*, "Wood on the mountainside." This is not a village but the name of sparsely populated area, called "town-land" in Ireland.

53   Ashis Nandy, quoted in Spivak, 94.

Inventing Ireland

Declan Kiberd

Declan Kiberd's magisterial *Inventing Ireland*, from which this piece is taken, attempts a wholesale revision of modern Irish literary history. In this essay, he focuses on an aspect of Irish nationalism (and, ultimately, postcolonialism) that is unique to the Irish experience: *deanglicization*. Because of its geographical proximity to England, Ireland developed as a "metropolitan colony" whose culture tended to be far more deeply affected by the English language and English literary and political traditions than more distant colonies. The process of "anglicization," which is inextricably associated with the decimation of the Gaelic language and culture, led to a situation that, by 1890, called for radical solutions. The key figure in this regard was Douglas Hyde, whose essay "The Necessity for De-Anglicizing Ireland," published in 1894, became the rallying cry for the nativist Gaelic League. As part of a postcolonial revisionist project, Kiberd's analysis of Hyde's work reveals the problems of nationalist programs of cultural revival. Hyde's unwillingness to embrace the political ramifications of his cultural project led to the Gaelic League's increasingly marginalized position in the years leading to the 1916 rebellion. The varying positions within Irish Revivalism toward the Gaelic language and the use of the Hiberno-English dialect are likened by Kiberd to the complicities and ambiguities of Salman Rushdie's India and **Frantz Fanon**'s Algeria. Yeats's theory of literature, articulated in *Samhain*, a periodical published by the Abbey Theatre, is described by Kiberd as "one of the first Irish articulations of the dialectics of postcolonial liberation." Students might want to compare Kiberd's account of "deanglicization" with **Partha Chatterjee**'s account of the "women's question" and consider both as problems unique to nationalist movements in eras of decolonization. Both **David Lloyd** and **Luke Gibbons** discuss the problem of Irish nationalism: **Lloyd**'s consideration of Gaelic ballads and their translation by Revivalists could usefully augment Kiberd's remarks about Hiberno-English.

Inventing Ireland

DEANGLICIZATION

The Irish writer has always been confronted with a choice. This is the dilemma of whether to write for the native audience – a risky, often thankless task – or to produce texts for consumption in Britain and North America. Through most of the nineteenth century, artists tended to exploit far more of Ireland than they expressed. Cruder performers resorted to stage-Irish effects, to the rollicking note and to "paddy-whack-ery", but even those who sought a subtler portraiture often failed, not so much through want of talent as through lack of a native audience. Most of these writers came, inevitably, from the upper classes and their commerce with the full range of Irish society was very limited.

The audience for most writing was primarily in England, and its expectations had to be satisfied. Occasionally, a writer like William Carleton might spring from the common people to real international success; but that success, in removing the artist from his own people into the ranks of the "classes", would often seem like a form of betrayal. This was why a group at the end of the century came to the conclusion that, if they were to create a truly national literature, they must also gather a national audience. If they were to invent Ireland, they must first invent the Irish. "Does not the greatest poetry always require a people to listen to it?" asked Yeats,[1] whose dream was to achieve with the Irish masses the sort of *rapport* enjoyed in the previous century only by the political leaders Daniel O'Connell and Charles Stewart Parnell.

The very success of both of these statesmen posed a problem, for neither had promoted the Irish language. O'Connell, though fluent in it, said that he could witness without a sigh the gradual disuse of Irish as it made way for the "superior utility" of English in matters of business and politics:[2] and Parnell, a Protestant gentleman educated at Cambridge, never had occasion to learn the language. O'Connell had chosen to use English at monster meetings attended by Irish speakers, on the shrewd understanding that his immediate audience was converted and that his need was to move English readers of his words in the next morning's newspaper. Almost inexorably, English had become *the* language in which the Irish nationalist case was made: a knowledge was essential for rebels who sought to defend themselves in court or for those agitators who wrote threatening letters to landlords.[3] The very notion of a modern nation is of a community, few of whose members can see or know one

Taken from *Inventing Ireland* (Cambridge, MT: Harvard University Press, 1996), pp. 136–65.

another, and who are thus bonded less by their massed bodies than by the abstract mechanism of print-technology. "Print language is what invents nationalism", observes Benedict Anderson, "and not a particular language *per se*":[4] and so Irish, being largely part of an oral culture, was supplanted by English, the logical medium of newspapers, and of those tracts and literary texts in which Ireland would be invented and imagined. If the colonial administration justified itself by waving pieces of paper bearing "titles" to occupied land, then the resistance movement would have to come up with its own set of documents to make its countervailing claim.

The literature so produced would base itself on a return to the people, the "hillside men" who were charmed by the *hauteur* of Parnell, a landlord who had gone against his own class. In this thrilling example, Yeats could find a model for the movement he hoped to lead: and so he wrote in October 1901:

> All Irish writers have to decide whether they will write as the upper classes have done, not to express but to exploit this country, or join the intellectual movement which has raised the cry that was heard in Russia in the seventies, the cry "to the people". Moses was little good to his people until he had killed an Egyptian; and for the most part a writer or public man of the upper classes is useless to this country till he has done something that separates him from his class.[5]

Accordingly, in the idealism of youth, Yeats had tried in *The Wanderings of Oisin* to recreate a Gaelic golden age, but working from "a version of a version" of the Gaelic original at his seat in the British Museum, he produced only the rather derivative "Celtic colourings" of a late-romantic English poem.[6] The problem was the same one that he had diagnosed in the patriotic ballads of Thomas Davis and Young Ireland: "they turned away from the unfolding of an Irish tradition, and borrowed the mature English methods of utterance and used them to sing of Irish wrongs or preach of Irish purposes. Their work was never wholly satisfactory, for what was Irish in it looked ungainly in an English garb and what was English was never perfectly mastered, never wholly absorbed into their being".[7] The themes might have been patriotic, but the forms were borrowed sedulously from the English romantics: a complaint which would be repeated by J. M. Synge, when he castigated the "bad art" often favoured by the Irish Irelander, "imitations of fourth-rate English poetry and nineteenth-century Irish novels".[8]

In exalting the fight against England into a self-sustaining tradition, the leaders of the previous century had largely forgotten what it was that they were fighting for: a distinctive culture of folktales, dances, sports, costumes, all seamlessly bound by the Irish language. This grave error became clear to a young Protestant named Douglas Hyde, a rectory child at Frenchpark, County Roscommon, who learned from humble cottiers in the fields around his parents' home the idioms and lore of a culture quite different from that of the Anglo-Irish drawing-room. By the time he had entered Trinity College, Hyde was an enthusiast: asked by a bemused fellow-student if he could actually speak this exotic language of which he talked so movingly, he responded "I dream in Irish".[9] In 1892, his ideas came to fruition in a famous lecture which was to be Ireland's declaration of cultural independence, analogous to Ralph Waldo Emerson's epoch-making address on "The American Scholar".

Hyde's gospel was epitomized by one word: deanglicization. He argued that previous leaders had confused politics and nationality, and had abandoned Irish civilization while professing with utter sincerity to fight for Irish nationalism. He sought to restore self-respect to Irish people, based on a shared rediscovery of the national culture: far from being "the badge of a beaten race", as Matthew Arnold had called it, the Irish language should be spoken henceforth with pride. Hyde's suggestion met with much cynicism and much amusement. Society ladies on meeting Hyde would whisper to friends that "he cannot be a gentleman because he speaks Irish": and even those more sympathetic to the language were often irritated by Hyde's wide-eyed fervour.[10] George Moore wickedly remarked that whenever in his public speeches Hyde reverted to his incoherent brand of English, it was easy to see why his greatest desire was to make Irish the first official language.[11]

But the young Yeats was profoundly impressed, on hearing Hyde's songs sung by haymakers in Connacht fields who were quite unaware that their author was passing: in such a moment, Yeats saw the return of a learned art to people's craft. Hyde truly had the capacity to make Ireland once again interesting to the Irish. Fired by his example, Yeats hoped for "a way of life in which the common man has some share in imaginative art. That this is the decisive element in the attempt to revive the Irish language I am quite certain".[12] He dreamed of a literary form so pure that it had not been indentured to any cause, whether of nation or of art, a form so fitted to a people's expressive ensemble that it would seem but an aspect of daily life.

Yeats wrote: "In Ireland, where the Gaelic tongue is still spoken, and to some little extent where it is not, the people live according to a tradition of life that existed before commercialism, and the vulgarity founded upon it; and we who would keep the Gaelic tongue and Gaelic memories and Gaelic habits of mind would keep them, as I think, that we may some day spread a tradition of life that makes neither great wealth nor great poverty, that makes the arts a natural expression of life, that permits even common men to understand good art and high thinking, and to have the fine manners these things can give". He went on:

> Almost everyone in Ireland, on the other hand, who comes from what are called the educated and wealthy classes . . . seeks . . . to establish a tradition of life, perfected and in part discovered by the English-speaking peoples, that has made great wealth and great poverty, that would make the arts impossible were it not for the sacrifice of a few who spend their lives in the bitterest of protest . . .[13]

This line of approach impressed many readers in England, too, who saw in it an interesting development of Matthew Arnold's critique of the specialist barbarism of the commercially-minded middle class. In seeking to express Ireland, these writers also hoped to challenge the culture of commercial exploitation in England: rather than have the Irish imitate the worst of English ways, they hoped to bring around a time when the English could emulate the finest Irish customs.

The invention of their idea of Ireland by Hyde and his friends happened, it should be noted, at the same time as English leaders were redesigning the image of England, in the decades between the 1880s and the Great War. These were the years when Queen Victoria, recovering from the republican challenge of Dilke and from her own grief after bereavement, restored a dimension of public pageantry to the monarchy, with much ancient costumery, archaic carriages and historical symbolism. Her 1887 jubilee proved so successful that it was repeated ten years later in 1897, and this prompted Irish nationalists in the following year, under the guidance of Maud Gonne, W. B. Yeats and James Connolly, to mount a similar counter-commemoration of the rebellion of 1798. Yeats said in March of 1898: "This year the Irish people will not celebrate, as England did last year, the establishment of an empire that has been built on the rapine of the world".[14] The new mania in England for erecting statues to historic figures was also emulated by the Irish, who began at once to collect funds for a massive monument to Wolfe Tone (as if a state which still did not exist were already rehearsing its consolidation by ceremonial recollections of the revolutionary struggle). Both the jubilee-cult and the statuary were relatively new phenomena, and mocked for their sentimentality by the young James Joyce in *Dubliners*, but it is easy to understand the function which they served.

The world was changing more in those thirty years than it had since the death of Christ. All over Europe leaders sought to reassure peoples, gone giddy from the speed of the changes, with images of stability. Part of the modernization process was the emergence of nation-states, which often arose out of the collapse of the old ways of life and so were badly in need of legitimation: this was afforded by the deliberate invention of traditions, which allowed leaders to ransack the past for a serviceable narrative.[15] In this way, by recourse to a few chosen symbols and simple ideas, random peoples could be transformed into Italians or Irish, and explain themselves by a highly-edited version of their history. Gaelic Ireland had retained few institutions or records after 1601 to act as a brake on these tendencies: all that remained were the notations of poets and the memories of the people. These played a far greater part in Hyde's remodelled Ireland than they did in many of the other emerging European countries. His lecture, rather cumbersomely titled "The Necessity for Deanglicizing Ireland", was delivered to the Irish Literary Society in November 1892, and it led, within a year, to the foundation of the Gaelic League, a movement for the preservation of Irish. The fall of Parnell, and subsequent split in the Irish Parliamentary Party at Westminster, may have left a number of unionists and landlords feeling free to express a cultural (as distinct from political) nationalism. If so, there was a real shrewdness in Hyde's strategy. He launched his appeal for Gaelic civilization as one coming from a man who could still feel the landlordly hankerings of a disappointed imperialist:

> It is the curious certainty that come what may Ireland will continue to resist English rule, even though it should be for their good, which prevents many of our nation from becoming unionists on the spot . . . It is just because there appears no earthly chance of their becoming good members of Empire that I argue that they should not remain in the anomalous position they are in, but since they absolutely refuse to become the one thing, that they become the other; cultivate what they have rejected, and build up an Irish nation on Irish lines.[16]

That subterranean pull back to all things English as touchstones of excellence is ironic in a text headed "deanglicization", but Hyde knew what he was about. He wanted to found Irish pride on something more positive and lasting than mere hatred of England. Yeats agreed: "I had dreamed of enlarging Irish hatred, till we had come to hate with a passion of patriotism what Morris and Ruskin hated".[17] The reactive patriotism which saw Ireland as not-England would have to give way to an identity which was self-constructed and existentially apt. Those peoples who *had* constructed themselves from within, the French for instance, never accused their bad citizens of being "unFrench": but throughout the nineteenth century delinquents were often called "un-Irish", because Irish nationalism too often defined itself by what it was against.

The Gaelic League might properly be seen as a response to the failure of a political attempt by nationalist leaders to shock English opinion by showing up the discrepancy between English order at home and misrule on the neighbouring island. The Irish resolved instead to instil in their people a self-belief which might in time lead to social and cultural prosperity. In its early years, the League received encouragement from the more enlightened colonial administrators like Augustine Birrell, who hoped that it might help to solve problems which the authorities had found intractable.

As a movement, the League was opposed to the antiquarianism of previous groups like the Gaelic Union, only six of whose members could speak Irish properly: it was, in fact, modern in its view of tradition as a yet-to-be-completed agenda, and in its insistence on combining ancient custom and contemporary method.

Some cynics accused Hyde of confusing Anglicization with modernization. Joyce's Stephen Hero, noting the willingness of the Catholic clergy to support the League, said that the priests hoped to find in Irish a bulwark against modern ideas, keeping "the wolves of unbelief" at bay and the people frozen in a past of "implicit faith".[18] This was a rather sour response from a Joyce whose experience of the League had been fatally narrowed by his attendance at the Irish classes of Patrick Pearse. (Pearse in his youthful days found it impossible to praise Irish without virulent denunciations of English, an approach much less ecumenical than Hyde's.) In the 1892 lecture, Hyde feared that people, ceasing to be Irish without becoming English, were falling into the vacuum between two admirable civilizations, as one nullified the other. His disgust was not caused by a baffling modernity or a difficult hybridity, so much as by the anomalous English element in every self-defeating document of Irish nationalism. He pointed to "the illogical position of men who drop their own language to speak English, of men who translate their euphonious Irish names into English monosyllables, of men who read English books and know nothing about Gaelic literature, nevertheless protesting as a matter of sentiment that they hate the country which at every hand's turn they rush to imitate".[19]

This was a subtle probing of Irish psychology: patriotic Anglophobia it attributed not to a troublesome difference with England so much as an abject similarity, leading like poles to repel one another with scientific predictability. Anglophobia seemed most extreme in those areas of maximum deference to English ways, while in the *Gaeltacht* itself physical-force nationalism made little headway. Hyde was merciless on the mentality which "continues to apparently hate the English, and at the same time continues to imitate them". Since people absolutely refused to become English, he concluded, they might as well resolve to be Irish.

This analysis had many salutary effects. Most important, it was the signal for a rebirth of cultural and literary criticism. Before the end of the decade, D. P. Moran could remark that "much [of] the perpetual flow of ridicule and largely unreasonable denunciation of England was turned from its course and directed back – where it was badly wanted – upon Irishmen themselves".[20] Moran went on: "From the great error that nationality is politics, a sea of corruption has sprung. Ireland was practically left unsubjected to wholesome native criticism, without which any collection of human-ity will corrupt . . . To find fault with your countryman was to play into the hands of England and act the traitor". For most of the previous century, a kind of national narcissism had pervaded debates: ever since O'Connell had told his followers that they were the finest peasantry in the world, even constructive criticism had been treated as sacrilege. Such a high-minded allergy to critique has been found in the early phases of most movements for cultural resistance – but this sentimentality had to be trans-cended. D. P. Moran suggested that an Ireland content to continue as a not-England would be indescribably boring: "Will a few soldiers dressed in green, and a republic, absolutely foreign to the genius of the Irish people, the humiliation of England, a hundred thousand English corpses with Irish bullets or pikes through them, satisfy the instinct within us that says 'Thou shalt be Irish'?"[21] It was Irish strength, rather than English weakness, which would count in the end.

What shocked Hyde about contemporary England was the apparent ease with which its people had endured the loss of so many of their traditions for the sake of material advancement. For English folk traditions he had, like Yeats, much respect and tenderness. When he spoke of "this awful idea of complete Anglicization", the phrase, if taken literally, could only offend unionists: if it were taken as a reference to the pollution and greyness of an environment despoiled by unplanned industrial-ism, it might win many over. Hyde insisted that the English would not finally be to blame if the Irish decided to abort their own traditions: "what the battleaxe of the Dane, the sword of the Norman, the wile of the Saxon were unable to perform, we have accomplished ourselves".[22] This was true in the sense that Irish declined in the nineteenth century only when large numbers of the people opted to learn English, as a prelude to emigration or to a more prosperous life at home. The tally-stick, later to be cited by chauvinist historians as a weapon of British cultural terror, had actually been devised for the schoolroom by Irish people themselves, as Sir William Wilde (father of Oscar) observed with dismay in a Galway schoolhouse of the midcentury:

> The man called the child to him, said nothing, but drawing forth from its dress a little stick, commonly called a scoreen or tally, which was suspended by a string round the neck, put an additional notch in it with his pen-knife. Upon our enquiring into the cause of their proceeding, we were told that it was done to prevent the child speaking Irish; for every time he attempted to do so a new nick was put in his tally, and, when these amounted to a certain number, summary punishment was inflicted on him by the schoolmaster.[23]

Hyde sensed that a purely economic or political freedom would be hollow, if the country was by the time of its attainment "despoiled of the bricks of nationality". The listless condition of dozens of post-colonies in the twentieth century was astutely anticipated by Hyde: "just at the moment when the Celtic race is presumably about to largely recover possession of its own country, it finds itself deprived and stript of its Celtic characteristics, cut off from its past, yet scarcely in touch with its present".[24] Equally familiar in the emergent states of Africa and Asia would be accounts of how young men and women were found to blush with shame when overheard speaking their own language. As would happen in some of these societies too, many children were not even aware of the existence in their culture of two languages: in the Connacht known to Hyde, parents often spoke Irish only to children who answered in English only, and when Hyde asked some children "Nach labhrann tú Gaeilge?" (Don't you speak Irish?), the answer was "And isn't it Irish that I'm speaking?" This domestic situation was repeated in *Gaeltacht* classrooms where schoolteachers spoke only English to children who spoke only Irish: Hyde wondered if there was any other country in the world where schoolteachers taught children who could not understand them, and children learned from instructors whose language they could not really follow.[25] There were many indeed.

His holistic method led Hyde to emphasize the intimate link between clothing and language. As Yeats could bewail the ways in which Irish sentiment looked ungainly in English garb, so Hyde regretted that men of the midland counties had grown "too proud" to wear homespun tweeds. The analysis anticipated by decades the strictures of Antonio Gramsci and John Berger on the crumpled, ill-fitting suits worn in photographs by peasants and labourers early this century: their vigorous actions simply spoiled the suits which were quite inappropriate to the lives they led, being designed for the sedentary administrators of the ruling class, but the suits signalled their acceptance of being "always, and recognizably to the classes above them, second-rate, clumsy, uncouth, defensive".[26]

The rhetorical guile of Hyde has been insufficiently recognized: the deanglicization lecture which began with an appeal to unionist-imperialists could nonetheless be brought to a climax with the Fenian trope of a call for a house-to-house visitation, "something – though with a very different purpose – analogous to the procedure that James Stephens adopted throughout Ireland when he found her like a corpse on a dissecting table".[27] Though he might steal some of these Phoenix fires and might use "west-Britonizing" as a term of jocular abuse, Hyde was no narrow-gauge nationalist: for he encouraged the "use of Anglo-Irish literature instead of English books, especially instead of English periodicals. We must set our face firmly against penny dreadfuls, shilling shockers, and, still more, the garbage of vulgar weeklies like *Bow Bells* and the *Police Intelligence*". This diagnosis has more in common with the future strictures of F. R. Leavis or, for that matter, Theodor Adorno, than might at first seem the case. The alleged anti-modern element in Irish revivalism, of which revisionist historians have made so much, turns out on inspection to be a prophetic critique of mass-culture and of the vulgarization of popular taste. The Gaelic League, acting on Hyde's precepts, became in effect one of the earliest examples of a Workers' Education Movement, at a time of limited opportunity for many. It was also, in some respects, a precursor of the movement for multiculturalism which, in later decades, would seek to revise and expand syllabi, with the introduction of subaltern cultures and oral literatures. In other respects, of course, its leaders were dismissive of many popular publications and magazines which current exponents of Cultural Studies find worthy of attention.

There were only six books in print in Irish at the founding of the League in 1893, and most Irish speakers in the countryside were still illiterate. Yet much was achieved very rapidly: in one year alone, according to Yeats, the League sold 50,000 text-books.[28] Thousands registered in language classes, and, in a decade which saw Fabian cyclists and suffragists take to the countryside for summer schools, the League was an interesting Irish version of the phenomenon. A civil rights agitation was mounted. Letters and parcels were addressed in Irish, much to the confusion of the postal authorities; and when a Donegal trader was prosecuted for inscribing his name in Irish on his wagon, he was defended in court by the young Patrick Pearse (his only appearance as a barrister, in what he called the ignoblest of professions).

Questions were raised in the House of Commons about such issues, but the crucial controversy arose in 1899, when evidence was taken by the Committee of Inter-mediate Education on whether or not it should ratify Irish as a valid school subject. The professors of Trinity College Dublin had taken fright at the League's success and warned Dublin Castle that it was a movement infiltrated by "separatists". Now they made a massive effort to remove Irish altogether from the secondary school system. John Pentland Mahaffy, a former tutor of Oscar Wilde and a Professor of Ancient History at Trinity, told the committee that, although it was sometimes useful to a man fishing for salmon or shooting game, it would be an unconscionable waste of time to teach it in schools, since it was "almost impossible to get hold of a text in Irish which is not religious or that is not silly or indecent".[29] Quite reasonably, Hyde asked how Mahaffy, a man ignorant of the Irish language, could make such sweeping claims: and he adduced evidence from a range of Celtic scholars to establish the value and scope of ancient Irish literature. Citations came from Windisch in Leipzig, Zimmer in Greifswald, Stern in Berlin, Meyer in Liverpool, Pedersen in Copenhagen, Dottin in Rennes; and York Powell of Oxford, a historian, wrote of the advantages to children of bilingualism. At this point in the controversy, Mahaffy revealed the source of his claims: Robert Atkinson, the Professor of Old Irish at Trinity who – in a remarkable anticipation of the line taken by prosecuting counsel in the 1960 trial of *Lady Chatterley's Lover* – declared that many Irish-language texts were unfit to have in the house alongside his daughters: if perused, they might cause a shock from which the young ladies might not recover for the rest of their lives.

Atkinson testified that the study of *Diarmuid and Gráinne*, then on the Intermediate course, was quite unsuitable for children: and he attacked one of Hyde's published stories as the doings of a common lout who never washed. He went on – with a tactic which would also be used by conservative academics in many emerging states – to denounce the native language for its alleged lack of a standard grammar and spelling. All in all, his evidence was a graphic illustration of the covert hatred among many exponents of Celticism for the peoples whose study made their professional reputa-tions. Stung by Atkinson's strictures on grammar and syntax, Fr. Peter O'Leary embarked, in the League's weekly paper *An Claidheamh Soluis* (The Sword of Light), on a detailed examination of Atkinson's own treatment of the copula *is* in his scholarly edition of *Trí Biorghaoithe an Bháis*, which he found so faulty that a couplet soon spread across the land:

Atkinson of TCD
Doesn't know the verb *to be*.

In later exposures, O'Leary showed that Atkinson's Irish was so shaky that "he had not the grasp of it that a gossoon in a Connemara bog has".[30]

For all its offence and inadvertent hilarity, this controversy was useful, for the battle with the Trinity dons brought public opinion solidly behind the Gaelic League. Yeats played a leading part in this: in February 1900, he called upon members of parliament to use the old Parnellite methods of obstruction to insert the teaching of Irish into the Education Bill. He condemned Trinity College as provincial, "which the Literary Society is not, and the Gaelic League is not; we must fight against provincialism and die fighting".[31] In *Beltaine*, the theoretical journal of the Irish Literary Theatre, the dramatist Edward Martyn wrote sardonically of "the efforts of certain persons and institutions whose aim seems to be to create in Ireland a sort of shabby England".[32] By 1906, the League had secured the use of Irish in Gaeltacht schools, as a subject in itself and, in addition, as the usual language of instruction, a campaign significantly assisted by the writings of J. M. Synge.[33] By 1909, Irish had been made compulsory for matriculation at the National University, just a year after Hyde's appointment to a professorship there.

In calling for a return to national traditions, Hyde had made a telling point: that far from being fixated on the past, the Irish were in danger of making an irreparable break with their inheritance. This blockage had its roots in the enforced migrations and interrupted family histories of the nineteenth century, which had disrupted the national archive. Hyde, by his promotion of Celtic scholarship and of Irish, was seeking to repair and restore it. He was dismayed by that weird blend of external deference and private rebellion which characterized the Irish relation to England. What remained of the Irish identity had been preserved through the spiritual leadership given to many people by the Catholic church, but that same church had also blocked the expression of that identity by the more militant nationalists and republicans.

Hyde, in unstopping the sentiment, was also careful to recognize the spiritual dimension in a collection like *Abhráin Diaga Chúige Chonnacht* (The Religious Songs of Connacht). He did indeed woo the Catholic clergy, though for subtler reasons than Joyce might have suspected: he needed their endorsement as an answer to those pious Catholics who condemned the mingling of sexes at League functions as "occasions of sin". Moreover, he was well aware that the careers of many Irish-language enthusiasts among the Catholic clergy had been stymied, in Maynooth and elsewhere, as a result of their high-profile activities. Men like Lorcán Ó Muireadhaigh, Dr. O'Hickey and Walter McDonald got into trouble with the ecclesiastical authorities for promoting Irish, for insisting on its central importance in the syllabus for matriculation, and so on. Far from abjectly toadying to such figures, Hyde may have been attempting to accord them a degree of respectability, by featuring them on platforms at successful mass-meetings. Those priests would undoubtedly have contained within their ranks a predictable proportion of conservative, anti-modern theologians, as Joyce alleged – but there were others, such as Walter McDonald, who were at the forefront of progressive movement, as well as being completely ecumenical.

Apart from being a great ecumenist and reconciler himself, Hyde was ever the cunning tactician – properly grateful to have the support of prestigious Catholic priests, whose presence could serve to glamorize the Irish language in the eyes of a peasantry for whom it had long been a token of shame. As the priests had once done, so now he – a Protestant gentleman-scholar – assumed leadership of a people whose traditions had been so disrupted that they were estranged from their very environment.

A major agent of that estrangement had been the Board of Education, which throughout the previous century, in Ireland as in India, had encouraged the materially ambitious natives to abandon their culture. These people had been encouraged to view their own great narratives as mere myths to be discarded (much as the Elizabethan historians like Stanyhurst had mocked the "unscientific" memorialists of Gaelic Ireland). If anything, the situation in Ireland was more extreme than that in India, for the Irish school texts were given to every child and brooked no nationalism, whereas the Indian books were intended only for the élites and *did* allow a modicum of national sentiment. The value of the new education, the British claimed, was that it would help the people to dismantle the myths which still bound them to their own culture, and instead, in the words of Lord Macaulay's minute on India, "make them look to this country with that veneration which the youthful student feels for the classical soul of Greece".[34] However, the pitched battle put up by Trinity College against the Gaelic League had precisely the reverse effect to that intended and had thrown this entire process into jeopardy. By 1903, the constitutional nationalist Stephen Gwynn, a member of parliament, could write that "I have heard the existence of an Irish literature denied by a roomful of professors, educated gentlemen, and, within a week, I have heard, in the same country, the classics of that literature recited by an Irish peasant who could neither write nor read. On which party should the stigma of illiteracy set the uglier brand?"[35]

The disarray of political nationalism in the 1890s had allowed some unionists to adopt a more relaxed attitude to the Gaelic tradition, and the League made an appeal to a much wider version of nationality. The movement was so powerful in Belfast by 1899 that it could cram a meeting-hall which called for the teaching of Irish in schools:

> All classes and creeds were represented at the gathering. The first resolution was proposed by an MA of Trinity College. Nationalists and Unionists, Protestants and Catholics, were equally earnest in their advocacy of the language – the Protestant Bishop of Ossory wrote in open approval of "a platform on which all lovers of our dear native land could meet as nationalists in the truest sense of the word".[36]

By 1904, it was the strongest democratic organization in the country, wooed by the directors of the Abbey Theatre and by John Redmond's Parliamentary Party which offered Hyde a seat in Westminster. He refused, but only on being cautioned that such a gesture would reduce the inflow of funds from nationalist sympathizers in the United States. The long-term implications of Hyde's position were by then becoming clear, and they were spelt out vividly by the Protestant canon James Hannay (*alias* George Birmingham, novelist) in 1907:

I take the Sinn Féin position to be the natural and inevitable development of the League principles. They couldn't lead to anything else...I do not myself believe that you will be able to straddle the fence for very much longer. You have, in my humble opinion, the chance of becoming a great Irish leader, with the alternative of relapsing into the position of a John Dillon. It will be intensely interesting to see which you choose. Either way, I think the movement you started will go on, whether you lead it or take the part of a poor Frankenstein who created a monster he could not control.[37]

Hyde did lose control. The Fenian sub-text of his own language impelled his more ardent supporters towards a brazenly political commitment: and Hyde, whose uninterest in politics helped to widen his initial support, now found that his political *naïveté* could lead to the League's decline or, at any rate, its co-option by other forces. Though thousands of students had enrolled in the League's classes, few ever got beyond the learning of a few token phrases. Without state support, there was a clear limit to what could be achieved. Equally, the *Gaeltacht*, the repository of unbroken traditions, could hardly be saved by a non-political organization which, by its own self-denying ordinance, could never expect to bring about industrial reform. The Gaelic League saw very clearly that if the *Gaeltacht* were left to survive on tourism, it would soon become a mere reservation, a museum: "the language, the industries, and the very existence of a people are all interdependent, and whoever has a living care for the one cannot be unmindful of the other".[38] So Patrick Pearse urged a programme of industrial development and called upon Leaguers to settle in the west, thereby making a real commitment over and above the use of ritual phrases. They did not go, preferring, as Sean O'Casey sarcastically noted, to stay in the more respectable Dublin suburbs of Donnybrook and Whitehall, "lisping Irish wrongly" and wincing at workmen like himself who frequented their meetings.[39]

O'Casey's portrait of Hyde in his autobiography is a vicious travesty of a kindly visionary, but there is truth in its retrospective suggestion that the League seemed at times to have confused "the fight for Irish" with "the fight for collars and ties". The lyrics studied in League classes often seemed to favour mental over physical labour:

> Aoibhinn beatha an scoláire
> bhíos ag deanamh léinn;
> is follas daoibh, a dhaoine,
> gur dó is aoibhne in Éirinn.
>
> Gan smacht rí air ná ruire
> ná tiarna dá threise,
> gan chuid cíosa ag caibidil,
> gan mochéirí, gan meirse.
>
> Mochéirí ná aoireacht
> ní thabhair uaidh choíche;
> is ní mó do-bheir dá aire
> fear na faire san oíche.[40]
>
> The life of a scholar is pleasant
> as he pursues his learning;

> it must be clear to you, O people,
> that his is the pleasantest life in Ireland.
>
> Neither king nor prince controls him,
> nor does any leader however strong,
> he does not have to pay dues to clergy,
> nor does he wake early or have to do hard labour.
>
> Early rising and animal-minding
> are things he never needs to do;
> and he never pays any heed
> to the watchmen in the nights.

Many Gaelic texts revived in the period were out-and-out attacks in the name of the Gaelic bards on the brutish parliamentarians of an earlier century. *Pairlement Chloinne Tomáis* (The Parliament of Clan Thomas), republished in 1912, probably helped to feed the forces of extra-parliamentary nationalism which gathered momentum in that year.

Some Leaguers projected an ideal self-image of the Gael as a descendant of ancient chieftains and kings. Irish Ireland countered the petty "*seoinín*" or West Briton, who asserted his superiority by imitating English manners, with its own form of invented Gaelic snobbery. Ireland became not-England, an apophatic construct which was as teasing to the mind as the notion of a horse as a wheelless car. Anything English was *ipso facto* not for the Irish, as it might appear to weaken the claim to separate nationhood, but any valued cultural possessions of the English were shown to have their Gaelic equivalents. Thus was born what Seán de Fréine has acutely called an ingenious device of national parallelism:[41]

English language – Irish language
English law   – Brehon law
Parliament   – Dáil
Prime Minister   – Taoiseach
Soccer   – Gaelic football
Hockey   – Hurling
Trousers   – Kilt

It mattered little whether those devices had a secure basis in Irish history, for if they had not previously existed they could be invented, Gaelic football being a classic case of instant archaeology but definitely not a game known to Cuchulain.

Equally, because Englishmen were sensible enough to wear trousers in their inclement climate, it followed that the romantic, impractical Irishman must have worn a kilt. This garment pleased the revivalists with its connotations of aristocracy, of Scottish chieftains and pipers marching into battle; but the garment never was Irish; and subsequent historians have shown that the Irish wore hip-hugging trousers long before the English (and were reviled for the barbarous fashion by the new invaders). The kilt wasn't properly Scottish either, having been devised by an English Quaker industrialist, seeking an outlet for unused tartan *after* the highland clearances: it was worn by Scottish workers in the new factories because it was cheaper than trousers.[42] None of these considerations, however, prevented a generation of enthusiasts from raising the cry "Down with trousers!" Some devious souls tried to have it both ways, as in George Moore's recommendation that tartan trousers be worn to his Gaelic lawn-party at Ely Place. *An Claidheamh Soluis* contributed to this pan-Celtic lunacy when it announced its own inspired compromise: "We condemn English-made evening dress, but evening dress of Irish manufacture is just as Irish as a Donegal cycling suit. Some people think we cannot be Irish unless we always wear tweeds and only occasionally wear collars".[43]

One historian has marvelled at how heated these debates could become and has suggested that the success of the League can be explained by "the opportunity it extended to a snobbishly-afficted middle and lower-middle class to assert a new social self-respect".[44] Sean O'Casey spoke corrosively of these pretensions to respectability, but it was left to James Joyce to write the most lethal account of the careerism of some Leaguers in his short story titled "A Mother". A respectable woman named Mrs. Kearney sees in the League a chance to promote not the cause of Irish but the musical prospects of her daughter:

> When the Irish Revival began to be appreciable, Mrs. Kearney determined to take advantage of her daughter's name and brought an Irish teacher to the house. Kathleen and her sister sent Irish picture postcards to their friends and those friends sent back other Irish picture postcards... People said that she was very clever at music and a very nice girl, and, moreover, that she was a believer in the language movement. Mrs. Kearney was well content with this.[45]

The daughter secures a position as accompanist at a series of concerts in aid of the Éire Abú Society, but when the functions are poorly attended and the society cannot afford to pay the fee, the mother creates a nasty scene and insists on every last penny. Joyce could see how, for some, the new social self-respect could verge on hard-nosed bourgeois materialism.

It was, however, the *unworldliness* of Hyde's analysis which led to the confrontation with radical Leaguers led by Pearse, who insisted that Ireland should not merely be free but Gaelic, not merely Gaelic but free, and that the two aspirations were inter-dependent. By its refusal to follow this logic, the League got left behind in the years leading up to the 1916 Rising. By 1913, Pearse was announcing that "the Gaelic League, as the Gaelic League, is a spent force", though he was careful to add in another speech of the following year that "what will be accomplished by the men of this generation, will be accomplished because the Gaelic League made it possible".[46] Hyde was disgusted by Pearse's support for James Larkin during the Lock-Out of 1913, though, in fairness, it should be said that he may have been motivated by concern for the hungry families of workers rather than the welfare of the bosses: but his break from the League came only in 1915, at a Dundalk conference which adopted a clear nationalist stance. He resigned the presidency amid tears and regret. "My own ideas had been quite different", he explained: "My own ambition had always been the language as a neutral ground upon which all Irishmen might meet... We were doing the only business that really counted, we were keeping Ireland Irish, and that in a way that the Government and Unionists, though they hated it, were powerless to oppose. So long as we remained non-political, there was no end to what we could do".[47]

By a wonderful irony, Hyde ended his days as first president of the Irish Free State, a golf-playing, grouse-shooting Anglo-Irish gentleman, who had never in his long life uttered a word from a public platform in support of Home Rule. His glory days had been the 1890s and the first decade of the new century, the heyday of the League, a period during which he supplied Synge and Lady Gregory with their literary dialect. He was described, with no exaggeration, as scholar-in-waiting to the Irish renaissance, furnishing Yeats with the figure of Hanrahan and a host of other *personae*. Sean O'Casey's rather savage comments on Hyde's snobbism and his "Déanta in Éirinn Irish" were tinged with the bitterness of retrospect, though it was noticeable that after Hyde's elevation to a university chair in 1908 references to him by writers became faintly mocking. George Russell was convinced that Hyde actively discouraged "the vital element"[48] in the League which would have been willing to challenge the conservative Catholic clergy. The man's popularity with crowds remained as great as ever, but rendered him a dubious quantity in the eyes of fastidious intellectuals. Yeats's poem "At the Abbey Theatre" is condescending rather than envious of that appeal; and George Moore depicted Hyde as the invertebrate kind of Catholic Protestant, "cunning, subtle, cajoling, superficial and affable".[49] This was rather too cynical an interpretation. In a land fissured along sectarian fault-lines, a "Catholic Protestant" was by no means an ignoble thing to be: the inclusiveness and ecumenism of Hyde's position would be a source of inspiration to many subsequent writers of Protestant background in later decades.

The real weaknesses of Hyde's position were to be found elsewhere: in his blithe assumption that a movement as opposed to mainstream unionism as the Gaelic League could somehow be non-political. Just as the League was weakened by its reluctance to examine the economic realities which underlay cultural policies (including the materialist motivations of some of its fair-weather enthusiasts), it was also blinded by a failure to examine the *political* assumptions of the movement. It was captured, as James Hannay so acutely predicted, not by the parliamentarians but by Sinn Féin, whose leaders took up the running after Dundalk. Cultural nationalism was soon supplanted by a more openly political movement, which in turn issued in the militarism of Easter 1916. Like many who partook in that uprising, Michael Collins had no doubt as to its intellectual sources: "we only succeeded after we had begun to get back our Irish ways; after we had made a serious effort to speak our own language; after we had striven again to govern ourselves".[50] It was not, however, the Easter Rising which put paid to the League's major influence and power. Rather, it was the unexamined contradictions in its programme which prevented it from gaining more unionist adherents and from keeping the militant nationalists at arm's length before the Rising. Later still, it would become redundant in the judgement of many because of the apparent embrace of its programme by the founders of the Free State. Nonetheless, of Hyde it could justly be said that he rescued the Irish element from absorption and made it, for a brilliant generation from 1893 to 1921, conscious of itself.

NATIONALITY OR COSMOPOLITANISM?

Even before the League held its founding meeting, Yeats had deflected the challenge which it posed to creative writers. Though many in decades to come would scoff at the patent contradiction of an Irish National Theatre staging plays in the English language, Yeats had solved that problem to his own satisfaction as far back as 1892:

> Is there then no hope for the de-Anglicizing of our people? Can we not build a national tradition, a national literature which shall be none the less Irish in spirit from being English in language?[51]

He answered that it could be done "by translating and retelling in English, which shall have an indefinable Irish quality of rhythm and style, all that is best in the ancient literature". Though the success of the League in the following decade would cause many English-speaking writers to learn Irish, and some to flirt with the idea of writing in it, the die was cast. Hyde was himself unwittingly to provide a spectacular example of the shape which events were taking: in his most successful collection, *Abhráin Ghrá Chúige Chonnacht: Love Songs of Connacht*, published in his *annus mirabilis* of 1893, he printed the Irish text on one side of the page and his own translation into Hiberno-English dialect on the other. It soon became clear, however, that the main appeal of this book to Yeats and his young contemporaries lay in Hyde's own translations, and especially in those translations written in prose rather than verse. The very success of the book caused the defeat of its initial purpose, for, along with popularizing Irish literature, it made the creation of a national literature in English seem all the more feasible.

Hyde's position was ambiguous from the start: in one sense, he was the leader of the movement to save Irish, but in another, he was a founder of the Anglo-Irish literary revival. Subsequent literary history was to emphasize the cruelty of the paradox: it was desperately unfortunate for him that his campaign to save Irish should have coincided with the emergence of a group of Irishmen destined to write masterpieces in English. The fact that, without the Gaelic *substratum*, few of them would have written so richly and some might not even have emerged, simply underlines the accuracy of Yeats's initial reading of the situation. George Moore might call for "a return to the language ... a mysterious inheritance in which resides the soul of the Irish people";[52] he might even threaten to disinherit his nephews if they failed to learn the native tongue; but when his own Irish teacher called at the appointed hour to his house in Ely Place, he had the butler tell him he was out.

The old *canard* that "the Gael must be the element that absorbs" was never seriously entertained by the writers: indeed, those who actually wrote in Irish were often more open to foreign (especially continental) influences than some who worked in English. It must be remembered that when D. P. Moran coined that polemical aphorism (in *The Philosophy of Irish Ireland* in 1905), it was at a time when the prestige of the Gael was still being restored after centuries of denial and when Irish speakers did not even enjoy the rights to education in their own language. Anyway, the declaration came with a notable qualification: it was prefaced by the more telling observation that "no one wants to fall out with Davis's comprehensive idea of the Irish people as a composite race drawn from various sources".[53] The real debate of the revivalist generation was about whether the literature it created should be national or cosmopolitan in tone.

At the outset, the options were not polarized in that rather simplified way. In 1893, Stopford Brooke said that a poetry which was national would "be able to become not only Irish, but also alive to the interests and passions of universal humanity".[54] The debate really took fire in 1899 with the publication of exchanges between John Eglinton, W. B. Yeats, George Russell and William Larminie in the *Dublin Daily Express*, a pro-union paper. Eglinton, a man of northern Protestant background and a humanist by inclination, questioned whether the use of Celtic heroic figures by dramatists could eventuate in anything more than *belles lettres*. He contended that Cuchulain or Deirdre would refuse to be translated out of their old environment into the world of modern sympathies, and such a use of "a subject outside experience" could produce only a mere exercise rather than "a strong interest in life itself".[55] Yeats countered with the claim that art is not an Arnoldian criticism of life so much as the sacred revelation of a hidden life. At this point, George Russell intervened with a characteristically ecumenical attempt to reconcile the national and the individual idea: the nation as a formation existed to enhance the expressive potential of the person, rather than the person existing as a mere illustration of some prior national essence. He offered a shrewd distinction between shallow cosmopolitanism and national individualism:

> ... there is little to distinguish the work of the best English writers or artists from that of their continental contemporaries ... If nationality is to justify itself in the face of all this, it must be because the country which preserves its individuality does so with the profound conviction that its peculiar ideal is nobler than that which the metropolitan spirit suggests.[56]

Russell acutely foresaw how mass communications would homogenize the whole of Europe into a dreary imitative provincialism. The imperial European powers had carved up Africa at the Congress of Berlin and he was not impressed by the results: "Empires do not permit the intensive cultivation of human life ... they destroy the richness and variety of existence by the extinction of personal and unique gifts".[57] Epic archetypes, on the other hand, would offset this objection, awakening each person to the heroism latent in the self: "it was this idea which led Whitman to 'exploit' himself as the typical American".[58] In all of his writings, Russell – most unusually, for the time – equated the cosmopolitan with the imperial.

In a rudimentary sense, the controversy established Yeats as the upholder of nationalism, Eglinton as the defender of cosmopolitanism, and Russell as the seeker of some vaguely-defined middle ground. But this is to underplay the interesting points of contact in their thought: all were agreed on the advisability of using the English language. Though Yeats pursued a diplomatic alliance with the Gaelic League, Russell complained of its "boyscoutish propaganda" and Eglinton contended that a "thought movement" rather than a "language movement" could provide a surer basis for a true Irish identity.[59] Eglinton misunderstood deanglicization when he argued that "there was something lacking in a mental and spiritual attitude so uncompromisingly negative".[60] Though he did not know Irish, he inferred with a strange confidence that as a language it lacked analytic power and "had never been to school". Fearing the division of Ireland into two armed camps, like the Jews and the Samaritans, he reminded the League that "it was among the lost sheep of the house of Israel – amongst those who had lost the use of the Hebrew tongue – that the Jewish Messiah appeared".[61] He denied that the word *Irish* accurately designated the language which "is no longer the language of Irish nationality" and "never was so"; and he wickedly but effectively questioned the revivalist use of the peasant for ulterior political purposes by those who "are for the most part ignorant of the old man personally". He was, however, notably vague in his definition of what his more ecumenical nationality might be constituted, preferring to ask that writers work from a "human" rather than an "Irish" standpoint.

Eglinton had not only an independent stance but a lively way of adopting it. Like many self-declared humanists and secularists, he was more concerned with the future than the past, and quite convinced that while most virtues are individual, most vices are national. He feared that a successful restoration of the Irish language would cut people off from the rest of Europe, condemning them to speak always in an Irish rather than a human capacity (and he had no scruple about presenting these as opposed concepts). Unable or unwilling to concede the modern element in the Gaelic League, he mockingly inverted Hyde's slogan and programme: "Literature must be free as the elements; if that is to be cosmopolitan, it must be cosmopolitan ... and I should like to see the day of what might be called ... the de-Davisization of Irish national literature, that is to say, the getting rid of the notion that in Ireland a writer is to think first and foremost of interpreting the nationality of his country, and not simply of the burden he is to deliver".[62] Eglinton badly underestimated the European dimension of Gaelic culture, past as well as present: after all, the *dánta grá* (love poems) were resolutely in the *amour courtois* tradition, and the revival in Irish-language writing led by Pearse had urged its followers to make contact with the Gaelic past *and also* "with the mind of contemporary Europe". Moreover, Eglinton seemed to have forgotten Mazzini's dictum that every people is bound to constitute itself a nation before it can occupy itself with the question of humanity, but that it does this in order to be free to move on to that question.

There are, nonetheless, wonderful moments in the writings of Eglinton when he exudes a real impatience with the nationalist process, an impatience which comes, as it were, from one who has moved on to better things and is impatient for companions to catch up and keep company with him on his journey. His strictures on the need of art to speak for the people of the present seem admirable: he was quite convinced that Yeats "lived back" in a nostalgic land of his imagination, a place unchastened by the real Ireland all around the living poet. This led Eglinton to mount a devastating, and wonderfully dialectical, critique of what he saw as the major contradiction of the Irish revival: "All the great literatures have seemed in retrospect to have risen like emanations from the life of a whole people, which has shared in a general exaltation: and this was not the case in Ireland. How could a literature movement be in any sense national when the interest of the whole nation lay in extirpating the conditions which produced it?"[63] Yet, somewhere along the line of his argument, Eglinton aborted the incipient dialectic: he failed to note that element in Irish nationalism which willed its own supersession by a humanism not unlike his, and he failed to recognize the genuine achievements of nationalism, albeit in sometimes outmoded forms.

That blind spot may have been caused by his refusal to adopt the Yeatsian strategy and to separate himself from his own class and background. He saw himself as opposed to those dogmatic patriots who were too ready to extinguish self in the service of a cause, but for all practical purposes this amounted to no more than the traditional Protestant aversion to the more demonstrative type of Catholic. If his understanding of the intricacies of Irish Ireland was limited, his grasp of the cultural effects of colonialism was non-existent. Many readers of the *United Irishman* of 1902 must have smiled at the simplicity of his analysis of the history of "The Island of Saints":

> Ireland will have to make up its mind that it is no longer the old Gaelic nation of the fifth or twelfth, or even of the eighteenth century, but one which has been in the making ever since these islands were drawn into the community of nations by the Normans.[64]

There is no recognition there of the European scope of Irish monasticism or of the commerce of scholars over many centuries: however, the marvellous euphemism for the Norman invasion tells all – what others might see as cultural conquest, Eglinton welcomes as a happy cosmopolitanism. A similar use of the word by Lord Cromer allowed him to describe Egypt as a land whose future lay not in narrow nationalism but in a more "cosmopolitan" mingling of identities, grounded not on race but on "the respect men have always accorded to superior talents and unselfish conduct".[65]

It was such thinking which allowed Eglinton to salute Edward Dowden (whom Yeats had judged the quintessential provincial) as the possessor of a cosmopolitan mind of the first rank, "probably the first point touched by anything new in the world of ideas outside Ireland".[66] Dowden, for his part, made no bones about the link between the imperial idea and literary cosmopolitanism. Long before African critics complained that "cosmopolitanism" was actually a code-word for the values of imperial Europe, he breezily conceded the point: "The direction of such work as I have done in literature has been (to give it a grand name) imperial or cosmopolitan, and though I think a literature ought to be rooted in the soil, I don't think a conscious effort to promote a provincial spirit tends in that direction".[67] The idea that the revival might be a revolt *against* imitative provincialism completely escaped Dowden, though it had been signalled by Thomas Davis in the refrain of his most famous song:

> And Ireland, long a province, be
> A nation once again.

Even less did it strike Dowden or Eglinton that this revolt was also a protest against *the provincialization of England* by the forces of industrial society. The leaders of that protest saw provincialism as taking one of two forms: the first and more obvious being found in people who looked to some faraway centre for approved patterns of cultural significance, the second and more insidious being found in those who were so smugly self-assured that they had lost all curiosity about any other forms of life beyond their own. The Irish in the previous century had suffered from the former provincialism, as had many parts of England; but it was the modern English who, even more than the nationalist Irish, were now suffering from the latter kind. While the former existed only as a comparison with a remote model, the latter refused any comparison at all. Neither Dowden nor Eglinton could concede what stared artists like Yeats and Joyce in the face: that England itself had grown smugly provincial in its imperial phase, because its citizens had lost the capacity to conceive of how they appeared in the eyes of others. They were psychologically driven to conquer largely because they had no sense of their own presence.

The English decline into the first form of deference had been diagnosed by George Eliot in the novel *Middlemarch* (1871–2), whose subtitle was "A study of provincial life". In it, the Middlemarchers all choose to define themselves in the distorting mirror of other people's opinions and this is the cause of their undoing: "Even Milton, looking for his portrait in a spoon, must submit to have the facial angle of a bumpkin".[68] By the new century, the decline into imperial smugness had fed massively off the earlier insecurity, but the underlying problem of provincialism remained to be documented by D. H. Lawrence: in *Women in Love* he shows lovers leaving home because "in England you can't let go", only for them to find that England is a state of mind which they bring with them wherever they travel. It was hardly a coincidence that, as English culture lapsed into this provincialism of spirit, Irish artists rediscovered their long-suppressed yearnings for the wider world. The moment might even be dated to 1892, when the Examiner of Plays in the Lord Chamberlain's office refused a licence for the performance of *Salomé*, a play in French by Oscar Wilde. The Examiner, E. F. Smyth Pigott, was called by Shaw "a walking compendium of vulgar, insular prejudice".[69] Wilde, for his part, responded with the assertion that Paris was now the true home of personal freedom. *Salomé* was published there in 1893 and performed in the city three years later.

From this point onwards, Irish thinkers turned to Europe, and beyond, as they had done so often in previous centuries, for ideas and audiences. The debate in Joyce's story "The Dead" is about whether the Irish person of the future will holiday for recreation on the Aran Islands or on continental Europe. All of a sudden, England was a bore: which was what George Moore meant by his famous telegram announcing that the centre of gravity in the literary world had shifted from London to Dublin. Certainly, the axis which had once run from Dublin to London now ran from Dublin to Paris instead.

Little of this seems to have borne in upon Dowden or Eglinton. As the years passed and the evidence mounted, Yeats made it perfectly clear that his Irish revival was a revolt against a provincialism of mind which can sometimes inhere in imitative nationalism, sometimes in complacent imperialism, but which always seeks to reproduce itself in facsimile wherever it is found. After the *Playboy* riots, Yeats discovered that, in order to protect his movement, he had to fight as hard against nationalist provincialism as he had once fought against the closed minds of Trinity College:

> Many are beginning to recognize the right of the individual mind to see the world in its own way, to cherish the thoughts which separate men from one another...instead of those thoughts that had made one man like another if they could, and have but

succeeded in setting up hysteria and insincerity in place of confidence and self-posses-
sion.[71]

The Gaelic obscurantist, the anti-intellectual priest, and the propagandist politician
were all as inimical to the revivalist ideal as were the empire men or the shallow
cosmopolitans. Yeats had believed that the language movement and the thought
movement could be reconciled; though remaining open to influences from Europe,
Asia and beyond, he based his doctrines on the conviction that there is no great
literature without nationality and no nationality without literature.

For all their blind spots, Eglinton's essays had a capital value: they alerted many to
a xenophobic element within the national movement, which often threatened to
negate its own better ideals. Synge became aware of certain insular Leaguers who,
"with their eyes glued on John Bull's navel, fear to be Europeans for fear the huckster
across the street will call them English".[72] For all the talk about deanglicization as a
fantasy of purification, it was the allegedly *French* decadence of Synge's plays, when
clothed in a rural Irish garb, which stung nationalist critics. These solemn commentators would object to a *boulevardier* element, while blithely ignoring the far more
potent English influence in Irish culture, an influence which went largely unnoticed
only because it was pervasive. The more probing Irish Ireland polemicists were
somewhat quicker to detect the English sub-text of many plays: D. P. Moran complained, for example, that Yeats and Moore in their version of *Diarmuid and Gráinne*
"have changed Diarmuid from a Fenian chief into a modern degenerate",[73] something, incidentally, which Eglinton had said could not be done; and Patrick Pearse
even more acutely heard echoes of Hamlet on the lips of the Cuchulain of *On Baile's
Strand*. To all of which the authors could say "but that effect was fully intended". In
the adaptation of Gaelic elements to English forms, both elements were vastly
changed, as Yeats had hoped, and changed also were the adaptors. The literature
which he and his colleagues produced arose not among the Irish speakers of the west
nor among the drawing-rooms of a self-enclosed gentry, but from the impact of one
civilization (Gaelic) upon another (English).

Davis's description of the Irish as "a composite race" had been borne out yet again.
What had been billed as the Battle of Two Civilizations was really, and more subtly,
the interpenetration of each by the other: and this led to the generation of a new
species of man and woman, who felt exalted by rather than ashamed of such
hybridity.

The essays put out by Yeats in the theoretical journals of his theatre elaborated on
this theme with a remarkable cogency and coherence of purpose. In October 1902,
for instance, he urged formal recognition of "that English idiom of the Irish-thinking
people of the west . . . the only good English spoken by any large numbers of Irish
people today".[74] With his tongue only partly in his cheek, he urged on the Inter-
mediate Board of Education ("a body that seems to benefit by advice") a novel scheme
to improve the written English of school-children:

> Let every child in Ireland be set to turn first a leading article, then a piece of what is called
> excellent English, written perhaps by some distinguished member of the Board, into the
> idiom of his own countryside.

The mind of official Ireland was, however, so colonized that it could not recognize that the people themselves had created a new idiom, neither standard Irish nor standard English, but something that "at its best is more vigorous, fresh and simple than either of the two languages between which it stands".[75] Had the argument been conceded, the dialect would have become the natural idiom of church sermons, newspaper editorials or university lectures, but these prestigious discourses remained unaffected by what Yeats mischievously called "the idiom of those who have rejected or of those who have never learned the base idiom of the newspapers".[76] He found in Hiberno-English that elusive style, that pressure of individual personality and that shared joy in free expression which was not available in official sources. Alert to the fact that writers of English faced more difficult problems than those which awaited artists in the Irish language, he pointed out that "English is the language in which the Irish cause has been debated and we have to struggle against traditional points of view",[77] in other words, the rollicking note thought peculiar to the stage Irishman. For that very reason, it was important to challenge these associations.

Over five decades later, but in an analogous situation, in French Algeria, Frantz Fanon, the revolutionary and psychiatrist, found that he too had to struggle against the "traditional points of view" embedded in French, "a language of occupation": this he did by broadcasting in French the programmes of Radio Fighting Algeria, "liberating the enemy language from its historic meanings".[78] It was doubtless a similar complex of feelings which, in more recent years still, led the Indian novelist Salman Rushdie to declare: "Those of us who use English do so in spite of our ambiguity towards it, or perhaps because of that, perhaps because we can find in that linguistic struggle a reflection of other struggles taking place in the real world". Like Yeats, Rushdie clung defiantly to the hope that something was gained rather than lost in the act of translation, one result of which might be "radically new types of human being".[79]

The deployment by postcolonial writers of historically-sanctioned English, and their speaking of it in a writerly, erudite fashion, have become much-remarked features of this process. Back in the 1890s, Walter Pater had said that he wished to write English as a learned language. This was precisely how the Irish actors of Yeats's theatre spoke it, as the London critic A. B. Walkley discovered on attending a performance: "The unexpected emphasis on the minor syllables has an air of not ungraceful pedantry, or, better still, of old world courtliness. We are listening to English spoken with a wonderful care and slightly timorous hesitation, as though it were a learned language".[80]

The decolonizing programme of the theatre was made very obvious in Yeats's repeated invocations of the writers of the American Renaissance as models for his own. His notions of a national literature were derived from Walt Whitman, but so also was his idea of the reception of such writers: "If one says a National Literature must be in the language of the country, there are many difficulties. Should it be written in the language that one's country does speak or the language it ought to speak?...Edgar Allan Poe and Walt Whitman are national writers of America, although the one had his first acceptance in France and the other in England and Ireland".[81] The man or woman of genius moulded the nation, rather than being made upon its mould: and because of their creative unpredictability, they encountered opposition, but they were embraced there "in the end". In the meantime, they might have to turn for protection to the despised police of the colonial power, as Yeats did during the *Playboy* riots and as Rushdie would decades later: expressing the people's life was far more dangerous than merely exploiting it.

Yet, though Yeats's *Samhain* articles and Rushdie's essays in *Imaginary Homelands* would be separated over time by eighty years, the experiences evoked in them did not markedly alter. Yeats's new species of man is recognizably one of Rushdie's hybrids, "people who root themselves in ideas rather than places, in memories as much as in material things; people who have been obliged to define themselves – because they are so defined by others – by their otherness; people in whose deepest selves strange fusions occur, unprecedented unions between what they were and where they find themselves". The experience recalled in the essays is one of *becoming*, identity being not so much a possession as a way of being in the world. For that reason, the image of the migrant or traveller features much in their work, not only because in his displacement he symbolizes the uprooted intellectual, but more especially because he is adaptive, one who moulds the new places that serve also to mould him. "The migrant is not simply transformed by his art; he also transforms his new world", writes Rushdie, who says that in consequence "migrants become mutants, but it is out of such hybridization that newness can emerge". The search is for a mode of expression, a fuller articulation, and this quest becomes its own point for the writer. It becomes clear that for such, reality is a mere artefact until it has been embodied in a style: what Rushdie calls "the sense of a writer feeling obliged to bring his new world into being by an act of pure will, the sense that if the world is not described into existence in the most minute detail, then it won't be there".[82]

Yeats, who had undergone these experiences so many years before Rushdie, was also led to the paradoxical conclusion that a nation could only achieve consciousness through exposure to others. Similarly, a self could only awaken by an act of hybridization: for nothing could create until first it was split in two:

> All literature in every country is derived from models, and as often as not these are foreign models, and it is the presence of a personal element alone that can give it nationality in a fine sense, the nationality of its maker. It is only before personality has been attained that a race struggling towards self-consciousness is the better for having, as in primitive times, nothing but native models, for before this has been attained, it can neither assimilate nor reject. It was precisely at this passive moment, attainment approaching but not yet come, that the Irish heart and mind surrendered to England, or rather to what is most temporary in England; and Irish patriotism, content that the names and opinions should be Irish, was deceived and satisfied. It is always necessary to affirm and reaffirm that nationality is in the things that escape analysis.[83]

This powerful and penetrating paragraph is one of the first Irish articulations of the dialectics of postcolonial liberation. It repeats the warnings of Hyde, Moran and others about a nationalism which would be no more than an imitation of its English begetter: but it transcends their diagnoses by offering a subtle account of *how* so many who dream of liberation become blocked at that mimic stage.

NOTES

1   W. B. Yeats, *Ideas of Good and Evil*, London 1903, 337.
2   W. J. O'Neill Daunt, *Personal Recollection of the late Daniel O'Connell*, London 1848, 14–15.
3   Maureen Wall, "The Decline of the Irish Language", *A View of the Irish Language*, ed. Brian Ó Cuív, Dublin 1969, 86.
4   Benedict Anderson, *Imagined Communities*, London 1983, 122.
5   W. B. Yeats, *Samhain*, October 1901, 9.
6   Harold Bloom, *Yeats*, New York 1970, 87.
7   W. B. Yeats, *Uncollected Prose 1*, ed. J. P. Frayne, London 1970, 361.
8   J. M. Synge, "National Drama: A Farce", *Plays 1*, ed. Ann Saddlemyer, Oxford 1968, 221–2.
9   Quoted by Diarmuid Coffey, *Douglas Hyde: President of Ireland*, Dublin 1938, 18.
10 On ascendancy attitudes to Irish, see Janet Egleson Dunleavy and Gareth W. Dunleavy, *Douglas Hyde: A Maker of Modern Ireland*, Berkeley 1991, 1–136.
11 George Moore, *Hail and Farewell*, ed. R. Cave, Gerrards Cross 1976, 238.
12 W. B. Yeats, *Samhain*, 1905, 5–6.
13 W. B. Yeats, postscript, *Ideals in Ireland*, ed. Lady Gregory, London 1901. See also *Essays and Controversies*, 10.
14 Ibid., 38.
15 Eric Hobsbawn and Terence Ranger eds., *The Invention of Tradition*, Cambridge 1983, 263–81.
16 Douglas Hyde, "The Necessity for Deanglicizing Ireland", *The Revival of Irish Literature*, London 1894, 120.
17 W. B. Yeats, *Essays and Introductions*, London 1961, 248.
18 James Joyce, *Stephen Hero*, London 1977, 52.
19 Hyde, "Necessity", 119.
20 D. P. Moran, "The Battle of Two Civilizations", *Ideals in Ireland*, 28, 30.
21 Ibid., 36.
22 Hyde, "Necessity", 123, 129.
23 Quoted by David Greene, "The Founding of the Gaelic League", *The Gaelic League Idea*, ed. Seán Ó Tuama, Cork 1972, 10.
24 Hyde, "Necessity", 129, 128.
25 *Ideals in Ireland*, 55.
26 John Berger, *About Looking*, London 1980, 35.
27 Hyde, "Necessity", 138, 159.
28 W. B. Yeats, "The Literary Movement in Ireland", *Ideals in Ireland*, 85–90.
29 Quoted by Tomás Ó Fiaich, "The Great Controversy", *The Gaelic League Idea*, 67. This is the best account and I rely on it accordingly.
30 Ibid., 68.
31 Augusta Gregory, *Seventy Years 1852–1922*, ed. Colin Smythe, Gerrards Cross 1974, 359.
32 Edward Martyn, *Beltaine*, No. 2, February 1900.
33 See Declan Kiberd, *Synge and the Irish Language*, London 1993, 224–5.
34 Thomas Babington Macaulay, "Indian Education", 2 February 1835 minute: in *Prose and Poetry*, ed. G. M. Young, Cambridge, Mass. 1967, 729.
35 Stephen Gwynn, *Today and Tomorrow in Ireland*, Dublin and London 1903, 59.
36 Kevin B. Nowlan, "The Gaelic League and Other National Movements", *The Gaelic League Idea*, 45.

37 Letter from J. O. Hannay to Hyde, 15 April 1907; Tadhg McGlinchey papers.
38 Nowlan quotes this, *The Gaelic League Idea*, 47.
39 Sean O'Casey, *Drums Under the Windows*, London 1945, 73.
40 Caoimhghín Ó Góilidhe ed., *Dánta Árdteastais*, Dublin 1967, 8.
41 Seán de Fréine, *The Great Silence*, Dublin 1965, 108.
42 Eric Hobsbawm, "Inventing Traditions", *The Invention of Tradition*, 15–22.
43 Quoted in *The United Irishman*, 22 June 1901.
44 Robert Kee, *The Green Flag*, London 1972, 432.
45 James Joyce, *Dubliners*, Harmondsworth 1992, 135.
46 Ruth Dudley Edwards, *Patrick Pearse: The Triumph of Failure*, London 1979, 178 (The Coming Revolution), 229 (From a Hermitage).
47 Quoted by Myles Dillon, "Douglas Hyde", *The Shaping of Modern Ireland*, ed. Conor Cruise O'Brien, London 1960, 59.
48 Quoted by Lady Gregory, *Seventy Years*, 417.
49 George Moore, *Hail and Farewell*, 587.
50 Michael Collins, *The Path to Freedom*, Dublin 1922. For a finely detailed study of the links between language revival and creative expression see Philip O'Leary, *The Prose Literature of the Gaelic Revival 1881–1921*, Pennsylvania 1994. Similar studies of poetry, sport, political discourse, and philosophy would in all likelihood yield equally rich results to researchers possessed of O'Leary's imaginative daring and scholarly scruple.
51 W. B. Yeats, *Uncollected Prose 1*, 255.
52 George Moore, "Literature and the Irish Language", *Ideals in Ireland*, 47.
53 D. P. Moran, *The Philosophy of Irish Ireland*, Dublin 1905, 37 ff.
54 Stopford A. Brooke, *The Need and Use of Getting Irish Literature into the English Tongue*, London 1893, 65.
55 John Eglinton, in *Literary Ideals in Ireland* (Eglinton et al.), London 1899, 11.
56 George Russell, ibid., 81–2.
57 George Russell, *Thoughts for a Convention*, Dublin and London 1917, 7.
58 *Literary Ideals in Ireland*, 86.
59 John Eglinton, *Bards and Saints*, Dublin 1906, 11.
60 John Eglinton, "A Word for Anglo-Irish Literature", *United Irishman*, 22 March 1902.
61 Quoted by Moore, *Hail and Farewell*, 166; Eglinton, *Bards and Saints*, 12, 7.
62 *United Irishman*, 31 March 1902.
63 John Eglinton, *Irish Literary Portraits*, 26.
64 *United Irishman*, 8 February 1902.
65 A. P. Thornton, *The Imperial Idea and Its Enemies*, London 1959, 210–11.
66 E. A. Boyd, *Appreciations and Depreciations*, Dublin 1918, 152.
67 Ibid., 157.
68 George Eliot, *Middlemarch*, Harmondsworth 1965, 110.
69 D. H. Lawrence, *Women in Love*, Harmondsworth 1960, 444.
70 Quoted by Hyde, *Oscar Wilde*, 506.
71 W. B. Yeats, *Plays and Controversies*, 197–8.
72 J. M. Synge, *Prose*, ed. Alan Price, Oxford 1968, 400.
73 D. P. Moran, *The Leader*, 2 November 1901.
74 W. B. Yeats, *Samhain*, October 1902, 8.
75 Thomas MacDonagh, *Literature in Ireland*, Dublin 1916, 47–8.
76 W. B. Yeats, *Samhain*, October 1902, 9.
77 W. B. Yeats, *Samhain*, October 1903, 8.
78 Frantz Fanon, *A Dying Colonialism*, Harmondsworth 1970, 73.

79 Salman Rushdie, *Imaginary Homelands*, London 1992, 124.
80 Quoted in *Samhain*, 1903, 35.
81 W. B. Yeats, *Samhain*, 1904, 20.
82 Rushdie, *Imaginary Homelands*, 124–5, 210, 149.
83 W. B. Yeats, *Samhain*, 1908, 7.

Race Against Time: Racial Discourse and Irish History

Luke Gibbons

Luke Gibbons's *Transformations in Irish Culture*, from which this essay is taken, is one of the most innovative studies of Irish colonial and postcolonial culture. In this piece, he concentrates on the intersection of racial discourse and Irish history. The main problem, as Gibbons sees it, is the way in which nineteenth-century Irish historians and other commentators on Irish cultural affairs drew on a discourse of race in order to advance the notion of "an original native purity," which nationalists could set against the "impure" influences of a coercive colonial discourse. Like **Declan Kiberd**, Gibbons's work is part of a revisionist postcolonial project that seeks to re-evaluate both nationalism and its relationship to the colonial discourse it putatively sets itself against. The influence of **Frantz Fanon**'s critique of nationalist movements is notable here, since racialist discourses were used (though for different ideological ends) by imperialist historians as well. And like **David Lloyd**, another revisionist critic, Gibbons draws on James Joyce's work in order to illustrate how postcolonial Irish modernists were able to evade the "transcendental essence" of both nationalist and imperialist historiography. The student may want to consider Gibbons, **Lloyd**, and **Kiberd** as exemplary in their adherence to Fanonian ideas about nationalism. Other possibilities include comparing Gibbons's historical approach with that of **Ranajit Guha**, or reading his argument about Irish racial discourse alongside the discussions of race offered in essays by **Chinua Achebe**, **George Lamming**, and **Moira Ferguson**.

Race Against Time: Racial Discourse and Irish History

> He was a young Irishman . . . he had the silent enduring beauty of a carved ivory negro mask, with his rather full eyes, and the strong queerly-arched brows, the immobile, compressed mouth; that momentary but revealed immobility, an immobility, a timelessness which the Buddha aims at, and which negroes express sometimes without ever aiming at it; something old, old, and acquiescent in the race! Aeons of acquiescence in race destiny, instead of our individual resistance. And thus a swimming through, like rats in a dark river.
>
> D. H. Lawrence, *Lady Chatterley's Lover*

During the twilight of colonialism, a children's toy circulated in the "Big Houses" of the Irish Ascendancy which purported to give the "British Empire at a Glance".[1] It took the form of a map of the world, mounted on a wheel complete with small apertures which revealed all that was worth knowing about the most distant corners of the Empire. One of the apertures gave a breakdown of each colony in terms of its "white" and "native" population, as if both categories were mutually exclusive. When it came to Ireland, the wheel ground to a halt for here was a colony whose subject population was both "native" and "white" at the same time. This was one corner of the Empire, apparently, that could not be taken in at a glance.

In his analysis of colonial discourse, Homi Bhabha has written that "colonial power produces the colonized as a fixed reality which is at once an 'other' and yet entirely knowable and visible": hence "in order to conceive of the colonial subject as the effect of power that is productive – disciplinary and 'pleasurable' – one has to see the surveillance of colonial power as functioning in relation to the regime of the scopic drive".[2] The apparent ease with which colonial discourse establishes its legitimacy derives from the paradox that it locates discrimination in a primal act of *visual* recognition – notwithstanding the fact that the visual, in this Lacanian sense of the Imaginary, obviated the very basis of difference in the first place. For this reason, it is clear that a native population which happened to be white was an affront to the very idea of the "white man's burden", and threw into disarray some of the constitutive categories of colonial discourse. The "otherness" and alien character of Irish experience was all the more disconcerting precisely because it did not lend itself to visible racial divisions, as is evident from Charles Kingsley's anxious ruminations on a visit to Sligo, Ireland, in 1860:

Taken from *Transformations in Irish Culture* (Notre Dame: University of Notre Dame Press; Cork: Cork University Press, 1996).

> I am haunted by the human chimpanzees I saw along that hundred miles of horrible country. I don't believe they are our fault. I believe . . . that they are happier, better, more comfortably fed and lodged under our rule than they ever were. But to see white chimpanzees is dreadful; if they were black, one would not feel it so much, but their skins, except where tanned by exposure, are as white as ours.[3]

Carlyle expressed similar impatience with the resistance of the Irish to neat classifications: "Black-lead them and put them over with the niggers" was his perfunctory solution to the Irish question.[4]

This lack of fixed boundaries, of clear racial markers, has led some commentators to conclude that there was no rational basis for the "ancient quarrel" between Ireland and England, and that the separatist movement was fuelled simply by the wilful obscurantism of Irish nationalism. In a trenchant discussion calling for a reappraisal of Irish colonial stereotypes, Sheridan Gilley argues that "since an objective criterion of race like skin colour is lacking to define Saxon dislike of the Celts, there is a difficulty of definition in deciding at what point vague talk about Celtic character amounts to 'racial prejudice'"[5] So far from evincing the kind of repulsion and hatred characteristic of racism, Gilley contends that English attitudes towards the Irish were distinguished by a spirit of toleration and a willingness to accommodate Irish difference. As *The Times* put it in an editorial after the Clerkenwell prison bombing in 1867:

> This is not a quarrel of race with race, nation with nation, or people with people, but between isolation, exclusion, inhospitality, and egotism, on the Irish side, and liberality, hospitality and neighbourliness on ours. . . . The Irish portion of this mixed community [in England] is quite as large as any that could call itself pure Saxon.[6]

Obvious to the irony in the phrase "Killing Home Rule with Kindness", Gilley proceeds to point out that apologists for imperial rule such as Matthew Arnold advocated a commingling of the Saxon and the Celt, and called for an infusion of Celtic blood into the enervated body politic of post-Benthamite England. This apparent magnanimity is hardly consistent with the fears about intermarriage and miscegenation which stalked the deep south in America, and as such it is an important corrective to a simplistic equation of the plight of the native Irish with that of the black population in the southern states of the USA, or in other British colonies. But while Gilley is right to emphasize that the analogy with the oppression of black people cannot be fully sustained, it does not follow that this was the only model of racism available to colonial regimes.[7] Far more important for understanding the distinctive character of Irish stereotypes was the analogy with the native Americans, or American Indians, an analogy, moreover, which had a foundation in the shared historical experience of being at the receiving end of the first systematic wave of colonial expansion. Research by historians such as D. B. Quinn and Nicholas Canny has suggested that it was Ireland – "that famous island in the Virginian sea", as Fynes Morison called it – which helped to turn the attention of the Elizabethan settlers towards America, and many of the earliest colonizers of the New World such as Humphrey Gilbert and Walter Raleigh alternated between Ireland and Virginia or

Newfoundland.[8] In this initial phase, there was far less confidence about the absorptive powers of English civilization, and Lord Mountjoy, for example, warned of the dangers of succumbing to the primitive native culture in Ireland (the fate of the previous settlers which he designates the English-Irish):

> Because the Irish and English-Irish were obstinate in Popish superstition, great care was thought fit to be taken that these new colonies should consist of such men as were most unlike to fall to the barbarous customs of the Irish, or the Popish superstition of Irish and English-Irish, so as no less cautions were to be observed for uniting them and keeping them from mixing with each other than if these new colonies were to be led to inhabit among the barbarous Indians.[9]

This type of comparison between the subject populations of both colonies established a network of affinities that was to recur in descriptions of both the Irish and the Indians. Referring to the "booleys" or wigwams built from the bark of walnut trees and mats, Thomas Morton remarked in 1632 that "the natives of New England are accustomed to build their houses much like the wild Irish" and this perception of a common primitive culture also extended to dress and sleeping habits. When Shane O'Neill presented himself at the court of Queen Elizabeth in 1562, decked out in a vivid saffron cloak, the historian Camden wrote that he was looked upon with as much wonderment as if he had come from "China and America". William Strachey frequently couched descriptions of the Indians in Irish terms, remarking of their sleeping habits that "some lie stark naked on the ground from six to twenty in a house, as do the Irish", and observing of their fashions that "the married women wear their hair all of a length, shaven, as the Irish, by a dish".[10] What is important for the purposes of understanding the implicit primitivist assumptions underlying these apparently casual observations on the state of the Irish peasantry is that comparisons with the American Indians persisted well beyond the initial period of conquest. Visiting Ireland on the eve of the Famine in 1839, Gustave de Beaumont, who had travelled widely in both the old and the new world, wrote ominously that the state of the Irish peasant was so wretched that he did not even have the redeeming qualities of the noble savage:

> I have seen the Indian in his forests and the negro in his irons, and I believed, in pitying their plight, that I saw the lowest ebb of human misery; but I did not then know the degree of poverty to be found in Ireland. Like the Indian, the Irishman is poor and naked; but he lives in the midst of a society which enjoys luxury, honours and wealth...The Indian retains a certain independence which has its attraction and a dignity of its own. Poverty-stricken and hungry he may be, but he is free in his desert places; and the feeling that he enjoys this liberty blunts the edge of his sufferings. But the Irishman undergoes the same deprivations without enjoying the same liberty, he is subjected to regulations: he dies of hunger. He is governed by laws; a sad condition, which combines the vices of civilization with those of primitive life. Today the Irishman enjoys neither the freedom of the savage nor the bread of servitude.[11]

There is even evidence that the comparison of the native Irish to American Indians as a justification of conquest has survived down to the present day in loyalist popular memory in Northern Ireland. As Anthony Buckley reports in his ethnographic study of Ulster Protestants:

> I have heard many individuals separately state, viz. "nobody expects that America should be given back to the Indians" (or Australia to the Aborigines). In part, this familiar statement is a plea to let bygones be bygones: "it all happened a long time ago". In part, however, it also contains an imperialist rhetoric that Protestants in Ireland, like white people in America, Australia, and elsewhere in the British Empire, have been the bringers of Christianity and civilization.[12]

De Beaumont's sympathetic observations show that the apparently carefree life-style of the Indian was not without its appeal to the white sensibility: yet there is little doubt that the American Indians were also the victims of some of the gravest acts of genocide ever perpetrated by white supremacist policies, policies, moreover, which owed a considerable amount of their impetus to the initial Irish pattern of conquest.[13] In a recent comparison of the image of the Indian and the black in American history, Michael Rogin has pointed out that Indians were not viewed with the kind of virulent hatred which whites reserved for blacks, but were often treated with bemused fascination and the type of paternalist affection which adults display towards child-ren. Like the Irish, and in marked contrast to blacks, fears of miscegenation and interracial contact did *not* figure prominently in the white demonology of the Indian. In fact, all the mitigating or "positive" features which, in Sheridan Gilley's view, extenuate the British from charges of racism with regard to Irish people, were evident in American attitudes towards the Indians, including the crucial expectation that they commingle with the whites and, in Andrew Jackson's words, "become merged in the mass of our population". The alternative to assimilation, however, was the stark prospect of annihilation: like Shakespearean drama, this particular racist scenario ended in either marriage or tragedy. As the US House Committee on Indian Affairs forecast in 1818: "In the present state of our country one of two things seem to be necessary, either that those sons of the forest should be moralized or exterminated."[14]

The extermination of the Indian way of life, if not the Indians themselves, was facilitated by the convenient belief that they were children of nature, "sons of the forest", and thus were bereft of even the most meagre forms of civilization:

> The Indian is hewn out of rock ... [wrote Francis Parkman] He will not learn the arts of civilization, and he and the forest must perish together. The stern, unchanging features of his mind excite our admiration from their very immutability; and we look with deep interest on the fate of this irreclaimable son of the wilderness, the child who will not be weaned from the breast of his rugged mother.[15]

The Indian remained at a primitive oral stage, and had not made the transition to the symbolic order of civilization. Ironically, this was the attribute of Indian society, translated into an opposition between speech or oral tradition on the one hand, and the acquisition of writing on the other, which led to its rehabilitation by Rousseau, and indeed by a tradition of romantic primitivism in anthropology extending down to Claude Lévi-Strauss at the present day. Oral culture, in this sense, is seen as a source of plenitude and stability, of a prelapsarian innocence or communion with nature before the fall brought about by the invention of letters. The primary of speech, the voice of experience, attests to the authenticity of a culture, presenting, as Derrida puts it, "the image of a community immediately present to itself, without difference, a community of speech where all the members are within earshot" of one another.[16]

The problem with this form of romantic primitivism, as it presented itself to native Irish historians in the eighteenth century, was that such a state of primordial innocence offered an open invitation to conquest. The plenitude of an original, oral state of nature, as Derrida argues, is paradoxically constituted by what it lacks, in this case the absence of "civilization": "the unity of nature or the identity of origin is shaped and undermined by a strange difference which constitutes it by breaching it".[17] If apologists for colonialism in the new world insisted on portraying America as "virgin" territory, as if its native inhabitants were simply hewn out of the rock formations which dominated the landscape, then it was decidedly in the interests of native Irish historians to deny that Ireland was ever in a state of nature, and that it was culturally inscribed from the dawn of antiquity. The difficulty with this position was that the testimony on which it was based depended to a large extent on an oral heritage, and thus had to contend with a prejudice *against* popular memory, derived ultimately from the Protestant valorization of the written word at the expense of custom and tradition. The *locus classicus* for this attack on oral culture was John Locke's argument that whereas an original text ("the attested copy of a record") bears witness to truth, in tradition *"each remove weakens the force of the proof*; and the more hands the tradition has successively passed through, the less evidence and strength does it receive from them".[18] In this schema, the *written* text enjoys the status of an originating presence, and is the standard against which the inferior claims to truth of speech and tradition may be judged.

Hence the relative ease with which those who opposed the enlisting of cultural nationalism in the cause of Catholic emancipation at the end of the eighteenth century could reject native pretensions to an ancient Irish civilization. According to David Hume, tradition lacked the clear-cut simplicity of scripture in that it was "complex, contradictory and, on many occasions doubtful". "Popish legends" not only led to a fragmentation of truth – "though every one, almost, believed a part of these stories, yet no one could believe or know the whole" – but also lacked foundations, the grounds of knowledge: "all must have acknowledged [of tradition], that no one part stood on a better foundation than the rest".[19] Hume lost little time in extending this critique to Irish culture, arguing that tradition and popular memory were indistinguishable from credulity and superstition:

> As the rudeness and ignorance of the Irish were extreme . . . The ancient superstitions, the practices and observations of their fathers, mingled and polluted with many wild opinions, still maintained an unshaken empire over them, and the example alone of the English was sufficient to render the reformation odious to the prejudices of the discontented Irish . . . The subduing and civilizing of that country seemed to become every day more difficult and impracticable.[20]

Faced with this dismissal of what they considered their intellectual birthright, it is not surprising that Irish historians, whether of native or old English stock, took considerable pains (and an even more considerable degree of poetic licence) to argue that the ancient Irish acquired literacy and kept written records in the pre-historic era. As early as 1633, in what is perhaps the pioneering work in Irish historiography, and the last great Irish book to be circulated in manuscript form, Geoffrey Keating wrote that both the accuracy and the extent of the ancient "chronicles of the Kingdom" was such that it procured for the Irish "a superior esteem to the antiquities of any other nation, except the Jewish, throughout the world".[21] By the eighteenth century, this had been transformed into an argument that the Irish, by virtue of their alleged Phoenician ancestry, had actually invented letters, and introduced the alphabet to classical Greece. In 1753, in the first systematic history of Ireland in the modern mode, Charles O'Conor could assert "that our nation and language are coeval":

> the annals of the nation were, from a very early age, committed to writing. Blind tradition, or ulterior invention, could never, in ages of simplicity, and so distant from each other, concur in so many marks of authenticity.

This was part of a general counter-offensive by a new wave of Irish historians which posited the existence of an *original* Irish civilization, rivalling Greece and Rome in its cultural attainments. If subsequent generations – indeed epochs – have receded from the plenitude of this founding moment, then there is at least the consolation, as O'Conor puts it in characteristically Lockean terms, "that our copy of the earliest times, is pretty just to the original".[22]

The difficulty with this argument was that it had to account for an extensive amount of mimetic shortfall to compensate for the gap between the glories of the past and the destitute condition of the mass of the Irish population in the eighteenth century. Native historians had to face Edmund Spenser's taunt, quoted with evident satisfaction by Thomas Campbell as part of an assault against native historians in 1789: "if such 'old scholars', why so unlearned still?"[23] Why, in other words, was there so little to show of the achievement of remote antiquity? The obvious answer was the destruction wrought by conquest; but to acknowledge the disruptive effect of successive invasions was to concede the discontinuous, fragmented nature of Irish history – the charge levelled at tradition by critics such as Hume. It was precisely for this reason that conservative minded nationalists sought to impose a coherent narrative form on the amorphous mass of Irish history, discerning a totalizing design in what A. M. Sullivan was later to refer to as "the Story of Ireland". As Charles Gavan Duffy expressed it in the 1840s: "The history of Ireland abounded in noble lessons, and had the unity and purpose of an epic poem".[24]

This provided a cue for *race* to enter the proceedings on the nationalist side, securing the image of an embattled people surviving intact and maintaining unity in the face of two thousand years of upheaval, invasion and oppression. The concept of race also helped to explain the persistence of continuity in the midst of change and, even more to the point, the racial notion of an original native purity allowed nationalists to cite the effects of conquest to explain away some of the less desirable aspects of Irish life, attributing them to the slave's propensity to mimic his master's vices. As Douglas Hyde expressed it in his lecture on "The Necessity for De-Anglicizing Ireland", one of the founding texts of the Literary Revival:

> The Irish race is at present in a most anomalous position, imitating England and yet apparently hating it. How can it produce anything good in literature, art, or institutions as long as it is actuated by motives so contradictory? Besides, I believe it is our Gaelic past which, though the Irish race does not recognize it just at present, is really at the bottom of the Irish heart, and prevents us becoming citizens of the Empire.[25]

In the hands of less astute propagandists, race became a scouring agent, removing from the Irish people all the impurities acquired through contamination by the "Saxon foe". In an unabashed tirade entitled *The Celt Above the Saxon*, published at the turn of the century, Fr. C. J. Herlihy sought to restore Ireland's reputation as an island of saints, scholars and sobriety:

> How many Englishmen ever reflect that England is responsible for [the] intemperance of the Irish? Our Celtic ancestors were a very temperate people before the English landed on their shores. In the time of St. Patrick drunkenness was unknown amongst them. In all his writings the great apostle does not even refer once to Irish intemperance. It was only after they lost their independence that this vice broke out among the Irish; and when we take into consideration all they suffered from English tyranny during the last seven hundred years, can we be astonished that they turned to drink?[26]

For Gilley this would exemplify the ambivalence and essentially contested nature of Irish colonial stereotypes, for here is clearly a case of attributing an English prove-nance to a trait of national character that was, unfortunately, home grown: "behind the English conception of the Irish", concludes Gilley, "lies the Irish idea of the Irishman", as if colonial rule had no role at all to play in fabricating the self-images of the Irish.[27] What Gilley conveniently over-looks, however, is that the process is a two-way (albeit unequal) transaction, and that many of the concepts requisitioned by nationalist propagandists in defence of Irish culture are, in fact, an extension of colonialism, rather than a repudiation of it. The racial concept of an Irish national character is a case in point: the mimicry of English life castigated by Douglas Hyde may have extended down to the concept of "the Irish race" which he posited to counteract alien influences. The "Celt", and by implication the Celtic revival, owed as much to eighteenth-century primitivism and the benevolent colonialism of Matthew Arnold as it did to the inner recesses of the hidden Ireland, and the facility with which Gilley construes the Arnoldian stereotype as benign – in fact, as not a stereotype at all – explains how it could be taken to heart by Irish revivalists. The racial mode is, moreover, the version of Irish nationalism which has passed into general academic circulation in recent years through the revisionist writings of Conor Cruise O'Brien and F. S. L. Lyons (among others) – largely, one suspects, because it redefines even resistance within a racist colonial frame and thus neutralizes the very idea of anti-colonial discourse.[28]

Yet not all the concepts of Irishness which emerged under the aegis of cultural nationalism were dependent on racial modes of identity. Indeed, it is worth noting that while moderate, anti-republican politicians such as Arthur Griffith voiced some of the most bigoted expressions of nationalism (to the point of condoning black slavery, for instance), others associated with militant republicanism rejected racial concepts out of hand on account of their exclusivity, and their simplistic approach to historical change.[29] In his posthumous work *Literature in Ireland* (published after his execution as one of the leaders of the 1916 Rising), the poet and critic Thomas MacDonagh took issue with the Arnoldian idea of "the Celtic Note" on the grounds that it carried with it unacceptable racial undertones:

> I have little sympathy with the criticism that marks off subtle qualities in literature as altogether racial, that refuses to admit natural exceptions in such a naturally exceptional thing as high literature, attributing only the central body to the national genius, the marginal portions to this alien strain or that.[30]

MacDonagh's thinking on this point was greatly influenced by the outstanding translator and scholar, Dr. George Sigerson (to whom, in fact, he dedicated his book). In a series of works beginning as early as 1868, Sigerson sought to remove the racial epithet "Celtic" entirely from the cultural canon, arguing that Irishness incorporated the residue of several cultural or "racial" strains, as befitted a country exposed to successive waves of invasion and internal strife over the centuries.[31] This carried with it the implication that history did not run in a straight line from the Milesians to the Celtic revival, but was closer to an alluvial deposit, secreting an unstable, porous version of Irish identity. As David Hume rightly observed, the lack of secure foundations prevented the most dynamic strands in Irish nationalism from succumbing to "fixed dogmas and principles".[32]

The construction of a continuous, unaltered tradition, stretching back to remote antiquity, can be seen, in fact, as precisely a colonial imposition, an attempt to emulate in an Irish context the Burkean model of the English constitution based on an organic theory of community and the inherited wisdom of the ages. The past can be eulogized when it is truly dead and gone and when even revolution leads to social stability, but these comforting sentiments were not so easily transferrable to a country such as Ireland in which history was still a matter of unfinished business. As a commentator in *The Nation* newspaper put it, writing at the height of the Famine in 1847, England's reassuring image of a common, unified past – a society in which "history knits together all ranks and sects" – is strangely at odds with the uneven, fractured course of Irish history.

> There are bright spots in our history; but of how few is the story common! and the contemplation of it, *as a whole*, does not tend to harmony, unless the conviction of past error produces wisdom for the future. We have no institution or idea that has been produced by all. We must look to the present or future for the foundations of concord and nationality.[33]

There was nothing organic about Irish history, despite the best attempts of the editors of *The Nation* to make it "racy of the soil".

Hence in the case of the Ossian controversy that raged in the latter half of the eighteenth century, it was precisely Macpherson's claim to faithfully reproduce the originals, to be in perfect communion with the past, which aroused the suspicions of his most perceptive Irish critics. Notwithstanding his emphasis elsewhere that "many volumes of well-authenticated records have escaped the ravages of time and of foreign spoils", the antiquarian Joseph Cooper Walker's comments on Oisin (as he was called in Ireland) show that he had no illusion about the preservative power of either antiquarian texts or traditions:

> Only a few fragments of his works, and those much mutilated and ill-authenticated, have come down to us. Indeed, had his productions reached us in a state of original perfection, our best Irish scholars would have found much difficulty in translating them; for there are many passages, in Irish poems of the fifth and sixth centuries, which seem at present, and *probably ever will remain*, inexplicable. Yet, we are told, that the poems of Oisin are recited and sung, at this day, by ignorant Scottish hinds, though the characters of the language, in which they were composed, are as unintelligible to the modern Scots, as the hieroglyphics of the Egyptians.[34]

The impossibility of gaining direct access to the past is not because it is sealed off, as in a time capsule, but because it is part of an unresolved historical process which engulfs the present. It is lived history that prevents the kind of omniscient narration envisaged by Locke which sees texts as transparent windows on the past. The romantic nostalgia for Ossian, and its vogue in the metropolitan centre, was not unrelated to the fact that after the Battle of Culloden, and the elimination of the Jacobite threat, it was relatively safe to rake over the embers of the Scottish past.[35] But such an option was not available in Ireland: the past was not simply part of recorded history but *remembered* history, an open-ended narrative which was not safely interred in texts (as Hume would have it) but continued to haunt contemporary political struggles. As Donal McCartney has written with reference to the constant invocation of key historical events such as the 1641 rebellion and the 1691 Treaty of Limerick, in the campaign that led to Catholic emancipation in 1829:

> With our eyes on the 1829 act, we may say that a single topic from Irish history kept constantly before an organized people and forced upon the intentions of parliament, had tremendous influence in altering the law of the United Kingdom. The treaty argument [of Limerick, 1691], which passed out of the written page and penetrated the walls of parliament, was more than the mere spearhead of the emancipation struggle. For, like 1641, the interpretations of 1691 never passed into history, inasmuch as they never passed out of politics.[36]

Texts, in other words, were not simply *about* history: they were part of history, fragments of a past that still awaited completion.

In his essay on "*Ulysses* in History", Fredric Jameson cites Roland Barthes in support of his observation that under the impact of modernity, the gap between meaning and existence, the representation and the real, has widened:

> The pure and simple "presentation" of the "real", the naked account of "what is" (or what has been), thus proves to resist meaning; such resistance reconfirms the great

mythic opposition between the vécu [that is, the experiential or what the existentialists called "lived experience"] and the intelligible...as though, by some de jure exclusion, what lives is structurally incapable of carrying a meaning – and vice versa.[37]

Reality has become dislocated from structures of signification, and takes the form of the random impression, the passing moment or the descent into the contingency of the detail. Yet, as David Frisby writes, if

modernity as a distinctive mode of experiencing (social) reality involves seeing society and the social relations within it as (temporally) transitory and (spatially) fleeting then this implies, conversely, that traditional, *permanent* structures are now absent from human experiences.[38]

As to the source of these "traditional, permanent structures", Nietzsche, for one, had no doubt where it lay: in history, or more accurately in historicism, precisely that view of the past which looks to tradition to confer a permanent structure on experience.[39] If we turn to Ireland, however, it will be seen that it is history itself which is irrevocably scarred with the traces of contingency. The fall from grace brought about by writing, the violent wrenching of tradition by the advent of the text, was present in Irish history from the very outset. In the novels of Walter Scott, or even in the Ossianic poems, the invocation of the past often had a therapeutic effect, the distance in time affording a common ground and a sense of stability which ensured that history was kept firmly in its place. This is the complacent historicism to which Nietzsche objected so strenuously. But in Ireland the recourse to history was the problem. As a writer in the appropriately entitled *The Voice of the Nation* expressed it in 1844.

In other countries the past is the neutral ground of the scholar and the antiquary; with us it is the battlefield.[40]

As a result of this, Irish culture did not have to await modernity to undergo the effects of fragmentation – the cult of the fragment was itself the stuff from which history was made. The sense of disintegration and "unconditional presentness" (Simmel) which exerted such a fascination for writers from Baudelaire to Benjamin was pre-eminently spatial, the result of a new topology of social relations in the metropolis. In Ireland, however, it was bound up with *temporality*, as the endless preoccupation with ruins and remnants of ancient manuscripts in cultural nationalism made all too evident. In mainstream romanticism (if such a generalization may be permitted), ruins represented the triumph of natural forces over human endeavour, and if at one level this was a process of destruction and decay, at another level it was redeemed as a higher totalizing moment, in the form of a trans-historical communion with nature. For George Simmel, the nature-encrusted ruin was of a piece with the organicist conception of history which came so easily to countries in control of their own destinies:

The charm of a ruin resides in the fact that it presents a work of man while giving the impression of being a work of nature....The upward thrust, the erection of the building, was the result of human will, while its present appearance results from the mechanical force of nature, whose power of decay draws things downwards.... Nature has used man's work of art as the material for its own creation, just as art had previously taken nature as its raw material.[41]

In Ireland, by contrast, as David Lloyd has shown, ruins were the result not of a clash between nature and culture, but between several opposing cultures, the debris of a history of invasions. In a state of seditious reverie, the United Irishman William Drennan meditated on the round tower of Glendalough, Co. Wicklow, which he saw as "raising its head above the surrounding fragments, as if moralizing on the ruins of the country, and the wreck of legislative independence."[42] Or as the narrator of James Clarence Mangan's lament on the ruins of the Abbey at Timoleague has it:

> – Tempest and Time – the drifting sands –
> The lightning and the rains – the seas that sweep around
> These hills in winter-nights, have awfully crowned
> The work of impious hands!...
>
> Where wert thou, Justice, in that hour?
> Where was thy smiting sword? What had those good men done,
> That thou shouldst tamely see them trampled on
> By brutal England's Power?[43]

The conviction that it was history in its refractory Irish variant which led to the shedding of experience formed the basis of one of the most powerful contemporary critiques of James Joyce, that formulated in Wyndham Lewis's *Time and Western Man*. Lewis was impatient enough with the accumulation of detail in naturalistic fiction as language sought to catch up with the proliferation of sense-data unleashed by modernity. But in Joyce, even this took a turn for the worse, for in his obsession with place and the relations between objects, his writing dispenses with the graphic clarity that is necessary to fix the contours of, and impart solidity to, the objects in our environment:

> The local colour, or locally coloured material, that was scraped together into a big variegated heap to make *Ulysses*, is – doctrinally even more than in fact – the material of the Past.... As a careful, even meticulous craftsman, with a long training of doctrinaire naturalism, the detail – the time detail as much as anything else – assumes an exaggerated importance for him...The painful preoccupation with the *exact* place of things in a room, for instance, could be mildly matched in his writing. The *things themselves* by which he is surrounded lose, for the hysterical subject, their importance, or even meaning. Their *position* absorbs all the attention of his mind.[44]

If Joyce's language dissolved the objective world into subjective experience, then that at least would offer the consolation of stabilizing the subject, of consolidating the ego of the narrator, the author and, indeed, the reader. But this is not what happens: the torrent of Joyce's prose carries all before it, leaving no room for a transcendental essence on either side: at the level of brute reality, or the numinous realm of the sovereign self. "No one who looks *at* it," Lewis writes, "will ever want to look *behind* it", and he continues, with reference to the persistence of history in related, aberrant forms of modernism:

> You lose not only the clearness of outline, the static beauty, of the things you commonly apprehend; you lose also the clearness of outline of your own individuality which apprehends them...."you" become the series of your temporal repetitions; you are no longer a centralized self, but a spun-out, strung along series...you are a *history*: there must be no Present for you. You are an historical object, since your mental or time-life has been as it were objectified. The valuable advantages of being a "subject" will perhaps scarcely be understood by the race of *historical objects* that may be expected to ensue.[45]

Joyce's use of language – in *Ulysses* at any rate – bears an inescapable resemblance to the fractured course of oral tradition which drew the fire of Lockean inspired critics of native Irish history in the eighteenth century. It is akin to the language of rumour, as analysed by Gayatri Chakravorty Spivak, that is to say, to a form of spoken utterance which carries back into its innermost structure the effects of spacing and rupturing which, according to Derrida, characterize written texts.[46] Rumour or tradition, in this sense, is not available to the detached reader or spectator but only to the active – one is tempted to say the *committed* – participant in social communication. Yet if it presupposes a face-to-face setting, it cannot be taken at face value for, unlike the phonocentric voice, it does not carry with it its own authenticity. As Spivak writes:

> Rumour evokes comradeship because it belongs to every "reader" or "transmitter". No one is its origin or source. Thus rumour is not error but primordially (originarily) errant, always in circulation with no assignable source. This illegitimacy makes it accessible to insurgency.[47]

The amorphousness which Barthes attributes to existence, to the surplus or excess of the real which constantly eludes signification, is here the hallmark of language itself, and it is this above all which threatens the imperious eye of Wyndham Lewis: "whatever I, for my part, say, can be traced back to an organ, but in my case it is *the eye*. It is in the service of the thing of vision that my ideas are mobilized."[48] The problem with Joyce, however, was that "*He thought in words*, not images", and this forfeited any chance of stabilizing the flux of events by discerning the organic totality of experience:[49]

> Where a multitude of little details or some obvious idiosyncracy are concerned, he may be said to be observant; but the secret of an *entire* organism escapes him.[50]

As Fredric Jameson has stated, "the visual, the spatially visible, the image is...the final form of the commodity itself, the ultimate terminus of reification", and yet, as he goes on to note, one of the minor but astonishing triumphs of Joyce's prose is that he succeeds in inserting even a sandwichboard man – the ultimate in both visual and human reification – back into a network of social and historical relations: "Everything seemingly material and solid in Dublin itself can presumably be dissolved back into the underlying reality of human relations and human praxis."[51]

Jameson's and Lewis's insistence on the unremitting temporality of Joyce's writing contrasts starkly with Franco Moretti's attempt to annex Joyce for the metropolitan centre, and to disenfranchise him of both his Irishness and his profound engagement with history:

> *Ulysses* is indeed static, and in its world nothing – absolutely nothing – is great. But this is not due to any technical or ideal shortcoming on Joyce's part, but rather to his subjection to English society: for Joyce, it is certainly the only society imaginable... (whatever has emerged from the studies that interpreted Joyce on the basis of Ireland?)[52]

Whatever about Moretti, Wyndham Lewis, for one, had no illusions about Joyce's Irishness, and it is difficult not to suspect that underneath the elaborate tracery of his critique of Joyce lay a colonial frustration with a form of cultural difference which offered intense resistance to what Homi Bhabha, following Freud, terms the scopic drive – or what an Irish dramatist has called "the artillery of the eye". In an extraordinary appendix to his study of Shakespeare, *The Lion and the Fox*, Lewis launched a sustained assault on those critics such as Renan, Lord Morley and Matthew Arnold who claimed that Shakespeare owed his genius to the Celtic strain in his personality. This was too much to take. Lewis heaped abuse on the exponents of this heresy and sought, in the process, to demolish the very foundations of the Celtic claim to be a separate race. Interestingly, these foundations, in his estimation, could only be based on *visual* characteristics, and their absence, for Lewis, was sufficient proof there was no difference at all between the Irish and the English. In a remarkable passage, he writes of his response to the funeral of Terence McSwiney, the republican lord mayor of Cork, whose death by hunger strike in 1920 proved a turning point in the Irish War of Independence:

> During the martyrdom of the Lord Mayor of Cork I had several opportunities of seeing considerable numbers of irish people [Lewis refused to capitalize adjectives referring to nationality] demonstrating among the London crowds. I was never able to distinguish which were irish and which were english, however. They looked to me exactly the same. With the best will in the world to discriminate the orderly groups of demonstrators from the orderly groups of spectators, and to satisfy the romantic proprieties on such an occasion, my eyes refused to effect the necessary separation, that the principle of "celt-ism" demanded, into chalk and cheese. I should have supposed that they were a lot of romantic english-people pretending to be irish people, and demonstrating with the assistance of a few priests and pipers, if it had not been that they all looked extremely depressed, and english-people when they are giving romance the rein are always very elated.[53]

There is a certain macabre irony in Lewis's persistence in adhering to an "epider-mal schema" (to cite Franz Fanon's phrase), to visible bodily differences, in a context in which the dematerialization of the body through hunger striking is itself a means of affording political resistance. Lewis's dogged refusal to register the traumatic rever-berations of McSwiney's funeral at anything other than a visual level is, in effect, an attempt to reduce it to *spectacle*. As such, it is consistent with his desire to remove all traces of history from the colonial experience, for it was precisely spectacle, in its collective modern variant, which sought to step outside history, transforming it into a set of horizontal, spatial relations.[54] As if to pre-empt this erasure of history, the nationalist response to McSwiney's funeral inserted history back into spectacle, seeing it as a means, in Benjamin's terms, of blasting open the centuries-old continuum of British rule in Ireland. As the anonymous writer of a contemporary pamphlet on the hunger strike wrote:

> A prominent man, occupying an eminent position, holding the chief office in one of the most important cities in his country, offers himself as a *spectacle* to the world that it may behold in him a *living document* of the secular injustice of England....The crisis has come...with a swiftness that is without parallel in our time. Old solutions are discarded. The new wine is bursting in old bottles....There may be other factors in the accomplishment of this astounding conversion, brought about as it has been in a space of time that is, compared to the slow march of events in history, phenomenally short. These other factors it will be for the historians to rehearse when the whole drama is unfolded.[55]

Lewis may have been indifferent to the impact of McSwiney's funeral, but it devastated Irish public opinion to such an extent that even James Joyce was forced to break his silence on the War of Independence, penning a scurrilous broadside against the English authorities. The difference between Irishness and Englishness escaped Lewis' notice, but it was all too plain to those Irish people who identified with the colonial administration in their own country. After all, it was the Unionist Provost of Trinity College, Dublin, J. P. Mahaffy, who remarked:

> James Joyce is a living argument in favour of my contention that it was a mistake to establish a separate university for the aborigines of this island – for the cornerboys who spit in the Liffey.[56]

Notes

1 This educational aid, along with other amusing board games such as "Trading with the Colonies", can be inspected at Strokestown Park House, Co. Roscommon. I am grateful to the curator of the house, Luke Dodd, for drawing my attention to these relics of "old decency".

2 Homi K. Bhabha, "Difference, Discrimination and the Discourse of Colonialism", *The Politics of Theory* (Colchester: University of Essex, 1983), pp. 199, 203–4. Revised versions of the essay appear in *Screen*, vol. 24: no. 6 (1983), and in Frances Barker et al., eds, *Literature, Politics and Theory, Papers from the Essex Conference, 1976–84* (London: Methuen, 1986).

3 Frances E. Kingsley, ed., *Charles Kingsley, His Letters and Memories of His Life*, vol. iii (London: Macmillan & Co. Ltd., 1901), p. 111 (cited in G. J. Watson, *Irish Identity and the Literary Revival* [London: Croom Helm, 1989] p. 17).

4 Cited in Francis Hackett, *Ireland: A Study in Nationalism* (New York: B. W. Huebsch, 1919), p. 227.

5 Sheridan Gilley, "English Attitudes to the Irish in England, 1780–1900", in C. Holmes, ed., *Immigrants and Minorities in British Society* (London: Croom Helm, 1978), p. 91. Gilley's work has been conscripted into the front ranks of contemporary polemical exchanges over

anti-Irish racism. As the historian Roy Foster expresses it: "Innocent and sometimes naively hilarious works of piety about the Fenians or Young Irelanders, written by amateur historians on the British left, fall into a much cruder category [of propaganda]. They are joined by the half-baked 'sociologists' employed on profitably never-ending research into 'anti-Irish racism', determined to prove what they have already decided to be the case. Historians like Sheridan Gilley may have scrupulously and sympathetically explored the definitions of historical 'racism' and rejected them for the Irish but this matters [little] to such zealots." (Roy Foster, " 'We are all Revisionists now' ", in *The Irish Review*, 1 (1986), p. 3.)

6 *The Times*, 17 December 1867 (cited in Gilley, op. cit. p. 96). These sentiments are endorsed by Gilley: "When the Irish conformed to English values they were quietly accepted in England. But that is surely the point: it was the Irish rejection of English values, which – rather than race – aroused English dislike of them" (p. 93). What this argument overlooks is the extent to which those who failed to conform to English values were not only deemed to be outside English civilization, but to be beyond "the pale of humanity", in Goldwyn Smith's felicitous phrase. For some of the less welcome implications of this acceptance of dominant English values, see the discussion below of how the Irish embraced racist ideologies, pp. 175–7.

7 Gilley's criticism is directed mainly at works such as L. P. Curtis's influential study *Apes and Angels: The Irishman in Victorian Caricature* (Newton Abbot: David & Charles, 1971).

8 See Nicholas Canny, *The Elizabethan Conquest of Ireland: A Pattern Established* (Hassocks, Sussex: Harvester Press, 1976): "Events in Ireland, 1565–76, have a significance in the general history of colonization that transcends English and Irish history. The involvement of men in Irish colonization who afterwards ventured to the New World suggests that their years in Ireland was a period of apprenticeship (p. 15). See also D. B. Quinn's pioneering work, *The Elizabethans and the Irish* (Ithaca: Cornell University Press, 1966), and K. R. Andrews, N. Canny and P. E. H. Hair, eds., *The Westward Enterprise: English Activities in Ireland, the Atlantic and America, 1480–1650* (Detroit: Wayne State University Press, 1979).

9 Cited in Quinn op. cit., p. 119. Mountjoy's statement was a response to a modest proposal that the entire native population of Ireland be transported to the Plantations of America.

10 Quinn, ibid., pp. 25, 153, 24.

11 Cited in Nicholas Mansergh, *The Irish Question, 1840–1921* (London: Unwin University Books, 1965), p. 23.

12 Anthony Buckley, " 'We're Trying to Find our Identity': Uses of History among Ulster Protestants", in Elizabeth Tonkin, Marion McDonald and Malcolm Chapman, eds., *History and Ethnicity*, ASA Monograph 27 (London: Routledge, 1989), p. 187.

13 According to Canny: "We find the colonists in Virginia using the same pretexts for the extermination of the Amerindians as their counterparts used in the 1560s and 1570s for the slaughter of segments of the native Irish population . . . no determined effort was ever made to reform the Irish, but rather, at the least pretext – generally resistance to the English – they were dismissed as a 'wicked and faythles peopoll' and put to the sword. This formula was repeated in the treatment of Indians in the New World" op. cit., (p. 160).

14 Michael Rogin, "Liberal Society and the Indian Question", in *Ronald Reagan the Movie and other Episodes in Political Demonology* (Berkeley: University of California Press, 1987), p. 153.

15 Ibid., p. 142.

16 Jacques Derrida, *Of Grammatology*, trans. Gayatri Chakravorty Spivak (Baltimore: The Johns Hopkins Press, 1977), p. 136.

17 Ibid., p. 198.

18 John Locke, *An Essay Concerning Human Understanding*, vol. 2 (London: Dent, 1974) p. 258. For a useful exposition of Locke's theory of history, see Ian Haywood, *The Making of History* (Rutherford: Fairleigh Dickinson University Press, 1986).

19 David Hume, "The Natural History of Religion", in Richard Wollheim, ed., *Hume on Religion* (London: Fontana, 1968), pp. 79–80.

20 David Hume, *A History of England*, new edition, vol. 5 (London, 1796), pp. 397–8.

21 Jeoffry [sic] Keating, *The General History of Ireland*, trans. Dermod O'Connor (Dublin, 1841), p. 53. Keating's history was composed in Irish and was first translated by O'Connor in 1723.

22 Charles O'Conor, *Dissertations on the History of Ireland* (1753), third edition (Dublin, 1812), pp. 78, ix, 77.

23 Thomas Campbell, *Strictures on the Ecclesiastical and Literary History of Ireland* (Dublin, 1789), p. 9.

24 Charles Gavan Duffy, *Young Ireland: A Fragment of Irish History, 1840–1850* (London, 1880), p. 44 (cited in David Lloyd, *Nationalism and Minor Literature: James Clarance Mangan and the Emergence of Irish Cultural Nationalism* [Berkeley: University of California Press, 1987], p. 68). It is worth pointing out that the title of Duffy's book – "Fragment" – belies the seamless unity he sought to impose on Irish history.

25 Douglas Hyde, "The Necessity for De-Anglicizing Ireland", in *The Revival of Irish Literature* (London, 1894), p. 121.

26 Rev. C. J. Herlihy, *The Celt Above the Saxon* (Boston: Angel Guardian Press, 1904), p. 171.

27 Gilley, op. cit., p. 81.

28 Conor Cruise O'Brien, *States of Ireland* (London: Hutchinson, 1972); F. S. L. Lyons, *Culture and Anarchy in Ireland, 1890–1939* (Oxford: Oxford University Press, 1979).

29 See Griffith's virulent defence of slavery in "Preface to the 1913 Edition" of John Mitchel's *Jail Journal*, reprinted, with critical introduction by Thomas Flanagan (Dublin: University Press of Ireland, 1982), pp. 370–1.

30 Thomas MacDonagh, *Literature in Ireland* (Dublin: The Talbot Press, 1919), p. 57.

31 George Sigerson, *Modern Ireland* (London, 1868); *Barla of the Gael and Gall* (London: Unwin, 1925), first published in 1897. I have dealt with MacDonagh and Sigerson at greater length in the sections which I have edited in vols. 2 and 3 of Seamus Deane, ed., *The Field Day Anthology of Irish Writing* (London: Faber and Faber, 1991).

32 Hume, "The Natural History of Religion", p. 80.

33 "The Individuality of a Native Literature," *The Nation*, 21 August 1847, p. 731 (cited in Lloyd, op. cit., p. 72).

34 Joseph Cooper Walker, *Historical Memoirs of the Irish Bards* (1786), 2nd edition, vol. 1 (Dublin, 1818), p. 55.

35 For the Jacobite background of Ossian, see Albert Boime, *Art in an Age of Revolution, 1750–1800* (Chicago: University of Chicago Press, 1987), pp. 214–27.

36 Donal McCartney, "The Writing of History in Ireland, 1800–30", in *Irish Historical Studies*, 10 (1957), p. 359. For an extended discussion of the differences between Irish and English conceptions of history, see Oliver MacDonagh, *States of Mind: A Study of Anglo-Irish Conflict, 1780–1980* (London: Allen and Unwin, 1983), ch. 1.

37 Fredric Jameson, "*Ulysses* in History", in W. J. McCormack and Alistair Stead. eds., *James Joyce and Modern Literature* (London: Routledge & Kegan Paul, 1982), p. 129.

38 David Frisby, *Fragments of Modernity* (London: Polity Press, 1985), p. 45.

39 For Nietzsche's aversion to historicism, see Frisby, op. cit., pp. 32 ff.

40 *The Voice of the Nation: A Manual of Nationality*, by the writers of *The Nation* newspaper (Dublin: James Duffy, 1844), p. 156.

41 George Simmel, "Die Ruine", in *Zur Philosophie der Kunst* (Potsdam, 1922) pp. 127–88 (cited in Louis Hawes, *Presences of Nature: British Landscape, 1780–1830* [New Haven: Yale Center for British Art, 1982]).

42 William Drennan, *Glendalloch and other Poems* (Dublin: William Robertson, 1859), p. 279.

43 "Lament over the Ruins of the Abbey of Teach Molaga", in D. J. O'Donoghue, ed., *Poems of James Clarence Mangan* (Dublin: O'Donoghue, 1903), pp. 26–7. For a detailed and perceptive reading of this poem, see Lloyd, op. cit., 90 ff.

44 Wyndham Lewis, *Time and Western Man* (London: Chatto and Windus, 1927), pp. 99–100, 106–7.

45 Lewis, ibid., pp. 109, 175, 181.

46 This is not to contradict Derrida's insistence that all speech carries with it the disruptive effects of writing: the point is, rather, that models of speech in societies which dominated Western thought operated, as Spivak puts it, "on an implicit phonocentrism, the presupposition that speech is the immediate expression of the self". The argument here is that the same powerful cultures were not so willing to grant this self-validating phonocentrism to the speech of subaltern cultures. It is precisely, therefore, the phonocentric presuppositions of dominant cultures, particularly in their imperial or colonial manifestations, which are thrown into disarray by subaltern modes of communication such as rumour. See the section on "Rumour" in Gayatri Chakravorty Spivak, "Subaltern Studies: Deconstructing Historiography", in *In Other Worlds: Essays in Cultural Politics* (New York: Methuen, 1987) pp. 211–15, as well as Jameson's remarks on gossip as a means of "dereification", op. cit., p. 135.

47 Spivak, ibid., p. 213. Spivak remarks in the course of her discussion that in certain cases, e.g. the codes of law, written texts operate on an implicit phonocentrism, a description that would seem to apply to the valorization of scripture and *written texts* in Locke's and Hume's approaches to religion and history.

48 Lewis, op. cit., pp. 7–8.

49 Lewis, ibid., p. 122 (quoting from his own book, *The Art of Being Ruled*, ch. vi, part xii).

50 Ibid., p. 118.

51 Jameson, op. cit., pp. 135–6.

52 Franco Moretti, "The Long Goodbye: *Ulysses* and the end of Liberal Capitalism", in *Signs Taken for Wonders* (London: Verso, 1983), pp. 189–90.

53 Wyndham Lewis, *The Lion and the Fox* (London: Grant Richards, 1927), p. 322.

54 See Guy Debord, *Society of the Spectacle* (Rebel Press, AIM Publications, 1987), paragraphs 158, 162: "The spectacle, as the present social organization of the paralysis of history and memory, of the abandonment of history built on the foundation of historical time, is the *false consciousness of time . . . thus spatial alienation*, the society that radically separates the subject from the activity it takes from him, separates him first of all from his own time".

55 *The Ethics of Hunger Striking*, by a Catholic priest (London: Sands, 1920), pp. 14–15.

56 G. J. Watson, op. cit., p. 28.

Glossary

This glossary is not meant to be inclusive but rather to provide the student with a quick reference point for commonly used terms and ideas in postcolonial theory. The index can be used to isolate places in *Postcolonial Discourses* where a particular term is defined and/or discussed. Please note: in the following entries, bold face type has been used to indicate cross references.

agency   This term refers to the power of a human subject to exert his or her will upon the social world. To have agency is to have social power; to lack it is to be the victim of that power. Typically, agency is associated with the **subject** of Western discourses, and historical agency is perhaps the most important form of agency for postcolonial theorists.

alienation   For many postcolonial writers, alienation refers to the social condition of colonialism, in which the colonized individual is condemned to live a way of life cut off from tradition. This general concept of alienation stems from the Marxian notion that the worker cannot enjoy the fruits of her labor and is thus alienated from the objective world she creates while working upon and transform[ing] nature (i.e., materiality). In many cases, this term is used with a psychoanalytic emphasis, often suggesting the self-alienation of individuals whose identity is shattered (when it is not annihilated) through colonial violence.

ambivalence   Ambivalence, as a term in postcolonial studies, is connected with the work of Homi K. Bhabha. He derives it from psychoanalysis, where the concept refers to the unstable nature of identity-formation when the norms governing sexual choice do not function predictably. There is a suggestion not only of a plurality of choices but also of the potential of choosing to balance or sustain two conflicting options. In postcolonial discourses, ambivalence has developed into a concept that attempts to explain the multiplicity of choices offered to colonial subjects for identity-formation, and to this extent, as in Frantz Fanon, it is psychoanalytically inflected. In Bhabha and elsewhere, it refers to the unstable, contradictory, non-identical nature of **colonial discourse**. It is antithetical to **universalism**.

authenticity, inauthenticity   See **primitivism**

colonial discourse   This term designates aggregates of texts, documents, art works, and other means of expression that relate directly and indirectly to colonial territories, colonial rule, or colonized peoples. Colonial discourse tends toward systematization at its foundation with a great deal of variety in its modes of textual and artistic expression. Colonial discourse includes everything from legal statutes to memoranda, from newspaper accounts to novels, from telegrams to poetry. Edward

Said's exploration of one form of colonial discourse, **Orientalism**, reveals both the complex interrelations of a vast spectrum of popular and scholarly texts as well as the authority and consistency of the system to which these texts contribute. Said's *Orientalism* is a good example of **colonial discourse analysis**, when it is employed by postcolonial intellectuals who wish both to understand and to deconstruct colonial discourse. In this way, analysis serves the needs of revisionist historians and social theorists who seek to offer native versions of history and the colonial process. Practitioners of this type of analysis, such as Peter Hulme, often discover startling relationships and dependencies between colonizers and the colonized.

colonial discourse analysis   See *colonial discourse*

colonialism   Broadly speaking, colonialism is a state-sanctioned social practice in which foreign territories are exploited for raw materials, slaves, and/or human labor by Western governments or commercial concerns. **Settler colonies** involve the extensive settlement of white Europeans in foreign territories, either through the imposition of penal colonies, as in Australia, or the appropriation of arable land, as in Ireland, the Caribbean, and parts of Africa. In one sense, colonialism functions as a part of global capitalist expansion at an early stage, when the non-Western world functioned primarily as a source of materials and labor or as a human warehouse for those individuals (criminals, Irish nationalists, displaced agricultural workers) left behind by that expansion. If colonization is the imposition of systematic exploitation of foreign territories, **decolonization** is the process in which the colonized begin to expel the colonizers and organize their desire for freedom into movements of national liberation. *Neo-colonialism* refers to the continuation of European exploitation of former colonies, and implies, on the part of those colonies, either economic help-lessness or collusion.

colonized, the   See *subaltern*

complicity   Complicity, as it is used in postcolonial theory, refers not to compromise, collaboration, or collusion at the level of political policy and practice (though these things do happen in postcolonial contexts). Rather, it usually refers to textual or discursive instances in which nationalist and postcolonial intellectuals appropriate or assimilate elements of the colonizer's social, political, or cultural traditions. But, as Fanon has shown, such instances are inevitable; thus, many postcolonial writers seek to give this complicity a more positive value and regard it as a potentially productive mode of social and cultural production. Increasingly, postcolonial intellectuals regard complicity as part of any contemporary vision of **authenticity**. See **Manicheaism**

construction   This is a term of wide currency in academic theory and refers to the conscious and deliberate act of building something, typically an identity, with the material provided by one's culture. To construct an identity, personal or national, is a matter of making choices from a wide array of models and combining choices in startling ways. This is most evident in the sphere of gender construction. An antithetical term to construction would be **essence**. Regarded in this fashion, identity is empowering because it gives individuals greater control over the social discourses around them and the way they influence their sense of themselves and of other people.

decolonization   See **colonialism**

deconstruction   Deconstruction is a mode of textual analysis associated initially with Jacques Derrida and Paul DeMan, but its influence has been felt in nearly all levels of the humanities. Simply put, deconstruction is a mode of analysis by which one seeks out the "blind spots" in a text, the moments in which the text seems to say something contrary to its manifest content. The author's intentions are here irrelevant, since deconstruction holds that it is the "play" of language that determines meaning, not the author. This play occurs by virtue of the arbitrary relationship between words and what they signify; we can never be sure, therefore, that our discourse refers to what we think it does. The deconstructionist critic points out the moments of rupture or aporias in which the text throws itself into doubt, and uses them as the starting point for a critique of the philosophical, scientific, moral, ethical, or critical assumptions underlying the text under analysis.

dialectic, dialectical method   These terms refer both to a kind of process and to a mode of analysis. The former goes back to Plato and the Socratic dialogues, in which logical propositions are formulated through the give-and-take of discussion. G. W. F. Hegel made famous the idea of an interplay between thesis and antithesis that yields a new synthesis, while Karl Marx put this idea into social terms when he theorized a dialectical struggle between classes that would yield a classless society. From Marx, a dialectical mode of analysis emerged that concentrated on the process of class struggle and its material effects. Much of what is sometimes called **materialist analysis** employs a dialectical method in which the critic seeks to understand the interplay of social and cultural forces in concrete material circumstances and to regard conflict within those circumstances as the sign not of an aberration but of a progressive struggle toward freedom. Fanon's method is exemplary, in that he focuses on both the situation of the colonized and the strategies of the colonizer, intervening on a dialectical process in a way that replicates that process discursively. Gayatri Chakravorty Spivak's notion of "assent" in the classroom is a dialectical process that makes students aware of the competing authorities behind the texts they read and teaches them how to understand the material implications of those conflicts.

disavowal   See **identity**

diaspora, diasporic identities   These terms refer to conditions of forced exile and/ or transportation, typically in slave or prison ships, to foreign territories. Caribbean peoples, many of whose ancestors began life in Africa, identify less with the ideal of a "homeland" equivalent to the nation-state than with a reality of shifting geographical locations in which contingency and emergency, migration and emigration, exile and "home" lessness figure as dominate realities and leitmotifs. The **identities** formed under these conditions are **hybridized** and pluralized, capable of the kinds of political action and cultural production that would be difficult to execute in Western cultures in which identity still implies *national* identity.

discrimination   See **identity**

essence, essentialism   Essence refers to the idea that an individual or a people is self-originating, immutable, and irreducible. When one strips away all social and cultural influences, what is left is one's "essence," one's core. One is either essentially civilized or savage, rational or superstitious, strong or weak. *Essentialism*, broadly, refers to the notion that an idea or statement implies the existence of an essence (an essential self or an essential nature, e.g., the essence of primitive tribes or of women). **Manichaean** oppositions (primitive/civilized, male/female, nature/culture) always assume the essential difference between two polarized terms. In postcolonial writing, a form of *anti-essentialism* emerges in which individuals, groups, and ideas are recognized as complex constructions with a genealogy that can be derived through critical analysis. In this view, essence is a fiction that has little value for people who have been denied an "essential nature" other than that of subhuman primitives.

figure   This term, like the similar term *trope*, refers to the turns of phrase used by writers that have solidified into conventions (e.g., metaphor is a "figure"). But in another sense – one that enjoys considerable currency in academic discourse – it is used strategically as an alternative to "image" (as in the phrase "figure of woman") in order to indicate the **constructedness** of the image one encounters in a text. Figure in this sense suggests *icon* and we are meant to understand its use in a more concrete sense than "image." In this sense, an **ironic** relationship is built between the "figure" and the human beings that it resembles, so that the "English Lady" described by Jenny Sharpe as a "figure" of womanhood has her analogues in very real English women living in India.

hegemony   This term refers to the formal exercise of ideology, whether in violent or nonviolent ways. According to Antonio Gramsci, hegemony is a practice whereby the ruling class achieves the consent of the governed through more or less non-coercive means. An ideology must be powerful if it is to achieve hegemony peacefully, since it must accommodate political dissent, minorities, and foreign influence. Often used to indicate an omnivorous imperial appetite, hegemony is, strictly speaking, more subtle and more insidious, since ruling elites often seek consent in part through mystification and misinformation. The critique of hegemony in postcolonial discourses is directed not only at the colonial rulers, who seek to impose the hegemony of the mother country, but also at nationalist leaders, who seek their own forms of nativist or *neo-imperialist* hegemony.

hybridity   This term, popularized by Homi Bhabha, refers to the process whereby native writers and intellectuals reveal the heterogeneous and contingent nature of a colonial discourse that comports itself as if it were monological and absolute. The effect is to render colonial discourse **ambivalent**. Hybridity or hybridization are the "affects" (as Bhabha puts it) of mimicry; a hybrid text, quite different from the "official" text of colonial discourse, is the product of an act of mimicry that is at bottom insurrectionary. Though limited to discursive contexts typically, **mimicry** and hybridity can be powerful tools in anti-colonial struggles because they create doubt as to the **universalism** and *self-identity* of colonial ideologies.

idealization   In postcolonial discourses, this term is linked to psychological notions of projection and fantasy, in which individuals invent an ideal (of one's own ego, of "woman") and project that invention onto the social world. In colonial and post-colonial contexts, natives (particularly those from the countryside) and women generally are frequently objects of idealization. In the hands of anti-colonial propagandists, such ideals can be deployed to represent nationalist aspirations (as Cathleen ni Houlihan represented the ambitions of Irish nationalism). When created by colonial discourse, they can distort and misrepresent those ambitions.

identity*, *identity formation   Identities and the ways we form them come in for a good deal of attention from postcolonial theorists. For them, identity is not an **essence** but is rather a **construct**, one for which each individual is more or less responsible. Rather than aspire to the ideal of *self-identity*, in which one's conception of oneself matches exactly one's social behavior, postcolonial writers exploit the disjunctions between conception and behavior, deriving an "identity(ies)" in the process. In this way, taking responsibility for one's own identity formation, in a postcolonial context, can be an anti-colonial act, one that seeks to bypass the mechanisms of **discrimination** and **disavowal** that colonialism puts into place in order to "type" native peoples. Another important insight from postcolonial theory is the *plurality* of identities that is necessitated by racial mixing, transportation, the slave trade, emigration, and migration. Identity becomes a pluralized process of "negotiation," a strategy by which one's identity(ies) shift and change, subject to social and cultural forces that transcend national, racial, ethnic, religious, and gender boundaries. See **subject**

ideology   Ideology is, in brief, a set of dominant beliefs, laws, statutes, principles, practices and traditions that govern any given society. Louis Althusser's definition – quite influential among postcolonial theorists – emphasizes the idea of *ideological state apparatuses* (e.g., state bureaucracies, schools, universities, the police and military, and so on). During the height of the colonial period in the nineteenth and twentieth centuries, *liberalism* was the dominant ideology in England. But with respect to the colonies, other ideologies prevailed. There, the discourses of race and **Orientalism** emerged as two dominant ideologies that came into conflict with the underlying principles of liberalism. Ideological conflict is therefore a prominent feature in colonial discourse and colonial discourse analysis.

imperialism   If **colonialism** refers to the imposition of exploitative administrations in foreign territories, imperialism refers, on the one hand, to the political objectives of such impositions at the level of state-sponsored territorial expansion and, on the other, to the competition between European states for control of foreign territories. Frequently, writers will use the terms interchangeably; and to some extent, there is no real confusion as a result. But it is useful to bear in mind the difference between the two, in part because they suggest a certain relationship of power. For it is at the level of empire – the level of political, economic, social, and cultural policy-making – that the ideology is formulated that will later govern the actions of colonial administrators. *Neo-imperialism* is a term that designates the continuation of economic and cultural relationships established during the imperial era. Neo-imperialism often manifests itself as an ideological influence, insidiously tied up with multinational capitalism and the ubiquity of Western commodities. Popular music, sports, and fashion are strong indicators of neo-imperialist forces at work.

implied reader   This term is associated with Wayne Booth's *Rhetoric of Fiction* and refers to the construct created by authors whenever they envision the reader of their texts. The implied reader is thus a theoretical category that enables writers to duplicate the conditions of a discursive exchange; by inventing an addressee, the position of addresser or narrator can be more fully explored. In Gayatri Chakravorty Spivak's use, the term is given a pedagogical importance; the implied reader is in this sense an ideological category as well as a rhetorical one, for the position of the implied reader is recognized as being determined by social forces beyond the control of the reading subject. Therefore tension crops up in the act of reading when the implied reader is at odds with the "actual" one in the classroom.

irony   Perhaps the most pervasive and ambiguous of rhetorical figures, irony is frequently pointed out and deployed by postcolonial writers. Simply put, irony is a gap between a thing said and a thing done. It indicates a displacement of meaning or intention, and runs the gamut from sarcasm to tragedy. In postcolonial writing, irony is often deployed as a means of upsetting conventional wisdom by alluding to its internal contradictions. Concepts such as **mimicry** and **ambivalence** are fundamentally ironic in that they point up the disparity between the foundational truths of colonial discourse and the effects of that discourse in the colonies.

Manichaeism   In its ancient Persian religious context, this term refers to the division of the world into good and evil forces that battle for the possession of humanity. In postcolonial theory, it refers to the dualism constituted by the colonizer/colonized dyad, with the implication that the former is the "good" seeking to dominate the latter, equated with "evil." Abdul JanMohamed coined the term "Manichaean allegory" to express the relations of power between colonizer and colonized. Generally speaking, Manichaeism is a binary relation of power characterized by polarization and inequality. Racial and ethnic difference contribute to the absolutist or **universalist** connotations behind this term. To some extent, **complicity** has proven to be a useful strategy for breaking the stranglehold that Manichaean thinking has had on the colonialist – and postcolonial – imagination.

Marxism   See *dialectic*

materialist analysis   See *dialectic*

mimicry   This concept was pioneered by Frantz Fanon in his *Black Skin, White Masks*, in which he argued that colonized people, forced to abandon traditional notions of selfhood and national identity, learn to mimic their own **identities**, often imitating their colonial masters. Homi Bhabha's treatment of the concept has influenced postcolonial theory to a great extent. For Bhabha, mimicry is a deconstructive practice whereby the colonized rewrite colonial discourse, simultaneously turning that discourse into a **hybrid** product of native intellectual labor and revealing the contradictions and inconsistencies that make that discourse available to the native in the first place.

nationalism   This term is fraught with difficulty. First, there is no consensus as to what constitutes nationalism, though many factors are deemed vitally important in determining this or that nation, particularly language, race, religion, ethnicity, and territorial occupation. Unlike European nationalisms, which developed more or less in tandem and with similar foundations, nationalism in the colonies developed unevenly and in reaction to varying social and political pressures. Further, postcolonial nationalism, especially insofar as it is anti-colonial in orientation, must resist the influence of Western nationalism. Frantz Fanon's term "national consciousness" is an attempt to define a national **identity** that is dependent neither on Western ideals of national sovereignty nor on a nostalgic vision of a pre-colonial past. The idea that postcolonial nationalism entails a commitment to international solidarity across the former colonies suggests that the postcolonial nation is something more than a replication of a European state. Nationalism, in a postcolonial context, is always misconceived if we look at it from the perspective of Europe. Overcoming such misconceptions might account for the tremendous emphasis postcolonial theorists place upon nationalism.

native   See **subaltern**

Orientalism   See **colonial discourse**

postcolonialism   As so many of the writers in this anthology suggest, postcolonialism is a problematic term. It refers both to an era after colonialism and to a set of critical attitudes taken toward colonialism. As the design of *Postcolonial Discourses* suggests, postcolonialism is region-specific and employs Western as well as native modes of expression. The reader is advised to read the editor's introduction and look at the essays by Stephen Slemon and Robert J. C. Young for a consideration of the term "postcolonialism."

postmodernism   Like postcolonialism, this term is complicated. On the one hand, it refers to an era after modernism; the problem here is that there is little consensus on when modernism ended. On the other hand, it refers to a set of practices, strategies, and theories that either refute modernist tendencies (i.e., expressive form, mythic structures, stream of consciousness) or develop those tendencies in extreme forms. In some cases – as in the pervasive use of **irony**, a certain flatness of affect, "blank" or objectless parody, citation, and other strategies of appropriation – postmodernism appears to offer something different from modernism. The "post" in postmodern is often thought to be related to the "post" in postcolonial; temporally, the two concepts coincide to some degree. In other ways, they diverge – namely, since postmodernism is the efflorescence of a European intellectual tradition, it is of doubtful usefulness to a postcolonial discourse that is profoundly anti-Western. Still, some writers – especially creative writers such as J. M. Coetzee and Salman Rushdie – evince a postmodern turn in their textual strategies. The debate may finally be academic, especially given the uncertainty with respect to the concept "postmodern."

post-structuralism   As a general term, post-structuralism refers to an intellectual movement in Europe and America in which the assumptions of **structuralism** – that human societies and their traditions can be understood according to universal and unchanging structures that are replicated in texts, rituals, and other modes of expression – are challenged by new theories of language and human consciousness. Grounded in a view of linguistics that saw language as governed by laws of structure rather than laws of reference, structuralism dominated intellectual innovation in the first half of the twentieth century. (Claude Lévi-Strauss's structuralist anthropology is a famous example.) Post-structuralists, on the other hand, held that language – as well as the societies in which it was used – was fundamentally unstable and that any discernable "structure" was the imposition of an author or reader who misunderstood the ambivalence of linguistic and ritual signs. Structures were the creation of the critic, not an intrinsic element of social or cultural phenomena. **Deconstruction**, for example, like Foucauldian genealogy and Lacanian psychoanalysis, is a post-structuralist theory that resists the influence of structural explanations, preferring to regard languages, societies, and individuals alike as complex assemblages of desire, intention, influence, coercion, and seduction.

primitivism   Primitivism is a colonial discourse that puts into play a **Manichaean** distinction between the civilized West and the savage East. It derives from scientific, historical, anthropological, philological, sociological, and imaginative texts whose common denominator is a vision of so-called primitive peoples as childlike, feminine, irrational, superstitious, violent, garrulous, and genetically inferior. As part of the ideological structure of colonialism, primitivism played an important role in establishing the *inhumanity* of non-Western peoples, thus making it easier to subjugate and exploit them. Artistically, primitivism had a profound impact on Western modernism. In this context, native art and rituals were appropriated by Western artists who sought to infuse their work with Eastern exoticism. A central attraction to the colonialist and artist alike was the guarantee of cultural or racial **authenticity** offered up by primitive people. This attraction, however, is an ambivalent one, for the **essential** nature of the primitive – the "noble savage," the genuine "man of nature" – served as both a sign of utter difference and as a balm for alienated modernists. Postcolonial theory has countered in recent years with notions of *inauthenticity* – like the idea of "diasporic identities" put forward by many writers – that celebrate contingency, non-essential identities, and historical change, rather than the static, ahistorical exoticism usually signified by "authentic."

problematic   Strictly speaking, this refers to a delimited set of social or textual phenomena – contradictions, aporias or gaps in logic, sudden discontinuities or juxtapositions, inequalities or asymmetries – which, when taken together, suggest an opportunity for critical intervention. A problematic, then, is a **constructed** set of phenomena prepared for analysis along the lines of a single proposition or theme. When used as an adjective – i.e., "the problematic relation between Ireland and England" – it is being used in a rather more commonsense way, as if to say "the relation between Ireland and England is a problem." Both are, needless to say, valid usages. What is important to note is that many postcolonial theorists use the term in the more complex sense and mean to indicate that certain apparently disparate texts or events may be understood differently or more deeply when considered as part of a single "problematic."

settler colonies   See ***colonialism***

structuralism   See ***post-structuralism***

subaltern, subaltern subject   These terms refer to those social groups – migrants, shantytown dwellers, displaced tribes, refugees, untouchable castes, the homeless – that either do not possess or are prevented from possessing class-consciousness and which are in any case prevented from mobilizing as an organized group. In this limited sense, subalternity refers to many but not all of those people who constitute the **colonized**. However, this term, like other related terms – e.g., peasant (and peasantry) and native – is often used to designate a collectivity or aggregate of individuals whose social existence is determined in more or less violent ways by colonialism. These terms are all grounded in the idea of *subject races*, an idea introduced by Lord Cromer in 1907 in order to differentiate between Europeans and non-Europeans on the basis of race, ethnicity, religion, and social conditions. The colonialist frame of reference that envisioned subject and subaltern races could do so only because it was supported by a **Manichaean** ideology of racial difference. And it is this ideology that subtends the various terms used to designate "the colonized."

subject, subjectivity   These terms, used in the context of postcolonial theory, typically refer to Western traditions of citizenship, selfhood, and consciousness. The subject, therefore, is an autonomous, free sovereign and self-determining individual who possesses social and historical **agency** and who aspires toward the ideal of *self-identity*. Subjectivity is that condition that characterizes a subject, specifically the condition of self-identity (i.e., self-awareness), and the ability not only to recognize oneself as a subject (agent or citizen) but also to regulate one's actions accordingly. To make a mark socially or politically, one needs to be a subject who already occupies a recognizable and legitimate place in a social structure. Subjectivity is the recognition of this occupancy, which in turn leads to actions that further legitimate the nature of "the subject." Such concepts have, of course, little value in colonial contexts where the rights and appurtenances that accrue to the subject in a Western society are abrogated. Consequently, postcolonial theorists critique these concepts, in part to reveal their false **universalism**, in part to account for their influence on postcolonial subject formation.

universalism   This term refers to the tendency in Western intellectual traditions to posit theories that claim to cover all practical implications, to explain all phenomena, and to predict all future results. Universal ideas – humanity, liberalism, racial difference – though formulated by European thinkers, are understood to have preceded such thinkers in the manner of an a priori "truth." In this way, Europe "discovered" the universal truths that it promulgated in the form of philosophy, anthropology, medicine, religion, and a host of other disciplines. Universalist thinking is paradoxically provincial: an idea is formulated under specific cultural conditions (e.g., individualism in nineteenth-century England) that quickly takes on the character of a universal: "all people are individuals and should cultivate their individuality." The fallacy of universals – that is, the fact of their **constructedness** – is revealed in the colonial context where different social conditions (e.g., those favoring collectivist or communal identities) prevail. One of the more effective results of **mimicry** is the exposure of bogus universals. It is interesting to note that some postcolonial theorists have attempted to counter the dominance of the universal as a concept by speaking of "contingent universals." This means that one employs an idea *as if* it were universal and does so self-consciously and temporarily and for a specific strategic effect.

Index